London Railway
ATLAS

4th Edition

Joe Brown

Ian Allan
PUBLISHING

Glossary

Aggregate	Stone, gravel, sand etc used for construction
Bay platform	Dedicated platform for terminating trains at an otherwise through station
Bi-directional	Single track signalled for train movements in both directions; Single-line working
Bradshaw	George Bradshaw's 'Monthly Railway Guide'; the industry standard of timetables published from December 1841 onwards
Chain	Unit of measurement still used on NR routes, approximately 20 metres
Chord	Short section of line connecting two joining or crossing routes
Clipped	Method of securing a set of points rendering one route out of use
Covered way	Section of line artificially covered over, usually for development above (in essence a tunnel not necessitated by topography)
Curve	See 'chord'
Down	Direction of travel, generally away from London ('Up to London, down to the country')
End-on junction	The line of demarcation between two railway companies on plain track (e.g. Barrington Road Junction)
Flat junction	Junction without diveunders / flyovers
Flying junction	Junction arranged with diveunders / flyovers to minimise conflicting train movements (also 'Grade separated junction')
Halt	Unstaffed platform where trains stop by request only
Head shunt	Dead-end siding provided for trains to reverse and shunt back into a depot or goods yard
Hump	Hump marshalling yards used gravity to sort wagons after being propelled over a hump (e.g. Feltham, Temple Mills)
Level crossing	Two railway lines or a railway line and road intersecting on the same level
Logistics	The management of the flow of goods
Loop	See 'chord'. Also a simple siding connected to a main line at both ends, typically to allow fast trains to overtake slow, or can refer to a much longer section of railway connected to a main line at both ends (e.g. Hertford Loop)
Mothballed	Disused infrastructure maintained for possible future use (e.g. North Pole Depot, Waterloo International, Post Office Railway)
Passing loop	Loop provided on single-track railway to allow 'up' and 'down' trains to pass each other
Plateway	Tramway formed of flanged cast iron plates to guide wheels (as opposed to conventional railway with flanged wheels on rails)
Run-around	Loop provided (usually at a terminus) to allow a locomotive to 'run around' its rake of coaches for the return journey
Single lead junction	Junction between two double track routes where one route merges to a single track before joining the other (e.g. Old Kew Junction)
Single-line working	See bi-directional
Stabling	'Parking' of rolling stock when not in use, e.g. overnight or between peak hours
Staggered	Where platforms on adjacent tracks are not parallel, usually either side of a level crossing (e.g. Mitcham Eastfields)
Terminal loop	A loop of track allowing trains to terminate without the need to reverse (e.g. Kennington, Heathrow Terminal 4)
Ticket platform	Platform, usually on approach to a terminus, where ticket inspectors would board to check tickets
Tramway	Railway line running along roadway
Turnback siding	Siding provided, usually between running lines, to allow terminating trains to reverse (e.g. Tooting Broadway, Archway)
Up	Direction of travel, generally towards London ('Up to London, down to the country')

Front cover: The larger-than-lifesize statue of Sir John Betjeman stares towards the roof of St Pancras station. Betjeman had been the driving force behind efforts to save the site when it was threatened by development plans during the 1960s. *Brian Morrison*

First published 2006
Reprinted 2006, 2007
Second edition 2009
Reprinted 2009, 2010
Third edition 2012
Reprinted 2013
This fourth edition first published 2015

ISBN 978 0 7110 3819 6

© Joe Brown 2015

Published by Ian Allan Publishing Ltd, Hersham, Surrey, KT12 4RG

Printed in Bulgaria

Visit the Ian Allan Publishing website at
www.ianallanpublishing.com

Preface to the Fourth edition

London, more than possibly any other city on Earth, owes its growth and continuing success to its intricate network of railways, which have been a part of the landscape for over 200 years and show no sign of losing their relevance or importance. Unlike much of the United Kingdom, London had lost relatively little of its passenger infrastructure during the 20th century and it could indeed be argued that with the recent additions of the Docklands Light Railway and Croydon Tramlink to the scene along with 'Heavy Rail' developments such as the Channel Tunnel Rail Link and East London Line Extensions, London's passenger rail network is today at its zenith. Despite this, there are many long-forgotten branch lines and abandoned stations dotted around London; casualties of war, route duplication, trams, buses and the car. London's freight and industrial facilities did not fare anywhere near as well as the passenger facilities during the late 20th century; changes to the way that freight was carried and the abandonment of domestic coal in favour of central heating, combined with industrial decline, decimated the hundreds of goods and coal yards and rail-served industrial sites in London.

I commenced this project in 2004 after searching for a publication like this one to no avail: one that provided a diagrammatic representation of London's railway history. What began as a light-hearted hobby has since become a serious project, which has taken up hundreds of hours' work through map-drawing, indexing and research. Following on from publication of the First edition nine years ago, I have continually striven to improve the cartography and to add ever more detail with each new edition, while of course keeping abreast of developments to London's railways. For the Fourth edition I have taken the opportunity to make more improvements to the format, the most significant being an improvement to the font size and overall clarity of the index. Whereas the previous two editions represented significant steps forwards in terms of detail and coverage, as I now am satisfied with the format, this Fourth edition bears a stronger resemblance to the Third than the Third did to the Second, or the Second to the First. A map of this scale can never be pin-point accurate, but I have attempted to achieve as closely as possible this goal while maintaining clarity. In some areas the railway infrastructure has changed repeatedly over time to the point that it is impossible to depict every historical permutation, so for some areas I have provided larger-scale maps giving the current layout alongside an historical snap-shot when pre-Beeching infrastructure was at its peak. I have broadened the scope of the atlas for this edition and have depicted several self-contained narrow gauge railways previously omitted, including the Post Office Railway (albeit in its 'mothballed' state), and I have also now included the very first London railways, the Surrey Iron, Croydon Canal, and Croydon, Merstham & Godstone Railways.

Despite many hours of research I am the first to acknowledge that there are quite probably some omissions (and dare I say it errors!), particularly regarding freight facilities on which available information is often scant. I have endeavoured to provide a hopefully near-complete history of London's passenger railways, although I have chosen to omit a handful of temporary, excursion and unadvertised stations which have had little bearing on London's railway history or for which I have been unable to find any significant information. Where dates were unobtainable, as a last resort I have used historical Ordnance survey maps to somewhat crudely infer an approximate date; I feel this is preferable to no date at all.

I very much regard this as a work in progress, and I would be delighted to hear from anyone who can provide me with further information. There are question marks against some dates in the index, and I would be very happy to receive locations and relevant dates for other goods, freight and industrial facilities that have been omitted, although I have had to be mindful in more complex areas not to overload the map with detail to the extent that it becomes a distraction. Regarding future developments, I have included those under construction such as 'Crossrail 1', the 'Croxley Link', 'Thameslink' improvement works, and also proposed developments such as High Speed Two and the Northern Line Battersea extension.

Please feel free to email me with any feedback or further information at: atlasupdate@blueyonder.co.uk

About the author:
I am a railway professional and near-lifelong London resident who since childhood had a keen interest in cartography as well as London's railway history. I joined London Underground as a Northern Line Guard in 1997 shortly after leaving school, and progressed to a 'Guard-Motorman' on that line in 1998 before transferring to be a District Line Train Operator at Parson's Green the following year. In 2001 I was promoted to Duty Manager Trains at Earl's Court, where I remained for six years before again being promoted to Train Operations Manager at Elephant & Castle (Bakerloo Line) in 2007. Since then I have gained experience managing station operations on the Marylebone Group of six Bakerloo Line stations, before returning to Trains management in 2011. I am currently Train Operations Manager at Wembley Park Depot on the Jubilee Line, with in excess of 200 drivers. I have produced the four editions of the London Railway Atlas around a busy work schedule on a home computer, self-taught on fairly basic software without any formal design training. Long-term I hope to continue updating this work every few years, perhaps with a view to tackling other cities or even the entire country in this same format, although the latter may be one for my retirement!

Thanks & dedications:
I would firstly like to thank Gary James for his never-ending patience and support during the ten years that it has taken for this fourth edition to be realised. Secondly a huge thank you to a multitude of people who offered feedback and information by email and post following publication of the first three editions; I cannot thank you all but special mention to Bob Allaway, David Bleicher, David Burnell, Alan Collis, Andy Cope, John Cousins, John Craig, John Edser, William Graveson, John Groves, Chris Harry, Claude Hart, Colin Hills, Geoff Hutton, Martin James, Phil Jones, Joel Kosminsky, Raj Kukadia, Mike Mellor, Simon Moore, Bill Munro, Brian Polley, A Porter, Dr Sunil Prasannan, D Roberts, Tony Roeder, John Sketcher, Stewart Smith, Frank Taylor, Steven Taylor, James Tinkler, Christopher Walker, Alan Walters, Ken Weston, Gordon Wickham and David Winter.

For my Nephews and Godsons Max & Felix Brown and Nephew and Niece Oscar & Jemima Thiagaraj.

In loving memory of Ruth Brown 1945-1989.

Joe Brown, London, January 2015

Abbreviations

AC	Alternating Current	
BAA	British Airports Authority	
BAK	Bakerloo Line	Abbreviated form of BSWR
BHR	Bexley Heath Railway	Absorbed by SECR 10.07.1900
BR	British Rail(ways)	Formed 01.01.1948 (Nationalisation)
BSWR	Baker Street & Waterloo Railway	Absorbed by UERL before opening, became Bakerloo Line
c.	circa	
CCEHR	Charing Cross, Euston & Hampstead Railway	Absorbed by UERL before opening, merged with CSLR to form Northern Line 13.09.1926
CCR	Croydon Canal Railway	Short branch off the SIR serving the Croydon Canal basin adjacent to present-day West Croydon
CE	Civil Engineers	
CEN	Central Line	Originally Central London Railway
Co.	Company	
CLR	Central London Railway	Absorbed by UERL 01.01.1913
CMGR	Croydon, Merstham & Godstone Railway	Extension of SIR (see below). Opened 24.07.1805, closed 28.09.1838 (last use 27.09.1838)
CR	Caterham Railway	Absorbed by SER 1859
CSLR	City & South London Railway	Absorbed by UERL 01.01.1913, merged with CCEHR to form Northern Line 13.09.1926
CTL	Croydon Tramlink	Renamed 'London Tramlink Croydon' 01.01.2009
CVR	Chipstead Valley Railway	Absorbed by SECR 13.07.1899
C.W.	Carriage Wash	
DBS	Deutsche Bahn Schenker	Formerly EWS, acquired 28.06.2007 and renamed 01.01.2009
DC	Direct Current	
DIS	District Line	Originally Metropolitan District Railway, absorbed by UERL 09.04.1902
DLR	Docklands Light Railway	Controlled by TfL since 03.07.2000
DMU	Diesel Multiple Unit	
E	East	
EB	Eastbound	
ECML	East Coast Main Line	Former GNR main line from King's Cross
ECR	Eastern Counties Railway	Absorbed by GER 01.07.1862
ECTJR	Eastern Counties & Thames Junction Railway	Absorbed by ECR 1847
EHLR	Edgware, Highgate & London Railway	Absorbed by GNR before opening, 07.1867
ELL	East London Line	Originally 'Metropolitan Line East London section', name came into use during 1980's
ELR	East London Railway	GER, LBSCR, SER, LCDR, MET & MDR joint (LNER / MET 01.01.1923), absorbed by SR 1925
EMU	Electric Multiple Unit	
EOR	Epping Ongar Railway	Preserved railway, commenced operation 10.10.2004
ES	Eurostar	
E.S.	Engine Shed	
EWIDBJR	East & West India Docks & Birmingham Junction Railway	Renamed NLR 01.01.1853
EWS	English, Welsh & Scottish Railway	Acquired by DBS 28.06.2007, renamed 01.01.2009
GCC	Gaslight & Coke Company	Leased to GER after 18.03.1874
GCR	Great Central Railway	Absorbed by LNER 01.01.1923
GER	Great Eastern Railway	Formed from ECR 01.07.1862, absorbed by LNER 01.01.1923
GNCR	Great Northern & City Railway	Absorbed by Metropolitan Railway 01.07.1913
GNPBR	Great Northern, Piccadilly & Brompton Railway	Absorbed by UERL before opening 09.04.1902, became Piccadilly Line
GNR	Great Northern Railway	Absorbed by LNER 01.01.1923
GRR	Gravesend & Rochester Railway	Absorbed by SER late 1845
GWR	Great Western Railway	Absorbed by BR 01.01.1948
HCL	Hammersmith & City Line	Formerly part of Metropolitan Line, given own name 30.07.1990
HCR	Hammersmith & City Railway	GWR & MET joint
HEX	Heathrow Express	Owned by BAA – British Airports Authority
HHR	Hundred of Hoo Railway	Absorbed by SER August 1880
HJR	Hampstead Junction Railway	Managed by NLR after 1864, absorbed by LNWR 1867
HS1	High Speed 1	High speed route between Channel Tunnel and St Pancras (LCOR)
HS2	High Speed 2	Proposed high speed route between London and Birmingham
HST	High Speed Train	
IEP	Intercity Express Programme	Programme to replace Class 43 (Intercity 125) fleet, first train in service expected 2017
Jcn.	Junction	
JUB	Jubilee Line	Formed 01.05.1979, partially from Bakerloo Line
km	Kilometres	
LBIR	London & Birmingham Railway	Absorbed by LNWR 16.07.1846
LBLR	London & Blackwall Railway	Leased to GER 18.03.1874, absorbed by LNER 01.01.1923
LBRR	London & Brighton Railway	Merged with LCRR to form LBSCR 27.02.1846
LBSCR	London, Brighton & South Coast Railway	Formed 27.02.1846 from LBRR and LCRR
LCC	London County Council	
LCDR	London, Chatham & Dover Railway	Merged with SER to form SECR 01.01.1899
LCOR	London & Continental Railway	Consortium that built Channel Tunnel Rail Link, leased to NR from outset
LCRR	London & Croydon Railway	Merged with LBRR to form LBSCR 27.02.1846
LGR	London & Greenwich Railway	Leased to SER 01.01.1845, absorbed by SR 01.01.1923
LMS	London, Midland & Scottish Railway	Formed 01.01.1923 from MID, LNWR & NLR

Abbreviation	Full name	Notes
LNER	London & North Eastern Railway	Formed 01.01.1923 from GNR, GCR & GER
LNWR	London & North Western Railway	Formed 16.07.1846 from LBIR
LOROL	London Overground Rail Operations Ltd	Took over former 'Silverlink' franchise, commenced operation 11.11.2007
LPTB	London Passenger Transport Board	Formed 01.07.1933, became LTE (1st) 01.01.1948
LRT	London Regional Transport	Formed 19.06.1984, became LUL 01.04.1985
LSKD	London St Katherine's Dock Company	Later became part of PLA, operated by GER after 01.07.1896
LSWR	London & South Western Railway	Absorbed by SR 01.01.1923, 'London & Southampton Railway' until opening day
LTB	London Transport Board	Formed 01.01.1963, became LTE (2nd) 01.01.1970
LTC	London Tramlink Croydon	Formerly Croydon Tramlink
LTE (1st)	London Transport Executive (1st incarnation)	Formed 01.01.1948, became LTB 01.01.1963
LTE (2nd)	London Transport Executive (2nd incarnation)	Formed 01.01.1970, became LRT 19.06.1984
LTSR	London, Tilbury & Southend Railway	ECR / LBLR joint, leased to its builders 03.07.1854, absorbed by MID 07.08.1912
LUL	London Underground Ltd	Formed 01.04.1985
m	metres	
MDR	Metropolitan District Railway	Absorbed by UERL 09.04.1902
MER	Millwall Extension Railway	LBLR, East & West India Dock Co. and Millwall Dock Co. joint
MET	Metropolitan Railway	Absorbed by LPTB 01.07.1933
MHPR	Muswell Hill & Palace Railway	Operated by GNR from outset, absorbed 09.1911
MID	Midland Railway	Absorbed by LMS 01.01.1923
MKR	Mid Kent Railway	Absorbed by SER 29.07.1864
MPD	Motive Power Depot	
MPV	Multi-purpose Vehicle	Purpose built vehicles used on Network Rail for activities such as water-jetting and de-icing
MSJWR	Metropolitan & St John's Wood Railway	Worked by MET from outset, formally absorbed by MET 01.01.1883
N	North	
NB	Northbound	
NCL	Northern City Line	Abbreviated form of GNCR, transferred to BR 16.08.1976
NER	Northern & Eastern Railway	Leased to ECR 01.01.1844, absorbed by GER 1902
NLR	North London Railway	Operated by LNWR after 01.02.1909, absorbed by LMS 01.01.1923
NOR	Northern Line	Formed from CCEHR & CSLR 13.09.1926, 'Northern Line' name not used until 08.1937
NR	Network Rail	Formed 03.10.2002 when Railtrack renationalised
NSWJR	North & South Western Junction Railway	LNWR & LSWR joint (LNWR, NLR & MID joint after 1871, LMS after 01.01.1923)
OHLE	Overhead Line Equipment	
OS	Ordnance Survey	
PIC	Piccadilly Line	Abbreviated form of GNPBR
PLA	Port of London Authority	
POR	Post Office Railway	Commenced operation 03.12.1927, mothballed 31.05.2003. Renamed 'Mail Rail' 1987
PRIV	Private	
RT	Railtrack	Formed from BR 01.04.1994 (privatisation)
Rwy.	Railway	
S	South	
S&T	Signal & Telegraph	
SB	Southbound	
Sdg.	Siding	
SECR	South Eastern & Chatham Railway	Formed from SER & LCDR 01.01.1899, absorbed by SR 01.01.1923
SER	South Eastern Railway	Absorbed by SECR 01.01.1899
SIR	Surrey Iron Railway	4ft 2in gauge plateway carrying goods, using horse traction. Opened 26.07.1803, closed 31.08.1846
SOR	Sevenoaks Railway	Later became Sevenoaks, Maidstone & Tunbridge Railway. Absorbed by LCDR 21.07.1879
Sq	Square	
SR	Southern Railway	Formed from LBSCR, LSWR & SECR 01.01.1923, absorbed by BR 01.01.1948
St	Saint or Street	
TFGR	Tottenham & Forest Gate Railway	MID & LTSR joint, LMS after 01.01.1923
TfL	Transport for London	Formed 03.07.2000, took control of LUL 15.07.2003, LOROL 11.11.2007
THJR	Tottenham & Hampstead Junction Railway	MID & GER joint, LMS & LNER joint after 01.01.1923
TMD	Traction maintenance depot	
TVR	Thames Valley Railway	Absorbed by LSWR 11.01.1867
UERL	Underground Electric Railways of London	Formed by merger of MDR, BSWR, GNPBR & CCEHR 1901-1902
VIC	Victoria Line	
VSPR	Victoria Station & Pimlico Railway	LBSCR, LCDR, GWR & LNWR joint
W	West	
WB	Westbound	
WBR	Whitechapel & Bow Railway	LTSR & MDR joint
WCIR	Waterloo & City Railway	Operated by LSWR from outset, Absorbed by 1906. Transferred to LUL 01.04.1994
WCL	Waterloo & City Line	
WCML	West Coast Main Line	Former LBIR (later LNWR) main line from Euston
WCRR	Wimbledon & Croydon Railway	Absorbed by LBSCR 01.01.1866
WELCPR	West End of London & Crystal Palace Railway	Absorbed by LBSCR 1860
WLER	West London Extension Railway	LNWR, GWR, LBSCR & LSWR joint, LMS & SR joint after 01.01.1923
WLR	West London Railway	Leased to LBIR & GWR 1846, absorbed by LNWR & GWR 31.07.1854
WRR	Watford & Rickmansworth Railway	Absorbed by LNWR 1881
WW1	World War One	
WW2	World War Two	
XRAIL	Crossrail 1	Projected opening 2018

References

It would be impossible to list every single reference source here, as they run into many hundreds in several formats. I have selected those upon which I have relied the most heavily and those whose accuracy I have the most confidence in.

Chronology of London Railways
H.V. Borley
Railway & Canal Historical Society 1982
ISBN 0-901461-33-4

Passenger Railway Stations in Great Britain – A Chronology
Michael Quick
Railway & Canal Historical Society 2009
ISBN 978-0-901461-57-5

London's Local Railways
Alan A. Jackson
Capital Transport 1999
ISBN 1-85414-209-7

The Railways of Great Britain – A Historical Atlas (Second Edition)
Colonel Michael H. Cobb
Ian Allan 2006
ISBN 07110-3236X

Railway Track Diagrams – Quail Track Diagrams

2 – Eastern	Third Edition	TRACKmaps 2006	ISBN 0-9549866-2-8
3 – Western	Fifth Edition	TRACKmaps 2010	ISBN 978-0-9549866-6-7
4 – Midlands & North West	Second Edition	TRACKmaps 2005	ISBN 0-9549866-0-1
5 – Southern & TfL	Third Edition	TRACKmaps 2008	ISBN 978-0-9549866-4-3

Capital Transport Illustrated Histories

The Jubilee Line – Mike Horne 2000	ISBN 1-85414-220-8
The Bakerloo Line – Mike Horne 2001	ISBN 1-85414-248-8
The Metropolitan Line – Mike Horne 2003	ISBN 1-85414-275-5
The First Tube: The Story of the Northern Line – Mike Horne & Bob Bayman 1990	ISBN 1-85414-128-7
The Circle Line – Desmond F. Croome 2003	ISBN 1-85414-267-4
The Piccadilly Line – Desmond F. Croome 1998	ISBN 1-85414-192-9
The Central Line – J Graeme Bruce & Desmond F. Croome 2006	ISBN 1-85414-297-6
Going Green: The Story of the District Line – Piers Connor 1994	ISBN 1-85414-162-7

Middleton Press Albums (unfortunately too many of these invaluable titles to list individual publication years and ISBN numbers)
Vic Mitchell and Keith Smith

Harrow to Watford, Marylebone to Rickmansworth, Paddington to Princes Risborough, Paddington to Ealing, Ealing to Slough, Willesden Junction to Richmond, Charing Cross to Dartford, Branch Lines of West London, West London Line, Victoria to Bromley South, East London Line, North London Line, South London Line, London Bridge to East Croydon, Waterloo to Windsor, Clapham Junction to Beckenham Junction, Lines around Wimbledon, Kingston and Hounslow Loops, London Bridge to Addiscombe, Mitcham Junction Lines, West Croydon to Epsom, Victoria to East Croydon, Surrey Narrow Gauge, Holborn Viaduct to Lewisham (in association with Leslie & Philip Davis), Crystal Palace (High level) and Catford Loop (in association with Leslie & Philip Davis)

J.E. Connor
Branch Lines around North Woolwich, Finsbury Park to Alexandra Palace, Branch Line to Ongar, Fenchurch Street to Barking, Branch Lines of East London, Liverpool Street to Ilford, St Pancras to Barking, Liverpool Street to Chingford

Dr Edwin Course	Barking to Southend, Tilbury Loop
Charlie and Jim Connor	King's Cross to Potters Bar
Geoff Goslin and J.E. Connor	St Pancras to St Albans
Dave Brennand	Ilford to Shenfield
Keith Scholey	Euston to Harrow & Wealdstone
Chalk Pits Museum	Industrial Railways of the South-East

The London Railway Record (Multiple editions) – Connor & Butler Ltd

Websites

Clive's Underground Line Guides (CULG)	http://www.davros.org/rail/culg/
Disused Stations – Closed railway stations in the UK	http://www.disused-stations.org.uk/sites.shtml
Kentrail.org.uk	http://www.kentrail.org.uk/index.htm
The Signal Box: Track layout diagrams	http://www.signalbox.org/diagrams.php
locosheds.co.uk	http://www.locosheds.co.uk/index.php
London Reconnections	http://www.londonreconnections.com/
old-maps.co.uk	http://www.old-maps.co.uk/index.html
Google Maps	http://maps.google.co.uk

EXPLANATION OF MAP SYMBOLS

Line symbols (each line depicts a single track):

Open, under construction, or disused but remaining in situ (Standard Gauge)

Closed / dismantled

Construction commenced but was abandoned

Proposed

Narrow Gauge

Platform symbols:

Open or under construction

Closed

Did not open

Proposed

Junction (In use)

Junction (Under construction)

Junction (Dismantled)

Tunnel (Bored deep level)

Tunnel (Shallow level)

Turntable

Trainshed (e.g. depot building, goods shed)
Note: station overall roofs omitted for clarity

Text principles:

Black text	= Open / current	PLAIN TEXT	= Passenger usage
Red text	= Closed / previous	*ITALIC TEXT*	= Non-passenger usage
Blue text	= Future (Under construction / Proposed)		

Naming principles:

All dates are in DD.MM.YYYY format and quoted as accurately as possible
Goods yards opened on same date as associated passenger station unless otherwise stated; the date quoted is that of closure

STATION (OPEN) — Current station name
Previous name (most recent)
Previous name (oldest)] Previous station names in reverse chronological order
(01.01.1900)
Date of opening

STATION (CLOSED) — Station name at point of closure
Previous name (most recent)
Previous name (oldest)] Previous station names in reverse chronological order
(01.01.1900 – 01.01.1950)
Date of opening   Date of closure

STATION (UNDER CONSTRUCTION / PROPOSED)] Proposed station name
(01.01.2020)
Estimated date of opening

NON-PASSENGER FACILITY (OPEN) — Current name
Previous name] Previous name
(01.01.1900)
Date of opening

NON-PASSENGER FACILITY (CLOSED) — Name at point of closure
Previous name] Previous name
(01.01.1900 – 01.01.1950)
Date of opening   Date of closure

Line chronology & parentage principles:

All lines currently open to passenger traffic are assumed to also be used for non-passenger purposes, e.g. stock movement, engineering, goods, etc
In some cases, the chronology / parentage of a stretch of line is too complex to be described as below, so an additional text box gives more detail on the map pages

Abbreviated name of company which opened line

MID
01.01.1900
Line currently open to all traffic, date of opening

MID
01.01.1890 (01.01.1900)
Date of opening to goods   Date of opening to passengers
Line currently open to all traffic, opened to non-passenger traffic before opening to passengers

MID
01.01.1900
Line currently open to non-passenger traffic which has never had regular passenger traffic, with date of opening

MID
01.01.1900 (01.01.1900 – 01.01.1950)
Date of opening to passengers   Date of closure to passengers
Line currently open to non-passenger traffic (with opening date) which has previously had passenger traffic, with dates of opening and closure to passenger traffic in red

LPTB 01.01.1950
ECR 01.01.1900 – 01.01.1970
Line currently open to all traffic which was built by a mainline railway company but subsequently transferred to present-day LUL, DLR or LTC. The black date / company refers to current use (e.g. in this case, LPTB services commenced 01.01.1950), the red date range refers to original use (e.g. opened by ECR 01.01.1900 and mainline services continued until 01.01.1970)

NR
01.01.2020
Line under construction or proposed, expected date of opening

MID
01.01.1910 – 01.01.1930
Date of opening to all traffic   Date of closure to all traffic
Closed line; date before hyphen denotes date of opening, date after hyphen denotes date of closure (if dates in italics, line never saw regular passenger services)

MID
01.01.1910 – 01.01.1930 *(01.01.1950)*
Line which closed to passenger traffic before closing to non-passenger traffic. Date before hyphen denotes date of opening to all traffic, dates after hyphen denote dates of closure in chronological order (passenger in plain text, non-passenger in italics)

MID
01.01.1910 (01.01.1920) – 01.01.1930 *(01.01.1950)*
Line which opened to non-passenger traffic before opening to passenger traffic, then closed to passenger traffic before closing to non-passenger traffic. The later opening / closure date is always quoted in brackets

MID
01.01.1900
Line where construction commenced but was abandoned, with company which abandoned line and date of abandonment (if known)

Line colour coding:

Network Rail (formerly Railtrack, British Rail, and predecessors)	LUL Hammersmith & City Line served by Circle Line
Network Rail served by LUL District Line	LUL Piccadilly Line
Network Rail served by LUL Bakerloo Line	LUL Victoria Line
LUL District Line	LUL Northern Line
LUL District Line served by Piccadilly Line	LUL Bakerloo Line
LUL District Line served by Circle Line	LUL Jubilee Line
LUL District Line served by Hammersmith & City Line	LUL Central Line
LUL Metropolitan & East London Lines	Docklands Light Railway (DLR)
LUL Metropolitan Line served by Hammersmith & City and Circle Lines	LUL Waterloo & City Line
LUL Metropolitan Line served by mainline 'Chiltern' trains	London Tramlink Croydon
LUL Metropolitan Line served by Piccadilly Line	Preserved & Miniature railways, Post Office Railway
LUL Circle Line	
LUL Hammersmith & City Line	

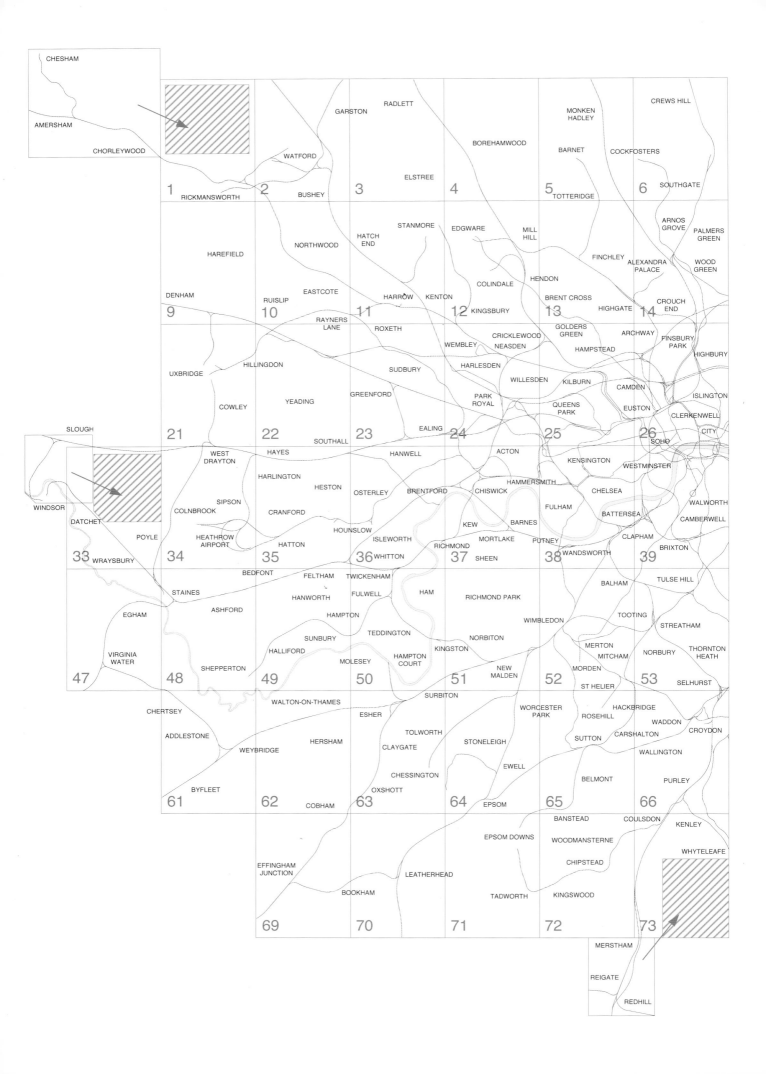

CHESHAM

AMERSHAM

CHORLEYWOOD

CREWS HILL

RADLETT

GARSTON

MONKEN
HADLEY

BOREHAMWOOD

WATFORD

BARNET

COCKFOSTERS

ELSTREE

1 RICKMANSWORTH   **2** BUSHEY   **3**   **4**   **5** TOTTERIDGE   **6** SOUTHGATE

STANMORE

EDGWARE

MILL
HILL

ARNOS
GROVE

PALMERS
GREEN

HATCH
END

NORTHWOOD

HAREFIELD

FINCHLEY

ALEXANDRA
PALACE

WOOD
GREEN

COLINDALE

HENDON

EASTCOTE

BRENT CROSS

CROUCH
END

DENHAM

RUISLIP

HARROW   KENTON

CROUCH
END

9   **10**   **11**   **12** KINGSBURY   **13**   HIGHGATE   **14**

RAYNERS
LANE

ROXETH

GOLDERS
GREEN

ARCHWAY

FINSBURY
PARK

HILLINGDON

WEMBLEY

CRICKLEWOOD
NEASDEN

HAMPSTEAD

HIGHBURY

UXBRIDGE

SUDBURY

HARLESDEN

WILLESDEN

KILBURN

CAMDEN

ISLINGTON

COWLEY

YEADING

GREENFORD

PARK
ROYAL

QUEENS
PARK

EUSTON

CLERKENWELL

SLOUGH

SOUTHALL

EALING

21   **22**   **23**   **24**   **25**   **26** SOHO   CITY

WEST
DRAYTON

HAYES

HANWELL

ACTON

KENSINGTON

WESTMINSTER

WINDSOR

HARLINGTON

HESTON

OSTERLEY

BRENTFORD

CHISWICK

HAMMERSMITH

CHELSEA

WALWORTH

DATCHET

SIPSON

CRANFORD

FULHAM

BATTERSEA

CAMBERWELL

POYLE

COLNBROOK

HOUNSLOW

KEW   BARNES

CLAPHAM

HEATHROW
AIRPORT

HATTON

ISLEWORTH

MORTLAKE

PUTNEY

33 WRAYSBURY   **34**   **35**   **36** WHITTON   RICHMOND   **37** SHEEN   **38** WANDSWORTH   **39** BRIXTON

BEDFONT

FELTHAM   TWICKENHAM

BALHAM   TULSE HILL

STAINES

HANWORTH

FULWELL

HAM

RICHMOND PARK

EGHAM

ASHFORD

HAMPTON

WIMBLEDON

TOOTING

SUNBURY

TEDDINGTON

STREATHAM

HALLIFORD

NORBITON

MERTON   NORBURY

THORNTON
HEATH

VIRGINIA
WATER

SHEPPERTON

MOLESEY

HAMPTON
COURT

KINGSTON

MITCHAM

MORDEN

47   **48**   **49**   **50**   **51** NEW
MALDEN   **52** ST HELIER   **53** SELHURST

WALTON-ON-THAMES

SURBITON

CHERTSEY

ESHER

WORCESTER
PARK

HACKBRIDGE

ROSEHILL

WADDON

ADDLESTONE

HERSHAM

TOLWORTH

STONELEIGH

SUTTON

CARSHALTON

CROYDON

WEYBRIDGE

CLAYGATE

WALLINGTON

EWELL

CHESSINGTON

BELMONT

PURLEY

BYFLEET

OXSHOTT

61   **62** COBHAM   **63**   **64** EPSOM   **65**   **66**

BANSTEAD   COULSDON   KENLEY

EPSOM DOWNS

WOODMANSTERNE

WHYTELEAFE

EFFINGHAM
JUNCTION

CHIPSTEAD

LEATHERHEAD

BOOKHAM

TADWORTH   KINGSWOOD

69   **70**   **71**   **72**   **73**

MERSTHAM

REIGATE

REDHILL

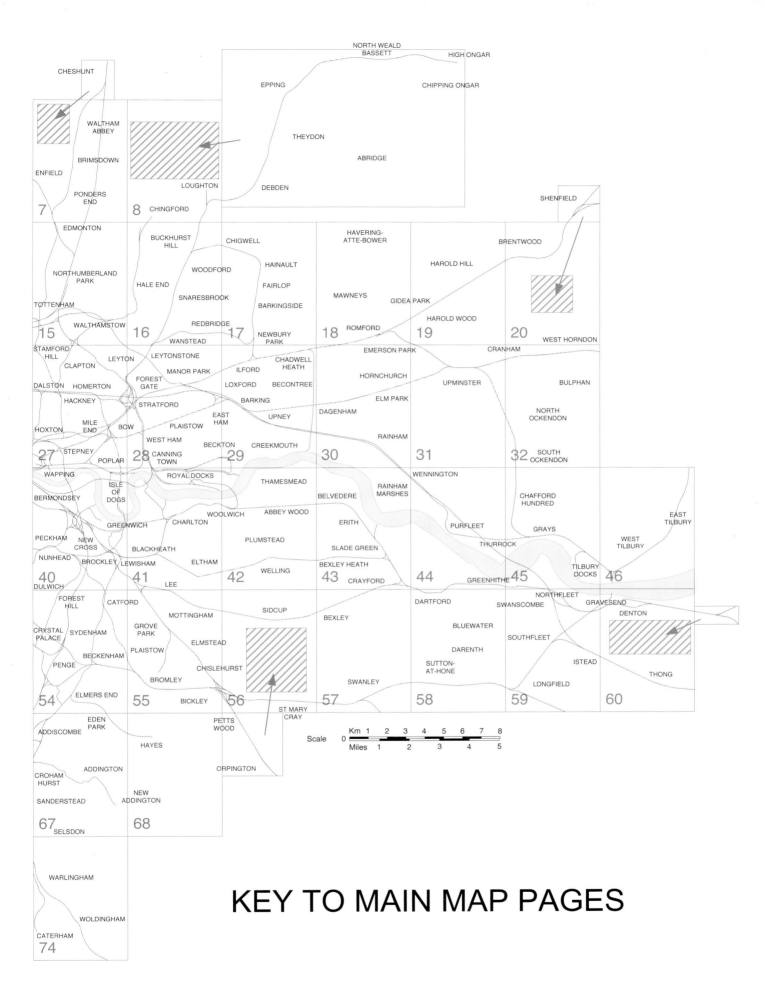

KEY TO MAIN MAP PAGES

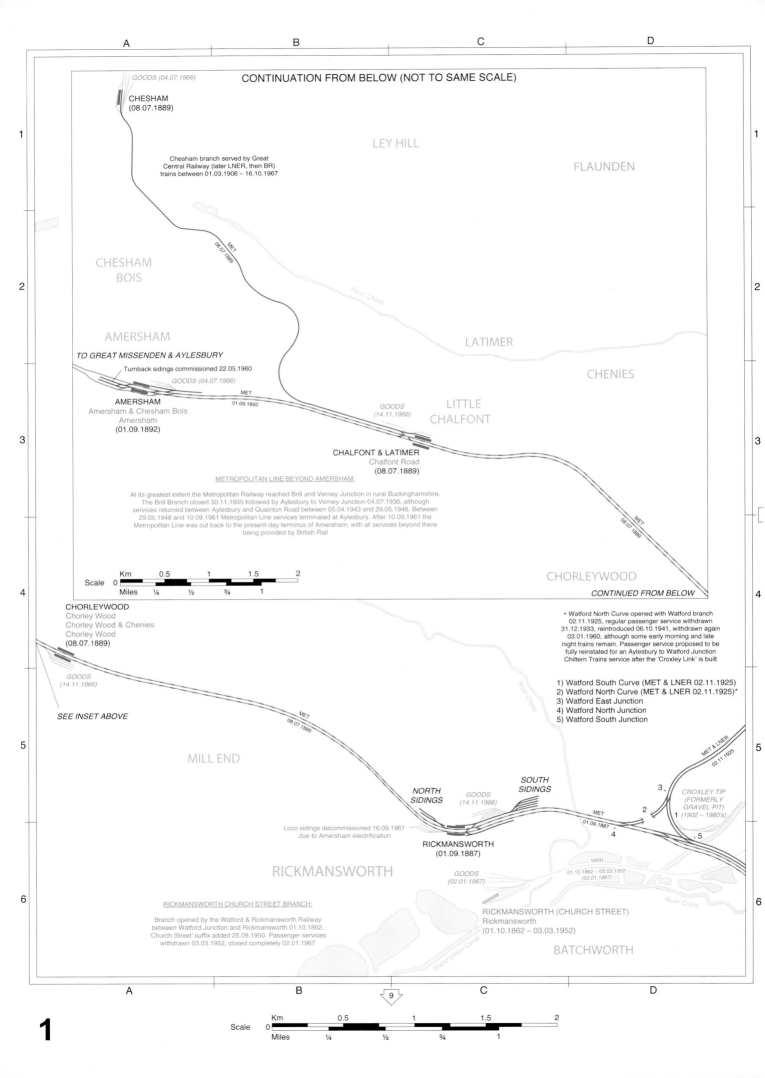

CONTINUATION FROM BELOW (NOT TO SAME SCALE)

GOODS (04.07.1966)

CHESHAM
(08.07.1889)

LEY HILL

FLAUNDEN

Chesham branch served by Great
Central Railway (later LNER, then BR)
trains between 01.03.1906 – 16.10.1967

CHESHAM
BOIS

MET
08.07.1889

River Chess

AMERSHAM

LATIMER

TO GREAT MISSENDEN & AYLESBURY

CHENIES

Turnback sidings commissioned 22.05.1960

GOODS (04.07.1966)

MET
01.09.1892

AMERSHAM
Amersham & Chesham Bois
Amersham
(01.09.1892)

GOODS
(14.11.1966)

LITTLE
CHALFONT

CHALFONT & LATIMER
Chalfont Road
(08.07.1889)

METROPOLITAN LINE BEYOND AMERSHAM:

At its greatest extent the Metropolitan Railway reached Brill and Verney Junction in rural Buckinghamshire.
The Brill Branch closed 30.11.1935 followed by Aylesbury to Verney Junction 04.07.1936, although
services returned between Aylesbury and Quainton Road between 05.04.1943 and 29.05.1948. Between
29.05.1948 and 10.09.1961 Metropolitan Line services terminated at Aylesbury. After 10.09.1961 the
Metropolitan Line was cut back to the present-day terminus of Amersham, with all services beyond there
being provided by British Rail

MET
08.07.1889

CHORLEYWOOD

Scale
Km   0   0.5   1   1.5   2
Miles   ¼   ½   ¾   1

CONTINUED FROM BELOW

CHORLEYWOOD
Chorley Wood
Chorley Wood & Chenies
Chorley Wood
(08.07.1889)

* Watford North Curve opened with Watford branch
02.11.1925, regular passenger service withdrawn
31.12.1933, reintroduced 06.10.1941, withdrawn again
03.01.1960, although some early morning and late
night trains remain. Passenger service proposed to be
fully reinstated for an Aylesbury to Watford Junction
Chiltern Trains service after the 'Croxley Link' is built

GOODS
(14.11.1966)

SEE INSET ABOVE

River Chess

1) Watford South Curve (MET & LNER 02.11.1925)
2) Watford North Curve (MET & LNER 02.11.1925)*
3) Watford East Junction
4) Watford North Junction
5) Watford South Junction

MET
08.07.1889

MET & LNER
02.11.1925

MILL END

NORTH
SIDINGS

SOUTH
SIDINGS

3

CROXLEY TIP
(FORMERLY
GRAVEL PIT)
(1902 – 1980's)

GOODS
(14.11.1966)

2

MET
01.09.1887

Loco sidings decommissioned 16.09.1961
due to Amersham electrification

4

RICKMANSWORTH
(01.09.1887)

5

RICKMANSWORTH

GOODS
(02.01.1967)

WRR

01.10.1862 – 03.03.1952
(02.01.1967)

River Colne

RICKMANSWORTH CHURCH STREET BRANCH:

Branch opened by the Watford & Rickmansworth Railway
between Watford Junction and Rickmansworth 01.10.1862.
'Church Street' suffix added 25.09.1950. Passenger services
withdrawn 03.03.1952, closed completely 02.01.1967

RICKMANSWORTH (CHURCH STREET)
Rickmansworth
(01.10.1862 – 03.03.1952)

BATCHWORTH

Grand Union Canal

9

1

Scale
Km   0   0.5   1   1.5   2
Miles   ¼   ½   ¾   1

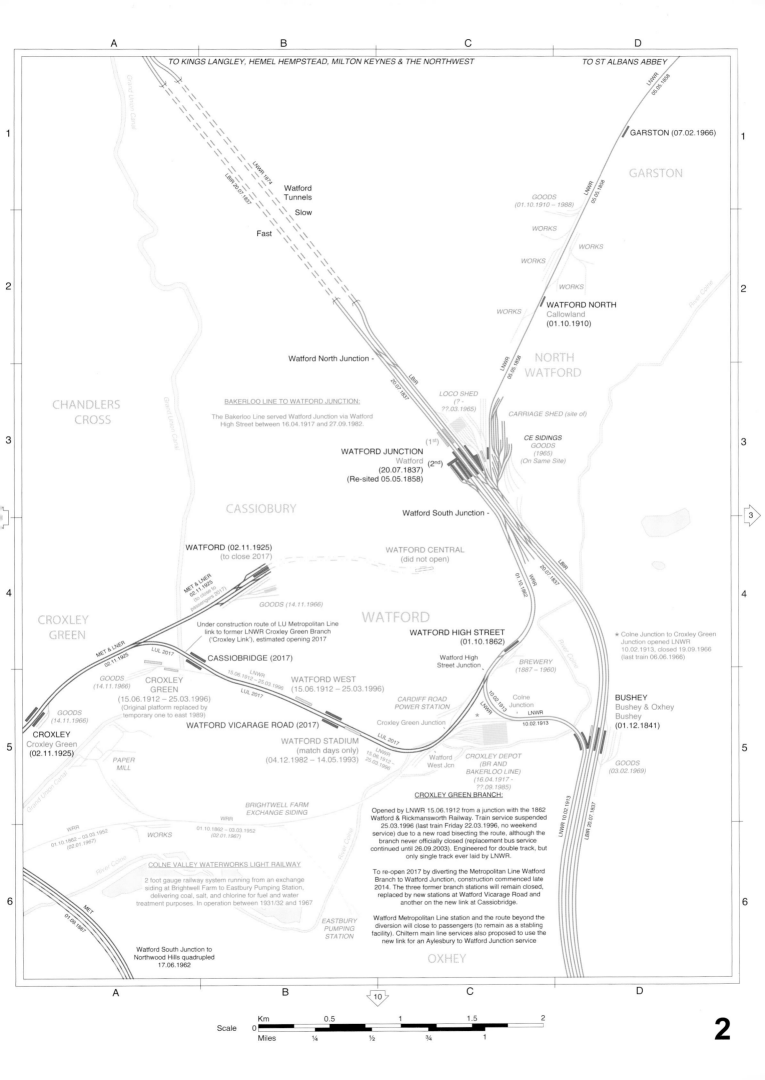

TO ST ALBANS, LUTON, AND THE MIDLANDS

09.09.1867 (13.07.1868)

MID

*GOODS
(initially named 'ALDENHAM'
until passenger station opened)
(pre-13.07.1868 – 25.03.1968)*

RADLETT (13.07.1868)

RADLETT

- Radlett Junction

09.09.1867 (13.07.1868)

MID

ALDENHAM

From below - LAYOUT OF BUSHEY HEATH DEPOT AS PROPOSED (1937)

BUSHEY
HEATH

ELSTREE SOUTH

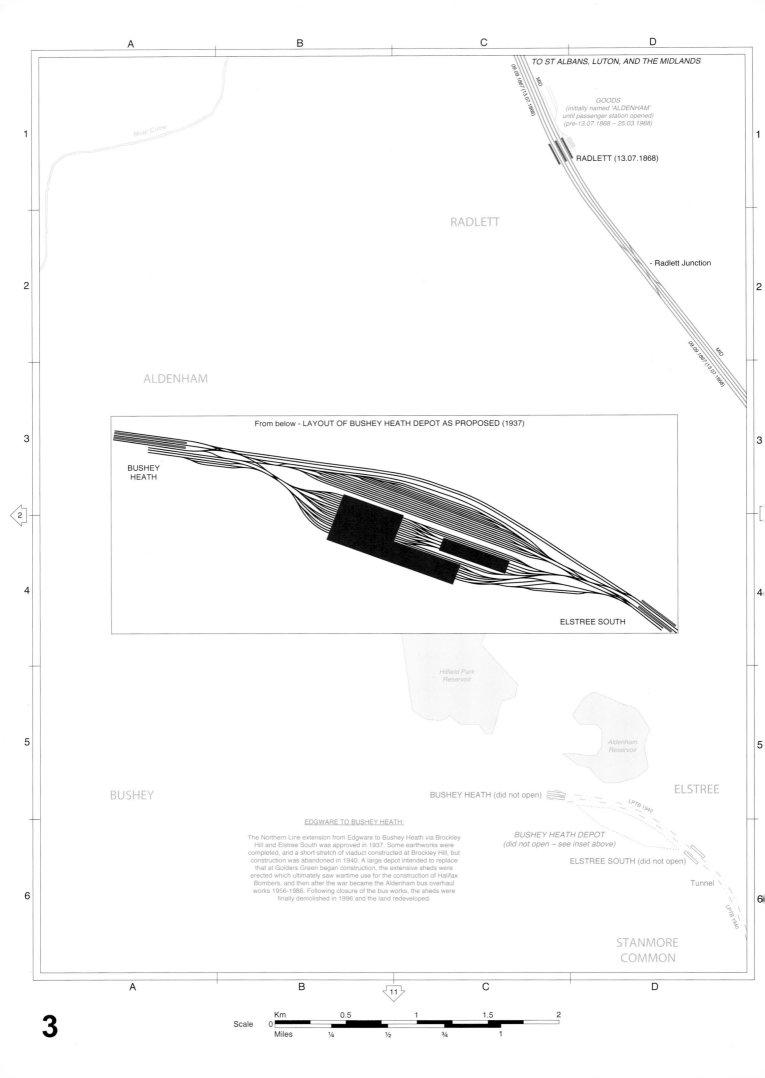

*Hilfield Park
Reservoir*

*Aldenham
Reservoir*

BUSHEY

BUSHEY HEATH (did not open)

LPTB 1940

ELSTREE

*BUSHEY HEATH DEPOT
(did not open – see inset above)*

ELSTREE SOUTH (did not open)

Tunnel

LPTB 1940

STANMORE
COMMON

EDGWARE TO BUSHEY HEATH:

The Northern Line extension from Edgware to Bushey Heath via Brockley
Hill and Elstree South was approved in 1937. Some earthworks were
completed, and a short stretch of viaduct constructed at Brockley Hill, but
construction was abandoned in 1940. A large depot intended to replace
that at Golders Green began construction, the extensive sheds were
erected which ultimately saw wartime use for the construction of Halifax
Bombers, and then after the war became the Aldenham bus overhaul
works 1956-1986. Following closure of the bus works, the sheds were
finally demolished in 1996 and the land redeveloped.

3

Scale

Km 0   0.5   1   1.5   2

Miles   ¼   ½   ¾   1

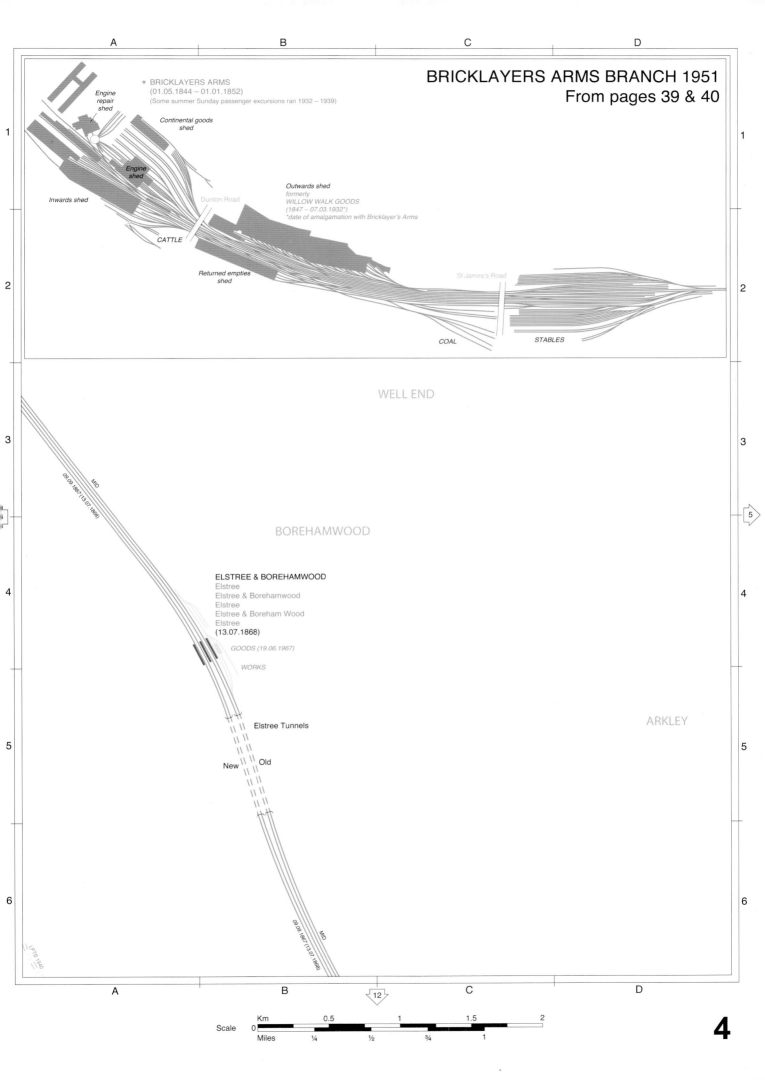

Engine repair shed

Engine shed

Continental goods shed

★ BRICKLAYERS ARMS
(01.05.1844 – 01.01.1852)
(Some summer Sunday passenger excursions ran 1932 – 1939)

Inwards shed

Dunton Road

CATTLE

Outwards shed
formerly
WILLOW WALK GOODS
(1847 – 07.03.1932*)
*date of amalgamation with Bricklayer's Arms

Returned empties shed

St James's Road

COAL

STABLES

WELL END

09.09.1867 (13.07.1868)

MID

BOREHAMWOOD

ELSTREE & BOREHAMWOOD
Elstree
Elstree & Borehamwood
Elstree
Elstree & Boreham Wood
Elstree
(13.07.1868)

GOODS (19.06.1967)

WORKS

ARKLEY

Elstree Tunnels

New   Old

09.09.1867 (13.07.1868)

MID

LPTB 1940

Scale
Km
0   0.5   1   1.5   2
Miles
¼   ½   ¾   1

4

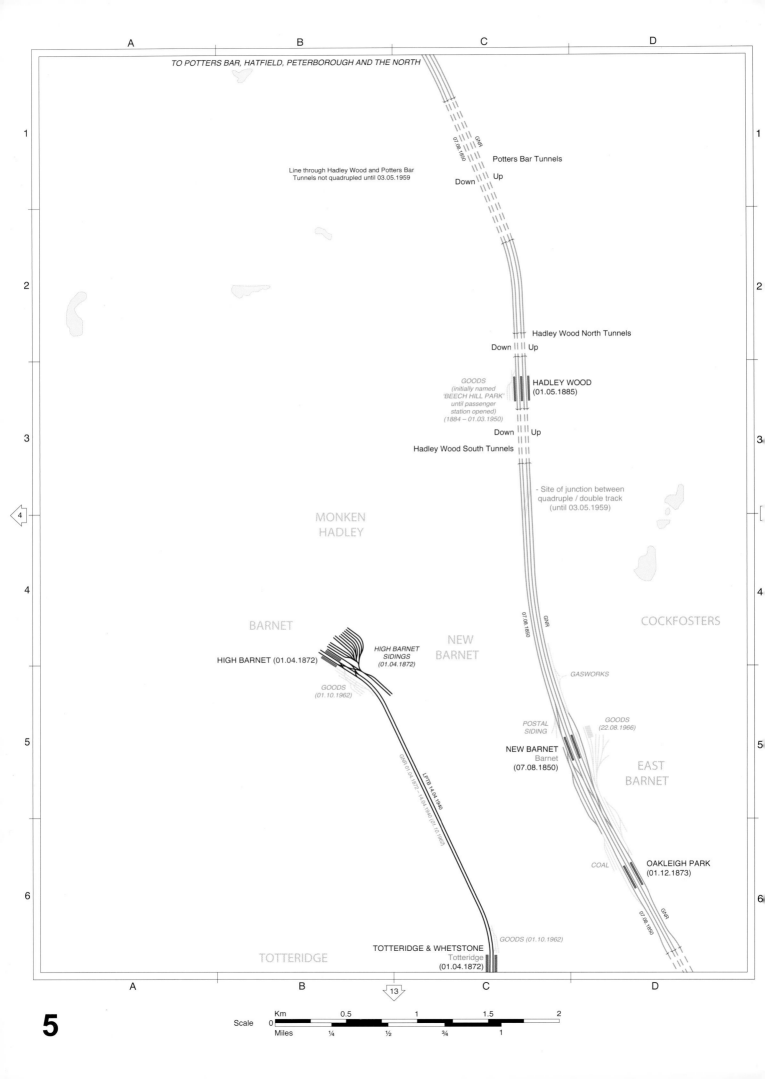

TO POTTERS BAR, HATFIELD, PETERBOROUGH AND THE NORTH

Line through Hadley Wood and Potters Bar
Tunnels not quadrupled until 03.05.1959

07.08.1850
GNR

Potters Bar Tunnels
Down   Up

Hadley Wood North Tunnels
Down   Up

GOODS
(initially named
'BEECH HILL PARK'
until passenger
station opened)
(1884 – 01.03.1950)

HADLEY WOOD
(01.05.1885)

Down   Up

Hadley Wood South Tunnels

- Site of junction between
quadruple / double track
(until 03.05.1959)

MONKEN
HADLEY

BARNET

COCKFOSTERS

NEW
BARNET

07.08.1850
GNR

HIGH BARNET (01.04.1872)

HIGH BARNET
SIDINGS
(01.04.1872)

GASWORKS

GOODS
(01.10.1962)

POSTAL
SIDING

GOODS
(22.08.1966)

NEW BARNET
Barnet
(07.08.1850)

EAST
BARNET

GNR 01.04.1872 – 14.04.1940 / 01.10.1962
LPTB 14.04.1940

COAL

OAKLEIGH PARK
(01.12.1873)

GOODS (01.10.1962)

07.08.1850
GNR

TOTTERIDGE

TOTTERIDGE & WHETSTONE
Totteridge
(01.04.1872)

13

Scale
Km
0   0.5   1   1.5   2
Miles
¼   ½   ¾   1

5

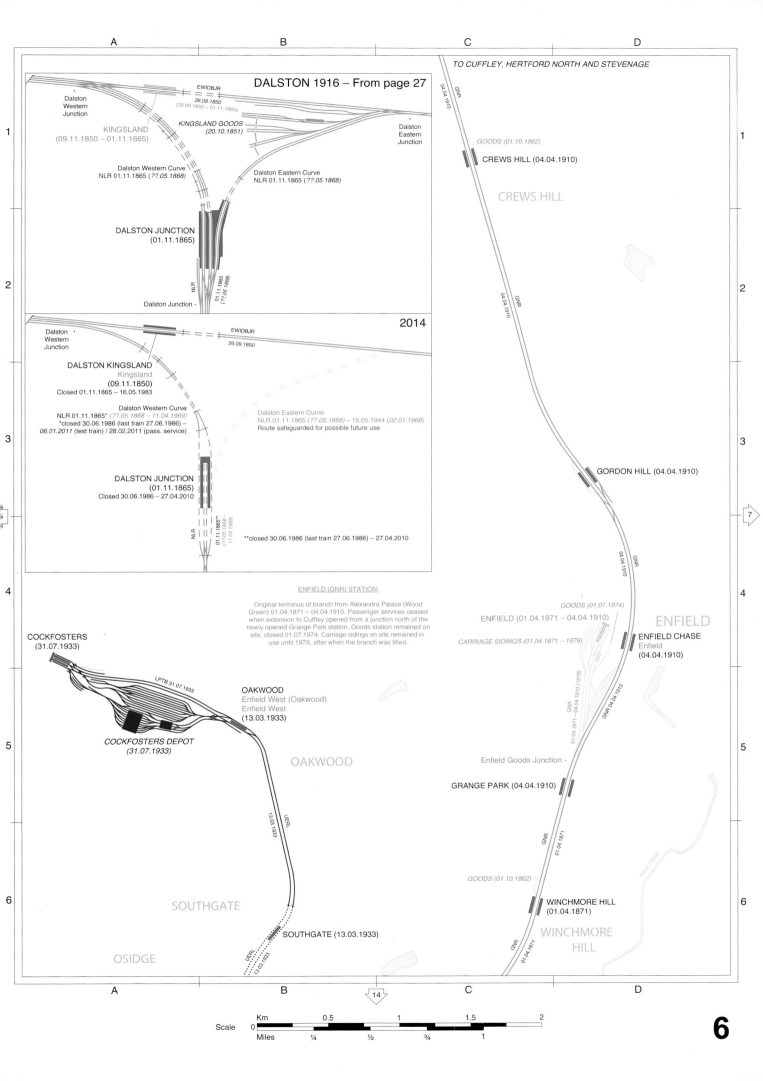

DALSTON 1916 – From page 27

Dalston Western Junction

KINGSLAND
(09.11.1850 – 01.11.1865)

EWIDBJR
26.09.1850
(26.09.1850 – 01.11.1865)

KINGSLAND GOODS
(20.10.1851)

Dalston Eastern Junction

Dalston Western Curve
NLR 01.11.1865 (??.05.1868)

Dalston Eastern Curve
NLR 01.11.1865 (??.05.1868)

DALSTON JUNCTION
(01.11.1865)

NLR

01.11.1865
(??.05.1868)

Dalston Junction -

2014

Dalston Western Junction

EWIDBJR
26.09.1850

DALSTON KINGSLAND
Kingsland
(09.11.1850)
Closed 01.11.1865 – 16.05.1983

Dalston Western Curve
NLR 01.11.1865* (??.05.1868 – 11.04.1969)
*closed 30.06.1986 (last train 27.06.1986) –
06.01.2011 (test train) / 28.02.2011 (pass. service)

Dalston Eastern Curve
NLR 01.11.1865 (??.05.1868) – 15.05.1944 (02.01.1966)
Route safeguarded for possible future use

DALSTON JUNCTION
(01.11.1865)
Closed 30.06.1986 – 27.04.2010

NLR

01.11.1865**
(??.05.1868 –
11.04.1969)

**closed 30.06.1986 (last train 27.06.1986) – 27.04.2010

TO CUFFLEY, HERTFORD NORTH AND STEVENAGE

04.04.1910

GNR

GOODS (01.10.1962)
CREWS HILL (04.04.1910)

CREWS HILL

04.04.1910
GNR

GORDON HILL (04.04.1910)

04.04.1910
GNR

ENFIELD (GNR) STATION:

Original terminus of branch from Alexandra Palace (Wood
Green) 01.04.1871 – 04.04.1910. Passenger services ceased
when extension to Cuffley opened from a junction north of the
newly opened Grange Park station. Goods station remained on
site, closed 01.07.1974. Carriage sidings on site remained in
use until 1979, after when the branch was lifted.

GOODS (01.07.1974)
ENFIELD (01.04.1871 – 04.04.1910)

CARRIAGE SIDINGS (01.04.1871 – 1979)

ENFIELD

ENFIELD CHASE
Enfield
(04.04.1910)

COCKFOSTERS
(31.07.1933)

LPTB 31.07.1933

OAKWOOD
Enfield West (Oakwood)
Enfield West
(13.03.1933)

COCKFOSTERS DEPOT
(31.07.1933)

OAKWOOD

GNR 01.04.1871 – 04.04.1910 (1979)

GNR 04.04.1910

Enfield Goods Junction -

GRANGE PARK (04.04.1910)

13.03.1933

UERL

SOUTHGATE

01.04.1871
GNR

GOODS (01.10.1962)

WINCHMORE HILL
(01.04.1871)

WINCHMORE HILL

OSIDGE

UERL
13.03.1933

SOUTHGATE (13.03.1933)

GNR
01.04.1871

14

7

Scale

Km
0   0.5   1   1.5   2

Miles
¼   ½   ¾   1

6

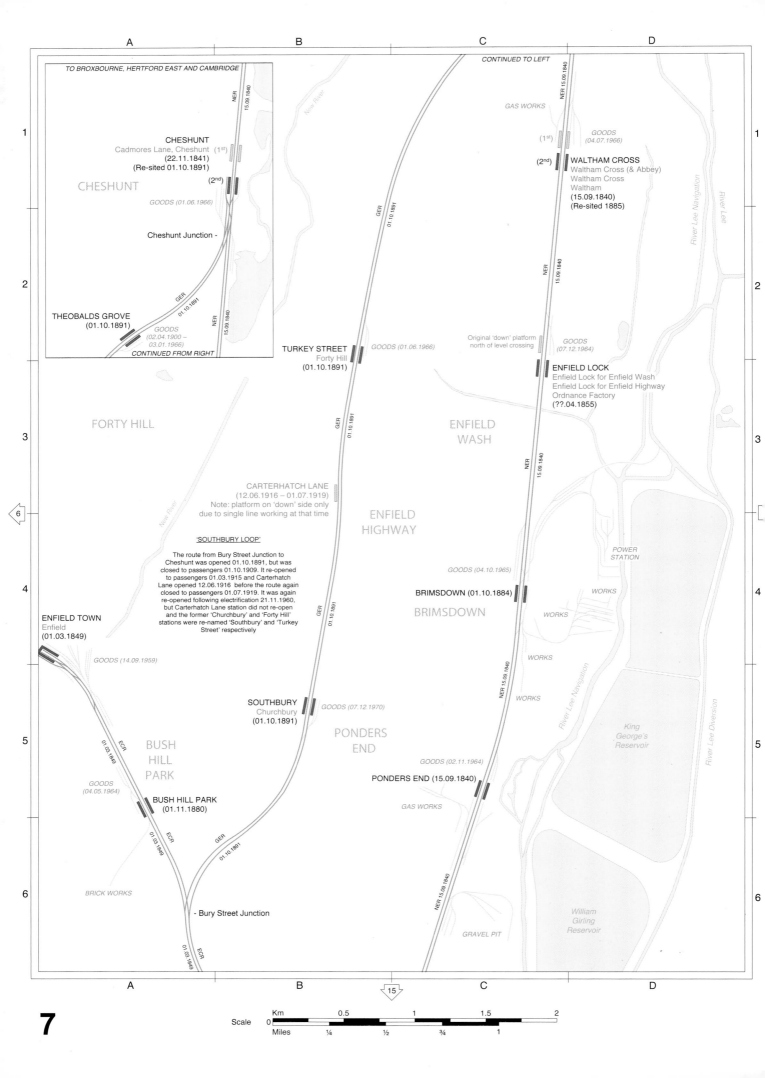

TO BROXBOURNE, HERTFORD EAST AND CAMBRIDGE

CONTINUED TO LEFT

NER 15.09.1840

GAS WORKS

GOODS
(04.07.1966)

(1st)

CHESHUNT
Cadmores Lane, Cheshunt (1st)
(22.11.1841)
(Re-sited 01.10.1891)

(2nd)   WALTHAM CROSS
Waltham Cross (& Abbey)
Waltham Cross
Waltham
(15.09.1840)
(Re-sited 1885)

CHESHUNT

(2nd)

GOODS (01.06.1966)

Cheshunt Junction -

NER 15.09.1840

THEOBALDS GROVE
(01.10.1891)

GER
01.10.1891

NER
15.09.1840

GOODS
(02.04.1900 –
03.01.1966)

CONTINUED FROM RIGHT

Original 'down' platform
north of level crossing

GOODS
(07.12.1964)

ENFIELD LOCK
Enfield Lock for Enfield Wash
Enfield Lock for Enfield Highway
Ordnance Factory
(??.04.1855)

TURKEY STREET
Forty Hill
(01.10.1891)

GOODS (01.06.1966)

FORTY HILL

GER
01.10.1891

ENFIELD
WASH

NER
15.09.1840

CARTERHATCH LANE
(12.06.1916 – 01.07.1919)
Note: platform on 'down' side only
due to single line working at that time

ENFIELD
HIGHWAY

New River

6

'SOUTHBURY LOOP'

The route from Bury Street Junction to
Cheshunt was opened 01.10.1891, but was
closed to passengers 01.10.1909. It re-opened
to passengers 01.03.1915 and Carterhatch
Lane opened 12.06.1916 before the route again
closed to passengers 01.07.1919. It was again
re-opened following electrification 21.11.1960,
but Carterhatch Lane station did not re-open
and the former 'Churchbury' and 'Forty Hill'
stations were re-named 'Southbury' and 'Turkey
Street' respectively

POWER
STATION

ENFIELD TOWN
Enfield
(01.03.1849)

GOODS (14.09.1959)

GER
01.10.1891

GOODS (04.10.1965)

BRIMSDOWN (01.10.1884)

BRIMSDOWN

WORKS

WORKS

WORKS

ECR
01.03.1849

BUSH
HILL
PARK

NER 15.09.1840

WORKS

River Lee Navigation

River Lee Diversion

SOUTHBURY
Churchbury
(01.10.1891)

GOODS (07.12.1970)

King
George's
Reservoir

PONDERS
END

GOODS
(04.05.1964)

BUSH HILL PARK
(01.11.1880)

GER
01.10.1891

GOODS (02.11.1964)

PONDERS END (15.09.1840)

GAS WORKS

ECR
01.03.1849

NER 15.09.1840

BRICK WORKS

- Bury Street Junction

William
Girling
Reservoir

GRAVEL PIT

ECR
01.03.1849

15

7

Scale

Km
0   0.5   1   1.5   2

Miles   ¼   ½   ¾   1

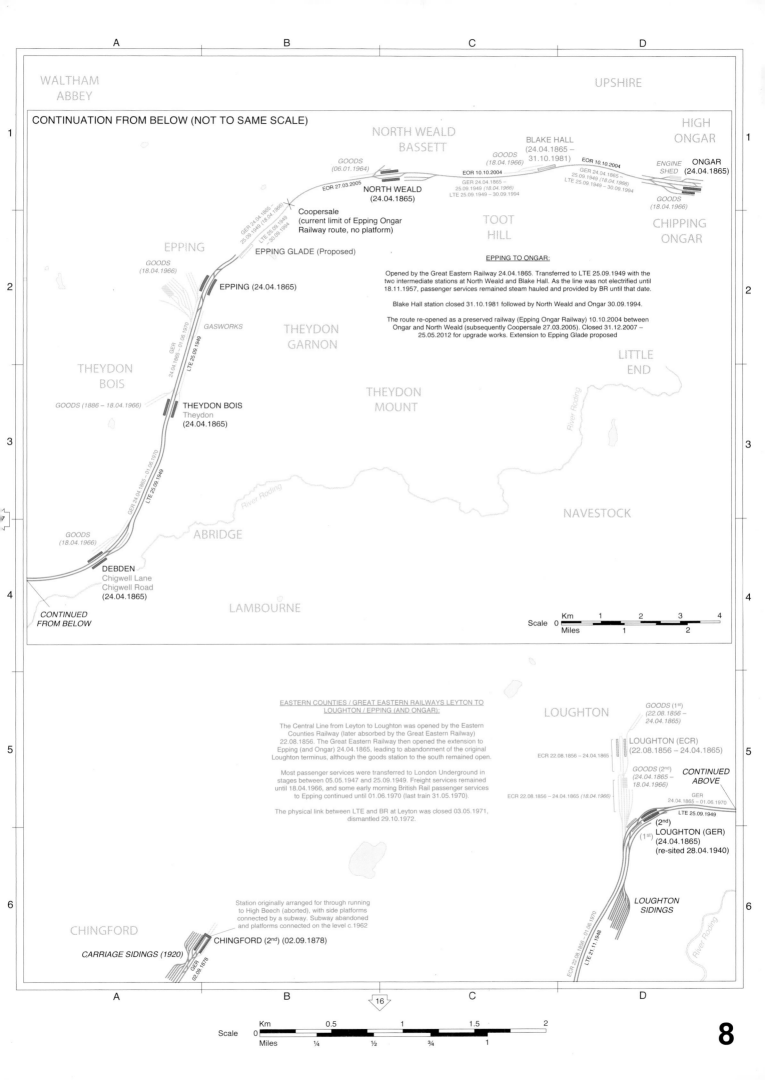

WALTHAM
ABBEY

UPSHIRE

HIGH
ONGAR

A   B   C   D

1

CONTINUATION FROM BELOW (NOT TO SAME SCALE)

NORTH WEALD
BASSETT

BLAKE HALL
(24.04.1865 –
31.10.1981)

*GOODS
(06.01.1964)*

*GOODS
(18.04.1966)*

EOR 10.10.2004

*ENGINE
SHED*

ONGAR
(24.04.1865)

EOR 10.10.2004

EOR 27.03.2005

GER 24.04.1865 –
25.09.1949 *(18.04.1966)*
LTE 25.09.1949 – 30.09.1994

GER 24.04.1865 –
25.09.1949 *(18.04.1966)*
LTE 25.09.1949 – 30.09.1994

NORTH WEALD
(24.04.1865)

Coopersale
(current limit of Epping Ongar
Railway route, no platform)

TOOT
HILL

*GOODS
(18.04.1966)*

CHIPPING
ONGAR

EPPING

EPPING GLADE (Proposed)

EPPING TO ONGAR:

*GOODS
(18.04.1966)*

EPPING (24.04.1865)

Opened by the Great Eastern Railway 24.04.1865. Transferred to LTE 25.09.1949 with the
two intermediate stations at North Weald and Blake Hall. As the line was not electrified until
18.11.1957, passenger services remained steam hauled and provided by BR until that date.

GASWORKS

THEYDON
GARNON

Blake Hall station closed 31.10.1981 followed by North Weald and Ongar 30.09.1994.

LITTLE
END

The route re-opened as a preserved railway (Epping Ongar Railway) 10.10.2004 between
Ongar and North Weald (subsequently Coopersale 27.03.2005). Closed 31.12.2007 –
25.05.2012 for upgrade works. Extension to Epping Glade proposed

THEYDON
BOIS

THEYDON
MOUNT

GOODS (1886 – 18.04.1966)

THEYDON BOIS
Theydon
(24.04.1865)

3

NAVESTOCK

River Roding

ABRIDGE

*GOODS
(18.04.1966)*

DEBDEN
Chigwell Lane
Chigwell Road
(24.04.1865)

*CONTINUED
FROM BELOW*

LAMBOURNE

Km   1   2   3   4
Scale 0
Miles   1   2

4

EASTERN COUNTIES / GREAT EASTERN RAILWAYS LEYTON TO
LOUGHTON / EPPING (AND ONGAR):

LOUGHTON

*GOODS (1st)
(22.08.1856 –
24.04.1865)*

The Central Line from Leyton to Loughton was opened by the Eastern
Counties Railway (later absorbed by the Great Eastern Railway)
22.08.1856. The Great Eastern Railway then opened the extension to
Epping (and Ongar) 24.04.1865, leading to abandonment of the original
Loughton terminus, although the goods station to the south remained open.

ECR 22.08.1856 – 24.04.1865

LOUGHTON (ECR)
(22.08.1856 – 24.04.1865)

*GOODS (2nd)
(24.04.1865 –
18.04.1966)*

*CONTINUED
ABOVE*

Most passenger services were transferred to London Underground in
stages between 05.05.1947 and 25.09.1949. Freight services remained
until 18.04.1966, and some early morning British Rail passenger services
to Epping continued until 01.06.1970 (last train 31.05.1970).

ECR 22.08.1856 – 24.04.1865 *(18.04.1966)*

GER
24.04.1865 – 01.06.1970

LTE 25.09.1949

The physical link between LTE and BR at Leyton was closed 03.05.1971,
dismantled 29.10.1972.

(2nd)
LOUGHTON (GER)
(1st) (24.04.1865)
(re-sited 28.04.1940)

5

*LOUGHTON
SIDINGS*

6

CHINGFORD

Station originally arranged for through running
to High Beech (aborted), with side platforms
connected by a subway. Subway abandoned
and platforms connected on the level c.1962

CARRIAGE SIDINGS (1920)

CHINGFORD (2nd) (02.09.1878)

A   B   16   C   D

Km   0.5   1   1.5   2
Scale 0
Miles   ¼   ½   ¾   1

8

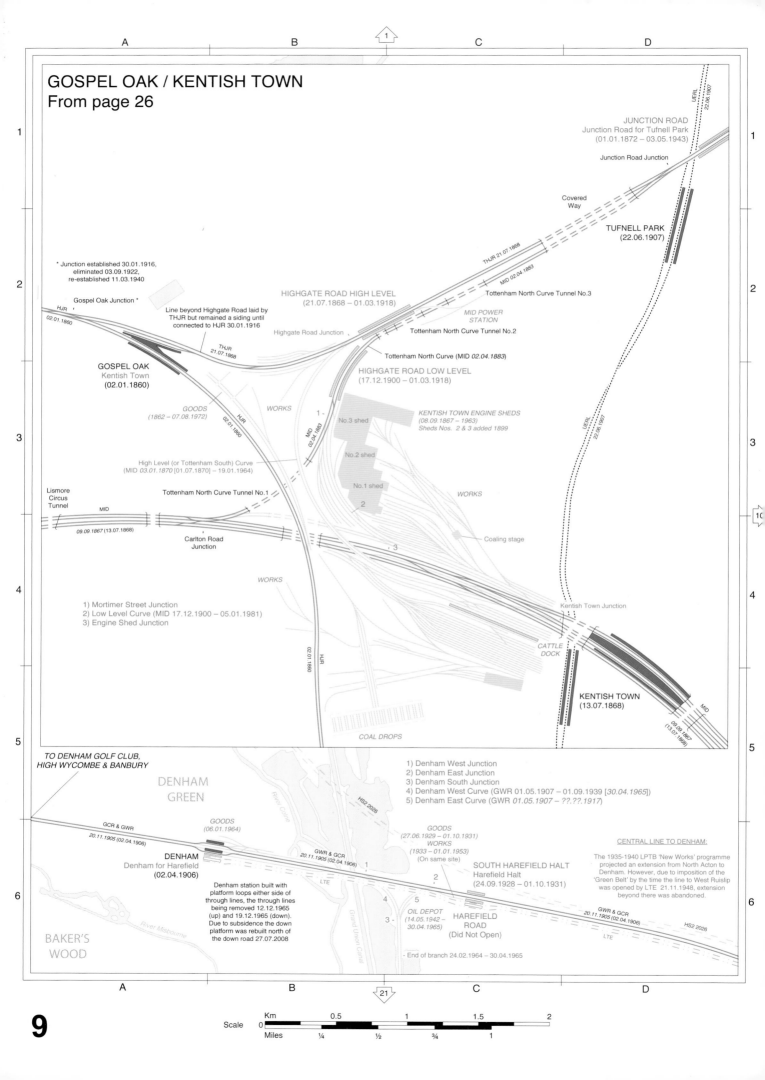

GOSPEL OAK / KENTISH TOWN
From page 26

From page 26

JUNCTION ROAD
Junction Road for Tufnell Park
(01.01.1872 – 03.05.1943)

Junction Road Junction

Covered
Way

TUFNELL PARK
(22.06.1907)

UERL
22.06.1907

THJR 21.07.1868

MID 02.04.1883

Tottenham North Curve Tunnel No.3

* Junction established 30.01.1916,
eliminated 03.09.1922,
re-established 11.03.1940

Gospel Oak Junction *

HIGHGATE ROAD HIGH LEVEL
(21.07.1868 – 01.03.1918)

Line beyond Highgate Road laid by
THJR but remained a siding until
connected to HJR 30.01.1916

MID POWER
STATION

HJR
02.01.1860

THJR
21.07.1868

Highgate Road Junction

Tottenham North Curve Tunnel No.2

Tottenham North Curve (MID 02.04.1883)

GOSPEL OAK
Kentish Town
(02.01.1860)

HIGHGATE ROAD LOW LEVEL
(17.12.1900 – 01.03.1918)

GOODS
(1862 – 07.08.1972)

WORKS

HJR
02.01.1860

MID
02.04.1883

KENTISH TOWN ENGINE SHEDS
(08.09.1867 – 1963)
Sheds Nos. 2 & 3 added 1899

No.3 shed

UERL
22.06.1907

High Level (or Tottenham South) Curve
(MID 03.01.1870 [01.07.1870] – 19.01.1964)

No.2 shed

Lismore
Circus
Tunnel

MID

Tottenham North Curve Tunnel No.1

No.1 shed

WORKS

09.09.1867 (13.07.1868)

Carlton Road
Junction

Coaling stage

1) Mortimer Street Junction
2) Low Level Curve (MID 17.12.1900 – 05.01.1981)
3) Engine Shed Junction

WORKS

Kentish Town Junction

02.01.1860

HJR

CATTLE
DOCK

KENTISH TOWN
(13.07.1868)

MID

09.09.1867
(13.07.1868)

COAL DROPS

**TO DENHAM GOLF CLUB,
HIGH WYCOMBE & BANBURY**

1) Denham West Junction
2) Denham East Junction
3) Denham South Junction
4) Denham West Curve (GWR 01.05.1907 – 01.09.1939 [30.04.1965])
5) Denham East Curve (GWR 01.05.1907 – ??.??.1917)

DENHAM
GREEN

HS2 2026

GCR & GWR
20.11.1905 (02.04.1906)

GOODS
(06.01.1964)

GWR & GCR
20.11.1905 (02.04.1906)

GOODS
(27.06.1929 – 01.10.1931)
WORKS
(1933 – 01.01.1953)
(On same site)

CENTRAL LINE TO DENHAM:

DENHAM
Denham for Harefield
(02.04.1906)

Denham station built with
platform loops either side of
through lines, the through lines
being removed 12.12.1965
(up) and 19.12.1965 (down).
Due to subsidence the down
platform was rebuilt north of
the down road 27.07.2008

LTE

SOUTH HAREFIELD HALT
Harefield Halt
(24.09.1928 – 01.10.1931)

The 1935-1940 LPTB 'New Works'
programme projected an extension from North Acton to
Denham. However, due to imposition of the
'Green Belt' by the time the line to West Ruislip
was opened by LTE 21.11.1948, extension
beyond there was abandoned.

BAKER'S
WOOD

River Misbourne

River Colne

Grand Union Canal

OIL DEPOT
(14.05.1942 –
30.04.1965)

HAREFIELD
ROAD
(Did Not Open)

GWR & GCR
20.11.1905 (02.04.1906)

LTE

HS2 2026

End of branch 24.02.1964 – 30.04.1965

Scale
Km 0 ... 0.5 ... 1 ... 1.5 ... 2
Miles ¼ ½ ¾ 1

9

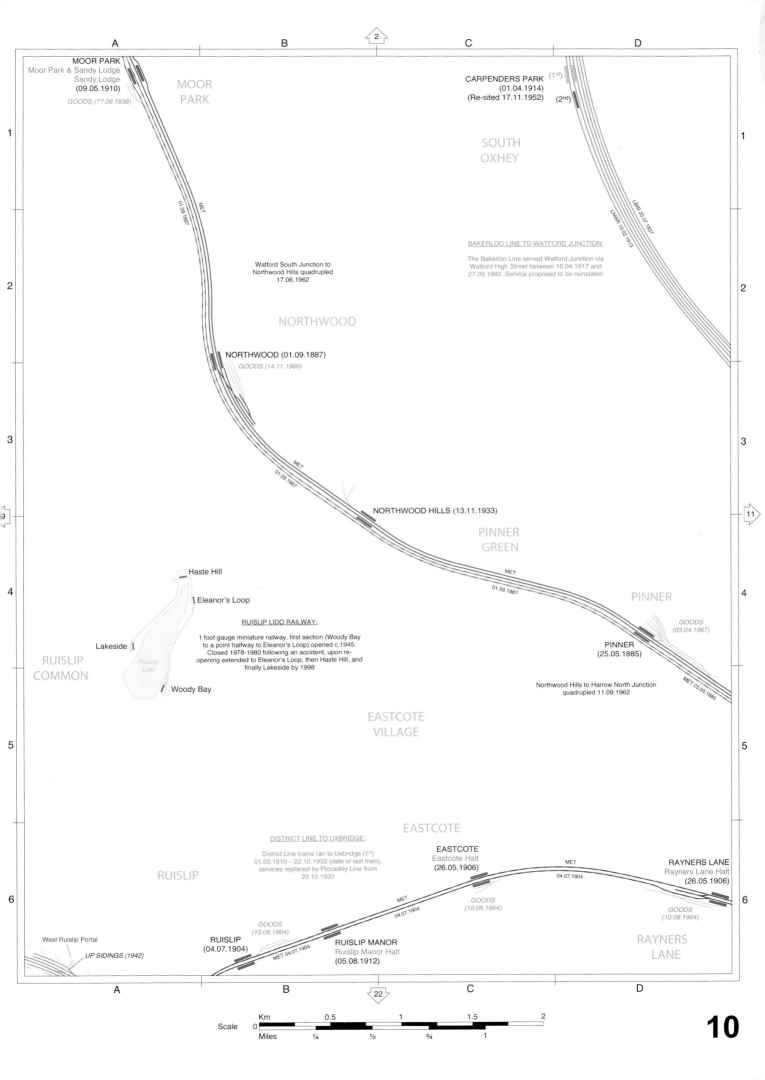

MOOR PARK
Moor Park & Sandy Lodge
Sandy Lodge
(09.05.1910)

GOODS (??.06.1938)

MOOR
PARK

CARPENDERS PARK (1ˢᵗ)
(01.04.1914)
(Re-sited 17.11.1952) (2ⁿᵈ)

SOUTH
OXHEY

01.09.1887
MET

LBIR 20.07.1837

LNWR 10.02.1913

Watford South Junction to
Northwood Hills quadrupled
17.06.1962

BAKERLOO LINE TO WATFORD JUNCTION:

The Bakerloo Line served Watford Junction via
Watford High Street between 16.04.1917 and
27.09.1982. Service proposed to be reinstated

NORTHWOOD

NORTHWOOD (01.09.1887)

GOODS (14.11.1966)

MET
01.09.1887

NORTHWOOD HILLS (13.11.1933)

PINNER
GREEN

MET
01.09.1887

PINNER

*GOODS
(03.04.1967)*

Haste Hill

Eleanor's Loop

RUISLIP LIDO RAILWAY:

1 foot gauge miniature railway, first section (Woody Bay
to a point halfway to Eleanor's Loop) opened c.1945.
Closed 1978-1980 following an accident, upon re-
opening extended to Eleanor's Loop, then Haste Hill, and
finally Lakeside by 1998

Lakeside

*Ruislip
Lido*

RUISLIP
COMMON

Woody Bay

PINNER
(25.05.1885)

MET 25.05.1885

Northwood Hills to Harrow North Junction
quadrupled 11.09.1962

EASTCOTE
VILLAGE

EASTCOTE

DISTRICT LINE TO UXBRIDGE:

District Line trains ran to Uxbridge (1ˢᵗ)
01.03.1910 – 22.10.1933 (date of last train),
services replaced by Piccadilly Line from
23.10.1933

RUISLIP

EASTCOTE
Eastcote Halt
(26.05.1906)

MET
04.07.1904

*GOODS
(10.08.1964)*

MET

RAYNERS LANE
Rayners Lane Halt
(26.05.1906)

*GOODS
(10.08.1964)*

MET
04.07.1904

*GOODS
(10.08.1964)*

West Ruislip Portal

UP SIDINGS (1942)

RUISLIP
(04.07.1904)

MET 04.07.1904

RUISLIP MANOR
Ruislip Manor Halt
(05.08.1912)

RAYNERS
LANE

Scale

Km 0   0.5   1   1.5   2

Miles ¼   ½   ¾   1

10

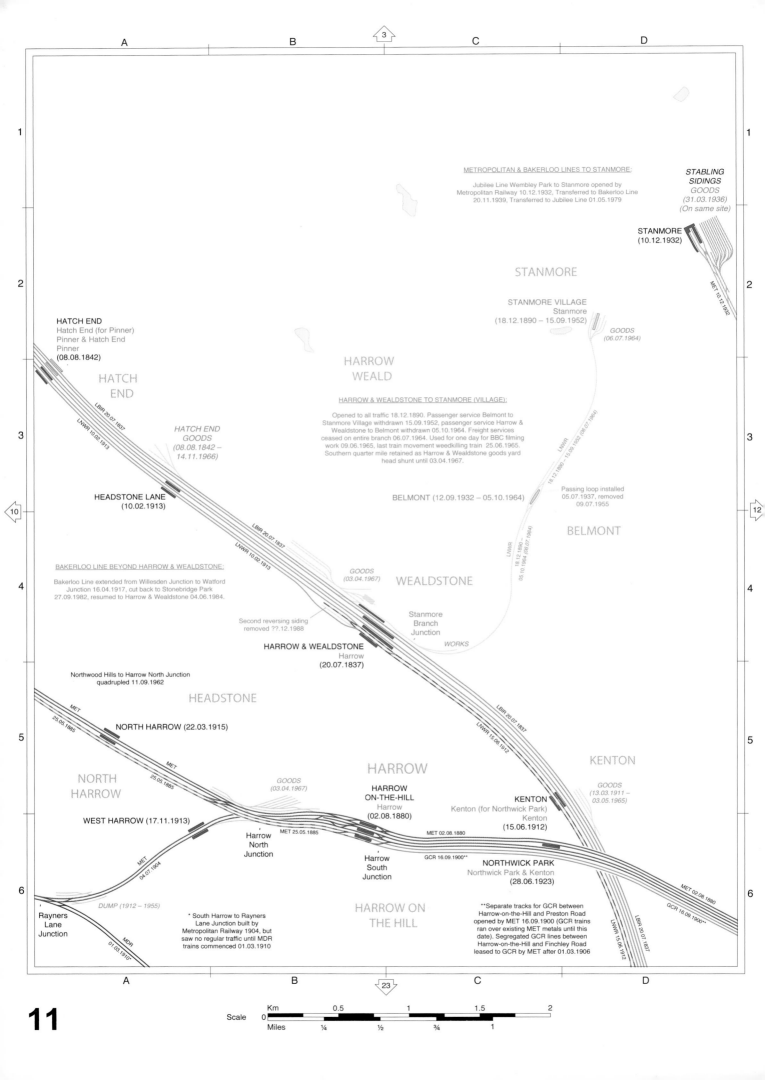

METROPOLITAN & BAKERLOO LINES TO STANMORE:

Jubilee Line Wembley Park to Stanmore opened by
Metropolitan Railway 10.12.1932, Transferred to Bakerloo Line
20.11.1939, Transferred to Jubilee Line 01.05.1979

*STABLING
SIDINGS
GOODS
(31.03.1936)
(On same site)*

STANMORE
(10.12.1932)

MET 10.12.1932

STANMORE

STANMORE VILLAGE
Stanmore
(18.12.1890 – 15.09.1952)

*GOODS
(06.07.1964)*

HATCH END
Hatch End (for Pinner)
Pinner & Hatch End
Pinner
(08.08.1842)

HATCH
END

HARROW
WEALD

HARROW & WEALDSTONE TO STANMORE (VILLAGE):

Opened to all traffic 18.12.1890. Passenger service Belmont to
Stanmore Village withdrawn 15.09.1952, passenger service Harrow &
Wealdstone to Belmont withdrawn 05.10.1964. Freight services
ceased on entire branch 06.07.1964. Used for one day for BBC filming
work 09.06.1965, last train movement weedkilling train 25.06.1965.
Southern quarter mile retained as Harrow & Wealdstone goods yard
head shunt until 03.04.1967.

LBIR 20.07.1837

LNWR 10.02.1913

*HATCH END
GOODS
(08.08.1842 –
14.11.1966)*

HEADSTONE LANE
(10.02.1913)

BELMONT (12.09.1932 – 05.10.1964)

Passing loop installed
05.07.1937, removed
09.07.1955

BELMONT

LNWR 18.12.1890 – 15.09.1952 (06.07.1964)
LNWR 18.12.1890 – 05.10.1964 (26.07.1964)

LBIR 20.07.1837

LNWR 10.02.1913

BAKERLOO LINE BEYOND HARROW & WEALDSTONE:

Bakerloo Line extended from Willesden Junction to Watford
Junction 16.04.1917, cut back to Stonebridge Park
27.09.1982, resumed to Harrow & Wealdstone 04.06.1984.

*GOODS
(03.04.1967)*

WEALDSTONE

Stanmore
Branch
Junction

WORKS

Second reversing siding
removed ??.12.1988

HARROW & WEALDSTONE
Harrow
(20.07.1837)

Northwood Hills to Harrow North Junction
quadrupled 11.09.1962

HEADSTONE

MET 25.05.1885

NORTH HARROW (22.03.1915)

MET 25.05.1885

KENTON

LBIR 20.07.1837

LNWR 15.06.1912

NORTH
HARROW

HARROW

*GOODS
(03.04.1967)*

HARROW
ON-THE-HILL
Harrow
(02.08.1880)

KENTON
Kenton (for Northwick Park)
Kenton
(15.06.1912)

*GOODS
(13.03.1911 –
03.05.1965)*

WEST HARROW (17.11.1913)

Harrow
North
Junction

MET 25.05.1885

MET 02.08.1880

Harrow
South
Junction

GCR 16.09.1900**

NORTHWICK PARK
Northwick Park & Kenton
(28.06.1923)

MET 02.08.1880

GCR 16.09.1900**

Rayners
Lane
Junction

MET
04.07.1904

DUMP (1912 – 1955)

* South Harrow to Rayners
Lane Junction built by
Metropolitan Railway 1904, but
saw no regular traffic until MDR
trains commenced 01.03.1910

HARROW ON
THE HILL

**Separate tracks for GCR between
Harrow-on-the-Hill and Preston Road
opened by MET 16.09.1900 (GCR trains
ran over existing MET metals until this
date). Segregated GCR lines between
Harrow-on-the-Hill and Finchley Road
leased to GCR by MET after 01.03.1906

MDR
01.03.1910*

LNWR 15.06.1912

LBIR 20.07.1837

Scale
Km 0   0.5   1   1.5   2
Miles   ¼   ½   ¾   1

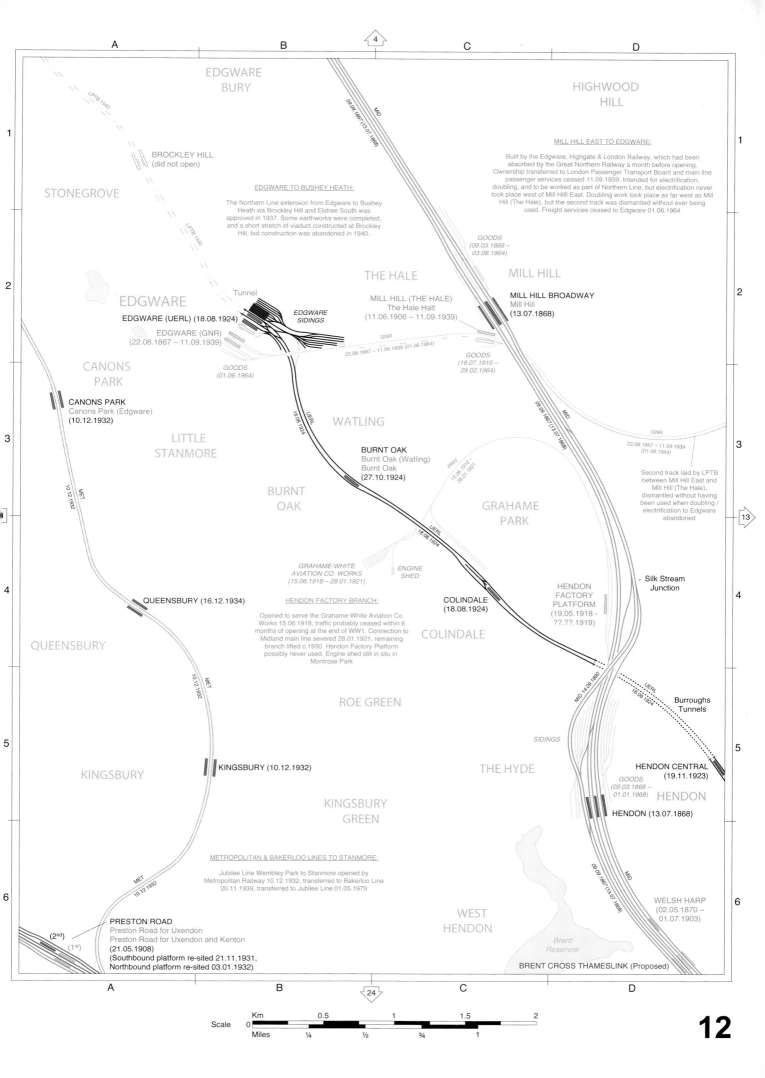

EDGWARE
BURY

HIGHWOOD
HILL

STONEGROVE

BROCKLEY HILL
(did not open)

MILL HILL EAST TO EDGWARE:

Built by the Edgware, Highgate & London Railway, which had been
absorbed by the Great Northern Railway a month before opening.
Ownership transferred to London Passenger Transport Board and main line
passenger services ceased 11.09.1939. Intended for electrification,
doubling, and to be worked as part of Northern Line, but electrification never
took place west of Mill Hill East. Doubling work took place as far west as Mill
Hill (The Hale), but the second track was dismantled without ever being
used. Freight services ceased to Edgware 01.06.1964

EDGWARE TO BUSHEY HEATH:

The Northern Line extension from Edgware to Bushey
Heath via Brockley Hill and Elstree South was
approved in 1937. Some earthworks were completed,
and a short stretch of viaduct constructed at Brockley
Hill, but construction was abandoned in 1940.

THE HALE

GOODS
(09.03.1868 –
03.08.1964)

MILL HILL

EDGWARE

Tunnel

MILL HILL (THE HALE)
The Hale Halt
(11.06.1906 – 11.09.1939)

MILL HILL BROADWAY
Mill Hill
(13.07.1868)

EDGWARE (UERL) (18.08.1924)

*EDGWARE
SIDINGS*

EDGWARE (GNR)
(22.08.1867 – 11.09.1939)

GNR

22.08.1867 – 11.09.1939 (01.06.1964)

GOODS
(18.07.1910 –
29.02.1964)

CANONS
PARK

GOODS
(01.06.1964)

CANONS PARK
Canons Park (Edgware)
(10.12.1932)

WATLING

GNR

22.08.1867 – 11.09.1939
(01.06.1964)

LITTLE
STANMORE

BURNT OAK
Burnt Oak (Watling)
Burnt Oak
(27.10.1924)

Second track laid by LPTB
between Mill Hill East and
Mill Hill (The Hale),
dismantled without having
been used when doubling /
electrification to Edgware
abandoned

⬅13➡

BURNT
OAK

GRAHAME
PARK

Silk Stream
Junction

QUEENSBURY (16.12.1934)

*GRAHAME-WHITE
AVIATION CO. WORKS
(15.06.1918 – 28.01.1921)*

*ENGINE
SHED*

HENDON
FACTORY
PLATFORM
(19.05.1918 –
??.??.1919)

HENDON FACTORY BRANCH:

Opened to serve the Grahame-White Aviation Co.
Works 15.06.1918, traffic probably ceased within 6
months of opening at the end of WW1. Connection to
Midland main line severed 28.01.1921, remaining
branch lifted c.1930. Hendon Factory Platform
possibly never used. Engine shed still in situ in
Montrose Park

COLINDALE
(18.08.1924)

QUEENSBURY

COLINDALE

Burroughs
Tunnels

ROE GREEN

SIDINGS

KINGSBURY

KINGSBURY (10.12.1932)

THE HYDE

HENDON CENTRAL
(19.11.1923)

GOODS
(09.03.1868 –
01.01.1968)

HENDON

KINGSBURY
GREEN

HENDON (13.07.1868)

METROPOLITAN & BAKERLOO LINES TO STANMORE:

Jubilee Line Wembley Park to Stanmore opened by
Metropolitan Railway 10.12.1932, transferred to Bakerloo Line
20.11.1939, transferred to Jubilee Line 01.05.1979

WELSH HARP
(02.05.1870 –
01.07.1903)

WEST
HENDON

*Brent
Reservoir*

(2nd)
(1st)

PRESTON ROAD
Preston Road for Uxendon
Preston Road for Uxendon and Kenton
(21.05.1908)
(Southbound platform re-sited 21.11.1931,
Northbound platform re-sited 03.01.1932)

BRENT CROSS THAMESLINK (Proposed)

Scale

Km 0   0.5   1   1.5   2

Miles   ¼   ½   ¾   1

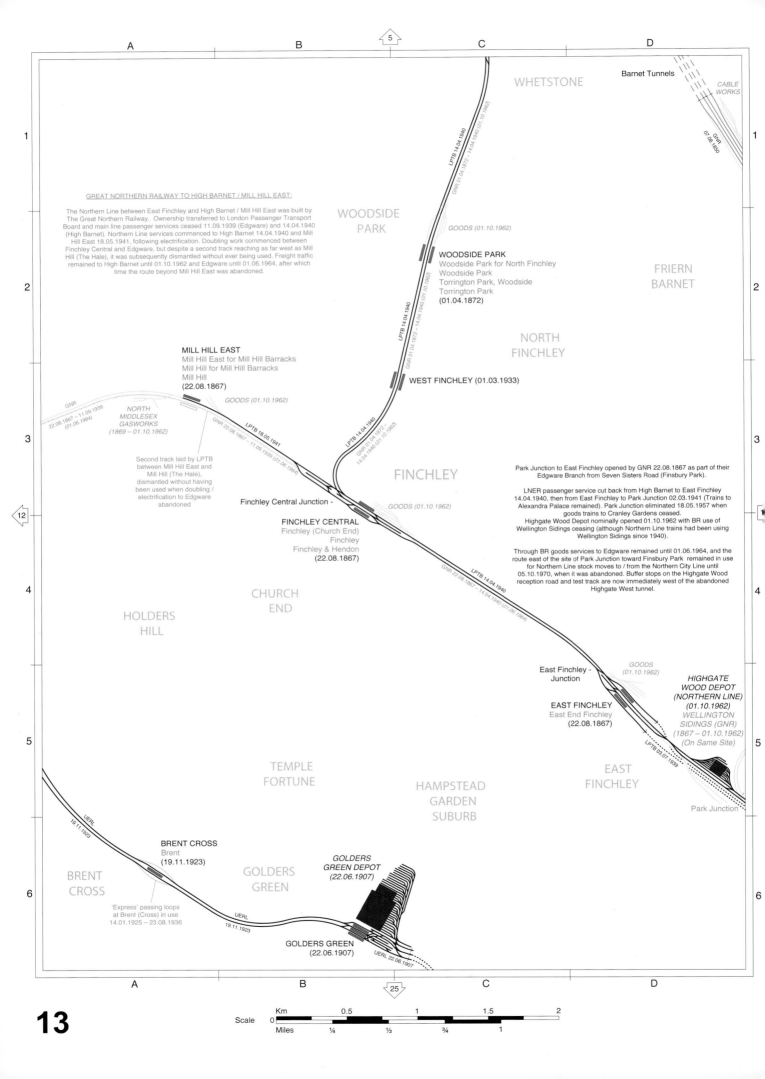

WHETSTONE

Barnet Tunnels

CABLE WORKS

07.08.1850

GNR

LPTB 14.04.1940
GNR 01.04.1872 – 14.04.1940 (01.10.1962)

WOODSIDE
PARK

FRIERN
BARNET

GREAT NORTHERN RAILWAY TO HIGH BARNET / MILL HILL EAST:

The Northern Line between East Finchley and High Barnet / Mill Hill East was built by The Great Northern Railway. Ownership transferred to London Passenger Transport Board and main line passenger services ceased 11.09.1939 (Edgware) and 14.04.1940 (High Barnet). Northern Line services commenced to High Barnet 14.04.1940 and Mill Hill East 18.05.1941, following electrification. Doubling work commenced between Finchley Central and Edgware, but despite a second track reaching as far west as Mill Hill (The Hale), it was subsequently dismantled without ever being used. Freight traffic remained to High Barnet until 01.10.1962 and Edgware until 01.06.1964, after which time the route beyond Mill Hill East was abandoned.

GOODS (01.10.1962)

WOODSIDE PARK
Woodside Park for North Finchley
Woodside Park
Torrington Park, Woodside
Torrington Park
(01.04.1872)

LPTB 14.04.1940
GNR 01.04.1872 – 14.04.1940 (01.10.1962)

NORTH
FINCHLEY

MILL HILL EAST
Mill Hill East for Mill Hill Barracks
Mill Hill for Mill Hill Barracks
Mill Hill
(22.08.1867)

WEST FINCHLEY (01.03.1933)

GNR
22.08.1867 – 11.09.1939
(01.06.1964)

*NORTH
MIDDLESEX
GASWORKS*
(1869 – 01.10.1962)

GNR 22.08.1867 – 11.09.1939 (01.06.1964)

LPTB 18.05.1941

Second track laid by LPTB between Mill Hill East and Mill Hill (The Hale), dismantled without having been used when doubling / electrification to Edgware abandoned

LPTB 14.04.1940
GNR 01.04.1872 – 14.04.1940 (01.10.1962)

FINCHLEY

GOODS (01.10.1962)

Finchley Central Junction -

FINCHLEY CENTRAL
Finchley (Church End)
Finchley
Finchley & Hendon
(22.08.1867)

Park Junction to East Finchley opened by GNR 22.08.1867 as part of their Edgware Branch from Seven Sisters Road (Finsbury Park).

LNER passenger service cut back from High Barnet to East Finchley 14.04.1940, then from East Finchley to Park Junction 02.03.1941 (Trains to Alexandra Palace remained). Park Junction eliminated 18.05.1957 when goods trains to Cranley Gardens ceased.
Highgate Wood Depot nominally opened 01.10.1962 with BR use of Wellington Sidings ceasing (although Northern Line trains had been using Wellington Sidings since 1940).

Through BR goods services to Edgware remained until 01.06.1964, and the route east of the site of Park Junction toward Finsbury Park remained in use for Northern Line stock moves to / from the Northern City Line until 05.10.1970, when it was abandoned. Buffer stops on the Highgate Wood reception road and test track are now immediately west of the abandoned Highgate West tunnel.

CHURCH
END

HOLDERS
HILL

GNR 22.08.1867 – 14.04.1940 (01.06.1964)
LPTB 14.04.1940

East Finchley -
Junction

GOODS
(01.10.1962)

**HIGHGATE
WOOD DEPOT
(NORTHERN LINE)**
(01.10.1962)
*WELLINGTON
SIDINGS (GNR)*
(1867 – 01.10.1962)
(On Same Site)

EAST FINCHLEY
East End Finchley
(22.08.1867)

LPTB 03.07.1939

TEMPLE
FORTUNE

HAMPSTEAD
GARDEN
SUBURB

EAST
FINCHLEY

Park Junction

UERL
19.11.1923

BRENT CROSS
Brent
(19.11.1923)

*GOLDERS
GREEN DEPOT
(22.06.1907)*

BRENT
CROSS

GOLDERS
GREEN

'Express' passing loops at Brent (Cross) in use 14.01.1925 – 23.08.1936

UERL
19.11.1923

UERL

GOLDERS GREEN
(22.06.1907)

UERL 22.06.1907

13

Scale
Km 0   0.5   1   1.5   2
Miles   ¼   ½   ¾   1

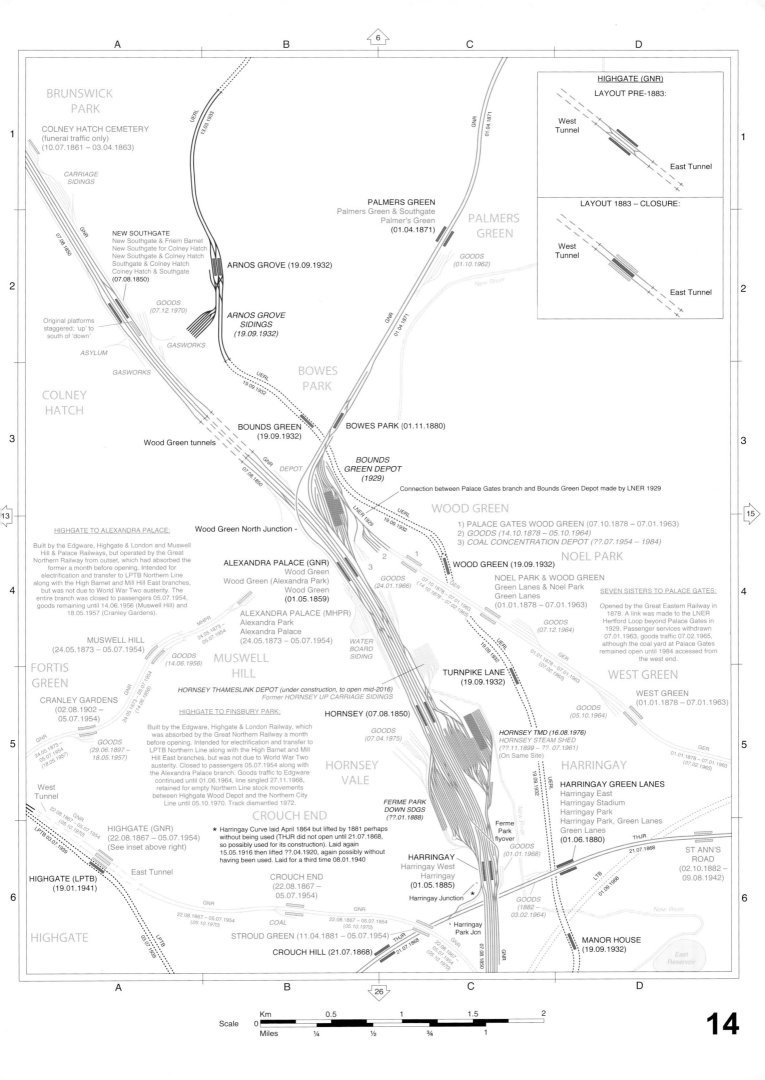

BRUNSWICK PARK

COLNEY HATCH CEMETERY
(funeral traffic only)
(10.07.1861 – 03.04.1863)

CARRIAGE SIDINGS

NEW SOUTHGATE
New Southgate & Friern Barnet
New Southgate for Colney Hatch
New Southgate & Colney Hatch
Southgate & Colney Hatch
Colney Hatch & Southgate
(07.08.1850)

Original platforms
staggered; 'up' to
south of 'down'

ASYLUM

GASWORKS

GASWORKS

COLNEY HATCH

ARNOS GROVE (19.09.1932)

ARNOS GROVE SIDINGS
(19.09.1932)

GOODS
(07.12.1970)

BOWES PARK

BOUNDS GREEN (19.09.1932)

Wood Green tunnels

BOWES PARK (01.11.1880)

BOUNDS GREEN DEPOT
(1929)

Connection between Palace Gates branch and Bounds Green Depot made by LNER 1929

WOOD GREEN

Wood Green North Junction –

1) *PALACE GATES WOOD GREEN* (07.10.1878 – 07.01.1963)
2) *GOODS* (14.10.1878 – 05.10.1964)
3) *COAL CONCENTRATION DEPOT* (??.07.1954 – 1984)

HIGHGATE TO ALEXANDRA PALACE:

Built by the Edgware, Highgate & London and Muswell
Hill & Palace Railways, but operated by the Great
Northern Railway from outset, which had absorbed the
former a month before opening. Intended for
electrification and transfer to LPTB Northern Line
along with the High Barnet and Mill Hill East branches,
but was not due to World War Two austerity. The
entire branch was closed to passengers 05.07.1954,
goods remaining until 14.06.1956 (Muswell Hill) and
18.05.1957 (Cranley Gardens).

ALEXANDRA PALACE (GNR)
Wood Green
Wood Green (Alexandra Park)
Wood Green
(01.05.1859)

ALEXANDRA PALACE (MHPR)
Alexandra Park
Alexandra Palace
(24.05.1873 – 05.07.1954)

GOODS
(24.01.1966)

WOOD GREEN (19.09.1932)

NOEL PARK

NOEL PARK & WOOD GREEN
Green Lanes & Noel Park
Green Lanes
(01.01.1878 – 07.01.1963)

GOODS
(07.12.1964)

SEVEN SISTERS TO PALACE GATES:

Opened by the Great Eastern Railway in
1878. A link was made to the LNER
Hertford Loop beyond Palace Gates in
1929. Passenger services withdrawn
07.01.1963, goods traffic 07.02.1965,
although the coal yard at Palace Gates
remained open until 1984 accessed from
the west end.

MUSWELL HILL
(24.05.1873 – 05.07.1954)

FORTIS GREEN

CRANLEY GARDENS
(02.08.1902 –
05.07.1954)

GOODS
(29.06.1897 –
18.05.1957)

MUSWELL HILL

GOODS
(14.06.1956)

HORNSEY THAMESLINK DEPOT (under construction, to open mid-2016)
Former HORNSEY UP CARRIAGE SIDINGS

HIGHGATE TO FINSBURY PARK:

Built by the Edgware, Highgate & London Railway, which
was absorbed by the Great Northern Railway a month
before opening. Intended for electrification and transfer to
LPTB Northern Line along with the High Barnet and Mill
Hill East branches, but was not due to World War Two
austerity. Closed to passengers 05.07.1954 along with
the Alexandra Palace branch. Goods traffic to Edgware
continued until 01.06.1964, line singled 27.11.1968,
retained for empty Northern Line stock movements
between Highgate Wood Depot and the Northern City
Line until 05.10.1970. Track dismantled 1972.

HORNSEY (07.08.1850)

GOODS
(07.04.1975)

TURNPIKE LANE
(19.09.1932)

HORNSEY TMD (16.08.1976)
HORNSEY STEAM SHED
(??.11.1899 – ??.07.1961)
(On Same Site)

HORNSEY VALE

FERME PARK DOWN SDGS
(??.01.1888)

Ferme Park flyover

WEST GREEN

WEST GREEN
(01.01.1878 – 07.01.1963)

GOODS
(05.10.1964)

HARRINGAY

HARRINGAY GREEN LANES
Harringay East
Harringay Stadium
Harringay Park
Harringay Park, Green Lanes
Green Lanes
(01.06.1880)

West
Tunnel

HIGHGATE (GNR)
(22.08.1867 – 05.07.1954)
(See inset above right)

★ Harringay Curve laid April 1864 but lifted by 1881 perhaps
without being used (THJR did not open until 21.07.1868,
so possibly used for its construction). Laid again
15.05.1916 then lifted ??.04.1920, again possibly without
having been used. Laid for a third time 08.01.1940

HIGHGATE (LPTB)
(19.01.1941)

East Tunnel

HIGHGATE

CROUCH END
(22.08.1867 –
05.07.1954)

HARRINGAY
Harringay West
Harringay
(01.05.1885)

Harringay Junction

Harringay Park Jcn

GOODS
(01.01.1968)

GOODS
(1882 –
03.02.1964)

ST ANN'S ROAD
(02.10.1882 –
09.08.1942)

COAL

STROUD GREEN (11.04.1881 – 05.07.1954)

CROUCH HILL (21.07.1868)

MANOR HOUSE
(19.09.1932)

East Reservoir

PALMERS GREEN
Palmers Green & Southgate
Palmer's Green
(01.04.1871)

GOODS
(01.10.1962)

New River

PALMERS GREEN

HIGHGATE (GNR)

LAYOUT PRE-1883:

West Tunnel

East Tunnel

LAYOUT 1883 – CLOSURE:

West Tunnel

East Tunnel

Scale

Km 0   0.5   1   1.5   2

Miles   ¼   ½   ¾   1

14

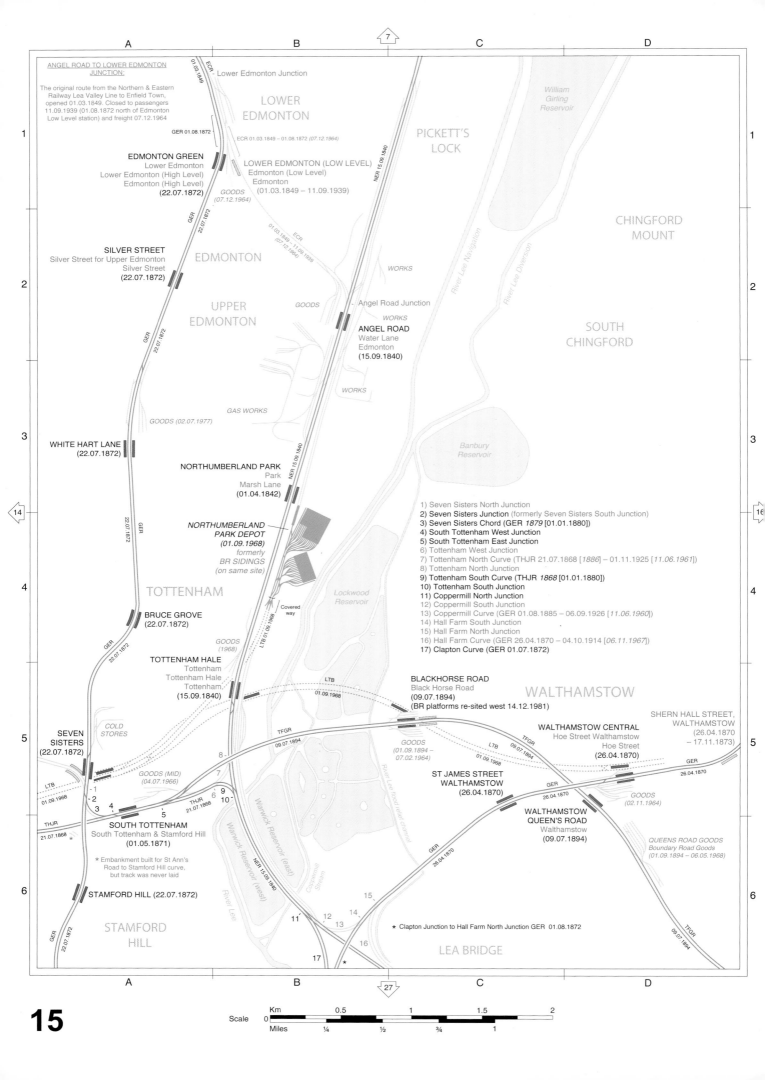

1

ANGEL ROAD TO LOWER EDMONTON JUNCTION:

The original route from the Northern & Eastern
Railway Lea Valley Line to Enfield Town,
opened 01.03.1849. Closed to passengers
11.09.1939 (01.08.1872 north of Edmonton
Low Level station) and freight 07.12.1964

01.03.1849 — Lower Edmonton Junction

LOWER
EDMONTON

ECR 01.03.1849 – 01.08.1872 (07.12.1964)

GER 01.08.1872

PICKETT'S
LOCK

EDMONTON GREEN
Lower Edmonton
Lower Edmonton (High Level)
Edmonton (High Level)
(22.07.1872)

LOWER EDMONTON (LOW LEVEL)
Edmonton (Low Level)
Edmonton
(01.03.1849 – 11.09.1939)

*GOODS
(07.12.1964)*

William
Girling
Reservoir

SILVER STREET
Silver Street for Upper Edmonton
Silver Street
(22.07.1872)

EDMONTON

UPPER
EDMONTON

CHINGFORD
MOUNT

WORKS

GOODS

Angel Road Junction

WORKS

ANGEL ROAD
Water Lane
Edmonton
(15.09.1840)

SOUTH
CHINGFORD

WORKS

GOODS (02.07.1977)

GAS WORKS

WHITE HART LANE
(22.07.1872)

NORTHUMBERLAND PARK
Park
Marsh Lane
(01.04.1842)

*Banbury
Reservoir*

*NORTHUMBERLAND
PARK DEPOT
(01.09.1968)
formerly
BR SIDINGS
(on same site)*

1) Seven Sisters North Junction
2) Seven Sisters Junction (formerly Seven Sisters South Junction)
3) Seven Sisters Chord (GER *1879* [01.01.1880])
4) South Tottenham West Junction
5) South Tottenham East Junction
6) Tottenham West Junction
7) Tottenham North Curve (THJR 21.07.1868 [*1886*] – 01.11.1925 [*11.06.1961*])
8) Tottenham North Junction
9) Tottenham South Curve (THJR *1868* [01.01.1880])
10) Tottenham South Junction
11) Coppermill North Junction
12) Coppermill South Junction
13) Coppermill Curve (GER 01.08.1885 – 06.09.1926 [*11.06.1960*])
14) Hall Farm South Junction
15) Hall Farm North Junction
16) Hall Farm Curve (GER 26.04.1870 – 04.10.1914 [*06.11.1967*])
17) Clapton Curve (GER 01.07.1872)

TOTTENHAM

*Lockwood
Reservoir*

*Covered
way*

BRUCE GROVE
(22.07.1872)

*GOODS
(1968)*

TOTTENHAM HALE
Tottenham
Tottenham Hale
Tottenham
(15.09.1840)

LTB
01.09.1968

BLACKHORSE ROAD
Black Horse Road
(09.07.1894)
(BR platforms re-sited west 14.12.1981)

WALTHAMSTOW

SHERN HALL STREET,
WALTHAMSTOW
(26.04.1870
– 17.11.1873)

SEVEN
SISTERS
(22.07.1872)

*COLD
STORES*

TFGR
09.07.1894

*GOODS
(01.09.1894 –
07.02.1964)*

LTB
01.09.1968

TFGR
09.07.1894

WALTHAMSTOW CENTRAL
Hoe Street Walthamstow
Hoe Street
(26.04.1870)

LTB
01.09.1968

*GOODS (MID)
(04.07.1966)*

8

7

9

10

THJR
21.07.1868

ST JAMES STREET
WALTHAMSTOW
(26.04.1870)

GER
26.04.1870

-1
-2
-3

4

5

6

5

GER

26.04.1870

*GOODS
(02.11.1964)*

SOUTH TOTTENHAM
South Tottenham & Stamford Hill
(01.05.1871)

* Embankment built for St Ann's
Road to Stamford Hill curve,
but track was never laid

WALTHAMSTOW
QUEEN'S ROAD
Walthamstow
(09.07.1894)

*QUEENS ROAD GOODS
Boundary Road Goods
(01.09.1894 – 06.05.1968)*

STAMFORD HILL (22.07.1872)

STAMFORD
HILL

Warwick Reservoir (west)

River Lee

River Lee flood relief channel

Warwick Reservoir (east)

Coppermill Stream

15

12

14

11

13

16

17

* Clapton Junction to Hall Farm North Junction GER 01.08.1872

LEA BRIDGE

TFGR
09.07.1894

15

Scale   Km   0   0.5   1   1.5   2

Miles   ¼   ½   ¾   1

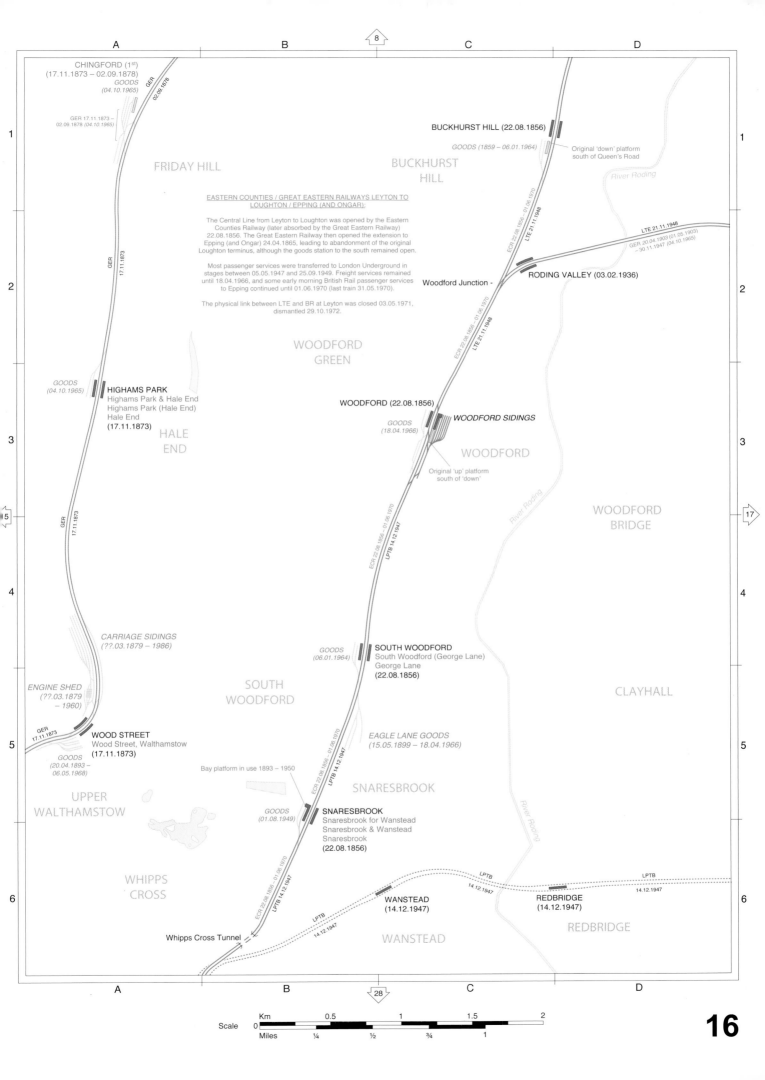

CHINGFORD (1st)
(17.11.1873 – 02.09.1878)
GOODS
(04.10.1965)

GER 17.11.1873 –
02.09.1878 *(04.10.1965)*

GER 02.09.1878

BUCKHURST HILL (22.08.1856)

GOODS (1859 – 06.01.1964)

Original 'down' platform
south of Queen's Road

River Roding

FRIDAY HILL

BUCKHURST
HILL

GER 17.11.1873

ECR 22.08.1856 – 01.06.1970

LTE 21.11.1948

LTE 21.11.1948

GER 20.04.1903 (01.05.1903)
– 30.11.1947 (04.10.1965)

EASTERN COUNTIES / GREAT EASTERN RAILWAYS LEYTON TO
LOUGHTON / EPPING (AND ONGAR):

The Central Line from Leyton to Loughton was opened by the Eastern
Counties Railway (later absorbed by the Great Eastern Railway)
22.08.1856. The Great Eastern Railway then opened the extension to
Epping (and Ongar) 24.04.1865, leading to abandonment of the original
Loughton terminus, although the goods station to the south remained open.

Most passenger services were transferred to London Underground in
stages between 05.05.1947 and 25.09.1949. Freight services remained
until 18.04.1966, and some early morning British Rail passenger services
to Epping continued until 01.06.1970 (last train 31.05.1970).

The physical link between LTE and BR at Leyton was closed 03.05.1971,
dismantled 29.10.1972.

WOODFORD
GREEN

Woodford Junction -

RODING VALLEY (03.02.1936)

ECR 22.08.1856 – 01.06.1970

LTE 21.11.1948

GOODS
(04.10.1965)

HIGHAMS PARK
Highams Park & Hale End
Highams Park (Hale End)
Hale End
(17.11.1873)

HALE
END

WOODFORD (22.08.1856)

GOODS
(18.04.1966)

WOODFORD SIDINGS

WOODFORD

Original 'up' platform
south of 'down'

River Roding

WOODFORD
BRIDGE

GER 17.11.1873

ECR 22.08.1856 – 01.06.1970

LPTB 14.12.1947

CARRIAGE SIDINGS
(??.03.1879 – 1986)

ENGINE SHED
(??.03.1879
– 1960)

SOUTH
WOODFORD

GOODS
(06.01.1964)

SOUTH WOODFORD
South Woodford (George Lane)
George Lane
(22.08.1856)

CLAYHALL

GER 17.11.1873

WOOD STREET
Wood Street, Walthamstow
(17.11.1873)

GOODS
(20.04.1893 –
06.05.1968)

EAGLE LANE GOODS
(15.05.1899 – 18.04.1966)

ECR 22.08.1856 – 01.06.1970

LPTB 14.12.1947

UPPER
WALTHAMSTOW

Bay platform in use 1893 – 1950

SNARESBROOK

GOODS
(01.08.1949)

SNARESBROOK
Snaresbrook for Wanstead
Snaresbrook & Wanstead
Snaresbrook
(22.08.1856)

WHIPPS
CROSS

ECR 22.08.1856 – 01.06.1970

LPTB 14.12.1947

LPTB
14.12.1947

WANSTEAD
(14.12.1947)

LPTB
14.12.1947

REDBRIDGE
(14.12.1947)

LPTB
14.12.1947

REDBRIDGE

Whipps Cross Tunnel

WANSTEAD

River Roding

Scale

Km
0   0.5   1   1.5   2

Miles
¼   ½   ¾   1

5
17

16

HAINAULT (FAIRLOP) LOOP:

The Central Line Woodford Junction to Newbury Park was opened by the Great Eastern Railway 20.04.1903 (through goods traffic) with passenger and local goods traffic commencing 01.05.1903.

Prior to transfer to LPTB (later LTE) the route was known as the Fairlop Loop. LNER passenger services were withdrawn 30.11.1947 and replaced by a bus service to allow electrification and transfer.

LPTB / LTE Central Line services commenced 14.12.1947 (Leytonstone to Newbury Park), 31.05.1948 (Newbury Park to Hainault) and 21.11.1948 (Hainault to Woodford Junction), however the Newbury Park to Hainault section was electrified and saw some empty stock workings between 14.12.1947 and 31.05.1948 to serve the partially-opened Hainault Depot (full opening 31.05.1948). Hainault Depot was ostensibly complete in 1939, and between June 1943 and January 1945 served as an assembly point for US Army Transportation Corps rolling stock.

Local goods services remained until 04.10.1965 serving yards at Grange Hill, Barkingside and Newbury Park. The LNER west curve at Ilford was closed 30.11.1947 and the BR connection between Newbury Park and Seven Kings was closed 19.03.1956, although the northernmost section was retained as a goods turnback siding, later engineers train turnback siding, before being lifted 16.08.1992.

TEMPLE MILLS MARSHALLING YARD 1958
From page 27

TEMPLE MILLS MARSHALLING YARD

The first railway use of the former marshland at Temple Mills was the 1897 GER wagon works, relocated from Stratford. The wagon works and later freight marshalling yard steadily grew throughout the first half of the 20th century.

Upon its opening in 1958, the modernised Temple Mills Marshalling Yard was the largest of its kind in Britain and the most modern in the world. Wagons were shunted over a 'hump' and proceeded into sorting sidings through gravity, being slowed by sets of 'retarders'. Sorting of wagons was achieved with electronic automatic controls orchestrated from a central control tower.

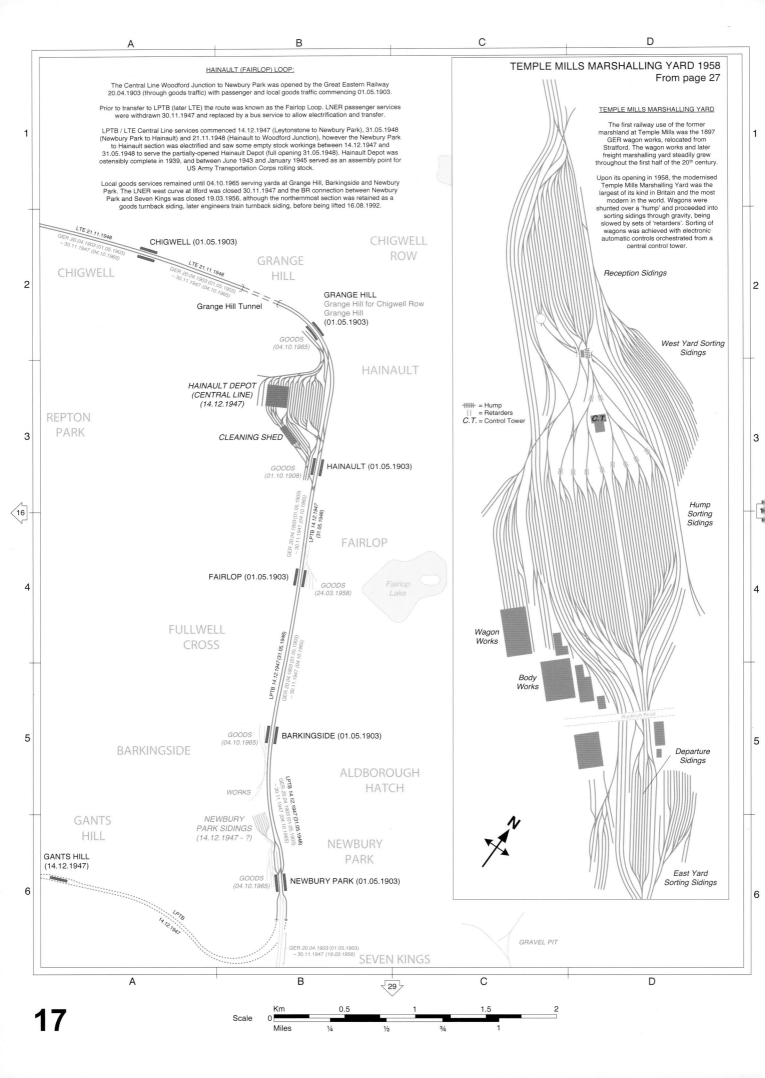

Reception Sidings

West Yard Sorting Sidings

〽〽〽 = Hump
〦 = Retarders
C.T. = Control Tower

C.T.

Hump Sorting Sidings

Wagon Works

Body Works

Ruckholt Road

Departure Sidings

East Yard Sorting Sidings

CHIGWELL (01.05.1903)

LTE 21.11.1948
GER 20.04.1903 (01.05.1903)
– 30.11.1947 (04.10.1965)

CHIGWELL

GRANGE HILL

CHIGWELL ROW

LTE 21.11.1948
GER 20.04.1903 (01.05.1903)
– 30.11.1947 (04.10.1965)

Grange Hill Tunnel

GRANGE HILL
Grange Hill for Chigwell Row
Grange Hill
(01.05.1903)

GOODS
(04.10.1965)

HAINAULT

REPTON PARK

HAINAULT DEPOT
(CENTRAL LINE)
(14.12.1947)

CLEANING SHED

GOODS
(01.10.1908)

HAINAULT (01.05.1903)

GER 20.04.1903 (01.05.1903)
– 30.11.1947 (04.10.1965)

LPTB 14.12.1947
(31.05.1948)

FAIRLOP

FAIRLOP (01.05.1903)

GOODS
(24.03.1958)

Fairlop Lake

FULLWELL CROSS

LPTB 14.12.1947 (31.05.1948)
GER 20.04.1903 (01.05.1903)
– 30.11.1947 (04.10.1965)

GOODS
(04.10.1965)

BARKINGSIDE (01.05.1903)

BARKINGSIDE

ALDBOROUGH HATCH

WORKS

LPTB 14.12.1947 (31.05.1948)
GER 20.04.1903 (01.05.1903)
– 30.11.1947 (04.10.1965)

GANTS HILL

NEWBURY PARK SIDINGS
(14.12.1947 - ?)

NEWBURY PARK

GANTS HILL
(14.12.1947)

GOODS
(04.10.1965)

NEWBURY PARK (01.05.1903)

LPTB
14.12.1947

GER 20.04.1903 (01.05.1903)
– 30.11.1947 (19.03.1956)

SEVEN KINGS

GRAVEL PIT

Km   0.5   1   1.5   2
Scale 0
Miles   ¼   ½   ¾   1

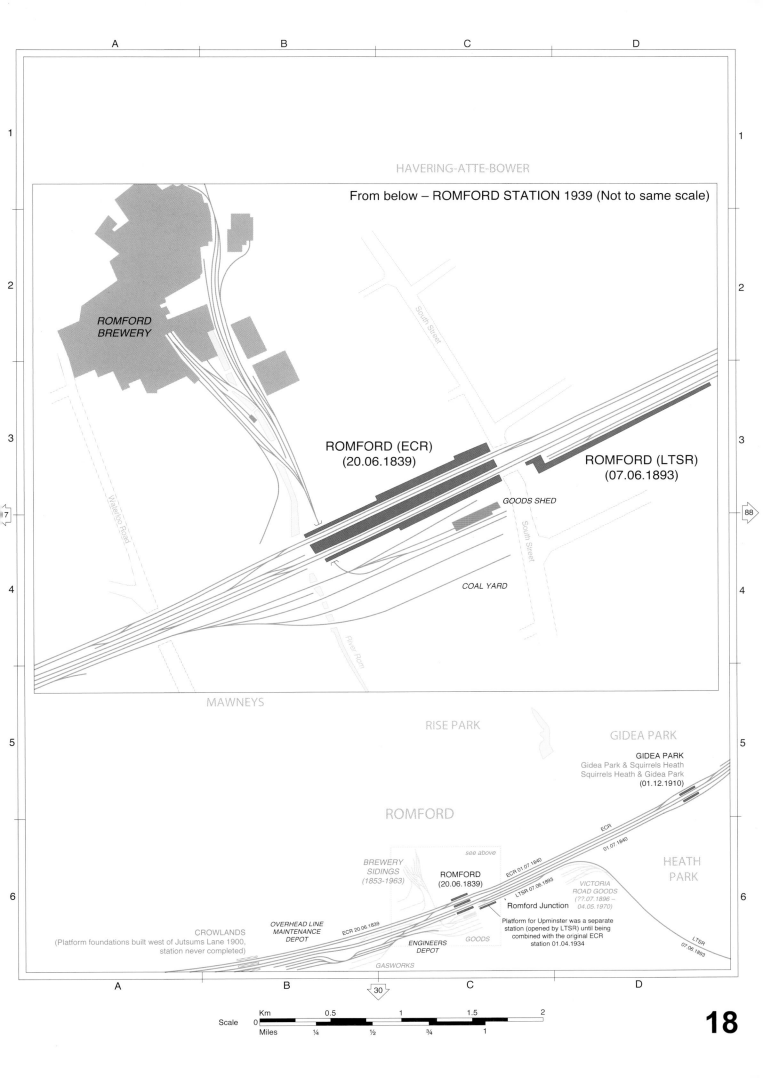

HAVERING-ATTE-BOWER

From below – ROMFORD STATION 1939 (Not to same scale)

ROMFORD BREWERY

South Street

ROMFORD (ECR)
(20.06.1839)

ROMFORD (LTSR)
(07.06.1893)

GOODS SHED

Waterloo Road

South Street

COAL YARD

River Rom

MAWNEYS

RISE PARK

GIDEA PARK

GIDEA PARK
Gidea Park & Squirrels Heath
Squirrels Heath & Gidea Park
(01.12.1910)

ROMFORD

see above

BREWERY
SIDINGS
(1853-1963)

ROMFORD
(20.06.1839)

Romford Junction

ECR 01.07.1840

LTSR 07.06.1893

ECR
01.07 1840

HEATH
PARK

VICTORIA
ROAD GOODS
(??.07.1896 –
04.05.1970)

Platform for Upminster was a separate
station (opened by LTSR) until being
combined with the original ECR
station 01.04.1934

CROWLANDS
(Platform foundations built west of Jutsums Lane 1900,
station never completed)

OVERHEAD LINE
MAINTENANCE
DEPOT

ECR 20.06.1839

ENGINEERS
DEPOT

GOODS

GASWORKS

LTSR
07.06.1893

Scale
Km   0   0.5   1   1.5   2
Miles   ¼   ½   ¾   1

18

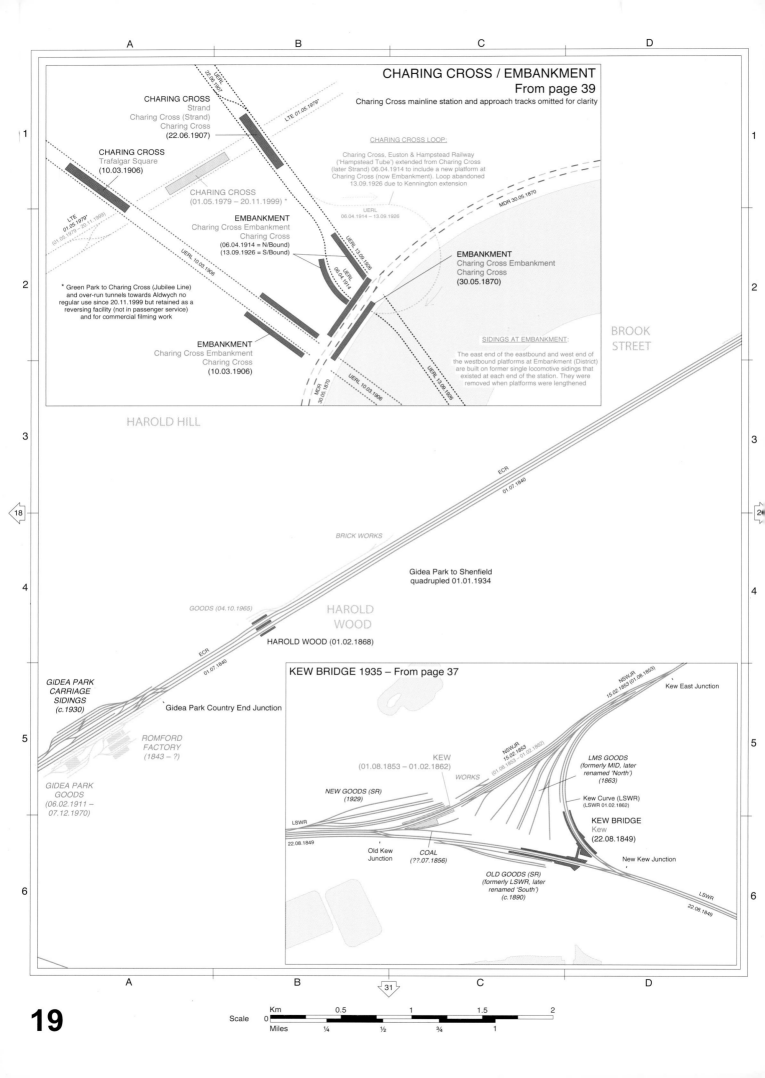

CHARING CROSS / EMBANKMENT
From page 39
Charing Cross mainline station and approach tracks omitted for clarity

CHARING CROSS LOOP:

Charing Cross, Euston & Hampstead Railway ('Hampstead Tube') extended from Charing Cross (later Strand) 06.04.1914 to include a new platform at Charing Cross (now Embankment). Loop abandoned 13.09.1926 due to Kennington extension

CHARING CROSS
Strand
Charing Cross (Strand)
Charing Cross
(22.06.1907)

CHARING CROSS
Trafalgar Square
(10.03.1906)

LTE 01.05.1979*

UERL 22.06.1907

CHARING CROSS
(01.05.1979 – 20.11.1999) *

EMBANKMENT
Charing Cross Embankment
Charing Cross
(06.04.1914 = N/Bound)
(13.09.1926 = S/Bound)

UERL 06.04.1914 – 13.09.1926

MDR 30.05.1870

EMBANKMENT
Charing Cross Embankment
Charing Cross
(30.05.1870)

LTE
01.05.1979*
(01.05.1979 – 20.11.1999)

UERL 10.03.1906

UERL 13.09.1926

UERL 06.04.1914

* Green Park to Charing Cross (Jubilee Line) and over-run tunnels towards Aldwych no regular use since 20.11.1999 but retained as a reversing facility (not in passenger service) and for commercial filming work

EMBANKMENT
Charing Cross Embankment
Charing Cross
(10.03.1906)

MDR 30.05.1870

UERL 10.03.1906

UERL 13.09.1926

SIDINGS AT EMBANKMENT:

The east end of the eastbound and west end of the westbound platforms at Embankment (District) are built on former single locomotive sidings that existed at each end of the station. They were removed when platforms were lengthened

BROOK STREET

HAROLD HILL

ECR
01.07.1840

BRICK WORKS

Gidea Park to Shenfield quadrupled 01.01.1934

GOODS (04.10.1965)

HAROLD WOOD

HAROLD WOOD (01.02.1868)

ECR
01.07.1840

GIDEA PARK CARRIAGE SIDINGS
(c.1930)

Gidea Park Country End Junction

ROMFORD FACTORY
(1843 – ?)

GIDEA PARK GOODS
(06.02.1911 – 07.12.1970)

KEW BRIDGE 1935 – From page 37

NSWJR
15.02.1853 (01.08.1853)

Kew East Junction

KEW
(01.08.1853 – 01.02.1862)

NSWJR
15.02.1853
(01.08.1853 – 01.02.1862)

LMS GOODS
(formerly MID, later renamed 'North')
(1863)

WORKS

NEW GOODS (SR)
(1929)

Kew Curve (LSWR)
(LSWR 01.02.1862)

KEW BRIDGE
Kew
(22.08.1849)

LSWR
22.08.1849

Old Kew Junction

COAL
(??.07.1856)

OLD GOODS (SR)
(formerly LSWR, later renamed 'South')
(c.1890)

New Kew Junction

LSWR
22.08.1849

Scale
Km 0   0.5   1   1.5   2
Miles ¼   ½   ¾   1

18   2

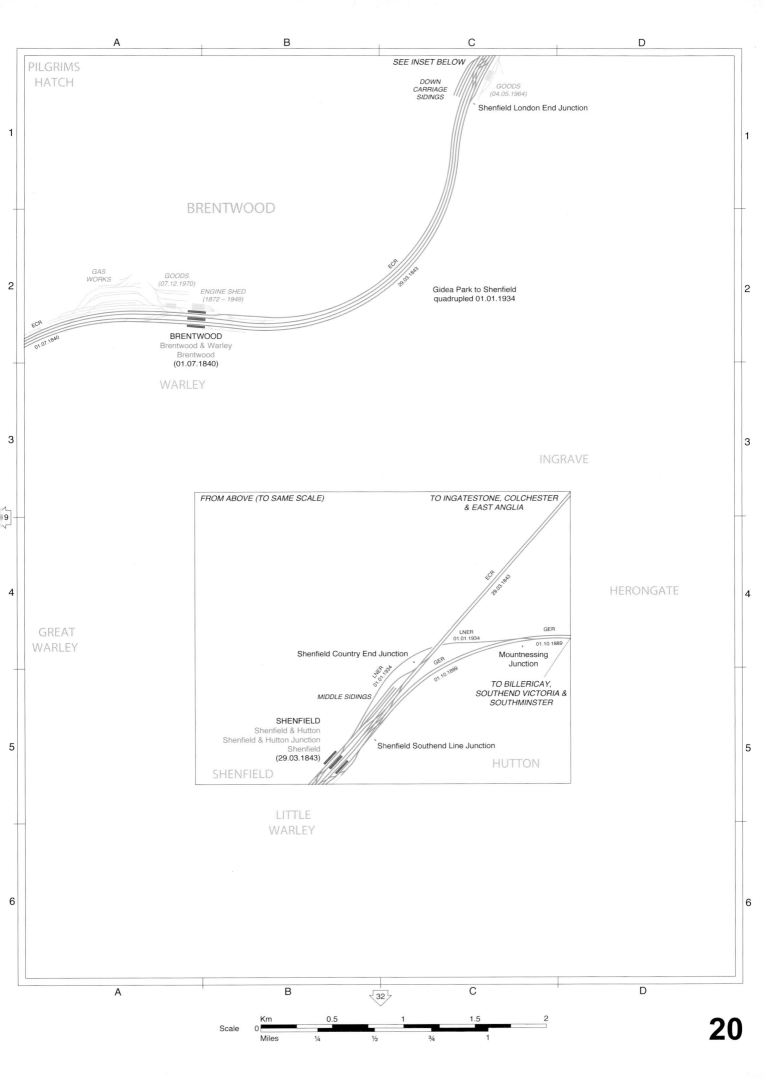

PILGRIMS
HATCH

BRENTWOOD

SEE INSET BELOW

DOWN
CARRIAGE
SIDINGS

GOODS
(04.05.1964)

Shenfield London End Junction

GAS
WORKS

GOODS
(07.12.1970)

ENGINE SHED
(1872 – 1949)

ECR
29.03.1843

Gidea Park to Shenfield
quadrupled 01.01.1934

ECR

01.07.1840

BRENTWOOD
Brentwood & Warley
Brentwood
(01.07.1840)

WARLEY

INGRAVE

9

FROM ABOVE (TO SAME SCALE)

TO INGATESTONE, COLCHESTER
& EAST ANGLIA

ECR
29.03.1843

HERONGATE

GREAT
WARLEY

LNER
01.01.1934

GER

Shenfield Country End Junction

LNER
01.01.1934

GER
01.10.1889

01.10.1889

Mountnessing
Junction

TO BILLERICAY,
SOUTHEND VICTORIA &
SOUTHMINSTER

MIDDLE SIDINGS

SHENFIELD
Shenfield & Hutton
Shenfield & Hutton Junction
Shenfield
(29.03.1843)

Shenfield Southend Line Junction

HUTTON

SHENFIELD

LITTLE
WARLEY

Scale

Km
0   0.5   1   1.5   2

Miles
¼   ½   ¾   1

32

20

DENHAM

ICKENHAM

UXBRIDGE HIGH STREET BRANCH:

Built by the Great Western Railway, opening
01.05.1907 (passengers) and 11.05.1914 (goods).
Denham South Junction to Denham East Junction
dismantled c.1917 and the entire branch singled.
Passenger services withdrawn 01.01.1917 –
03.05.1920 and again for good 01.09.1939. Coal traffic
remained to Uxbridge until 24.02.1964, and oil traffic at
the extreme northern end of the branch until 30.04.1965

HILLINGDON
Hillingdon (Swakeleys)
Hillingdon
(10.12.1923) (1st)
(Re-sited 28.06.1992) (1st)
(2nd)

GOODS
(11.05.1914 – 24.02.1964)

GOODS
(10.08.1964)

UXBRIDGE HIGH STREET
(01.05.1907 – 01.09.1939)

UXBRIDGE (1st)
(04.07.1904 – 04.12.1938)

MET 04.07.1904 – 04.12.1938

UXBRIDGE
SIDINGS
(1942)
GOODS
(04.07.1904 –
01.05.1939)
(On Same Site)

DISTRICT LINE TO UXBRIDGE:

District Line trains ran to Uxbridge (1st)
01.03.1910 – 22.10.1933 (date of last train),
services replaced by Piccadilly Line from
23.10.1933

Uxbridge High Street branch originally intended
to continue to a point south of Uxbridge Vine
Street, but construction was abandoned

LPTB 04.12.1938

UXBRIDGE (2nd) (04.12.1938)

UXBRIDGE

GOODS
(13.07.1964)

UXBRIDGE VINE STREET
Uxbridge
(08.09.1856 – 10.09.1962)

HILLINGDON

WEST DRAYTON TO UXBRIDGE VINE STREET:

Opened by the Great Western Railway 08.09.1856. Intermediate
station at Cowley added 01.10.1904. Closed to passengers
10.09.1962, then singled the following month. Closed to goods
13.07.1964 except the southernmost section serving Middlesex Oil
& Chemical works, to where rail traffic ceased in 1976.

**HILLINGDON
HEATH**

IVER
HEATH

COWLEY (01.10.1904 – 10.09.1962)

COWLEY

**COLHAM
GREEN**

**COWLEY
PEACHEY**

IVER

**GOULDS
GREEN**

MIDDLESEX OIL & CHEMICAL WORKS
(c.1964 – 1976)

**STOCKLEY
PARK**

WEST DRAYTON COAL
(CELTIC ENERGY)
(18.12.1963 – 07.04.1999)

YIEWSLEY

GOODS SHED

West Drayton to Slough quadrupled 08.09.1884,
5th road (up goods) added Iver to West Drayton
22.03.1914

LAFARGE AGGREGATES

GWR 04.06.1838

21

Scale

Km
0   0.5   1   1.5   2

Miles
¼   ½   ¾   1

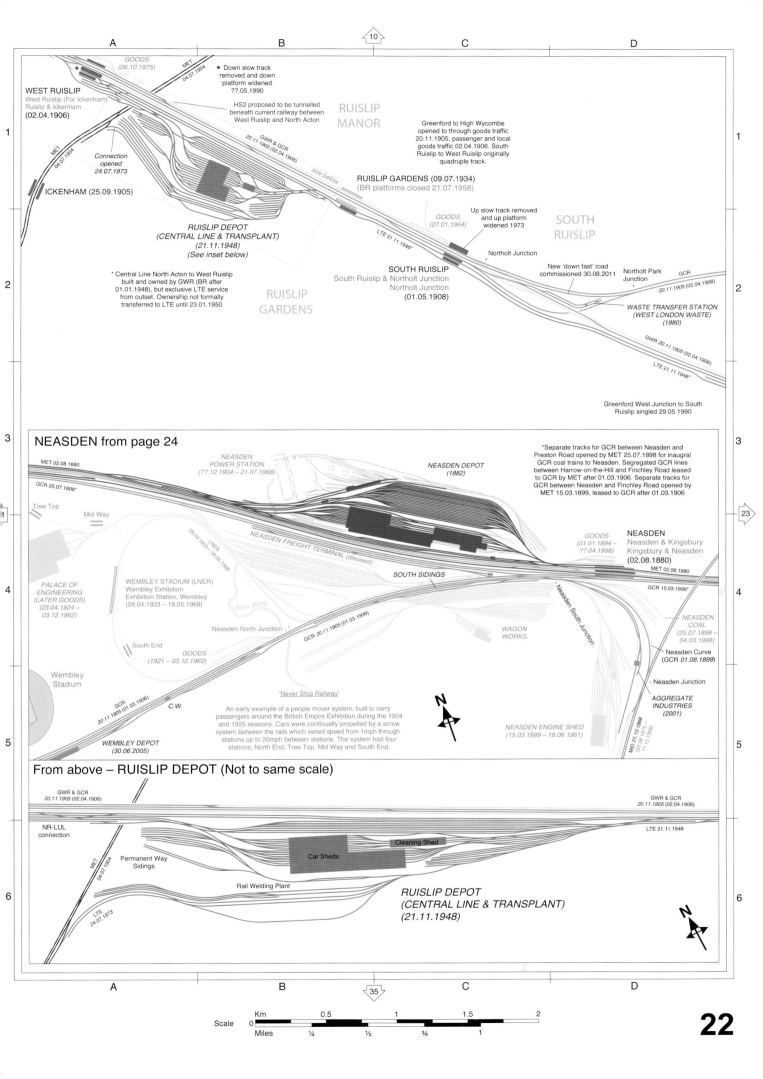

WEST RUISLIP
West Ruislip (For Ickenham)
Ruislip & Ickenham
(02.04.1906)

GOODS
(06.10.1975)

MET
04.07.1904

★ Down slow track
removed and down
platform widened
??.05.1990

HS2 proposed to be tunnelled
beneath current railway between
West Ruislip and North Acton

**RUISLIP
MANOR**

MET
04.07.1904

Connection
opened
24.07.1973

ICKENHAM (25.09.1905)

GWR & GCR
20.11.1905 (02.04.1906)

see below

Greenford to High Wycombe
opened to through goods traffic
20.11.1905, passenger and local
goods traffic 02.04.1906. South
Ruislip to West Ruislip originally
quadruple track.

RUISLIP GARDENS (09.07.1934)
(BR platforms closed 21.07.1958)

**SOUTH
RUISLIP**

GOODS
(27.01.1964)

Up slow track removed
and up platform
widened 1973

RUISLIP DEPOT
(CENTRAL LINE & TRANSPLANT)
(21.11.1948)
(See inset below)

LTE 21.11.1948*

Northolt Junction

New 'down fast' road
commissioned 30.08.2011

Northolt Park
Junction

GCR
20.11.1905 (02.04.1906)

* Central Line North Acton to West Ruislip
built and owned by GWR (BR after
01.01.1948), but exclusive LTE service
from outset. Ownership not formally
transferred to LTE until 23.01.1950

**RUISLIP
GARDENS**

SOUTH RUISLIP
South Ruislip & Northolt Junction
Northolt Junction
(01.05.1908)

WASTE TRANSFER STATION
(WEST LONDON WASTE)
(1980)

GWR 20.11.1905 (02.04.1906)

LTE 21.11.1948*

Greenford West Junction to South
Ruislip singled 29.05.1990

NEASDEN from page 24

MET 02.08.1880

GCR 25.07.1898*

Tree Top

Mid Way

**NEASDEN
POWER STATION**
(??.12.1904 – 21.07.1968)

NEASDEN DEPOT
(1882)

*Separate tracks for GCR between Neasden and
Preston Road opened by MET 25.07.1898 for inaugral
GCR coal trains to Neasden. Segregated GCR lines
between Harrow-on-the-Hill and Finchley Road leased
to GCR by MET after 01.03.1906. Separate tracks for
GCR between Neasden and Finchley Road opened by
MET 15.03.1899, leased to GCR after 01.03.1906

**PALACE OF
ENGINEERING
(LATER GOODS)**
(23.04.1924 –
03.12.1962)

28.04.1923 – 18.05.1968 LNER

NEASDEN FREIGHT TERMINAL (disused)

GOODS
(01.01.1894 –
??.04.1958)

NEASDEN
Neasden & Kingsbury
Kingsbury & Neasden
(02.08.1880)

MET 02.08.1880

GCR 15.03.1899*

WEMBLEY STADIUM (LNER)
Wembley Exhibition
Exhibition Station, Wembley
(28.04.1923 – 18.05.1968)

SOUTH SIDINGS

River Brent

Neasden North Junction

GCR 20.11.1905 (01.03.1906)

**WAGON
WORKS**

**NEASDEN
COAL**
(25.07.1898 –
04.03.1968)

Neasden South Junction

South End

GOODS
(1921 – 03.12.1962)

Neasden Curve
(GCR 01.08.1899)

- Neasden Junction

Wembley
Stadium

GCR
20.11.1905 (01.03.1906)

C.W.

'Never Stop Railway'

**AGGREGATE
INDUSTRIES**
(2001)

WEMBLEY DEPOT
(30.06.2005)

An early example of a people mover system, built to carry
passengers around the British Empire Exhibition during the 1924
and 1925 seasons. Cars were continually propelled by a screw
system between the rails which varied speed from 1mph through
stations up to 20mph between stations. The system had four
stations; North End, Tree Top, Mid Way and South End.

N

NEASDEN ENGINE SHED
(15.03.1899 – 18.06.1961)

MID 01.10.1868
(03.08.1875 –
17.10.1906)

From above – RUISLIP DEPOT (Not to same scale)

GWR & GCR
20.11.1905 (02.04.1906)

GWR & GCR
20.11.1905 (02.04.1906)

NR-LUL
connection

LTE 21.11.1948

MET
04.07.1904

Permanent Way
Sidings

Car Sheds

Cleaning Shed

Rail Welding Plant

RUISLIP DEPOT
(CENTRAL LINE & TRANSPLANT)
(21.11.1948)

LTE
24.07.1973

N

Scale

Km
0   0.5   1   1.5   2

Miles
¼   ½   ¾   1

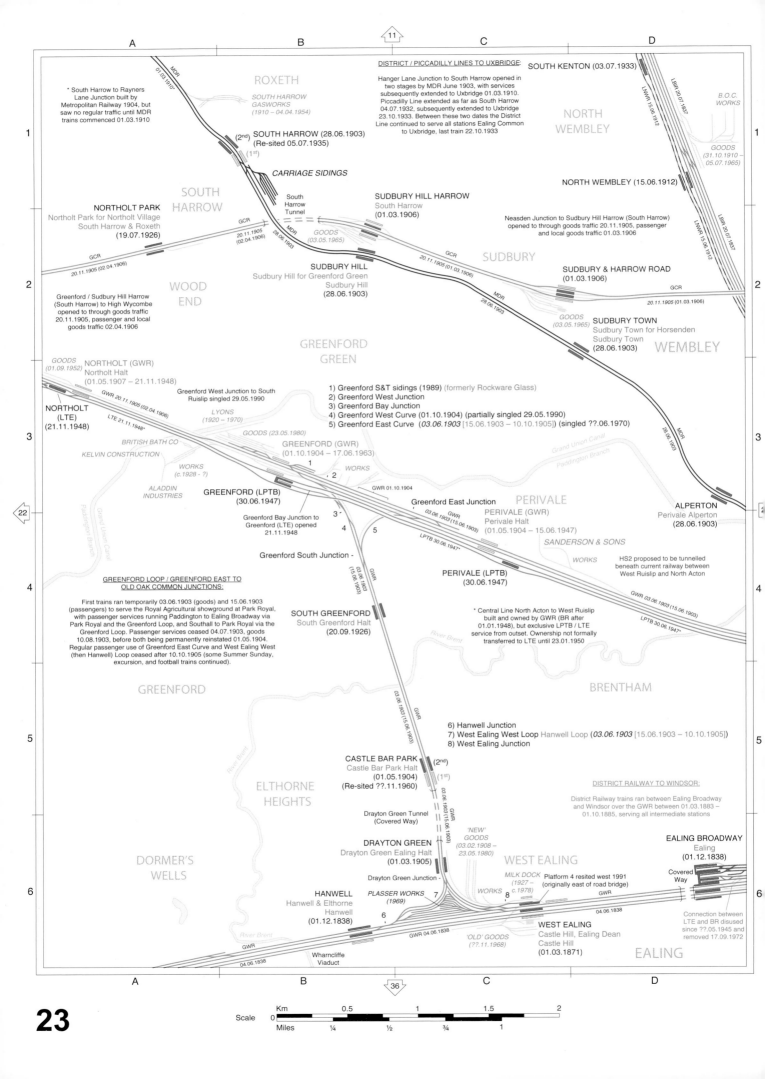

A   B   C   D

ROXETH

SOUTH HARROW
GASWORKS
(1910 – 04.04.1954)

* South Harrow to Rayners Lane Junction built by Metropolitan Railway 1904, but saw no regular traffic until MDR trains commenced 01.03.1910

DISTRICT / PICCADILLY LINES TO UXBRIDGE:
Hanger Lane Junction to South Harrow opened in two stages by MDR June 1903, with services subsequently extended to Uxbridge 01.03.1910. Piccadilly Line extended as far as South Harrow 04.07.1932, subsequently extended to Uxbridge 23.10.1933. Between these two dates the District Line continued to serve all stations Ealing Common to Uxbridge, last train 22.10.1933

SOUTH KENTON (03.07.1933)

NORTH WEMBLEY

B.O.C. WORKS

(2nd) SOUTH HARROW (28.06.1903)
(Re-sited 05.07.1935)
(1st)

CARRIAGE SIDINGS

South Harrow Tunnel

NORTH WEMBLEY (15.06.1912)

GOODS
(31.10.1910 – 05.07.1965)

NORTHOLT PARK
Northolt Park for Northolt Village
South Harrow & Roxeth
(19.07.1926)

SOUTH HARROW

SUDBURY HILL HARROW
South Harrow
(01.03.1906)

GOODS
(03.05.1965)

Neasden Junction to Sudbury Hill Harrow (South Harrow) opened to through goods traffic 20.11.1905, passenger and local goods traffic 01.03.1906

GCR
20.11.1905 (02.04.1906)

GCR
20.11.1905 (02.04.1906)

WOOD END

SUDBURY HILL
Sudbury Hill for Greenford Green
Sudbury Hill
(28.06.1903)

GCR
20.11.1905 (01.03.1906)

SUDBURY

SUDBURY & HARROW ROAD
(01.03.1906)

GCR
20.11.1905 (01.03.1906)

Greenford / Sudbury Hill Harrow (South Harrow) to High Wycombe opened to through goods traffic 20.11.1905, passenger and local goods traffic 02.04.1906

GREENFORD GREEN

GOODS
(03.05.1965)

SUDBURY TOWN
Sudbury Town for Horsenden
Sudbury Town
(28.06.1903)

WEMBLEY

GOODS
(01.09.1952)
NORTHOLT (GWR)
Northolt Halt
(01.05.1907 – 21.11.1948)

GWR 20.11.1905 (02.04.1906)

LTE 21.11.1948*

NORTHOLT
(LTE)
(21.11.1948)

LYONS
(1920 – 1970)

GOODS (23.05.1980)

1) Greenford S&T sidings (1989) (formerly Rockware Glass)
2) Greenford West Junction
3) Greenford Bay Junction
4) Greenford West Curve (01.10.1904) (partially singled 29.05.1990)
5) Greenford East Curve (03.06.1903 [15.06.1903 – 10.10.1905]) (singled ??.06.1970)

Greenford West Junction to South Ruislip singled 29.05.1990

GREENFORD (GWR)
(01.10.1904 – 17.06.1963)

WORKS

BRITISH BATH CO

KELVIN CONSTRUCTION

WORKS
(c. 1928 - ?)

ALADDIN INDUSTRIES

GREENFORD (LPTB)
(30.06.1947)

Greenford Bay Junction to Greenford (LTE) opened 21.11.1948

PERIVALE

GWR 01.10.1904

Greenford East Junction
03.06.1903 GWR (15.06.1903)

PERIVALE (GWR)
Perivale Halt
(01.05.1904 – 15.06.1947)

ALPERTON
Perivale Alperton
(28.06.1903)

LPTB 30.06.1947*

SANDERSON & SONS

WORKS

Greenford South Junction -

PERIVALE (LPTB)
(30.06.1947)

HS2 proposed to be tunnelled beneath current railway between West Ruislip and North Acton

GREENFORD LOOP / GREENFORD EAST TO OLD OAK COMMON JUNCTIONS:

First trains ran temporarily 03.06.1903 (goods) and 15.06.1903 (passengers) to serve the Royal Agricultural showground at Park Royal, with passenger services running Paddington to Ealing Broadway via Park Royal and the Greenford Loop, and Southall to Park Royal via the Greenford Loop. Passenger services ceased 04.07.1903, goods 10.08.1903, before both being permanently reinstated 01.05.1904. Regular passenger use of Greenford East Curve and West Ealing West (then Hanwell) Loop ceased after 10.10.1905 (some Summer Sunday, excursion, and football trains continued).

SOUTH GREENFORD
South Greenford Halt
(20.09.1926)

* Central Line North Acton to West Ruislip built and owned by GWR (BR after 01.01.1948), but exclusive LPTB / LTE service from outset. Ownership not formally transferred to LTE until 23.01.1950

GREENFORD

BRENTHAM

6) Hanwell Junction
7) West Ealing West Loop Hanwell Loop (03.06.1903 [15.06.1903 – 10.10.1905])
8) West Ealing Junction

ELTHORNE HEIGHTS

CASTLE BAR PARK
Castle Bar Park Halt
(01.05.1904)
(Re-sited ??.11.1960)
(2nd)
(1st)

DISTRICT RAILWAY TO WINDSOR:
District Railway trains ran between Ealing Broadway and Windsor over the GWR between 01.03.1883 – 01.10.1885, serving all intermediate stations

Drayton Green Tunnel
(Covered Way)

DRAYTON GREEN
Drayton Green Ealing Halt
(01.03.1905)

'NEW' GOODS
(03.02.1908 – 23.05.1980)

EALING BROADWAY
Ealing
(01.12.1838)

WEST EALING

DORMER'S WELLS

Drayton Green Junction -

HANWELL
Hanwell & Elthorne
Hanwell
(01.12.1838)

PLASSER WORKS
(1969)

MILK DOCK
(1927 – c.1978)

WORKS

Platform 4 resited west 1991
(originally east of road bridge)

Covered Way

Connection between LTE and BR disused since ??.05.1945 and removed 17.09.1972

WEST EALING
Castle Hill, Ealing Dean
Castle Hill
(01.03.1871)

Wharncliffe Viaduct

GWR 04.06.1838

'OLD' GOODS
(??.11.1968)

EALING

River Brent

23

Scale
Km 0   0.5   1   1.5   2
Miles ¼ ½ ¾ 1

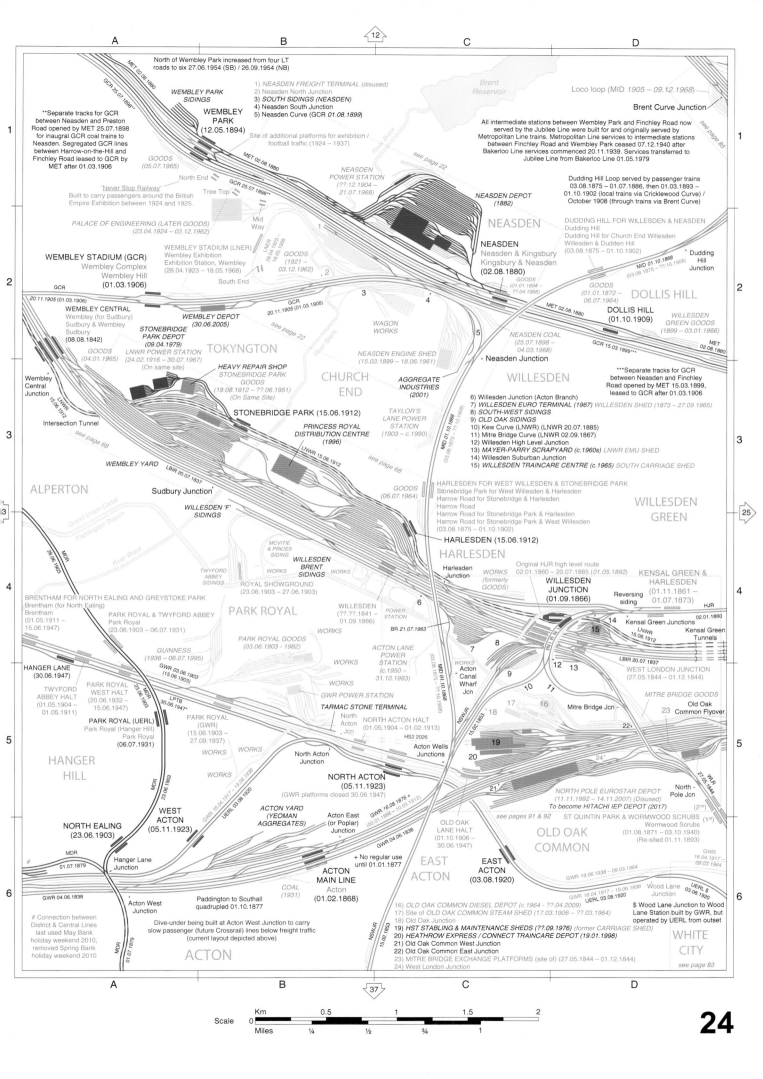

North of Wembley Park increased from four LT
roads to six 27.06.1954 (SB) / 26.09.1954 (NB)

MET 02.08.1880
*GCR 25.07.1898***

WEMBLEY PARK
SIDINGS

WEMBLEY
PARK
(12.05.1894)

1) NEASDEN FREIGHT TERMINAL (disused)
2) Neasden North Junction
3) SOUTH SIDINGS (NEASDEN)
4) Neasden South Junction
5) Neasden Curve (GCR 01.08.1899)

*Brent
Reservoir*

Loco loop (MID 1905 – 09.12.1968)

Brent Curve Junction

All intermediate stations between Wembley Park and Finchley Road now
served by the Jubilee Line were built for and originally served by
Metropolitan Line trains. Metropolitan Line services to intermediate stations
between Finchley Road and Wembley Park ceased 07.12.1940 after
Bakerloo Line services commenced 20.11.1939. Services transferred to
Jubilee Line from Bakerloo Line 01.05.1979

**Separate tracks for GCR
between Neasden and Preston
Road opened by MET 25.07.1898
for inaugural GCR coal trains to
Neasden. Segregated GCR lines
between Harrow-on-the-Hill and
Finchley Road leased to GCR by
MET after 01.03.1906

*GOODS
(05.07.1965)*

North End

MET 02.08.1880

*GCR 25.07.1898***

NEASDEN
POWER STATION
(??.12.1904 –
21.07.1968)

see page 22

River Brent

NEASDEN DEPOT
(1882)

NEASDEN

Dudding Hill Loop served by passenger trains
03.08.1875 – 01.07.1886, then 01.03.1893 –
01.10.1902 (local trains via Cricklewood Curve) /
October 1908 (through trains via Brent Curve)

'Never Stop Railway'
Built to carry passengers around the British
Empire Exhibition between 1924 and 1925.

Tree Top

Mid
Way

*PALACE OF ENGINEERING (LATER GOODS)
(23.04.1924 – 03.12.1962)*

WEMBLEY STADIUM (GCR)
Wembley Complex
Wembley Hill
(01.03.1906)

WEMBLEY STADIUM (LNER)
Wembley Exhibition
Exhibition Station, Wembley
(28.04.1923 – 18.05.1968)

LNER 28.04.1923 – 18.05.1968

*GOODS
(1921 –
03.12.1962)*

South End

NEASDEN
Neasden & Kingsbury
Kingsbury & Neasden
(02.08.1880)

*GOODS
(01.01.1894 –
??.04.1958)*

DUDDING HILL FOR WILLESDEN & NEASDEN
Dudding Hill
Dudding Hill for Church End Willesden
Willesden & Dudden Hill
(03.08.1875 – 01.10.1902)

*MID 01.10.1868
(03.08.1875 – ??.10.1908)*

Dudding
Hill
Junction

*GOODS
(01.01.1872 –
06.07.1964)*

DOLLIS HILL

DOLLIS HILL
(01.10.1909)

*WILLESDEN
GREEN GOODS
(1899 – 03.01.1966)*

*MET
02.08.1880*

*GCR
20.11.1905 (01.03.1906)*

WEMBLEY CENTRAL
Wembley (for Sudbury)
Sudbury & Wembley
Sudbury
(08.08.1842)

WEMBLEY DEPOT
(30.06.2005)

STONEBRIDGE
PARK DEPOT
(09.04.1979)

*GCR
20.11.1905 (01.03.1906)*

WAGON
WORKS

MET 02.08.1880

NEASDEN COAL
(25.07.1898 –
04.03.1968)

*GCR 15.03.1899***

WILLESDEN

***Separate tracks for GCR
between Neasden and Finchley
Road opened by MET 15.03.1899,
leased to GCR after 01.03.1906

*GOODS
(04.01.1965)*

GCR

LNWR POWER STATION
(24.02.1916 – 30.07.1967)
(On same site)

TOKYNGTON

CHURCH
END

NEASDEN ENGINE SHED
(15.03.1899 – 18.06.1961)

- Neasden Junction

HEAVY REPAIR SHOP
STONEBRIDGE PARK
(19.08.1912 – ??.06.1951)
(On Same Site)

River Brent

AGGREGATE
INDUSTRIES
(2001)

6) Willesden Junction (Acton Branch)
7) WILLESDEN EURO TERMINAL (1967) WILLESDEN SHED (1873 – 27.09.1965)
8) SOUTH-WEST SIDINGS
9) OLD OAK SIDINGS
10) Kew Curve (LNWR 20.07.1885)
11) Mitre Bridge Curve (LNWR 02.09.1867)
12) Willesden High Level Junction
13) MAYER-PARRY SCRAPYARD (c.1960s) LNWR EMU SHED
14) Willesden Suburban Junction
15) WILLESDEN TRAINCARE CENTRE (c.1965) SOUTH CARRIAGE SHED

Wembley
Central
Junction

*LNWR
15.06.1912*

Intersection Tunnel

see page 68

STONEBRIDGE PARK (15.06.1912)

PRINCESS ROYAL
DISTRIBUTION CENTRE
(1996)

TAYLOR'S
LANE POWER
STATION
(1903 – c.1990)

see page 68

WEMBLEY YARD

LBIR 20.07.1837

LNWR 15.06.1912

Sudbury Junction

WILLESDEN 'F'
SIDINGS

GOODS
(06.07.1964)

HARLESDEN FOR WEST WILLESDEN & STONEBRIDGE PARK
Stonebridge Park for West Willesden & Harlesden
Harrow Road for Stonebridge & Harlesden
Harrow Road
Harrow Road for Stonebridge Park & Harlesden
Harrow Road for Stonebridge Park & West Willesden
(03.08.1875 – 01.10.1902)

WILLESDEN
GREEN

ALPERTON

*MDR
28.06.1903*

*Grand Union Canal
Paddington Branch*

River Brent

MCVITIE
& PRICES
SIDING

WILLESDEN
BRENT SIDINGS

WORKS

HARLESDEN (15.06.1912)

HARLESDEN

Original HJR high level route
02.01.1860 – 20.07.1885 (01.05.1892)

KENSAL GREEN &
HARLESDEN
(01.11.1861 –
01.07.1873)

*TWYFORD
ABBEY
SIDINGS*

ROYAL SHOWGROUND
(23.06.1903 – 27.06.1903)

WORKS

Harlesden
Junction

*WORKS
(formerly
GOODS)*

WILLESDEN
JUNCTION
(01.09.1866)

Reversing
siding

HJR

BRENTHAM FOR NORTH EALING AND GREYSTOKE PARK
Brentham (for North Ealing)
Brentham
(01.05.1911 –
15.06.1947)

PARK ROYAL & TWYFORD ABBEY
Park Royal
(23.06.1903 – 06.07.1931)

PARK ROYAL

WILLESDEN
(??.??.1841 –
01.09.1866)

*POWER
STATION*

BR 21.07.1963

Kensal Green Junctions
02.01.1860

*LNWR
15.06.1912*

14

15

Kensal Green
Tunnels

LBIR 20.07.1837

WEST LONDON JUNCTION
(27.05.1844 – 01.12.1844)

HANGER LANE
(30.06.1947)

*GUINNESS
(1936 – 06.07.1995)*

*GWR 03.06.1903
(15.06.1903)*

PARK ROYAL GOODS
(03.06.1903 – 1982)

ACTON LANE
POWER
STATION
(c.1950 –
31.10.1983)

*MID 01.10.1868
(03.08.1875 – ??.10.1908)*

WORKS

Acton
Canal
Wharf
Jcn

7

8

9

12 13

MITRE BRIDGE GOODS

Mitre Bridge Jcn

Old Oak
Common Flyover

23

TWYFORD
ABBEY HALT
(01.05.1904 –
01.05.1911)

PARK ROYAL
WEST HALT
(20.06.1932 –
15.06.1947)

*MDR
23.06.1903*

*LPTB
30.06.1947*

PARK ROYAL (UERL)
Park Royal (Hanger Hill)
Park Royal
(06.07.1931)

PARK ROYAL
(GWR)
(15.06.1903 –
27.09.1937)

WORKS

GWR POWER STATION

TARMAC STONE TERMINAL

North
Acton
Jcn

NORTH ACTON HALT
(01.05.1904 – 01.02.1913)

HS2 2026

Acton Wells
Junctions

NSWJR

15.02.1853

10

11

16

17

18

19

20

21

22

24

MITRE BRIDGE GOODS

North Pole Jcn

HANGER
HILL

*MDR
23.06.1903*

WEST
ACTON
(05.11.1923)

GWR 16.04.1917 – 18.06.1938
UERL 03.06.1920

ACTON YARD
(YEOMAN
AGGREGATES)

Acton East
(or Poplar)
Junction

*GWR 16.08.1876 +
(02.01.1888 – 10.03.1912)*

NORTH ACTON
(05.11.1923)
(GWR platforms closed 30.06.1947)

NORTH EALING
(23.06.1903)

NORTH ACTON
Junction

OLD OAK
LANE HALT
(01.10.1906 –
30.06.1947)

NORTH POLE EUROSTAR DEPOT
(11.11.1992 – 14.11.2007) (Disused)
To become HITACHI IEP DEPOT (2017)

see pages 91 & 92

ST QUINTIN PARK & WORMWOOD SCRUBS
Wormwood Scrubs
(01.08.1871 – 03.10.1940)
(Re-sited 01.11.1893)

WLR 27.05.1844

North -
Pole Jcn

(2nd)

OLD OAK
COMMON

*GWR
16.04.1917 –
09.03.1964*

Hanger Lane
Junction

*MDR
01.07.1879*

GWR 04.06.1838

+ No regular use
until 01.01.1877

ACTON
MAIN LINE
Acton
(01.02.1868)

EAST
ACTON

EAST
ACTON
(03.08.1920)

GWR 19.06.1938 – 09.03.1964

GWR 16.04.1917 – 19.06.1938
UERL 03.06.1920

Wood Lane
Junction

*UERL
03.08.1920*

WHITE
CITY

Connection between
District & Central Lines
last used May Bank
holiday weekend 2010,
removed Spring Bank
holiday weekend 2010

GWR 04.06.1838

Acton West
Junction

Paddington to Southall
quadrupled 01.10.1877

*COAL
(1931)*

Dive-under being built at Acton West Junction to carry
slow passenger (future Crossrail) lines below freight traffic
(current layout depicted above)

16) OLD OAK COMMON DIESEL DEPOT (c.1964 – ??.04.2009)
17) Site of OLD OAK COMMON STEAM SHED (17.03.1906 – ??.03.1964)
18) Old Oak Junction
19) HST STABLING & MAINTENANCE SHEDS (??.09.1976) (former CARRIAGE SHED)
20) HEATHROW EXPRESS / CONNECT TRAINCARE DEPOT (19.01.1998)
21) Old Oak Common West Junction
22) Old Oak Common East Junction
23) MITRE BRIDGE EXCHANGE PLATFORMS (site of) (27.05.1844 – 01.12.1844)
24) West London Junction

NSWJR

15.02.1853

$ Wood Lane Junction to Wood
Lane Station built by GWR, but
operated by UERL from outset

see page 83

ACTON

Km
Scale 0   0.5   1   1.5   2

Miles ¼   ½   ¾   1

24

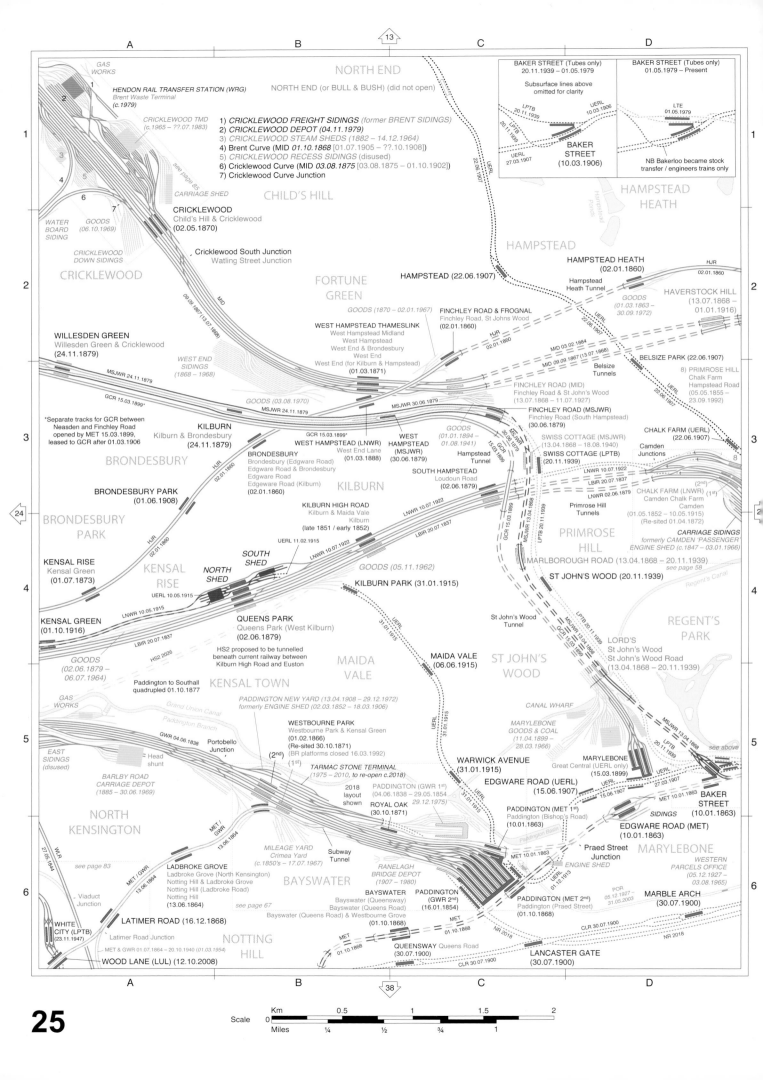

GAS WORKS

HENDON RAIL TRANSFER STATION (WRG)
Brent Waste Terminal
(c.1979)

NORTH END

NORTH END (or BULL & BUSH) (did not open)

CRICKLEWOOD TMD
(c.1965 – ??.07.1983)

1) *CRICKLEWOOD FREIGHT SIDINGS* (former BRENT SIDINGS)
2) *CRICKLEWOOD DEPOT* (04.11.1979)
3) *CRICKLEWOOD STEAM SHEDS* (1882 – 14.12.1964)
4) Brent Curve (MID *01.10.1868* [01.07.1905 – ??.10.1908])
5) *CRICKLEWOOD RECESS SIDINGS* (disused)
6) Cricklewood Curve (MID *03.08.1875* [03.08.1875 – 01.10.1902])
7) Cricklewood Curve Junction

BAKER STREET (Tubes only)
20.11.1939 – 01.05.1979
Subsurface lines above
omitted for clarity

BAKER STREET (Tubes only)
01.05.1979 – Present

LPTB
20.11.1939

UERL
10.03.1906

LTE
01.05.1979

UERL
22.08.1907

UERL
27.03.1907

BAKER
STREET
(10.03.1906)

NB Bakerloo became stock
transfer / engineers trains only

CRICKLEWOOD TMD
see page 85

CARRIAGE SHED

CHILD'S HILL

HAMPSTEAD
HEATH

CRICKLEWOOD

WATER
BOARD
SIDING

GOODS
(06.10.1969)

CRICKLEWOOD
DOWN SIDINGS

CRICKLEWOOD
Child's Hill & Cricklewood
(02.05.1870)

Cricklewood South Junction
Watling Street Junction

HAMPSTEAD (22.06.1907)

HAMPSTEAD HEATH
(02.01.1860)

HAMPSTEAD

Hampstead
Heath Tunnel

HJR
02.01.1860

HAVERSTOCK HILL
(13.07.1868 –
01.01.1916)

FORTUNE
GREEN

GOODS (1870 – 02.01.1967)

FINCHLEY ROAD & FROGNAL
Finchley Road, St Johns Wood
(02.01.1860)

GOODS
(01.03.1863 –
30.09.1972)

WILLESDEN GREEN
Willesden Green & Cricklewood
(24.11.1879)

WEST HAMPSTEAD THAMESLINK
West Hampstead Midland
West Hampstead
West End & Brondesbury
West End
West End (for Kilburn & Hampstead)
(01.03.1871)

HJR
02.01.1860

BELSIZE PARK (22.06.1907)

MID 03.02.1884

Belsize
Tunnels

8) PRIMROSE HILL
Chalk Farm
Hampstead Road
(05.05.1855 –
23.09.1992)

MSJWR 24.11.1879

GCR 15.03.1899*

GOODS (03.08.1970)

MSJWR 24.11.1879

MID 09.09.1867 (13.07.1868)

FINCHLEY ROAD (MID)
Finchley Road & St John's Wood
(13.07.1868 – 11.07.1927)

CHALK FARM (UERL)
(22.06.1907)

*Separate tracks for GCR between
Neasden and Finchley Road
opened by MET 15.03.1899,
leased to GCR after 01.03.1906

KILBURN
Kilburn & Brondesbury
(24.11.1879)

GCR 15.03.1899*

WEST HAMPSTEAD (LNWR)
West End Lane
(01.03.1888)

WEST
HAMPSTEAD
(MSJWR)
(30.06.1879)

FINCHLEY ROAD (MSJWR)
Finchley Road (South Hampstead)
(30.06.1879)

GOODS
(01.01.1894 –
01.08.1941)

SWISS COTTAGE (MSJWR)
(13.04.1868 – 18.08.1940)

Camden
Junctions

BRONDESBURY

BRONDESBURY
Brondesbury (Edgware Road)
Edgware Road & Brondesbury
Edgware Road
Edgeware Road (Kilburn)
(02.01.1860)

Hampstead Tunnel

SOUTH HAMPSTEAD
Loudoun Road
(02.06.1879)

SWISS COTTAGE (LPTB)
(20.11.1939)

CHALK FARM (LNWR)
(2nd)
Camden Chalk Farm
Camden
(01.05.1852 – 10.05.1915)
(Re-sited 01.04.1872)

(1st)

KILBURN

BRONDESBURY PARK
(01.06.1908)

LNWR 10.07.1922

LBIR 20.07.1837

PRIMROSE
HILL

CARRIAGE SIDINGS
formerly CAMDEN 'PASSENGER'
ENGINE SHED (c.1847 – 03.01.1966)

KILBURN HIGH ROAD
Kilburn & Maida Vale
Kilburn
(late 1851 / early 1852)

LNWR 10.07.1922

LNWR 02.06.1879

Primrose Hill
Tunnels

MARLBOROUGH ROAD (13.04.1868 – 20.11.1939)
see page 58

KENSAL RISE
Kensal Green
(01.07.1873)

UERL 11.02.1915

SOUTH
SHED

ST JOHN'S WOOD (20.11.1939)

REGENT'S
PARK

KENSAL
RISE

NORTH
SHED

KILBURN PARK (31.01.1915)

GOODS (05.11.1962)

St John's Wood
Tunnel

LORD'S
St John's Wood
St John's Wood Road
(13.04.1868 – 20.11.1939)

UERL 10.05.1915

KENSAL GREEN
(01.10.1916)

LNWR 10.05.1915

QUEENS PARK
Queens Park (West Kilburn)
(02.06.1879)

LBIR 20.07.1837

MAIDA VALE
(06.06.1915)

ST JOHN'S
WOOD

GOODS
(02.06.1879 –
06.07.1964)

HS2 2026

HS2 proposed to be tunnelled
beneath current railway between
Kilburn High Road and Euston

MAIDA
VALE

Paddington to Southall
quadrupled 01.10.1877

KENSAL TOWN

PADDINGTON NEW YARD (13.04.1908 – 29.12.1972)
formerly ENGINE SHED (02.03.1852 – 18.03.1906)

CANAL WHARF

MARYLEBONE
GOODS & COAL
(11.04.1899 –
28.03.1966)

GAS
WORKS

Grand Union Canal

Paddington Branch

GWR 04.06.1838

Portobello
Junction

WESTBOURNE PARK
Westbourne Park & Kensal Green
(01.02.1866)
(Re-sited 30.10.1871)
(BR platforms closed 16.03.1992)

WARWICK AVENUE
(31.01.1915)

MARYLEBONE
Great Central (UERL only)
(15.03.1899)

EAST
SIDINGS
(disused)

BARLBY ROAD
CARRIAGE DEPOT
(1885 – 30.06.1969)

Head
shunt

(2nd)

(1st)

TARMAC STONE TERMINAL
(1975 – 2010, to re-open c.2018)

EDGWARE ROAD (UERL)
(15.06.1907)

BAKER
STREET
(10.01.1863)

NORTH
KENSINGTON

2018
layout
shown

PADDINGTON (GWR 1st)
(04.06.1838 – 29.05.1854)
29.12.1975)

ROYAL OAK
(30.10.1871)

PADDINGTON (MET 1st)
Paddington (Bishop's Road)
(10.01.1863)

EDGWARE ROAD (MET)
(10.01.1863)

SIDINGS

see page 83

MET / GWR
13.06.1864

LADBROKE GROVE
Ladbroke Grove (North Kensington)
Notting Hill & Ladbroke Grove
Notting Hill (Ladbroke Road)
Notting Hill
(13.06.1864)

MILEAGE YARD
Crimea Yard
(c.1850's – 17.07.1967)

Subway
Tunnel

Praed Street
Junction

ENGINE SHED

WESTERN
PARCELS OFFICE
(05.12.1927 –
18.05.1965)

27.05.1844

WLR

Viaduct
Junction

BAYSWATER

RANELAGH
BRIDGE DEPOT
(1907 – 1980)

PADDINGTON
(GWR 2nd)
(16.01.1854)

PADDINGTON (MET 2nd)
Paddington (Praed Street)
(01.10.1868)

MARBLE ARCH
(30.07.1900)

MARYLEBONE

LATIMER ROAD (16.12.1868)

see page 67

BAYSWATER
Bayswater (Queensway)
Bayswater (Queens Road)
Bayswater (Queens Road) & Westbourne Grove
(01.10.1868)

POR
05.12.1927 –
31.05.2003

WHITE
CITY (LPTB)
(23.11.1947)

Latimer Road Junction

NOTTING
HILL

MET
01.10.1868

QUEENSWAY Queens Road
(30.07.1900)

LANCASTER GATE
(30.07.1900)

NR 2018

WOOD LANE (LUL) (12.10.2008)

MET & GWR 01.07.1864 – 20.10.1940 (01.03.1954)

MET
01.10.1868

CLR 30.07.1900

Scale

Km
0   0.5   1   1.5   2

Miles
¼   ½   ¾   1

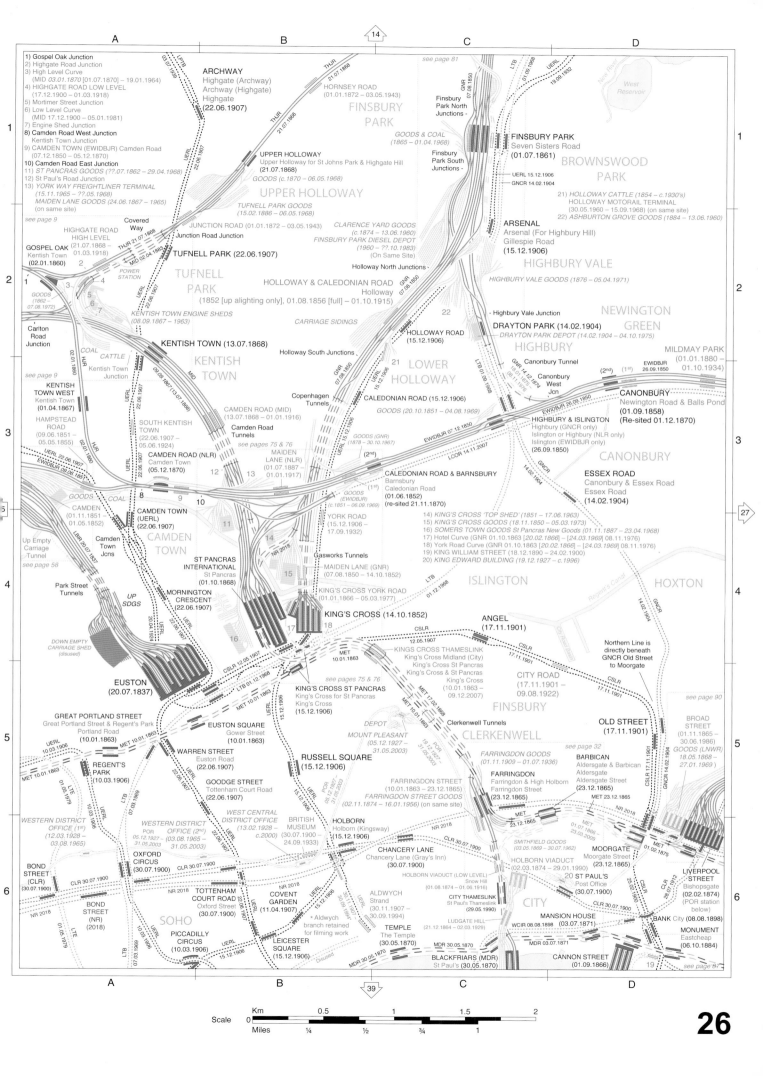

A   B   14   C   D

1   1

see page 81

THJR 21.07.1868

ARCHWAY
Highgate (Archway)
Archway (Highgate)
Highgate
(22.06.1907)

HORNSEY ROAD
(01.01.1872 – 03.05.1943)

FINSBURY PARK

GNR 07.08.1850

LTB 01.09.1868   UERL 19.09.1932

Finsbury Park North Junctions –

FINSBURY PARK
Seven Sisters Road
(01.07.1861)

BROWNSWOOD PARK

UERL 15.12.1906
GNCR 14.02.1904

21) HOLLOWAY CATTLE (1854 – c.1930's)
HOLLOWAY MOTORAIL TERMINAL
(30.05.1960 – 15.09.1968) (on same site)
22) ASHBURTON GROVE GOODS (1884 – 13.06.1960)

THJR 21.07.1868

UPPER HOLLOWAY
Upper Holloway for St Johns Park & Highgate Hill
(21.07.1868)

GOODS (c.1870 – 06.05.1968)

UPPER HOLLOWAY

GOODS & COAL
(1865 – 01.04.1908)

Finsbury Park South Junctions –

ARSENAL
Arsenal (For Highbury Hill)
Gillespie Road
(15.12.1906)

HIGHBURY VALE

UERL 22.06.1907

1) Gospel Oak Junction
2) Highgate Road Junction
3) High Level Curve
(MID 03.01.1870 [01.07.1870] – 19.01.1964)
4) HIGHGATE ROAD LOW LEVEL
(17.12.1900 – 01.03.1918)
5) Mortimer Street Junction
6) Low Level Curve
(MID 17.12.1900 – 05.01.1981)
7) Engine Shed Junction
8) Camden Road West Junction
Kentish Town Junction
9) CAMDEN TOWN (EWIDBJR) Camden Road
(07.12.1850 – 05.12.1870)
10) Camden Road East Junction
11) ST PANCRAS GOODS (??.07.1862 – 29.04.1968)
12) St Paul's Road Junction
13) YORK WAY FREIGHTLINER TERMINAL
(15.11.1965 – ??.05.1968)
MAIDEN LANE GOODS (24.06.1867 – 1965)
(on same site)

TUFNELL PARK GOODS
(15.02.1888 – 06.05.1968)

JUNCTION ROAD (01.01.1872 – 03.05.1943)

CLARENCE YARD GOODS
(c.1874 – 13.06.1960)
FINSBURY PARK DIESEL DEPOT
(1960 – ??.10.1983)
(On Same Site)

Holloway North Junctions –

HIGHBURY VALE GOODS (1876 – 05.04.1971)

NEWINGTON GREEN

see page 9

Covered Way

HIGHGATE ROAD
HIGH LEVEL
(21.07.1868 –
01.03.1918)

THJR 21.07.1868

Junction Road Junction

TUFNELL PARK (22.06.1907)

MID 02.04.1883

POWER STATION

TUFNELL PARK

KENTISH TOWN ENGINE SHEDS
(08.09.1867 – 1963)

HOLLOWAY & CALEDONIAN ROAD
Holloway
(1852 [up alighting only], 01.08.1856 [full] – 01.10.1915)

CARRIAGE SIDINGS

GNR 07.08.1850

- Highbury Vale Junction

DRAYTON PARK (14.02.1904)
DRAYTON PARK DEPOT (14.02.1904 – 04.10.1975)

HIGHBURY

MILDMAY PARK
(01.01.1880 –
01.10.1934)

2   2

GOSPEL OAK
Kentish Town
(02.01.1860)

GOODS
(1862 –
07.08.1972)

Carlton Road Junction

see page 9

Carlton Road Junction

02.01.1860
HJR

KENTISH TOWN WEST
Kentish Town
(01.04.1867)

HAMPSTEAD ROAD
(09.06.1851 –
05.05.1855)

CATTLE
Kentish Town
Junction

Kentish Town
Junction

KENTISH TOWN (13.07.1868)

MID 02.09.1867 (13.07.1868)

KENTISH TOWN

HOLLOWAY ROAD
(15.12.1906)

Holloway South Junctions –

Copenhagen Tunnels

CALEDONIAN ROAD (15.12.1906)

GOODS (20.10.1851 – 04.08.1969)

21

LOWER HOLLOWAY

GNR 07.08.1850

UERL 15.12.1906

Canonbury Tunnel

GNR 14.12.1874

Canonbury West Jcn

(2nd)   (1st)
EWIDBJR
26.09.1850

CANONBURY
Newington Road & Balls Pond
(01.09.1858) (Re-sited 01.12.1870)

HIGHBURY VALE

CANONBURY

3   3

HAMPSTEAD
ROAD
(09.06.1851 –
05.05.1855)

UERL 22.06.1907

HJR 02.01.1860

SOUTH KENTISH TOWN
(22.06.1907 –
05.06.1924)

EWIDBJR 09.06.1851

CAMDEN ROAD (MID)
(13.07.1868 – 01.01.1916)

Camden Road Tunnels

CAMDEN ROAD (NLR)
Camden Town
(05.12.1870)

MAIDEN LANE (NLR)
(01.07.1887 –
01.01.1917)

see pages 75 & 76

GOODS (GNR)
(1878 – 30.10.1967)

(2nd)

EWIDBJR 07.12.1850

LCOR 14.11.2007

14.02.1904
GNCR

HIGHBURY & ISLINGTON
Highbury (GNCR only)
Islington or Highbury (NLR only)
Islington (EWIDBJR only)
(26.09.1850)

ESSEX ROAD
Canonbury & Essex Road
Essex Road
(14.02.1904)

CAMDEN TOWN (UERL)
(22.06.1907)

12   13

MAIDEN LANE (NLR)
(01.07.1887 –
01.01.1917)

GOODS
(EWIDBJR)
(c.1851 – 06.09.1969)

CALEDONIAN ROAD & BARNSBURY
Barnsbury
Caledonian Road
(01.06.1852)
(re-sited 21.11.1870)

(1st)

14) KING'S CROSS 'TOP SHED' (1851 – 17.06.1963)
15) KING'S CROSS GOODS (18.11.1850 – 05.03.1973)
16) SOMERS TOWN GOODS St Pancras New Goods (01.11.1887 – 23.04.1968)
17) Hotel Curve (GNR 01.10.1863 [20.02.1866] – [24.03.1969] 08.11.1976)
18) York Road Curve (GNR 01.10.1863 [20.02.1866] – [24.03.1969] 08.11.1976)
19) KING WILLIAM STREET (18.12.1890 – 24.02.1900)
20) KING EDWARD BUILDING (19.12.1927 – c.1996)

GOODS   COAL

CAMDEN
(01.11.1851 –
01.05.1852)

CAMDEN TOWN (UERL)
(22.06.1907)

Camden Town Jcns

8

9   10

11

YORK ROAD
(15.12.1906 –
17.09.1932)

Gasworks Tunnels

14

NR 2018

ISLINGTON

HOXTON

4   4

Park Street Tunnels

UP SDGS

MORNINGTON CRESCENT
(22.06.1907)

ST PANCRAS INTERNATIONAL
St Pancras
(01.10.1868)

15

MAIDEN LANE (GNR)
(07.08.1850 – 14.10.1852)

KING'S CROSS YORK ROAD
(01.01.1866 – 05.03.1977)

KING'S CROSS (14.10.1852)

17

16   18

ANGEL
(17.11.1901)

CITY ROAD
(17.11.1901 –
09.08.1922)

Northern Line is
directly beneath
GNCR Old Street
to Moorgate

DOWN EMPTY
CARRIAGE SHED
(disused)

see page 58

EUSTON
(20.07.1837)

UERL 22.06.1907

UERL 20.04.1924

CSLR 12.05.1907

12.05.1907

KINGS CROSS THAMESLINK
King's Cross Midland (City)
King's Cross St Pancras
King's Cross & St Pancras
King's Cross
(10.01.1863 –
09.12.2007)

CSLR 17.11.1901

CSLR 17.11.1901

5   27

MET 10.01.1863

MET 17.02.1866

KING'S CROSS ST PANCRAS
King's Cross for St Pancras
King's Cross
(15.12.1906)

MET 10.01.1863

Clerkenwell Tunnels

FINSBURY

CLERKENWELL

see page 90

OLD STREET
(17.11.1901)

BROAD STREET
(01.11.1865 –
30.06.1986)
GOODS (LNWR)
(18.05.1868 –
27.01.1969)

5   5

GREAT PORTLAND STREET
Great Portland Street & Regent's Park
Portland Road
(10.01.1863)

EUSTON SQUARE
Gower Street
(10.01.1863)

WARREN STREET
Euston Road
(22.06.1907)

REGENT'S PARK
(10.03.1906)

GOODGE STREET
Tottenham Court Road
(22.06.1907)

RUSSELL SQUARE
(15.12.1906)

DEPOT
MOUNT PLEASANT
(05.12.1927 –
31.05.2003)

19.12.1927
31.05.2003

FARRINGDON GOODS
(01.11.1909 – 01.07.1936)

FARRINGDON
Farringdon & High Holborn
Farringdon Street
(23.12.1865)

BARBICAN
Aldersgate & Barbican
Aldersgate
Aldersgate Street
(23.12.1865)

MET 23.12.1865

MOORGATE
Moorgate Street
(23.12.1865)

MET 01.02.1875

NR 2018

01.07.1866
23.03.2009

LIVERPOOL STREET
Bishopsgate
(02.02.1874)
(POR station below)

6   6

WESTERN DISTRICT
OFFICE (1st)
(12.03.1928 –
03.08.1965)

WESTERN DISTRICT
OFFICE (2nd)
POR
(05.12.1927 –
31.05.2003)

WEST CENTRAL
DISTRICT OFFICE
(13.02.1928 –
c.2000)

BOND STREET (CLR)
(30.07.1900)

OXFORD CIRCUS
(30.07.1900)

BOND STREET (NR)
(2018)

TOTTENHAM COURT ROAD
Oxford Street
(30.07.1900)

COVENT GARDEN
(11.04.1907)

BRITISH MUSEUM
(30.07.1900 –
24.09.1933)

HOLBORN
Holborn (Kingsway)
(15.12.1906)

CHANCERY LANE
Chancery Lane (Gray's Inn)
(30.07.1900)

CLR 30.07.1900

NR 2018

HOLBORN VIADUCT (LOW LEVEL)
Snow Hill
(01.08.1874 – 01.06.1916)

CITY THAMESLINK
St Paul's Thameslink
(29.05.1990)

20 ST PAUL'S
Post Office
(30.07.1900)

SMITHFIELD GOODS
(03.05.1869 – 30.07.1962)

HOLBORN VIADUCT
(02.03.1874 – 29.01.1990)

CITY

LIVERPOOL STREET

CLR 28.07.1912

BANK City (08.08.1898)

SOHO

PICCADILLY CIRCUS
(10.03.1906)

LEICESTER SQUARE
(15.12.1906)

* Aldwych
branch retained
for filming work

ALDWYCH
Strand
(30.11.1907 –
30.09.1994)

TEMPLE
The Temple
(30.05.1870)

LUDGATE HILL
(21.12.1864 – 02.03.1929)

MDR 30.05.1870

WCIR 08.08.1898

MANSION HOUSE
(03.07.1871)

MDR 03.07.1871

MONUMENT
Eastcheap
(06.10.1884)

Disused

MDR 30.05.1870

BLACKFRIARS (MDR)
St Paul's
(30.05.1870)

CANNON STREET
(01.09.1866)

19

see page 87

Km   Scale   0   0.5   1   1.5   2
Miles   ¼   ½   ¾   1

26

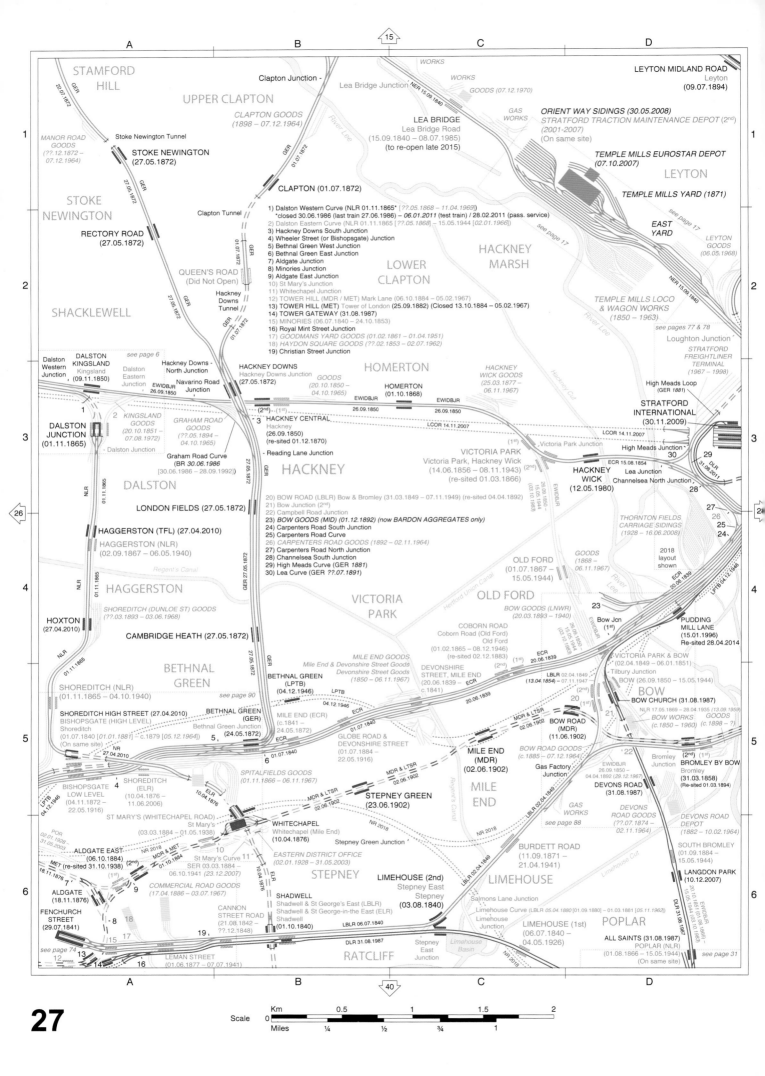

STAMFORD HILL

UPPER CLAPTON

CLAPTON GOODS
(1898 – 07.12.1964)

Clapton Junction –

WORKS

WORKS

GOODS (07.12.1970)

LEYTON MIDLAND ROAD
Leyton
(09.07.1894)

GER 22.07.1872

MANOR ROAD
GOODS
(??.12.1872 –
07.12.1964)

Stoke Newington Tunnel

STOKE NEWINGTON
(27.05.1872)

GER 27.05.1872

Lea Bridge Junction
NER 15.09.1840

LEA BRIDGE
Lea Bridge Road
(15.09.1840 – 08.07.1985)
(to re-open late 2015)

GAS
WORKS

ORIENT WAY SIDINGS (30.05.2008)
STRATFORD TRACTION MAINTENANCE DEPOT (2nd)
(2001-2007)
(On same site)

TEMPLE MILLS EUROSTAR DEPOT
(07.10.2007)

LEYTON

see page 17

STOKE
NEWINGTON

GER 27.05.1872

CLAPTON (01.07.1872)

GER 01.07.1872

TEMPLE MILLS YARD (1871)

LEYTON
GOODS
(06.05.1968)

EAST
YARD

RECTORY ROAD
(27.05.1872)

Clapton Tunnel

GER 01.07.1872

GER

QUEEN'S ROAD
(Did Not Open)

Hackney
Downs
Tunnel

GER 01.07.1872

1) Dalston Western Curve (NLR 01.11.1865* [*??.05.1868 – 11.04.1969*])
   *closed 30.06.1986 (last train 27.06.1986) – 06.01.2011 (test train) / 28.02.2011 (pass. service)
2) Dalston Eastern Curve (NLR 01.11.1865 [*??.05.1868*] – 15.05.1944 [*02.01.1966*])
3) Hackney Downs South Junction
4) Wheeler Street (or Bishopsgate) Junction
5) Bethnal Green West Junction
6) Bethnal Green East Junction
7) Aldgate Junction
8) Minories Junction
9) Aldgate East Junction
10) St Mary's Junction
11) Whitechapel Junction
12) TOWER HILL (MDR / MET) Mark Lane (06.10.1884 – 05.02.1967)
13) TOWER HILL (MET) Tower of London (25.09.1882) (Closed 13.10.1884 – 05.02.1967)
14) TOWER GATEWAY (31.08.1987)
15) MINORIES (06.07.1840 – 24.10.1853)
16) Royal Mint Street Junction
17) *GOODMANS YARD GOODS (01.02.1861 – 01.04.1951)*
18) *HAYDON SQUARE GOODS (??.02.1853 – 02.07.1962)*
19) Christian Street Junction

SHACKLEWELL

HACKNEY
MARSH

LOWER
CLAPTON

see pages 77 & 78

Loughton Junction

Dalston
Western Junction

see page 6

DALSTON
KINGSLAND
Kingsland
(09.11.1850)

Dalston
Eastern
Junction

Navarino Road
Junction

EWIDBJR
26.09.1850

HACKNEY DOWNS –
NORTH JUNCTION

HACKNEY DOWNS
Hackney Downs Junction
(27.05.1872)

HOMERTON

GOODS
(20.10.1850 –
04.10.1965)

HACKNEY
WICK GOODS
(25.03.1877 –
06.11.1967)

*STRATFORD
FREIGHTLINER
TERMINAL*
(1967 – 1998)

High Meads Loop
(GER 1881)

STRATFORD
INTERNATIONAL
(30.11.2009)

KINGSLAND
GOODS
(20.10.1851 –
07.08.1972)

EWIDBJR
26.09.1850

HOMERTON
(01.10.1868)

EWIDBJR
26.09.1850

LCOR 14.11.2007

DALSTON
JUNCTION
(01.11.1865)

1

2

3

GRAHAM ROAD
GOODS
(??.05.1894 –
04.10.1965)

HACKNEY CENTRAL
Hackney
(26.09.1850)
(re-sited 01.12.1870)

LCOR 14.11.2007

High Meads Junction

30

Dalston Junction

Graham Road Curve
(BR 30.06.1986)
[30.06.1986 – 28.09.1992]

Reading Lane Junction

VICTORIA
PARK
Victoria Park, Hackney Wick
(14.06.1856 – 08.11.1943)
(re-sited 01.03.1866)

(1st)
Victoria Park Junction

ECR 15.08.1854
Lea Junction
Channelsea North Junction

29

DLR
31.08.2011

28

26

DALSTON

HACKNEY

HACKNEY
WICK
(12.05.1980)

27

LONDON FIELDS (27.05.1872)

26

GER 27.05.1872

20) BOW ROAD (LBLR) Bow & Bromley (31.03.1849 – 07.11.1949) (re-sited 04.04.1892)
21) Bow Junction
22) Campbell Road Junction
23) BOW GOODS (MID) (01.12.1892) (now BARDON AGGREGATES only)
24) Carpenters Road South Junction
25) Carpenters Road Curve
26) CARPENTERS ROAD GOODS (1892 – 02.11.1964)
27) Carpenters Road North Junction
28) Channelsea South Junction
29) High Meads Curve (GER 1881)
30) Lea Curve (GER ??.07.1891)

*THORNTON FIELDS
CARRIAGE SIDINGS
(1928 – 16.06.2008)*

25

24

HAGGERSTON (TFL) (27.04.2010)

HAGGERSTON (NLR)
(02.09.1867 – 06.05.1940)

2018
layout
shown

HOXTON
(27.04.2010)

Regent's Canal

VICTORIA
PARK

OLD FORD

*GOODS
(1868 –
06.11.1967)*

HAGGERSTON

*SHOREDITCH (DUNLOE ST) GOODS
(??.03.1893 – 03.06.1968)*

OLD FORD
(01.07.1867 –
15.05.1944)

ECR
20.06.1839

LPTB 04.12.1846

CAMBRIDGE HEATH (27.05.1872)

BOW GOODS (LNWR)
(20.03.1893 – 1940)

Bow Jcn
(1st)

23

PUDDING
MILL LANE
(15.01.1996)
Re-sited 28.04.2014

BETHNAL
GREEN

COBURN ROAD
Coburn Road (Old Ford)
Old Ford
(01.02.1865 – 08.12.1946)
(re-sited 02.12.1883)

VICTORIA PARK & BOW
(02.04.1849 – 06.01.1851)

SHOREDITCH (NLR)
(01.11.1865 – 04.10.1940)

BETHNAL GREEN
(LPTB)
(04.12.1946)

*MILE END GOODS
Mile End & Devonshire Street Goods
Devonshire Street Goods
(1850 – 06.11.1967)*

DEVONSHIRE
STREET, MILE END
(20.06.1839 –
c.1841)

ECR
20.06.1839

Tilbury Junction

BOW (26.09.1850 – 15.05.1944)

see page 90

LPTB
12.04.1946

BOW CHURCH (31.08.1987)

SHOREDITCH HIGH STREET (27.04.2010)
BISHOPSGATE (HIGH LEVEL)
Shoreditch
(01.07.1840 [01.01.1881] – c.1879 [05.12.1964])
(On same site)

BETHNAL GREEN
(GER)
(24.05.1872)

MILE END (ECR)
(c.1841 –
24.05.1872)

01.07.1840

20.06.1839

LBLR 02.04.1849
(13.04.1854) – 07.11.1947

MDR & LTSR
02.06.1902

BOW ROAD
(MDR)
(11.06.1902)

NLR 17.05.1869 – 28.04.1935 (13.09.1959)

BOW WORKS
(c.1850 – 1960)

GOODS
(c.1898 – ?)

BISHOPSGATE
LOW LEVEL
(04.11.1872 –
22.05.1916)

SHOREDITCH
(ELR)
(10.04.1876 –
11.06.2006)

GLOBE ROAD &
DEVONSHIRE STREET
(01.07.1884 –
22.05.1916)

MDR & LTSR
02.06.1902

MILE END
(MDR)
(02.06.1902)

Gas Factory
Junction

BOW ROAD GOODS
(c.1885 – 07.12.1964)

Bromley
Junction

BOW WORKS

BROMLEY BY BOW
Bromley
(31.03.1858)
(Re-sited 01.03.1894)

LPTB
04.12.1946

*SPITALFIELDS GOODS
(01.11.1866 – 06.11.1967)*

ELR
10.04.1876

MDR & LTSR
02.06.1902

STEPNEY GREEN
(23.06.1902)

NR 2018

DEVONS ROAD
(31.08.1987)

NR
27.04.2010

ST MARY'S (WHITECHAPEL ROAD)
St Mary's
(03.03.1884 – 01.05.1938)

WHITECHAPEL
Whitechapel (Mile End)
(10.04.1876)

Stepney Green Junction

*DEVONS
ROAD GOODS
(??.07.1874 –
02.11.1964)*

DEVONS ROAD
DEPOT
(1882 – 10.02.1964)

ALDGATE EAST
(06.10.1884)
MET (re-sited 31.10.1938)

St Mary's Curve
SER 03.03.1884 –
06.10.1941 (23.12.2007)

11

*EASTERN DISTRICT OFFICE
(02.01.1928 – 31.05.2003)*

BURDETT ROAD
(11.09.1871 –
21.04.1941)

SOUTH BROMLEY
(01.09.1884 –
15.05.1944)

MET
18.11.1876

10

NR 2018

MDR & MET
01.10.1884

ELR
10.04.1876

STEPNEY

LIMEHOUSE (2nd)
Stepney East
Stepney
(03.08.1840)

LANGDON PARK
(10.12.2007)

ALDGATE
(18.11.1876)

*COMMERCIAL ROAD GOODS
(17.04.1886 – 03.07.1967)*

SHADWELL
Shadwell & St George's East (LBLR)
Shadwell & St George-in-the-East (ELR)
Shadwell
(01.10.1840)

Salmons Lane Junction

LIMEHOUSE

POPLAR

FENCHURCH
STREET
(29.07.1841)

*POR
02.01.1928 –
31.05.2003*

18

CANNON
STREET ROAD
(21.08.1842 –
??.12.1848)

19

Limehouse Curve (LBLR 05.04.1880 [01.09.1880] – 01.03.1881 [05.11.1962])
Limehouse
Junction

LIMEHOUSE (1st)
(06.07.1840 –
04.05.1926)

ALL SAINTS (31.08.1987)
POPLAR (NLR)
(01.08.1866 – 15.05.1944)
(On same site)

see page 74

15

17

LEMAN STREET
(01.06.1877 – 07.07.1941)

LBLR 06.07.1840

Stepney
East
Junction

RATCLIFF

LBLR 02.04.1849

NR 2018

DLR 31.08.1987

see page 31

12

13

14

16

27

Scale

Km
0   0.5   1   1.5   2

Miles
¼   ½   ¾   1

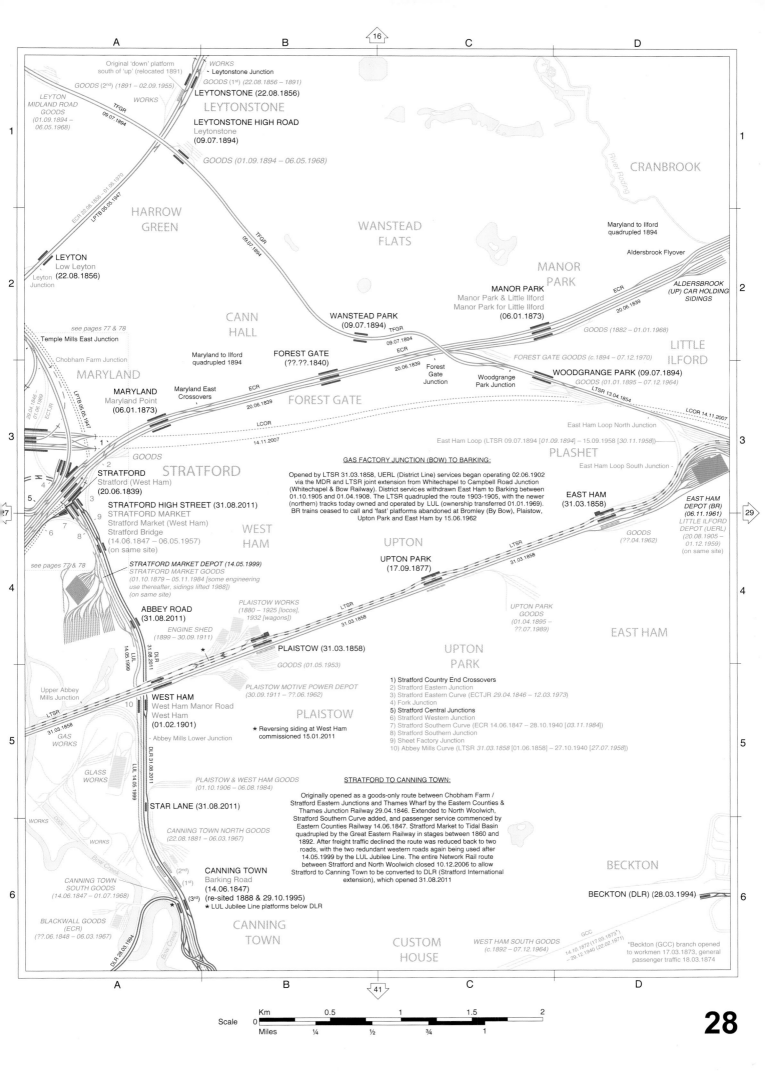

A   B   C   D

Original 'down' platform
south of 'up' (relocated 1891)

WORKS
~ Leytonstone Junction
GOODS (1st) (22.08.1856 – 1891)

GOODS (2nd) (1891 – 02.09.1955)
WORKS

LEYTONSTONE (22.08.1856)

LEYTON
MIDLAND ROAD
GOODS
(01.09.1894 –
06.05.1968)

TFGR
09.07.1894

LEYTONSTONE

LEYTONSTONE HIGH ROAD
Leytonstone
(09.07.1894)

CRANBROOK

River Roding

GOODS (01.09.1894 – 06.05.1968)

ECR 22.06.1856 – 01.06.1970
LPTB 05.05.1947

HARROW
GREEN

WANSTEAD
FLATS

TFGR
09.07.1894

Maryland to Ilford
quadrupled 1894

Aldersbrook Flyover

MANOR
PARK

LEYTON
Low Leyton
(22.08.1856)
Leyton
Junction

MANOR PARK
Manor Park & Little Ilford
Manor Park for Little Ilford
(06.01.1873)

ECR
20.06.1839

ALDERSBROOK
(UP) CAR HOLDING
SIDINGS

CANN
HALL

WANSTEAD PARK
(09.07.1894)

TFGR
09.07.1894

LITTLE
ILFORD

see pages 77 & 78
Temple Mills East Junction

Maryland to Ilford
quadrupled 1894

FOREST GATE
(??.??.1840)

ECR
20.06.1839

Forest
Gate
Junction

GOODS (1882 – 01.01.1968)

FOREST GATE GOODS (c.1894 – 07.12.1970)

WOODGRANGE PARK (09.07.1894)
GOODS (01.01.1895 – 07.12.1964)

Chobham Farm Junction

MARYLAND

Woodgrange
Park Junction

LTSR 13.04.1854

29.04.1846 –
01.06.1969

LPTB 05.05.1947

MARYLAND
Maryland Point
(06.01.1873)

Maryland East
Crossovers

ECR
20.06.1839

FOREST GATE

LCOR 14.11.2007

ECTJR

LCOR
14.11.2007

East Ham Loop North Junction

PLASHET

East Ham Loop (LTSR 09.07.1894 [01.09.1894] – 15.09.1958 [30.11.1958])

STRATFORD

GOODS

STRATFORD
Stratford (West Ham)
(20.06.1839)

East Ham Loop South Junction

27

see pages 77 & 78

STRATFORD HIGH STREET (31.08.2011)
STRATFORD MARKET
Stratford Market (West Ham)
Stratford Bridge
(14.06.1847 – 06.05.1957)
(on same site)

**WEST
HAM**

UPTON

GAS FACTORY JUNCTION (BOW) TO BARKING:

Opened by LTSR 31.03.1858, UERL (District Line) services began operating 02.06.1902
via the MDR and LTSR joint extension from Whitechapel to Campbell Road Junction
(Whitechapel & Bow Railway). District services withdrawn East Ham to Barking between
01.10.1905 and 01.04.1908. The LTSR quadrupled the route 1903-1905, with the newer
(northern) tracks today owned and operated by LUL (ownership transferred 01.01.1969).
BR trains ceased to call and 'fast' platforms abandoned at Bromley (By Bow), Plaistow,
Upton Park and East Ham by 15.06.1962

EAST HAM
(31.03.1858)

GOODS
(??.04.1962)

EAST HAM
DEPOT (BR)
(06.11.1961)
LITTLE ILFORD
DEPOT (UERL)
(20.08.1905 –
01.12.1959)
(on same site)

29

STRATFORD MARKET DEPOT (14.05.1999)
STRATFORD MARKET GOODS
(01.10.1879 – 05.11.1984 [some engineering
use thereafter, sidings lifted 1988])
(on same site)

UPTON PARK
(17.09.1877)

LTSR
31.03.1858

ABBEY ROAD
(31.08.2011)

PLAISTOW WORKS
(1880 – 1925 [locos],
1932 [wagons])

LTSR
31.03.1858

UPTON PARK
GOODS
(01.04.1895 –
??.07.1989)

EAST HAM

ENGINE SHED
(1899 – 30.09.1911)

LUL
14.05.1999

DLR
31.08.2011

PLAISTOW (31.03.1858)

**UPTON
PARK**

WEST HAM
West Ham Manor Road
West Ham
(01.02.1901)

GOODS (01.05.1953)

1) Stratford Country End Crossovers
2) Stratford Eastern Junction
3) Stratford Eastern Curve (ECTJR 29.04.1846 – 12.03.1973)
4) Fork Junction
5) Stratford Central Junctions
6) Stratford Western Junction
7) Stratford Southern Curve (ECR 14.06.1847 – 28.10.1940 [03.11.1984])
8) Stratford Southern Junction
9) Sheet Factory Junction
10) Abbey Mills Curve (LTSR 31.03.1858 [01.06.1858] – 27.10.1940 [27.07.1958])

Upper Abbey
Mills Junction

LTSR
31.03.1858

GAS
WORKS

DLR 31.08.2011

LUL 14.05.1999

PLAISTOW MOTIVE POWER DEPOT
(30.09.1911 – ??.06.1962)

PLAISTOW

★ Reversing siding at West Ham
commissioned 15.01.2011

- Abbey Mills Lower Junction

GLASS
WORKS

PLAISTOW & WEST HAM GOODS
(01.10.1906 – 06.08.1984)

STRATFORD TO CANNING TOWN:

Originally opened as a goods-only route between Chobham Farm /
Stratford Eastern Junctions and Thames Wharf by the Eastern Counties &
Thames Junction Railway 29.04.1846. Extended to North Woolwich,
Stratford Southern Curve added, and passenger service commenced by
Eastern Counties Railway 14.06.1847. Stratford Market to Tidal Basin
quadrupled by the Great Eastern Railway in stages between 1860 and
1892. After freight traffic declined the route was reduced back to two
roads, with the two redundant western roads again being used after
14.05.1999 by the LUL Jubilee Line. The entire Network Rail route
between Stratford and North Woolwich closed 10.12.2006 to allow
Stratford to Canning Town to be converted to DLR (Stratford International
extension), which opened 31.08.2011

WORKS

STAR LANE (31.08.2011)

CANNING TOWN NORTH GOODS
(22.08.1881 – 06.03.1967)

BECKTON

WORKS

CANNING TOWN
SOUTH GOODS
(14.06.1847 – 01.07.1968)

Bow Creek

(2nd)

(1st)

CANNING TOWN
Barking Road
(14.06.1847)

(3rd) (re-sited 1888 & 29.10.1995)
★ LUL Jubilee Line platforms below DLR

BECKTON (DLR) (28.03.1994)

DLR 28.03.1994

BLACKWALL GOODS
(ECR)
(??.06.1848 – 06.03.1967)

**CANNING
TOWN**

**CUSTOM
HOUSE**

WEST HAM SOUTH GOODS
(c.1892 – 07.12.1964)

GCC
14.10.1872 (17.03.1873*)
– 29.12.1940 (22.02.1971)

*Beckton (GCC) branch opened
to workmen 17.03.1873, general
passenger traffic 18.03.1874

A   B   C   D

Scale
Km
0   0.5   1   1.5   2
Miles
¼   ½   ¾   1

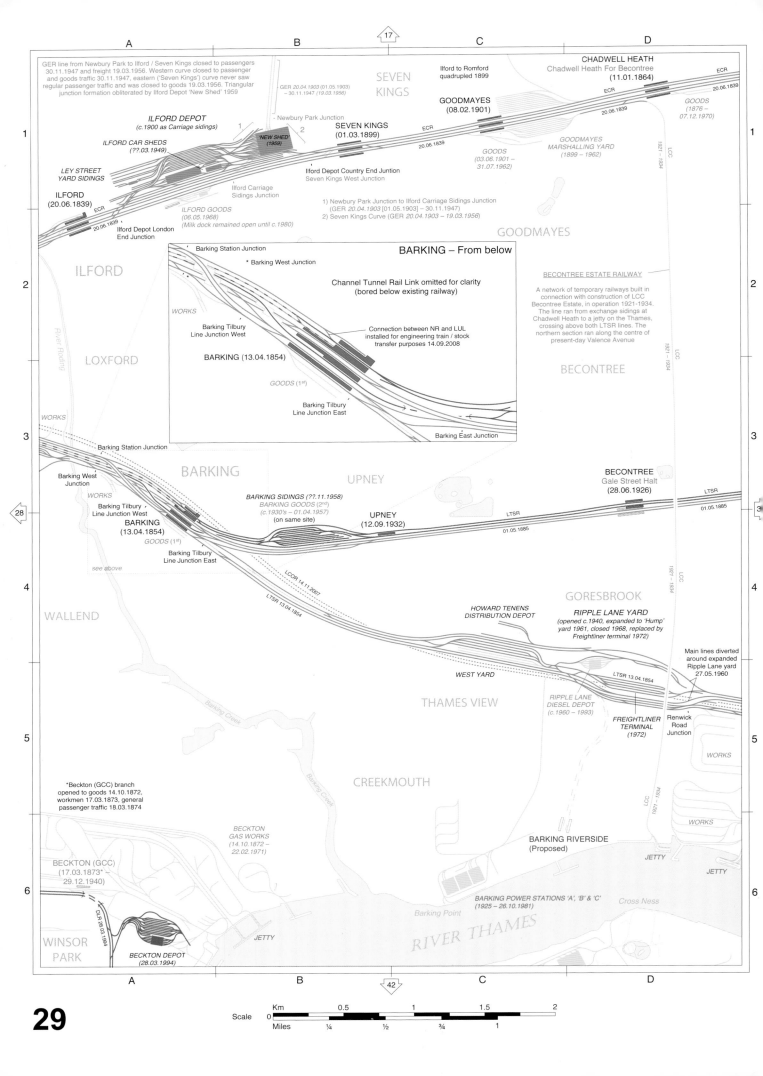

GER line from Newbury Park to Ilford / Seven Kings closed to passengers
30.11.1947 and freight 19.03.1956. Western curve closed to passenger
and goods traffic 30.11.1947, eastern ('Seven Kings') curve never saw
regular passenger traffic and was closed to goods 19.03.1956. Triangular
junction formation obliterated by Ilford Depot 'New Shed' 1959

SEVEN
KINGS

Ilford to Romford
quadrupled 1899

CHADWELL HEATH
Chadwell Heath For Becontree
(11.01.1864)

ECR

GER *20.04.1903 (01.05.1903)*
– 30.11.1947 (19.03.1956)

GOODMAYES
(08.02.1901)

ECR

ECR

20.06.1839

GOODS
*(1876 –
07.12.1970)*

ILFORD DEPOT
(c.1900 as Carriage sidings)

- Newbury Park Junction

SEVEN KINGS
(01.03.1899)

ECR

20.06.1839

'NEW SHED'
(1959)

ILFORD CAR SHEDS
(??.03.1949)

1

2

20.06.1839

GOODMAYES
MARSHALLING YARD
(1899 – 1962)

1

LEY STREET
YARD SIDINGS

Ilford Depot Country End Juntion
Seven Kings West Junction

GOODS
*(03.06.1901 –
31.07.1962)*

1921 – 1934

LCC

ILFORD
(20.06.1839)

ECR

Ilford Carriage
Sidings Junction

GOODMAYES

20.06.1839

ILFORD GOODS
(06.05.1968)
(Milk dock remained open until c.1980)

1) Newbury Park Junction to Ilford Carriage Sidings Junction
(GER *20.04.1903* [*01.05.1903*] *– 30.11.1947*)
2) Seven Kings Curve (GER *20.04.1903 – 19.03.1956*)

Ilford Depot London
End Junction

ILFORD

2

LOXFORD

River Roding

BARKING – From below

Barking Station Junction

* Barking West Junction

Channel Tunnel Rail Link omitted for clarity
(bored below existing railway)

2

BECONTREE ESTATE RAILWAY

A network of temporary railways built in
connection with construction of LCC
Becontree Estate, in operation 1921-1934.
The line ran from exchange sidings at
Chadwell Heath to a jetty on the Thames,
crossing above both LTSR lines. The
northern section ran along the centre of
present-day Valence Avenue

WORKS

WORKS

Barking Tilbury
Line Junction West

BARKING (13.04.1854)

Connection between NR and LUL
installed for engineering train / stock
transfer purposes 14.09.2008

BECONTREE

GOODS (1st)

1921 – 1934

LCC

Barking Tilbury
Line Junction East

WORKS

Barking Station Junction

Barking East Junction

3

3

3

Barking West
Junction

BARKING

UPNEY

BECONTREE
Gale Street Halt
(28.06.1926)

LTSR

WORKS

BARKING SIDINGS (??.11.1958)
BARKING GOODS (2nd)
(c.1930's – 01.04.1957)
(on same site)

UPNEY
(12.09.1932)

LTSR

01.05.1885

28

Barking Tilbury
Line Junction West

BARKING
(13.04.1854)

01.05.1885

3

GOODS (1st)

Barking Tilbury
Line Junction East

LCOR 14.11.2007

GORESBROOK

Main lines diverted
around expanded
Ripple Lane yard
27.05.1960

4

see above

LTSR 13.04.1854

HOWARD TENENS
DISTRIBUTION DEPOT

RIPPLE LANE YARD
(opened c.1940, expanded to 'Hump'
yard 1961, closed 1968, replaced by
Freightliner terminal 1972)

4

WALLEND

WEST YARD

LTSR 13.04.1854

1921 – 1934

LCC

WORKS

THAMES VIEW

RIPPLE LANE
DIESEL DEPOT
(c.1960 – 1993)

LTSR 13.04.1854

Renwick
Road
Junction

Barking Creek

FREIGHTLINER
TERMINAL
(1972)

5

*Beckton (GCC) branch
opened to goods 14.10.1872,
workmen 17.03.1873, general
passenger traffic 18.03.1874

CREEKMOUTH

WORKS

5

Barking Creek

*BECKTON
GAS WORKS
(14.10.1872 –
22.02.1971)*

BARKING RIVERSIDE
(Proposed)

1921 – 1934

LCC

WORKS

JETTY

BECKTON (GCC)
(17.03.1873* –
29.12.1940)

JETTY

JETTY

6

DLR 28.03.1994

BECKTON DEPOT
(28.03.1994)

JETTY

BARKING POWER STATIONS 'A', 'B' & 'C'
(1925 – 26.10.1981)

Barking Point

Cross Ness

RIVER THAMES

6

WINSOR
PARK

29

Km

0.5

1

1.5

2

Scale

0

Miles

¼

½

¾

1

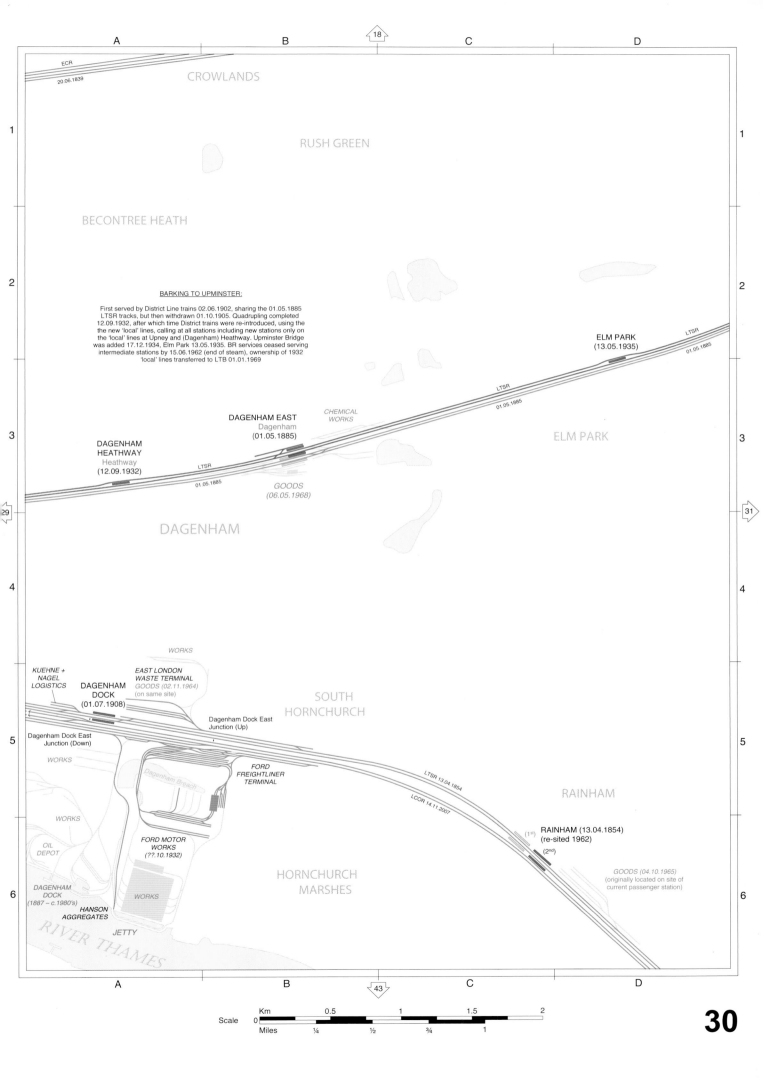

ECR
20.06.1839

CROWLANDS

RUSH GREEN

BECONTREE HEATH

BARKING TO UPMINSTER:

First served by District Line trains 02.06.1902, sharing the 01.05.1885
LTSR tracks, but then withdrawn 01.10.1905. Quadrupling completed
12.09.1932, after which time District trains were re-introduced, using the
the new 'local' lines, calling at all stations including new stations only on
the 'local' lines at Upney and (Dagenham) Heathway. Upminster Bridge
was added 17.12.1934, Elm Park 13.05.1935. BR services ceased serving
intermediate stations by 15.06.1962 (end of steam), ownership of 1932
'local' lines transferred to LTB 01.01.1969

ELM PARK
(13.05.1935)

LTSR
01.05.1885

LTSR
01.05.1885

ELM PARK

CHEMICAL
WORKS

DAGENHAM EAST
Dagenham
(01.05.1885)

DAGENHAM
HEATHWAY
Heathway
(12.09.1932)

LTSR
01.05.1885

GOODS
(06.05.1968)

DAGENHAM

WORKS

KUEHNE +
NAGEL
LOGISTICS

DAGENHAM
DOCK
(01.07.1908)

EAST LONDON
WASTE TERMINAL
GOODS (02.11.1964)
(on same site)

SOUTH
HORNCHURCH

Dagenham Dock East
Junction (Up)

Dagenham Dock East
Junction (Down)

WORKS

FORD
FREIGHTLINER
TERMINAL

LTSR 13.04.1854

LCOR 14.11.2007

RAINHAM

WORKS

FORD MOTOR
WORKS
(??.10.1932)

HORNCHURCH
MARSHES

RAINHAM (13.04.1854)
(re-sited 1962)

(1st)

(2nd)

OIL
DEPOT

GOODS (04.10.1965)
(originally located on site of
current passenger station)

DAGENHAM
DOCK
(1887 – c.1980's)

HANSON
AGGREGATES

WORKS

JETTY

RIVER THAMES

Km   0.5   1   1.5   2
Scale   0
Miles   ¼   ½   ¾   1

30

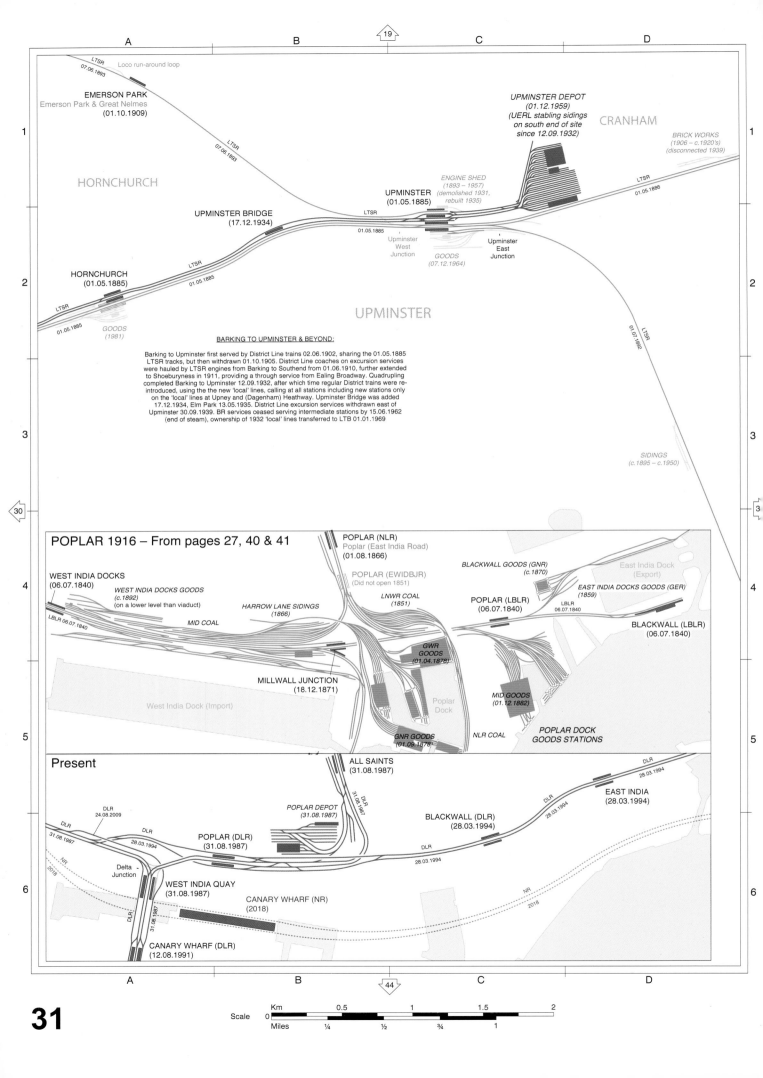

Loco run-around loop

LTSR
07.06.1893

EMERSON PARK
Emerson Park & Great Nelmes
(01.10.1909)

LTSR
07.06.1893

HORNCHURCH

UPMINSTER DEPOT
(01.12.1959)
(UERL stabling sidings
on south end of site
since 12.09.1932)

CRANHAM

BRICK WORKS
(1906 – c.1920's)
(disconnected 1939)

ENGINE SHED
(1893 – 1957)
(demolished 1931,
rebuilt 1935)

UPMINSTER
(01.05.1885)

UPMINSTER BRIDGE
(17.12.1934)

LTSR
01.05.1885

LTSR
01.05.1886

LTSR
01.05.1885

Upminster
West
Junction

Upminster
East
Junction

HORNCHURCH
(01.05.1885)

LTSR

LTSR
01.05.1885

GOODS
(07.12.1964)

UPMINSTER

LTSR
01.05.1885

GOODS
(1981)

LTSR
01.07.1892

BARKING TO UPMINSTER & BEYOND:

Barking to Upminster first served by District Line trains 02.06.1902, sharing the 01.05.1885
LTSR tracks, but then withdrawn 01.10.1905. District Line coaches on excursion services
were hauled by LTSR engines from Barking to Southend from 01.06.1910, further extended
to Shoeburyness in 1911, providing a through service from Ealing Broadway. Quadrupling
completed Barking to Upminster 12.09.1932, after which time regular District trains were re-
introduced, using the the new 'local' lines at Upney and (Dagenham) Heathway. Upminster
Bridge was added 17.12.1934, Elm Park 13.05.1935. District Line excursion services withdrawn east of
Upminster 30.09.1939. BR services ceased serving intermediate stations by 15.06.1962
(end of steam), ownership of 1932 'local' lines transferred to LTB 01.01.1969

SIDINGS
(c.1895 – c.1950)

30

3

POPLAR 1916 – From pages 27, 40 & 41

POPLAR (NLR)
Poplar (East India Road)
(01.08.1866)

POPLAR (EWIDBJR)
Did not open 1851

BLACKWALL GOODS (GNR)
(c.1870)

East India Dock
(Export)

WEST INDIA DOCKS
(06.07.1840)

WEST INDIA DOCKS GOODS
(c.1892)
(on a lower level than viaduct)

HARROW LANE SIDINGS
(1866)

LNWR COAL
(1851)

EAST INDIA DOCKS GOODS (GER)
(1859)

LBLR 06.07.1840

MID COAL

POPLAR (LBLR)
(06.07.1840)

LBLR
06.07.1840

BLACKWALL (LBLR)
(06.07.1840)

MILLWALL JUNCTION
(18.12.1871)

GWR
GOODS
(01.04.1878)

MID GOODS
(01.12.1882)

West India Dock (Import)

Poplar
Dock

NLR COAL

POPLAR DOCK
GOODS STATIONS

GNR GOODS
(01.09.1878)

Present

ALL SAINTS
(31.08.1987)

DLR
31.08.1987

DLR
28.03.1994

DLR
24.08.2009

POPLAR DEPOT
(31.08.1987)

DLR
31.08.1987

BLACKWALL (DLR)
(28.03.1994)

DLR
28.03.1994

EAST INDIA
(28.03.1994)

DLR
31.08.1987

POPLAR (DLR)
(31.08.1987)

DLR
28.03.1994

NR
2018

Delta
Junction

WEST INDIA QUAY
(31.08.1987)

CANARY WHARF (NR)
(2018)

DLR
31.08.1987

NR
2018

DLR

CANARY WHARF (DLR)
(12.08.1991)

Scale

Km
0   0.5   1   1.5   2

Miles
¼   ½   ¾   1

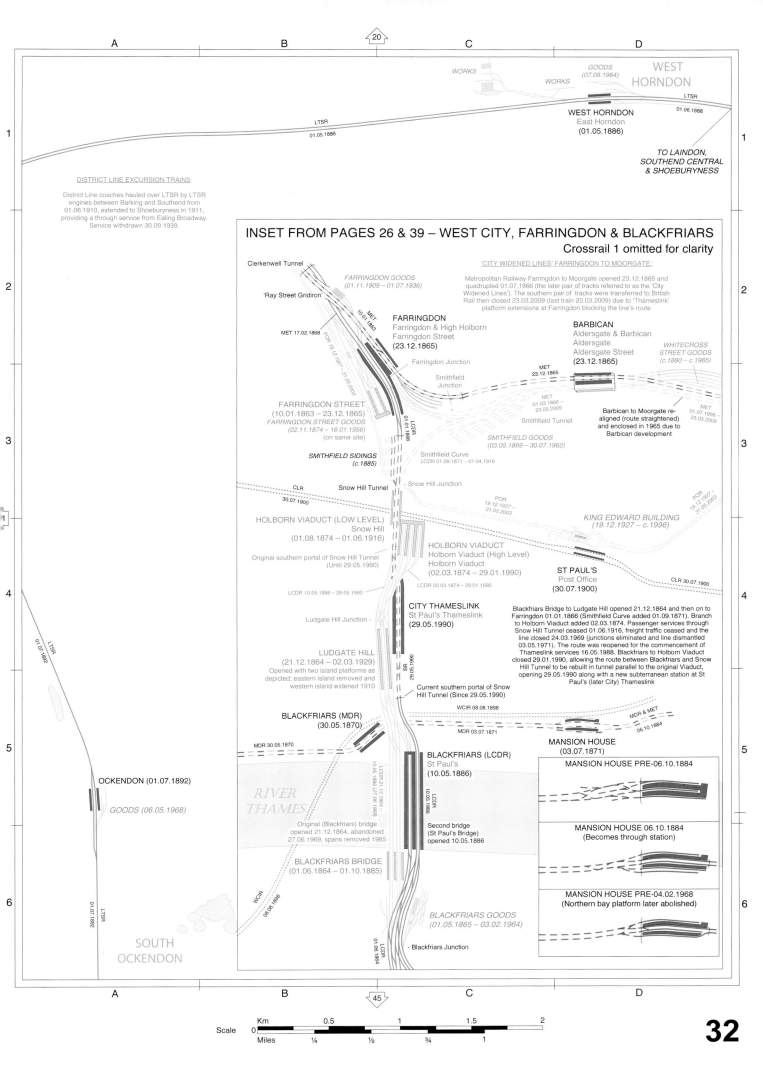

WEST HORNDON

WORKS

WORKS

GOODS
(07.09.1964)

LTSR
01.06.1888

WEST HORNDON
East Horndon
(01.05.1886)

LTSR
01.05.1886

*TO LAINDON,
SOUTHEND CENTRAL
& SHOEBURYNESS*

DISTRICT LINE EXCURSION TRAINS:

District Line coaches hauled over LTSR by LTSR
engines between Barking and Southend from
01.06.1910, extended to Shoeburyness in 1911,
providing a through service from Ealing Broadway.
Service withdrawn 30.09.1939.

INSET FROM PAGES 26 & 39 – WEST CITY, FARRINGDON & BLACKFRIARS
Crossrail 1 omitted for clarity

'CITY WIDENED LINES' FARRINGDON TO MOORGATE:

Metropolitan Railway Farringdon to Moorgate opened 23.12.1865 and
quadrupled 01.07.1866 (the later pair of tracks referred to as the 'City
Widened Lines'). The southern pair of tracks were transferred to British
Rail then closed 23.03.2009 (last train 20.03.2009) due to 'Thameslink'
platform extensions at Farringdon blocking the line's route

Clerkenwell Tunnel

*FARRINGDON GOODS
(01.11.1909 – 01.07.1936)*

'Ray Street Gridiron'

MET
10.01.1863

MET 17.02.1868

POR 19.12.1927 – 31.05.2003

FARRINGDON
Farringdon & High Holborn
Farringdon Street
(23.12.1865)

Farringdon Junction

Smithfield
Junction

MET
23.12.1865

BARBICAN
Aldersgate & Barbican
Aldersgate
Aldersgate Street
(23.12.1865)

*WHITECROSS
STREET GOODS
(c.1880 – c.1965)*

MET
01.03.1866 –
23.03.2009

MET
01.07.1866 –
23.03.2009

FARRINGDON STREET
(10.01.1863 – 23.12.1865)
*FARRINGDON STREET GOODS
(02.11.1874 – 16.01.1956)
(on same site)*

LCDR
01.01.1866

Smithfield Tunnel

Barbican to Moorgate re-
aligned (route straightened)
and enclosed in 1965 due to
Barbican development

*SMITHFIELD SIDINGS
(c.1885)*

*SMITHFIELD GOODS
(03.05.1869 – 30.07.1962)*

CLR
30.07.1900

Snow Hill Tunnel

Smithfield Curve
LCDR 01.09.1871 – 01.04.1916

Snow Hill Junction

POR
19.12.1927 –
31.05.2003

POR
19.12.1927 –
31.05.2003

HOLBORN VIADUCT (LOW LEVEL)
Snow Hill
(01.08.1874 – 01.06.1916)

*KING EDWARD BUILDING
(19.12.1927 – c.1996)*

Original southern portal of Snow Hill Tunnel
(Until 29.05.1990)

HOLBORN VIADUCT
Holborn Viaduct (High Level)
Holborn Viaduct
(02.03.1874 – 29.01.1990)

ST PAUL'S
Post Office
(30.07.1900)

CLR 30.07.1900

LCDR 10.05.1886 – 29.05.1990

LCDR 02.03.1874 – 29.01.1990

CITY THAMESLINK
St Paul's Thameslink
(29.05.1990)

Ludgate Hill Junction -

BR
29.05.1990

LUDGATE HILL
(21.12.1864 – 02.03.1929)
Opened with two island platforms as
depicted; eastern island removed and
western island widened 1910

Blackfriars Bridge to Ludgate Hill opened 21.12.1864 and then on to
Farringdon 01.01.1866 (Smithfield Curve added 01.09.1871). Branch
to Holborn Viaduct added 02.03.1874. Passenger services through
Snow Hill Tunnel ceased 01.06.1916, freight traffic ceased and the
line closed 24.03.1969 (junctions eliminated and line dismantled
03.05.1971). The route was reopened for the commencement of
Thameslink services 16.05.1988. Blackfriars to Holborn Viaduct
closed 29.01.1990, allowing the route between Blackfriars and Snow
Hill Tunnel to be rebuilt in tunnel parallel to the original Viaduct,
opening 29.05.1990 along with a new subterranean station at St
Paul's (later City) Thameslink

Current southern portal of Snow
Hill Tunnel (Since 29.05.1990)

WCIR 08.08.1898

MDR & MET
06.10.1884

BLACKFRIARS (MDR)
(30.05.1870)

MDR 30.05.1870

MDR 03.07.1871

MANSION HOUSE
(03.07.1871)

BLACKFRIARS (LCDR)
St Paul's
(10.05.1886)

LCDR 21.12.1864 –
10.05.1886 (27.06.1969)

LCDR
10.05.1886

Second bridge
(St Paul's Bridge)
opened 10.05.1886

MANSION HOUSE PRE-06.10.1884

*RIVER
THAMES*

OCKENDON (01.07.1892)

GOODS (06.05.1968)

LTSR
01.07.1892

LTSR
01.07.1892

Original (Blackfriars) bridge
opened 21.12.1864, abandoned
27.06.1969, spans removed 1985

MANSION HOUSE 06.10.1884
(Becomes through station)

BLACKFRIARS BRIDGE
(01.06.1864 – 01.10.1885)

WCIR
08.08.1898

MANSION HOUSE PRE-04.02.1968
(Northern bay platform later abolished)

*BLACKFRIARS GOODS
(01.05.1865 – 03.02.1964)*

LCDR
01.06.1864

- Blackfriars Junction

*SOUTH
OCKENDON*

Km
Scale 0   0.5   1   1.5   2
Miles   ¼   ½   ¾   1

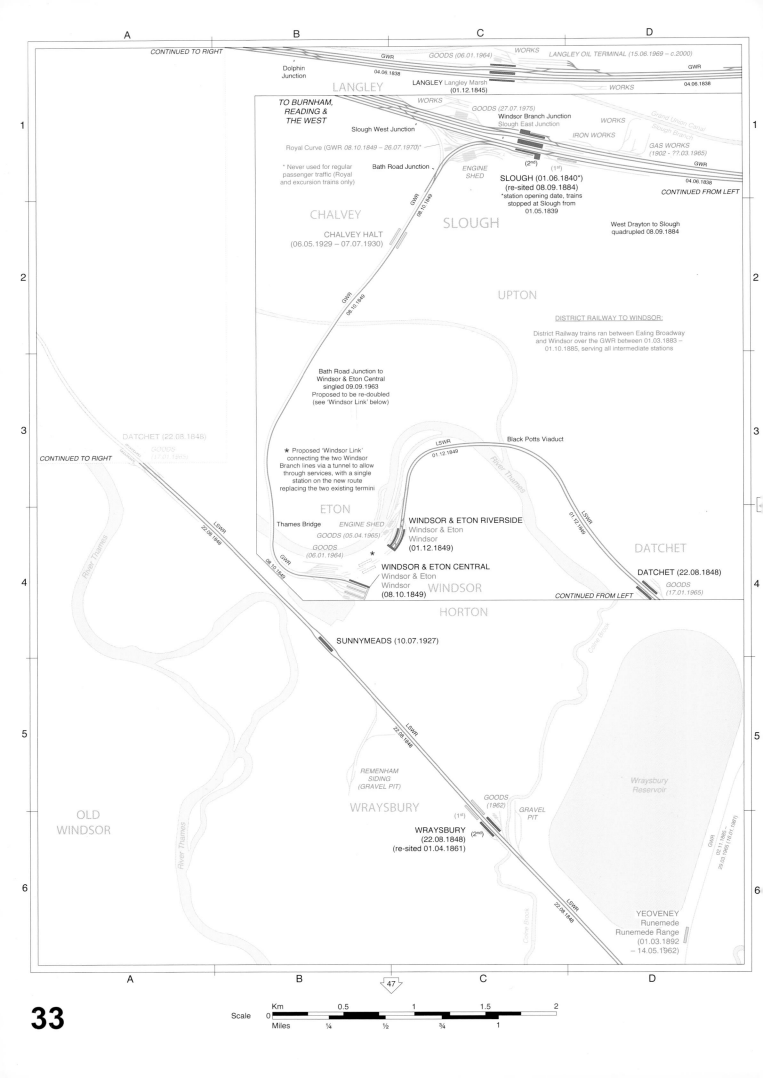

CONTINUED TO RIGHT

LANGLEY

Dolphin
Junction

GWR
04.06.1838

GOODS (06.01.1964)

WORKS

LANGLEY OIL TERMINAL (15.06.1969 – c.2000)

GWR

WORKS

04.06.1838

LANGLEY Langley Marsh
(01.12.1845)

TO BURNHAM,
READING &
THE WEST

WORKS

GOODS (27.07.1975)

Windsor Branch Junction
Slough East Junction

WORKS

IRON WORKS

Grand Union Canal

Slough Branch

Slough West Junction

Royal Curve (GWR 08.10.1849 – 26.07.1970)*

(2nd)

(1st)

GAS WORKS
(1902 - ??.03.1965)

GWR

* Never used for regular
passenger traffic (Royal
and excursion trains only)

Bath Road Junction

ENGINE
SHED

04.06.1838

SLOUGH (01.06.1840*)
(re-sited 08.09.1884)
*station opening date, trains
stopped at Slough from
01.05.1839

CONTINUED FROM LEFT

CHALVEY

GWR
08.10.1849

SLOUGH

West Drayton to Slough
quadrupled 08.09.1884

CHALVEY HALT
(06.05.1929 – 07.07.1930)

UPTON

GWR
08.10.1849

DISTRICT RAILWAY TO WINDSOR:

District Railway trains ran between Ealing Broadway
and Windsor over the GWR between 01.03.1883 –
01.10.1885, serving all intermediate stations

Bath Road Junction to
Windsor & Eton Central
singled 09.09.1963
Proposed to be re-doubled
(see 'Windsor Link' below)

DATCHET (22.08.1848)

GOODS
(17.01.1965)

CONTINUED TO RIGHT

★ Proposed 'Windsor Link'
connecting the two Windsor
Branch lines via a tunnel to allow
through services, with a single
station on the new route
replacing the two existing termini

Black Potts Viaduct

LSWR
01.12.1849

River Thames

LSWR
01.12.1849

ETON

LSWR
22.08.1848

Thames Bridge

ENGINE SHED

GOODS (05.04.1965)

WINDSOR & ETON RIVERSIDE
Windsor & Eton
Windsor
(01.12.1849)

DATCHET

River Thames

GOODS
(06.01.1964)

★

WINDSOR & ETON CENTRAL
Windsor & Eton
Windsor
(08.10.1849)

DATCHET (22.08.1848)

GWR
08.10.1849

WINDSOR

GOODS
(17.01.1965)

CONTINUED FROM LEFT

HORTON

**OLD
WINDSOR**

SUNNYMEADS (10.07.1927)

Colne Brook

Wraysbury
Reservoir

LSWR
22.08.1848

REMENHAM
SIDING
(GRAVEL PIT)

WRAYSBURY

GOODS
(1962)

GRAVEL
PIT

River Thames

(1st)

WRAYSBURY
(22.08.1848)
(re-sited 01.04.1861)

(2nd)

Colne Brook

GWR
02.11.1885 –
29.03.1965 (16.01.1981)

LSWR
22.08.1848

YEOVENEY
Runemede
Runemede Range
(01.03.1892
– 14.05.1962)

47

Scale

Km
0 0.5 1 1.5 2

Miles
¼ ½ ¾ 1

33

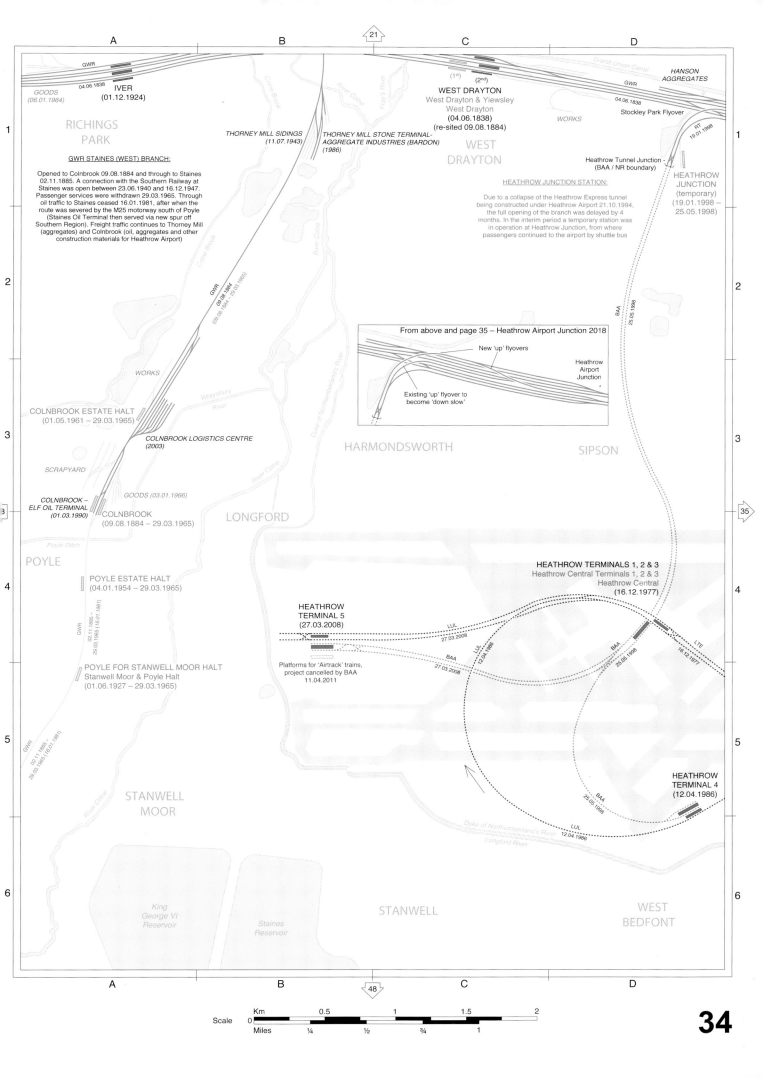

GWR

GOODS
(06.01.1964)

04.06.1838

IVER
(01.12.1924)

RICHINGS
PARK

GWR STAINES (WEST) BRANCH:

Opened to Colnbrook 09.08.1884 and through to Staines
02.11.1885. A connection with the Southern Railway at
Staines was open between 23.06.1940 and 16.12.1947.
Passenger services were withdrawn 29.03.1965. Through
oil traffic to Staines ceased 16.01.1981, after when the
route was severed by the M25 motorway south of Poyle
(Staines Oil Terminal then served via new spur off
Southern Region). Freight traffic continues to Thorney Mill
(aggregates) and Colnbrook (oil, aggregates and other
construction materials for Heathrow Airport)

THORNEY MILL SIDINGS
(11.07.1943)

*THORNEY MILL STONE TERMINAL-
AGGREGATE INDUSTRIES (BARDON)*
(1986)

GWR
09.08.1884
(09.08.1884 - 29.03.1965)

(1st)   *(2nd)*

WEST DRAYTON
West Drayton & Yiewsley
West Drayton
(04.06.1838)
(re-sited 09.08.1884)

WEST
DRAYTON

HEATHROW JUNCTION STATION:

Due to a collapse of the Heathrow Express tunnel
being constructed under Heathrow Airport 21.10.1994,
the full opening of the branch was delayed by 4
months. In the interim period a temporary station was
in operation at Heathrow Junction, from where
passengers continued to the airport by shuttle bus

Grand Union Canal

HANSON
AGGREGATES

GWR

04.06.1838

Stockley Park Flyover

RT
19.01.1998

WORKS

Heathrow Tunnel Junction -
(BAA / NR boundary)

HEATHROW
JUNCTION
(temporary)
(19.01.1998 –
25.05.1998)

BAA
25.05.1998

From above and page 35 – Heathrow Airport Junction 2018

New 'up' flyovers

Heathrow
Airport
Junction

Existing 'up' flyover to
become 'down slow'

WORKS

COLNBROOK ESTATE HALT
(01.05.1961 – 29.03.1965)

COLNBROOK LOGISTICS CENTRE
(2003)

SCRAPYARD

GOODS (03.01.1966)

HARMONDSWORTH

SIPSON

*COLNBROOK –
ELF OIL TERMINAL*
(01.03.1990)

COLNBROOK
(09.08.1884 – 29.03.1965)

Poyle Ditch

POYLE

LONGFORD

POYLE ESTATE HALT
(04.01.1954 – 29.03.1965)

GWR
02.11.1895 –
29.03.1965 (16.01.1981)

HEATHROW
TERMINAL 5
(27.03.2008)

Platforms for 'Airtrack' trains,
project cancelled by BAA
11.04.2011

LUL
27.03.2008

LUL
27.03.2008

BAA

LUL
12.04.1986

HEATHROW TERMINALS 1, 2 & 3
Heathrow Central Terminals 1, 2 & 3
Heathrow Central
(16.12.1977)

BAA
25.05.1998

LTE
16.12.1977

POYLE FOR STANWELL MOOR HALT
Stanwell Moor & Poyle Halt
(01.06.1927 – 29.03.1965)

GWR
02.11.1895 –
29.03.1965 (16.01.1981)

STANWELL
MOOR

HEATHROW
TERMINAL 4
(12.04.1986)

BAA
25.05.1998

LUL
12.04.1986

*King
George VI
Reservoir*

*Staines
Reservoir*

STANWELL

WEST
BEDFONT

Scale   Km   0   0.5   1   1.5   2
Miles   ¼   ½   ¾   1

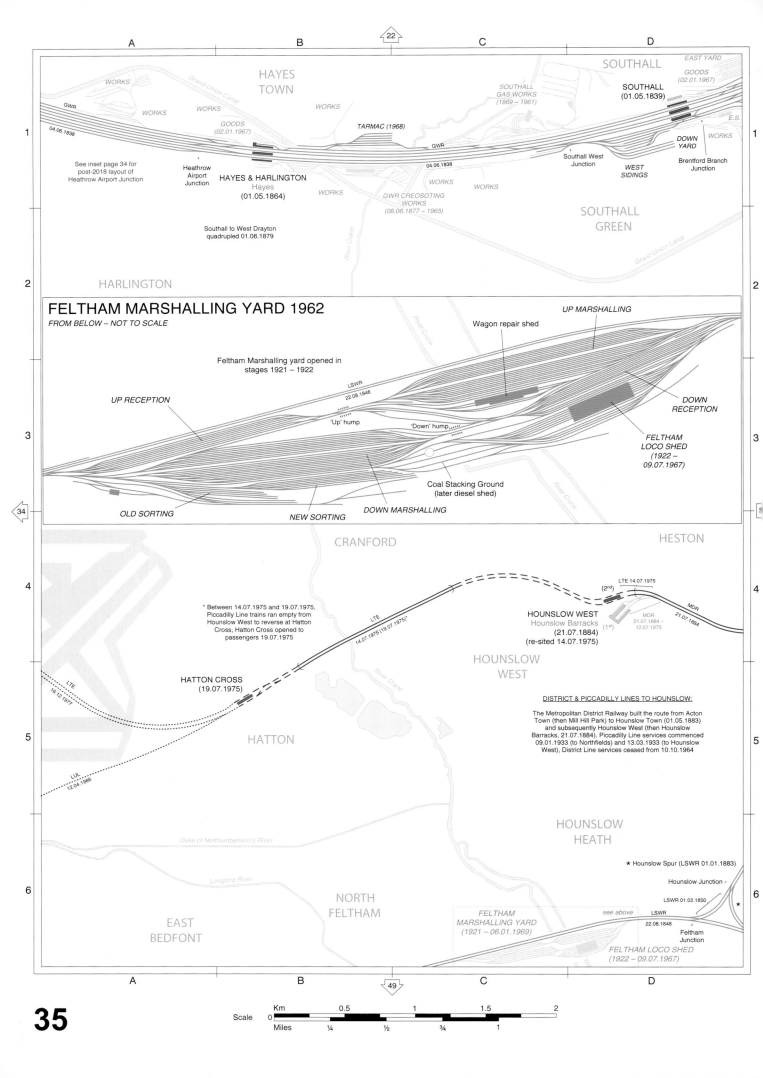

HAYES
TOWN

SOUTHALL

WORKS

WORKS

EAST YARD

GOODS
(02.01.1967)

WORKS

GWR

WORKS

WORKS

WORKS

SOUTHALL
GAS WORKS
(1869 – 1961)

SOUTHALL
(01.05.1839)

E.S.

1

04.06.1838

GOODS
(02.01.1967)

TARMAC (1968)

GWR

DOWN
YARD

1

See inset page 34 for
post-2018 layout of
Heathrow Airport Junction

Heathrow
Airport
Junction

HAYES & HARLINGTON
Hayes
(01.05.1864)

04.06.1838

Southall West
Junction

WEST
SIDINGS

Brentford Branch
Junction

WORKS

SOUTHALL
GREEN

WORKS

WORKS

Southall to West Drayton
quadrupled 01.06.1879

GWR CREOSOTING
WORKS
(06.06.1877 – 1965)

2

HARLINGTON

2

FELTHAM MARSHALLING YARD 1962

FROM BELOW – NOT TO SCALE

Wagon repair shed

UP MARSHALLING

Feltham Marshalling yard opened in
stages 1921 – 1922

DOWN
RECEPTION

UP RECEPTION

LSWR
22.08.1848

'Up' hump

'Down' hump

FELTHAM
LOCO SHED
(1922 –
09.07.1967)

3

3

Coal Stacking Ground
(later diesel shed)

OLD SORTING

NEW SORTING

DOWN MARSHALLING

34

CRANFORD

HESTON

4

LTE 14.07.1975

(2nd)

4

* Between 14.07.1975 and 19.07.1975,
Piccadilly Line trains ran empty from
Hounslow West to reverse at Hatton
Cross, Hatton Cross opened to
passengers 19.07.1975

LTE

14.07.1975 (19.07.1975)

HOUNSLOW WEST
Hounslow Barracks
(21.07.1884)
(re-sited 14.07.1975)

MDR
21.07.1884 –
12.07.1975

MDR
21.07.1884

(1st)

HOUNSLOW
WEST

LTE
16.12.1977

HATTON CROSS
(19.07.1975)

DISTRICT & PICCADILLY LINES TO HOUNSLOW:

The Metropolitan District Railway built the route from Acton
Town (then Mill Hill Park) to Hounslow Town (01.05.1883)
and subsequently Hounslow West (then Hounslow
Barracks, 21.07.1884). Piccadilly Line services commenced
09.01.1933 (to Northfields) and 13.03.1933 (to Hounslow
West), District Line services ceased from 10.10.1964

5

HATTON

5

LUL
12.04.1986

Duke of Northumberland's River

HOUNSLOW
HEATH

Longford River

* Hounslow Spur (LSWR 01.01.1883)

Hounslow Junction -

6

NORTH
FELTHAM

FELTHAM
MARSHALLING YARD
(1921 – 06.01.1969)

see above

LSWR 01.02.1850

LSWR

*

6

EAST
BEDFONT

22.08.1848

Feltham
Junction

FELTHAM LOCO SHED
(1922 – 09.07.1967)

Scale

Km
0   0.5   1   1.5   2

Miles
¼   ½   ¾   1

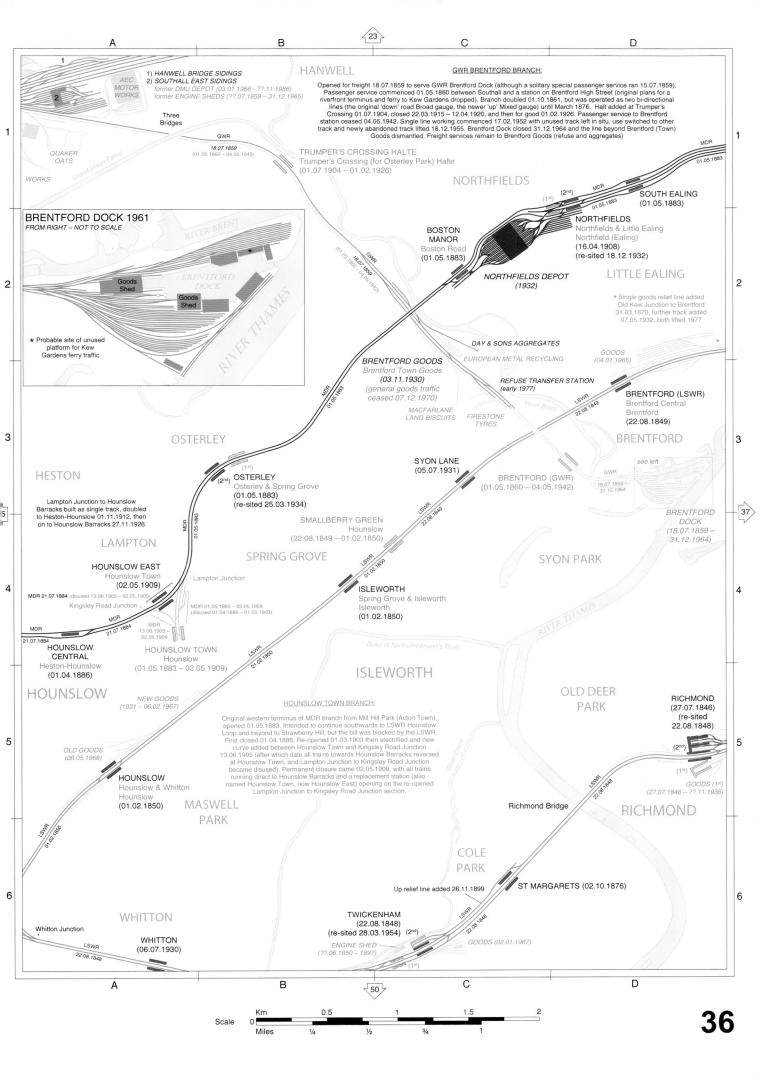

1) *HANWELL BRIDGE SIDINGS*
2) *SOUTHALL EAST SIDINGS*
former DMU DEPOT (03.01.1966 – ??.11.1986)
former ENGINE SHEDS (??.07.1859 – 31.12.1965)

AEC MOTOR WORKS

Three Bridges

QUAKER OATS

WORKS

GWR
18.07.1859
(01.05.1860 – 04.05.1942)

GWR BRENTFORD BRANCH:

Opened for freight 18.07.1859 to serve GWR Brentford Dock (although a solitary special passenger service ran 15.07.1859). Passenger service commenced 01.05.1860 between Southall and a station on Brentford High Street (original plans for a riverfront terminus and ferry to Kew Gardens dropped). Branch doubled 01.10.1861, but was operated as two bi-directional lines (the original 'down' road Broad gauge, the newer 'up' Mixed gauge) until March 1876. Halt added at Trumper's Crossing 01.07.1904, closed 22.03.1915 – 12.04.1920, and then for good 01.02.1926. Passenger service to Brentford station ceased 04.05.1942. Single line working commenced 17.02.1952 with unused track left in situ, use switched to other track and newly abandoned track lifted 18.12.1955. Brentford Dock closed 31.12.1964 and the line beyond Brentford (Town) Goods dismantled. Freight services remain to Brentford Goods (refuse and aggregates)

TRUMPER'S CROSSING HALTE
Trumper's Crossing (for Osterley Park) Halte
(01.07.1904 – 01.02.1926)

MDR
01.05.1883

MDR
01.05.1883

NORTHFIELDS

SOUTH EALING
(01.05.1883)

BOSTON MANOR
Boston Road
(01.05.1883)

(1st) (2nd)
01.05.1883

MDR
01.05.1883

NORTHFIELDS
Northfields & Little Ealing
Northfield (Ealing)
(16.04.1908)
(re-sited 18.12.1932)

BRENTFORD DOCK 1961
FROM RIGHT – NOT TO SCALE

RIVER BRENT

BRENTFORD DOCK

Goods Shed

Goods Shed

RIVER THAMES

★ *Probable site of unused platform for Kew Gardens ferry traffic*

NORTHFIELDS DEPOT
(1932)

LITTLE EALING

* Single goods relief line added
Old Kew Junction to Brentford
31.03.1870, further track added
07.05.1932, both lifted 1977

DAY & SONS AGGREGATES
EUROPEAN METAL RECYCLING

GOODS
(04.01.1965)

GWR
(01.05.1860 – 04.05.1942)

GWR

BRENTFORD GOODS
Brentford Town Goods
(03.11.1930)
(general goods traffic ceased 07.12.1970)

MACFARLANE LANG BISCUITS

REFUSE TRANSFER STATION
(early 1977)

River Brent

LSWR
22.08.1849

BRENTFORD (LSWR)
Brentford Central
Brentford
(22.08.1849)

BRENTFORD

FIRESTONE TYRES

MDR
01.05.1883

OSTERLEY

SYON LANE
(05.07.1931)

BRENTFORD (GWR)
(01.05.1860 – 04.05.1942)

see left

GWR
18.07.1859 –
31.12.1964

HESTON

Lampton Junction to Hounslow Barracks built as single track, doubled to Heston-Hounslow 01.11.1912, then on to Hounslow Barracks 27.11.1926

(1st)
(2nd)

OSTERLEY
Osterley & Spring Grove
(01.05.1883)
(re-sited 25.03.1934)

SMALLBERRY GREEN
Hounslow
(22.08.1849 – 01.02.1850)

LSWR
22.08.1849

BRENTFORD DOCK
(18.07.1859 – 31.12.1964)

37

LAMPTON

MDR
01.05.1883

SPRING GROVE

SYON PARK

HOUNSLOW EAST
Hounslow Town
(02.05.1909)

- Lampton Junction

LSWR
01.02.1850

ISLEWORTH
Spring Grove & Isleworth
Isleworth
(01.02.1850)

MDR 21.07.1884 (disused 13.06.1905 – 02.05.1909)
Kingsley Road Junction

MDR 01.05.1883 – 02.05.1909
(disused 01.04.1886 – 01.03.1903)

MDR
13.06.1905 –
02.05.1909

MDR
21.07.1884

MDR
21.07.1884

HOUNSLOW CENTRAL
Heston-Hounslow
(01.04.1886)

HOUNSLOW TOWN
Hounslow
(01.05.1883 – 02.05.1909)

Duke of Northumberland's River

ISLEWORTH

OLD DEER PARK

RICHMOND
(27.07.1846)
(re-sited 22.08.1848)

HOUNSLOW

NEW GOODS
(1931 – 06.02.1967)

HOUNSLOW TOWN BRANCH:

Original western terminus of MDR branch from Mill Hill Park (Acton Town), opened 01.05.1883. Intended to continue southwards to LSWR Hounslow Loop and beyond to Strawberry Hill, but the bill was blocked by the LSWR. First closed 01.04.1886. Re-opened 01.03.1903 then electrified and new curve added between Hounslow Town and Kingsley Road Junction 13.06.1905 (after which date all trains towards Hounslow Barracks reversed at Hounslow Town, and Lampton Junction to Kingsley Road Junction became disused). Permanent closure came 02.05.1909, with all trains running direct to Hounslow Barracks and a replacement station (also named Hounslow Town, now Hounslow East) opening on the re-opened Lampton Junction to Kingsley Road Junction section.

OLD GOODS
(06.05.1968)

River Crane

(2nd)

(1st)

GOODS (1st)
(27.07.1846 – ??.11.1936)

RICHMOND

HOUNSLOW
Hounslow & Whitton
Hounslow
(01.02.1850)

MASWELL PARK

Richmond Bridge

LSWR
22.08.1848

LSWR
01.02.1850

COLE PARK

ST MARGARETS (02.10.1876)

Up relief line added 26.11.1899

WHITTON

Whitton Junction

WHITTON
(06.07.1930)

LSWR
22.08.1848

TWICKENHAM
(22.08.1848)
(re-sited 28.03.1954) (2nd)

ENGINE SHED
(??.06.1850 – 1897)

(1st)

LSWR
22.08.1848

GOODS (02.01.1967)

Km
Scale 0   0.5   1   1.5   2
Miles   ¼   ½   ¾   1

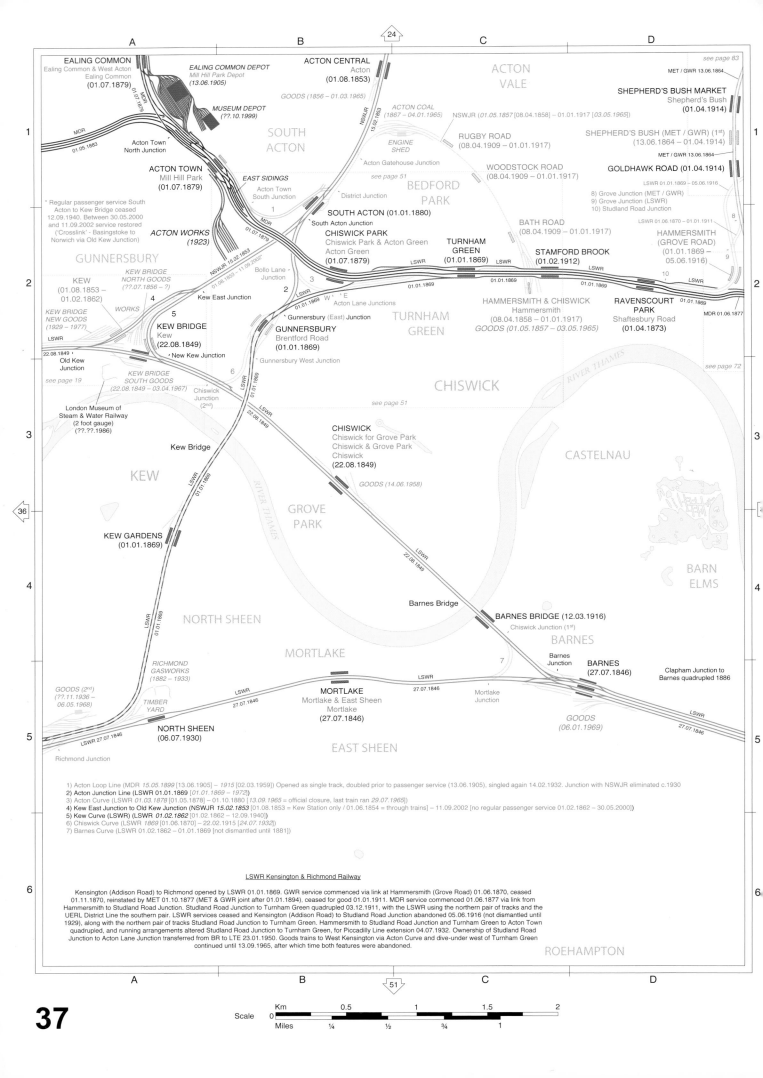

EALING COMMON
Ealing Common & West Acton
Ealing Common
(01.07.1879)

EALING COMMON DEPOT
Mill Hill Park Depot
(13.06.1905)

MUSEUM DEPOT
(??.10.1999)

ACTON CENTRAL
Acton
(01.08.1853)

GOODS (1856 – 01.03.1965)

ACTON COAL
(1867 – 04.01.1965)

NSWJR *(01.05.1857 [08.04.1858] – 01.01.1917 [03.05.1965])*

SHEPHERD'S BUSH MARKET
Shepherd's Bush
(01.04.1914)

MET / GWR 13.06.1864

see page 83

ENGINE SHED

RUGBY ROAD
(08.04.1909 – 01.01.1917)

SHEPHERD'S BUSH (MET / GWR) (1st)
(13.06.1864 – 01.04.1914)

GOLDHAWK ROAD (01.04.1914)

Acton Gatehouse Junction

WOODSTOCK ROAD
(08.04.1909 – 01.01.1917)

LSWR 01.01.1869 – 05.06.1916

8) Grove Junction (MET / GWR)
9) Grove Junction (LSWR)
10) Studland Road Junction

LSWR 01.06.1870 – 01.01.1911

**HAMMERSMITH
(GROVE ROAD)**
(01.01.1869 –
05.06.1916)

ACTON TOWN
Mill Hill Park
(01.07.1879)

EAST SIDINGS

Acton Town
South Junction

District Junction

SOUTH ACTON (01.01.1880)

South Acton Junction

CHISWICK PARK
Chiswick Park & Acton Green
Acton Green
(01.07.1879)

**TURNHAM
GREEN**
(01.01.1869)

BATH ROAD
(08.04.1909 – 01.01.1917)

STAMFORD BROOK
(01.02.1912)

LSWR 01.01.1869

ACTON WORKS
(1923)

* Regular passenger service South
Acton to Kew Bridge ceased
12.09.1940. Between 30.05.2000
and 11.09.2002 service restored
('Crosslink' - Basingstoke to
Norwich via Old Kew Junction)

GUNNERSBURY

KEW
(01.08.1853 –
01.02.1862)

*KEW BRIDGE
NEW GOODS
(1929 – 1977)*

*KEW BRIDGE
NORTH GOODS
(??.07.1856 – ?)*

Kew East Junction

Bollo Lane
Junction

HAMMERSMITH & CHISWICK
Hammersmith
(08.04.1858 – 01.01.1917)
GOODS (01.05.1857 – 03.05.1965)

**RAVENSCOURT
PARK**
Shaftesbury Road
(01.04.1873)

WORKS

LSWR

22.08.1849
Old Kew
Junction

see page 19

KEW BRIDGE
Kew
(22.08.1849)

New Kew Junction

*KEW BRIDGE
SOUTH GOODS*
(22.08.1849 – 03.04.1967)

London Museum of
Steam & Water Railway
(2 foot gauge)
(??.??.1986)

Gunnersbury West Junction

GUNNERSBURY
Brentford Road
(01.01.1869)

Chiswick
Junction
(2nd)

see page 51

Acton Lane Junctions

Gunnersbury (East) Junction

**TURNHAM
GREEN**

CHISWICK

MDR 01.06.1877

see page 72

CHISWICK
Chiswick for Grove Park
Chiswick & Grove Park
Chiswick
(22.08.1849)

GOODS (14.06.1958)

CASTELNAU

Kew Bridge

KEW

**GROVE
PARK**

**BARN
ELMS**

KEW GARDENS
(01.01.1869)

Barnes Bridge

BARNES BRIDGE (12.03.1916)

Chiswick Junction (1st)

NORTH SHEEN

*RICHMOND
GASWORKS
(1882 – 1933)*

MORTLAKE

Barnes
Junction

BARNES

*TIMBER
YARD*

MORTLAKE
Mortlake & East Sheen
Mortlake
(27.07.1846)

LSWR 27.07.1846

Mortlake
Junction

BARNES
(27.07.1846)

Clapham Junction to
Barnes quadrupled 1886

*GOODS (2nd)
(??.11.1936 –
06.05.1968)*

NORTH SHEEN
(06.07.1930)

Richmond Junction

EAST SHEEN

*GOODS
(06.01.1969)*

1) Acton Loop Line (MDR *15.05.1899* [13.06.1905] *– 1915* [02.03.1959]) Opened as single track, doubled prior to passenger service (13.06.1905), singled again 14.02.1932. Junction with NSWJR eliminated c.1930
2) Acton Junction Line (LSWR 01.01.1869 *[01.01.1869 – 1972]*)
3) Acton Curve (LSWR *01.03.1878* [01.05.1878] *– 01.10.1880* [*13.09.1965* = official closure, last train ran *29.07.1965*])
4) Kew East Junction to Old Kew Junction (NSWJR *15.02.1853* [01.08.1853 = Kew Station only / 01.06.1854 = through trains] – 11.09.2002 [no regular passenger service 01.02.1862 – 30.05.2000])
5) Kew Curve (LSWR *01.02.1862* [01.02.1862 – 12.09.1940])
6) Chiswick Curve (LSWR *1869* [01.06.1870] *– 22.02.1915* [*24.07.1932*])
7) Barnes Curve (LSWR 01.02.1862 – 01.01.1869 [not dismantled until 1881])

LSWR Kensington & Richmond Railway

Kensington (Addison Road) to Richmond opened by LSWR 01.01.1869. GWR service commenced via link at Hammersmith (Grove Road) 01.06.1870, ceased
01.11.1870, reinstated by MET 01.10.1877 (MET & GWR joint after 01.01.1894), ceased for good 01.01.1911. MDR service commenced 01.06.1877 via link from
Hammersmith to Studland Road Junction. Studland Road Junction to Turnham Green quadrupled 03.12.1911, with the LSWR using the northern pair of tracks and the
UERL District Line the southern pair. LSWR services ceased and Kensington (Addison Road) to Studland Road Junction abandoned 05.06.1916 (not dismantled until
1929), along with the northern pair of tracks Studland Road Junction to Turnham Green. Hammersmith to Studland Road Junction and Turnham Green to Acton Town
quadrupled, and running arrangements altered Studland Road Junction to Turnham Green, for Piccadilly Line extension 04.07.1932. Ownership of Studland Road
Junction to Acton Lane Junction transferred from BR to LTE 23.01.1950. Goods trains to West Kensington via Acton Curve and dive-under west of Turnham Green
continued until 13.09.1965, after which time both features were abandoned.

ROEHAMPTON

Scale

Km   0.5   1   1.5   2
Miles   ¼   ½   ¾   1

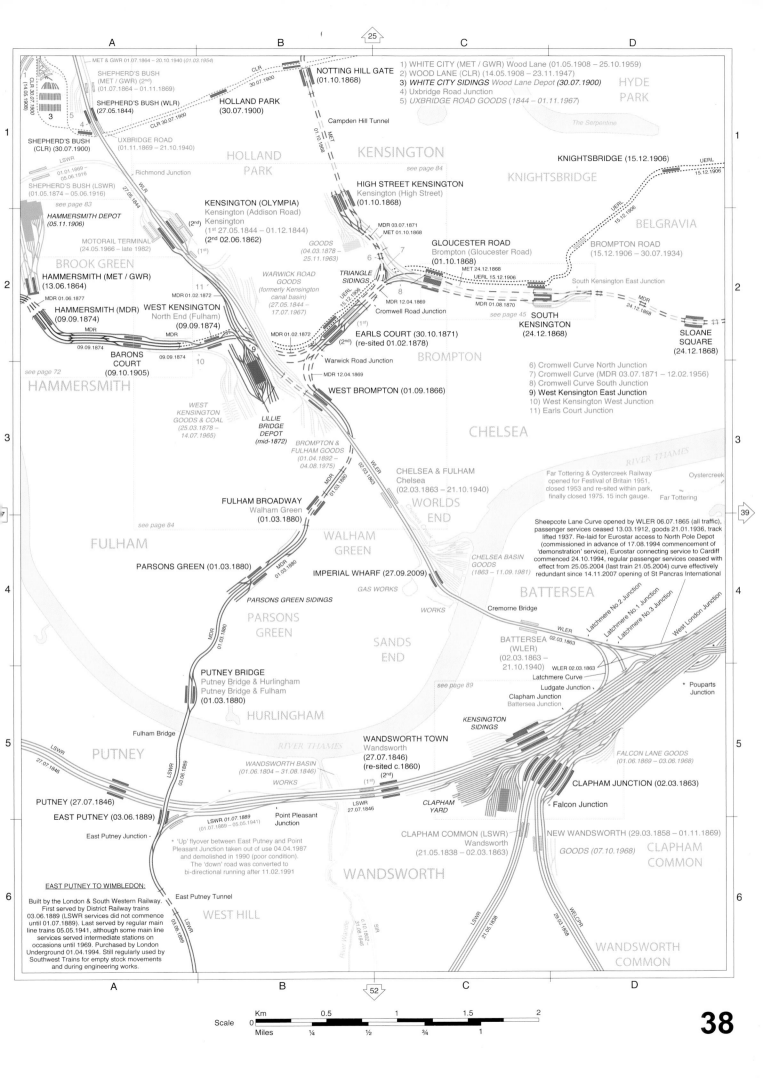

A   **B**   **C**   **D**

MET & GWR 01.07.1864 – 20.10.1940 *(01.03.1954)*

SHEPHERD'S BUSH
(MET / GWR) (2nd)
(01.07.1864 – 01.11.1869)

SHEPHERD'S BUSH (WLR)
(27.05.1844)

CLR 30.07.1900

NOTTING HILL GATE
(01.10.1868)

1) WHITE CITY (MET / GWR) Wood Lane (01.05.1908 – 25.10.1959)
2) WOOD LANE (CLR) (14.05.1908 – 23.11.1947)
3) *WHITE CITY SIDINGS* Wood Lane Depot **(30.07.1900)**
4) Uxbridge Road Junction
5) *UXBRIDGE ROAD GOODS (1844 – 01.11.1967)*

HOLLAND PARK
(30.07.1900)

Campden Hill Tunnel

HYDE
PARK

The Serpentine

SHEPHERD'S BUSH
(CLR) (30.07.1900)

1
CLR 30.07.1900
3
5
4

UXBRIDGE ROAD
(01.11.1869 – 21.10.1940)

LSWR

Richmond Junction

HOLLAND
PARK

see page 84

KENSINGTON

HIGH STREET KENSINGTON
Kensington (High Street)
(01.10.1868)

KNIGHTSBRIDGE (15.12.1906)

UERL
15.12.1906

KNIGHTSBRIDGE

BELGRAVIA

SHEPHERD'S BUSH (LSWR)
(01.05.1874 – 05.06.1916)

01.01.1869 –
05.06.1916

see page 83

HAMMERSMITH DEPOT
(05.11.1906)

MOTORAIL TERMINAL
(24.05.1966 – late 1982)

KENSINGTON (OLYMPIA)
Kensington (Addison Road)
Kensington
(1st 27.05.1844 – 01.12.1844)
(2nd 02.06.1862)

(2nd)

(1st)

GOODS
(04.03.1878 –
25.11.1963)

MDR 03.07.1871
MET 01.10.1868

GLOUCESTER ROAD
Brompton (Gloucester Road)
(01.10.1868)

MET 24.12.1868

UERL 15.12.1906

BROMPTON ROAD
(15.12.1906 – 30.07.1934)

UERL
15.12.1906

South Kensington East Junction

BROOK GREEN

HAMMERSMITH (MET / GWR)
(13.06.1864)

MDR 01.06.1877

HAMMERSMITH (MDR)
(09.09.1874)

MDR

09.09.1874

WEST KENSINGTON
North End (Fulham)
(09.09.1874)

MDR 01.02.1872

11

WARWICK ROAD
GOODS
(formerly Kensington
canal basin)
(27.05.1844 –
17.07.1967)

6
7
TRIANGLE
SIDINGS

8
UERL
15.12.1906

MDR 12.04.1869

Cromwell Road Junction

MDR 01.08.1870

see page 45

MDR 01.02.1872

EARLS COURT (30.10.1871)
(2nd) (re-sited 01.02.1878)

SOUTH
KENSINGTON
(24.12.1868)

MDR
24.12.1868

SLOANE
SQUARE
(24.12.1868)

MDR

09.09.1874

BARONS
COURT
(09.10.1905)

MDR

see page 72

HAMMERSMITH

10

9

WEST
KENSINGTON
GOODS & COAL
(25.03.1878 –
14.07.1965)

LILLIE
BRIDGE
DEPOT
(mid-1872)

(1st)

MDR 01.02.1872

Warwick Road Junction

MDR 12.04.1869

WEST BROMPTON (01.09.1866)

BROMPTON

CHELSEA

6) Cromwell Curve North Junction
7) Cromwell Curve (MDR 03.07.1871 – 12.02.1956)
8) Cromwell Curve South Junction
9) West Kensington East Junction
10) West Kensington West Junction
11) Earls Court Junction

7

39

BROMPTON &
FULHAM GOODS
(01.04.1892 –
04.08.1975)

WLER
02.03.1863

CHELSEA & FULHAM
Chelsea
(02.03.1863 – 21.10.1940)

WORLDS
END

RIVER THAMES

Oystercreek

Far Tottering & Oystercreek Railway
opened for Festival of Britain 1951,
closed 1953 and re-sited within park,
finally closed 1975. 15 inch gauge.

Far Tottering

FULHAM

FULHAM BROADWAY
Walham Green
(01.03.1880)

MDR
01.03.1880

see page 84

WALHAM
GREEN

Sheepcote Lane Curve opened by WLER 06.07.1865 (all traffic),
passenger services ceased 13.03.1912, goods 21.01.1936, track
lifted 1937. Re-laid for Eurostar access to North Pole Depot
(commissioned in advance of 17.08.1994 commencement of
'demonstration' service), Eurostar connecting service to Cardiff
commenced 24.10.1994, regular passenger services ceased with
effect from 25.05.2004 (last train 21.05.2004) curve effectively
redundant since 14.11.2007 opening of St Pancras International

PARSONS GREEN (01.03.1880)

MDR
01.03.1880

IMPERIAL WHARF (27.09.2009)

GAS WORKS

WORKS

CHELSEA BASIN
GOODS
(1863 – 11.09.1981)

BATTERSEA

Cremorne Bridge

Latchmere No. 2 Junction
Latchmere No 1 Junction
Latchmere No 3 Junction

West London Junction

PARSONS GREEN SIDINGS

PARSONS
GREEN

SANDS
END

WLER
02.03.1863

BATTERSEA
(WLER)
(02.03.1863 –
21.10.1940)

WLER 02.03.1863

Pouparts
Junction

PUTNEY BRIDGE
Putney Bridge & Hurlingham
Putney Bridge & Fulham
(01.03.1880)

MDR

01.03.1880

see page 89

Latchmere Curve

Ludgate Junction

Clapham Junction
Battersea Junction

KENSINGTON
SIDINGS

HURLINGHAM

Fulham Bridge

WANDSWORTH TOWN
Wandsworth
(27.07.1846)
(re-sited c.1860)

FALCON LANE GOODS
(01.06.1869 – 03.06.1968)

PUTNEY

LSWR

27.07.1846

RIVER THAMES

WANDSWORTH BASIN
(01.06.1804 – 31.08.1846)

WORKS

(1st)

(2nd)

LSWR

27.07.1846

CLAPHAM JUNCTION (02.03.1863)

Falcon Junction

LSWR

03.06.1889

CLAPHAM
YARD

PUTNEY (27.07.1846)

EAST PUTNEY (03.06.1889)

East Putney Junction -

LSWR 01.07.1889
(01.07.1889 – 05.05.1941)

Point Pleasant
Junction

CLAPHAM COMMON (LSWR)
Wandsworth
(21.05.1838 – 02.03.1863)

NEW WANDSWORTH (29.03.1858 – 01.11.1869)

GOODS (07.10.1968)

CLAPHAM
COMMON

* 'Up' flyover between East Putney and Point
Pleasant Junction taken out of use 04.04.1987
and demolished in 1990 (poor condition).
The 'down' road was converted to
bi-directional running after 11.02.1991

WANDSWORTH

EAST PUTNEY TO WIMBLEDON:

Built by the London & South Western Railway.
First served by District Railway trains
03.06.1889 (LSWR services did not commence
until 01.07.1889). Last served by regular main
line trains 05.05.1941, although some main line
services served intermediate stations on
occasions until 1969. Purchased by London
Underground 01.04.1994. Still regularly used by
Southwest Trains for empty stock movements
and during engineering works.

East Putney Tunnel

WEST HILL

River Wandle

c.10.1802 –
31.08.1846

SIR

LSWR
21.05.1838

WLCPR
29.03.1858

WANDSWORTH
COMMON

A   **B**   **C**   **D**

Scale

Km
0   0.5   1   1.5   2

Miles
¼   ½   ¾   1

38

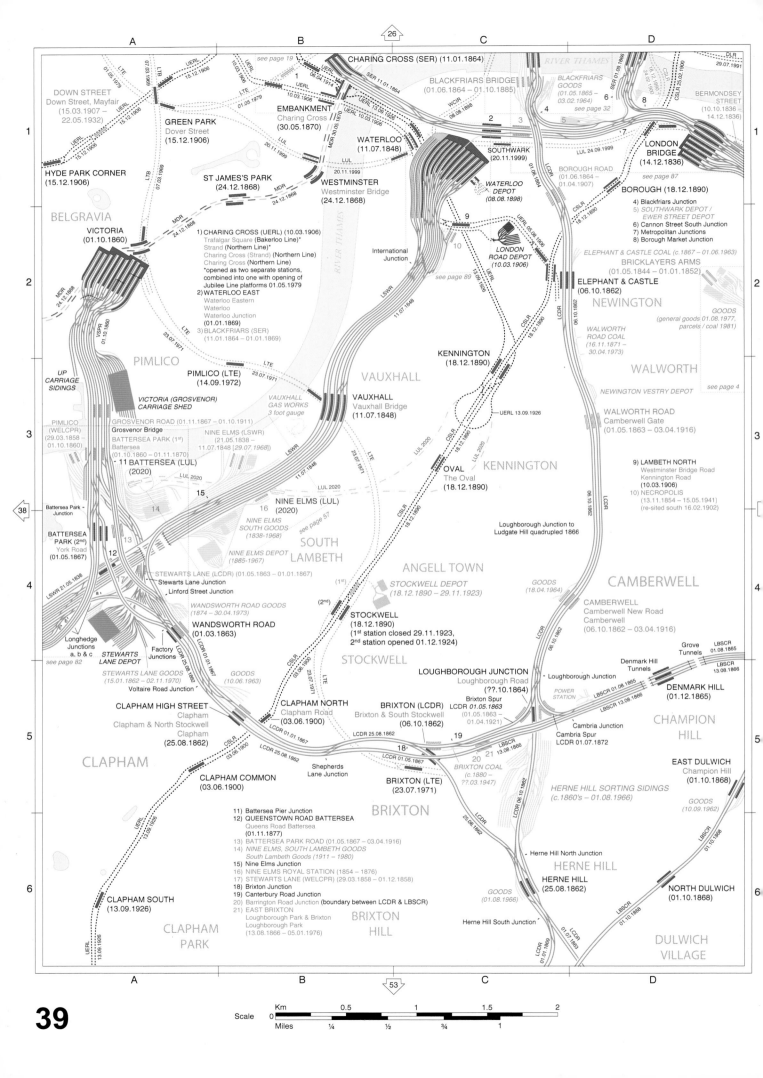

A B C D

DOWN STREET
Down Street, Mayfair
(15.03.1907 –
22.05.1932)

GREEN PARK
Dover Street
(15.12.1906)

HYDE PARK CORNER
(15.12.1906)

BELGRAVIA

VICTORIA
(01.10.1860)

PIMLICO

ST JAMES'S PARK
(24.12.1868)

see page 19

CHARING CROSS (SER) (11.01.1864)

EMBANKMENT
Charing Cross
(30.05.1870)

WESTMINSTER
Westminster Bridge
(24.12.1868)

WATERLOO
(11.07.1848)

BLACKFRIARS BRIDGE
(01.06.1864 – 01.10.1885)

BLACKFRIARS
GOODS
(01.05.1865 –
03.02.1964)
see page 32

SOUTHWARK
(20.11.1999)

WATERLOO
DEPOT
(08.08.1898)

RIVER THAMES

BERMONDSEY
STREET
(10.10.1836 –
14.12.1836)

LONDON
BRIDGE
(14.12.1836)

see page 87

BOROUGH (18.12.1890)

BOROUGH ROAD
(01.06.1864 –
01.04.1907)

1) CHARING CROSS (UERL) (10.03.1906)
Trafalgar Square (Bakerloo Line)*
Strand (Northern Line)*
Charing Cross (Strand) (Northern Line)
Charing Cross (Northern Line)
*opened as two separate stations,
combined into one with opening of
Jubilee Line platforms 01.05.1979
2) WATERLOO EAST
Waterloo Eastern
Waterloo
Waterloo Junction
(01.01.1869)
3) BLACKFRIARS (SER)
(11.01.1864 – 01.01.1869)

International
Junction

LONDON
ROAD DEPOT
(10.03.1906)

see page 89

4) Blackfriars Junction
5) SOUTHWARK DEPOT /
EWER STREET DEPOT
6) Cannon Street South Junction
7) Metropolitan Junctions
8) Borough Market Junction

ELEPHANT & CASTLE COAL (c.1867 – 01.06.1963)

ELEPHANT & CASTLE
(06.10.1862)

NEWINGTON

BRICKLAYERS ARMS
(01.05.1844 – 01.01.1852)

GOODS
(general goods 01.08.1977,
parcels / coal 1981)

WALWORTH

WALWORTH
ROAD COAL
(16.11.1871 –
30.04.1973)

NEWINGTON VESTRY DEPOT

see page 4

WALWORTH ROAD
Camberwell Gate
(01.05.1863 – 03.04.1916)

PIMLICO (LTE)
(14.09.1972)

UP
CARRIAGE
SIDINGS

PIMLICO
(WELCPR)
(29.03.1858 –
01.10.1860)

VICTORIA (GROSVENOR)
CARRIAGE SHED

GROSVENOR ROAD (01.11.1867 – 01.10.1911)
Grosvenor Bridge
BATTERSEA PARK (1st)
Battersea
(01.10.1860 – 01.11.1870)

11 BATTERSEA (LUL)
(2020)

VAUXHALL
GAS WORKS
3 foot gauge

VAUXHALL
Vauxhall Bridge
(11.07.1848)

VAUXHALL

NINE ELMS (LSWR)
(21.05.1838 –
11.07.1848 [29.07.1968])

NINE ELMS (LUL)
(2020)

SOUTH
LAMBETH

NINE ELMS
SOUTH GOODS
(1838-1968)

NINE ELMS DEPOT
(1885-1967)

see page 57

KENNINGTON
(18.12.1890)

UERL 13.09.1926

OVAL
The Oval
(18.12.1890)

KENNINGTON

9) LAMBETH NORTH
Westminster Bridge Road
Kennington Road
(10.03.1906)
10) NECROPOLIS
(13.11.1854 – 15.05.1941)
(re-sited south 16.02.1902)

Loughborough Junction to
Ludgate Hill quadrupled 1866

CAMBERWELL

GOODS
(18.04.1964)

CAMBERWELL
Camberwell New Road
Camberwell
(06.10.1862 – 03.04.1916)

STEWARTS LANE (LCDR) (01.05.1863 – 01.01.1867)
Stewarts Lane Junction
Linford Street Junction

WANDSWORTH ROAD GOODS
(1874 – 30.04.1973)

BATTERSEA
PARK (2nd)
York Road
(01.05.1867)

Longhedge
Junctions
a, b & c
see page 82

STEWARTS
LANE DEPOT

STEWARTS LANE GOODS
(15.01.1862 – 02.11.1970)
Voltaire Road Junction

Factory
Junctions

WANDSWORTH ROAD
(01.03.1863)

GOODS
(10.06.1963)

ANGELL TOWN

STOCKWELL DEPOT
(18.12.1890 – 29.11.1923)

STOCKWELL
(18.12.1890)
(1st station closed 29.11.1923,
2nd station opened 01.12.1924)

STOCKWELL

LOUGHBOROUGH JUNCTION
Loughborough Road
(??.10.1864)

Loughborough Junction

POWER
STATION

Denmark Hill
Tunnels

Grove
Tunnels

DENMARK HILL
(01.12.1865)

CHAMPION
HILL

CLAPHAM HIGH STREET
Clapham
Clapham & North Stockwell
Clapham
(25.08.1862)

CLAPHAM

CLAPHAM NORTH
Clapham Road
(03.06.1900)

BRIXTON (LCDR)
Brixton & South Stockwell
(06.10.1862)

Brixton Spur
LCDR 01.05.1863
(01.05.1863 –
01.04.1921)

Cambria Junction
Cambria Spur
LCDR 01.07.1872

EAST DULWICH
Champion Hill
(01.10.1868)

CLAPHAM COMMON
(03.06.1900)

Shepherds
Lane Junction

BRIXTON (LTE)
(23.07.1971)

BRIXTON
HILL

BRIXTON COAL
(c.1880 –
??.03.1947)

HERNE HILL SORTING SIDINGS
(c.1860's – 01.08.1966)

GOODS
(10.09.1962)

11) Battersea Pier Junction
12) QUEENSTOWN ROAD BATTERSEA
Queens Road Battersea
(01.11.1877)
13) BATTERSEA PARK ROAD (01.05.1867 – 03.04.1916)
14) NINE ELMS, SOUTH LAMBETH GOODS
South Lambeth Goods (1911 – 1980)
15) Nine Elms Junction
16) NINE ELMS ROYAL STATION (1854 – 1876)
17) STEWARTS LANE (WELCPR) (29.03.1858 – 01.12.1858)
18) Brixton Junction
19) Canterbury Road Junction
20) Barrington Road Junction (boundary between LCDR & LBSCR)
21) EAST BRIXTON
Loughborough Park & Brixton
Loughborough Park
(13.08.1866 – 05.01.1976)

Herne Hill North Junction

HERNE HILL
(25.08.1862)

GOODS
(01.08.1966)

NORTH DULWICH
(01.10.1868)

HERNE HILL

Herne Hill South Junction

DULWICH
VILLAGE

CLAPHAM SOUTH
(13.09.1926)

CLAPHAM
PARK

Scale

Km 0.5 1 1.5 2

Miles ¼ ½ ¾ 1

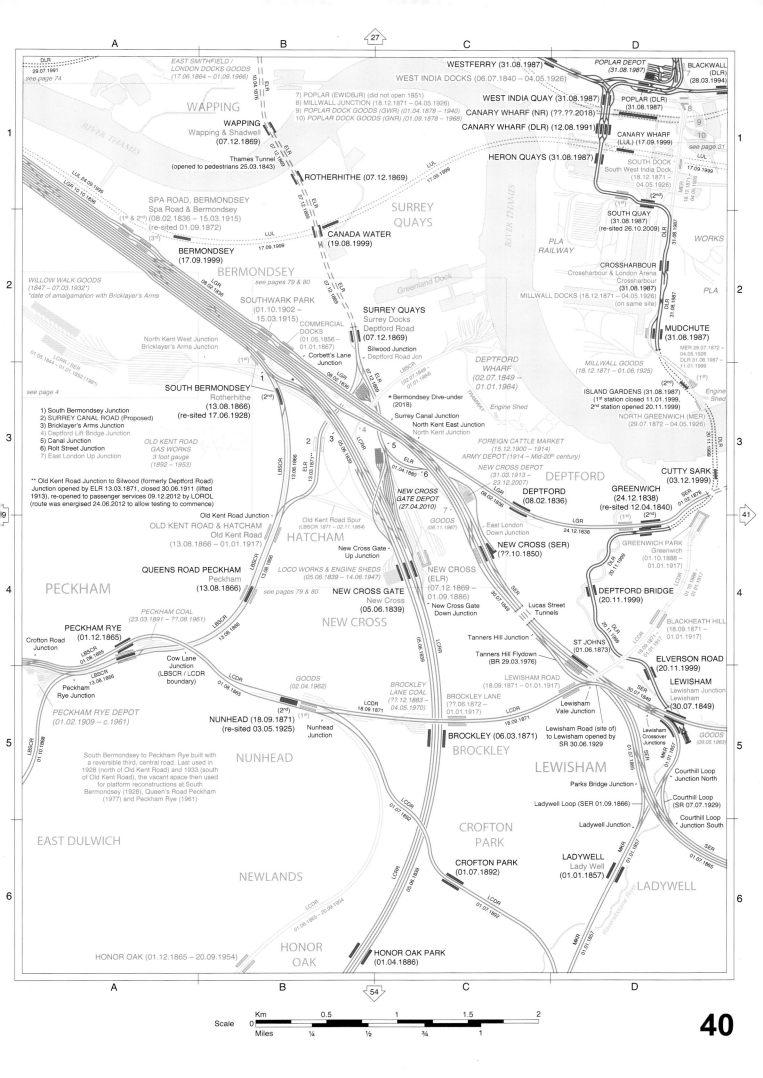

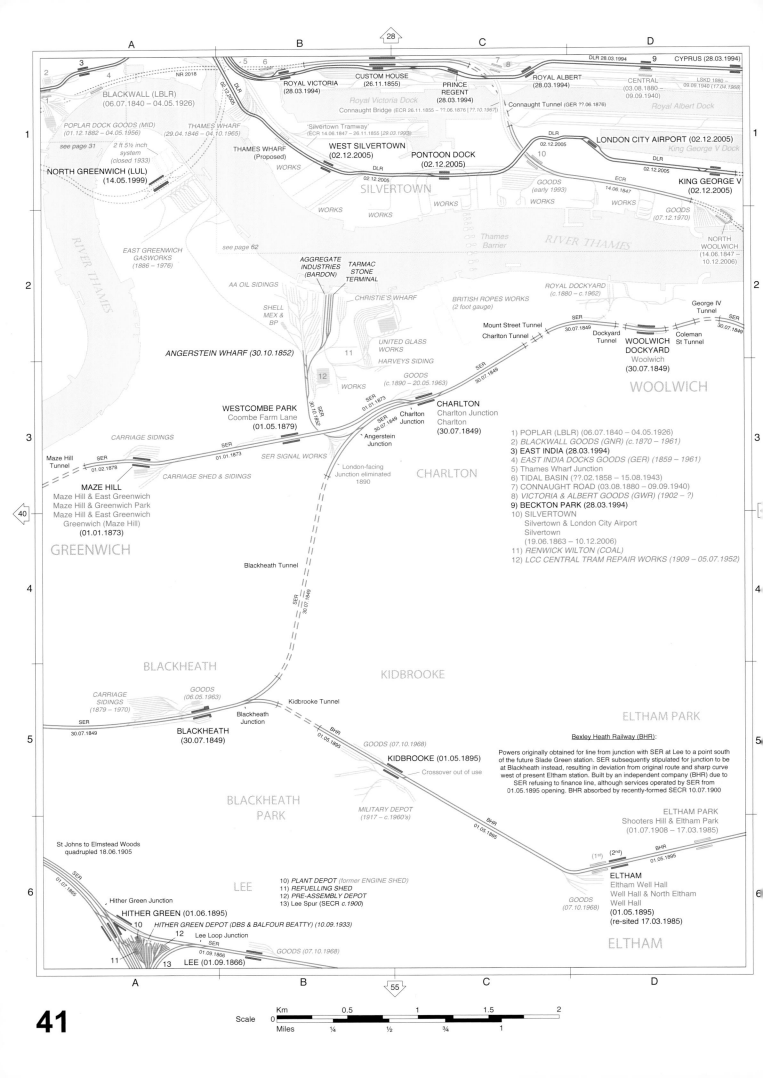

NR 2018

DLR 28.03.1994   9   CYPRUS (28.03.1994)

3

2

4

BLACKWALL (LBLR)
(06.07.1840 – 04.05.1926)

5 6

ROYAL VICTORIA
(28.03.1994)

CUSTOM HOUSE
(26.11.1855)

7 8

PRINCE
REGENT

ROYAL ALBERT
(28.03.1994)

CENTRAL
(03.08.1880 –
09.09.1940)

LSKD 1880 –
09.09.1940 (17.04.1966)

1

POPLAR DOCK GOODS (MID)
(01.12.1882 – 04.05.1956)

see page 31

THAMES WHARF
(29.04.1846 – 04.10.1965)

Royal Victoria Dock

Connaught Bridge (ECR 26.11.1855 – ??.06.1876 [??.10.1967])

Royal Albert Dock

2 ft 5½ inch
system
(closed 1933)

THAMES WHARF
(Proposed)

'Silvertown Tramway'
(ECR 14.06.1847 – 26.11.1855 [29.03.1993])

Connaught Tunnel (GER ??.06.1876)

02.12.2005

DLR

LONDON CITY AIRPORT (02.12.2005)
King George V Dock

1

NORTH GREENWICH (LUL)
(14.05.1999)

WEST SILVERTOWN
(02.12.2005)

PONTOON DOCK
(02.12.2005)

DLR

02.12.2005

10

02.12.2005

DLR

KING GEORGE V
(02.12.2005)

DLR

WORKS

SILVERTOWN

ECR
14.06.1847

*GOODS
(early 1993)*

WORKS

*GOODS
(07.12.1970)*

EAST GREENWICH
GASWORKS
(1886 – 1976)

see page 62

AGGREGATE
INDUSTRIES
(BARDON)

TARMAC
STONE
TERMINAL

WORKS

WORKS

WORKS

*Thames
Barrier*

RIVER THAMES

NORTH
WOOLWICH
(14.06.1847 –
10.12.2006)

2

RIVER THAMES

AA OIL SIDINGS

CHRISTIE'S WHARF

*BRITISH ROPES WORKS
(2 foot gauge)*

*ROYAL DOCKYARD
(c.1880 – c.1962)*

George IV
Tunnel

SER
30.07.1849

2

SHELL
MEX &
BP

*UNITED GLASS
WORKS*

Mount Street Tunnel

SER

Dockyard
Tunnel

WOOLWICH
DOCKYARD

Coleman
St Tunnel

ANGERSTEIN WHARF (30.10.1852)

11

HARVEYS SIDING

Charlton Tunnel

30.07.1849

Woolwich
Tunnel

Woolwich
(30.07.1849)

WOOLWICH

12

*GOODS
(c.1890 – 20.05.1963)*

SER
30.07.1849

WESTCOMBE PARK
Coombe Farm Lane
(01.05.1879)

WORKS

SER
30.10.1852

SER
01.01.1873

Charlton
Junction

CHARLTON
Charlton Junction
Charlton
(30.07.1849)

CARRIAGE SIDINGS

SER
01.01.1873

SER
30.07.1849

Charlton
Junction

3

Maze Hill
Tunnel

SER
01.02.1878

CARRIAGE SHED & SIDINGS

SER

Angerstein
Junction

SER SIGNAL WORKS

London-facing
Junction eliminated
1890

CHARLTON

1) POPLAR (LBLR) (06.07.1840 – 04.05.1926)
2) *BLACKWALL GOODS (GNR) (c.1870 – 1961)*
3) **EAST INDIA (28.03.1994)**
4) *EAST INDIA DOCKS GOODS (GER) (1859 – 1961)*
5) Thames Wharf Junction
6) *TIDAL BASIN (??.02.1858 – 15.08.1943)*
7) CONNAUGHT ROAD (03.08.1880 – 09.09.1940)
8) *VICTORIA & ALBERT GOODS (GWR) (1902 – ?)*
9) BECKTON PARK (28.03.1994)
10) SILVERTOWN
    Silvertown & London City Airport
    Silvertown
    (19.06.1863 – 10.12.2006)
11) *RENWICK WILTON (COAL)*
12) *LCC CENTRAL TRAM REPAIR WORKS (1909 – 05.07.1952)*

MAZE HILL
Maze Hill & East Greenwich
Maze Hill & Greenwich Park
Maze Hill & East Greenwich
Greenwich (Maze Hill)
(01.01.1873)

3

40

GREENWICH

SER
01.01.1873

Blackheath Tunnel

SER
30.07.1849

BLACKHEATH

KIDBROOKE

ELTHAM PARK

4

4

Bexley Heath Railway (BHR):

Powers originally obtained for line from junction with SER at Lee to a point south
of the future Slade Green station. SER subsequently stipulated for junction to be
at Blackheath instead, resulting in deviation from original route and sharp curve
west of present Eltham station. Built by an independent company (BHR) due to
SER refusing to finance line, although services operated by SER from
01.05.1895 opening. BHR absorbed by recently-formed SECR 10.07.1900

CARRIAGE SIDINGS
(1879 – 1970)

*GOODS
(06.05.1963)*

SER

Blackheath
Junction

Kidbrooke Tunnel

BHR
01.05.1895

5

SER
30.07.1849

BLACKHEATH
(30.07.1849)

GOODS (07.10.1968)

KIDBROOKE (01.05.1895)

Crossover out of use

ELTHAM PARK
Shooters Hill & Eltham Park
(01.07.1908 – 17.03.1985)

5

*BLACKHEATH
PARK*

*MILITARY DEPOT
(1917 – c.1960's)*

BHR
01.05.1895

St Johns to Elmstead Woods
quadrupled 18.06.1905

(1st) (2nd)

BHR
01.05.1895

SER
01.07.1895

LEE

10) *PLANT DEPOT (former ENGINE SHED)*
11) *REFUELLING SHED*
12) *PRE-ASSEMBLY DEPOT*
13) Lee Spur (SECR c.1900)

*GOODS
(07.10.1968)*

ELTHAM
Eltham Well Hall
Well Hall & North Eltham
Well Hall
(01.05.1895)
(re-sited 17.03.1985)

6

SER
01.07.1895

Hither Green Junction

10

HITHER GREEN (01.06.1895)
HITHER GREEN DEPOT (DBS & BALFOUR BEATTY) (10.09.1933)

12

Lee Loop Junction

SER
01.09.1866

GOODS (07.10.1968)

ELTHAM

6

11

13

SER
01.09.1866

LEE (01.09.1866)

Scale

Km	0		0.5		1		1.5		2

Miles   ¼   ½   ¾   1

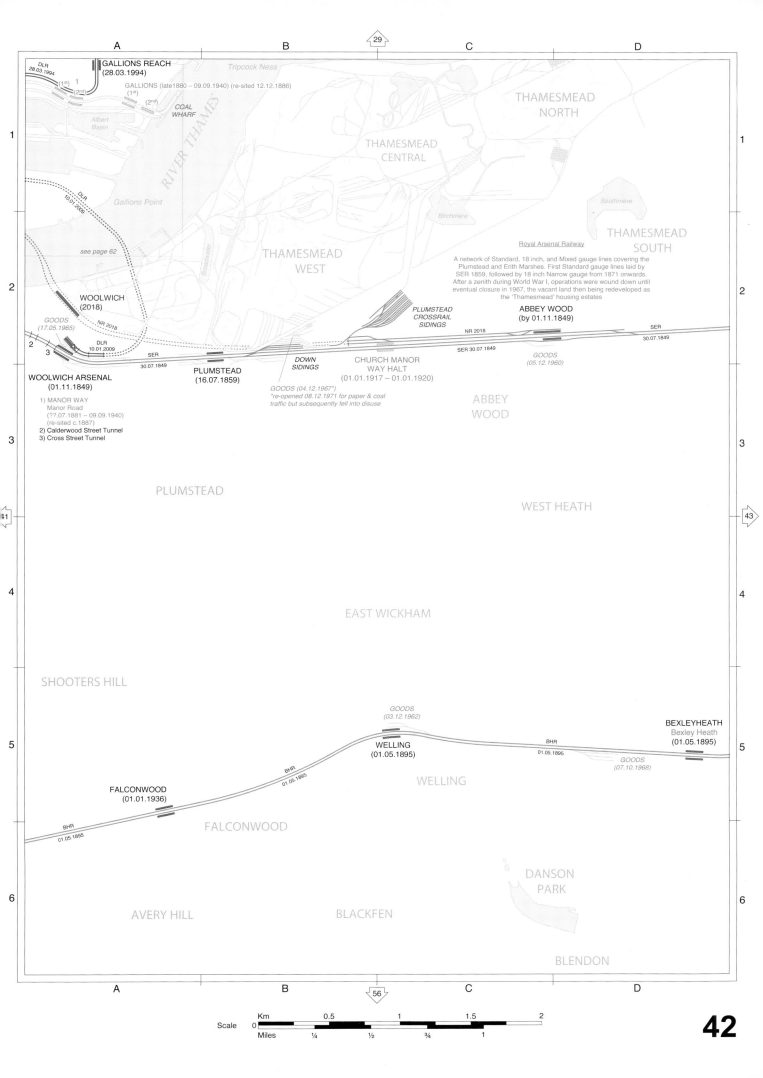

DLR
28.03.1994

GALLIONS REACH
(28.03.1994)

(1st) 1
(2nd)

GALLIONS (late1880 – 09.09.1940) (re-sited 12.12.1886)
(1st)
(2nd)

Tripcock Ness

**THAMESMEAD
NORTH**

*COAL
WHARF*

*Albert
Basin*

RIVER THAMES

**THAMESMEAD
CENTRAL**

DLR
10.01.2009

Gallions Point

Southmere

**THAMESMEAD
SOUTH**

see page 62

Broadwater

Birchmere

**THAMESMEAD
WEST**

Royal Arsenal Railway

A network of Standard, 18 inch, and Mixed gauge lines covering the
Plumstead and Erith Marshes. First Standard gauge lines laid by
SER 1859, followed by 18 inch Narrow gauge from 1871 onwards.
After a zenith during World War I, operations were wound down until
eventual closure in 1967, the vacant land then being redeveloped as
the 'Thamesmead' housing estates

WOOLWICH
(2018)

NR 2018

*GOODS
(17.05.1965)*

2

3

DLR
10.01.2009

WOOLWICH ARSENAL
(01.11.1849)

1) MANOR WAY
Manor Road
(??.07.1881 – 09.09.1940)
(re-sited c.1887)
2) Calderwood Street Tunnel
3) Cross Street Tunnel

SER
30.07.1849

PLUMSTEAD
(16.07.1859)

*PLUMSTEAD
CROSSRAIL
SIDINGS*

*DOWN
SIDINGS*

**CHURCH MANOR
WAY HALT**
(01.01.1917 – 01.01.1920)

GOODS (04.12.1967)
*re-opened 08.12.1971 for paper & coal
traffic but subsequently fell into disuse*

NR 2018

SER 30.07.1849

ABBEY WOOD
(by 01.11.1849)

SER
30.07.1849

*GOODS
(05.12.1960)*

**ABBEY
WOOD**

PLUMSTEAD

WEST HEATH

EAST WICKHAM

SHOOTERS HILL

*GOODS
(03.12.1962)*

BEXLEYHEATH
Bexley Heath
(01.05.1895)

WELLING
(01.05.1895)

BHR
01.05.1895

BHR
01.05.1895

*GOODS
(07.10.1968)*

WELLING

FALCONWOOD
(01.01.1936)

BHR
01.05.1895

BHR
01.05.1895

FALCONWOOD

**DANSON
PARK**

AVERY HILL

BLACKFEN

BLENDON

Scale

Km 0   0.5   1   1.5   2
Miles ¼   ½   ¾   1

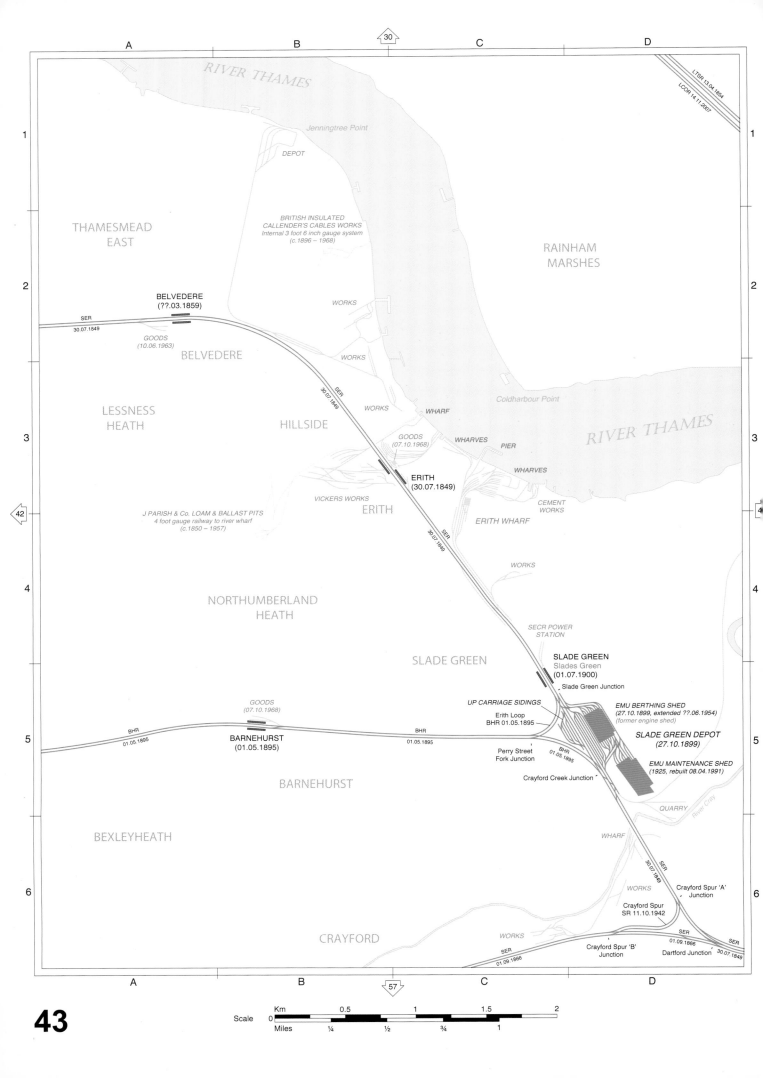

RIVER THAMES

LTSR 13.04.1854
LCOR 14.11.2007

Jenningtree Point

DEPOT

THAMESMEAD
EAST

BRITISH INSULATED
CALLENDER'S CABLES WORKS
Internal 3 foot 6 inch gauge system
(c.1896 – 1968)

RAINHAM
MARSHES

WORKS

BELVEDERE
(??.03.1859)

SER
30.07.1849

WORKS

GOODS
(10.06.1963)

BELVEDERE

LESSNESS
HEATH

HILLSIDE

30.07.1849 SER

WORKS

Coldharbour Point

RIVER THAMES

WHARF

WORKS

WHARVES

GOODS
(07.10.1968)

PIER

ERITH
(30.07.1849)

WHARVES

42

VICKERS WORKS

ERITH

CEMENT
WORKS

J PARISH & Co. LOAM & BALLAST PITS
4 foot gauge railway to river wharf
(c.1850 – 1957)

SER
30.07.1849

ERITH WHARF

42

WORKS

NORTHUMBERLAND
HEATH

SECR POWER
STATION

SLADE GREEN

SLADE GREEN
Slades Green
(01.07.1900)

Slade Green Junction

UP CARRIAGE SIDINGS

EMU BERTHING SHED
(27.10.1899, extended ??.06.1954)
(former engine shed)

GOODS
(07.10.1968)

Erith Loop
BHR 01.05.1895

SLADE GREEN DEPOT
(27.10.1899)

BHR
01.05.1895

BARNEHURST
(01.05.1895)

BHR
01.05.1895

Perry Street
Fork Junction

BHR
01.05.1895

Crayford Creek Junction

EMU MAINTENANCE SHED
(1925, rebuilt 08.04.1991)

BARNEHURST

QUARRY

River Cray

BEXLEYHEATH

WHARF

Crayford Spur 'A'
Junction

WORKS

Crayford Spur
SR 11.10.1942

SER
30.07.1849

WORKS

SER
01.09.1866

CRAYFORD

SER
01.09.1866

Crayford Spur 'B'
Junction

Dartford Junction

SER
30.07.1849

43

Scale
Km   0   0.5   1   1.5   2
Miles   ¼   ½   ¾   1

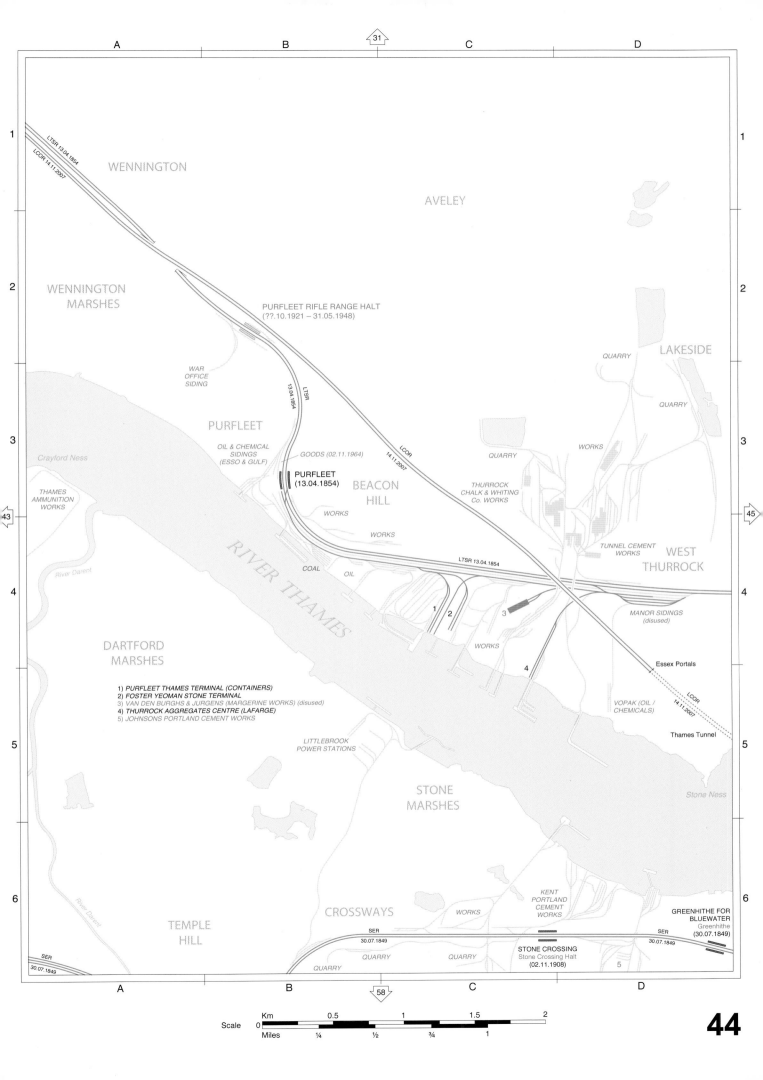

A B C D

1

WENNINGTON

LTSR 13.04.1854
LCOR 14.11.2007

AVELEY

2

WENNINGTON
MARSHES

PURFLEET RIFLE RANGE HALT
(??.10.1921 – 31.05.1948)

LAKESIDE

QUARRY

WAR
OFFICE
SIDING

13.04.1854
LTSR

QUARRY

3

Crayford Ness

PURFLEET

OIL & CHEMICAL
SIDINGS
(ESSO & GULF)

GOODS (02.11.1964)

LCOR
14.11.2007

WORKS

QUARRY

43

THAMES
AMMUNITION
WORKS

PURFLEET
(13.04.1854)

BEACON
HILL

THURROCK
CHALK & WHITING
Co. WORKS

45

River Darent

WORKS

WORKS

TUNNEL CEMENT
WORKS

WEST
THURROCK

LTSR 13.04.1854

4

COAL

OIL

1 2

3

MANOR SIDINGS
(disused)

DARTFORD
MARSHES

WORKS

Essex Portals

1) PURFLEET THAMES TERMINAL (CONTAINERS)
2) FOSTER YEOMAN STONE TERMINAL
3) VAN DEN BURGHS & JURGENS (MARGERINE WORKS) (disused)
4) THURROCK AGGREGATES CENTRE (LAFARGE)
5) JOHNSONS PORTLAND CEMENT WORKS

4

VOPAK (OIL /
CHEMICALS)

LCOR
14.11.2007

Thames Tunnel

5

LITTLEBROOK
POWER STATIONS

STONE
MARSHES

Stone Ness

River Darent

6

TEMPLE
HILL

CROSSWAYS

KENT
PORTLAND
CEMENT
WORKS

GREENHITHE FOR
BLUEWATER
Greenhithe
(30.07.1849)

SER
30.07.1854

SER
30.07.1849

WORKS

SER
30.07.1849

SER
30.07.1849

STONE CROSSING
Stone Crossing Halt
(02.11.1908)

QUARRY

QUARRY

QUARRY

5

A B C D

Scale
Km 0 0.5 1 1.5 2
Miles ¼ ½ ¾ 1

44

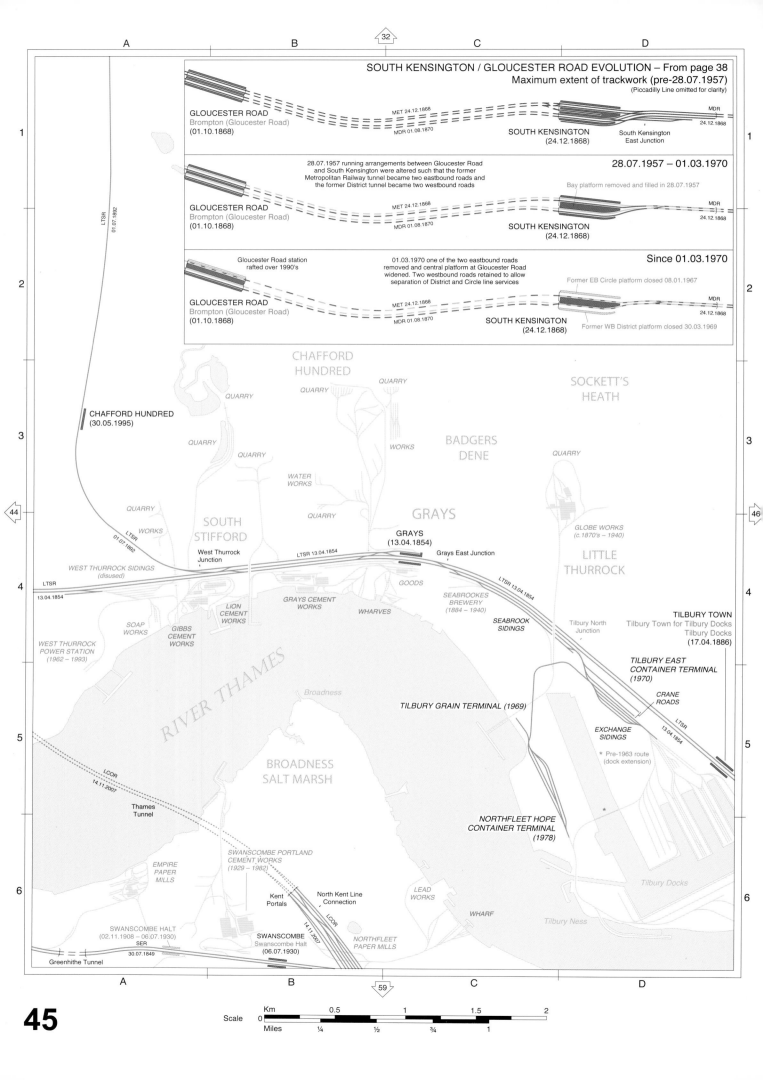

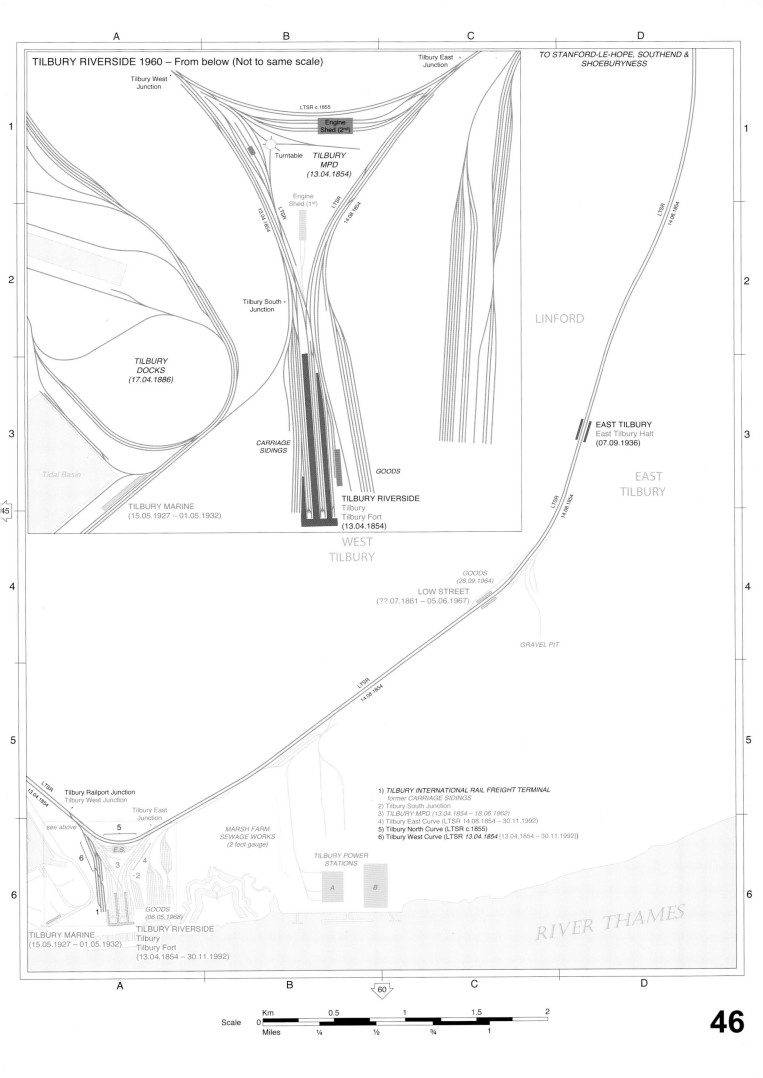

TILBURY RIVERSIDE 1960 – From below (Not to same scale)

Tilbury West Junction

Tilbury East Junction

TO STANFORD-LE-HOPE, SOUTHEND & SHOEBURYNESS

LTSR c.1855

Engine Shed (2nd)

Turntable

TILBURY MPD
(13.04.1854)

Engine Shed (1st)

13.04.1854

LTSR

LTSR

14.08.1854

LTSR
14.08.1854

LINFORD

Tilbury South - Junction

TILBURY DOCKS
(17.04.1886)

EAST TILBURY
East Tilbury Halt
(07.09.1936)

EAST TILBURY

Tidal Basin

CARRIAGE SIDINGS

GOODS

45

TILBURY MARINE
(15.05.1927 – 01.05.1932)

TILBURY RIVERSIDE
Tilbury
Tilbury Fort
(13.04.1854)

WEST TILBURY

GOODS
(28.09.1964)

LOW STREET
(??.07.1861 – 05.06.1967)

LTSR
14.08.1854

GRAVEL PIT

LTSR
14.08.1854

LTSR
13.04.1854

Tilbury Railport Junction
Tilbury West Junction

see above

5

Tilbury East Junction

E.S.

6

3

4

-2

1

GOODS
(06.05.1968)

MARSH FARM
SEWAGE WORKS
(2 foot gauge)

TILBURY POWER
STATIONS

A

B

1) TILBURY INTERNATIONAL RAIL FREIGHT TERMINAL
   former CARRIAGE SIDINGS
2) Tilbury South Junction
3) TILBURY MPD (13.04.1854 – 18.06.1962)
4) Tilbury East Curve (LTSR 14.08.1854 – 30.11.1992)
5) Tilbury North Curve (LTSR c.1855)
6) Tilbury West Curve (LTSR 13.04.1854 [13.04.1854 – 30.11.1992])

TILBURY MARINE
(15.05.1927 – 01.05.1932)

TILBURY RIVERSIDE
Tilbury
Tilbury Fort
(13.04.1854 – 30.11.1992)

RIVER THAMES

60

Scale
Km 0   0.5   1   1.5   2
Miles   ¼   ½   ¾   1

46

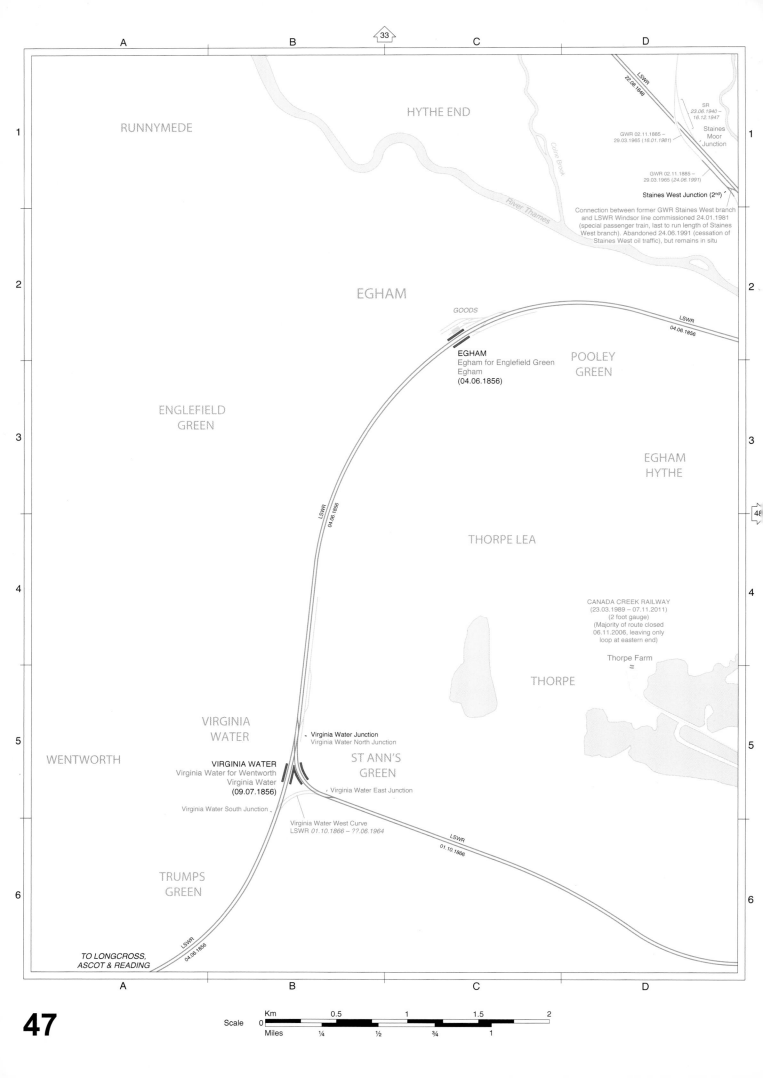

A   B   C   D

1   RUNNYMEDE   HYTHE END   1

Colne Brook

River Thames

LSWR
22.06.1848

SR
23.06.1940 –
16.12.1947

Staines
Moor
Junction

GWR 02.11.1885 –
29.03.1965 *(16.01.1981)*

GWR 02.11.1885 –
29.03.1965 *(24.06.1991)*

Staines West Junction (2ⁿᵈ)

Connection between former GWR Staines West branch
and LSWR Windsor line commissioned 24.01.1981
(special passenger train, last to run length of Staines
West branch). Abandoned 24.06.1991 (cessation of
Staines West oil traffic), but remains in situ

2   EGHAM   2

GOODS

EGHAM
Egham for Englefield Green
Egham
(04.06.1856)

POOLEY
GREEN

LSWR
04.06.1856

ENGLEFIELD
GREEN

3   3

EGHAM
HYTHE

LSWR
04.06.1856

THORPE LEA

48

4   4

CANADA CREEK RAILWAY
(23.03.1989 – 07.11.2011)
(2 foot gauge)
(Majority of route closed
06.11.2006, leaving only
loop at eastern end)

Thorpe Farm

THORPE

5   VIRGINIA
WATER   5

Virginia Water Junction
Virginia Water North Junction

WENTWORTH

VIRGINIA WATER
Virginia Water for Wentworth
Virginia Water
(09.07.1856)

ST ANN'S
GREEN

Virginia Water East Junction

Virginia Water South Junction

Virginia Water West Curve
LSWR *01.10.1866 – ??.06.1964*

LSWR
01.10.1866

6   TRUMPS
GREEN   6

TO LONGCROSS,
ASCOT & READING

LSWR
04.06.1856

A   B   C   D

47

Scale   Km   0   0.5   1   1.5   2
Miles   ¼   ½   ¾   1

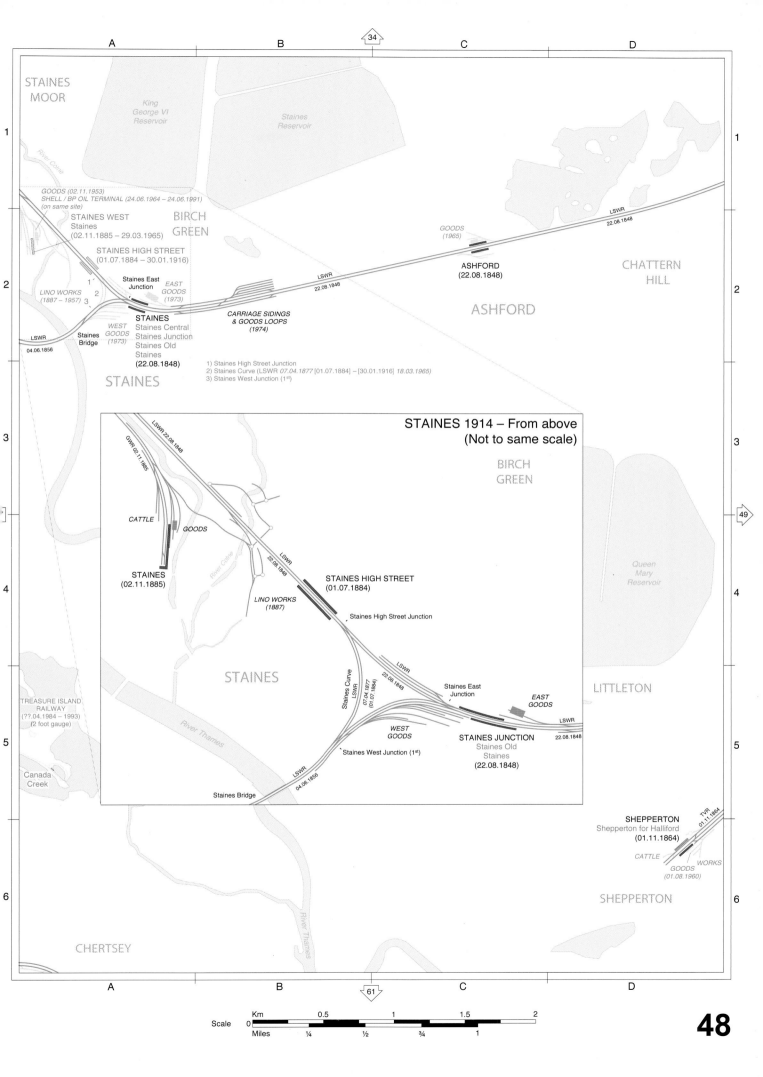

A   B   C   D

1

STAINES
MOOR

King
George VI
Reservoir

Staines
Reservoir

GOODS (02.11.1953)
SHELL / BP OIL TERMINAL (24.06.1964 – 24.06.1991)
(on same site)

STAINES WEST
Staines
(02.11.1885 – 29.03.1965)

BIRCH
GREEN

LSWR
22.08.1848

CHATTERN
HILL

STAINES HIGH STREET
(01.07.1884 – 30.01.1916)

GOODS
(1965)

ASHFORD
(22.08.1848)

Staines East
Junction

EAST
GOODS
(1973)

LSWR
22.08.1848

ASHFORD

2

LINO WORKS
(1887 – 1957)

1
2
3

CARRIAGE SIDINGS
& GOODS LOOPS
(1974)

LSWR
04.06.1856

Staines
Bridge

WEST
GOODS
(1973)

STAINES
Staines Central
Staines Junction
Staines Old
Staines
(22.08.1848)

1) Staines High Street Junction
2) Staines Curve (LSWR 07.04.1877 [01.07.1884] – [30.01.1916] 18.03.1965)
3) Staines West Junction (1st)

STAINES

3

**STAINES 1914 – From above
(Not to same scale)**

LSWR 22.08.1848

GWR 02.11.1885

BIRCH
GREEN

49

CATTLE

GOODS

Queen
Mary
Reservoir

STAINES
(02.11.1885)

LSWR
22.08.1848

STAINES HIGH STREET
(01.07.1884)

4

LINO WORKS
(1887)

River Colne

Staines High Street Junction

TREASURE ISLAND
RAILWAY
(??.04.1984 – 1993)
(2 foot gauge)

STAINES

Staines Curve

LSWR
07.04.1877
(01.07.1884)

LSWR
22.08.1848

Staines East
Junction

EAST
GOODS

LITTLETON

5

Canada
Creek

River Thames

WEST
GOODS

Staines West Junction (1st)

STAINES JUNCTION
Staines Old
Staines
(22.08.1848)

LSWR
22.08.1848

LSWR

LSWR
04.06.1856

Staines Bridge

SHEPPERTON
Shepperton for Halliford
(01.11.1864)

TVR
01.11.1864

CATTLE

WORKS

GOODS
(01.08.1960)

6

CHERTSEY

River Thames

SHEPPERTON

A   B   C   D

Scale

Km
0   0.5   1   1.5   2
Miles
¼   ½   ¾   1

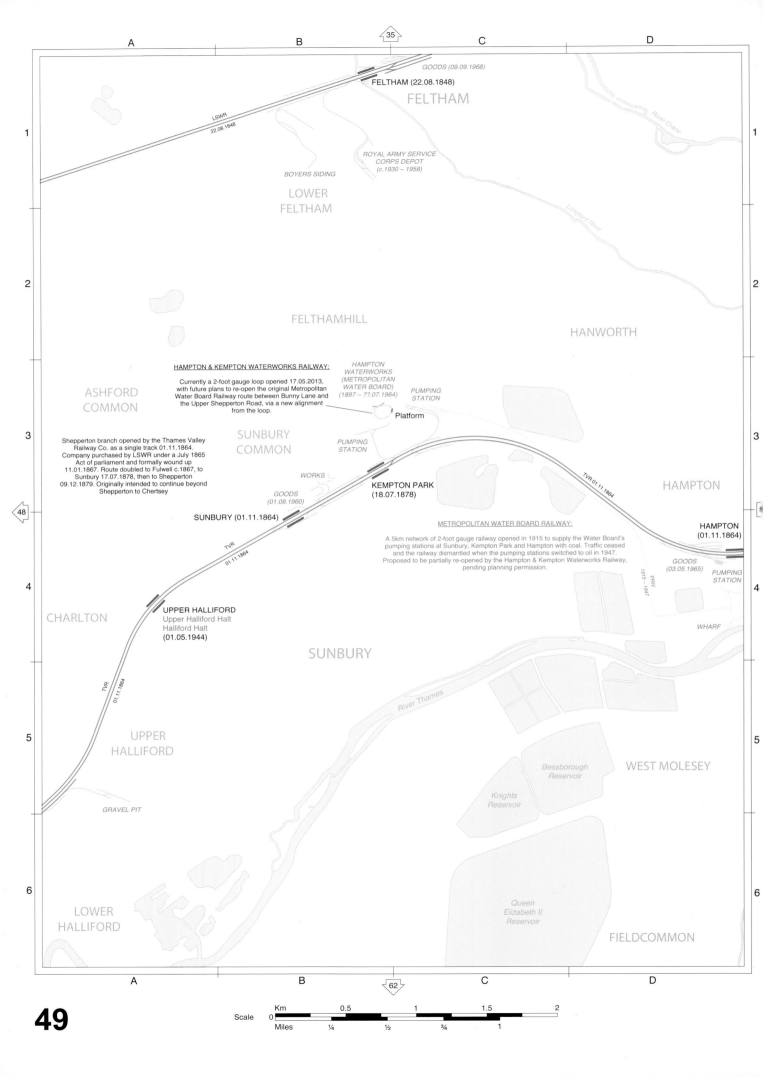

A   B   C   D

GOODS (09.09.1968)

FELTHAM (22.08.1848)

FELTHAM

LSWR
22.08.1848

1

ROYAL ARMY SERVICE
CORPS DEPOT
(c.1930 – 1958)

River Crane

BOYERS SIDING

LOWER
FELTHAM

Longford River

2

FELTHAMHILL

HANWORTH

HAMPTON & KEMPTON WATERWORKS RAILWAY:

Currently a 2-foot gauge loop opened 17.05.2013,
with future plans to re-open the original Metropolitan
Water Board Railway route between Bunny Lane and
the Upper Shepperton Road, via a new alignment
from the loop.

HAMPTON
WATERWORKS
(METROPOLITAN
WATER BOARD)
(1897 – ??.07.1964)

PUMPING
STATION

ASHFORD
COMMON

Platform

3

Shepperton branch opened by the Thames Valley
Railway Co. as a single track 01.11.1864.
Company purchased by LSWR under a July 1865
Act of parliament and formally wound up
11.01.1867. Route doubled to Fulwell c.1867, to
Sunbury 17.07.1878, then to Shepperton
09.12.1879. Originally intended to continue beyond
Shepperton to Chertsey

SUNBURY
COMMON

PUMPING
STATION

WORKS

TVR 01.11.1864

HAMPTON

KEMPTON PARK
(18.07.1878)

GOODS
(01.08.1960)

48

SUNBURY (01.11.1864)

METROPOLITAN WATER BOARD RAILWAY:

A 5km network of 2-foot gauge railway opened in 1915 to supply the Water Board's
pumping stations at Sunbury, Kempton Park and Hampton with coal. Traffic ceased
and the railway dismantled when the pumping stations switched to oil in 1947.
Proposed to be partially re-opened by the Hampton & Kempton Waterworks Railway,
pending planning permission.

HAMPTON
(01.11.1864)

TVR
01.11.1864

GOODS
(03.05.1965)

PRIV
1915 – 1947

PUMPING
STATION

4

CHARLTON

UPPER HALLIFORD
Upper Halliford Halt
Halliford Halt
(01.05.1944)

WHARF

SUNBURY

TVR
01.11.1864

River Thames

5

UPPER
HALLIFORD

Bessborough
Reservoir

WEST MOLESEY

GRAVEL PIT

Knights
Reservoir

6

LOWER
HALLIFORD

Queen
Elizabeth II
Reservoir

FIELDCOMMON

Scale

Km   0.5   1   1.5   2
0
Miles   ¼   ½   ¾   1

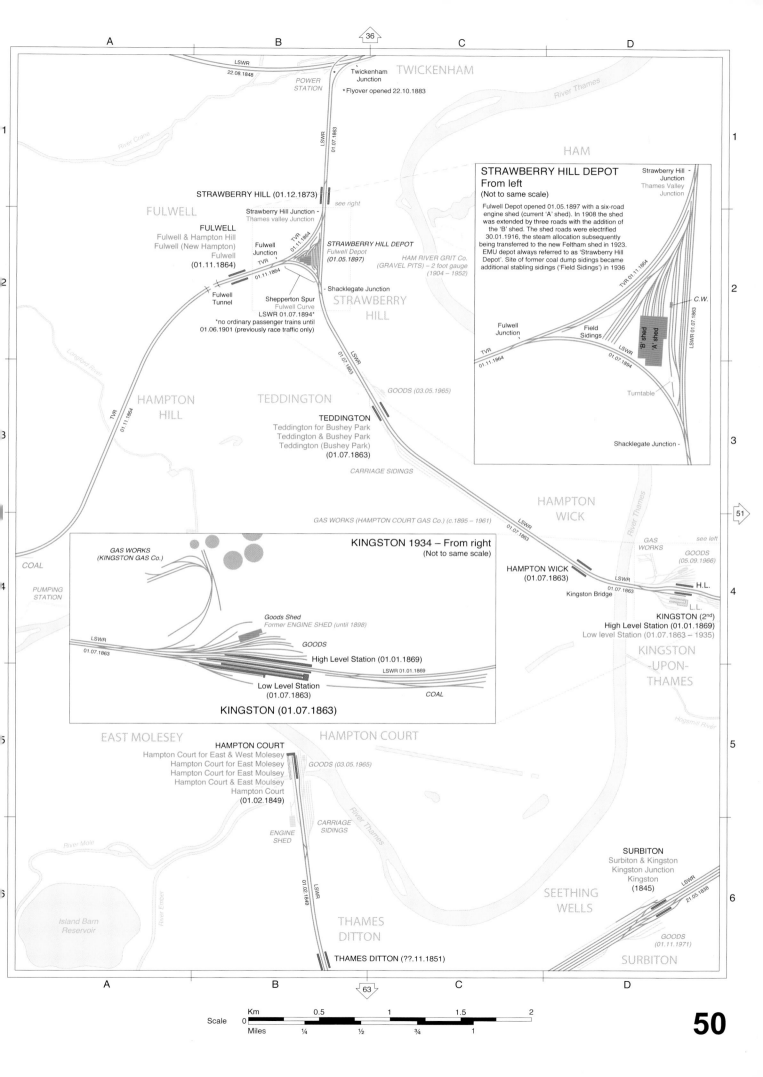

TWICKENHAM

LSWR
22.08.1848

POWER
STATION

Twickenham
Junction
• Flyover opened 22.10.1883

River Thames

HAM

LSWR
01.07.1863

STRAWBERRY HILL (01.12.1873)

FULWELL

FULWELL
Fulwell & Hampton Hill
Fulwell (New Hampton)
Fulwell
(01.11.1864)

Strawberry Hill Junction -
Thames valley Junction

Fulwell
Junction

TVR
01.11.1864

TVR
01.11.1864

Fulwell Junction

Fulwell
Tunnel

Shepperton Spur
Fulwell Curve
LSWR 01.07.1894*
*no ordinary passenger trains until
01.06.1901 (previously race traffic only)

STRAWBERRY HILL DEPOT
Fulwell Depot
(01.05.1897)

HAM RIVER GRIT Co.
(GRAVEL PITS) – 2 foot gauge
(1904 – 1952)

- Shacklegate Junction

STRAWBERRY
HILL

STRAWBERRY HILL DEPOT
From left
(Not to same scale)

Fulwell Depot opened 01.05.1897 with a six-road
engine shed (current 'A' shed). In 1908 the shed
was extended by three roads with the addition of
the 'B' shed. The shed roads were electrified
30.01.1916, the steam allocation subsequently
being transferred to the new Feltham shed in 1923.
EMU depot always referred to as 'Strawberry Hill
Depot'. Site of former coal dump sidings became
additional stabling sidings ('Field Sidings') in 1936.

Strawberry Hill -
Junction
Thames Valley
Junction

TVR 01.11.1864

LSWR 01.07.1863

Fulwell
Junction

C.W.

Field
Sidings

'B' shed 'A' shed

TVR
01.11.1864

LSWR
01.07.1894

Turntable

Shacklegate Junction -

HAMPTON
HILL

TVR
01.11.1864

LSWR
01.07.1863

TEDDINGTON

GOODS (03.05.1965)

TEDDINGTON
Teddington for Bushey Park
Teddington & Bushey Park
Teddington (Bushey Park)
(01.07.1863)

CARRIAGE SIDINGS

HAMPTON
WICK

Longford River

COAL

PUMPING
STATION

GAS WORKS (HAMPTON COURT GAS Co.) (c.1895 – 1961)

LSWR
01.07.1863

River Thames

51

GAS
WORKS

see left

GOODS
(05.09.1966)

KINGSTON 1934 – From right
(Not to same scale)

GAS WORKS
(KINGSTON GAS Co.)

Goods Shed
Former ENGINE SHED (until 1898)

GOODS

High Level Station (01.01.1869)

LSWR 01.01.1869

Low Level Station
(01.07.1863)

COAL

KINGSTON (01.07.1863)

LSWR
01.07.1863

HAMPTON WICK
(01.07.1863)

Kingston Bridge

LSWR
01.07.1863

H.L.

L.L.

KINGSTON (2nd)
High Level Station (01.01.1869)
Low level Station (01.07.1863 – 1935)

KINGSTON-
UPON-
THAMES

Hogsmill River

EAST MOLESEY

HAMPTON COURT

HAMPTON COURT
Hampton Court for East & West Molesey
Hampton Court for East Molesey
Hampton Court for East Moulsey
Hampton Court & East Moulsey
Hampton Court
(01.02.1849)

GOODS (03.05.1965)

CARRIAGE
SIDINGS

River Thames

ENGINE
SHED

River Mole

River Ember

Island Barn
Reservoir

LSWR
01.02.1849

THAMES
DITTON

THAMES DITTON (??.11.1851)

SURBITON
Surbiton & Kingston
Kingston Junction
Kingston
(1845)

SEETHING
WELLS

LSWR
21.05.1838

GOODS
(01.11.1971)

SURBITON

Scale
Km 0 0.5 1 1.5 2
Miles ¼ ½ ¾ 1

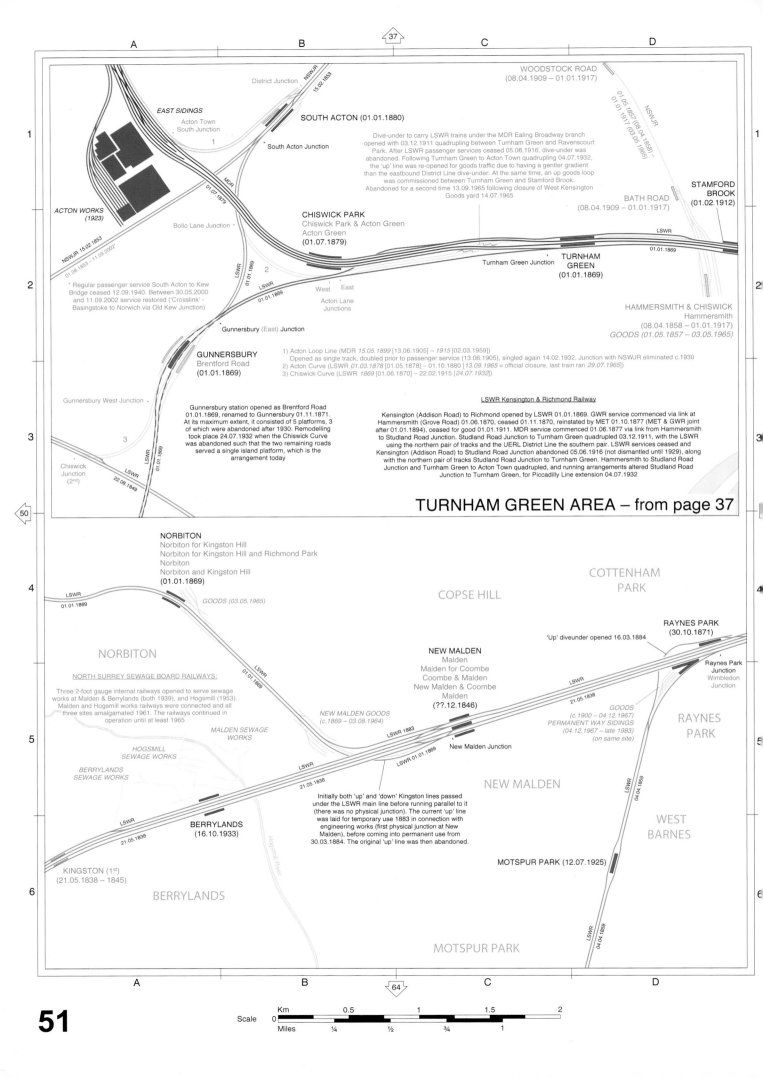

WOODSTOCK ROAD
(08.04.1909 – 01.01.1917)

EAST SIDINGS

Acton Town
South Junction

District Junction

NSWJR
15.02.1853

SOUTH ACTON (01.01.1880)

South Acton Junction

01.05.1857 (08.04.1858) –
01.01.1917 (03.05.1965)

NSWJR

STAMFORD
BROOK
(01.02.1912)

BATH ROAD
(08.04.1909 – 01.01.1917)

Dive-under to carry LSWR trains under the MDR Ealing Broadway branch
opened with 03.12.1911 quadrupling between Turnham Green and Ravenscourt
Park. After LSWR passenger services ceased 05.06.1916, dive-under was
abandoned. Following Turnham Green to Acton Town quadrupling 04.07.1932,
the 'up' line was re-opened for goods traffic due to having a gentler gradient
than the eastbound District Line dive-under. At the same time, an up goods loop
was commissioned between Turnham Green and Stamford Brook.
Abandoned for a second time 13.09.1965 following closure of West Kensington
Goods yard 14.07.1965

ACTON WORKS
(1923)

MDR
01.07.1879

Bollo Lane Junction

CHISWICK PARK
Chiswick Park & Acton Green
Acton Green
(01.07.1879)

LSWR
01.01.1869

Turnham Green Junction

TURNHAM
GREEN
(01.01.1869)

LSWR
01.01.1869

NSWJR 15.02.1853

01.08.1853 - 11.09.2002

LSWR
01.01.1869

* Regular passenger service South Acton to Kew
Bridge ceased 12.09.1940. Between 30.05.2000
and 11.09.2002 service restored ('Crosslink' -
Basingstoke to Norwich via Old Kew Junction)

2

West   East

Acton Lane
Junctions

HAMMERSMITH & CHISWICK
Hammersmith
(08.04.1858 – 01.01.1917)
GOODS (01.05.1857 – 03.05.1965)

Gunnersbury (East) Junction

GUNNERSBURY
Brentford Road
(01.01.1869)

1) Acton Loop Line (MDR 15.05.1899 [13.06.1905] – 1915 [02.03.1959])
   Opened as single track, doubled prior to passenger service (13.06.1905), singled again 14.02.1932. Junction with NSWJR eliminated c.1930
2) Acton Curve (LSWR 01.03.1878 [01.05.1878] – 01.10.1880 [13.09.1965 = official closure, last train ran 29.07.1965])
3) Chiswick Curve (LSWR 1869 [01.06.1870] – 22.02.1915 [24.07.1932])

Gunnersbury West Junction

LSWR
01.01.1869

LSWR
22.08.1849

Chiswick
Junction
(2nd)

Gunnersbury station opened as Brentford Road
01.01.1869, renamed to Gunnersbury 01.11.1871.
At its maximum extent, it consisted of 5 platforms, 3
of which were abandoned after 1930. Remodelling
took place 24.07.1932 when the Chiswick Curve
was abandoned such that the two remaining roads
served a single island platform, which is the
arrangement today

LSWR Kensington & Richmond Railway

Kensington (Addison Road) to Richmond opened by LSWR 01.01.1869. GWR service commenced via link at
Hammersmith (Grove Road) 01.06.1870, ceased 01.11.1870, reinstated by MET 01.10.1877 (MET & GWR joint
after 01.01.1894), ceased for good 01.01.1911. MDR service commenced 01.06.1877 via link from Hammersmith
to Studland Road Junction. Studland Road Junction to Turnham Green quadrupled 03.12.1911, with the LSWR
using the northern pair of tracks and the UERL District Line the southern pair. LSWR services ceased and
Kensington (Addison Road) to Studland Road Junction abandoned 05.06.1916 (not dismantled until 1929), along
with the northern pair of tracks Studland Road Junction to Turnham Green. Hammersmith to Studland Road
Junction and Turnham Green to Acton Town quadrupled, and running arrangements altered Studland Road
Junction to Turnham Green, for Piccadilly Line extension 04.07.1932

TURNHAM GREEN AREA – from page 37

50

NORBITON
Norbiton for Kingston Hill
Norbiton for Kingston Hill and Richmond Park
Norbiton
Norbiton and Kingston Hill
(01.01.1869)

COTTENHAM
PARK

COPSE HILL

LSWR
01.01.1869

GOODS (03.05.1965)

RAYNES PARK
(30.10.1871)

'Up' diveunder opened 16.03.1884

NEW MALDEN
Malden
Malden for Coombe
Coombe & Malden
New Malden & Coombe
Malden
(??.12.1846)

Raynes Park
Junction
Wimbledon
Junction

NORBITON

NORTH SURREY SEWAGE BOARD RAILWAYS:

Three 2-foot gauge internal railways opened to serve sewage
works at Malden & Berrylands (both 1939), and Hogsmill (1953).
Malden and Hogsmill works railways were connected and all
three sites amalgamated 1961. The railways continued in
operation until at least 1965

LSWR
01.01.1869

MALDEN SEWAGE
WORKS

LSWR
21.05.1838

NEW MALDEN GOODS
(c.1869 – 03.08.1964)

New Malden Junction

LSWR 1883

LSWR 01.01.1869

GOODS
(c.1900 – 04.12.1967)
PERMANENT WAY SIDINGS
(04.12.1967 – late 1983)
(on same site)

RAYNES
PARK

HOGSMILL
SEWAGE WORKS

BERRYLANDS
SEWAGE WORKS

NEW MALDEN

LSWR
21.05.1838

Hogsmill River

LSWR
04.04.1859

WEST
BARNES

Initially both 'up' and 'down' Kingston lines passed
under the LSWR main line before running parallel to it
(there was no physical junction). The current 'up' line
was laid for temporary use 1883 in connection with
engineering works (first physical junction at New
Malden), before coming into permanent use from
30.03.1884. The original 'up' line was then abandoned.

LSWR
21.05.1838

BERRYLANDS
(16.10.1933)

MOTSPUR PARK (12.07.1925)

KINGSTON (1st)
(21.05.1838 – 1845)

BERRYLANDS

LSWR
04.04.1859

MOTSPUR PARK

Scale
Km   0   0.5   1   1.5   2
Miles   ¼   ½   ¾   1

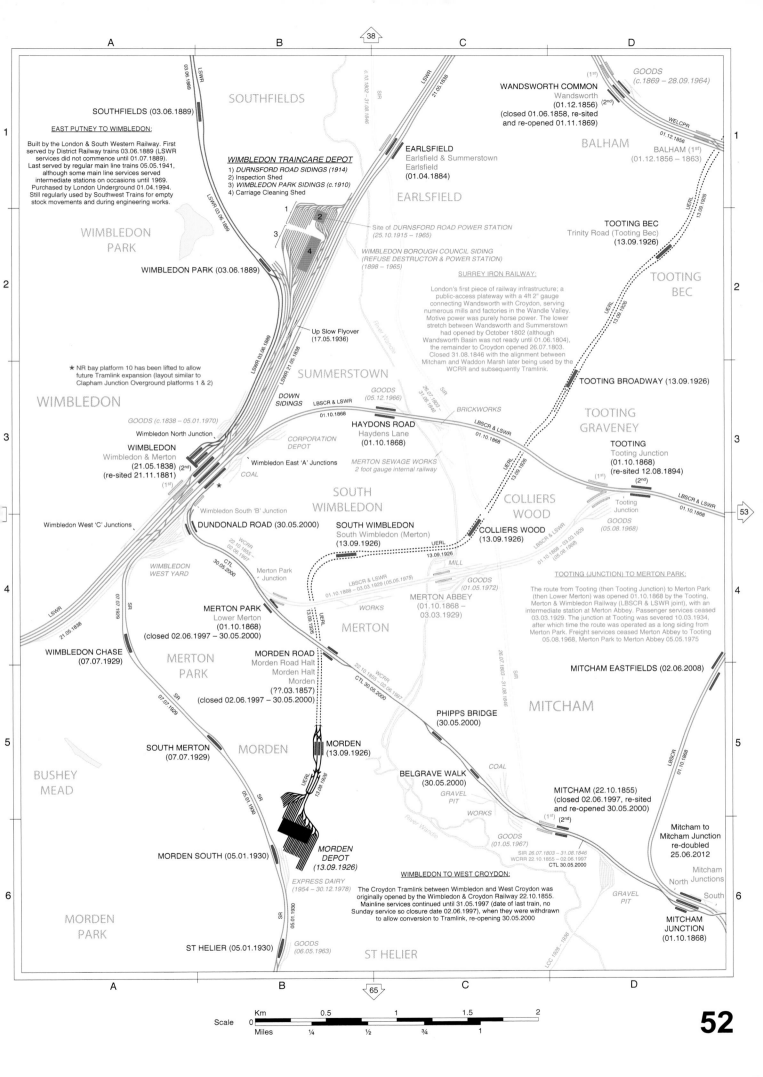

SOUTHFIELDS

SOUTHFIELDS (03.06.1889)

EAST PUTNEY TO WIMBLEDON:

Built by the London & South Western Railway. First
served by District Railway trains 03.06.1889 (LSWR
services did not commence until 01.07.1889).
Last served by regular main line trains 05.05.1941,
although some main line services served
intermediate stations on occasions until 1969.
Purchased by London Underground 01.04.1994.
Still regularly used by Southwest Trains for empty
stock movements and during engineering works.

WIMBLEDON TRAINCARE DEPOT
1) *DURNSFORD ROAD SIDINGS* (1914)
2) *Inspection Shed*
3) *WIMBLEDON PARK SIDINGS (c.1910)*
4) *Carriage Cleaning Shed*

EARLSFIELD
Earlsfield & Summerstown
Earlsfield
(01.04.1884)

EARLSFIELD

WANDSWORTH COMMON
Wandsworth
(01.12.1856)
(closed 01.06.1858, re-sited
and re-opened 01.11.1869)

GOODS
(c.1869 – 28.09.1964)

BALHAM

BALHAM (1st)
(01.12.1856 – 1863)

Site of *DURNSFORD ROAD POWER STATION*
(25.10.1915 – 1965)

WIMBLEDON BOROUGH COUNCIL SIDING
(REFUSE DESTRUCTOR & POWER STATION)
(1898 – 1965)

TOOTING BEC
Trinity Road (Tooting Bec)
(13.09.1926)

TOOTING
BEC

SURREY IRON RAILWAY:

London's first piece of railway infrastructure; a
public-access plateway with a 4ft 2" gauge
connecting Wandsworth with Croydon, serving
numerous mills and factories in the Wandle Valley.
Motive power was purely horse power. The lower
stretch between Wandsworth and Summerstown
had opened by October 1802 (although
Wandsworth Basin was not ready until 01.06.1804),
the remainder to Croydon opened 26.07.1803.
Closed 31.08.1846 with the alignment between
Mitcham and Waddon Marsh later being used by the
WCRR and subsequently Tramlink.

Up Slow Flyover
(17.05.1936)

★ NR bay platform 10 has been lifted to allow
future Tramlink expansion (layout similar to
Clapham Junction Overground platforms 1 & 2)

WIMBLEDON

GOODS (c.1838 – 05.01.1970)

Wimbledon North Junction

WIMBLEDON
Wimbledon & Merton
(21.05.1838) (2nd)
(re-sited 21.11.1881)
(1st)

DOWN
SIDINGS

LBSCR & LSWR
01.10.1868

SUMMERSTOWN

GOODS
(05.12.1966)

CORPORATION
DEPOT

HAYDONS ROAD
Haydens Lane
(01.10.1868)

BRICKWORKS

LBSCR & LSWR
01.10.1868

COAL

Wimbledon East 'A' Junctions

MERTON SEWAGE WORKS
2 foot gauge internal railway

SOUTH
WIMBLEDON

TOOTING
Tooting Junction
(01.10.1868)
(re-sited 12.08.1894)
(2nd)

TOOTING
GRAVENEY

(1st)

Tooting
Junction

LBSCR & LSWR
01.10.1868

Wimbledon South 'B' Junction

DUNDONALD ROAD (30.05.2000)

SOUTH WIMBLEDON
South Wimbledon (Merton)
(13.09.1926)

COLLIERS WOOD
(13.09.1926)

COLLIERS
WOOD

GOODS
(05.08.1968)

Wimbledon West 'C' Junctions

WCRR
22.10.1855 –
02.06.1997

CTL
30.05.2000

WIMBLEDON
WEST YARD

Merton Park
Junction

MILL

GOODS
(01.05.1972)

TOOTING (JUNCTION) TO MERTON PARK:

The route from Tooting (then Tooting Junction) to Merton Park
(then Lower Merton) was opened 01.10.1868 by the Tooting,
Merton & Wimbledon Railway (LBSCR & LSWR joint), with an
intermediate station at Merton Abbey. Passenger services ceased
03.03.1929. The junction at Tooting was severed 10.03.1934,
after which time the route was operated as a long siding from
Merton Park. Freight services ceased Merton Abbey to Tooting
05.08.1968, Merton Park to Merton Abbey 05.05.1975

MERTON ABBEY
(01.10.1868 –
03.03.1929)

MERTON

WORKS

LSWR
21.05.1838

SR
07.07.1929

WIMBLEDON CHASE
(07.07.1929)

MERTON
PARK

MERTON PARK
Lower Merton
(01.10.1868)
(closed 02.06.1997 – 30.05.2000)

MORDEN ROAD
Morden Road Halt
Morden Halt
Morden
(??.03.1857)
(closed 02.06.1997 – 30.05.2000)

WCRR
22.10.1855 – 02.06.1997

CTL 30.05.2000

MITCHAM EASTFIELDS (02.06.2008)

MITCHAM

PHIPPS BRIDGE
(30.05.2000)

BUSHEY
MEAD

SOUTH MERTON
(07.07.1929)

MORDEN

MORDEN
(13.09.1926)

BELGRAVE WALK
(30.05.2000)

COAL

GRAVEL
PIT

WORKS

MITCHAM (22.10.1855)
(closed 02.06.1997, re-sited
and re-opened 30.05.2000)

(1st) **(2nd)**

Mitcham to
Mitcham Junction
re-doubled
25.06.2012

MORDEN SOUTH (05.01.1930)

MORDEN DEPOT
(13.09.1926)

EXPRESS DAIRY
(1954 – 30.12.1978)

MORDEN
PARK

WIMBLEDON TO WEST CROYDON:

The Croydon Tramlink between Wimbledon and West Croydon was
originally opened by the Wimbledon & Croydon Railway 22.10.1855.
Mainline services continued until 31.05.1997 (date of last train, no
Sunday service so closure date 02.06.1997), when they were withdrawn
to allow conversion to Tramlink, re-opening 30.05.2000

GOODS
(01.05.1967)

SIR 26.07.1803 – 31.08.1846
WCRR 22.10.1855 – 02.06.1997
CTL 30.05.2000

GRAVEL
PIT

Mitcham
North
Junctions
South

**MITCHAM
JUNCTION
(01.10.1868)**

ST HELIER (05.01.1930)

ST HELIER

GOODS
(06.05.1963)

Scale

Km
0   0.5   1   1.5   2

Miles
¼   ½   ¾   1

52

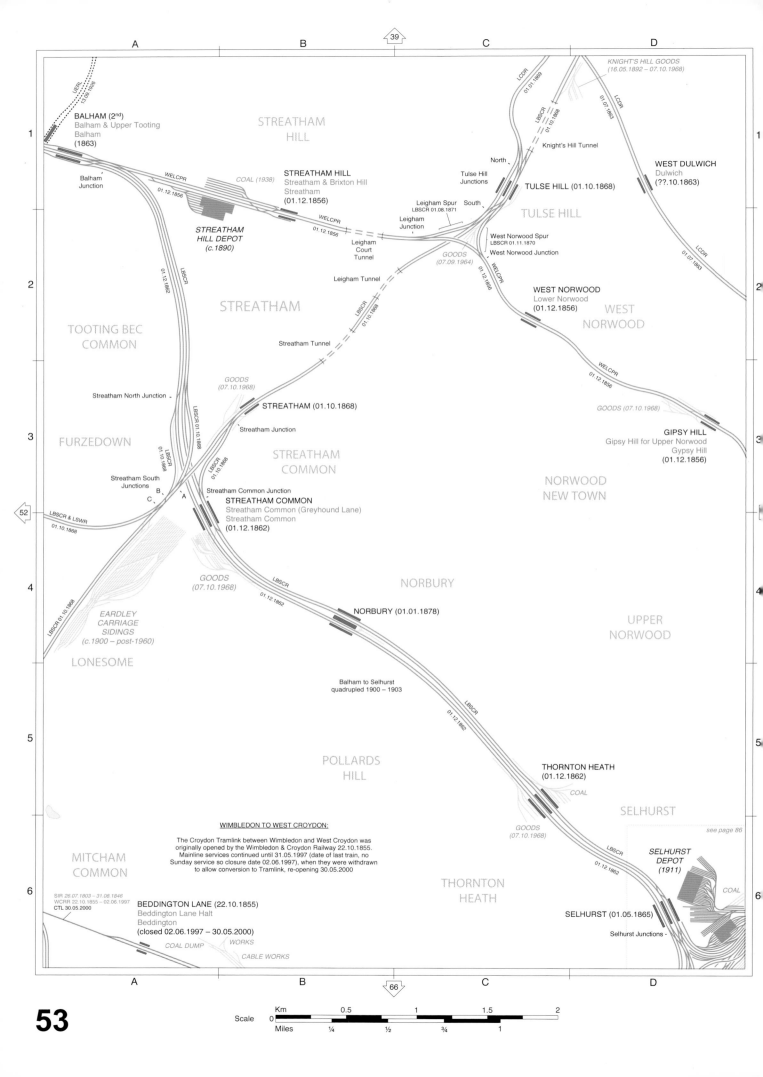

A   B   C   D

UERL 13.09.1926

BALHAM (2nd)
Balham & Upper Tooting
Balham
(1863)

STREATHAM
HILL

*KNIGHT'S HILL GOODS
(16.05.1892 – 07.10.1968)*

Balham
Junction

WELCPR
01.12.1856

COAL (1938)

STREATHAM HILL
Streatham & Brixton Hill
Streatham
(01.12.1856)

WELCPR
01.12.1856

LCDR
01.01.1869

LBSCR
01.10.1868

LCDR
01.07.1863

North

Tulse Hill
Junctions

TULSE HILL (01.10.1868)

Knight's Hill Tunnel

WEST DULWICH
Dulwich
(??.10.1863)

*STREATHAM
HILL DEPOT
(c.1890)*

Leigham Spur
LBSCR 01.08.1871

Leigham
Junction

Leigham
Court
Tunnel

South

TULSE HILL

LCDR
01.07.1863

West Norwood Spur
LBSCR 01.11.1870

West Norwood Junction

LBSCR
01.12.1862

Leigham Tunnel

LBSCR
01.10.1868

WELCPR
01.12.1856

WEST NORWOOD
Lower Norwood
(01.12.1856)

WEST
NORWOOD

TOOTING BEC
COMMON

STREATHAM

Streatham Tunnel

*GOODS
(07.09.1964)*

*GOODS
(07.10.1968)*

STREATHAM (01.10.1868)

Streatham North Junction

FURZEDOWN

LBSCR 01.10.1868

Streatham Junction

STREATHAM
COMMON

WELCPR
01.12.1856

GOODS (07.10.1968)

GIPSY HILL
Gipsy Hill for Upper Norwood
Gypsy Hill
(01.12.1856)

NORWOOD
NEW TOWN

Streatham South
Junctions

LBSCR
01.10.1868

B
C   A

Streatham Common Junction

STREATHAM COMMON
Streatham Common (Greyhound Lane)
Streatham Common
(01.12.1862)

LBSCR & LSWR
01.10.1868

LBSCR 01.10.1868

*GOODS
(07.10.1968)*

LBSCR
01.12.1862

NORBURY

UPPER
NORWOOD

*EARDLEY
CARRIAGE
SIDINGS
(c.1900 – post-1960)*

NORBURY (01.01.1878)

LONESOME

Balham to Selhurst
quadrupled 1900 – 1903

LBSCR
01.12.1862

POLLARDS
HILL

THORNTON HEATH
(01.12.1862)

COAL

SELHURST

see page 86

WIMBLEDON TO WEST CROYDON:

The Croydon Tramlink between Wimbledon and West Croydon was
originally opened by the Wimbledon & Croydon Railway 22.10.1855.
Mainline services continued until 31.05.1997 (date of last train, no
Sunday service so closure date 02.06.1997), when they were withdrawn
to allow conversion to Tramlink, re-opening 30.05.2000

*GOODS
(07.10.1968)*

LBSCR
01.12.1862

*SELHURST
DEPOT
(1911)*

COAL

MITCHAM
COMMON

SIR 26.07.1803 – 31.08.1846
WCRR 22.10.1855 – 02.06.1997
CTL 30.05.2000

BEDDINGTON LANE (22.10.1855)
Beddington Lane Halt
Beddington
(closed 02.06.1997 – 30.05.2000)

THORNTON
HEATH

SELHURST (01.05.1865)

Selhurst Junctions

COAL DUMP

WORKS

CABLE WORKS

A   B   C   D

53

Scale
Km
0   0.5   1   1.5   2
Miles
¼   ½   ¾   1

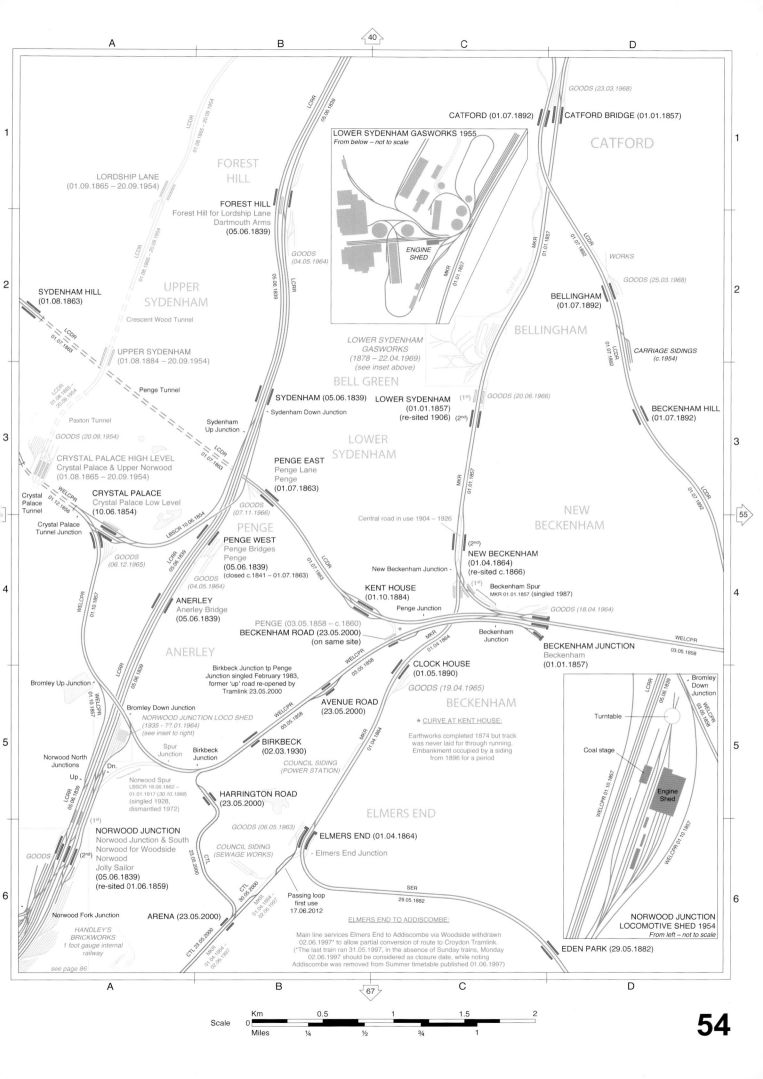

CATFORD (01.07.1892)
CATFORD BRIDGE (01.01.1857)

GOODS (23.03.1968)

CATFORD

LCRR
05.06.1839

LORDSHIP LANE
(01.09.1865 – 20.09.1954)

FOREST HILL

FOREST HILL
Forest Hill for Lordship Lane
Dartmouth Arms
(05.06.1839)

LOWER SYDENHAM GASWORKS 1955
From below – not to scale

ENGINE
SHED

MKR
01.01.1857

MKR
01.01.1857

LCDR
01.07.1892

WORKS

GOODS (25.03.1968)

BELLINGHAM
(01.07.1892)

BELLINGHAM

UPPER
SYDENHAM

SYDENHAM HILL
(01.08.1863)

Crescent Wood Tunnel

GOODS
(04.05.1964)

LCRR
05.06.1839

LCDR
01.07.1863

LCDR
01.07.1863

CARRIAGE SIDINGS
(c.1954)

LCDR
01.07.1892

UPPER SYDENHAM
(01.08.1884 – 20.09.1954)

Penge Tunnel

LOWER SYDENHAM
GASWORKS
(1878 – 22.04.1969)
(see inset above)

BELL GREEN

BECKENHAM HILL
(01.07.1892)

Paxton Tunnel

SYDENHAM (05.06.1839)

LOWER SYDENHAM
(01.01.1857)
(re-sited 1906)

(1st)

(2nd)

GOODS (20.06.1966)

LCDR
01.07.1892

GOODS (20.09.1954)

CRYSTAL PALACE HIGH LEVEL
Crystal Palace & Upper Norwood
(01.08.1865 – 20.09.1954)

Sydenham Down Junction

LOWER
SYDENHAM

Crystal
Palace
Tunnel

CRYSTAL PALACE
Crystal Palace Low Level
(10.06.1854)

WELCPR
01.12.1856

Sydenham
Up Junction

PENGE EAST
Penge Lane
Penge
(01.07.1863)

MKR
01.01.1857

NEW
BECKENHAM

Crystal Palace
Tunnel Junction

LBSCR 10.06.1854

GOODS
(07.11.1966)

PENGE

GOODS
(06.12.1965)

LCRR
05.06.1839

PENGE WEST
Penge Bridges
Penge
(05.06.1839)
(closed c.1841 – 01.07.1863)

Central road in use 1904 – 1926

(2nd)

NEW BECKENHAM
(01.04.1864)
(re-sited c.1866)

GOODS
(04.05.1964)

New Beckenham Junction

WELCPR
01.10.1857

ANERLEY
Anerley Bridge
(05.06.1839)

KENT HOUSE
(01.10.1884)

(1st)

Beckenham Spur
MKR 01.01.1857 (singled 1987)

GOODS (18.04.1964)

WELCPR
03.05.1858

Penge Junction

ANERLEY

LCDR
01.07.1863

PENGE (03.05.1858 – c.1860)
BECKENHAM ROAD (23.05.2000)
(on same site)

*

MKR
01.04.1864

Beckenham
Junction

BECKENHAM JUNCTION
Beckenham
(01.01.1857)

Bromley Up Junction

LCRR
05.06.1839

Birkbeck Junction tp Penge
Junction singled February 1983,
former 'up' road re-opened by
Tramlink 23.05.2000

WELCPR
03.05.1858

CLOCK HOUSE
(01.05.1890)

WELCPR
03.05.1858

WELCPR
01.10.1857

Bromley Down Junction

NORWOOD JUNCTION LOCO SHED
(1935 - ??.01.1964)
(see inset to right)

AVENUE ROAD
(23.05.2000)

GOODS (19.04.1965)

BECKENHAM

Bromley
Down
Junction

LCRR
05.06.1839

Turntable

WELCPR
03.05.1858

Norwood North
Junctions

Dn.

Spur
Junction

Birkbeck
Junction

BIRKBECK
(02.03.1930)

MKR
01.04.1864

* CURVE AT KENT HOUSE:

Earthworks completed 1874 but track
was never laid for through running.
Embankment occupied by a siding
from 1896 for a period

Coal stage

WELCPR 01.10.1857

WELCPR 01.10.1857

Up

COUNCIL SIDING
(POWER STATION)

Engine
Shed

LCRR
05.06.1839

Norwood Spur
LBSCR 18.06.1862 –
01.01.1917 (30.10.1966)
(singled 1928,
dismantled 1972)

HARRINGTON ROAD
(23.05.2000)

23.05.2000

GOODS (06.05.1963)

ELMERS END

(1st)

NORWOOD JUNCTION
Norwood Junction & South
Norwood for Woodside
Norwood
Jolly Sailor
(05.06.1839)
(re-sited 01.06.1859)

GOODS

(2nd)

COUNCIL SIDING
(SEWAGE WORKS)

ELMERS END (01.04.1864)

- Elmers End Junction

NORWOOD JUNCTION
LOCOMOTIVE SHED 1954
From left – not to scale

Norwood Fork Junction

HANDLEY'S
BRICKWORKS
1 foot gauge internal
railway

see page 86

CTL
23.05.2000

CTL
30.05.2000

MKR
01.04.1864 –
02.06.1997

ARENA (23.05.2000)

CTL 23.05.2000

Passing loop
first use
17.06.2012

SER
29.05.1882

GOODS
29.05.1882

ELMERS END TO ADDISCOMBE:

Main line services Elmers End to Addiscombe via Woodside withdrawn
02.06.1997* to allow partial conversion of route to Croydon Tramlink.
(*The last train ran 31.05.1997, in the absence of Sunday trains, Monday
02.06.1997 should be considered as closure date, while noting
Addiscombe was removed from Summer timetable published 01.06.1997)

EDEN PARK (29.05.1882)

Scale
Km
0   0.5   1   1.5   2

Miles
¼   ½   ¾   1

54

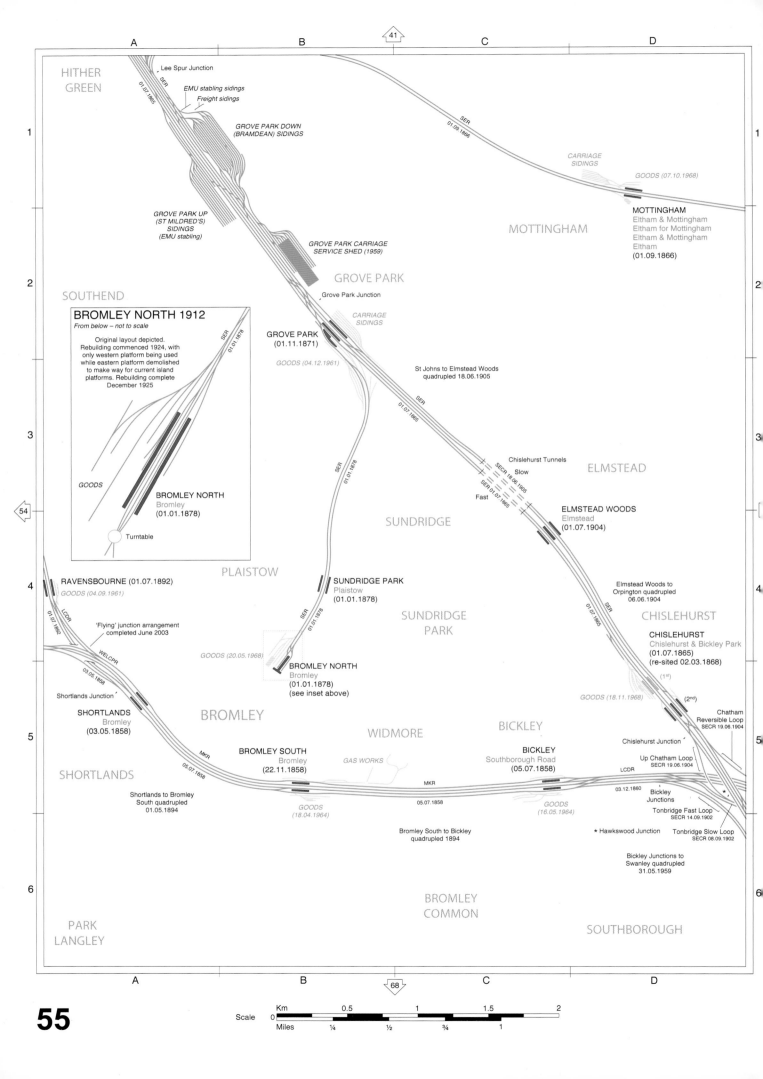

HITHER
GREEN

Lee Spur Junction

01.07.1865
SER

EMU stabling sidings
Freight sidings

GROVE PARK DOWN
(BRAMDEAN) SIDINGS

SER
01.09.1866

CARRIAGE
SIDINGS

GOODS (07.10.1968)

MOTTINGHAM
Eltham & Mottingham
Eltham for Mottingham
Eltham & Mottingham
Eltham
(01.09.1866)

MOTTINGHAM

GROVE PARK UP
(ST MILDRED'S)
SIDINGS
(EMU stabling)

GROVE PARK CARRIAGE
SERVICE SHED (1959)

GROVE PARK

Grove Park Junction

SOUTHEND

BROMLEY NORTH 1912
From below – not to scale

Original layout depicted.
Rebuilding commenced 1924, with
only western platform being used
while eastern platform demolished
to make way for current island
platforms. Rebuilding complete
December 1925

01.01.1878
SER

CARRIAGE
SIDINGS

GROVE PARK
(01.11.1871)

GOODS (04.12.1961)

St Johns to Elmstead Woods
quadrupled 18.06.1905

SER
01.07.1865

BROMLEY NORTH
Bromley
(01.01.1878)

GOODS

Turntable

54

Chislehurst Tunnels
Slow
SECR 18.06.1905

Fast
SER 01.07.1865

ELMSTEAD

ELMSTEAD WOODS
Elmstead
(01.07.1904)

SER
01.01.1878

SUNDRIDGE

RAVENSBOURNE (01.07.1892)
GOODS (04.09.1961)

PLAISTOW

SUNDRIDGE PARK
Plaistow
(01.01.1878)

SUNDRIDGE
PARK

Elmstead Woods to
Orpington quadrupled
06.06.1904

CHISLEHURST

LCDR
01.07.1892

SER
01.01.1878

CHISLEHURST
Chislehurst & Bickley Park
(01.07.1865)
(re-sited 02.03.1868)

SER
01.07.1865

'Flying' junction arrangement
completed June 2003

WELCPR

GOODS (20.05.1968)

BROMLEY NORTH
Bromley
(01.01.1878)
(see inset above)

(1st)

GOODS (18.11.1968)

(2nd)

03.05.1858

Shortlands Junction

SHORTLANDS
Bromley
(03.05.1858)

BROMLEY

WIDMORE

BICKLEY

Chislehurst Junction

Chatham
Reversible Loop
SECR 19.06.1904

Up Chatham Loop
SECR 19.06.1904

Chislehurst Junction

SHORTLANDS

BROMLEY SOUTH
Bromley
(22.11.1858)

GAS WORKS

BICKLEY
Southborough Road
(05.07.1858)

LCDR
03.12.1860

Bickley
Junctions

MKR
05.07.1858

Shortlands to Bromley
South quadrupled
01.05.1894

GOODS
(18.04.1964)

MKR
05.07.1858

GOODS
(16.05.1964)

*

Tonbridge Fast Loop
SECR 14.09.1902

Tonbridge Slow Loop
SECR 08.09.1902

Bromley South to Bickley
quadrupled 1894

* Hawkswood Junction

Bickley Junctions to
Swanley quadrupled
31.05.1959

BROMLEY
COMMON

SOUTHBOROUGH

PARK
LANGLEY

55

Km
Scale
0   0.5   1   1.5   2

Miles
¼   ½   ¾   1

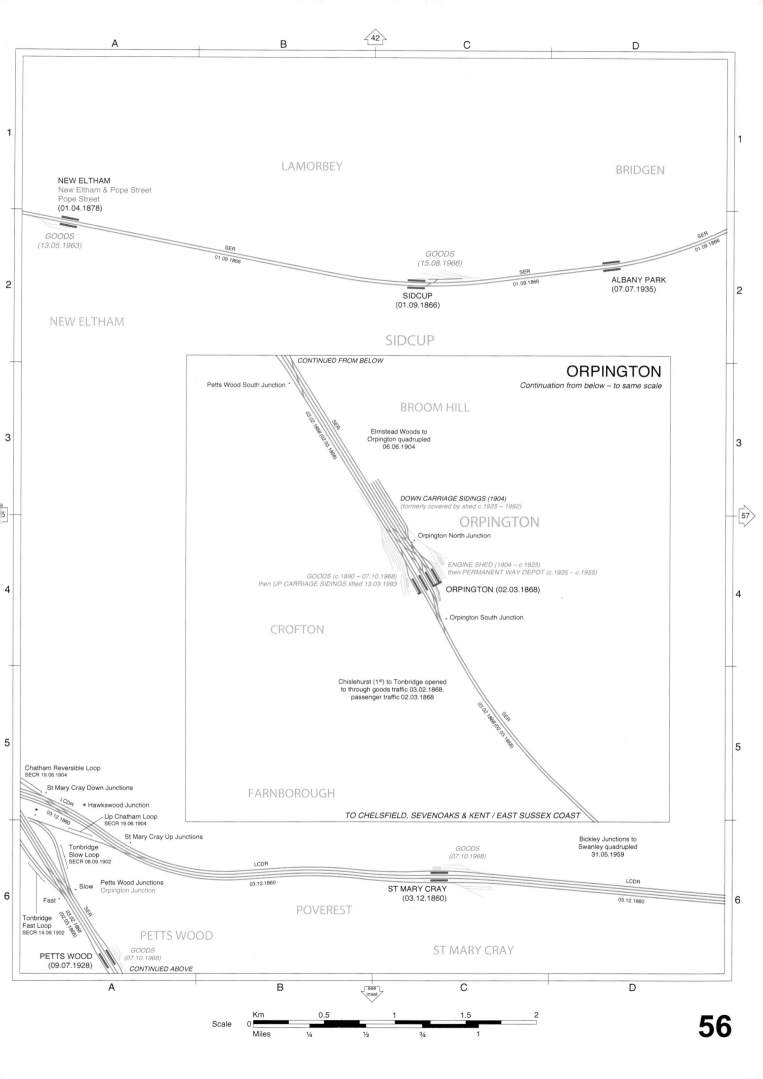

A   B   C   D

1

LAMORBEY

BRIDGEN

NEW ELTHAM
New Eltham & Pope Street
Pope Street
(01.04.1878)

GOODS
(13.05.1963)

SER
01.09.1866

SER
01.09.1866

GOODS
(15.08.1966)

SER
01.09.1866

ALBANY PARK
(07.07.1935)

2

NEW ELTHAM

SIDCUP
(01.09.1866)

SIDCUP

CONTINUED FROM BELOW

Petts Wood South Junction

ORPINGTON
Continuation from below – to same scale

BROOM HILL

03.02.1868 (02.03.1868)

SER

Elmstead Woods to
Orpington quadrupled
06.06.1904

3

DOWN CARRIAGE SIDINGS (1904)
(formerly covered by shed c.1925 – 1992)

ORPINGTON

Orpington North Junction

ENGINE SHED (1904 – c.1925)
then PERMANENT WAY DEPOT (c.1925 – c.1955)

57

GOODS (c.1890 – 07.10.1968)
then UP CARRIAGE SIDINGS lifted 13.03.1993

ORPINGTON (02.03.1868)

4

Orpington South Junction

CROFTON

Chislehurst (1st) to Tonbridge opened
to through goods traffic 03.02.1868.
passenger traffic 02.03.1868

03.02.1868 (02.03.1868)
SER

5

Chatham Reversible Loop
SECR 19.06.1904

St Mary Cray Down Junctions

LCDR
03.12.1860

✱ Hawkswood Junction

Up Chatham Loop
SECR 19.06.1904

St Mary Cray Up Junctions

FARNBOROUGH

TO CHELSFIELD, SEVENOAKS & KENT / EAST SUSSEX COAST

Tonbridge
Slow Loop
SECR 08.09.1902

Slow

Petts Wood Junctions
Orpington Junction

LCDR
03.12.1860

GOODS
(07.10.1968)

Bickley Junctions to
Swanley quadrupled
31.05.1959

Fast

LCDR
03.12.1860

ST MARY CRAY
(03.12.1860)

LCDR
03.12.1860

6

Tonbridge
Fast Loop
SECR 14.09.1902

03.02.1868
(02.03.1868)

SER

POVEREST

ST MARY CRAY

PETTS WOOD
(09.07.1928)

PETTS WOOD

GOODS
(07.10.1968)

CONTINUED ABOVE

A   B   C   D

see
inset

Scale
Km   0   0.5   1   1.5   2
Miles   ¼   ½   ¾   1

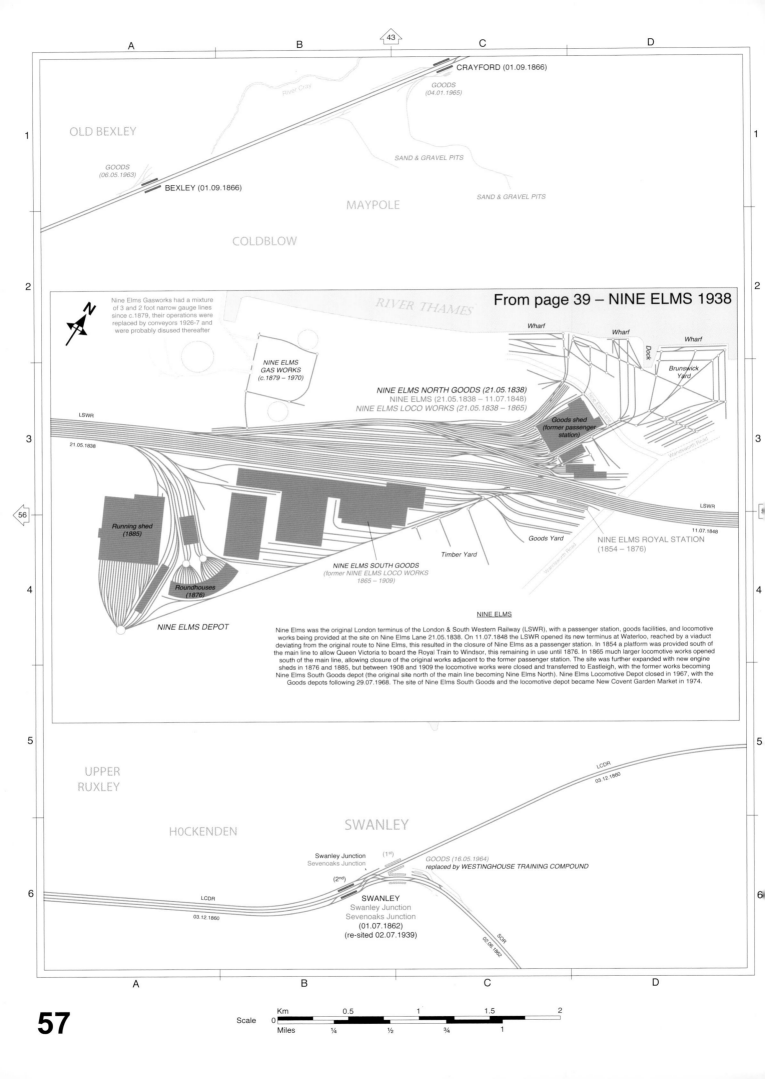

A B C D

CRAYFORD (01.09.1866)

GOODS
(04.01.1965)

River Cray

OLD BEXLEY

1

SAND & GRAVEL PITS

GOODS
(06.05.1963)

BEXLEY (01.09.1866)

MAYPOLE

SAND & GRAVEL PITS

COLDBLOW

2

Nine Elms Gasworks had a mixture
of 3 and 2 foot narrow gauge lines
since c.1879, their operations were
replaced by conveyors 1926-7 and
were probably disused thereafter

RIVER THAMES

From page 39 – NINE ELMS 1938

Wharf   Wharf   Wharf

Dock

Brunswick
Yard

NINE ELMS
GAS WORKS
(c.1879 – 1970)

NINE ELMS NORTH GOODS (21.05.1838)
NINE ELMS (21.05.1838 – 11.07.1848)
NINE ELMS LOCO WORKS (21.05.1838 – 1865)

Goods shed
(former passenger
station)

LSWR

21.05.1838

3

Wandsworth Road

LSWR

56

11.07.1848

Running shed
(1885)

NINE ELMS ROYAL STATION
(1854 – 1876)

Goods Yard

Wandsworth Road

Roundhouses
(1876)

Timber Yard

NINE ELMS SOUTH GOODS
(former NINE ELMS LOCO WORKS
1865 – 1909)

4

NINE ELMS DEPOT

NINE ELMS

Nine Elms was the original London terminus of the London & South Western Railway (LSWR), with a passenger station, goods facilities, and locomotive
works being provided at the site on Nine Elms Lane 21.05.1838. On 11.07.1848 the LSWR opened its new terminus at Waterloo, reached by a viaduct
deviating from the original route to Nine Elms, this resulted in the closure of Nine Elms as a passenger station. In 1854 a platform was provided south of
the main line to allow Queen Victoria to board the Royal Train to Windsor, this remaining in use until 1876. In 1865 much larger locomotive works opened
south of the main line, allowing closure of the original works adjacent to the former passenger station. The site was further expanded with new engine
sheds in 1876 and 1885, but between 1908 and 1909 the locomotive works were closed and transferred to Eastleigh, with the former works becoming
Nine Elms South Goods depot (the original site north of the main line becoming Nine Elms North). Nine Elms Locomotive Depot closed in 1967, with the
Goods depots following 29.07.1968. The site of Nine Elms South Goods and the locomotive depot became New Covent Garden Market in 1974.

5

UPPER
RUXLEY

LCDR

03.12.1860

HOCKENDEN

SWANLEY

Swanley Junction
Sevenoaks Junction

(1st)

GOODS (16.05.1964)
replaced by WESTINGHOUSE TRAINING COMPOUND

(2nd)

6

LCDR

03.12.1860

SWANLEY
Swanley Junction
Sevenoaks Junction
(01.07.1862)
(re-sited 02.07.1939)

SOR

02.06.1862

A B C D

57

Scale

Km   0   0.5   1   1.5   2
Miles   0   ¼   ½   ¾   1

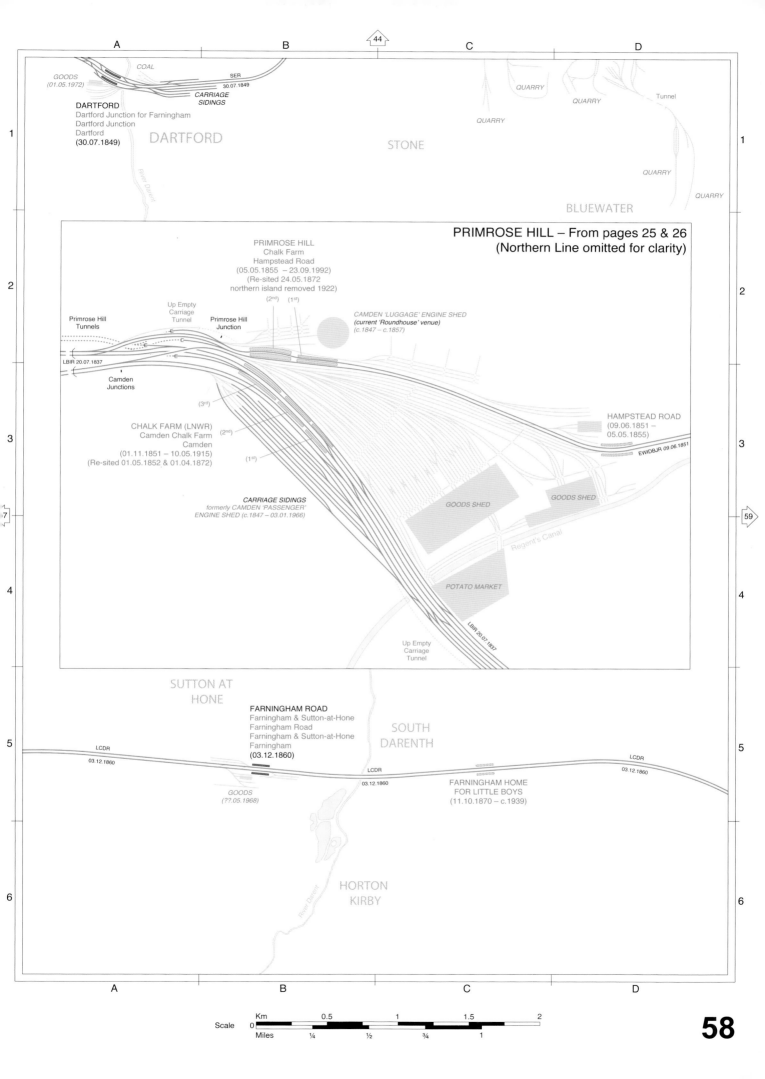

GOODS
(01.05.1972)

COAL

SER
30.07.1849

*CARRIAGE
SIDINGS*

1

DARTFORD
Dartford Junction for Farningham
Dartford Junction
Dartford
(30.07.1849)

DARTFORD

STONE

QUARRY

QUARRY

QUARRY

Tunnel

BLUEWATER

QUARRY

QUARRY

PRIMROSE HILL – From pages 25 & 26
(Northern Line omitted for clarity)

PRIMROSE HILL
Chalk Farm
Hampstead Road
(05.05.1855 – 23.09.1992)
(Re-sited 24.05.1872
northern island removed 1922)

(2ⁿᵈ)　(1ˢᵗ)

*CAMDEN 'LUGGAGE' ENGINE SHED
(current 'Roundhouse' venue)
(c.1847 – c.1857)*

2

Primrose Hill
Tunnels

Up Empty
Carriage
Tunnel

Primrose Hill
Junction

LBIR 20.07.1837

Camden
Junctions

HAMPSTEAD ROAD
(09.06.1851 –
05.05.1855)

(3ʳᵈ)

CHALK FARM (LNWR)
Camden Chalk Farm
Camden
(01.11.1851 – 10.05.1915)
(Re-sited 01.05.1852 & 01.04.1872)

(2ⁿᵈ)

(1ˢᵗ)

EWIDBJR 09.06.1851

3

*CARRIAGE SIDINGS
formerly CAMDEN 'PASSENGER'
ENGINE SHED (c.1847 – 03.01.1966)*

GOODS SHED

GOODS SHED

POTATO MARKET

Regent's Canal

LBIR 20.07.1837

4

Up Empty
Carriage
Tunnel

SUTTON AT
HONE

FARNINGHAM ROAD
Farningham & Sutton-at-Hone
Farningham Road
Farningham & Sutton-at-Hone
Farningham
(03.12.1860)

SOUTH
DARENTH

5

LCDR
03.12.1860

LCDR
03.12.1860

LCDR
03.12.1860

*GOODS
(??.05.1968)*

FARNINGHAM HOME
FOR LITTLE BOYS
(11.10.1870 – c.1939)

HORTON
KIRBY

6

River Darent

Scale

Km
0　　　　0.5　　　　1　　　　1.5　　　　2

Miles
¼　　　½　　　¾　　　1

SWANSCOMBE

Tunnels

QUARRY

QUARRY

GOODS (09.09.1968)

NORTHFLEET
(01.11.1849)

14.11.2007

LCOR

SER 30.07.1849

WORKS

NORTHFLEET CROSSRAIL LOGISTICS CENTRE
(27.04.2012)
To become LAFARGE AGGREGATES TERMINAL
NORTHFLEET CEMENT WORKS
(14.12.1970 – 13.03.1993)

Western
Tunnel

EBBSFLEET INTERNATIONAL
(19.11.2007)

NR
13.12.2009

Eastern Tunnel

CHURCH PATH SIDINGS

Up '   ' Down

Springhead Junctions

SER
30.07.1849

LCDR
10.05.1886 –
03.08.1953 (24.03.1968)

PERRY
STREET

GRAVESEND WEST BRANCH

Opened by the LCDR 10.05.1886 (public opening; ceremonial opening had occurred 17.04.1886),
with two intermediate stations at Southfleet and Rosherville (Longfield Halt added 01.07.1913).
Closed to passengers 03.08.1953 (Rosherville had already closed 16.07.1933), singled 1959 (passing
loop retained at Southfleet), then closed to goods 24.03.1968 and the branch formally abandoned.
Branch re-opened to coal traffic between Fawkham Junction and a terminal on the site of Southfleet
station to serve APCM (later Blue Circle) Northfleet Cement works in 1972, but this then closed in
1976 and the branch was again abandoned, but with track left in situ for much of its length.
On 05.10.1998 construction in the area commenced on Section 1 of High Speed 1, resulting in the
remaining original track being lifted and track bed south of Southfleet being re-used, this opened
28.09.2003. When Section 2 of High Speed 1 opened 14.11.2007, the Southfleet Junction to
Fawkham Junction section became effectively redundant, although it remains in situ albeit rarely used.

14.11.2007

LCOR

LCDR
10.05.1886 –
03.08.1953 (1976)

End of Gravesend West branch 1972 – 1976
(head shunt beyond Southfleet APCM coal terminal)

Pepper Hill Tunnel

GOODS (11.06.1962)

SOUTHFLEET
(10.05.1886 – 03.08.1953)
APCM COAL TERMINAL
(1972 – 1976)
(on same site)

LCOR
28.09.2003
(28.09.2003 – 14.11.2007)

Southfleet Junction

BETSHAM

LCOR
28.09.2003

SOUTHFLEET

NORTHFLEET
GREEN

LCDR
10.05.1886 –
14.11.2007

HOOK GREEN

ISTEAD

LONGFIELD HALT
(01.07.1913 – 03.08.1953)

LCDR
10.05.1886 –
14.11.2007

Fawkham
Junction

GOODS (??.05.1962)

LONGFIELD

NEW BARN

LONGFIELD
Longfield for Fawkham and Hartley
Longfield
Fawkham for Hartley and Longfield
Fawkham
Fawkham Road
(12.06.1872)

LCDR
03.12.1860

HARTLEY

Scale

Km
0   0.5   1   1.5   2

Miles
¼   ½   ¾   1

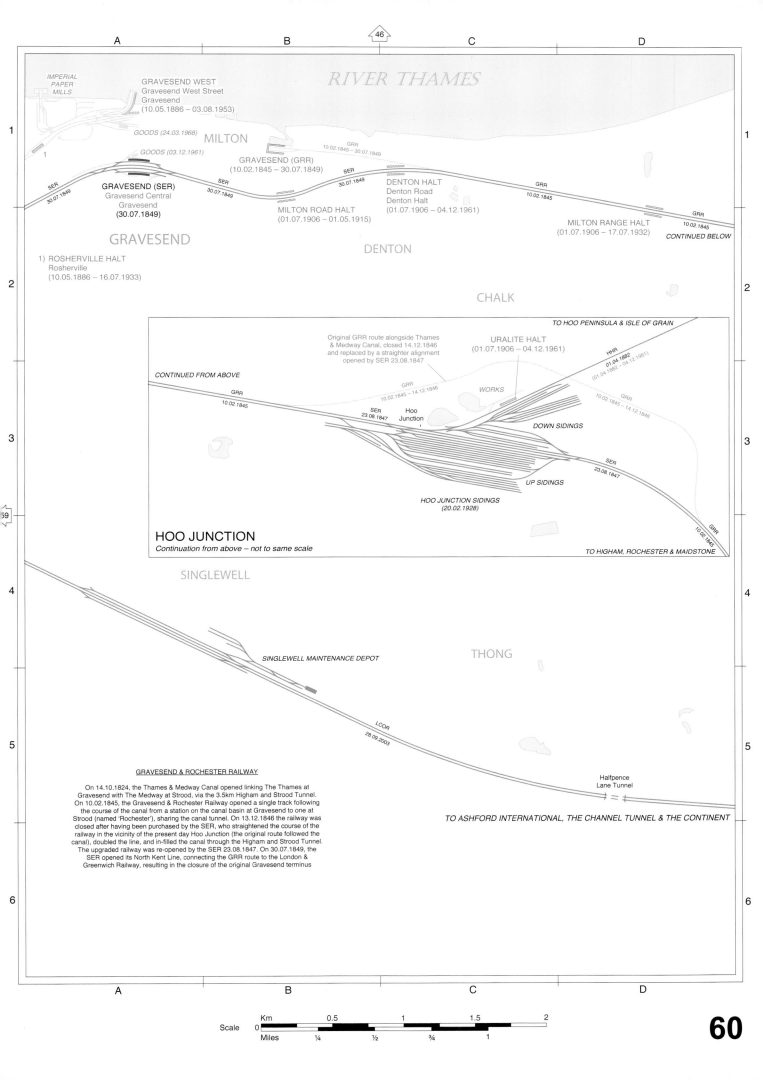

IMPERIAL
PAPER
MILLS

RIVER THAMES

GRAVESEND WEST
Gravesend West Street
Gravesend
(10.05.1886 – 03.08.1953)

GOODS (24.03.1968)

MILTON

GOODS (03.12.1961)

GRR
10.02.1845 – 30.07.1849

SER
30.07.1849

GRAVESEND (GRR)
(10.02.1845 – 30.07.1849)

SER
30.07.1849

SER
30.07.1849

DENTON HALT
Denton Road
Denton Halt
(01.07.1906 – 04.12.1961)

GRR
10.02.1845

GRR
10.02.1845

GRAVESEND (SER)
Gravesend Central
Gravesend
(30.07.1849)

MILTON ROAD HALT
(01.07.1906 – 01.05.1915)

MILTON RANGE HALT
(01.07.1906 – 17.07.1932)

CONTINUED BELOW

GRAVESEND

DENTON

1) ROSHERVILLE HALT
Rosherville
(10.05.1886 – 16.07.1933)

CHALK

Original GRR route alongside Thames
& Medway Canal, closed 14.12.1846
and replaced by a straighter alignment
opened by SER 23.08.1847

URALITE HALT
(01.07.1906 – 04.12.1961)

TO HOO PENINSULA & ISLE OF GRAIN

HHR
01.04.1882
(01.04.1882 – 04.12.1961)

CONTINUED FROM ABOVE

GRR
10.02.1845

GRR
10.02.1845 – 14.12.1846

WORKS

GRR
10.02.1845 – 14.12.1846

SER
23.08.1847

Hoo
Junction

DOWN SIDINGS

SER
23.08.1847

UP SIDINGS

GRR
10.02.1845

HOO JUNCTION SIDINGS
(20.02.1928)

HOO JUNCTION

Continuation from above – not to same scale

TO HIGHAM, ROCHESTER & MAIDSTONE

SINGLEWELL

THONG

SINGLEWELL MAINTENANCE DEPOT

LCOR
28.09.2003

Halfpence
Lane Tunnel

GRAVESEND & ROCHESTER RAILWAY

On 14.10.1824, the Thames & Medway Canal opened linking The Thames at
Gravesend with The Medway at Strood, via the 3.5km Higham and Strood Tunnel.
On 10.02.1845, the Gravesend & Rochester Railway opened a single track following
the course of the canal from a station on the canal basin at Gravesend to one at
Strood (named 'Rochester'), sharing the canal tunnel. On 13.12.1846 the railway was
closed after having been purchased by the SER, who straightened the course of the
railway in the vicinity of the present day Hoo Junction (the original route followed the
canal), doubled the line, and in-filled the canal through the Higham and Strood Tunnel.
The upgraded railway was re-opened by the SER 23.08.1847. On 30.07.1849, the
SER opened its North Kent Line, connecting the GRR route to the London &
Greenwich Railway, resulting in the closure of the original Gravesend terminus

TO ASHFORD INTERNATIONAL, THE CHANNEL TUNNEL & THE CONTINENT

Scale

Km
0   0.5   1   1.5   2

Miles
¼   ½   ¾   1

60

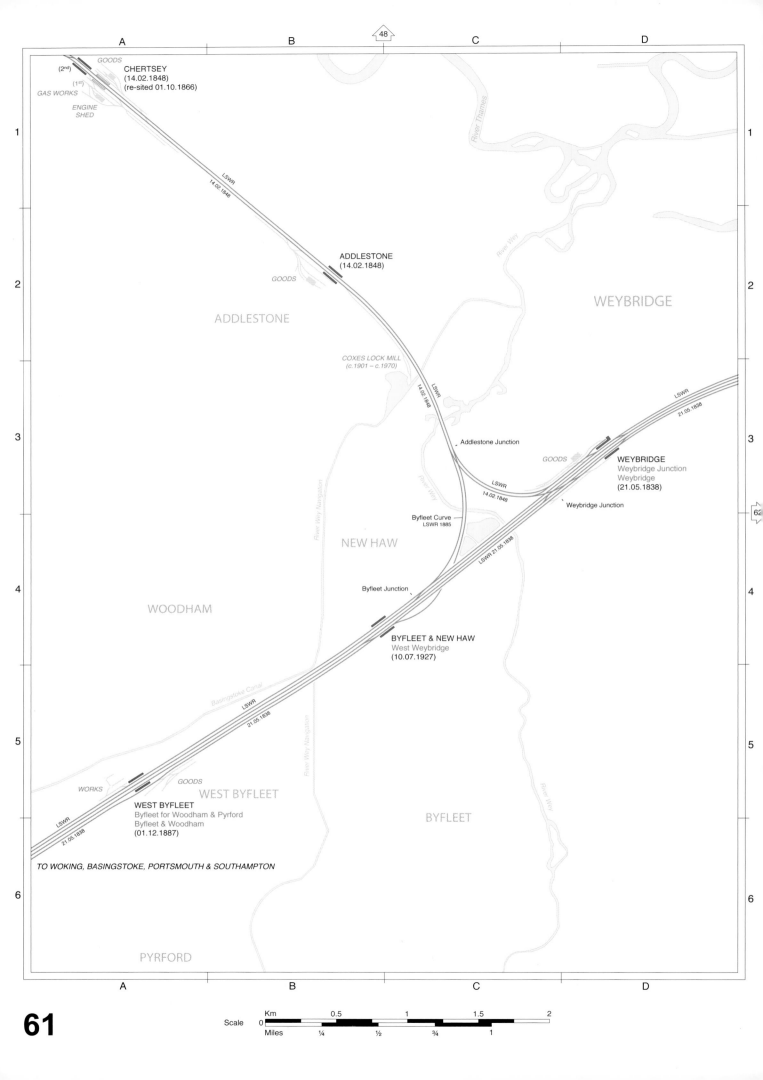

GOODS
(2nd)
CHERTSEY
(14.02.1848)
(re-sited 01.10.1866)
(1st)
GAS WORKS
ENGINE
SHED

LSWR
14.02.1848

River Thames

River Wey

WEYBRIDGE

ADDLESTONE
(14.02.1848)

GOODS

ADDLESTONE

COXES LOCK MILL
(c.1901 – c.1970)

LSWR
14.02.1848

LSWR
21.05.1838

Addlestone Junction

River Wey Navigation

River Wey

GOODS

WEYBRIDGE
Weybridge Junction
Weybridge
(21.05.1838)

LSWR
14.02.1848

Weybridge Junction

NEW HAW

Byfleet Curve
LSWR 1885

LSWR 21.05.1838

WOODHAM

Byfleet Junction

BYFLEET & NEW HAW
West Weybridge
(10.07.1927)

Basingstoke Canal

LSWR
21.05.1838

River Wey Navigation

River Wey

WORKS

GOODS

WEST BYFLEET

BYFLEET

WEST BYFLEET
Byfleet for Woodham & Pyrford
Byfleet & Woodham
(01.12.1887)

LSWR
21.05.1838

TO WOKING, BASINGSTOKE, PORTSMOUTH & SOUTHAMPTON

PYRFORD

61

Scale

Km
0   0.5   1   1.5   2

Miles
¼   ½   ¾   1

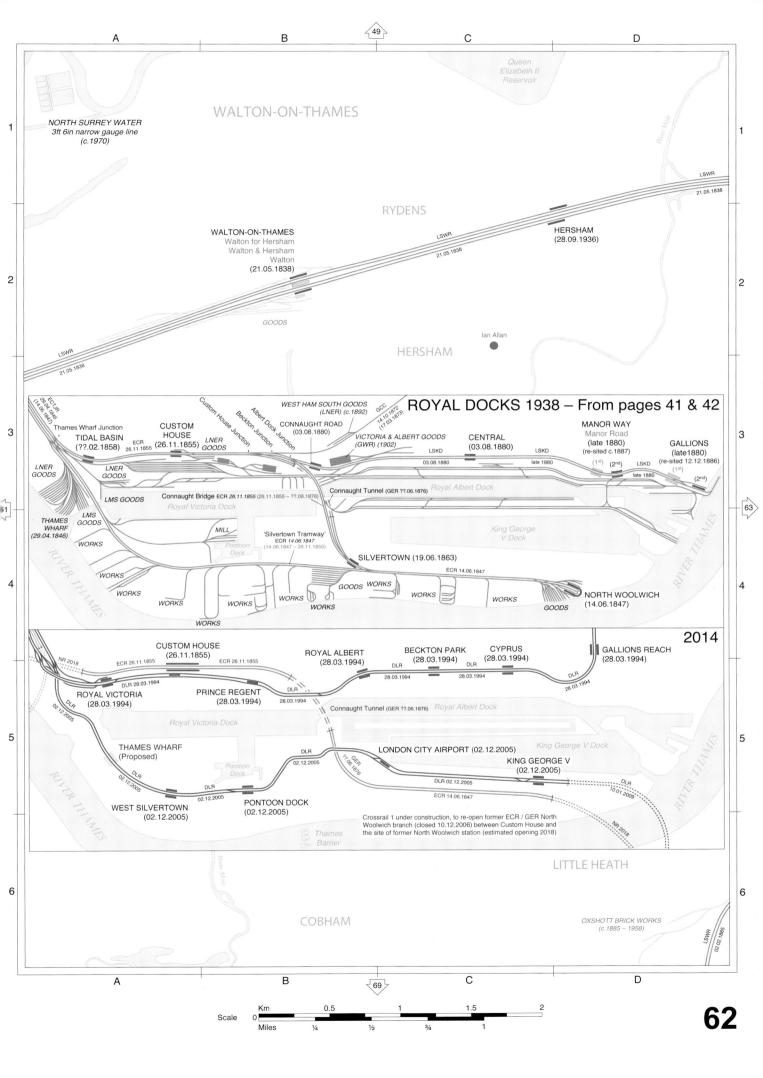

NORTH SURREY WATER
3ft 6in narrow gauge line
(c.1970)

WALTON-ON-THAMES

Queen
Elizabeth II
Reservoir

RYDENS

LSWR
21.05.1838

WALTON-ON-THAMES
Walton for Hersham
Walton & Hersham
Walton
(21.05.1838)

LSWR
21.05.1838

HERSHAM
(28.09.1936)

GOODS

HERSHAM

Ian Allan

LSWR
21.05.1838

ROYAL DOCKS 1938 – From pages 41 & 42

ECT J.R
29.04.1846
(14.06.1847)

Thames Wharf Junction

TIDAL BASIN
(??.02.1858)

CUSTOM
HOUSE
(26.11.1855)

ECR
26.11.1855

Custom House Junction

LNER
GOODS

Beckton Junction

Albert Dock Junction

WEST HAM SOUTH GOODS
(LNER) (c.1892)

CONNAUGHT ROAD
(03.08.1880)

VICTORIA & ALBERT GOODS
(GWR) (1902)

GCC
14.10.1872
(17.03.1873)

CENTRAL
(03.08.1880)

MANOR WAY
Manor Road
(late 1880)
(re-sited c.1887)

GALLIONS
(re-sited 12.12.1886)

LNER
GOODS

LNER
GOODS

LSKD
03.08.1880

LSKD
late 1880

(1st) (2nd)

LSKD
late 1880

(1st)

(2nd)

LMS GOODS

Connaught Bridge ECR 26.11.1855 (26.11.1855 – ??.06.1876)

Connaught Tunnel (GER ??.06.1876)

Royal Albert Dock

THAMES
WHARF
(29.04.1846)

LMS
GOODS

Royal Victoria Dock

King George
V Dock

61

63

MILL

Pontoon
Dock

'Silvertown Tramway'
ECR 14.06.1847
(14.06.1847 – 26.11.1855)

SILVERTOWN (19.06.1863)

ECR 14.06.1847

WORKS

WORKS

WORKS

WORKS

WORKS

WORKS

GOODS

WORKS

WORKS

WORKS

NORTH WOOLWICH
(14.06.1847)

GOODS

RIVER THAMES

RIVER THAMES

2014

NR 2018

CUSTOM HOUSE
(26.11.1855)

ECR 26.11.1855

ECR 26.11.1855

ROYAL ALBERT
(28.03.1994)

DLR
28.03.1994

BECKTON PARK
(28.03.1994)

DLR
28.03.1994

CYPRUS
(28.03.1994)

DLR
28.03.1994

GALLIONS REACH
(28.03.1994)

DLR
28.03.1994

DLR 28.03.1994

ROYAL VICTORIA
(28.03.1994)

PRINCE REGENT
(28.03.1994)

DLR
28.03.1994

Royal Victoria Dock

Connaught Tunnel (GER ??.06.1876)

Royal Albert Dock

THAMES WHARF
(Proposed)

Pontoon
Dock

DLR
02.12.2005

GER
??.06.1876

LONDON CITY AIRPORT (02.12.2005)

King George V Dock

KING GEORGE V
(02.12.2005)

DLR
10.01.2009

DLR
02.12.2005

DLR
02.12.2005

DLR
02.12.2005

WEST SILVERTOWN
(02.12.2005)

PONTOON DOCK
(02.12.2005)

Thames
Barrier

DLR 02.12.2005

ECR 14.06.1847

NR 2018

Crossrail 1 under construction, to re-open former ECR / GER North
Woolwich branch (closed 10.12.2006) between Custom House and
the site of former North Woolwich station (estimated opening 2018)

LITTLE HEATH

River Mole

COBHAM

OXSHOTT BRICK WORKS
(c.1885 – 1958)

LSWR
02.02.1885

Km

0.5

1

1.5

2

Scale
0

Miles

¼

½

¾

1

62

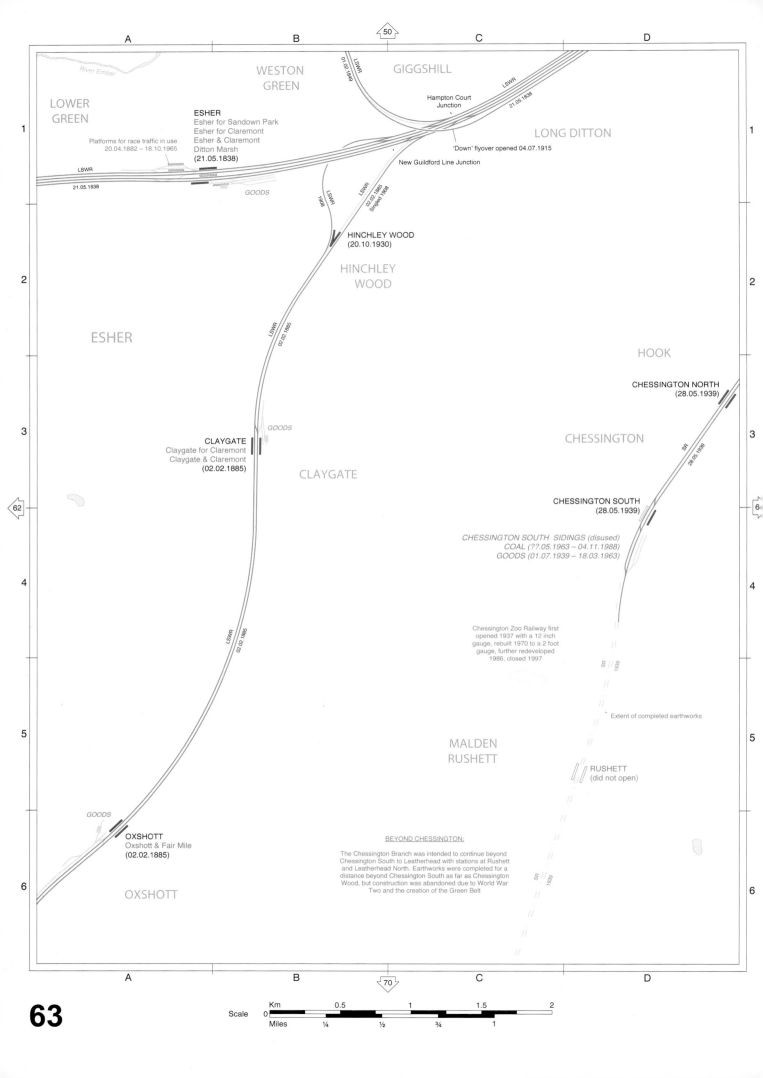

River Ember

WESTON
GREEN

GIGGSHILL

01.02.1849

LSWR

LOWER
GREEN

ESHER
Esher for Sandown Park
Esher for Claremont
Esher & Claremont
Ditton Marsh
(21.05.1838)

Platforms for race traffic in use
20.04.1882 – 18.10.1965

Hampton Court
Junction

LSWR
21.05.1838

LONG DITTON

LSWR
21.05.1838

'Down' flyover opened 04.07.1915

New Guildford Line Junction

LSWR
1908

LSWR
02.02.1885
Singled 1908

GOODS

LSWR
1908

HINCHLEY WOOD
(20.10.1930)

HINCHLEY
WOOD

ESHER

LSWR
02.02.1885

HOOK

CHESSINGTON NORTH
(28.05.1939)

CLAYGATE
Claygate for Claremont
Claygate & Claremont
(02.02.1885)

GOODS

CHESSINGTON

SR
28.05.1939

CLAYGATE

62

CHESSINGTON SOUTH
(28.05.1939)

6

CHESSINGTON SOUTH SIDINGS (disused)
COAL (??.05.1963 – 04.11.1988)
GOODS (01.07.1939 – 18.03.1963)

LSWR
02.02.1885

Chessington Zoo Railway first
opened 1937 with a 12 inch
gauge, rebuilt 1970 to a 2 foot
gauge, further redeveloped
1986, closed 1997

SR
1939

Extent of completed earthworks

MALDEN
RUSHETT

RUSHETT
(did not open)

GOODS

OXSHOTT
Oxshott & Fair Mile
(02.02.1885)

BEYOND CHESSINGTON:

The Chessington Branch was intended to continue beyond
Chessington South to Leatherhead with stations at Rushett
and Leatherhead North. Earthworks were completed for a
distance beyond Chessington South as far as Chessington
Wood, but construction was abandoned due to World War
Two and the creation of the Green Belt

SR
1939

OXSHOTT

63

Scale

Km
0   0.5   1   1.5   2

Miles
   ¼   ½   ¾   1

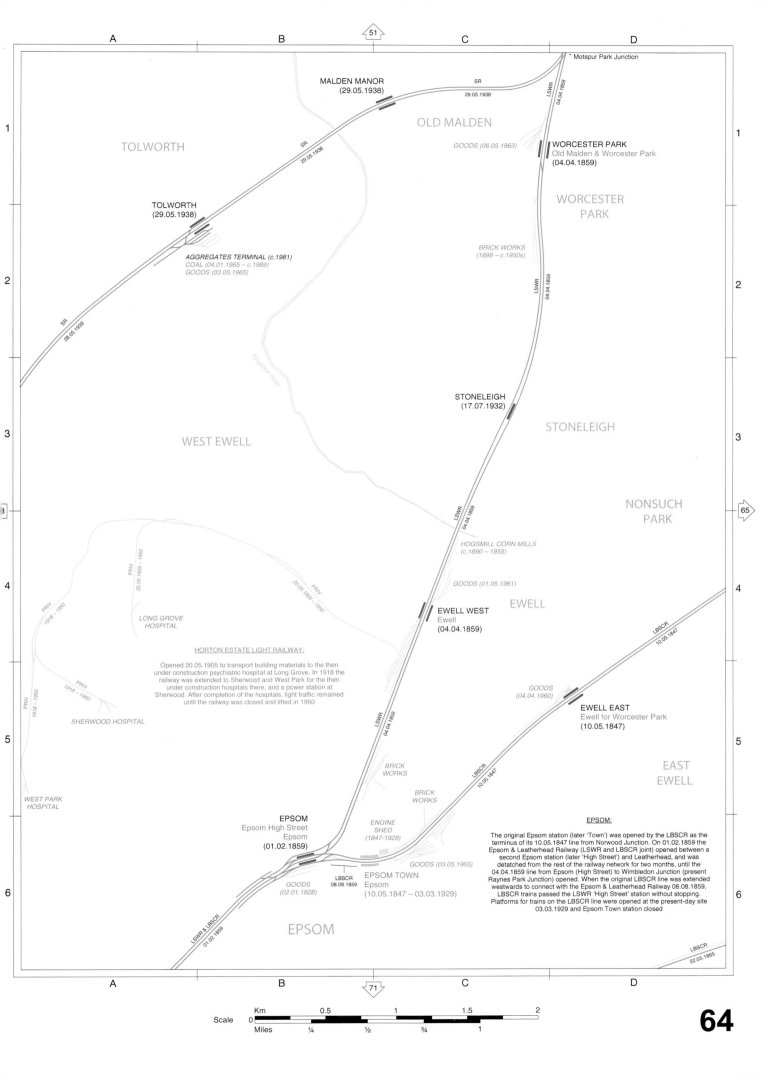

MALDEN MANOR
(29.05.1938)

OLD MALDEN

SR
29.05.1938

Motspur Park Junction

LSWR
04.04.1859

TOLWORTH

1

SR
29.05.1938

GOODS (06.05.1963)

WORCESTER PARK
Old Malden & Worcester Park
(04.04.1859)

WORCESTER
PARK

TOLWORTH
(29.05.1938)

2

SR
28.05.1859

AGGREGATES TERMINAL (c.1981)
COAL (04.01.1965 – c.1989)
GOODS (03.05.1965)

BRICK WORKS
(1898 – c.1950s)

LSWR
04.04.1859

2

Hogsmil River

STONELEIGH
(17.07.1932)

STONELEIGH

WEST EWELL

3

NONSUCH
PARK

65

LSWR
04.04.1859

HOGSMILL CORN MILLS
(c.1890 – 1955)

PRIV
20.05.1905 – 1950

PRIV
20.05.1905 – 1950

GOODS (01.05.1961)

EWELL

4

PRIV
1918 – 1950

LONG GROVE
HOSPITAL

EWELL WEST
Ewell
(04.04.1859)

LBSCR
10.05.1847

PRIV
1918 – 1950

HORTON ESTATE LIGHT RAILWAY:

Opened 20.05.1905 to transport building materials to the then
under construction psychiatric hospital at Long Grove. In 1918 the
railway was extended to Sherwood and West Park for the then
under construction hospitals there, and a power station at
Sherwood. After completion of the hospitals, light traffic remained
until the railway was closed and lifted in 1950

GOODS
(04.04.1960)

EWELL EAST
Ewell for Worcester Park
(10.05.1847)

PRIV
1918 – 1950

SHERWOOD HOSPITAL

LSWR
04.04.1859

EAST
EWELL

5

WEST PARK
HOSPITAL

BRICK
WORKS

BRICK
WORKS

LBSCR
10.05.1847

EPSOM:

The original Epsom station (later 'Town') was opened by the LBSCR as the
terminus of its 10.05.1847 line from Norwood Junction. On 01.02.1859 the
Epsom & Leatherhead Railway (LSWR and LBSCR joint) opened between a
second Epsom station (later 'High Street') and Leatherhead, and was
detatched from the rest of the railway network for two months, until the
04.04.1859 line from Epsom (High Street) to Wimbledon Junction (present
Raynes Park Junction) opened. When the original LBSCR line was extended
westwards to connect with the Epsom & Leatherhead Railway 08.08.1859,
LBSCR trains passed the LSWR 'High Street' station without stopping.
Platforms for trains on the LBSCR line were opened at the present-day site
03.03.1929 and Epsom Town station closed

EPSOM
Epsom High Street
Epsom
(01.02.1859)

ENGINE
SHED
(1847-1929)

GOODS (03.05.1965)

6

LBSCR
08.08.1859

EPSOM TOWN
Epsom
(10.05.1847 – 03.03.1929)

GOODS
(02.01.1928)

EPSOM

LSWR & LBSCR
01.02.1859

LBSCR
22.05.1865

Km 0.5 1 1.5 2
Scale 0
Miles ¼ ½ ¾ 1

64

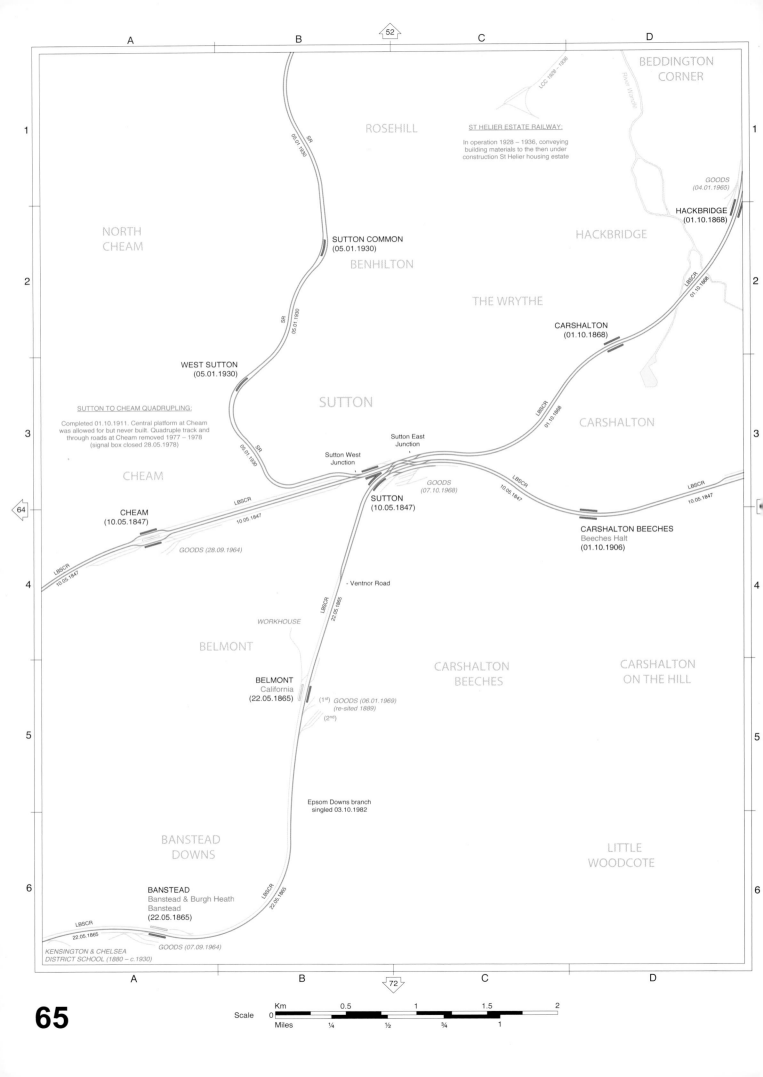

ROSEHILL

BEDDINGTON
CORNER

ST HELIER ESTATE RAILWAY:

In operation 1928 – 1936, conveying
building materials to the then under
construction St Helier housing estate

LCC 1928 – 1936

River Wandle

GOODS
(04.01.1965)

NORTH
CHEAM

SUTTON COMMON
(05.01.1930)

BENHILTON

HACKBRIDGE

HACKBRIDGE
(01.10.1868)

THE WRYTHE

LBSCR
01.10.1868

SR
05.01.1930

SR
05.01.1930

WEST SUTTON
(05.01.1930)

SUTTON

CARSHALTON
(01.10.1868)

LBSCR
01.10.1868

CARSHALTON

SUTTON TO CHEAM QUADRUPLING:

Completed 01.10.1911. Central platform at Cheam
was allowed for but never built. Quadruple track and
through roads at Cheam removed 1977 – 1978
(signal box closed 28.05.1978)

SR
05.01.1930

Sutton East
Junction

CHEAM

Sutton West
Junction

GOODS
(07.10.1968)

LBSCR
10.05.1847

LBSCR
10.05.1847

CHEAM
(10.05.1847)

LBSCR
10.05.1847

GOODS (28.09.1964)

SUTTON
(10.05.1847)

LBSCR
10.05.1847

CARSHALTON BEECHES
Beeches Halt
(01.10.1906)

LBSCR
10.05.1847

- Ventnor Road

LBSCR
22.05.1865

WORKHOUSE

BELMONT

BELMONT
California
(22.05.1865)

(1st) GOODS (06.01.1969)
(re-sited 1889)

(2nd)

CARSHALTON
BEECHES

CARSHALTON
ON THE HILL

LITTLE
WOODCOTE

Epsom Downs branch
singled 03.10.1982

BANSTEAD
DOWNS

LBSCR
22.05.1865

BANSTEAD
Banstead & Burgh Heath
Banstead
(22.05.1865)

LBSCR
22.05.1865

LBSCR
22.05.1865

GOODS (07.09.1964)

KENSINGTON & CHELSEA
DISTRICT SCHOOL (1880 – c.1930)

65

Scale

Km
0   0.5   1   1.5   2

Miles
¼   ½   ¾   1

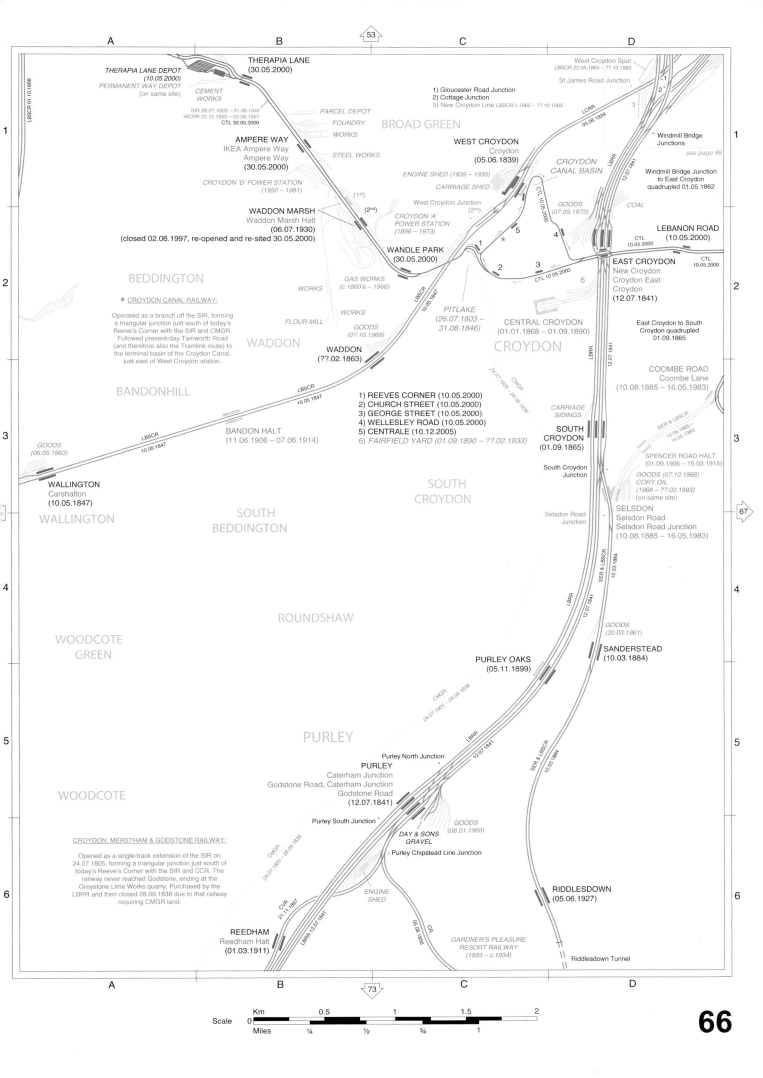

THERAPIA LANE DEPOT
(10.05.2000)
PERMANENT WAY DEPOT
(on same site)

THERAPIA LANE
(30.05.2000)

*CEMENT
WORKS*

West Croydon Spur
LBSCR 22.05.1865 – ??.10.1983

St James Road Junction

1) Gloucester Road Junction
2) Cottage Junction
3) New Croydon Line LBSCR c.1865 – ??.10.1983

*Windmill Bridge
Junctions*

see page 86

SIR 26.07.1803 – 31.08.1846
WCRR 22.10.1855 – 02.06.1997
CTL 30.05.2000

PARCEL DEPOT

FOUNDRY

WORKS

BROAD GREEN

LCRR
05.06.1839

AMPERE WAY
IKEA Ampere Way
Ampere Way
(30.05.2000)

STEEL WORKS

WEST CROYDON
Croydon
(05.06.1839)

*CROYDON
CANAL BASIN*

*Windmill Bridge Junction
to East Croydon
quadrupled 01.05.1862*

CROYDON 'B' POWER STATION
(1950 – 1981)

(1st)

ENGINE SHED (1839 – 1935)

CARRIAGE SHED

LBRR

12.07.1841

COAL

LEBANON ROAD
(10.05.2000)

WADDON MARSH
Waddon Marsh Halt
(06.07.1930)

(2nd)

West Croydon Junction
(2nd)

CROYDON 'A'
POWER STATION
(1896 – 1973)

*GOODS
(07.05.1973)*

CTL 10.05.2000

1

5

4

CTL
10.05.2000

CTL
10.05.2000

(closed 02.06.1997, re-opened and re-sited 30.05.2000)

WANDLE PARK
(30.05.2000)

2

3

*

EAST CROYDON
New Croydon
Croydon East
Croydon
(12.07.1841)

CTL 10.05.2000

6

BEDDINGTON

✶ CROYDON CANAL RAILWAY:

Operated as a branch off the SIR, forming
a triangular junction just south of today's
Reeve's Corner with the SIR and CMGR.
Followed present-day Tamworth Road
(and therefore also the Tramlink route) to
the terminal basin of the Croydon Canal,
just east of West Croydon station.

GAS WORKS
(c.1860's – 1966)

WORKS

PITLAKE
(26.07.1803 –
31.08.1846)

CENTRAL CROYDON
(01.01.1868 – 01.09.1890)

*East Croydon to South
Croydon quadrupled
01.09.1865*

LBSCR
10.05.1847

LBRR

12.07.1841

WADDON
BANDONHILL

WORKS

FLOUR MILL

CROYDON

COOMBE ROAD
Coombe Lane
(10.08.1885 – 16.05.1983)

WADDON
(??.02.1863)

*GOODS
(07.10.1968)*

CMGR
24.07.1805 – 28.09.1838

*CARRIAGE
SIDINGS*

SER & LBSCR
10.08.1885 –
16.05.1983

SOUTH
CROYDON

LBSCR
10.05.1847

1) REEVES CORNER (10.05.2000)
2) CHURCH STREET (10.05.2000)
3) GEORGE STREET (10.05.2000)
4) WELLESLEY ROAD (10.05.2000)
5) CENTRALE (10.12.2005)
6) *FAIRFIELD YARD (01.09.1890 – ??.02.1933)*

SOUTH
CROYDON
(01.09.1865)

SPENCER ROAD HALT
(01.09.1906 – 15.03.1915)

*GOODS (07.10.1968)
CORY OIL
(1968 – ??.03.1993)
(on same site)*

*GOODS
(06.05.1963)*

South Croydon
Junction

SELSDON
Selsdon Road
Selsdon Road Junction
(10.08.1885 – 16.05.1983)

LBSCR
10.05.1847

BANDON HALT
(11.06.1906 – 07.06.1914)

Selsdon Road
Junction

WALLINGTON
Carshalton
(10.05.1847)

SOUTH
CROYDON

WALLINGTON

SOUTH
BEDDINGTON

SER & LBSCR
10.03.1884

ROUNDSHAW

WOODCOTE
GREEN

LBRR

12.07.1841

*GOODS
(20.03.1961)*

SANDERSTEAD
(10.03.1884)

PURLEY OAKS
(05.11.1899)

CMGR
24.07.1805 – 28.09.1838

PURLEY

Purley North Junction

LBRR
12.07.1841

SER & LBSCR
10.03.1884

WOODCOTE

PURLEY
Caterham Junction
Godstone Road, Caterham Junction
Godstone Road
(12.07.1841)

Purley South Junction

*GOODS
(06.01.1969)*

*DAY & SONS
GRAVEL*

CROYDON, MERSTHAM & GODSTONE RAILWAY:

Opened as a single-track extension of the SIR on
24.07.1805, forming a triangular junction just south of
today's Reeve's Corner with the SIR and CCR. The
railway never reached Godstone, ending at the
Greystone Lime Works quarry. Purchased by the
LBRR and then closed 28.09.1838 due to that railway
requiring CMGR land.

CMGR
24.07.1805 – 28.09.1838

- Purley Chipstead Line Junction

*ENGINE
SHED*

RIDDLESDOWN
(05.06.1927)

CVR
21.11.1897

LBRR 12.07.1841

CR
05.08.1856

REEDHAM
Reedham Halt
(01.03.1911)

*GARDNER'S PLEASURE
RESORT RAILWAY
(1893 – c.1934)*

Riddlesdown Tunnel

Km
Scale
0   0.5   1   1.5   2
Miles
    ¼   ½   ¾   1

66

LBSCR 01.10.1868

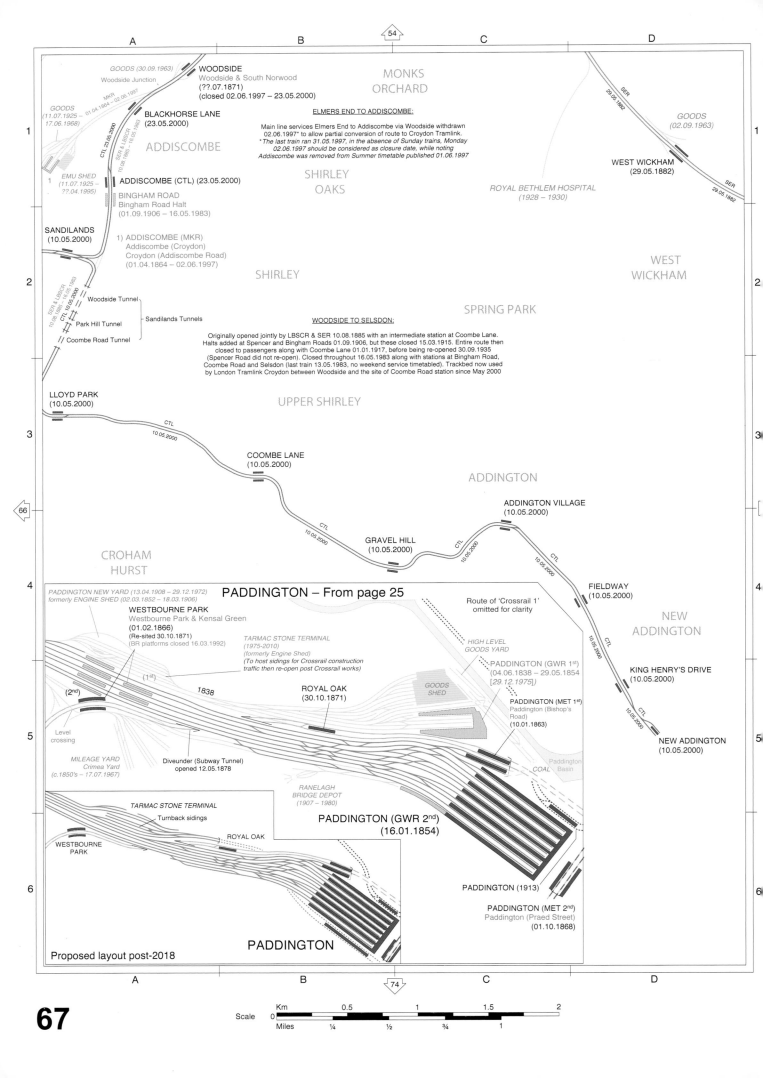

GOODS (30.09.1963)
Woodside Junction

GOODS (11.07.1925 – 17.06.1968)

MKR
01.04.1864 – 02.06.1997

CTL 23.05.2000

SER & LBSCR
10.08.1885 – 16.05.1983

WOODSIDE
Woodside & South Norwood
(??.07.1871)
(closed 02.06.1997 – 23.05.2000)

BLACKHORSE LANE
(23.05.2000)

ADDISCOMBE

EMU SHED
(11.07.1925 – ??.04.1995)

1

ADDISCOMBE (CTL) (23.05.2000)

BINGHAM ROAD
Bingham Road Halt
(01.09.1906 – 16.05.1983)

1) ADDISCOMBE (MKR)
Addiscombe (Croydon)
Croydon (Addiscombe Road)
(01.04.1864 – 02.06.1997)

SANDILANDS
(10.05.2000)

SER & LBSCR
10.08.1885 – 16.05.1983
CTL 10.05.2000

Woodside Tunnel

Park Hill Tunnel — Sandilands Tunnels

Coombe Road Tunnel

LLOYD PARK
(10.05.2000)

CTL
10.05.2000

COOMBE LANE
(10.05.2000)

CTL
10.05.2000

GRAVEL HILL
(10.05.2000)

CTL
10.05.2000

ADDINGTON VILLAGE
(10.05.2000)

CTL
10.05.2000

FIELDWAY
(10.05.2000)

CTL
10.05.2000

NEW ADDINGTON

KING HENRY'S DRIVE
(10.05.2000)

CTL
10.05.2000

NEW ADDINGTON
(10.05.2000)

MONKS ORCHARD

SHIRLEY OAKS

SHIRLEY

SPRING PARK

UPPER SHIRLEY

ADDINGTON

CROHAM HURST

WEST WICKHAM

ROYAL BETHLEM HOSPITAL
(1928 – 1930)

SER
29.05.1882

GOODS
(02.09.1963)

WEST WICKHAM
(29.05.1882)

SER
29.05.1882

ELMERS END TO ADDISCOMBE:
Main line services Elmers End to Addiscombe via Woodside withdrawn
02.06.1997* to allow partial conversion of route to Croydon Tramlink.
*The last train ran 31.05.1997, in the absence of Sunday trains, Monday
02.06.1997 should be considered as closure date, while noting
Addiscombe was removed from Summer timetable published 01.06.1997

WOODSIDE TO SELSDON:
Originally opened jointly by LBSCR & SER 10.08.1885 with an intermediate station at Coombe Lane.
Halts added at Spencer and Bingham Roads 01.09.1906, but these closed 15.03.1915. Entire route then
closed to passengers along with Coombe Lane 01.01.1917, before being re-opened 30.09.1935
(Spencer Road did not re-open). Closed throughout 16.05.1983 along with stations at Bingham Road,
Coombe Road and Selsdon (last train 13.05.1983, no weekend service timetabled). Trackbed now used
by London Tramlink Croydon between Woodside and the site of Coombe Road station since May 2000

66

PADDINGTON – From page 25

PADDINGTON NEW YARD (13.04.1908 – 29.12.1972)
formerly ENGINE SHED (02.03.1852 – 18.03.1906)

WESTBOURNE PARK
Westbourne Park & Kensal Green
(01.02.1866)
(Re-sited 30.10.1871)
(BR platforms closed 16.03.1992)

(1st)

(2nd)

Level crossing

MILEAGE YARD
Crimea Yard
(c.1850's – 17.07.1967)

1838

Diveunder (Subway Tunnel)
opened 12.05.1878

TARMAC STONE TERMINAL
(1975-2010)
(formerly Engine Shed)
(To host sidings for Crossrail construction
traffic then re-open post Crossrail works)

ROYAL OAK
(30.10.1871)

RANELAGH
BRIDGE DEPOT
(1907 – 1980)

Route of 'Crossrail 1'
omitted for clarity

HIGH LEVEL
GOODS YARD

GOODS SHED

PADDINGTON (GWR 1st)
(04.06.1838 – 29.05.1854
[29.12.1975])

PADDINGTON (MET 1st)
Paddington (Bishop's Road)
(10.01.1863)

Paddington Basin

COAL

PADDINGTON (GWR 2nd)
(16.01.1854)

PADDINGTON (1913)

PADDINGTON (MET 2nd)
Paddington (Praed Street)
(01.10.1868)

TARMAC STONE TERMINAL
Turnback sidings

ROYAL OAK

WESTBOURNE PARK

PADDINGTON

Proposed layout post-2018

74

Scale
Km 0   0.5   1   1.5   2
Miles   ¼   ½   ¾   1

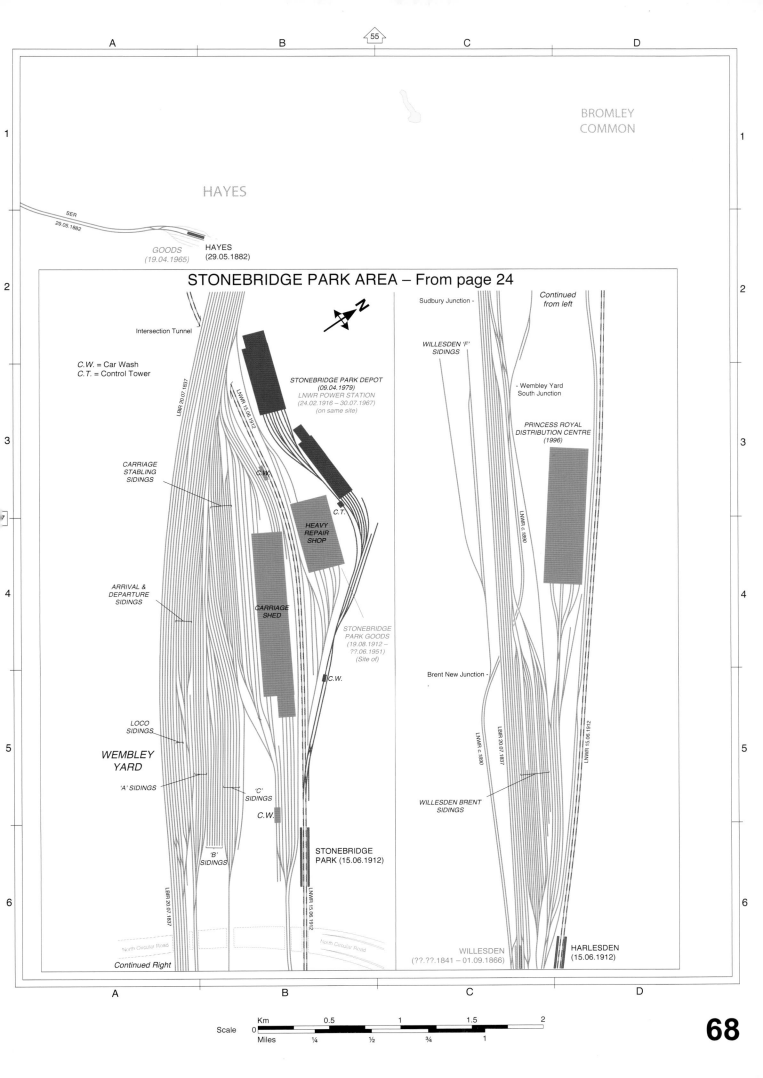

55

A   B   C   D

1

BROMLEY
COMMON

HAYES

SER
29.05.1882

GOODS   HAYES
(19.04.1965)   (29.05.1882)

2

STONEBRIDGE PARK AREA – From page 24

Sudbury Junction -

Continued
from left

Intersection Tunnel

WILLESDEN 'F'
SIDINGS

C.W. = Car Wash
C.T. = Control Tower

STONEBRIDGE PARK DEPOT
(09.04.1979)
LNWR POWER STATION
(24.02.1916 – 30.07.1967)
(on same site)

- Wembley Yard
South Junction

LBIR 20.07.1837

LNWR 15.06.1912

PRINCESS ROYAL
DISTRIBUTION CENTRE
(1996)

3

CARRIAGE
STABLING
SIDINGS

C.W.

C.T.

HEAVY
REPAIR
SHOP

LNWR c.1890

4

ARRIVAL &
DEPARTURE
SIDINGS

CARRIAGE
SHED

STONEBRIDGE
PARK GOODS
(19.08.1912 –
??.06.1951)
(Site of)

C.W.

Brent New Junction -

5

LOCO
SIDINGS

**WEMBLEY
YARD**

'A' SIDINGS

'C'
SIDINGS

C.W.

LNWR c.1890

LBIR 20.07.1837

LNWR 15.06.1912

WILLESDEN BRENT
SIDINGS

6

'B'
SIDINGS

LBIR 20.07.1837

STONEBRIDGE
PARK (15.06.1912)

LNWR 15.06.1912

North Circular Road

North Circular Road

Continued Right

WILLESDEN
(??.??.1841 – 01.09.1866)

HARLESDEN
(15.06.1912)

A   B   C   D

Scale   Km   0.5   1   1.5   2
0
Miles   ¼   ½   ¾   1

68

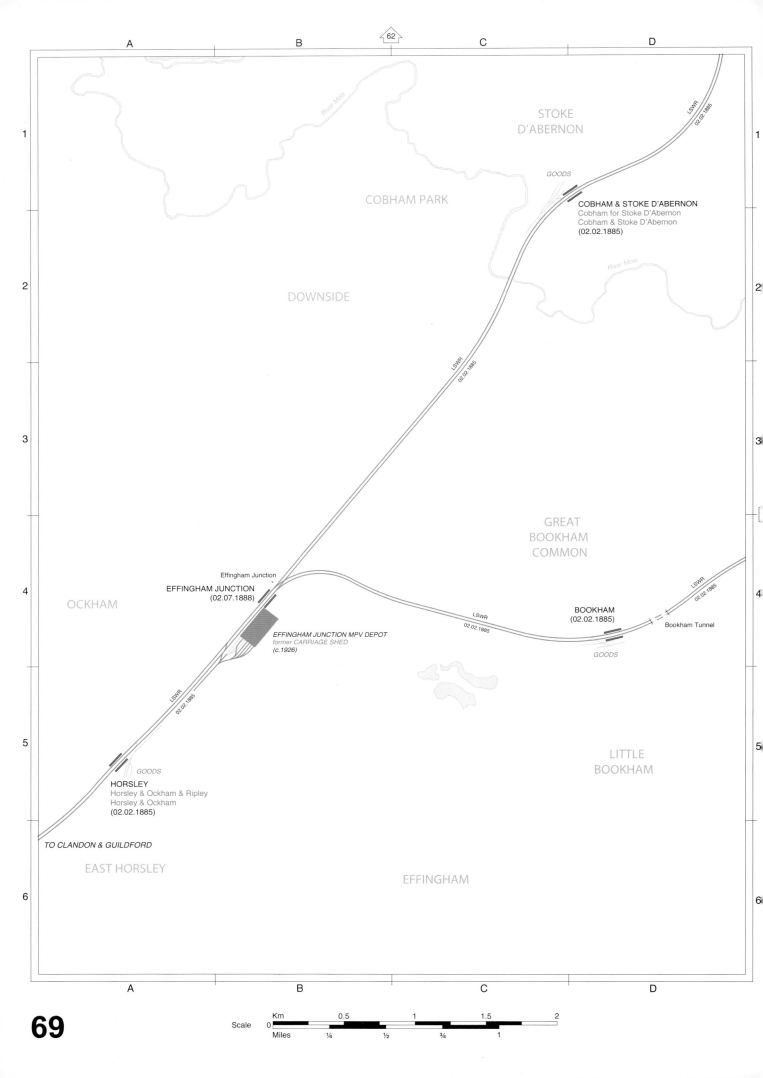

STOKE
D'ABERNON

COBHAM PARK

River Mole

GOODS

LSWR
02.02.1885

COBHAM & STOKE D'ABERNON
Cobham for Stoke D'Abernon
Cobham & Stoke D'Abernon
(02.02.1885)

River Mole

DOWNSIDE

LSWR
02.02.1885

GREAT
BOOKHAM
COMMON

Effingham Junction

EFFINGHAM JUNCTION
(02.07.1888)

OCKHAM

EFFINGHAM JUNCTION MPV DEPOT
former *CARRIAGE SHED*
(c.1926)

LSWR
02.02.1885

BOOKHAM
(02.02.1885)

Bookham Tunnel

LSWR
02.02.1885

GOODS

LSWR
02.02.1885

LITTLE
BOOKHAM

GOODS

HORSLEY
Horsley & Ockham & Ripley
Horsley & Ockham
(02.02.1885)

TO CLANDON & GUILDFORD

EAST HORSLEY

EFFINGHAM

69

Scale

Km
0   0.5   1   1.5   2

Miles
¼   ½   ¾   1

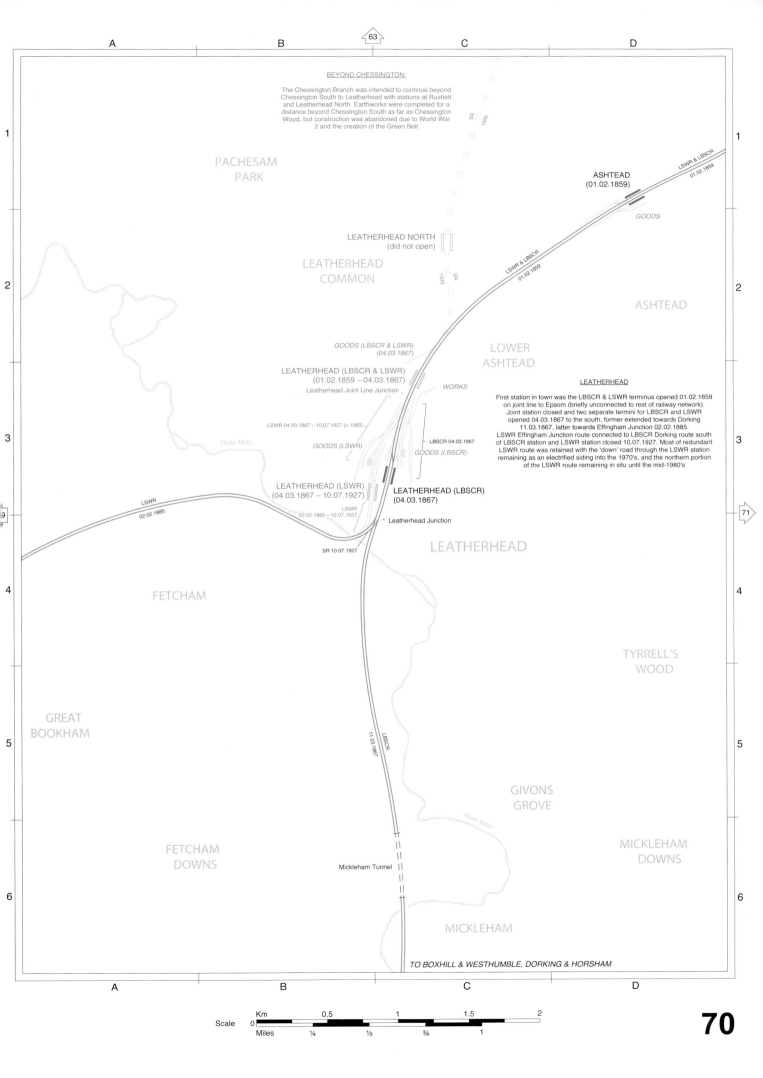

A B C D

1

BEYOND CHESSINGTON:

The Chessington Branch was intended to continue beyond
Chessington South to Leatherhead with stations at Rushett
and Leatherhead North. Earthworks were completed for a
distance beyond Chessington South as far as Chessington
Wood, but construction was abandoned due to World War
2 and the creation of the Green Belt

PACHESAM
PARK

ASHTEAD
(01.02.1859)

LSWR & LBSCR
01.02.1859

GOODS

LEATHERHEAD NORTH
(did not open)

LEATHERHEAD
COMMON

SR 1939

LSWR & LBSCR
01.02.1859

ASHTEAD

2

GOODS (LBSCR & LSWR)
(04.03.1867)

LOWER
ASHTEAD

LEATHERHEAD (LBSCR & LSWR)
(01.02.1859 – 04.03.1867)

Leatherhead Joint Line Junction

WORKS

LEATHERHEAD

First station in town was the LBSCR & LSWR terminus opened 01.02.1859
on joint line to Epsom (briefly unconnected to rest of railway network).
Joint station closed and two separate termini for LBSCR and LSWR
opened 04.03.1867 to the south, former extended towards Dorking
11.03.1867, latter towards Effingham Junction 02.02.1885.
LSWR Effingham Junction route connected to LBSCR Dorking route south
of LBSCR station and LSWR station closed 10.07.1927. Most of redundant
LSWR route was retained with the 'down' road through the LSWR station
remaining as an electrified siding into the 1970's, and the northern portion
of the LSWR route remaining in situ until the mid-1980's

LSWR 04.03.1867 – 10.07.1927 (c.1985)

River Mole

GOODS (LSWR)

LBSCR 04.03.1867

GOODS (LBSCR)

3

LSWR
02.02.1885

LEATHERHEAD (LSWR)
(04.03.1867 – 10.07.1927)

LEATHERHEAD (LBSCR)
(04.03.1867)

LSWR
02.02.1885 – 10.07.1927

Leatherhead Junction

71

LEATHERHEAD

SR 10.07.1927

FETCHAM

4

TYRRELL'S
WOOD

GREAT
BOOKHAM

GIVONS
GROVE

11.03.1867 LBSCR

5

FETCHAM
DOWNS

River Mole

MICKLEHAM
DOWNS

Mickleham Tunnel

6

MICKLEHAM

TO BOXHILL & WESTHUMBLE, DORKING & HORSHAM

A B C D

Scale 0   Km   0.5   1   1.5   2

Miles ¼   ½   ¾   1

70

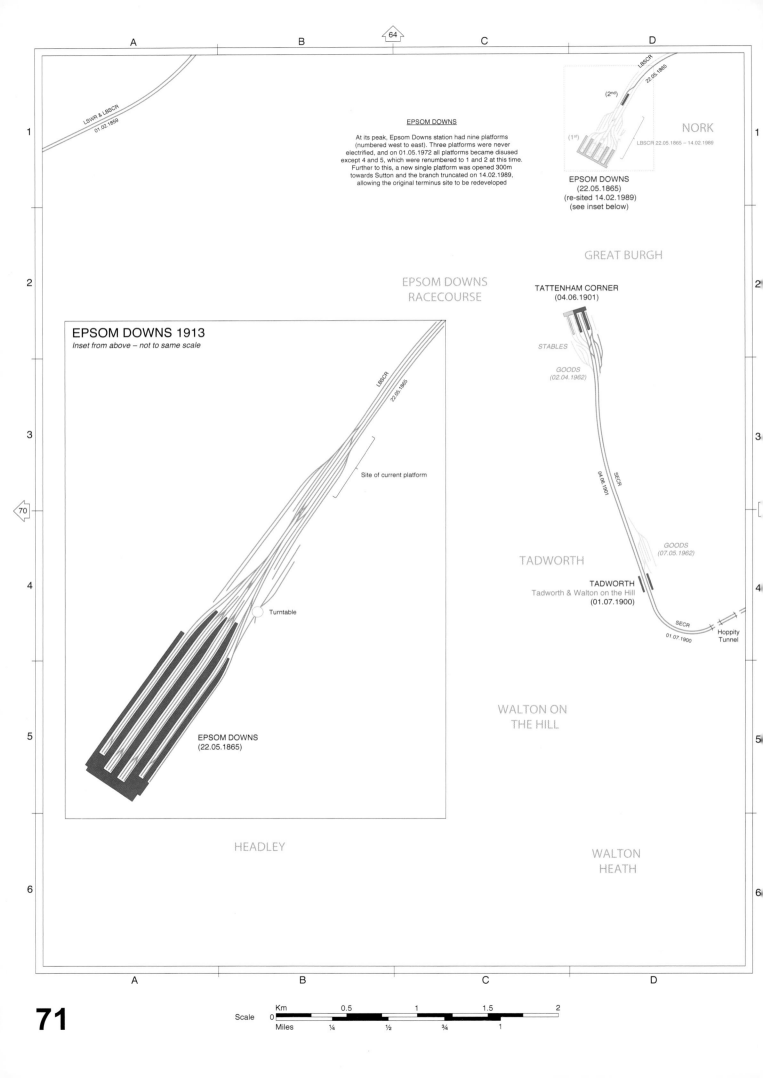

EPSOM DOWNS

At its peak, Epsom Downs station had nine platforms (numbered west to east). Three platforms were never electrified, and on 01.05.1972 all platforms became disused except 4 and 5, which were renumbered to 1 and 2 at this time. Further to this, a new single platform was opened 300m towards Sutton and the branch truncated on 14.02.1989, allowing the original terminus site to be redeveloped

LSWR & LBSCR
01.02.1859

NORK

LBSCR 22.05.1865

(2nd)

(1st)

LBSCR 22.05.1865 – 14.02.1989

EPSOM DOWNS
(22.05.1865)
(re-sited 14.02.1989)
(see inset below)

GREAT BURGH

EPSOM DOWNS
RACECOURSE

TATTENHAM CORNER
(04.06.1901)

STABLES

GOODS
(02.04.1962)

EPSOM DOWNS 1913
Inset from above – not to same scale

LBSCR
22.05.1865

Site of current platform

SECR
04.06.1901

TADWORTH

GOODS
(07.05.1962)

TADWORTH
Tadworth & Walton on the Hill
(01.07.1900)

Turntable

EPSOM DOWNS
(22.05.1865)

SECR
01.07.1900

Hoppity
Tunnel

WALTON ON
THE HILL

WALTON
HEATH

HEADLEY

70

Scale
Km 0   0.5   1   1.5   2
Miles   ¼   ½   ¾   1

HAMMERSMITH / BARONS COURT
From pages 37 & 38

HAMMERSMITH (GROVE ROAD)
(01.01.1869)

HAMMERSMITH (MET / GWR)
(13.06.1864)

GOODS

MDR
01.06.1877

HAMMERSMITH (MDR)
(09.09.1874)

UERL 15.12.1906

MDR 09.09.1874

BARONS COURT
(09.10.1905)

UERL 15.12.1906

MDR 09.09.1874

15.12.1906

HAMMERSMITH (GROVE ROAD)
(01.01.1869 – 05.06.1916)

HAMMERSMITH (MET / GWR)
(13.06.1864)
GOODS (01.02.1960)

UERL
04.07.1932

MDR
01.06.1877

HAMMERSMITH (MDR)
(09.09.1874)

UERL 15.12.1906

MDR 09.09.1874

BARONS COURT
(09.10.1905)

UERL 15.12.1906

MDR 09.09.1874

Sidings / loops for freight trains
entering / leaving West Kensington
Goods Yard

04.07.1932 - Present

WOODMANSTERNE

WOODMANSTERNE
(17.07.1932)

CVR
02.11.1897

GOODS
(07.05.1962)

CHIPSTEAD
Chipstead & Banstead Downs
(02.11.1897)

CVR
02.11.1897

73

HOOLEY

GOODS
(07.05.1962)

KINGSWOOD
Kingswood & Burgh Heath
(02.11.1897)

SECR
01.07.1900

Kingswood
Tunnel

LOWER
KINGSWOOD

CMGR
24.07.1805 –
28.09.1838

CHIPSTEAD VALLEY RAILWAY

Initially an independent company with trains provided by SER (SECR
after 01.01.1899), absorbed by SECR 13.07.1899.
Opened 02.11.1897 between Purley and Kingswood (& Burgh Heath)
with one intermediate stop at Chipstead (& Banstead Downs),
although regular passenger service did not commence until
09.11.1897. Initially a single line, doubling took place during 1899.
Extended to Tadworth (& Walton on the Hill) 01.07.1900, again as a
single track (doubled by November 1900), and finally to Tattenham
Corner 04.06.1901

MUGSWELL

KINGSWOOD

Scale

Km   0   0.5   1   1.5   2

Miles   ¼   ½   ¾   1

72

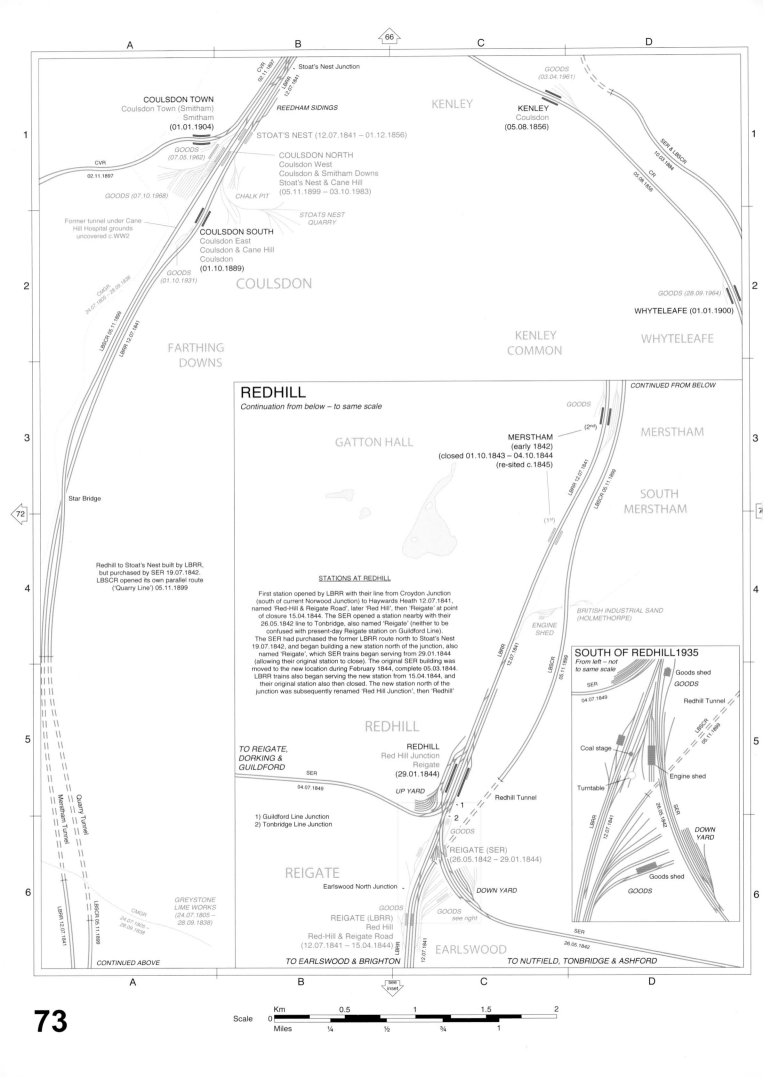

COULSDON TOWN
Coulsdon Town (Smitham)
Smitham
(01.01.1904)

CVR
02.11.1897

Stoat's Nest Junction

REEDHAM SIDINGS

GOODS
(03.04.1961)

KENLEY

KENLEY
Coulsdon
(05.08.1856)

STOAT'S NEST (12.07.1841 – 01.12.1856)

CVR
02.11.1897

GOODS
(07.05.1962)

COULSDON NORTH
Coulsdon West
Coulsdon & Smitham Downs
Stoat's Nest & Cane Hill
(05.11.1899 – 03.10.1983)

SER & LBSCR
10.03.1884

CR
05.08.1856

GOODS (07.10.1968)

CHALK PIT

STOATS NEST QUARRY

Former tunnel under Cane
Hill Hospital grounds
uncovered c.WW2

COULSDON SOUTH
Coulsdon East
Coulsdon & Cane Hill
Coulsdon
(01.10.1889)

GOODS
(01.10.1931)

COULSDON

GOODS (28.09.1964)

WHYTELEAFE (01.01.1900)

CMGR
24.07.1805 – 28.09.1838

LBSCR 05.11.1899

LBRR 12.07.1841

FARTHING
DOWNS

KENLEY
COMMON

WHYTELEAFE

Star Bridge

Redhill to Stoat's Nest built by LBRR,
but purchased by SER 19.07.1842.
LBSCR opened its own parallel route
('Quarry Line') 05.11.1899

REDHILL
Continuation from below – to same scale

CONTINUED FROM BELOW

GOODS

GATTON HALL

MERSTHAM
(early 1842)
(closed 01.10.1843 – 04.10.1844
(re-sited c.1845)

(2nd)

MERSTHAM

LBRR 12.07.1841

LBSCR 05.11.1899

SOUTH
MERSTHAM

(1st)

STATIONS AT REDHILL

First station opened by LBRR with their line from Croydon Junction
(south of current Norwood Junction) to Haywards Heath 12.07.1841,
named 'Red-Hill & Reigate Road', later 'Red Hill', then 'Reigate' at point
of closure 15.04.1844. The SER opened a station nearby with their
26.05.1842 line to Tonbridge, also named 'Reigate' (neither to be
confused with present-day Reigate station on Guildford Line).
The SER had purchased the former LBRR route north to Stoat's Nest
19.07.1842, and began building a new station north of the junction, also
named 'Reigate', which SER trains began serving from 29.01.1844
(allowing their original station to close). The original SER building was
moved to the new location during February 1844, complete 05.03.1844.
LBRR trains also began serving the new station from 15.04.1844, and
their original station also then closed. The new station north of the
junction was subsequently renamed 'Red Hill Junction', then 'Redhill'

BRITISH INDUSTRIAL SAND
(HOLMETHORPE)

ENGINE
SHED

LBRR
12.07.1841

LBSCR
05.11.1899

SOUTH OF REDHILL 1935
From left – not
to same scale

Goods shed
GOODS

Redhill Tunnel

LBSCR
05.11.1899

Coal stage

SER
04.07.1849

Engine shed

Turntable

26.05.1842

DOWN
YARD

LBRR
12.07.1841

Goods shed

GOODS

REDHILL

REDHILL
Red Hill Junction
Reigate
(29.01.1844)

**TO REIGATE,
DORKING &
GUILDFORD**

SER
04.07.1849

UP YARD

LBRR
12.07.1841

LBSCR
05.11.1899

Redhill Tunnel

1
2

GOODS

1) Guildford Line Junction
2) Tonbridge Line Junction

REIGATE (SER)
(26.05.1842 – 29.01.1844)

REIGATE

Earlswood North Junction

DOWN YARD

Merstham Tunnel

Quarry Tunnel

LBRR
12.07.1841

LBSCR
05.11.1899

CMGR
24.07.1805 –
28.09.1838

*GREYSTONE
LIME WORKS*
(24.07.1805 –
28.09.1838)

GOODS

REIGATE (LBRR)
Red Hill
Red-Hill & Reigate Road
(12.07.1841 – 15.04.1844)

GOODS

GOODS
see right

LBRR
12.07.1841

SER
26.05.1842

EARLSWOOD

CONTINUED ABOVE

TO EARLSWOOD & BRIGHTON

TO NUTFIELD, TONBRIDGE & ASHFORD

Scale

Km 0.5 1 1.5 2

Miles ¼ ½ ¾ 1

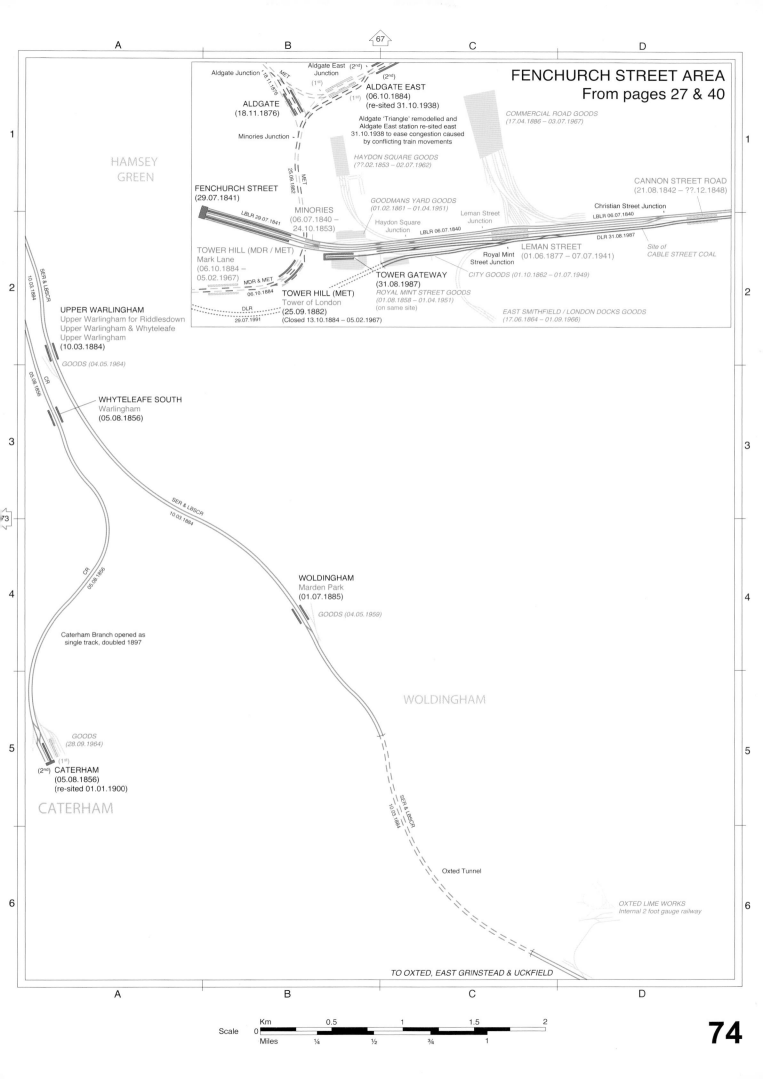

A   B   C   D

1

FENCHURCH STREET AREA
From pages 27 & 40

Aldgate Junction
18.11.1876

MET

Aldgate East (2nd)
Junction
(1st)

(2nd)

ALDGATE EAST
(06.10.1884)
(re-sited 31.10.1938)
(1st)

ALDGATE
(18.11.1876)

Minories Junction

Aldgate 'Triangle' remodelled and
Aldgate East station re-sited east
31.10.1938 to ease congestion caused
by conflicting train movements

COMMERCIAL ROAD GOODS
(17.04.1886 – 03.07.1967)

HAMSEY
GREEN

MET
25.09.1882

HAYDON SQUARE GOODS
(??.02.1853 – 02.07.1962)

CANNON STREET ROAD
(21.08.1842 – ??.12.1848)

FENCHURCH STREET
(29.07.1841)

LBLR 29.07.1841

GOODMANS YARD GOODS
(01.02.1861 – 01.04.1951)

MINORIES
(06.07.1840 –
24.10.1853)

Haydon Square
Junction

Leman Street
Junction

Christian Street Junction

LBLR 06.07.1840

LBLR 06.07.1840

DLR 31.08.1987

Site of
CABLE STREET COAL

TOWER HILL (MDR / MET)
Mark Lane
(06.10.1884 –
05.02.1967)

MDR & MET
06.10.1884

Royal Mint
Street Junction

LEMAN STREET
(01.06.1877 – 07.07.1941)

TOWER GATEWAY
(31.08.1987)

CITY GOODS (01.10.1862 – 01.07.1949)

TOWER HILL (MET)
Tower of London
(25.09.1882)
(Closed 13.10.1884 – 05.02.1967)

DLR
29.07.1991

ROYAL MINT STREET GOODS
(01.08.1858 – 01.04.1951)
(on same site)

EAST SMITHFIELD / LONDON DOCKS GOODS
(17.06.1864 – 01.09.1966)

2

SER & LBSCR
10.03.1884

UPPER WARLINGHAM
Upper Warlingham for Riddlesdown
Upper Warlingham & Whyteleafe
Upper Warlingham
(10.03.1884)

CR
05.08.1856

GOODS (04.05.1964)

WHYTELEAFE SOUTH
Warlingham
(05.08.1856)

73

3

SER & LBSCR
10.03.1884

CR
05.08.1856

4

WOLDINGHAM
Marden Park
(01.07.1885)

GOODS (04.05.1959)

Caterham Branch opened as
single track, doubled 1897

WOLDINGHAM

5

GOODS
(28.09.1964)

(1st)

(2nd) **CATERHAM**
(05.08.1856)
(re-sited 01.01.1900)

CATERHAM

SER & LBSCR
10.03.1884

6

Oxted Tunnel

OXTED LIME WORKS
Internal 2 foot gauge railway

TO OXTED, EAST GRINSTEAD & UCKFIELD

A   B   C   D

Scale
Km 0   0.5   1   1.5   2
Miles ¼   ½   ¾   1

74

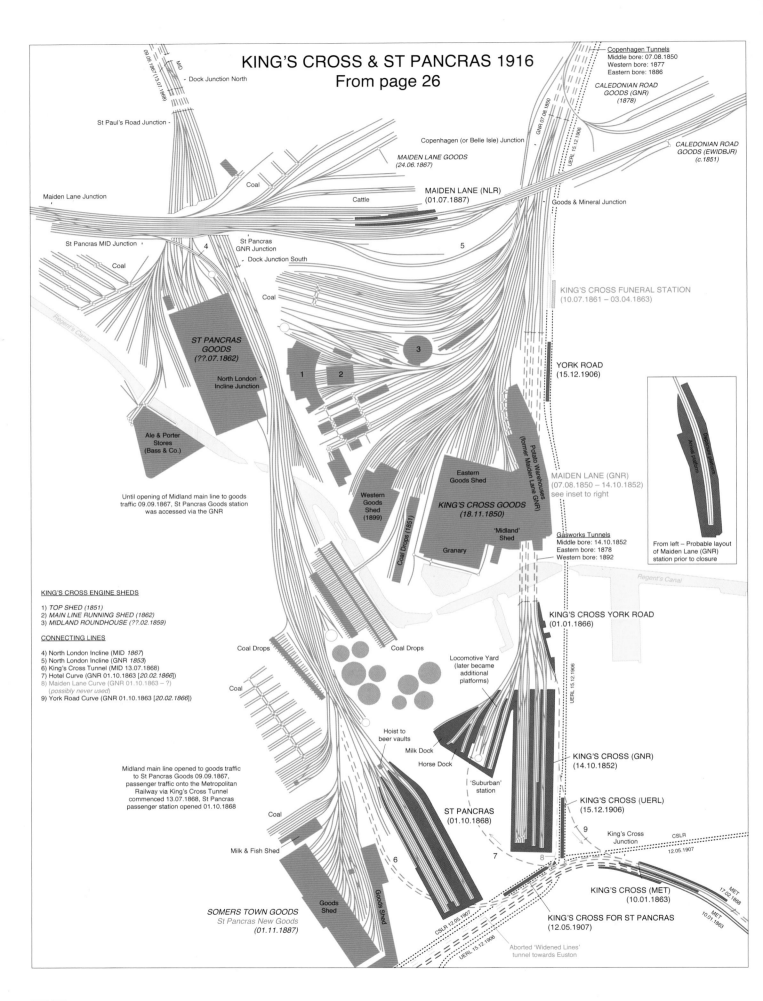

KING'S CROSS & ST PANCRAS 1916
From page 26

09.09.1867 (13.07.1868)

MID

- Dock Junction North

St Paul's Road Junction -

Maiden Lane Junction

Copenhagen (or Belle Isle) Junction

MAIDEN LANE GOODS
(24.06.1867)

Coal

Cattle

St Pancras MID Junction ·

St Pancras
GNR Junction

- Dock Junction South

Coal

4

Coal

5

MAIDEN LANE (NLR)
(01.07.1887)

Goods & Mineral Junction

Copenhagen Tunnels
Middle bore: 07.08.1850
Western bore: 1877
Eastern bore: 1886

*CALEDONIAN ROAD
GOODS (GNR)
(1878)*

GNR 07.08.1850

UERL 15.12.1906

*CALEDONIAN ROAD
GOODS (EWIDBJR)
(c.1851)*

KING'S CROSS FUNERAL STATION
(10.07.1861 – 03.04.1863)

**ST PANCRAS
GOODS
(??.07.1862)**

North London
Incline Junction

Ale & Porter
Stores
(Bass & Co.)

3

1   2

YORK ROAD
(15.12.1906)

Until opening of Midland main line to goods
traffic 09.09.1867, St Pancras Goods station
was accessed via the GNR

Eastern
Goods Shed

Western
Goods
Shed
(1899)

Coal Drops (1851)

KING'S CROSS GOODS
(18.11.1850)

'Midland'
Shed

Granary

Potato Warehouses
(former Maiden Lane GNR)

MAIDEN LANE (GNR)
(07.08.1850 – 14.10.1852)
see inset to right

Gasworks Tunnels
Middle bore: 14.10.1852
Eastern bore: 1878
Western bore: 1892

Regent's Canal

Departure platform

Arrival platform

From left – Probable layout
of Maiden Lane (GNR)
station prior to closure

KING'S CROSS ENGINE SHEDS

1) *TOP SHED (1851)*
2) *MAIN LINE RUNNING SHED (1862)*
3) *MIDLAND ROUNDHOUSE (??.02.1859)*

CONNECTING LINES

4) North London Incline (MID *1867*)
5) North London Incline (GNR *1853*)
6) King's Cross Tunnel (MID 13.07.1868)
7) Hotel Curve (GNR 01.10.1863 [*20.02.1866*])
8) Maiden Lane Curve (GNR 01.10.1863 – ?)
   (possibly never used)
9) York Road Curve (GNR 01.10.1863 [*20.02.1866*])

Coal Drops

Coal Drops

Coal

KING'S CROSS YORK ROAD
(01.01.1866)

UERL 15.12.1906

Locomotive Yard
(later became
additional
platforms)

Midland main line opened to goods traffic
to St Pancras Goods 09.09.1867,
passenger traffic onto the Metropolitan
Railway via King's Cross Tunnel
commenced 13.07.1868, St Pancras
passenger station opened 01.10.1868

Hoist to
beer vaults

Milk Dock

Horse Dock

'Suburban'
station

KING'S CROSS (GNR)
(14.10.1852)

KING'S CROSS (UERL)
(15.12.1906)

9

King's Cross
Junction

CSLR
12.05.1907

Coal

Milk & Fish Shed

ST PANCRAS
(01.10.1868)

6

7

8

KING'S CROSS (MET)
(10.01.1863)

MET
17.02.1868

MET
10.01.1863

SOMERS TOWN GOODS
St Pancras New Goods
(01.11.1887)

Goods
Shed

Goods Shed

CSLR 12.05.1907

UERL 15.12.1906

KING'S CROSS FOR ST PANCRAS
(12.05.1907)

Aborted 'Widened Lines'
tunnel towards Euston

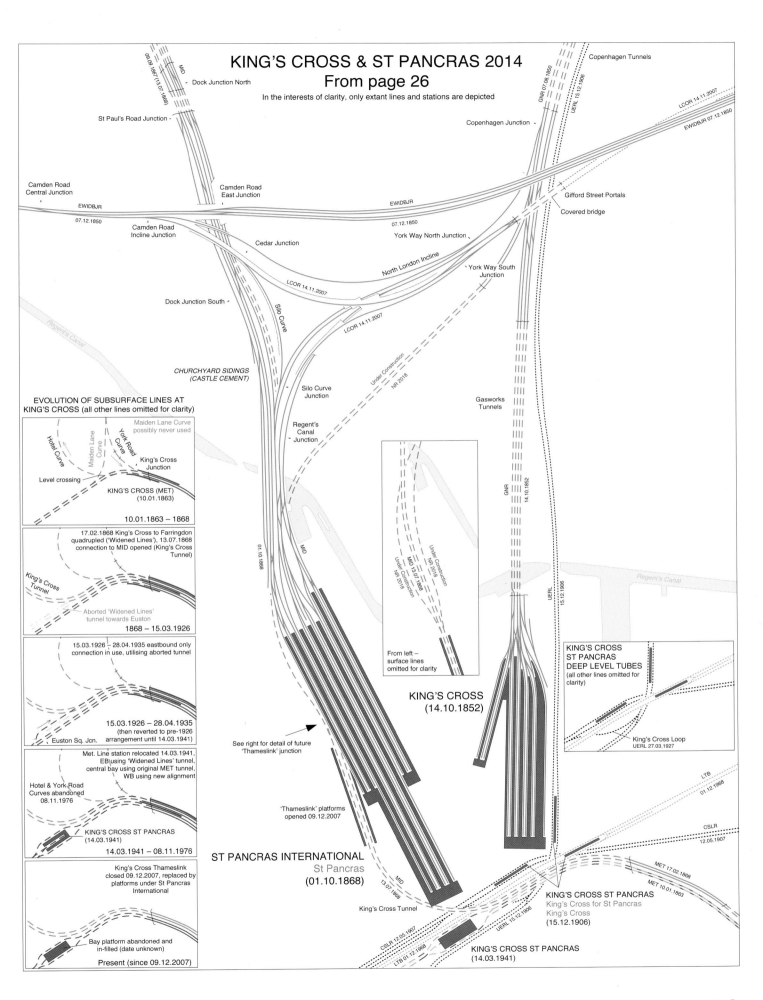

KING'S CROSS & ST PANCRAS 2014
From page 26
In the interests of clarity, only extant lines and stations are depicted

Copenhagen Tunnels

09.09.1867 (13.07.1868)
MID
Dock Junction North
GNR 07.08.1850
UERL 15.12.1906
LCOR 14.11.2007

St Paul's Road Junction

Copenhagen Junction
EWIDBJR 07.12.1850

Camden Road
Central Junction
Camden Road
East Junction
Gifford Street Portals
EWIDBJR
EWIDBJR
Covered bridge

07.12.1850
07.12.1850
York Way North Junction

Camden Road
Incline Junction
Cedar Junction
North London Incline
York Way South
Junction

LCOR 14.11.2007
Dock Junction South
Silo Curve
LCOR 14.11.2007
Under Construction
NR 2018
Gasworks
Tunnels

CHURCHYARD SIDINGS
(CASTLE CEMENT)
Silo Curve
Junction

EVOLUTION OF SUBSURFACE LINES AT
KING'S CROSS (all other lines omitted for clarity)
Regent's
Canal
Junction

Maiden Lane Curve
possibly never used

Hotel Curve
Maiden Lane Curve
York Road Curve
King's Cross
Junction
Level crossing
KING'S CROSS (MET)
(10.01.1863)

10.01.1863 – 1868

17.02.1868 King's Cross to Farringdon
quadrupled ('Widened Lines'), 13.07.1868
connection to MID opened (King's Cross
Tunnel)
King's Cross
Tunnel

Aborted 'Widened Lines'
tunnel towards Euston

1868 – 15.03.1926

15.03.1926 – 28.04.1935 eastbound only
connection in use, utilising aborted tunnel

Under Construction
NR 2018
MID 13.07.1868
Under Construction
NR 2018

From left –
surface lines
omitted for clarity

GNR
14.10.1852

KING'S CROSS
ST PANCRAS
DEEP LEVEL TUBES
(all other lines omitted for
clarity)

Euston Sq. Jcn.

15.03.1926 – 28.04.1935
(then reverted to pre-1926
arrangement until 14.03.1941)

01.10.1868
MID

UERL
15.12.1906

Met. Line station relocated 14.03.1941,
EB using 'Widened Lines' tunnel,
central bay using original MET tunnel,
WB using new alignment

Hotel & York Road
Curves abandoned
08.11.1976

KING'S CROSS
(14.10.1852)

KING'S CROSS ST PANCRAS
(14.03.1941)

14.03.1941 – 08.11.1976

King's Cross Thameslink
closed 09.12.2007, replaced by
platforms under St Pancras
International

See right for detail of future
'Thameslink' junction

'Thameslink' platforms
opened 09.12.2007

ST PANCRAS INTERNATIONAL
St Pancras
(01.10.1868)

King's Cross Tunnel

MID
13.07.1868

King's Cross Loop
UERL 27.03.1927

LTB
01.12.1968

CSLR
12.05.1907

MET 17.02.1868
MET 10.01.1863

KING'S CROSS ST PANCRAS
King's Cross for St Pancras
King's Cross
(15.12.1906)

Bay platform abandoned and
in-filled (date unknown)

Present (since 09.12.2007)

CSLR 12.05.1907
LTB 01.12.1968
UERL 15.12.1906

KING'S CROSS ST PANCRAS
(14.03.1941)

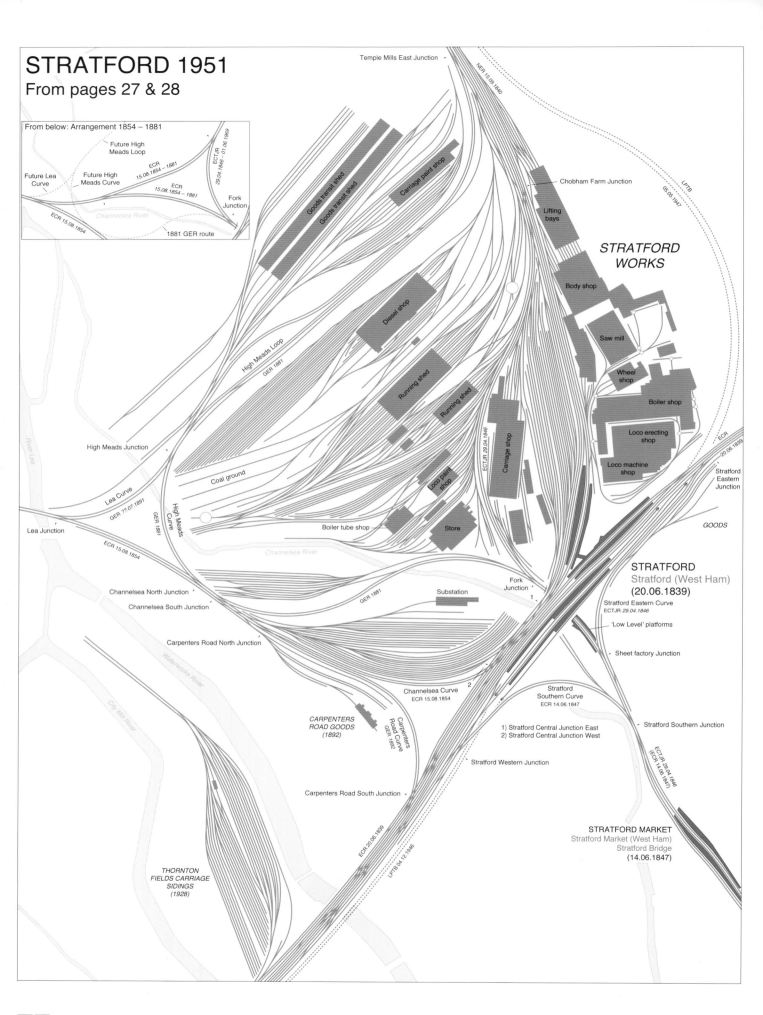

STRATFORD 1951
From pages 27 & 28

From below: Arrangement 1854 – 1881

Future High Meads Loop

Future High Meads Curve

Future Lea Curve

ECR 15.08.1854 – 1881

ECTJR 29.04.1846 – 01.06.1969

ECR 15.08.1854 – 1881

Channelsea River

ECR 15.08 1854

1881 GER route

Fork Junction

Temple Mills East Junction

NER 15.08.1840

LPTB 05.05.1947

Chobham Farm Junction

Lifting bays

STRATFORD WORKS

Goods transit shed

Goods transit shed

Carriage paint shop

Body shop

Saw mill

Diesel shop

Wheel shop

High Meads Loop

GER 1881

Running shed

Running shed

Boiler shop

Loco erecting shop

Loco machine shop

High Meads Junction

Carriage shop

ECTJR 29.04.1846

ECR 20.06.1839

Stratford Eastern Junction

Lea Curve

GER ??.07.1891

Coal ground

Loco paint shop

GER 1881

High Meads Curve

GOODS

Lea Junction

Boiler tube shop

Store

ECR 15.08.1854

Channelsea River

Substation

GER 1881

Fork Junction

1

STRATFORD
Stratford (West Ham)
(20.06.1839)

Channelsea North Junction

Stratford Eastern Curve
ECTJR 29.04.1846

Channelsea South Junction

'Low Level' platforms

Carpenters Road North Junction

Sheet factory Junction

Waterworks River

Channelsea Curve
ECR 15.08.1854

2

Stratford Southern Curve
ECR 14.06.1847

Stratford Southern Junction

City Mill River

CARPENTERS ROAD GOODS
(1892)

Carpenters Road Curve GER 1892

1) Stratford Central Junction East
2) Stratford Central Junction West

ECTJR 29.04.1846 (ECR 14.06.1847)

Carpenters Road South Junction

Stratford Western Junction

ECR 20.06.1839

LPTB 04.12.1946

STRATFORD MARKET
Stratford Market (West Ham)
Stratford Bridge
(14.06.1847)

THORNTON FIELDS CARRIAGE SIDINGS
(1928)

River Lea

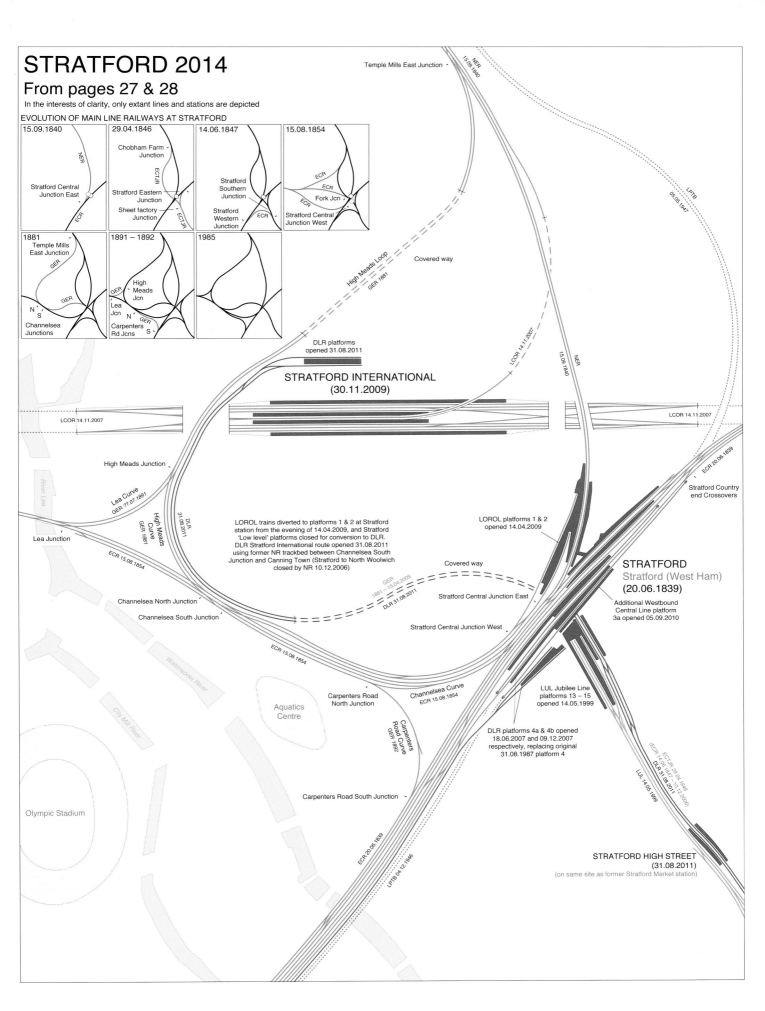

STRATFORD 2014
From pages 27 & 28
In the interests of clarity, only extant lines and stations are depicted

EVOLUTION OF MAIN LINE RAILWAYS AT STRATFORD

15.09.1840
NER
Stratford Central Junction East
ECR

29.04.1846
Chobham Farm Junction
ECT/R
Stratford Eastern Junction
Sheet factory Junction
ECT/R

14.06.1847
Stratford Southern Junction
Stratford Western Junction
ECR
Fork Jcn
ECR

15.08.1854
ECR
ECR
ECR
Fork Jcn
Stratford Central Junction West

1881
Temple Mills East Junction
GER
GER
N S
Channelsea Junctions

1891 – 1892
GER
High Meads Jcn
Lea Jcn
N GER S
Carpenters Rd Jcns

1985

Temple Mills East Junction

NER 15.09.1840

LPTB 05.05.1947

High Meads Loop
GER 1881

Covered way

LCOR 14.11.2007

NER 15.09.1840

DLR platforms
opened 31.08.2011

STRATFORD INTERNATIONAL
(30.11.2009)

LCOR 14.11.2007

LCOR 14.11.2007

ECR 20.06.1839

High Meads Junction

Lea Curve
GER 27.07.1891

High Meads Curve
GER 1881

DLR 31.08.2011

Stratford Country end Crossovers

River Lea

LOROL platforms 1 & 2
opened 14.04.2009

Lea Junction

ECR 15.08.1854

LOROL trains diverted to platforms 1 & 2 at Stratford station from the evening of 14.04.2009, and Stratford 'Low level' platforms closed for conversion to DLR. DLR Stratford International route opened 31.08.2011 using former NR trackbed between Channelsea South Junction and Canning Town (Stratford to North Woolwich closed by NR 10.12.2006)

Covered way

GER 1881 – 15.04.2009
DLR 31.08.2011

STRATFORD
Stratford (West Ham)
(20.06.1839)

Additional Westbound Central Line platform 3a opened 05.09.2010

Channelsea North Junction

Channelsea South Junction

Stratford Central Junction East

Stratford Central Junction West

ECR 15.08.1854

Channelsea Curve
ECR 15.08.1854

LUL Jubilee Line platforms 13 – 15 opened 14.05.1999

Waterworks River

Carpenters Road North Junction

Aquatics Centre

City Mill River

Carpenters Road Curve
GER 1892

DLR platforms 4a & 4b opened 18.06.2007 and 09.12.2007 respectively, replacing original 31.08.1987 platform 4

ECT/R 29.04.1846 / ECR 14.06.1847 / 10.12.2006
DLR 31.08.2011

LUL 14.05.1999

Carpenters Road South Junction

Olympic Stadium

ECR 20.06.1839

LPTB 04.12.1946

STRATFORD HIGH STREET
(31.08.2011)
(on same site as former Stratford Market station)

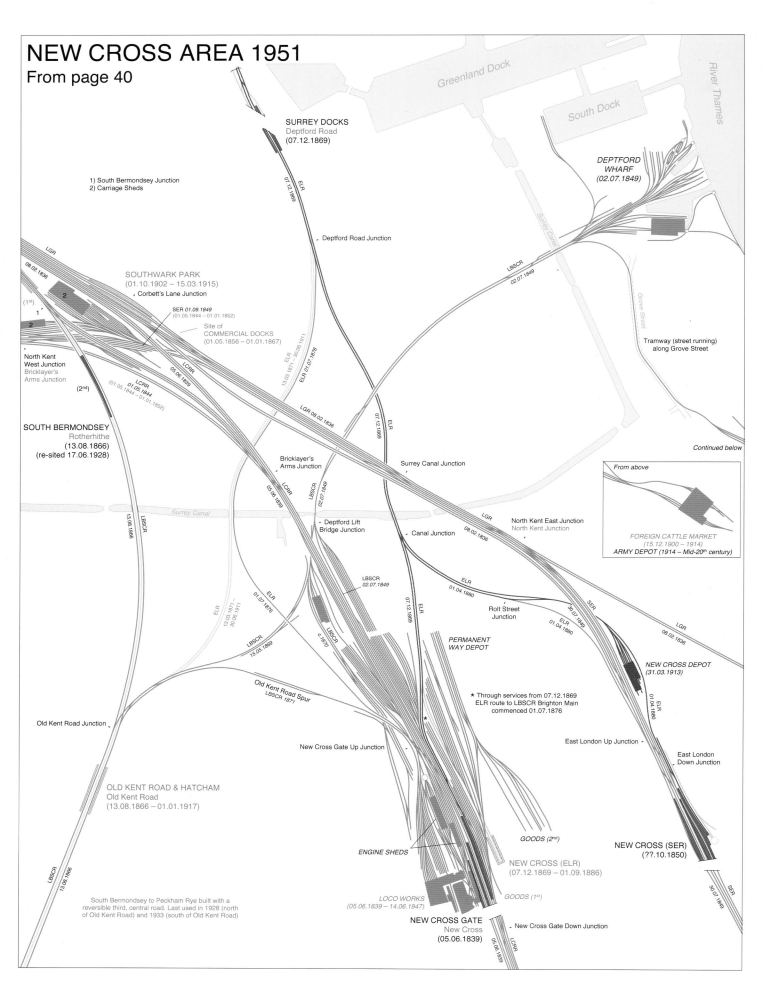

NEW CROSS AREA 1951
From page 40

Greenland Dock

South Dock

River Thames

SURREY DOCKS
Deptford Road
(07.12.1869)

DEPTFORD
WHARF
(02.07.1849)

07.12.1869

ELR

Deptford Road Junction

Surrey Canal

Grove Street

1) South Bermondsey Junction
2) Carriage Sheds

LGR

08.02.1836

(1st)

2

1

2

SOUTHWARK PARK
(01.10.1902 – 15.03.1915)
Corbett's Lane Junction

SER 01.09.1849
(01.05.1844 – 01.01.1852)

Site of
COMMERCIAL DOCKS
(01.05.1856 – 01.01.1867)

LBSCR
02.07.1849

Tramway (street running)
along Grove Street

North Kent
West Junction
Bricklayer's
Arms Junction

(2nd)

LCRR
05.06.1839

ELR 13.03.1871 – 30.06.1911

ELR 01.07.1876

LGR 08.02.1836

07.12.1869 ELR

Continued below

LCRR 01.05.1844
(01.05.1844 – 01.01.1852)

SOUTH BERMONDSEY
Rotherhithe
(13.08.1866)
(re-sited 17.06.1928)

Bricklayer's
Arms Junction

Surrey Canal Junction

From above

LCRR
05.06.1839

LBSCR
02.07.1849

LGR
08.02.1836

North Kent East Junction
North Kent Junction

FOREIGN CATTLE MARKET
(15.12.1900 – 1914)
ARMY DEPOT (1914 – Mid-20th century)

13.08.1866

LBSCR

Surrey Canal

Deptford Lift
Bridge Junction

Canal Junction

ELR 13.03.1871 – 30.06.1911

ELR 01.04.1880

ELR 01.07.1876

LBSCR
02.07.1849

Rolt Street
Junction

30.07.1849

SER

LGR
08.02.1836

01.05.1869 LBSCR

PERMANENT
WAY DEPOT

c. 1870 LBSCR

NEW CROSS DEPOT
(31.03.1913)

01.04.1880 ELR

Old Kent Road Spur
LBSCR 1871

* Through services from 07.12.1869
ELR route to LBSCR Brighton Main
commenced 01.07.1876

Old Kent Road Junction

East London Up Junction

East London
Down Junction

New Cross Gate Up Junction

OLD KENT ROAD & HATCHAM
Old Kent Road
(13.08.1866 – 01.01.1917)

ENGINE SHEDS

GOODS (2nd)

NEW CROSS (SER)
(??.10.1850)

NEW CROSS (ELR)
(07.12.1869 – 01.09.1886)

30.07.1849 SER

13.08.1866 LBSCR

South Bermondsey to Peckham Rye built with a
reversible third, central road. Last used in 1928 (north
of Old Kent Road) and 1933 (south of Old Kent Road)

LOCO WORKS
(05.06.1839 – 14.06.1947)

GOODS (1st)

NEW CROSS GATE
New Cross
(05.06.1839)

New Cross Gate Down Junction

05.06.1839 LCRR

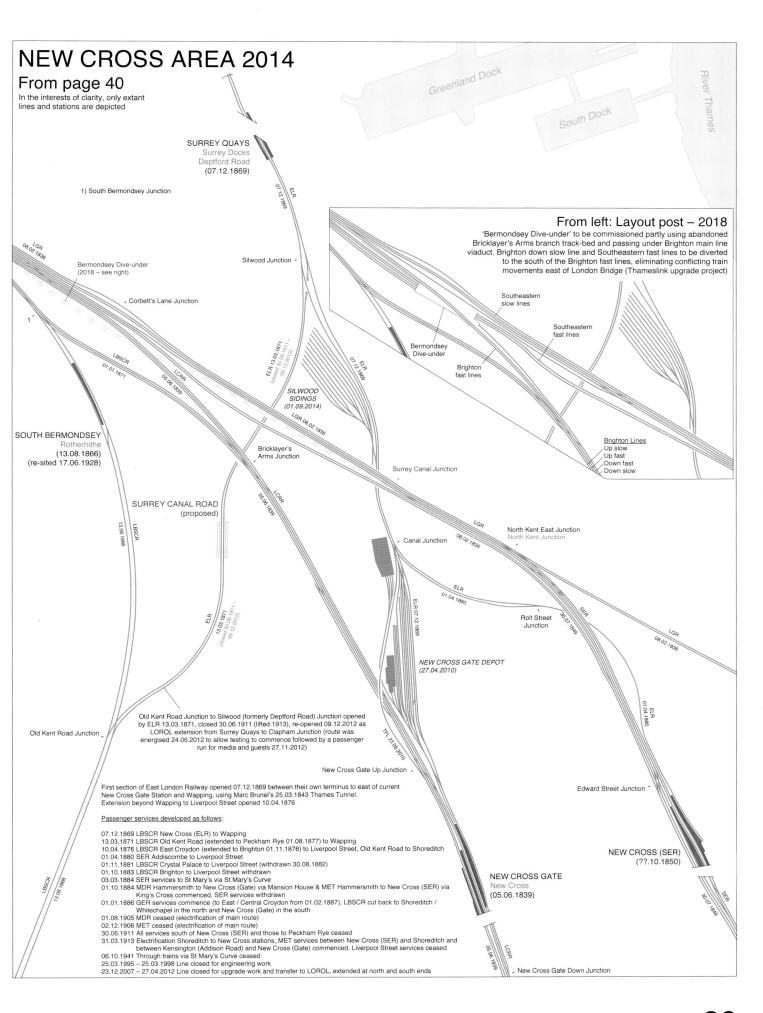

NEW CROSS AREA 2014
From page 40
In the interests of clarity, only extant
lines and stations are depicted

Greenland Dock

South Dock

River Thames

SURREY QUAYS
Surrey Docks
Deptford Road
(07.12.1869)

ELR 07.12.1869

1) South Bermondsey Junction

Silwood Junction

From left: Layout post – 2018
'Bermondsey Dive-under' to be commissioned partly using abandoned
Bricklayer's Arms branch track-bed and passing under Brighton main line
viaduct. Brighton down slow line and Southeastern fast lines to be diverted
to the south of the Brighton fast lines, eliminating conflicting train
movements east of London Bridge (Thameslink upgrade project)

Southeastern
slow lines

Southeastern
fast lines

Bermondsey
Dive-under

Brighton
fast lines

ELR 07.12.1869

Brighton Lines
Up slow
Up fast
Down fast
Down slow

LGR 08.02.1836

Bermondsey Dive-under
(2018 - see right)

Corbett's Lane Junction

LBSCR 01.01.1871

LCRR 05.06.1839

ELR 13.03.1871
(closed 30.06.1911 –
09.12.2012)

LGR 08.02.1836

**SILWOOD
SIDINGS**
(01.09.2014)

Bricklayer's
Arms Junction

Surrey Canal Junction

SOUTH BERMONDSEY
Rotherhithe
(13.08.1866)
(re-sited 17.06.1928)

LBSCR 13.08.1866

SURREY CANAL ROAD
(proposed)

LCRR 05.06.1839

LGR 08.02.1836

North Kent East Junction
North Kent Junction

Canal Junction

ELR 01.04.1880

SER 30.07.1849

LGR 08.02.1836

ELR 07.12.1869

Rolt Street
Junction

ELR 01.04.1880

NEW CROSS GATE DEPOT
(27.04.2010)

ELR 13.03.1871
(closed 30.06.1911 –
09.12.2012)

TFL 23.05.2010

Old Kent Road Junction to Silwood (formerly Deptford Road) Junction opened
by ELR 13.03.1871, closed 30.06.1911 (lifted 1913), re-opened 09.12.2012 as
LOROL extension from Surrey Quays to Clapham Junction (route was
energised 24.06.2012 to allow testing to commence followed by a passenger
run for media and guests 27.11.2012)

Old Kent Road Junction

New Cross Gate Up Junction

Edward Street Junction

First section of East London Railway opened 07.12.1869 between their own terminus to east of current
New Cross Gate Station and Wapping, using Marc Brunel's 25.03.1843 Thames Tunnel.
Extension beyond Wapping to Liverpool Street opened 10.04.1876

Passenger services developed as follows:

07.12.1869 LBSCR New Cross (ELR) to Wapping
13.03.1871 LBSCR Old Kent Road (extended to Peckham Rye 01.08.1877) to Wapping
10.04.1876 LBSCR East Croydon (extended to Brighton 01.11.1876) to Liverpool Street, Old Kent Road to Shoreditch
01.04.1880 SER Addiscombe to Liverpool Street
01.11.1881 LBSCR Crystal Palace to Liverpool Street (withdrawn 30.08.1882)
01.10.1883 LBSCR Brighton to Liverpool Street withdrawn
03.03.1884 SER services to St Mary's via St Mary's Curve
01.10.1884 MDR Hammersmith to New Cross (Gate) via Mansion House & MET Hammersmith to New Cross (SER) via
             King's Cross commenced, SER services withdrawn
01.01.1886 GER services commence (to East / Central Croydon from 01.02.1887), LBSCR cut back to Shoreditch /
             Whitechapel in the north and New Cross (Gate) in the south
01.08.1905 MDR ceased (electrification of main route)
02.12.1906 MET ceased (electrification of main route)
30.06.1911 All services south of New Cross (SER) and those to Peckham Rye ceased
31.03.1913 Electrification Shoreditch to New Cross stations, MET services between New Cross (SER) and Shoreditch and
             between Kensington (Addison Road) and New Cross (Gate) commenced. Liverpool Street services ceased
06.10.1941 Through trains via St Mary's Curve ceased
25.03.1995 – 25.03.1998 Line closed for engineering work
23.12.2007 – 27.04.2012 Line closed for upgrade work and transfer to LOROL, extended at north and south ends

LBSCR 13.08.1866

NEW CROSS (SER)
(??.10.1850)

NEW CROSS GATE
New Cross
(05.06.1839)

SER 30.07.1849

LCRR 05.06.1839

New Cross Gate Down Junction

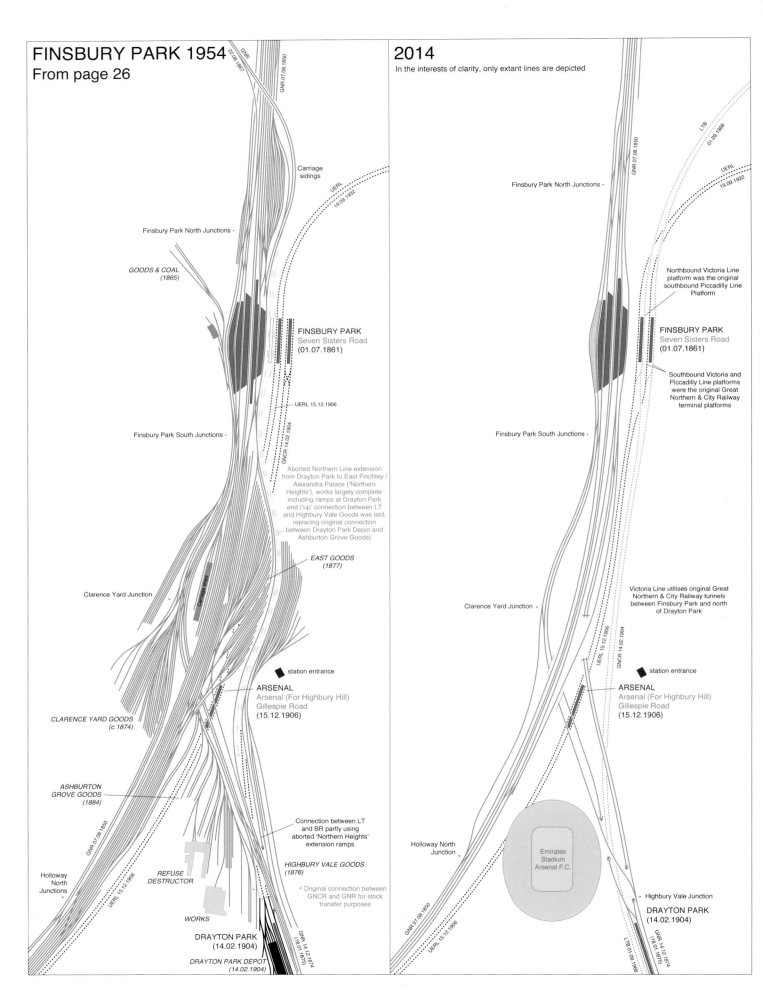

FINSBURY PARK 1954
From page 26

GNR
22.08.1867

GNR
GNR 07.08.1850

Carriage
sidings

UERL
19.09.1932

Finsbury Park North Junctions -

GOODS & COAL
(1865)

FINSBURY PARK
Seven Sisters Road
(01.07.1861)

UERL 15.12.1906

Finsbury Park South Junctions -

GNCR 14.02.1904

Aborted Northern Line extension
from Drayton Park to East Finchley /
Alexandra Palace ('Northern
Heights'), works largely complete
including ramps at Drayton Park
end ('up' connection between LT
and Highbury Vale Goods was laid,
replacing original connection
between Drayton Park Depot and
Ashburton Grove Goods)

EAST GOODS
(1877)

Clarence Yard Junction

Carriage Shed

■ station entrance

ARSENAL
Arsenal (For Highbury Hill)
Gillespie Road
(15.12.1906)

CLARENCE YARD GOODS
(c.1874)

ASHBURTON
GROVE GOODS
(1884)

GNR 07.08.1850

Connection between LT
and BR partly using
aborted 'Northern Heights'
extension ramps

HIGHBURY VALE GOODS
(1876)

Holloway
North
Junctions

UERL 15.12.1906

REFUSE
DESTRUCTOR

* Original connection between
GNCR and GNR for stock
transfer purposes

WORKS

DRAYTON PARK
(14.02.1904)

GNR 14.12.1874
(18.01.1875)

DRAYTON PARK DEPOT
(14.02.1904)

2014
In the interests of clarity, only extant lines are depicted

GNR 07.08.1850

LTB
01.09.1968

UERL
19.09.1932

Finsbury Park North Junctions -

Northbound Victoria Line
platform was the original
southbound Piccadilly Line
Platform

FINSBURY PARK
Seven Sisters Road
(01.07.1861)

Southbound Victoria and
Piccadilly Line platforms
were the original Great
Northern & City Railway
terminal platforms

Finsbury Park South Junctions -

Victoria Line utilises original Great
Northern & City Railway tunnels
between Finsbury Park and north
of Drayton Park

Clarence Yard Junction -

UERL 15.12.1906
GNCR 14.02.1904

■ station entrance

ARSENAL
Arsenal (For Highbury Hill)
Gillespie Road
(15.12.1906)

Holloway North
Junction

Emirates
Stadium
Arsenal F.C.

- Highbury Vale Junction

DRAYTON PARK
(14.02.1904)

GNR 07.08.1850

UERL 15.12.1906

LTB 01.09.1968

GNR 14.12.1874
(18.01.1875)

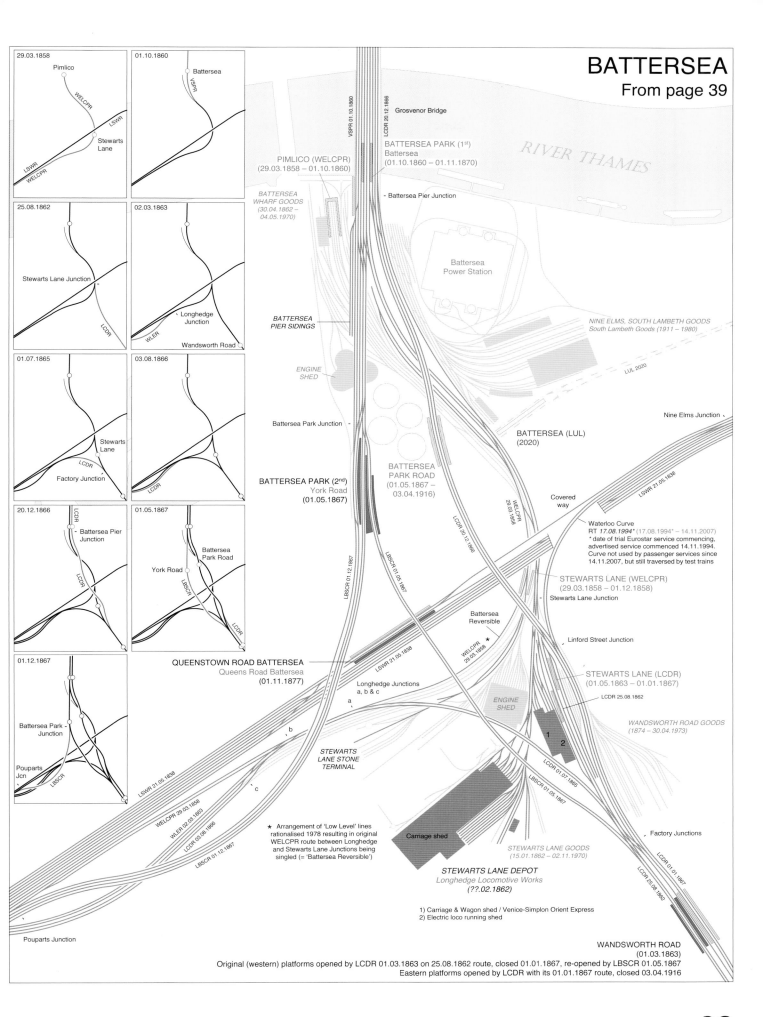

29.03.1858
Pimlico
WELCPR
LSWR
Stewarts Lane
LSWR
WELCPR

01.10.1860
Battersea
VSPR

25.08.1862
Stewarts Lane Junction
LCDR

02.03.1863
Longhedge Junction
WLER
Wandsworth Road

01.07.1865
Stewarts Lane
LCDR
Factory Junction

03.08.1866
LCDR

20.12.1866
LCDR
Battersea Pier Junction
LCDR

01.05.1867
Battersea Park Road
York Road
LBSCR
LCDR

01.12.1867
LCDR
Battersea Park Junction
Pouparts Jcn
LBSCR

RIVER THAMES

VSPR 01.10.1860

LCDR 20.12.1866

Grosvenor Bridge

PIMLICO (WELCPR)
(29.03.1858 – 01.10.1860)

BATTERSEA PARK (1st)
Battersea
(01.10.1860 – 01.11.1870)

- Battersea Pier Junction

BATTERSEA
WHARF GOODS
(30.04.1862 –
04.05.1970)

Battersea Power Station

BATTERSEA
PIER SIDINGS

NINE ELMS, SOUTH LAMBETH GOODS
South Lambeth Goods (1911 – 1980)

ENGINE
SHED

LUL 2020

Battersea Park Junction -

BATTERSEA (LUL)
(2020)

Nine Elms Junction -

BATTERSEA
PARK ROAD
(01.05.1867 –
03.04.1916)

LSWR 21.05.1838

BATTERSEA PARK (2nd)
York Road
(01.05.1867)

LCDR 20.12.1866

WELCPR 29.03.1858

Covered way

Waterloo Curve
RT *17.08.1994** (17.08.1994* – 14.11.2007)
* date of trial Eurostar service commencing,
advertised service commenced 14.11.1994.
Curve not used by passenger services since
14.11.2007, but still traversed by test trains

STEWARTS LANE (WELCPR)
(29.03.1858 – 01.12.1858)

Stewarts Lane Junction

Linford Street Junction

Battersea
Reversible

WELCPR
29.03.1858 *

STEWARTS LANE (LCDR)
(01.05.1863 – 01.01.1867)

LCDR 25.08.1862

WANDSWORTH ROAD GOODS
(1874 – 30.04.1973)

LBSCR 01.12.1867

LBSCR 01.05.1867

QUEENSTOWN ROAD BATTERSEA
Queens Road Battersea
(01.11.1877)

LSWR 21.05.1838

Longhedge Junctions
a, b & c

a

b

STEWARTS
LANE STONE
TERMINAL

c

ENGINE
SHED

1
2

LCDR 01.07.1865

LBSCR 01.05.1867

Factory Junctions

LCDR 01.01.1867

Carriage shed

STEWARTS LANE GOODS
(15.01.1862 – 02.11.1970)

STEWARTS LANE DEPOT
Longhedge Locomotive Works
(??.02.1862)

LCDR 25.08.1862

LSWR 21.05.1838

WELCPR 29.03.1858

WLER 02.03.1863

LCDR 03.08.1866

LBSCR 01.12.1867

★ Arrangement of 'Low Level' lines
rationalised 1978 resulting in original
WELCPR route between Longhedge
and Stewarts Lane Junctions being
singled (= 'Battersea Reversible')

1) Carriage & Wagon shed / Venice-Simplon Orient Express
2) Electric loco running shed

Pouparts Junction

WANDSWORTH ROAD
(01.03.1863)

Original (western) platforms opened by LCDR 01.03.1863 on 25.08.1862 route, closed 01.01.1867, re-opened by LBSCR 01.05.1867
Eastern platforms opened by LCDR with its 01.01.1867 route, closed 03.04.1916

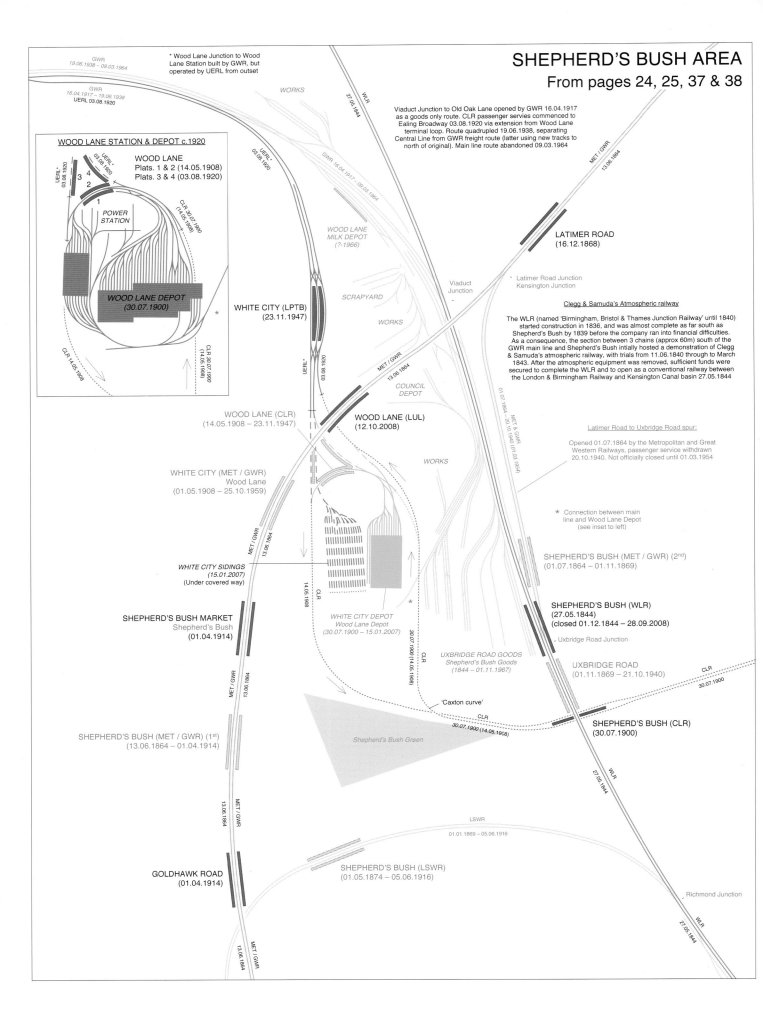

GWR
19.06.1938 – 09.03.1964

GWR
16.04.1917 – 19.06.1938
UERL 03.08.1920

* Wood Lane Junction to Wood
Lane Station built by GWR, but
operated by UERL from outset

WORKS

27.05.1844 WLR

MET / GWR

13.06.1864

Viaduct Junction to Old Oak Lane opened by GWR 16.04.1917
as a goods only route. CLR passenger servies commenced to
Ealing Broadway 03.08.1920 via extension from Wood Lane
terminal loop. Route quadrupled 19.06.1938, separating
Central Line from GWR freight route (latter using new tracks to
north of original). Main line route abandoned 09.03.1964

WOOD LANE STATION & DEPOT c.1920

UERL *
03.08.1920

UERL
03.08.1920

3 4
2
1

WOOD LANE
Plats. 1 & 2 (14.05.1908)
Plats. 3 & 4 (03.08.1920)

POWER
STATION

CLR 30.07.1920
(14.05.1908)

WOOD LANE DEPOT
(30.07.1900)

CLR 30.07.1900
(14.05.1908)

CLR 14.05.1908

GWR 16.04.1917 – 06.03.1964

WOOD LANE
MILK DEPOT
(?-1966)

SCRAPYARD

WORKS

Viaduct
Junction

LATIMER ROAD
(16.12.1868)

Latimer Road Junction
Kensington Junction

Clegg & Samuda's Atmospheric railway

The WLR (named 'Birmingham, Bristol & Thames Junction Railway' until 1840)
started construction in 1836, and was almost complete as far south as
Shepherd's Bush by 1839 before the company ran into financial difficulties.
As a consequence, the section between 3 chains (approx 60m) south of the
GWR main line and Shepherd's Bush intially hosted a demonstration of Clegg
& Samuda's atmospheric railway, with trials from 11.06.1840 through to March
1843. After the atmospheric equipment was removed, sufficient funds were
secured to complete the WLR and to open as a conventional railway between
the London & Birmingham Railway and Kensington Canal basin 27.05.1844

WHITE CITY (LPTB)
(23.11.1947)

MET / GWR
13.06.1864

COUNCIL
DEPOT

UERL
03.08.1920

MET & GWR
01.07.1864 – 20.10.1940 (01.03.1954)

WOOD LANE (CLR)
(14.05.1908 – 23.11.1947)

WOOD LANE (LUL)
(12.10.2008)

WORKS

Latimer Road to Uxbridge Road spur:

Opened 01.07.1864 by the Metropolitan and Great
Western Railways, passenger service withdrawn
20.10.1940. Not officially closed until 01.03.1954

WHITE CITY (MET / GWR)
Wood Lane
(01.05.1908 – 25.10.1959)

MET / GWR
13.06.1864

* Connection between main
line and Wood Lane Depot
(see inset to left)

SHEPHERD'S BUSH (MET / GWR) (2nd)
(01.07.1864 – 01.11.1869)

WHITE CITY SIDINGS
(15.01.2007)
(Under covered way)

CLR
14.05.1908

SHEPHERD'S BUSH (WLR)
(27.05.1844)
(closed 01.12.1844 – 28.09.2008)

SHEPHERD'S BUSH MARKET
Shepherd's Bush
(01.04.1914)

MET / GWR
13.06.1864

WHITE CITY DEPOT
Wood Lane Depot
(30.07.1900 – 15.01.2007)

30.07.1900 (14.05.1908)
CLR

Uxbridge Road Junction

UXBRIDGE ROAD GOODS
Shepherd's Bush Goods
(1844 – 01.11.1967)

UXBRIDGE ROAD
(01.11.1869 – 21.10.1940)

CLR
30.07.1900

SHEPHERD'S BUSH (MET / GWR) (1st)
(13.06.1864 – 01.04.1914)

MET / GWR
13.06.1864

'Caxton curve'

CLR
30.07.1900 (14.05.1908)

Shepherd's Bush Green

SHEPHERD'S BUSH (CLR)
(30.07.1900)

27.05.1844 WLR

MET / GWR
13.06.1864

LSWR
01.01.1869 – 05.06.1916

GOLDHAWK ROAD
(01.04.1914)

SHEPHERD'S BUSH (LSWR)
(01.05.1874 – 05.06.1916)

Richmond Junction

MET / GWR
13.06.1864

27.05.1844 WLR

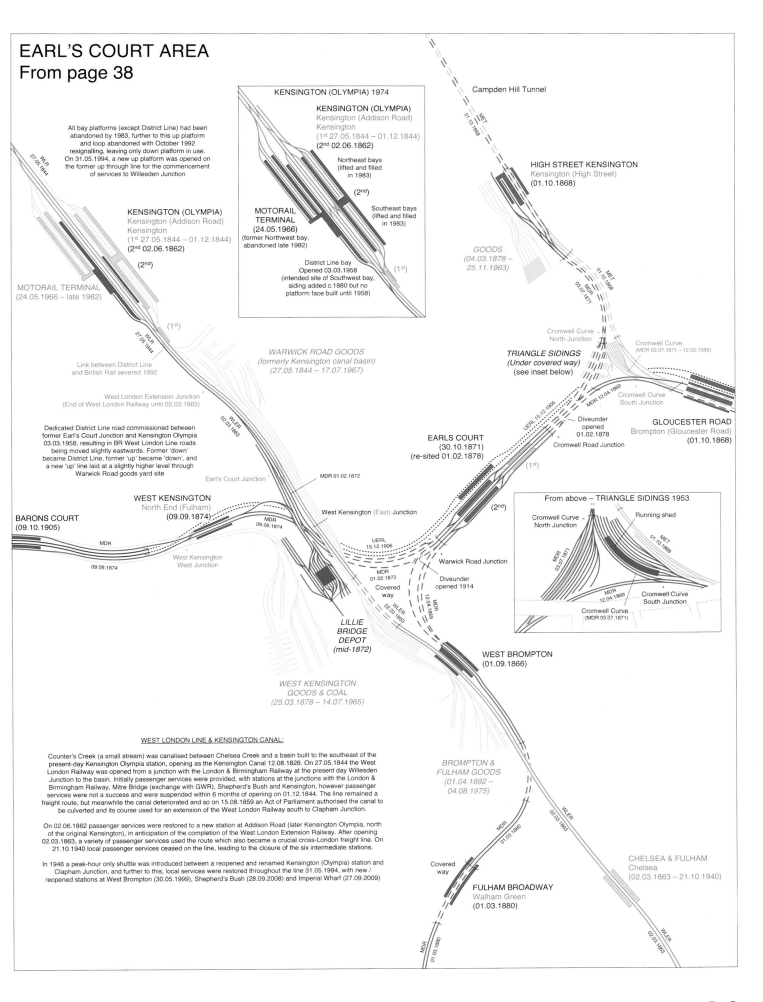

All bay platforms (except District Line) had been abandoned by 1983, further to this up platform and loop abandoned with October 1992 resignalling, leaving only down platform in use. On 31.05.1994, a new up platform was opened on the former up through line for the commencement of services to Willesden Junction

KENSINGTON (OLYMPIA) 1974

KENSINGTON (OLYMPIA)
Kensington (Addison Road)
Kensington
(1st 27.05.1844 – 01.12.1844)
(2nd 02.06.1862)

Campden Hill Tunnel

MET
01.10.1868

HIGH STREET KENSINGTON
Kensington (High Street)
(01.10.1868)

KENSINGTON (OLYMPIA)
Kensington (Addison Road)
Kensington
(1st 27.05.1844 – 01.12.1844)
(2nd 02.06.1862)

Northeast bays
(lifted and filled
in 1983)

(2nd)

MOTORAIL
TERMINAL
(24.05.1966)
(former Northwest bay,
abandoned late 1982)

Southeast bays
(lifted and filled
in 1983)

District Line bay
Opened 03.03.1958
(intended site of Southwest bay,
siding added c.1880 but no
platform face built until 1958)

(1st)

MOTORAIL TERMINAL
(24.05.1966 – late 1982)

(1st)

GOODS
(04.03.1878 –
25.11.1963)

MDR
01.10.1868

MET
01.10.1868

MDR
03.07.1871

27.05.1844
WLR

WLR
27.05.1844

Link between District Line
and British Rail severed 1992

WARWICK ROAD GOODS
(formerly Kensington canal basin)
(27.05.1844 – 17.07.1967)

Cromwell Curve
North Junction

TRIANGLE SIDINGS
(Under covered way)
(see inset below)

Cromwell Curve
(MDR 03.07.1871 – 12.02.1956)

West London Extension Junction
(End of West London Railway until 02.03.1863)

WLER
02.03.1863

UERL 15.12.1906

MDR 12.04.1869

Cromwell Curve
South Junction

GLOUCESTER ROAD
Brompton (Gloucester Road)
(01.10.1868)

Dedicated District Line road commissioned between former Earl's Court Junction and Kensington Olympia 03.03.1958, resulting in BR West London Line roads being moved slightly eastwards. Former 'down' became District Line, former 'up' became 'down', and a new 'up' line laid at a slightly higher level through Warwick Road goods yard site

EARLS COURT
(30.10.1871)
(re-sited 01.02.1878)

Diveunder
opened
01.02.1878

Cromwell Road Junction

Earl's Court Junction

MDR 01.02.1872

(1st)

From above – TRIANGLE SIDINGS 1953

WEST KENSINGTON
North End (Fulham)
(09.09.1874)

West Kensington (East) Junction

(2nd)

Cromwell Curve
North Junction

Running shed

BARONS COURT
(09.10.1905)

MDR
09.09.1874

UERL
15.12.1906

MDR
01.02.1872

MDR
03.07.1871

MET
01.10.1868

MDR
MDR

West Kensington
West Junction

Warwick Road Junction

Diveunder
opened 1914

MDR
12.04.1869

Cromwell Curve
South Junction

09.09.1874

Covered
way

WLER
02.03.1863

MDR
12.04.1869

Cromwell Curve
(MDR 03.07.1871)

LILLIE
BRIDGE
DEPOT
(mid-1872)

WEST BROMPTON
(01.09.1866)

WEST KENSINGTON
GOODS & COAL
(25.03.1878 – 14.07.1965)

WEST LONDON LINE & KENSINGTON CANAL:

Counter's Creek (a small stream) was canalised between Chelsea Creek and a basin built to the southeast of the present-day Kensington Olympia station, opening as the Kensington Canal 12.08.1828. On 27.05.1844 the West London Railway was opened from a junction with the London & Birmingham Railway at the present day Willesden Junction to the basin. Initially passenger services were provided, with stations at the junctions with the London & Birmingham Railway, Mitre Bridge (exchange with GWR), Shepherd's Bush and Kensington, however passenger services were not a success and were suspended within 6 months of opening on 01.12.1844. The line remained a freight route, but meanwhile the canal deteriorated and so on 15.08.1859 an Act of Parliament authorised the canal to be culverted and its course used for an extension of the West London Railway south to Clapham Junction.

On 02.06.1862 passenger services were restored to a new station at Addison Road (later Kensington Olympia, north of the original Kensington), in anticipation of the completion of the West London Extension Railway. After opening 02.03.1863, a variety of passenger services used the route which also became a crucial cross-London freight line. On 21.10.1940 local passenger services ceased on the line, leading to the closure of the six intermediate stations.

In 1946 a peak-hour only shuttle was introduced between a reopened and renamed Kensington (Olympia) station and Clapham Junction, and further to this, local services were restored throughout the line 31.05.1994, with new / reopened stations at West Brompton (30.05.1999), Shepherd's Bush (28.09.2008) and Imperial Wharf (27.09.2009)

BROMPTON &
FULHAM GOODS
(01.04.1892 –
04.08.1975)

WLER
02.03.1863

CHELSEA & FULHAM
Chelsea
(02.03.1863 – 21.10.1940)

MDR
01.03.1880

Covered
way

FULHAM BROADWAY
Walham Green
(01.03.1880)

MDR
01.03.1880

WLER
02.03.1863

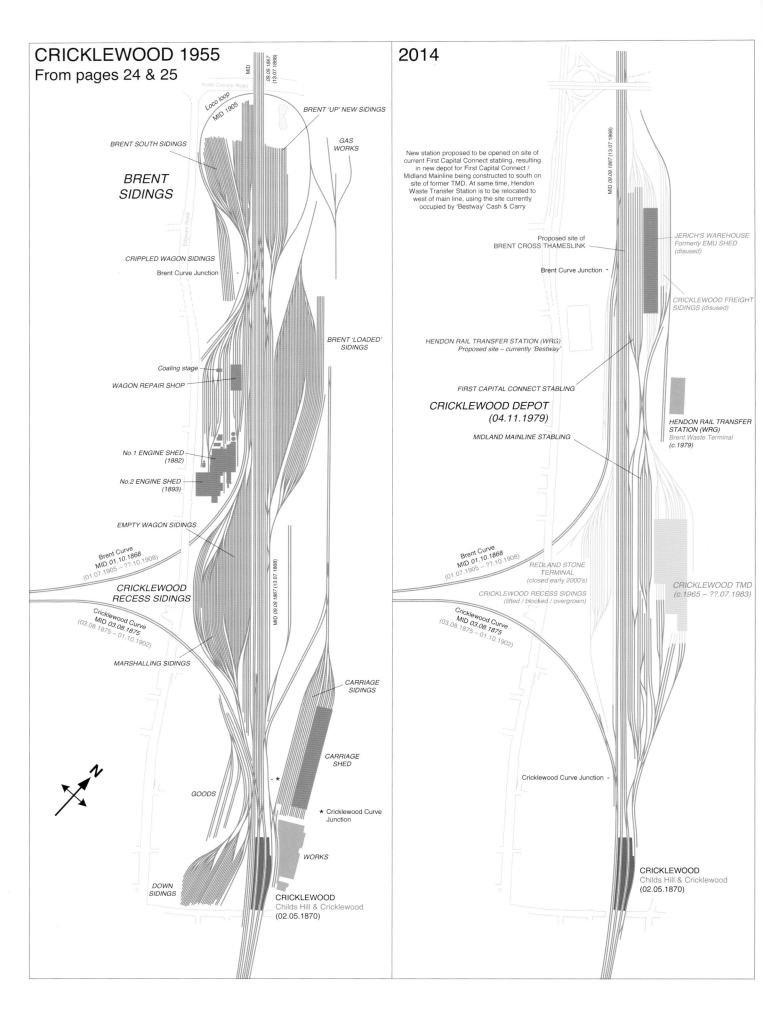

CRICKLEWOOD 1955
From pages 24 & 25

MID

09.09.1867
(13.07.1868)

North Circular Road

Loco loop
MID 1905

BRENT SOUTH SIDINGS

GAS
WORKS

BRENT 'UP' NEW SIDINGS

BRENT
SIDINGS

Edgware Road

CRIPPLED WAGON SIDINGS

Brent Curve Junction

BRENT 'LOADED'
SIDINGS

Coaling stage

WAGON REPAIR SHOP

No.1 ENGINE SHED
(1882)

No.2 ENGINE SHED
(1893)

EMPTY WAGON SIDINGS

MID 09.09.1867 (13.07.1868)

Brent Curve
MID 01.10.1868
(01.07.1905 – ??.10.1908)

CRICKLEWOOD
RECESS SIDINGS

Cricklewood Curve
MID 03.08.1875
(03.08.1875 – 01.10.1902)

MARSHALLING SIDINGS

N

CARRIAGE
SIDINGS

CARRIAGE
SHED

*

★ Cricklewood Curve
Junction

GOODS

WORKS

DOWN
SIDINGS

CRICKLEWOOD
Childs Hill & Cricklewood
(02.05.1870)

2014

New station proposed to be opened on site of
current First Capital Connect stabling, resulting
in new depot for First Capital Connect /
Midland Mainline being constructed to south on
site of former TMD. At same time, Hendon
Waste Transfer Station is to be relocated to
west of main line, using the site currently
occupied by 'Bestway' Cash & Carry

MID 09.09.1867 (13.07.1868)

Proposed site of
BRENT CROSS THAMESLINK

JERICH'S WAREHOUSE
Formerly EMU SHED
(disused)

Brent Curve Junction

CRICKLEWOOD FREIGHT
SIDINGS (disused)

HENDON RAIL TRANSFER STATION (WRG)
Proposed site – currently 'Bestway'

FIRST CAPITAL CONNECT STABLING

HENDON RAIL TRANSFER
STATION (WRG)
Brent Waste Terminal
(c.1979)

CRICKLEWOOD DEPOT
(04.11.1979)

MIDLAND MAINLINE STABLING

Brent Curve
MID 01.10.1868
(01.07.1905 – ??.10.1908)

REDLAND STONE
TERMINAL
(closed early 2000's)

CRICKLEWOOD RECESS SIDINGS
(lifted / blocked / overgrown)

CRICKLEWOOD TMD
(c.1965 – ??.07.1983)

Cricklewood Curve
MID 03.08.1875
(03.08.1875 – 01.10.1902)

Cricklewood Curve Junction

CRICKLEWOOD
Childs Hill & Cricklewood
(02.05.1870)

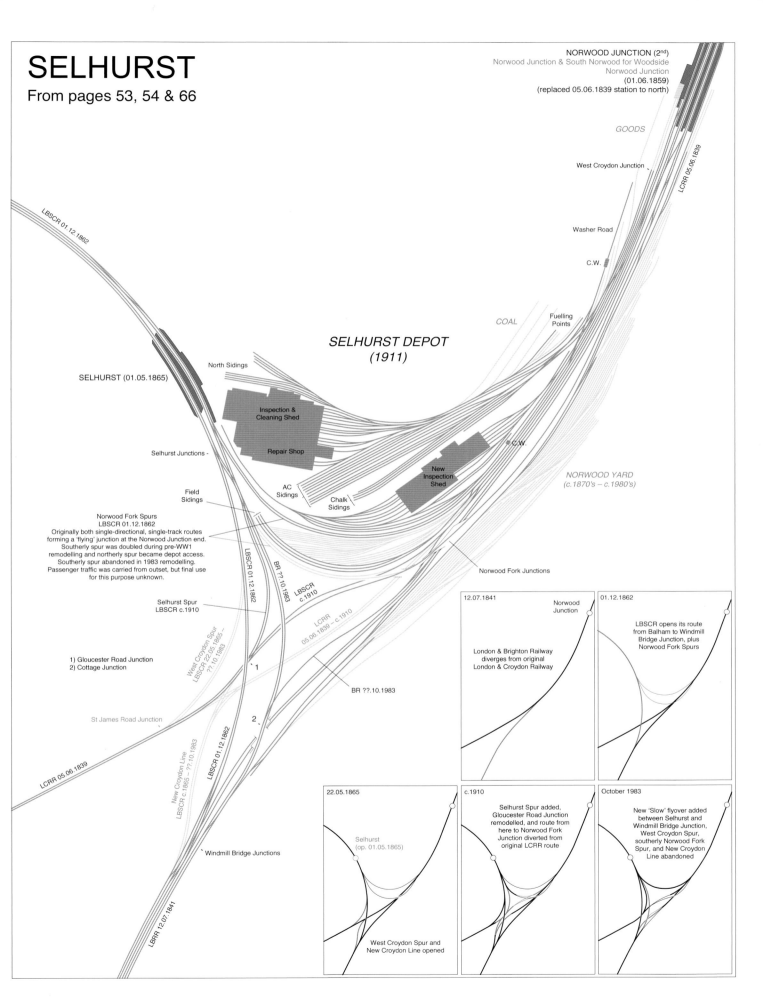

SELHURST

From pages 53, 54 & 66

GOODS

West Croydon Junction

Washer Road

C.W.

COAL

Fuelling
Points

SELHURST DEPOT
(1911)

North Sidings

SELHURST (01.05.1865)

Inspection &
Cleaning Shed

Repair Shop

Selhurst Junctions -

AC
Sidings

Chalk
Sidings

New
Inspection
Shed

C.W.

NORWOOD YARD
(c.1870's – c.1980's)

Field
Sidings

Norwood Fork Spurs
LBSCR 01.12.1862
Originally both single-directional, single-track routes
forming a 'flying' junction at the Norwood Junction end.
Southerly spur was doubled during pre-WW1
remodelling and northerly spur became depot access.
Southerly spur abandoned in 1983 remodelling.
Passenger traffic was carried from outset, but final use
for this purpose unknown.

Norwood Fork Junctions

Selhurst Spur
LBSCR c.1910

1) Gloucester Road Junction
2) Cottage Junction

St James Road Junction

Windmill Bridge Junctions

12.07.1841		01.12.1862
London & Brighton Railway diverges from original London & Croydon Railway	Norwood Junction	LBSCR opens its route from Balham to Windmill Bridge Junction, plus Norwood Fork Spurs

22.05.1865	c.1910	October 1983
Selhurst (op. 01.05.1865)	Selhurst Spur added, Gloucester Road Junction remodelled, and route from here to Norwood Fork Junction diverted from original LCRR route	New 'Slow' flyover added between Selhurst and Windmill Bridge Junction, West Croydon Spur, southerly Norwood Fork Spur, and New Croydon Line abandoned
West Croydon Spur and New Croydon Line opened		

86

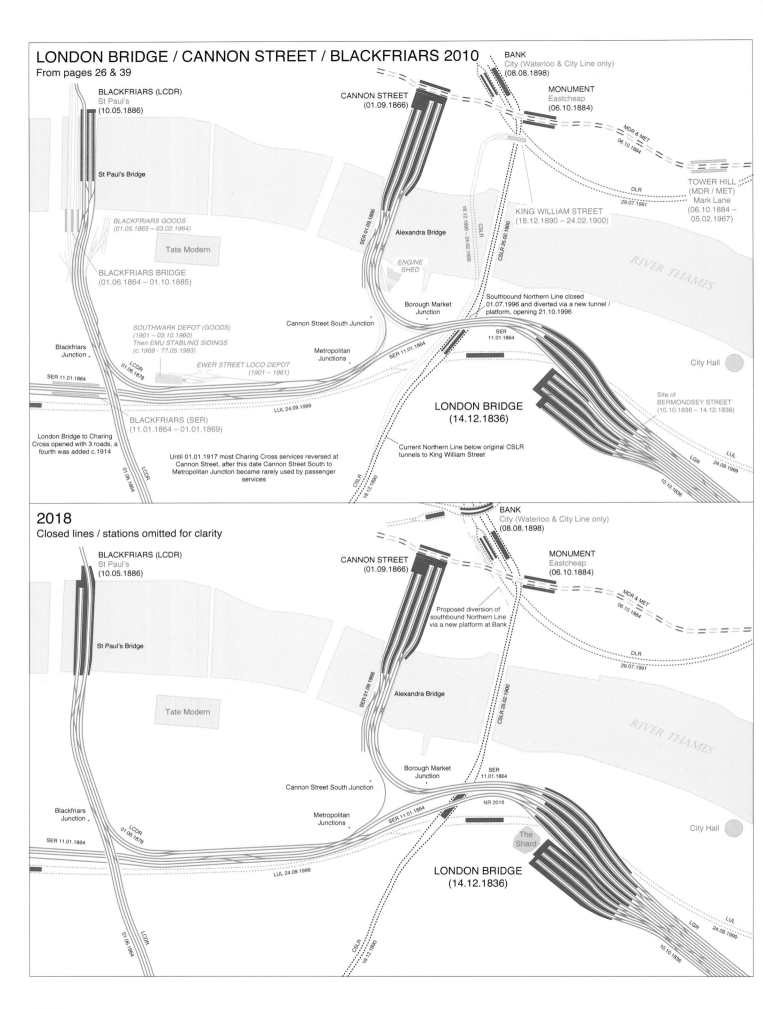

LONDON BRIDGE / CANNON STREET / BLACKFRIARS 2010
From pages 26 & 39

BANK
City (Waterloo & City Line only)
(08.08.1898)

BLACKFRIARS (LCDR)
St Paul's
(10.05.1886)

CANNON STREET
(01.09.1866)

MONUMENT
Eastcheap
(06.10.1884)

St Paul's Bridge

MDR & MET
06.10.1884

TOWER HILL
(MDR / MET)
Mark Lane
(06.10.1884 –
05.02.1967)

DLR
29.07.1991

BLACKFRIARS GOODS
(01.05.1865 – 03.02.1964)

Tate Modern

KING WILLIAM STREET
(18.12.1890 – 24.02.1900)

Alexandra Bridge

ENGINE
SHED

RIVER THAMES

BLACKFRIARS BRIDGE
(01.06.1864 – 01.10.1885)

Borough Market
Junction

Cannon Street South Junction

Southbound Northern Line closed
01.07.1996 and diverted via a new tunnel /
platform, opening 21.10.1996

SER
11.01.1864

City Hall

Blackfriars
Junction

SOUTHWARK DEPOT (GOODS)
(1901 – 03.10.1960)
Then EMU STABLING SIDINGS
(c.1969 - ??.05.1983)

Metropolitan
Junctions

SER 11.01.1864

Site of
BERMONDSEY STREET
(10.10.1836 – 14.12.1836)

LCDR
01.06.1878

EWER STREET LOCO DEPOT
(1901 – 1961)

LONDON BRIDGE
(14.12.1836)

LUL
24.09.1999

SER 11.01.1864

LUL 24.09.1999

BLACKFRIARS (SER)
(11.01.1864 – 01.01.1869)

London Bridge to Charing
Cross opened with 3 roads, a
fourth was added c.1914

Until 01.01.1917 most Charing Cross services reversed at
Cannon Street, after this date Cannon Street South to
Metropolitan Junction became rarely used by passenger
services

Current Northern Line below original CSLR
tunnels to King William Street

LGR
10.10.1836

01.06.1864

CSLR
18.12.1890

2018
Closed lines / stations omitted for clarity

BANK
City (Waterloo & City Line only)
(08.08.1898)

BLACKFRIARS (LCDR)
St Paul's
(10.05.1886)

CANNON STREET
(01.09.1866)

MONUMENT
Eastcheap
(06.10.1884)

St Paul's Bridge

Proposed diversion of
southbound Northern Line
via a new platform at Bank

MDR & MET
06.10.1884

DLR
29.07.1991

Tate Modern

Alexandra Bridge

RIVER THAMES

Borough Market
Junction

SER
11.01.1864

Cannon Street South Junction

Blackfriars
Junction

Metropolitan
Junctions

SER 11.01.1864

NR 2018

City Hall

LCDR
01.06.1878

The
Shard

SER 11.01.1864

LUL 24.09.1999

LONDON BRIDGE
(14.12.1836)

LUL
24.09.1999

LGR
10.10.1836

01.06.1864

CSLR
18.12.1890

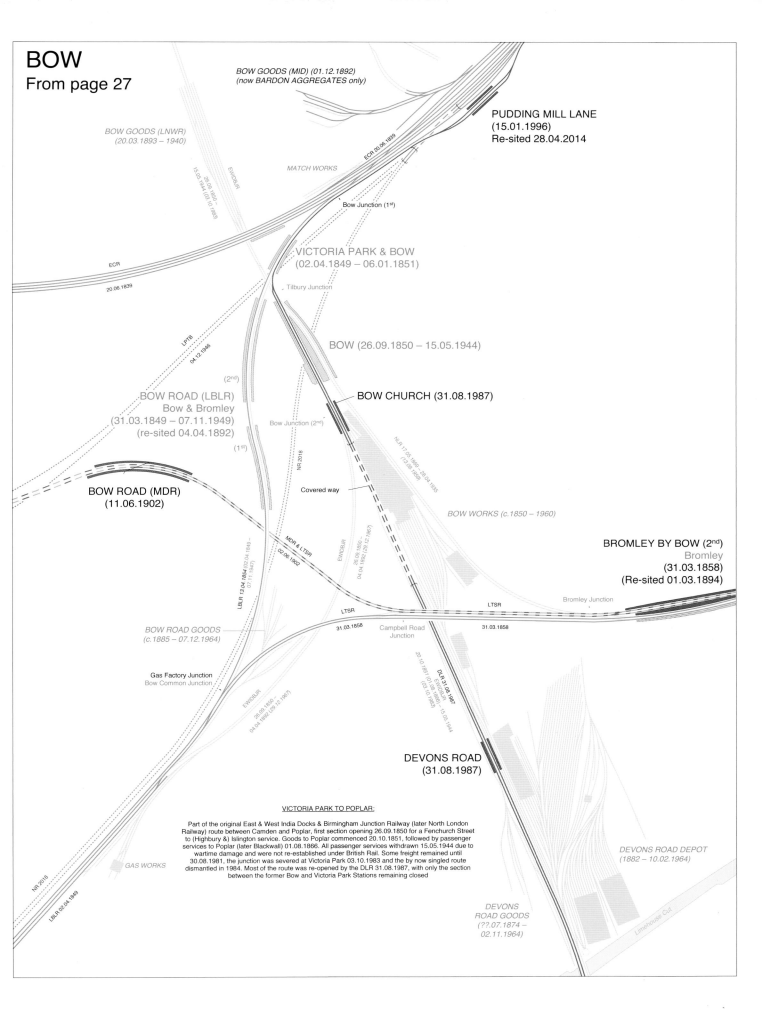

BOW
From page 27

BOW GOODS (MID) (01.12.1892)
(now BARDON AGGREGATES only)

PUDDING MILL LANE
(15.01.1996)
Re-sited 28.04.2014

BOW GOODS (LNWR)
(20.03.1893 – 1940)

MATCH WORKS

ECR 20.06.1839

ECR

20.06.1839

Bow Junction (1st)

VICTORIA PARK & BOW
(02.04.1849 – 06.01.1851)

Tilbury Junction

LPTB

04.12.1946

BOW (26.09.1850 – 15.05.1944)

(2nd)

BOW ROAD (LBLR)
Bow & Bromley
(31.03.1849 – 07.11.1949)
(re-sited 04.04.1892)

BOW CHURCH (31.08.1987)

Bow Junction (2nd)

(1st)

NR 2018

Covered way

BOW ROAD (MDR)
(11.06.1902)

BOW WORKS (c.1850 – 1960)

BROMLEY BY BOW (2nd)
Bromley
(31.03.1858)
(Re-sited 01.03.1894)

MDR & LTSR

02.06.1902

EWIDBJR
26.09.1850 –
04.04.1892 (29.12.1967)

LBLR 13.04.1854 (02.04.1849 –
07.11.1947)

Bromley Junction

LTSR

LTSR

31.03.1858

Campbell Road
Junction

31.03.1858

BOW ROAD GOODS
(c.1885 – 07.12.1964)

Gas Factory Junction
Bow Common Junction

EWIDBJR
26.09.1850 –
04.04.1892 (29.12.1967)

DLR 31.08.1987
EWIDBJR
20.10.1851 (01.08.1866) –
(03.10.1983)
15.05.1944

DEVONS ROAD
(31.08.1987)

VICTORIA PARK TO POPLAR:

Part of the original East & West India Docks & Birmingham Junction Railway (later North London
Railway) route between Camden and Poplar, first section opening 26.09.1850 for a Fenchurch Street
to (Highbury &) Islington service. Goods to Poplar commenced 20.10.1851, followed by passenger
services to Poplar (later Blackwall) 01.08.1866. All passenger services withdrawn 15.05.1944 due to
wartime damage and were not re-established under British Rail. Some freight remained until
30.08.1981, the junction was severed at Victoria Park 03.10.1983 and the by now singled route
dismantled in 1984. Most of the route was re-opened by the DLR 31.08.1987, with only the section
between the former Bow and Victoria Park Stations remaining closed

GAS WORKS

NR 2018

LBLR 02.04.1849

DEVONS ROAD DEPOT
(1882 – 10.02.1964)

DEVONS
ROAD GOODS
(??.07.1874 –
02.11.1964)

Limehouse Cut

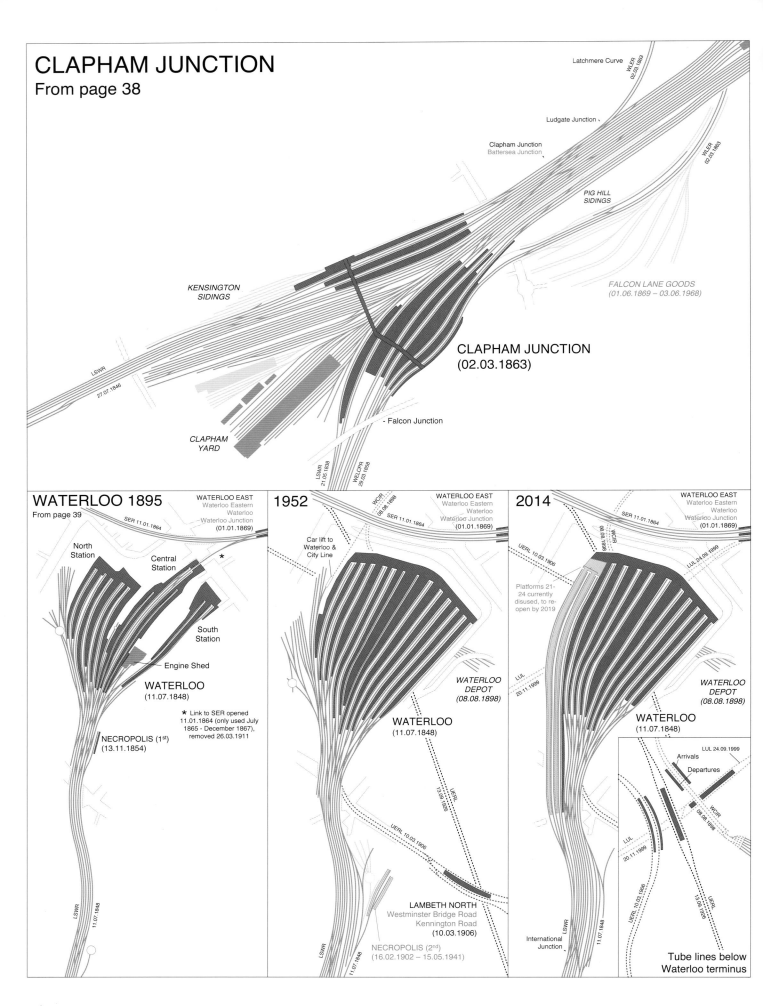

CLAPHAM JUNCTION
From page 38

Latchmere Curve

WLER 02.03.1863

Ludgate Junction

Clapham Junction
Battersea Junction

WLER 02.03.1863

PIG HILL
SIDINGS

*KENSINGTON
SIDINGS*

*FALCON LANE GOODS
(01.06.1869 – 03.06.1968)*

**CLAPHAM JUNCTION
(02.03.1863)**

LSWR 27.07.1846

- Falcon Junction

*CLAPHAM
YARD*

LSWR 21.05.1838

WELCPR 29.03.1858

WATERLOO 1895
From page 39

WATERLOO EAST
Waterloo Eastern
Waterloo
Waterloo Junction
(01.01.1869)

SER 11.01.1864

North
Station

Central
Station

★

South
Station

Engine Shed

**WATERLOO
(11.07.1848)**

★ Link to SER opened
11.01.1864 (only used July
1865 - December 1867),
removed 26.03.1911

NECROPOLIS (1st)
(13.11.1854)

LSWR 11.07.1848

1952

WCIR 08.08.1898

WATERLOO EAST
Waterloo Eastern
Waterloo
Waterloo Junction
(01.01.1869)

SER 11.01.1864

Car lift to
Waterloo &
City Line

*WATERLOO
DEPOT
(08.08.1898)*

**WATERLOO
(11.07.1848)**

UERL 13.09.1926

UERL 10.03.1906

LAMBETH NORTH
Westminster Bridge Road
Kennington Road
(10.03.1906)

NECROPOLIS (2nd)
(16.02.1902 – 15.05.1941)

LSWR 11.07.1848

2014

WATERLOO EAST
Waterloo Eastern
Waterloo
Waterloo Junction
(01.01.1869)

SER 11.01.1864

WCIR 08.08.1898

UERL 10.03.1906

LUL 24.09.1999

Platforms 21-
24 currently
disused, to re-
open by 2019

*WATERLOO
DEPOT
(08.08.1898)*

LUL 20.11.1999

**WATERLOO
(11.07.1848)**

International
Junction

LSWR 11.07.1848

LUL 24.09.1999

Arrivals

Departures

WCIR 08.08.1898

LUL 20.11.1999

UERL 10.03.1906

UERL 13.09.1926

Tube lines below
Waterloo terminus

89

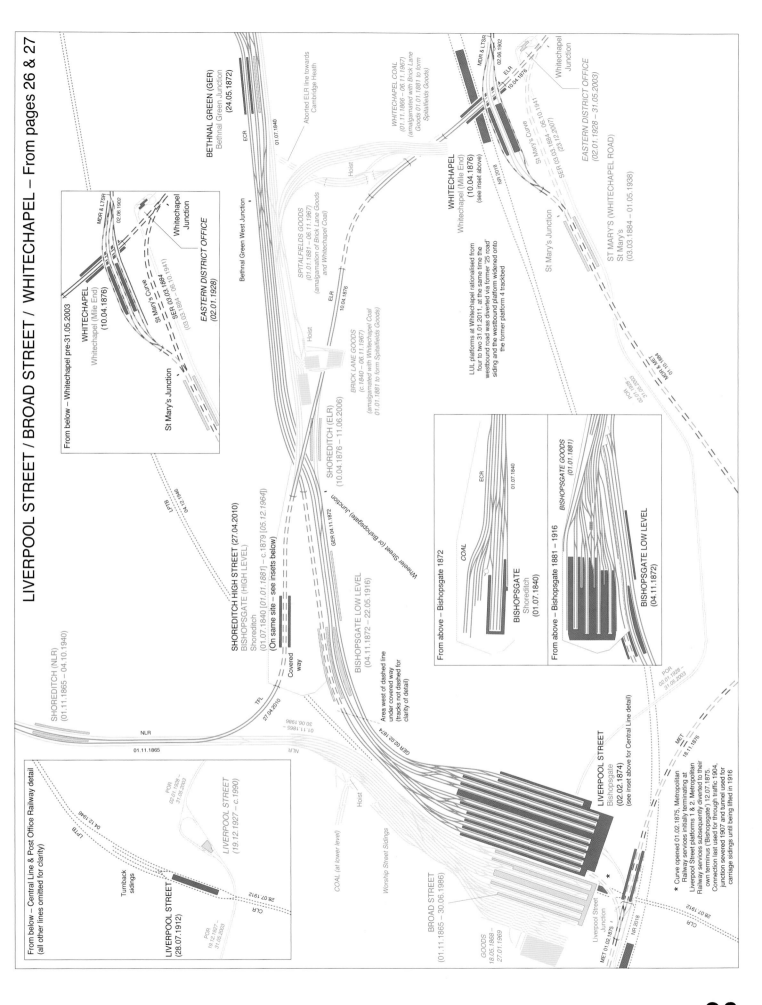

LIVERPOOL STREET / BROAD STREET / WHITECHAPEL – From pages 26 & 27

From below – Whitechapel pre-31.05.2003

WHITECHAPEL
Whitechapel (Mile End)
(10.04.1876)

MDR & LTSR
02.06.1902

Whitechapel Junction

St Mary's Curve
SER 03.03.1884
(03.03.1884 – 06.10.1941)

St Mary's Junction

EASTERN DISTRICT OFFICE
(02.01.1928)

BETHNAL GREEN (GER)
Bethnal Green Junction
(24.05.1872)

ECR
01.07.1840

Aborted ELR line towards Cambridge Heath

Bethnal Green West Junction

Hoist

SPITALFIELDS GOODS
(01.01.1881 – 06.11.1967)
(amalgamation of Brick Lane Goods and Whitechapel Coal)

Hoist

ELR
10.04.1876

BRICK LANE GOODS
(c.1840 – 06.11.1967)
(amalgamated with Whitechapel Coal
01.01.1881 to form Spitalfields Goods)

WHITECHAPEL COAL
(01.11.1866 – 06.11.1967)
(amalgamated with Brick Lane Goods 01.01.1881 to form Spitalfields Goods)

WHITECHAPEL
Whitechapel (Mile End)
(10.04.1876)
(see inset above)

MDR & LTSR
02.06.1902

ELR
10.04.1876

Whitechapel Junction

St Mary's Curve
06.10.1941

NR 2018

SER 03.03.1884
(23.12.2007)

EASTERN DISTRICT OFFICE
(02.01.1928 – 31.05.2003)

ST MARY'S (WHITECHAPEL ROAD)
St Mary's
(03.03.1884 – 01.05.1938)

St Mary's Junction

MDR & MET
07.10.1884

POR
02.01.1928
31.05.2003

LUL platforms at Whitechapel rationalised from four to two 31.01.2011, at the same time the westbound road was diverted via former '25 road' siding and the westbound platform widened onto the former platform 4 trackbed

SHOREDITCH (NLR)
(01.11.1865 – 04.10.1940)

NLR
01.11.1865

LIVERPOOL STREET
(28.07.1912)

POR
19.12.1927 –
31.05.2003

CLR
28.07.1912

From below – Central Line & Post Office Railway detail
(all other lines omitted for clarity)

Turnback sidings

LIVERPOOL STREET
(19.12.1927 – c.1990)

LPTB
04.12.1946

SHOREDITCH HIGH STREET (27.04.2010)
BISHOPSGATE (HIGH LEVEL)
Shoreditch
(01.07.1840 (01.01.1881) – c.1879 [05.12.1964])
(On same site – see insets below)

TFL
27.04.2010

Covered way

BISHOPSGATE LOW LEVEL
(04.11.1872 – 22.05.1916)

SHOREDITCH (ELR)
(10.04.1876 – 11.06.2006)

GER 04.11.1872

Wheeler Street (or Bishopsgate) Junction

NLR
01.11.1865 –
30.06.1986

GER 02.02.1874

Area west of dashed line under covered way (tracks not dashed for clarity of detail)

From above – Bishopsgate 1872

COAL

ECR
01.07.1840

BISHOPSGATE
Shoreditch
(01.07.1840)

From above – Bishopsgate 1881 – 1916

BISHOPSGATE GOODS
(01.01.1881)

BISHOPSGATE LOW LEVEL
(04.11.1872)

BROAD STREET
(01.11.1865 – 30.06.1986)

Hoist

Worship Street Sidings

COAL (at lower level)

GOODS
18.05.1868 –
27.01.1969

LIVERPOOL STREET
Bishopsgate
(02.02.1874)
(see inset above for Central Line detail)

Liverpool Street

*

MET 01.02.1875

NR 2018

POR
02.01.1928 –
31.05.2003

MET
18.11.1876

CLR
28.07.1912

Liverpool Street Junction

* Curve opened 01.02.1875, Metropolitan Railway services initially terminating at Liverpool Street platforms 1 & 2. Metropolitan Railway services subsequently diverted to their own terminus (Bishopsgate) 12.07.1875. Connection last used for through traffic 1904, junction severed 1907 and tunnel used for carriage sidings until being lifted in 1916

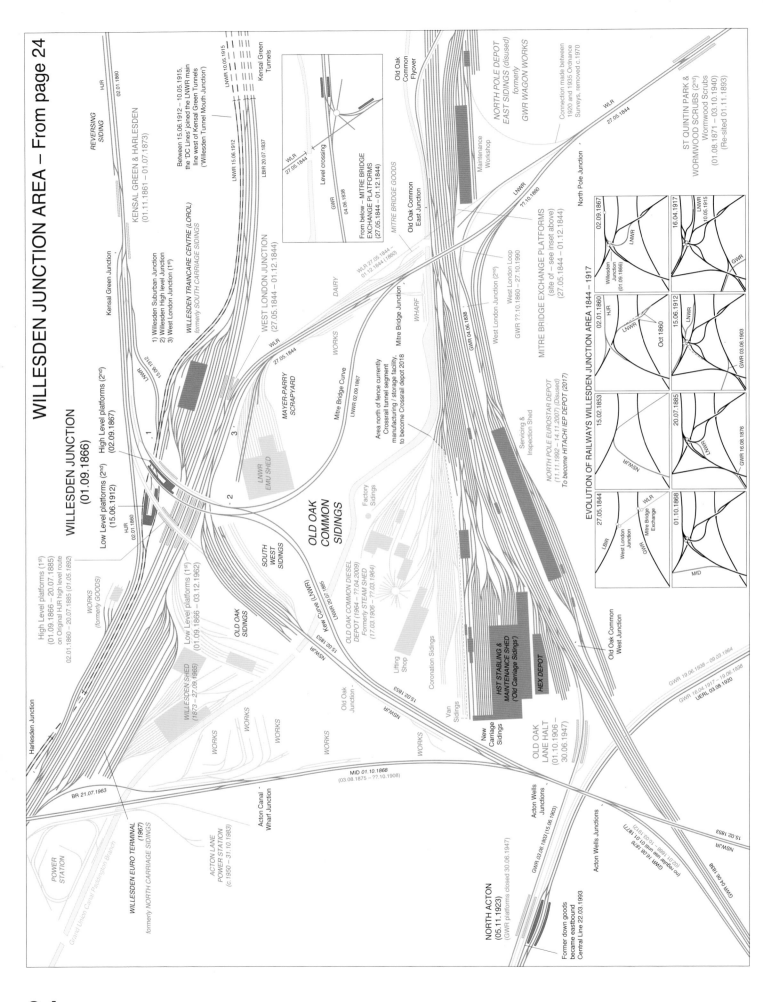

WILLESDEN JUNCTION
(01.09.1866)

High Level platforms (2nd)
(01.09.1866 – 20.07.1885)
on Original HJR high level route
02.01.1860 – 20.07.1885 (01.05.1892)

High Level platforms (1st)
(01.09.1866 – 20.07.1885)

WORKS
(formerly GOODS)

Low Level platforms (2nd)
(15.06.1912)

Low Level platforms (1st)
(01.09.1866 – 03.12.1962)

REVERSING SIDING

02.01.1860

HJR

Kensal Green Junction

KENSAL GREEN & HARLESDEN
(01.11.1861 – 01.07.1873)

1) Willesden Suburban Junction
2) Willesden High level Junction
3) West London Junction (1st)

WILLESDEN TRAINCARE CENTRE (LOROL)
formerly SOUTH CARRIAGE SIDINGS

Between 15.06.1912 – 10.05.1915,
the 'DC Lines' joined the LNWR main
line west of Kensal Green Tunnels
('Willesden Tunnel Mouth Junction')

LNWR 10.05.1915

Kensal Green
Tunnels

LNWR 15.06.1912

LBIR 20.07.1837

GWR
04.06.1838

Level crossing

WLR
27.05.1844

From below – MITRE BRIDGE
EXCHANGE PLATFORMS
(27.05.1844 – 01.12.1844)

Old Oak
Common
Flyover

Old Oak Common
East Junction

NORTH POLE DEPOT
EAST SIDINGS (disused)
formerly
GWR WAGON WORKS

Connection made between
1920 and 1935 Ordnance
Surveys, removed c.1970

Maintenance
Workshop

ST QUINTIN PARK &
WORMWOOD SCRUBS (2nd)
Wormwood Scrubs
(01.08.1871 – 03.10.1940)
(Re-sited 01.11.1893)

WLR 27.05.1844

North Pole Junction

LNWR

LNWR 27.10.1860

MITRE BRIDGE GOODS

DAIRY

WORKS

WEST LONDON JUNCTION
(27.05.1844 – 01.12.1844)

WLR
27.05.1844

LNWR

15.06.1912

MAYER-PARRY
SCRAPYARD

Mitre Bridge Curve

LNWR 02.09.1867

WHARF

Mitre Bridge Junction

GWR 04.06.1838

West London Junction (2nd)
GWR ??.10.1860 – 27.10.1990

West London Loop

MITRE BRIDGE EXCHANGE PLATFORMS
(site of – see inset above)
(27.05.1844 – 01.12.1844)

NORTH POLE EUROSTAR DEPOT
(11.11.1992 – 14.11.2007) (Disused)
To become HITACHI IEP DEPOT (2017)

Area north of fence currently
Crossrail tunnel segment
manufacturing / storage facility,
to become Crossrail depot 2018

Servicing &
Inspection Shed

OLD OAK
COMMON
SIDINGS

SOUTH
WEST
SIDINGS

LNWR
EMU SHED

Factory
Sidings

OLD OAK COMMON DIESEL
DEPOT (1964 – ??.04.2009)
Formerly STEAM SHED
(17.03.1906 – ??.03.1964)

Kew Curve (LNWR)

LNWR 20.07.1885

OLD OAK
SIDINGS

WILLESDEN SHED
(1873 – 27.09.1965)

Old Oak
Junction

NSWJR

Lifting
Shop

Coronation Sidings

Van
Sidings

New
Carriage
Sidings

HST STABLING &
MAINTENANCE SHED
(Old Carriage Sidings?)

HEX DEPOT

Old Oak Common
West Junction

OLD OAK
LANE HALT
(01.10.1906 –
30.06.1947)

GWR 19.06.1938 – 09.03.1964

GWR 16.04.1917 – 19.06.1938

UERL 03.08.1920

Harlesden Junction

BR 21.07.1963

WILLESDEN EURO TERMINAL
(1967)
formerly NORTH CARRIAGE SIDINGS

ACTON LANE
POWER STATION
(c.1950 – 31.10.1983)

POWER
STATION

Grand Union Canal Paddington Branch

WORKS

WORKS

WORKS

WORKS

Acton Canal
Wharf Junction

MID 01.10.1868
(03.08.1875 – ??.10.1908)

Acton Wells
Junctions

NORTH ACTON
(05.11.1923)
(GWR platforms closed 30.06.1947)

Former down goods
became eastbound
Central Line 22.03.1993

GWR 03.06.1923 (15.06.1903)

NSWJR 15.02.1853

GWR 16.08.1876
(no regular use until 01.10.1871)
(02.01.1888 – 10.08.1913)

GWR 04.06.1838

Acton Wells Junctions

NSWJR 15.02.1853

EVOLUTION OF RAILWAYS WILLESDEN JUNCTION AREA 1844 – 1917

27.05.1844

LBIR

West London
Junction

Mitre Bridge
Exchange

WLR

GWR

MID

01.10.1868

15.02.1853

NSWJR

HJR

02.09.1867

Willesden
Junction
(01.09.1866)

LNWR

HJR

LNWR

Oct 1860

16.04.1917

LNWR
10.05.1915

GWR

15.06.1912

LNWR

GWR 03.06.1903

20.07.1885

LNWR

GWR 16.08.1876

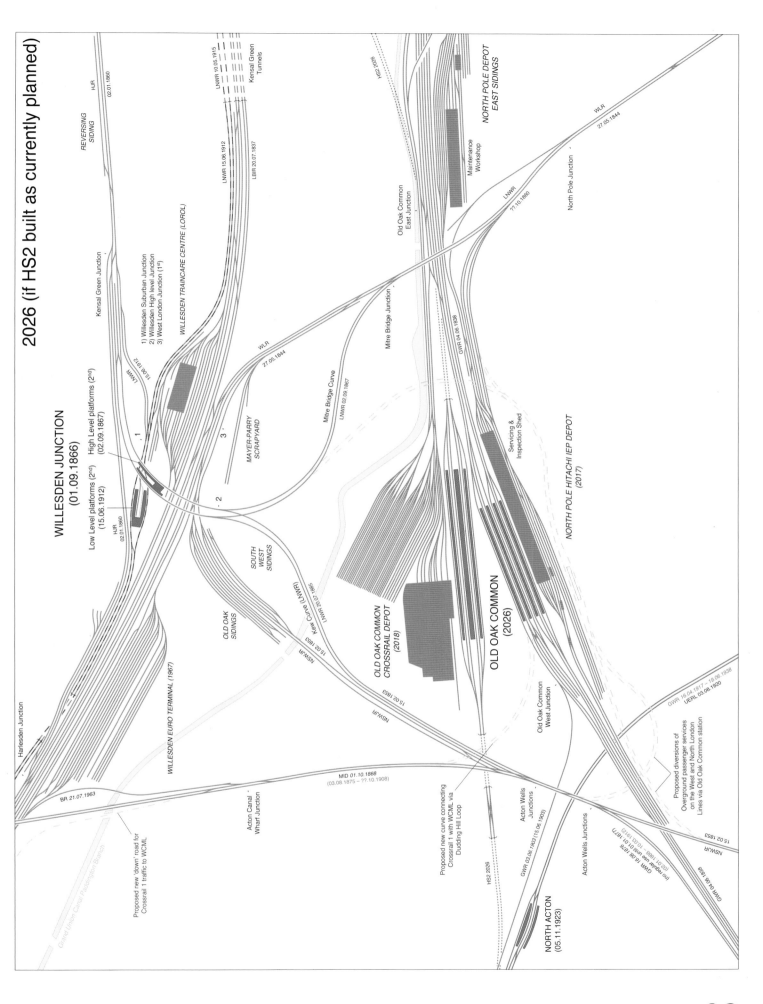

2026 (if HS2 built as currently planned)

Index

Names quoted are the current names or the name at the point of closure. As many alternative names are quoted as possible with dates of name changes noted, but please note that at any given time names could vary between different timetables and station name boards, even between name boards on different platforms of the same station. If two stations shared the same name, they are differentiated through the addition of the abbreviated railway company name which opened that station in brackets. Where more than one station shared the same name and were built by the same railway company, they are differentiated chronologically through the suffix (1st), (2nd), etc.

Entries in black plain capital text denote open passenger stations, red closed, blue under construction or proposed (2014). Previous names are listed in reverse chronological order in red lower-case indented text below. Entries in black italic capital text denote open non-passenger facilities, red closed, blue under construction or proposed (2014). Entries in black lower-case text denote in-use railway features, e.g. junctions, curves, or tunnels, red disused.

Dates are given as accurately as possible. Italic dates refer to non-passenger usage. Goods yards are listed with the associated passenger station if applicable, unless the location of the goods yard was significantly remote from the passenger station. Where a station had a goods yard associated with it, dates of opening and closing are stated for both passenger and goods facilities, differentiated by 'P' and 'G'. The same principle applies to connecting curves / loops, although in this case 'G' relates to any non-passenger usage. In some cases approximate dates are quoted where no reliable source can be found, these are generally inferred from Ordnance Survey maps with the rationale stated in the notes. In some cases research established conflicting information. Where sufficient doubt remains about which information is correct, all is stated with their respective sources noted.

Opening dates are the first full day of normal service unless otherwise indicated, closure dates are the first full traffic day without trains unless otherwise indicated. For example, if a station was only open Monday-Friday and was last served on a Friday, the following Monday's date is quoted as the closure date. Minor periods of closure (e.g. due to engineering works, terrorism, enemy action etc.) are generally omitted, although some of significant length or interest are recorded. Some stations (e.g. Dalston Junction, Homerton, Shepherds Bush [WLR]) were closed for long periods of their existence, but as they were ultimately rebuilt on the same site, the original opening date is given with the period of closure recorded in the notes. Minor re-siting of stations is recorded in the notes under a single index entry.

Name	Page / grid		Date opened	Date closed	Opened by	Notes
A						
Abbey Mills Curve	28 / 5A	P	01/06/1858	27/10/1940	LTSR	Abbey Mills Curve open to passengers 01/06/1858 – 27/10/1940.
		G	31/03/1858	27/07/1958		
Abbey Mills Lower Junction	28 / 5A		31/03/1858	27/07/1958	LTSR	Junction at south end of Abbey Mills Curve.
ABBEY ROAD	28 / 4A		31/08/2011	N/A	DLR	
ABBEY WOOD	42 / 2C	P	??/??/1849	N/A	SER	Opening date unknown, either on or by 01/11/1849, does not appear to have opened with rest of line (30/07/1849). Goods yard closed 05/12/1960. To be rebuilt with four platforms as an eastern terminus of Crossrail 1 2018.
		G	??/??/1849	05/12/1960		
Acton Canal Wharf Junction	24 / 5C 91 & 92		21/07/1963	N/A	BR	Date is that of opening of curve to WCML, access to various works alongside canal existed before this date.
ACTON CENTRAL	37 / 1B	P	01/08/1853	N/A	NSWJR	Bay platform formerly on 'up' side. 'Central' suffix added 01/11/1925. Goods yard opened 1856, closed 01/03/1965.
Acton		G	??/??/1856	01/03/1965		
ACTON COAL	37 / 1C		??/??/1867	04/01/1965	NSWJR	
Acton Curve	37 / 2B	P	01/05/1878	01/10/1880	LSWR	Briefly carried passenger traffic 01/05/1878 - 01/10/1880. Last used for access to West Kensington Goods & coal, last train 29/07/1965, 13/09/1965 is official closure date.
	51 / 2B	G	01/03/1878	13/09/1965		
Acton East (or Poplar) Junction	24 / 6B		16/08/1876	N/A	GWR	Curve to NSWJR opened 16/08/1876, but saw no regular use until 01/01/1877.
Acton Gatehouse Junction	37 / 1B		01/05/1857	03/05/1965	NSWJR	Junction between NSWJR main line and their Hammersmith & Chiswick Branch.
Acton Lane East Junction	37 / 2B 51 / 2B		03/12/1911	13/09/1965	LSWR	LSWR dive-under opened due to quadrupling works Ravenscourt Park to Turnham Green, later goods use only.
ACTON LANE POWER STATION	24 / 5C 91		c.1950	31/10/1983	PRIV	
Acton Lane West Junction	37 / 2B 51 / 2B		01/03/1878	13/09/1965	LSWR	Junction at east end of Acton Curve.
Acton Loop Line	37 / 2B 51 / 1A	P	13/06/1905	02/03/1959	MDR	First used for construction traffic for MDR extension to South Harrow. Doubled shortly before passenger services commenced 13/06/1905. Goods traffic ceased 22/02/1915 and connection at north end 'clipped' out of use (not physically removed until c.1930). Branch singled 14/02/1932. Service withdrawn and branch dismantled 02/03/1959.
		G	15/05/1899	22/02/1915		
ACTON MAIN LINE	24 / 6B	P	01/02/1868	N/A	GWR	Coal yard closed 1931. 'Main Line' suffix added 01/11/1949.
Acton		G	01/02/1868	??/??/1931		
ACTON TOWN	37 / 1B		01/07/1879	N/A	MDR	Rebuilt and renamed 01/03/1910, further rebuilt 1933. First served by Piccadilly Line 04/07/1932. South Acton Shuttle served bay platform 5 until 28/02/1959.
Mill Hill Park						
Acton Town North Junction	37 / 1A		01/05/1883	N/A	MDR	Extensively remodelled 1932 during Turnham Green to Northfields quadrupling.
Acton Town South Junction	37 / 2B 51 / 1A		15/05/1899	01/03/1959	MDR	First passenger use 13/06/1905, last freight use 1915.
Acton Wells Junctions	24 / 5C 91 & 92		01/10/1868	N/A	MID / NSWJR	Junction between MID Dudding Hill Loop and NSWJR. Junction with GWR curve to Acton added 01/01/1877.
Acton West Junction	24 / 6A		c.1931	N/A	GWR	Seemingly established during the yard's 1931 expansion. Currently being reconstructed with a dive-under for 2018.
ACTON WORKS (REW)	37 / 2A 51 / 1A		??/??/1923	N/A	UERL	Works for heavy overhaul of LUL rolling stock. REW = Railway Engineering Works.
ACTON YARD (YEOMAN AGGREGATES)	24 / 6B		??/01/1877	N/A	GWR	Yard established by GWR January 1877. Expanded 03/06/1901 and again 1931. Closed as a marshalling yard 24/05/1984, remaining in use for stone traffic (Yeoman Aggregates).
ADDINGTON VILLAGE	67 / 4C		10/05/2000	N/A	CTL	
ADDISCOMBE (MKR)	67 / 1A	P	01/04/1864	02/06/1997	MKR	Opened as 'Croydon (Addiscombe Road)', renamed 'Croydon (Addiscombe)' 01/04/1925, 'Addiscombe (Croydon)' ??/03/1926, 'Croydon' suffix dropped 13/06/1955. Goods yard did not open until 11/07/1925, closed 17/06/1968. Reduced to one operational platform (platform 2) March 1996 due to signal box being destroyed by arson. Elmers End to Addiscombe last train 31/05/1997, but as no Sunday service timetabled, Monday 02/06/1997 is given as closure date (station removed from 1997 Summer timetable published 01/06/1997).
Addiscombe (Croydon)		G	11/07/1925	17/06/1968		
Croydon (Addiscombe)						
Croydon (Addiscombe Road)						
ADDISCOMBE (CTL)	67 / 1A		23/05/2000	N/A	CTL	
ADDISCOMBE EMU SHED	67 / 1A		11/07/1925	??/04/1995	SR	Shed commissioned on 11/07/1925 according to kentrail.org.uk, electrification of branch planned for 01/12/1925 but was delayed until 28/02/1926, so presumably no regular use for EMU stabling before this date. Closed as a traincrew depot 12/04/1993, although stabling of 4EPB units continued until withdrawal April 1995 (shed was never cleared for stabling of 'Networker' EMUs).

Name	Page / grid		Date opened	Date closed	Opened by	Notes
ADDLESTONE	61 / 2B	P	14/02/1848	N/A	LSWR	
		G	14/02/1848	c.1965		
Addlestone Junction	61 / 3C		??/??/1885	N/A	LSWR	Junction at north end of Byfleet Curve.
AEC MOTOR WORKS	36 / 1A		?	?	PRIV	
AGGREGATE INDUSTRIES LTD (NEASDEN)	24 / 3C 22		??/??/2001	N/A	PRIV	
ALBANY PARK	56 / 2D		07/07/1935	N/A	SR	
Albert Dock Junction	62 / 3B		03/08/1880	08/09/1940	LSKD / GER	Junction of Gallions branch.
Aldersbrook Flyover	28 / 2D		06/10/1947	N/A	LNER	
ALDERSBROOK (UP) CAR HOLDING SIDINGS	28 / 2D		c.1894	N/A	GER	Appear on OS maps after 1895, may have been opened at same time as GER quadrupling work (c.1894).
ALDGATE	27 / 6A 74 / 1B		18/11/1876	N/A	MET	
Aldgate Junction	27 / 6A 74 / 1B		01/10/1884	N/A	MET	
ALDGATE EAST	27 / 6A 74 / 1B		06/10/1884	N/A	MDR / MET	Relocated East 30/10/1938 (Junction remodelling to ease congestion around Aldgate Triangle).
Aldgate East Junction	27 / 6A 74 / 1B		06/10/1884	N/A	MDR / MET	Relocated East 30/10/1938 (Junction remodelling to ease congestion around Aldgate Triangle).
ALDWYCH Strand	26 / 6B		30/11/1907	30/09/1994	UERL (GNPBR)	Opened as 'Strand', renamed 'Aldwych' 09/05/1915. Closed 21/09/1940 - 01/07/1946 (World War II). Aldwych Branch closed to passengers 30/09/1994, but track / a 1972 Mk1 Stock train retained for filming work.
Alexandra Bridge	87		01/09/1866	N/A	SER	
ALEXANDRA PALACE (GNR) Wood Green Wood Green (Alexandra Park) Wood Green	14 / 4B	P	01/05/1859	N/A	GNR	Opened as 'Wood Green', suffix '(Alexandra Park)' added 01/08/1864, dropped 18/03/1971. Renamed 'Alexandra Palace' 17/05/1982. Goods yard closed 24/01/1966.
		G	01/05/1859	24/01/1966		
ALEXANDRA PALACE (MHPR) Alexandra Park (1891-1892 only) Alexandra Palace	14 / 4B		24/05/1873	05/07/1954	MHPR	Nominally opened by Muswell Hill & Palace Railway, but operated by GNR from opening. Closed and re-opened several times; closed 01/08/1873 - 01/05/1875 plus on several other occasions thereafter (mostly during Winter), known as Alexandra Park 1891-1892. Open without interruption 01/04/1898 to 29/10/1951, when closed again until 07/01/1952. Permanently closed 05/07/1954. Had been intended for electrification and transfer to LT, but works abandoned post-WW2.
ALL SAINTS	27 / 6D		31/08/1987	N/A	DLR	On Site of former NLR Poplar Station. Poplar to Stratford no service 18/04/2014 until 22:00 25/04/2014.
ALPERTON Perivale Alperton	23 / 3D		28/06/1903	N/A	MDR	Renamed 'Alperton' 07/10/1910. First served Piccadilly Line 04/07/1932, last served District Line 23/10/1933.
AMERSHAM Amersham & Chesham Bois Amersham	1 / 3A	P	01/09/1892	N/A	MET	Suffix '& Chesham Bois' 12/03/1922 - ??/??/1934. Metropolitan Line services beyond Amersham ceased 10/09/1961. Goods yard closed 04/07/1966.
		G	01/09/1892	04/07/1966		
AMPERE WAY IKEA Ampere Way Ampere Way	66 / 1B		10/05/2000	N/A	CTL	'IKEA' Prefix 18/10/2006 - ??/03/2008 (Sponsorship deal).
ANERLEY Anerley Bridge	54 / 4A		05/06/1839	N/A	LCRR	Suffix 'Bridge' dropped c.1840. According to Mitchell & Smith, initially spelt 'Annerley'. Rebuilt 1853-4 (quadrupling).
ANGEL	26 / 4C		17/11/1901	N/A	CSLR	Terminus from opening until 12/05/1907. Closed 09/08/1922 - 20/04/1924 (tunnel widening). Rebuilt with Northbound road routed via new tunnel 19/10/1992.
ANGEL ROAD Water Lane Edmonton	15 / 2B	P	15/09/1840	N/A	NER	Opened as 'Edmonton', renamed 'Water Lane' 01/03/1849, 'Angel Road' 01/01/1864. Goods yard opened with passenger station, but closure date unknown.
		G	15/09/1840	?		
Angel Road Junction Edmonton Junction	15 / 2B		01/03/1849	07/12/1964	ECR	Originally 'Edmonton Junction'; junction of ECR Enfield (Town) branch with NER Lea Valley line. Angel Road Junction to Lower Edmonton Junction closed 07/12/1964.
Angerstein Junction	41 / 3B		30/10/1852	N/A	SER / PRIV	Junction between Angerstein Wharf branch and SER North Kent Line. London-facing junction eliminated 1890.
ANGERSTEIN WHARF	41 / 2B		30/10/1852	N/A	PRIV	Angerstein Wharf Branch privately built by John Angerstein, but leased to SER from outset. Purchased by SER 1898. Several industrial were present for various purposes: AA Oil Co. and BP / Shell Mex (oil), Christie's (sleeper & telegraph pole works), United Glass works, Renwick Wilton (coal), as well as giving access to East Greenwich gasworks and the LCC Central Tram repair works. Today the wharf handles solely aggregates traffic (Bardon and Tarmac).
APCM COAL TERMINAL (SOUTHFLEET)	59 / 3C		??/??/1972	??/??/1976	PRIV	Established on site of former Southfleet station at end of branch from Fawkham Junction (former LCDR Gravesend West branch, closed 24/03/1968). Supplied coal to nearby Northfleet Cement works (APCM, later Blue Circle).
ARCHWAY Highgate (Archway) Archway (Highgate) Highgate	26 / 1A		22/06/1907	N/A	UERL (CCEHR)	Terminus 22/06/1907 - 03/07/1939, opened as 'Highgate'. 'Archway' prefix added 11/06/1939, reversed 19/01/1941, 'Highgate' prefix dropped ??/12/1947.
ARENA	54 / 6B		23/05/2000	N/A	CTL	Became a junction a week after opening (30/05/2000) with addition of branch to Elmers End.
ARNOS GROVE	14 / 2B		19/09/1932	N/A	UERL (GNPBR)	Terminus of extension from Finsbury Park 19/09/1932 - 13/03/1933.
ARNOS GROVE SIDINGS	14 / 2A		19/09/1932	N/A	UERL (GNPBR)	Stabling Sidings for Piccadilly Line.
ARSENAL Arsenal (for Highbury Hill) Gillespie Road	26 / 2C 81		15/12/1906	N/A	UERL (GNPBR)	Opened as 'Gillespie Road', renamed 'Arsenal (for Highbury Hill)' 31/10/1932, suffix gradually dropped.
ASHBURTON GROVE GOODS	26 / 2C 81		??/??/1884	13/06/1960	GNR	
ASHFORD	48 / 2C	P	22/08/1848	N/A	LSWR	Goods yard closed 1965.
		G	22/08/1848	??/??/1965		
ASHTEAD	70 / 1D	P	01/02/1859	N/A	LBSCR / LSWR	
		G	01/02/1859	c.1965		
AVENUE ROAD	54 / 5B		23/05/2000	N/A	CTL	

Name	Page / grid		Date opened	Date closed	Opened by	Notes
B						
BAKER STREET	25 / 5D		10/01/1863	N/A	MET	MSJWR platforms to Swiss Cottage opened 13/04/1868 (Now Metropolitan Line Platforms), BSWR platforms open 10/03/1906. Bakerloo Line platforms to Stanmore opened 20/11/1939, Jubilee Line opened 01/05/1979 using existing southbound Bakerloo platform ex-Stanmore and a new northbound.

BALHAM
    Balham & Upper Tooting
    Balham
	52 / 1D
	53 / 1A
			01/12/1856	N/A	WELCPR	Original station west of road, re-sited east 1863. UERL (later Northern Line) station opened 06/12/1926. '& Upper Tooting' suffix added ??/03/1927, dropped 06/10/1969 (applied to main line station only).

Balham Junction	53 / 1A		01/12/1862	N/A	LBSCR	
BANDON HALT	66 / 3B		11/06/1906	07/06/1914	LBSCR	
BANK City (WCIR only)	26 / 6D 87		08/08/1898	N/A	WCIR	Opened by WCIR as 'City' 08/08/1898. CSLR and CLR platforms opened 25/02/1900 and 30/07/1900 respectively as 'Bank'. Waterloo & City platforms renamed from 'City' to 'Bank' 1940, DLR platforms opened 29/07/1991. Southbound Northern Line tunnel proposed to be re-bored to serve a new platform to alleviate overcrowding. Transport and Works Act Order application late 2012, construction to start 2015, completion 2021.

BANSTEAD
    Banstead & Burgh Heath
    Banstead
	65 / 6A	P
		G
			22/05/1865
			22/05/1865
				N/A
				07/09/1964
					LBSCR	Suffix '& Burgh Heath' 01/06/1898 - ??/08/1928. Goods yard closed 07/09/1964 (note: Jackson refers to goods not being into use until 'about 1880', but Borley gives goods opening on same date as passenger, and goods yard is visible on 1871 OS). Former 'up' platform closed and branch singled 03/10/1982.

BARBICAN
    Aldersgate & Barbican
    Aldersgate
    Aldersgate Street
	26 / 6D
	32 / 3D
			23/12/1865	N/A	MET	Opened as 'Aldersgate Street', City Widened Lines platforms (later Network Rail) added 01/03/1866, 'Street' suffix dropped 01/11/1910. '& Barbican' suffix added ??/??/1923, 'Aldersgate' prefix dropped 01/12/1968. Network Rail platforms closed 23/03/2009 (last train 20/03/2009), although westbound NR services had ceased stopping at Barbican prior to this date.

BARKING	29 / 4A	P G	13/04/1854 13/04/1854	N/A 01/04/1957	LTSR	Served by District Railway since 02/06/1902 (no service 30/09/1905 - 01/04/1908), Served by Metropolitan Railway since 04/05/1936 ('Hammersmith & City Line' since 30/07/1990). Goods yard originally on 'up' side of station, relocated to east c.1930 to present site of Barking LUL Sidings, closed 01/04/1957. Station rebuilt 1959-1961.
Barking East Junction	29 / 4B		11/05/1959	N/A	LTSR	All junctions in Barking area extensively remodelled 1959.
BARKING POWER STATIONS 'A', 'B' & 'C'	29 / 6C		??/??/1925	26/10/1981	PRIV	Station 'A' opened 1925, extended via Station 'B', both closed 15/03/1976. Station 'C' built 1954, closed 26/10/1981.
BARKING RIVERSIDE	29 / 5D		TBA	N/A	DLR	Gallions Reach to Dagenham Dock DLR was proposed to open c.2017, but funding removed November 2008. Further proposed to be served by London Overground extension from Barking via Tilbury Loop Line.
BARKING SIDINGS	29 / 4B		??/11/1958	N/A	LTE (DIS)	Stabling sidings for District and Hammersmith & City Line trains, opened on site of Barking Goods (2nd).
Barking Station Junction	29 / 3A		11/05/1959	N/A	BR	All junctions in Barking area extensively remodelled and new flyovers commissioned 11/05/1959.
Barking Tilbury Line Junction East	29 / 4A		01/06/1888	N/A	BR	All junctions in Barking area extensively remodelled 1959.
Barking Tilbury Line Junction West	29 / 3A		11/05/1959	N/A	BR	All junctions in Barking area extensively remodelled and new flyovers commissioned 11/05/1959.
Barking West Junction	29 / 3A		11/05/1959	N/A	BR	All junctions in Barking area extensively remodelled and new flyovers commissioned 11/05/1959.
BARKINGSIDE	17 / 5B	P G	01/05/1903 01/05/1903	N/A 04/10/1965	GER	Closed 22/05/1916 - 01/07/1919. LNER passenger trains ceased on Fairlop Loop 30/11/1947 to allow electrification & transfer to LTE. First served by LTE Central Line 31/05/1948. Goods yard closed 04/10/1965.
BARLBY ROAD CARRIAGE DEPOT	25 / 5A		??/??/1885	30/06/1969	GWR	Site partially re-used for North Pole Depot (disused).
BARNEHURST	43 / 5B	P G	01/05/1895 01/05/1895	N/A 07/10/1968	BHR	Goods yard closed 07/10/1968.
BARNES	37 / 5D	P G	27/07/1846 27/07/1846	N/A 06/01/1969	LSWR	Expanded to 4 platforms during quadrupling 1886. Goods yard closed 06/01/1969.
BARNES BRIDGE	37 / 4C		12/03/1916	N/A	LSWR	Opening coincided with electrification of Hounslow Loop.
Barnes Bridge	37 / 4C		22/08/1849	N/A	LSWR	Rebuilt 1894 - 1895 (strengthening).
Barnes Junction	37 / 5C		22/08/1849	N/A	LSWR	
Barnet Tunnels	13 / 1D		07/08/1850	N/A	GNR	
BARONS COURT	38 / 2A 84 & 87		09/10/1905	N/A	UERL (MDR)	UERL (GNPBR) platforms opened 15/12/1906 to north of District platforms, reconfigured with Piccadilly Line between District Line platforms 04/07/1932.
Barrington Road Junction	39 / 5C		01/08/1865	01/01/1923	LBSCR / LCDR	'End on' junction between LBSCR and LCDR west of East Brixton station, demarcation eliminated at Grouping.
BATH ROAD	37 / 2C 51 / 1D		08/04/1909	01/01/1917	NSWJR	
Bath Road Junction	33 / 1C		08/10/1849	N/A	GWR	Originally junction at southern end of Royal Curve (closed 26/07/1970), today point where Windsor Branch becomes single track (branch singled 09/09/1963).
BATTERSEA (LUL)	39 / 3A 82		c.2020	N/A	LUL (NOR)	Proposed terminus of Northern Line extension from Kennington.
BATTERSEA (WLER)	38 / 4C		02/03/1863	21/10/1940	WLER	Passenger service withdrawn Willesden Junction to Clapham Junction 21/10/1940.
BATTERSEA PARK (1st) Battersea	39 / 3A 82		01/10/1860	01/11/1870	LBSCR	Renamed 01/07/1862. Also referred to as 'Battersea Park & Steamboat Pier'.

BATTERSEA PARK (2nd)
    Battersea Park & York Road
    York Road & Battersea Park
    York Road
	39 / 4A 82		01/05/1867	N/A	LBSCR	Opened as 'York Road', renamed 'York Road & Battersea Park' 01/11/1870, 'Battersea Park & York Road' 01/01/1877, suffix dropped 01/06/1885.

Battersea Park Junction	39 / 3A 82		01/12/1867	N/A	LBSCR	
BATTERSEA PARK ROAD Battersea Park (York Road)	39 / 4A 82		01/05/1867	03/04/1916	LCDR	Renamed 01/11/1877.
Battersea Pier Junction	39 / 3A 82		01/12/1860	N/A	LCDR / VSPR	
BATTERSEA PIER SIDINGS	82		?	N/A	LBSCR	
BATTERSEA WHARF GOODS	82		30/04/1862	04/05/1970	LBSCR	

Name	Page / grid		Date opened	Date closed	Opened by	Notes

BAYSWATER
  Bayswater (Queensway)
  Bayswater (Queens Road)
  Bayswater (Queens Road) & Westbourne Grove
  Bayswater
	25 / 6C		01/10/1868	N/A	MET	Opened as 'Bayswater', renamed 'Bayswater (Queens Road) & Westbourne Grove' 1923, suffix '& Westbourne Grove' dropped 1933, renamed 'Bayswater (Queensway)' 01/09/1946, suffix gradually dropped. First served by District Line to Edgware Road 01/11/1926, 'Circle Line' service provided by a combination of Metropolitan and District Line trains and did not receive its own identity as a line until c.1949. Closed 23/07/2011 - 23/08/2011 (engineering work).

BECKENHAM HILL	54 / 3D		01/07/1892	N/A	LCDR	
BECKENHAM JUNCTION Beckenham	54 / 4D	P G	01/01/1857 *01/01/1857*	N/A *18/04/1964*	MKR	Initially terminus of MKR from Lewisham, WELCPR from Bromley Junction to Shortlands added 03/05/1858. Suffix 'Junction' added 01/04/1864. Originally two goods yards, north and south of passenger station, south yard closed c.1928 (now Tramlink platforms). North yard closed 18/04/1964, but remained in use as a coal concentration depot until 1982. Croydon Tramlink terminus platforms opened 23/05/2000 on former south goods yard site.
Beckenham Junction	54 / 4C		03/05/1858	N/A	WELCPR / MKR	
BECKENHAM ROAD	54 / 4C		23/05/2000	N/A	CTL	On site of former Penge station (WELCPR), closed c.1860.
Beckenham Spur	54 / 4C	P G	01/01/1857 *01/01/1857*	N/A N/A	MKR	Regular passenger traffic ceased after 15/10/1939. Singled 1987. Passenger services re-introduced 29/05/1995.
BECKTON (GCC)	29 / 6A		17/03/1873	29/12/1940	GCC	Opened 17/03/1873 (workmen only), general passenger traffic commenced 18/03/1874. Passenger services withdrawn from Beckton and Gallions 29/12/1940.
BECKTON (DLR)	28 / 6D		28/03/1994	N/A	DLR	
BECKTON DEPOT	29 / 6A		*28/03/1994*	N/A	DLR	DLR Depot.
BECKTON GAS WORKS	29 / 6B		*14/10/1872*	*22/02/1971*	GCC	Last train from works departed 01/06/1970, 22/02/1971 is official date of closure. Track lifted by 1973.
Beckton Junction	62 / 3B		03/08/1880	07/09/1940	LSKD	Divergence of Beckton and Gallions Branches.
BECKTON PARK	41 / 1D 62 / 5C		28/03/1994	N/A	DLR	
BECKTON RIVERSIDE	29 / 6A		TBA	N/A	DLR	Gallions Reach to Dagenham Dock was proposed to open c.2017, but funding removed November 2008.
BECONTREE Gale Street Halt	29 / 3D		28/06/1926	N/A	LMS	Opened on existing LTSR Main Line (now 'fast' tracks). Renamed 18/07/1932. First served by regular District Line trains after quadrupling and addition of platforms on new 'local' tracks 12/09/1932, although through excursion trains to Shoeburyness had called from opening until 30/09/1939. Last served British Rail 15/06/1962 and 'fast' platforms abandoned. Transferred to LTB 01/01/1969.
BECONTREE ESTATE RAILWAY	29 / 2D		*??/??/1921*	*??/??/1934*	LCC	Transported building materials during construction of Becontree Estate. Extended to a wharf on The Thames.

BEDDINGTON LANE
  Beddington Lane Halt
  Beddington
	53 / 6A		22/10/1855	N/A	WCRR	Opened as 'Beddington', 'Lane' suffix added January 1887. 'Halt' suffix added 1919, dropped 06/05/1969. Wimbledon to West Croydon closed by Railtrack 31/05/1997 (date of last train; official date of closure 02/06/1997). Re-opened as Tramlink stop also named 'Beddington Lane' towards the west of original site, opening 30/05/2000.

BELGRAVE WALK	52 / 5C		30/05/2000	N/A	CTL	
BELLINGHAM	54 / 2D	P G	01/07/1892 *c.1900*	N/A *25/03/1968*	LCDR SECR ?	Goods yard stated as opening with passenger station in Borley, but no evidence on 1897 OS (present by 1916). Closed 25/03/1968, also accessed Robertson's jam factory. Carriage sidings south of station laid out c.1954 to replace stabling facilities closed at Crystal Palace (High Level).
BELMONT (LMS)	11 / 3C		12/09/1932	05/10/1964	LMS	Passing loop in use 05/07/1937 - 09/07/1955. Became passenger terminus 15/09/1952. Belmont to Harrow & Wealdstone service withdrawn 05/10/1964, branch previously closed to goods 06/07/1964.
BELMONT (LBSCR) California	65 / 5B	P G	22/05/1865 *22/05/1865*	N/A *06/01/1969*	LBSCR	Renamed 01/10/1875. Goods yard relocated south 1889, closed 06/01/1969 (note: Jackson refers to goods not being into use until 'about 1880', but Borley gives goods opening on same date as passenger, and goods yard is visible on 1866 OS). Former 'up' platform closed and branch singled 03/10/1982.
BELSIZE PARK	25 / 3D		22/06/1907	N/A	UERL (CCEHR)	
Belsize Tunnels	25 / 3D		07/09/1867	N/A	MID	Midland Main line first goods train ran 07/09/1867, first passenger 13/07/1868 (to King's Cross MET). Second tunnel added 03/02/1884 (today's 'slow' tunnel, with original tunnel now 'fast').
BELVEDERE	43 / 2A	P G	??/03/1859 *??/03/1859*	N/A *10/06/1963*	SER	Exact opening date unknown: first appeared in timetables March 1859. Goods yard closed 10/06/1963.
BERMONDSEY	40 / 2A		17/09/1999	N/A	LUL (JUB)	Terminus of services from Stratford 17/07/1999 - 24/09/1999.
Bermondsey Dive-under	40 / 3B 80		??/??/2018	N/A	NR	New diver-under to open in conjunction with 'Thameslink' upgrade 2018, using part of former Bricklayers Arms branch to remove conflicting train movements approaching London Bridge.
BERMONDSEY STREET	39 / 1D 87		10/10/1836	14/12/1836	LGR	Temporary London terminus of London & Greenwich Railway.
BERRYLANDS	51 / 5B		16/10/1933	N/A	SR	
BETHNAL GREEN (GER) Bethnal Green Junction	27 / 5B 90		24/05/1872	N/A	GER	Referred to as '-Junction' at times until 1895. Platforms on Stratford lines closed 08/12/1946.
BETHNAL GREEN (LPTB)	27 / 5B		04/12/1946	N/A	LPTB (CEN)	
Bethnal Green East Junction	27 / 5B		27/05/1872	N/A	GER	
Bethnal Green West Junction	27 / 5B 90		04/11/1872	N/A	GER	Divergence of GER extension to Bishopsgate Low Level (later Liverpool Street) from original ECR route to Bishopsgate High Level (latter abandoned 05/12/1964). Junction remains as set of crossovers.
BEXLEY	57 / 1A	P G	01/09/1866 *01/09/1866*	N/A *06/05/1963*	SER	Goods yard closed 06/05/1963.
BEXLEYHEATH Bexley Heath	42 / 5D	P G	01/05/1895 *01/05/1895*	N/A *07/10/1968*	BHR	Initially referred to as either 'Bexleyheath' or 'Bexley Heath'. Goods yard situated 400m West of passenger station, closed 07/10/1968.
BICKLEY Southborough Road	55 / 5C	P G	05/07/1858 *05/07/1858*	N/A *16/05/1964*	MKR	Terminus of MKR extension from Shortlands. Renamed 01/10/1860. Line extended to Rochester Bridge by LCDR 03/12/1860. Rebuilt 1893-4 (quadrupling). Goods yard closed 16/05/1964.
Bickley Junctions	55 / 5D		08/09/1902	N/A	SECR	Junctions at north end of Tonbridge Loops, 'slow' junction opened 08/09/1902, 'fast' 14/09/1902.

Name	Page / grid		Date opened	Date closed	Opened by	Notes
BINGHAM ROAD	67 / 1A		01/09/1906	16/05/1983	LBSCR / SER	Closed 15/03/1915 - 30/09/1935, permanently closed 16/05/1983, later replaced by CTL 'Addiscombe' station to north.
BIRKBECK	54 / 5B		02/03/1930	N/A	SR	'Up' platform closed and route singled ??/02/1983. Croydon Tramlink opened 23/05/2000 using 'Up' alignment, with the former BR 'up' platform consequently rebuilt and re-opened.
Birkbeck Junction	54 / 5B		??/02/1983	N/A	BR	Commencement of single NR track to Penge Junction (originally double track throughout).
BISHOPSGATE (HIGH LEVEL) Bishopsgate Shoreditch	27 / 5A 90	P G	01/07/1840 01/01/1881	c.1879 05/12/1964	ECR	Passenger terminus for ECR 01/07/1840 - 01/11/1875 although occasional passenger services remained until c.1879. Renamed 'Bishopsgate' 27/07/1846. 'High level' suffix 04/11/1872. Goods traffic commenced 01/01/1881, lasting until 05/12/1964. LOROL station 'Shoreditch High Street' opened on same site 27/04/2010.
BISHOPSGATE (LOW LEVEL)	27 / 5A 90		04/11/1872	22/05/1916	GER	Functioned as an additional GER terminus to the 'High Level' station until Liverpool Street opened 02/02/1874.
Black Potts Viaduct	33 / 3C		01/12/1849	N/A	LSWR	
BLACKFRIARS (MDR) St Paul's (LCDR only)	26 / 6C 32 / 5B 87		30/05/1870	N/A	MDR	Main Line station opened by LCDR 10/05/1886 as 'St Paul's', renamed 'Blackfriars' 01/02/1937. LU platforms closed 27/02/2009 - 20/02/2012 due to redevelopment works, NR platforms extensively rebuilt during same period and consequently closed 20/11/2010 - 16/01/2011. New entrance on South bank of The Thames opened 06/12/2011, new bay platforms opened 19/05/2012.
BLACKFRIARS (SER) Great Surrey Street	39 / 1C 87		11/01/1864	01/01/1869	SER	Former name of 'Great Surrey Street' referred to in Dewick, but no mention in Borley or Quick. Replaced by Waterloo Junction (= East) to west.
BLACKFRIARS BRIDGE	39 / 1C 32 / 6C 87		01/06/1864	01/10/1885	LCDR	Terminus until 21/12/1864. Replaced by St Paul's (= Blackfriars) on north bank of Thames (opened 10/05/1886).
Blackfriars Bridge	32 / 6C		21/12/1864	27/06/1969	LCDR	Spans removed 1985, piers remain. Easternmost piers re-used for Blackfriars station redevelopment.
BLACKFRIARS GOODS	39 / 1C 32 / 6C 87		01/05/1865	03/02/1964	LCDR	
Blackfriars Junction	39 / 1C 32 & 87		01/06/1878	N/A	LCDR	Western end of curve between LCDR and SER.
BLACKHEATH	41 / 5A	P G	30/07/1849 30/07/1849	N/A 06/05/1963	SER	Opened with west-facing bay platforms on both 'up' and 'down' sides. Extensive carriage sidings laid out to west 1879, but were not electrified with main line 06/06/1926. Goods yard closed 06/05/1963, bays and sidings all decommissioned with rationalisation 15/03/1970 and signal boxes closed.
BLACKHEATH HILL	40 / 4D		18/09/1871	01/01/1917	LCDR	Terminus 18/09/1871 - 01/10/1888. Passenger service withdrawn Nunhead to Greenwich Park 01/01/1917.
Blackheath Junction	41 / 5B		01/05/1895	N/A	SER / BHR	Junction between SER North Kent Line and Bexleyheath Railway.
Blackheath Tunnel	41 / 4B		30/07/1849	N/A	SER	
BLACKHORSE LANE	67 / 1A		23/05/2000	N/A	CTL	
BLACKHORSE ROAD Black Horse Road	15 / 5C	P G	09/07/1894 01/09/1894	N/A 07/12/1964	TFGR	Goods yard open 01/09/1894 - 07/12/1964. Victoria Line opened 01/09/1968. BR platforms re-sited west 14/12/1981 to improve interchange. Main line platforms originally referred to as either 'Black Horse Road' or 'Blackhorse Road', usually the former, until the 14/12/1981 re-siting when they became 'Blackhorse Road' permanently.
BLACKWALL (DLR)	40 / 1D 31 / 6C		28/03/1994	N/A	DLR	
BLACKWALL (LBLR)	41 / 1A 31 / 4D		06/07/1840	04/05/1926	LBLR	Served by NLR 01/09/1870 - 01/07/1890. Passenger service Stepney East to Blackwall withdrawn 04/05/1926.
BLACKWALL GOODS (ECR) Blackwall Pepper Warehouses	28 / 6A		??/06/1848	06/03/1967	ECR	Accessed by a branch off the ECR North Woolwich Branch and bridge across The River Lea. Also referred to as 'Blackwall Pepper Warehouses'.
BLACKWALL GOODS (GNR)	41 / 1A 31 / 4C		c.1870	c.1961	GNR	Borley gives c.1870 (shipping traffic only) and 1900 (general goods) for opening, and c.1961 for closure. Jackson gives years of opening / closing as 1860 / 1961.
BLAKE HALL	8 / 1C	P G	24/04/1865 24/04/1865	31/10/1981 18/04/1966	GER	Epping to Ongar transferred to LTE 25/09/1949, Electrified 18/11/1957. Goods yard closed 18/04/1966. Was not re-opened by the Epping-Ongar Railway on account of now being a private residence.
Bollo Lane Junction	37 / 2B 51 / 2B		01/03/1878	13/09/1965	LSWR	Junction at West end of Acton Curve.
BOND STREET (CLR)	26 / 6A		24/09/1900	N/A	CLR	'Davies Street' until opening. Jubilee Line platforms opened 01/05/1979. Central Line platforms closed 23/04/2014 – 18/06/2014, Jubilee Line platforms closed 30/06/2014 (last train 27/06/2014) – 30/11/2014 (station upgrade works).
BOND STREET (NR)	26 / 6A		??/??/2018	N/A	NR (XRAIL)	Station on 'Crossrail 1', under construction for 2018 opening.
BOOKHAM	69 / 4D	P G	02/02/1885 02/02/1885	N/A c.1965	LSWR	Referred to as 'Bookham Common' in opening notice, but had always been 'Bookham' in Bradshaw.
BOROUGH	39 / 1D		18/12/1890	N/A	CSLR	Named 'Great Dover Street' until opening. Closed 16/07/1922 - 23/02/1925 (tunnel widening), and 02/07/1999 - 05/09/1999 (tunnel works).
Borough Market Junction	39 / 1D 87		01/09/1866	N/A	SER	Junction for Cannon Street.
BOROUGH ROAD	39 / 1C		01/06/1864	01/04/1907	LCDR	
BOSTON MANOR Boston Road	36 / 2C		01/05/1883	N/A	MDR	Renamed 11/12/1911. First served by Piccadilly Line 13/03/1933. District Line service ceased 10/10/1964.
BOUNDS GREEN	14 / 3B		19/09/1932	N/A	UERL (GNPBR)	
BOUNDS GREEN DEPOT	14 / 3B		??/??/1929	N/A	LNER	
BOW	27 / 5D 88		26/09/1850	15/05/1944	EWIDBJR	Platforms on line to Bromley (LTSR) added 17/05/1869, closed to regular traffic 01/01/1915 (Plaistow to Bow shuttle). Passenger service Dalston Junction to Poplar withdrawn 15/05/1944 (enemy action), official closure 23/04/1945.
BOW CHURCH	27 / 5D 88		31/08/1987	N/A	DLR	Poplar to Stratford no service 18/04/2014 until 22:00 25/04/2014.
BOW GOODS (MID)	27 / 4D 88		01/12/1892	N/A	MID	Opened by MID, transferred to BR Eastern c.1956. Currently serves Bardon Aggregates only.

Name	Page / grid		Date opened	Date closed	Opened by	Notes
BOW GOODS (LNWR)	27 / 4D 88		*20/03/1893*	*??/??/1940*	LNWR	
Bow Junction (1st)	27 / 4D 88		02/04/1849	N/A	LBLR / ECR	Junction between ECR and LBLR (Blackwall Extension Railway).
Bow Junction (2nd)	27 / 5D 88		20/10/1851	29/12/1967	EWIDBJR	Junction of EWIDBJR (later NLR) routes to Poplar and Fenchurch Street (via Gas Factory Junction).
BOW ROAD (LBLR) Bow & Bromley	27 / 5D 88		02/04/1849	07/11/1949	LBLR	Opened with Blackwall Extension Railway (LBLR) 02/04/1849 as 'Bow & Bromley', closed 29/09/1850. Re-opened 10/10/1876 on same site as 'Bow Road', re-sited north of Bow Road 04/04/1892. Closed 21/04/1941 -09/12/1946 & 06/01/1947 - 06/10/1947. Passenger services Fenchurch Street to Stratford withdrawn 07/11/1949.
BOW ROAD (MDR)	27 / 5D 88		11/06/1902	N/A	MDR / LTSR	Served by Metropolitan Line since 30/03/1936 ('Hammersmith & City Line' since 30/07/1990).
BOW ROAD GOODS	27 / 5D 88		*??/??/1885*	07/12/1964	GER	
BOW WORKS	27 / 5D 88		*c.1850*	*??/??/1960*	NLR	North London Railway Loco Works, enlarged 1863 & 1882.
BOYERS SIDING (FELTHAM)	49 / 1B		*c.1900*	*c.1935*	PRIV	Market garden. Sidings not present on 1895 OS, but had appeared by 1914. Housing built on site by WW2.
BOWES PARK	14 / 3B		01/11/1880	N/A	GNR	Terminating siding added 1911, removed 1950, re-laid 1974.
BRENT CROSS Brent	13 / 6A		19/11/1923	N/A	UERL (CCEHR)	Express passing loops commissioned 04/01/1925, abolished 23/08/1936, used by a handful of timetabled trains daily. Renamed 20/07/1976.
BRENT CROSS THAMESLINK	12 / 6D 85		TBA	N/A	NR	Proposed new station in connection with regeneration project.
Brent Curve	25 / 1A 85	P G	01/07/1905 *01/10/1868*	*??/10/1908* N/A	MID	Opened to goods, along with rest of Dudding Hill Loop, 01/10/1868. Some through passenger services operated between 01/07/1905 - October 1908.
Brent Curve Junction	24 / 1D 85		01/10/1868	N/A	MID	Junction between Midland Main Line and Dudding Hill Loop.
Brent New Junction	68 / 5C		c.1940	N/A	LMS	Junction with Willesden 'F' sidings.
BRENTFORD (GWR)	36 / 3D		01/05/1860	04/05/1942	GWR	Closed 22/03/1915 - 12/04/1920. Passenger service on GWR Brentford Branch withdrawn 04/05/1942.
BRENTFORD (LSWR) Brentford Central Brentford	36 / 3D	P G	22/08/1849 22/08/1849	N/A 04/01/1965	LSWR	'Brentford Central' 05/06/1950 - 12/05/1980. Goods yard closed 04/01/1965, parcels traffic ceased 07/09/1980.
Brentford Branch Junction	35 / 1D		18/07/1859	N/A	GWR	
BRENTFORD DOCK	36 / 3D		*18/07/1859*	*31/12/1964*	GWR	Originally intended to have a passenger station to serve ferries to Kew Gardens; platform may have been constructed for this purpose on north side of dock. Special passenger service ran on branch 15/07/1859, regular goods traffic commenced three days later.
BRENTFORD GOODS *Brentford Town Goods*	36 / 3C		*03/11/1930*	N/A	GWR	Opened as 'Brentford Town' goods as distinct from LSWR goods station, today known as 'Brentford Goods'. Closed to general goods traffic 07/12/1970, but stone (Day & sons) and domestic waste traffic remain. The domestic waste terminal opened in early 1977.
BRENTHAM FOR NORTH EALING AND GREYSTOKE PARK Brentham (for North Ealing) Brentham	24 / 4A		01/05/1911	15/06/1947	GWR	Replaced Twyford Abbey Halt. Closed 01/02/1915 - 29/03/1920. Suffix 'for North Ealing' added 1932, with further suffix 'and Greystoke Park' subsequently added, until closure.
BRENTWOOD Brentwood & Warley Brentwood	20 / 2A	P G	01/07/1840 01/07/1840	N/A 07/12/1970	ECR	Country terminus of ECR from opening until 29/03/1843. Name carried suffix '& Warley' 01/11/1882 - 20/02/1969. Engine shed opened 1872, closed 1949. Rebuilt through quadrupling work 01/01/1934. Goods yard closed 07/12/1970.
BREWERY SIDINGS (ROMFORD)	18 / 6C		*??/??/1853*	*??/??/1963*	PRIV	Originally accessed via a wagon hoist and turntable, tunnel under and incline up to main line added in 1860s.
BRICKLAYERS ARMS	39 / 2D 4	P G	01/05/1844 01/05/1844	01/01/1852 *??/??/1981*	SER / LCRR	Closed to passengers 01/01/1852, although some Summer Sunday excursion trains operated 1932-1939. Amalgamated with Willow Walk Goods 07/03/1932. Remained in use for general goods until 01/08/1977, some parcels & coal traffic remained until 1981.
Bricklayers Arms Junction	40 / 3B 79 & 80		01/05/1844	N/A	LCRR	Originally junction between LCRR and LCRR / SER Bricklayers Arms branch (traffic ceased by 1981). Today junction where spur leaves former LCRR to join South London Line (opened 01/01/1871).
BRIMSDOWN	7 / 4C	P G	01/10/1884 01/10/1884	N/A 04/10/1965	GER	Goods yard closed 04/10/1965.
BRITISH INDUSTRIAL SAND (Holmethorpe)	73 / 4D		*c.1870*	*c.1990s*	PRIV	Rail-served brickworks had existed on site since at least 1871 (OS). Later became Standard Brick Co., then British Industrial Sand. Complex included exchange sidings with three shunters and engine shed, closure date unknown, extant in 1990 edition of Baker, disused and disconnected but in situ in 2002 edition of Quail. 2 foot gauge internal system also present until c.1965.
BRITISH INSULATED CALLENDER'S CABLES	43 / 2B		*c.1896*	*??/??/1968*	PRIV	3 foot 6 inch narrow gauge internal system within cable works. Works and railway absent from 1895 OS but present on 1897, so opening date for railway of c.1896 presumed. System closed 1968.
BRITISH MUSEUM	26 / 6B		*30/07/1900*	*24/09/1933*	CLR	Replaced by Central Line platforms at Holborn (Kingsway) (opened 25/09/1933).
BRITISH ROPES WORKS	41 / 2C		*c.1930*	*c.1970*	PRIV	2 foot gauge internal system. Not present on 1920 OS, but had opened by 1939. Still operational 1965 but not on 1971 OS.
BRIXTON (LCDR) Brixton & South Stockwell Brixton	39 / 5C		06/10/1862	N/A	LCDR	Suffix '& South Stockwell' 01/05/1863 - 09/07/1934. Platforms on route to Denmark Hill closed 1929, demolished during 1930.
BRIXTON (LTE)	39 / 5C		23/07/1971	N/A	LTE (VIC)	Southern terminus of Victoria Line.
BRIXTON COAL	39 / 5C		*c.1880*	*??/03/1947*	MID	
Brixton Junction	39 / 5C		01/05/1863	N/A	LCDR	Junction between 1862 LCDR route from Herne Hill to Stewarts Lane and 01/05/1863 line to Loughborough Junction.
Brixton Spur	39 / 5C	P G	01/05/1863 01/05/1863	01/04/1921 N/A	LCDR	Previously closed to passengers 02/04/1916 - 04/10/1920, remains in use primarily for stock transfer. Also referred to as 'West Curve'.
BROAD STREET	26 / 6D 90	P G	01/11/1865 18/05/1868	30/06/1986 27/01/1969	NLR LNWR	Ex-Richmond trains diverted to North Woolwich 13/05/1985, remaining ex-Watford Junction services diverted to temporary platform north of original station July 1985, allowing demolition to commence. Temporary platform closed due to diversion of remaining trains to Liverpool Street via Graham Road Curve 30/06/1986 (last train 27/06/1986).

Name	Page / grid		Date opened	Date closed	Opened by	Notes
BROCKLEY	40 / 5C		06/03/1871	N/A	LBSCR	
BROCKLEY HILL	12 / 1A		N/A	N/A	LPTB (NOR)	On Northern Line extension to Bushey Heath from Edgware. Construction abandoned 1940.
BROCKLEY LANE	40 / 5C		??/06/1872	01/01/1917	LCDR	Exact opening date unknown (June 1872). Passenger service withdrawn Nunhead to Greenwich Park 01/01/1917.
BROCKLEY LANE COAL	40 / 5C		??/12/1883	04/05/1970	GNR	'Martins Siding' on down side became LNWR Coal Yard 1885.
BROMLEY-BY-BOW Bromley	27 / 5D 88	P G	31/03/1858 c.1898	N/A ?	LTSR	Opened by LTSR as 'Bromley', damaged by fire 1892, rebuilt to West 01/03/1894. Goods yard opened c.1898. First served by District Railway 02/06/1902, line quadrupled 1905, District trains then using 'Slow' lines. Served by Metropolitan Line since 30/03/1936 ('Hammersmith & City Line' since 30/07/1990). 'Fast' platforms abandoned 15/06/1962. Renamed 18/05/1967. Ownership transferred to LTB 01/01/1969. Goods yard closure date unknown.
Bromley Down Junction	54 / 5A		03/05/1858	N/A	WELCPR	
Bromley Junction	27 / 5D 88		17/05/1869	13/09/1959	NLR / LTSR	Re-sited to the West with Bromley Station 01/03/1894.
BROMLEY NORTH Bromley	55 / 5B	P G	01/01/1878 01/01/1878	N/A 20/05/1968	SER	Renamed 01/06/1899. Originally two side platforms astride three roads terminating at a turntable. In 1924 rebuilding commenced, with the western platform remaining in use while the eastern was demolished, replaced by current island platforms. Completed December 1925, remaining original platform abandoned. Goods yard closed 20/05/1968.
BROMLEY SOUTH Bromley	55 / 5B	P G	22/11/1858 22/11/1858	N/A 18/04/1964	MKR	Opening date given as 22/11/1858 in Borley but 05/07/1858 in Quick (latter is date line through station opened). Alternative original name of 'Bromley Common' given in Dewick, but not mentioned in any other publication. Renamed 'Bromley South' 01/06/1899. Rebuilt 1893-1894 (quadrupling). Goods yard closed 18/04/1964.
Bromley Up Junction	54 / 5A		03/05/1858	N/A	WELCPR	
BROMPTON & FULHAM GOODS	38 / 3B 84		01/04/1892	04/08/1975	LNWR	
BROMPTON ROAD	38 / 2D		15/12/1906	30/07/1934	UERL (GNPBR)	
BRONDESBURY Brondesbury (Edgware Road) Edgware Road & Brondesbury Edgware Road Edgeware Road (Kilburn)	25 / 3A		02/01/1860	N/A	HJR	Opened as 'Edgeware Road (Kilburn)', '& Brondesbury' suffix added 01/01/1872, renamed 'Brondesbury (Edgware Road)' 01/01/1873, renamed 'Brondesbury' 01/01/1883. Closed 29/10/1995 - 29/09/1996.
BRONDESBURY PARK	25 / 3A		01/06/1908	N/A	LNWR	Closed 29/10/1995 - 29/09/1996 (engineering works).
BRUCE GROVE	15 / 4A		22/07/1872	N/A	GER	
BUCKHURST HILL	16 / 1D	P G	22/08/1856 ??/??/1859	N/A 06/01/1964	ECR	'Down' platform originally south of Queen's Road. Majority of Passenger services transferred to LTE 21/11/1948. First Trains in the morning remained British Rail services until 01/06/1970. Goods yard open 1859 - 06/01/1964.
BURDETT ROAD	27 / 6C		11/09/1871	21/04/1941	LBLR	Closed 29/12/1940 - 05/01/1941 (enemy action), closed again 10/04/1941 (enemy action) and did not re-open. 21/04/1941 is the 'official' closure date.
BURNT OAK Burnt Oak (Watling) Burnt Oak	12 / 3B		27/10/1924	N/A	UERL (CCEHR)	'Watling' suffix introduced c.1928, gradually dropped.
Burroughs Tunnels	12 / 5D		18/08/1924	N/A	UERL (CCEHR)	
Bury Street Junction	7 / 6A		01/10/1891	N/A	GER	No passenger service Bury Street Junction to Cheshunt Junction 01/10/1909 - 01/03/1915 & 01/07/1919 - 21/11/1960.
BUSHEY Bushey & Oxhey Bushey	2 / 5D	P G	01/12/1841 01/12/1841	N/A 03/02/1969	LBIR	Served by London Underground Bakerloo Line Trains 16/04/1917 - 24/09/1982. '& Oxhey' dropped 06/05/1974. Goods yard closed 03/02/1969.
BUSHEY HEATH	3 / 5C		N/A	N/A	LPTB (NOR)	Intended terminus of Northern Line extension from Edgware. Construction abandoned 1940.
BUSHEY HEATH DEPOT	3 / 6D		N/A	N/A	LPTB (NOR)	Was to replace Golders Green Depot. Sheds constructed but track never laid, sheds used for construction of Halifax Bombers during WW2, and then later became Aldenham bus overhaul works 1956-1986.
BUSH HILL PARK	7 / 5A	P G	01/11/1880 01/11/1880	N/A 04/05/1964	GER	Goods yard closed 04/05/1964.
BYFLEET & NEW HAW West Weybridge	61 / 4C		01/07/1927	N/A	SR	Opened as 'West Weybridge', renamed 12/06/1961.
Byfleet Curve	61 / 4C	P G	??/??/1885 ??/??/1885	N/A N/A	LSWR	Lightly used by passenger services.
Byfleet Junction	61 / 4C		??/??/1885	N/A	LSWR	Junction at south end of Byfleet Curve.

C

Name	Page / grid		Date opened	Date closed	Opened by	Notes
CABLE STREET COAL	74 / 2D		c.1893	post-1954	PRIV	On south side of LBLR viaduct between Grove St and Cannon St Rd. Not noted in Borley, but illustrated in Connor 'Fenchurch St to Barking', which notes wagon traversers supplied in 1893 and shows yard open in 1954.
Calderwood Street Tunnel	42 / 2A		30/07/1849	N/A	SER	
CALEDONIAN ROAD	26 / 3B		15/12/1906	N/A	UERL (GNPBR)	
CALEDONIAN ROAD & BARNSBURY Barnsbury Caledonian Road	26 / 3C		10/06/1852	N/A	EWIDBJR	Opened as 'Caledonian Road', renamed 'Barnsbury' 01/07/1870, Re-sited to east as 'Barnsbury' 21/11/1870. Prefix 'Caledonian Road' added 22/05/1893. Closed 20/02/2010 - 01/06/2010, upon re-opening, platforms reconfigured with new island platform 2 & 3 in between two pairs of tracks, and platform 1 to south abandoned.
CALEDONIAN ROAD GOODS (GNR)	26 / 3B 75		??/??/1878	30/10/1967	GNR	Adjacent to North London Railway but no physical connection to it.
CALEDONIAN ROAD GOODS (EWIDBJR)	26 / 3B 75		c.1851	06/09/1969	EWIDBJR	Originally on north side of line, relocated to south side 1869, transferred to LNWR 01/09/1871.
CAMBERWELL Camberwell New Road Camberwell	39 / 4D	P G	06/10/1862 06/10/1862	03/04/1916 18/04/1964	LCDR	Opened as 'Camberwell', 'New Road' suffix added 01/05/1863, dropped 01/10/1908. Passenger station closed 03/04/1916, goods & coal yard closed 18/04/1964.
Cambria Junction	39 / 5D		01/07/1872	N/A	LCDR / LBSCR	Junction at southern end of Cambria Spur. Sometimes referred to 'Cambria Road Junction'.

Name	Page / grid		Date opened	Date closed	Opened by	Notes
Cambria Spur	39 / 5C	P G	01/07/1872 01/07/1872	N/A N/A	LCDR	Also referred to as 'East Curve'.
CAMBRIDGE HEATH 17/02/1986 - 16/03/1986 (rebuilding).	27 / 4B		27/05/1872	N/A	GER	Closed 22/05/1916 - 05/05/1919, 27/07/1984 - September 1984 (fire),
CAMDEN	26 / 3A 58	P G	01/11/1851 c.1839	01/05/1852 ?	LNWR	Opened as a ticket platform c.1844, full opening 01/11/1851. Replaced by station of same name slightly to north 01/05/1852 (see entry for 'Chalk Farm LNWR'). Borley states goods opened 'probably' 1839, gives no closure date.
CAMDEN CARRIAGE SIDINGS	25 / 4D 58		c.1960s	N/A	LNWR	Formerly Camden Engine shed.
CAMDEN CHALK FARM Camden	25 / 3D 58	.	01/05/1852	01/04/1872	LNWR	Replaced Camden (1st) to south, replaced by Camden Chalk Farm (2nd) to north (later 'Chalk Farm').
CAMDEN 'PASSENGER' ENGINE SHED	25 / 4D 58		*c.1847*	*03/01/1966*	LNWR	Built at same time as Camden Roundhouse, both replacing earlier LBIR structure on Roundhouse site. Extended 1932, closed to steam 09/09/1963 then diesel 03/01/1966. Demolished, became Camden carriage sidings.
Camden Junctions	25 / 3D		09/06/1851	N/A	LNWR / EWIDBJR	Extensively remodelled with the addition of 'flying' junctions to the 'DC' lines 10/07/1922.
CAMDEN 'LUGGAGE' ENGINE SHED	58		*c.1847*	*c.1857*	LNWR	Replaced earlier LBIR engine shed on same site, became obsolete within 10 years (too small for engines). Utilised as warehouse for approx. 100 years, became cultural / music venue 1964 (Camden Roundhouse).
CAMDEN ROAD (MID)	26 / 3B		13/07/1868	01/01/1916	MID	
CAMDEN ROAD (NLR) Camden Town	26 / 3A		05/12/1870	N/A	NLR	Replaced first Camden Town station to east. Renamed 'Camden Road' 25/09/1950. Reduced from 4 tracks to 2 in 1984. Closed 20/02/2010 - 01/06/2010 (LOROL upgrade works).
Camden Road Central Junction	76		14/11/2007	N/A	LCOR / NR	
Camden Road East Junction	26 / 3A 76		??/??/1984	N/A	BR	Junction formed when quadruple track through Camden Road reduced to double in 1984.
Camden Road Incline Junction	76		14/11/2007	N/A	LCOR / NR	
Camden Road Tunnels	26 / 3B		07/09/1867	N/A	MID	Midland Main line first goods train ran 07/09/1867, first passenger 13/07/1868 (to King's Cross MET).
Camden Road West Junction Kentish Town Junction	26 / 3A		03/01/1860	N/A	HJR / NLR	Junction renamed 26/03/1955.
CAMDEN TOWN (CCEHR)	26 / 4A		22/06/1907	N/A	UERL (CCEHR)	
CAMDEN TOWN (EWIDBJR) Camden Road Camden Town	26 / 3A		07/12/1850	05/12/1870	EWIDBJR	Original station on St Pancras Way, opened as 'Camden Town'. Renamed 'Camden Road' 1853, reverted to 'Camden Town' 01/07/1870 Replaced by Camden Town (NLR) Station to West 05/12/1870.
Camden Town Junctions	26 / 4A		22/06/1907	N/A	UERL (CCEHR)	Extensively remodelled 20/04/1924 due to extension of Bank Branch from Euston.
Campbell Road Junction	27 / 5D 88		02/06/1902	13/09/1959	LTSR / MDR	Junction between LTSR and MDR, physical connection removed 13/09/1959 (although name still in use).
Campden Hill Tunnel	38 / 1B 84		01/10/1868	N/A	MET	
CANADA CREEK RAILWAY	48 / 5A		23/03/1989	07/11/2011	PRIV	2 foot gauge railway within Thorpe Park, last ran 06/11/2011. Originally a 2km route connecting the theme park with Thorpe Farm, truncated to a 350m loop at the eastern end of the original route after end of 2006 season (last train ran 05/11/2006).
CANADA WATER	40 / 2B		19/08/1999	N/A	LUL (ELL)	Jubilee Line platforms opened 17/09/1999. East London Line platforms closed 22/12/2007, re-opened 27/04/2010 as TfL (LOROL).
Canal Junction	40 / 3C 79 / 80		01/04/1880	N/A	ELR	Junction formed when spur from ELR to New Cross (SER) opened.
CANARY WHARF (DLR)	40 / 1D 31 / 6A		12/08/1991	N/A	DLR	Opened to construction workers 02/04/1991, date given is public opening. Closed 09/02/1996 - 09/03/1996 (bomb).
CANARY WHARF (LUL)	40 / 1D		17/09/1999	N/A	LUL (JUB)	
CANARY WHARF (NR)	40 / 1D 31 / 6B		??/??/2018	N/A	NR (XRAIL)	Station on Crossrail 1 Abbey Wood branch, to open 2018.
CANNING TOWN Barking Road	28 / 6A		14/06/1847	N/A	ECTJR	Renamed 01/07/1873, originally on south side of Barking Road, relocated to north side 1888 in connection with quadrupling works. Closed 29/05/1994 in connection with Jubilee Line extension works, re-opened 29/10/1995 on a new site again south of Barking Road and to south of original 1847 site. DLR platforms opened 05/03/1998, LUL Jubilee Line platforms opened 14/05/1999. NR platforms closed 09/12/2006, re-opened as DLR 31/08/2011.
CANNING TOWN NORTH GOODS	28 / 6A		*22/08/1881*	*06/03/1967*	LNWR	Renamed 'North' by BR 01/07/1950 to distinguish from 'South'.
CANNING TOWN SOUTH GOODS	28 / 6A		*14/06/1847*	*01/07/1968*	GER	Renamed 'South' by BR 01/07/1950 to distinguish from 'North'.
CANNON STREET	26 / 6D 87		01/09/1866	N/A	SER	Metropolitan & District Railways joint station opened 06/10/1884.
CANNON STREET ROAD	27 / 6A 74 / 2D		21/08/1842	??/12/1848	LBLR	
Cannon Street South Junction	39 / 1D 87		01/09/1866	N/A	SER	
CANONBURY Newington Road & Balls Pond	26 / 3D		01/09/1858	N/A	NLR	Opened as 'Newington Road & Balls Pond' 01/09/1858, re-sited west and renamed 'Canonbury' 01/12/1870. Closed 20/02/2010 - 01/06/2010 (LOROL upgrade works), upon re-opening trains called at northern platforms 3 & 4 (previously southern 1 & 2 used), all four platforms restored to use from 06/01/2011.
Canonbury Tunnel	26 / 3C	P G	18/01/1875 14/12/1874	08/11/1976 N/A	GNR	Line through tunnel singled 1988 due to electrification (clearance for overhead wires).
Canonbury West Junction	26 / 3D		14/12/1874	N/A	NLR / GNR	
CANONS PARK Canons Park (Edgware)	12 / 3A		10/12/1932	N/A	MET	Opened by Metropolitan Railway. 'Edgware' Suffix dropped ??/09/1933. Transferred to Bakerloo Line 20/11/1939, Jubilee Line 01/05/1979.
Canterbury Road Junction	39 / 5C		01/08/1865	N/A	LCDR	Junction between 01/05/1863 LCDR line Brixton to Loughborough Junction and 01/08/1865 line to Crystal Palace (High Level).
Carlton Road Junction	26 / 2A 9		02/04/1883	N/A	MID	
CARPENDERS PARK	10 / 1D		01/04/1914	N/A	LNWR	Re-sited south 17/11/1952. Served by London Underground Bakerloo Line Trains 16/04/1917 - 24/09/1982.

Name	Page / grid		Date opened	Date closed	Opened by	Notes
Carpenters Road Curve	27 / 4D 77 / 78	P G	N/A ??/??/1892	N/A N/A	GER	No regular passenger traffic carried.
CARPENTERS ROAD GOODS	27 / 4D 77		??/??/1892	02/11/1964	GER	
Carpenters Road North Junction	27 / 3D 77 / 78		??/??/1892	N/A	GER	Junction at north end of Carpenters Road Curve.
Carpenters Road South Junction	27 / 4D 77 / 78		??/??/1892	N/A	GER	Junction at south end of Carpenters Road Curve.
CARSHALTON	65 / 2D		01/10/1868	N/A	LBSCR	
CARSHALTON BEECHES Beeches Halt	65 / 4D .		01/10/1906	N/A	LBSCR	Renamed 01/04/1925
CARTERHATCH LANE	7 / 3B		12/06/1916	01/07/1919	GER	Single platform on current 'down' side only due to line being subject to single line working at this time.
CASSIOBRIDGE	2 / 4A		??/??/2017	N/A	LUL (MET)	Proposed station on Metropolitan Line Watford Junction extension, estimated opening 2017.
CASTLE BAR PARK Castle Bar Park Halt	23 / 5C		01/05/1904	N/A	GWR	Original wooden platforms replaced by concrete structures to north ??/11/1960. 'Halt' suffix dropped 05/05/1969.
CATERHAM	74 / 5A	P G	05/08/1856 05/08/1856	N/A 28/09/1964	CR	Rebuilt slightly to the west 01/01/1900. Goods yard closed 28/09/1964.
CATFORD	54 / C1		01/07/1892	N/A	LCDR	
CATFORD BRIDGE	54 / D1	P G	01/01/1857 01/01/1857	N/A 23/03/1968	MKR	Goods yard closed 23/03/1968.
Cedar Junction	76		14/11/2007	N/A	LCOR / NR	
CENTRAL	41 / 1D 62 / 3C		03/08/1880	09/09/1940	LSKD	Initially temporary terminus per Quick, Connor and Jackson ('for first few weeks' in latter), precise date of services to Gallions commencing unknown, but had appeared in Bradshaw by November 1880. Gallions branch single until 14/11/1881. Operated by GER after 1896, ownership later transferred to PLA. Branch closed from 09/09/1940 due to 'Black Saturday' air raid 07/09/1940 (no Sunday service after 27/06/1915). Listed as 'Royal Albert Dock Central' in Borley, also referred to as such in 1914 GER timetable per Quick. Became a 'halt' 01/11/1933.
CENTRAL CROYDON	66 / 2C		01/01/1868	01/09/1890	LBSCR	Closed 01/12/1871 - 01/06/1886. Between 1886 re-opening and 1890 final closure often also 'Croydon Central'.
CENTRALE	66 / 2C		10/12/2005	N/A	CTL	

CHADWELL HEATH
  Chadwell Heath for Becontree
  Chadwell Heath
	29 / 1D
	.
	.
		P
		G
			11/01/1864
			??/??/1876
				N/A
				07/12/1970
					GER	Suffix 'for Becontree' used between 1927 and 1955. Goods yard opened 1876, closed 07/12/1970

CHAFFORD HUNDRED	45 / 3A		30/05/1995	N/A	RT	Ceremonial opening 29/05/1995.
CHALFONT & LATIMER Chalfont Road	1 / 3C	P G	08/07/1889 08/07/1889	N/A 14/11/1966	MET	Renamed 01/11/1915. Goods yard closed 14/11/1966.
CHALK FARM (UERL)	25 / 3D		22/06/1907	N/A	UERL (CCEHR)	Named 'Adelaide Road' until opening.

CHALK FARM (LNWR)
  Camden (Chalk Farm)
  Camden
	25 / 3D		01/05/1852	10/05/1915	LNWR	Replaced first 'Camden' to south. Suffix '(Chalk Farm)' added 1866. Re-sited north 01/04/1872 for better interchange with NLR. Renamed 'Chalk Farm' 1876.

CHALVEY HALT	33 / 2C		06/05/1929	07/07/1930	GWR	

CHANCERY LANE
  Chancery Lane (Gray's Inn)
  Chancery Lane
	26 / 6C		30/07/1900	N/A	CLR	'Gray's Inn' suffix introduced 25/06/1934, gradually dropped.

Channelsea Curve	77	P G	15/08/1854 15/08/1854	N/A N/A	GER	No regular passenger traffic 1881 - 30/05/2000, then 11/09/2002 - 14/04/2009. Quadrupled 14/04/2009.
Channelsea North Junction	27 / 3D 77 / 78		??/??/1881	N/A	GER	Junction at south end of High Meads Loop.
Channelsea South Junction	27 / 3D 77 / 78		??/??/1881	N/A	GER	Re-arranged due to new Stratford platforms 1 & 2 opening from the evening of 14/04/2009.
CHARING CROSS (SER)	39 / 1B		11/01/1864	N/A	SER	Closed 05/12/1905 - 19/03/1906 (roof collapse) & 24/07/1993 - 16/08/1993 (track remodelling).

CHARING CROSS (UERL)
  Strand (*Northern Line*)
  Charing Cross (Strand) (*Northern Line*)
  Charing Cross (*Northern Line*)
  Trafalgar Square (*Bakerloo Line*)
	39 / 1B
	19
			10/06/1906	N/A	UERL
					(BSWR)
						Bakerloo Line platforms opened 10/06/1906 as 'Trafalgar Square', retaining this name until 01/05/1979. Northern Line platforms opened as separate station 'Charing Cross' 22/06/1907, renamed 'Charing Cross (Strand)' 06/04/1914, then 'Strand' 01/05/1915. Northern Line platforms closed 16/06/1973 - 01/05/1979 in connection with Jubilee Line construction. Jubilee Line platforms opened, Northern Line platforms re-opened, and station combined as 'Charing Cross' 01/05/1979. Jubilee Line platforms closed when line diverted at Green Park to Westminster 20/11/1999, retained for emergency train turnback (out of service) and for filming work.

CHARLTON
  Charlton Junction
  Charlton
	41 / 3B	P
		G
			30/07/1849
			c.1890
				N/A
				20/05/1963
					SER	Goods yard does not appear to have opened with passenger station: Borley gives goods opening date of c.1904, but a coal yard is depicted on 1895 OS map (none apparent on the 1882 survey), so opening date c.1890 assumed. Suffix 'Junction' often added between 1877/8 and 1928/9, with this name appearing on station nameboards and OS maps. Bay platform on 'down' side added when branch to Greenwich (Maze Hill) opened 01/01/1873. At some point the bay road was incorporated into the goods yard and fenced off. Goods yard closed 20/05/1963.

Charlton Junction	41 / 3B		01/01/1873	N/A	SER	Junction between SER North Kent Line and branch to Greenwich (Maze Hill).
Charlton Tunnel	41 / 2C		30/07/1849	N/A	SER	
Chatham Loops	55 / 5D 56 / 6A	P G	19/06/1904 19/06/1904	N/A N/A	SECR	Originally 'up' and 'down', but former 'down' loop resignalled for bidirectional working 1983 (= 'Reversible'). Referred to as 'Chislehurst Loops' until 1959.
CHEAM	65 / 4A	P G	10/05/1847 10/05/1847	N/A 28/09/1964	LBSCR	Line through station quadrupled 01/10/1911, central island platform allowed for but never built. Through roads removed 1977-8 (signal box closed 28/05/1978). Goods yard closed 28/09/1964.
CHELSEA & FULHAM Chelsea	38 / 3C 84		02/03/1863	14/09/1940	WLER	'& Fulham' after 01/01/1902. Passenger service withdrawn Willesden Junction to Clapham Junction 14/09/1940.
CHELSEA BASIN GOODS	38 / 4C		??/??/1863	11/09/1981	LNWR / GWR	

Name	Page / grid		Date opened	Date closed	Opened by	Notes
CHERTSEY	61 / 1A	P	14/02/1848	N/A	LSWR	Re-sited north 01/10/1866 to opposite side of level crossing when line extended to Virginia Water.
		G	14/02/1848	c.1965		
CHESHAM	1 / 1A	P	08/07/1889	N/A	MET	Served by GCR trains (later LNER, later BR) 01/03/1906 - 16/10/1967. Goods yard closed 04/07/1966.
		G	08/07/1889	04/07/1966		
CHESHUNT	7 / 1B	P	22/11/1841	N/A	NER	Original station 150m north of present site. Opened as 'Cadmores Lane Cheshunt' by NER 22/11/1841, closed 1842. Re-opened 31/05/1846 as 'Cheshunt', re-sited to present site 01/10/1891. Goods yard closed 01/06/1966.
Cadmores Lane, Cheshunt		G	22/11/1841	01/06/1966		
Cheshunt Junction	7 / 2B		01/10/1891	N/A	GER	
CHESSINGTON NORTH	63 / 3D		28/05/1939	N/A	SR	
CHESSINGTON SOUTH	63 / 4D	P	28/05/1939	N/A	SR	Intended to be a through station en route to Leatherhead, but line never completed beyond goods yard and 'up' platform never used (footbridge not completed). Goods yard opened 01/07/1939 (per Jackson, Borley states goods yard opened with passenger station), closed 18/03/1963 (see Chessington South Sidings).
		G	01/07/1939	18/03/1963		
CHESSINGTON SOUTH SIDINGS (disused)	63 / 4D		01/07/1939	N/A	SR	Originally Chessington South goods yard, closed to general goods 18/03/1963. Re-opened as coal concentration depot May 1963, closed 04/11/1988. Some sidings remain in situ (continuation of branch), but are disused.
CHESSINGTON ZOO RAILWAY	63 / 5C		??/??/1937	??/??/1997	PRIV	Opened 1937 with a 12 inch gauge, rebuilt 1970 to a 2 foot gauge, closed 1985. Redeveloped as 'Chessington Railroad' (also 2 foot gauge) and re-opened 1986, closed for good 1997.
CHIGWELL	17 / 2A		01/05/1903	N/A	GER	Fairlop Loop closed by LNER 30/11/1947 for electrification and transfer to LTE Central Line, re-opened 21/11/1948.
CHINGFORD (1st)	16 / 1A	P	17/11/1873	02/09/1878	GER	Original terminus of extension from Walthamstow. Closed to passengers 02/09/1878, goods 04/10/1965. Often referred to as 'Bull Lane'.
		G	17/11/1873	04/10/1965		
CHINGFORD (2nd)	8 / 6B		02/09/1878	N/A	GER	New passenger terminus opened to north of original, which closed the same day. Arranged for through running on an aborted extension to High Beech; stub of extension blocked and platforms connected beyond buffers c.1962. Carriage sidings added 1920, and subsequently expanded.
CHIPSTEAD	72 / 2D	P	02/11/1897	N/A	CVR	02/11/1897 is given as opening date for Chipstead Valley Railway (Purley to Kingswood) in Borley, but it also states regular passenger service 'probably' commenced 09/11/1897, Quick states first train 09/11/1897, so 02/11/1897 may have been official / ceremonial opening. Suffix dropped 09/07/1923. Goods yard closed 07/05/1962.
Chipstead & Banstead Downs		G	02/11/1897	07/05/1962		
CHISLEHURST	55 / 5D	P	01/07/1865	N/A	SER	Renamed 01/09/1866. Passenger station re-sited to the south 02/03/1868. Goods yard closed 18/11/1968.
Chislehurst & Bickley Park		G	01/07/1865	18/11/1968		
Chislehurst Junction	55 / 5D		19/06/1904	N/A	SECR	Junctions at north end of Chatham Loops.
Chislehurst Tunnels	55 / 3C		01/07/1865	N/A	SER	Fast tunnel opened 01/07/1865, Slow tunnel added by SECR 18/06/1905 (St Johns to Elmstead Woods quadrupling).
CHISWICK	37 / 3B	P	22/08/1849	N/A	LSWR	Suffix in use 01/11/1872 - 1955 ('for Grove Park' after c.1920). Goods yard closed 14/06/1958.
Chiswick for Grove Park		G	22/08/1849	14/06/1958		
Chiswick & Grove Park						
Chiswick						
Chiswick Curve	37 / 3B	P	01/06/1870	22/02/1915	LSWR	Opened at same time as Kensington (Addison Road) to Richmond, passenger service 01/06/1870 - 22/02/1915.
	51 / 3A	G	01/01/1869	24/07/1932		
Chiswick Junction (1st)	37 / 4C		01/02/1862	01/01/1869	LSWR	Junction at north end of Barnes Curve. Barnes Curve disused since 01/01/1869 but not dismantled until 1881.
Chiswick Junction (2nd)	37 / 3A		01/01/1869	24/07/1932	LSWR	Junction at south end of Chiswick Curve.
	51 / 3A					
CHISWICK PARK	37 / 2B		01/07/1879	N/A	MDR	Opened as 'Acton Green', renamed 'Chiswick Park & Acton Green' ??/03/1887, renamed 'Chiswick Park' 01/03/1910. Completely rebuilt 1932-33 due to quadrupling works. Served by Piccadilly Line 26/12/2013 – 30/12/2013 due to District Line engineering works.
Chiswick Park & Acton Green	51 / 2B					
Acton Green						
Chobham Farm Junction	28 / 3A		29/04/1846	01/06/1969	ECTJR / NER	
	77					
CHORLEYWOOD	1 / 4A	P	08/07/1889	N/A	MET	Opened as 'Chorley Wood', '& Chenies' suffix in use 01/11/1915 - c.1934 (LPTB) and c.1950 (BR). Became 'Chorleywood' c.1964 (LTB) and 1987 (BR). Goods yard closed 14/11/1966.
Chorley Wood		G	08/07/1889	14/11/1966		
Chorley Wood & Chenies						
Chorley Wood						
Christian Street Junction	27 / 6A		17/04/1886	N/A	LTSR	Originally Junction for Commercial Road Goods, Now point where 4 tracks become 2.
	74 / 2D					
CHURCH MANOR WAY HALT	42 / 2C		01/01/1917	01/01/1920	SECR	Provided for munitions workers.
CHURCH PATH SIDINGS	59 / 1D		14/11/2007	N/A	LCOR	Stabling / turnback sidings built in connection with HS1..
CHURCH STREET	66 / 2C		10/05/2000	N/A	CTL	
CHURCHYARD SIDINGS	76		??/??/1868	N/A	MID	Now Castle Cement terminal.
CITY GOODS	74 / 2C		01/10/1862	01/07/1949	MID	Site subsequently used for DLR Bank extension tunnel portals. Hydraulic accumulator tower remains in situ (listed).
CITY ROAD	26 / 5C		17/11/1901	09/08/1922	CSLR	
CITY THAMESLINK	26 / 6C		29/05/1990	N/A	BR	Renamed 30/09/1991.
St Paul's Thameslink	32 / 4C					
CLAPHAM COMMON (LSWR)	38 / 5C		21/05/1838	02/03/1863	LSWR	Renamed ??/07/1846. Replaced by Clapham Junction Station to North.
Wandsworth						
CLAPHAM COMMON (CSLR)	39 / 5A		03/06/1900	N/A	CSLR	Terminus of City & South London Railway 03/06/1900 - 13/09/1926. Closed 28/11/1923 - 01/12/1924.
CLAPHAM HIGH STREET	39 / 5B	P	25/08/1862	N/A	LCDR	Suffix '& North Stockwell' in use between 01/05/1863 and 27/09/1937. Northern platforms opened 01/01/1867, closed 03/04/1916. Station also referred to as 'Clapham Road' or 'Clapham Road & North Stockwell'. LSWR timetable for trains serving here to / from Ludgate Hill referred to 'Clapham Town' (distinct from 'Junction'). Goods yard closed 10/06/1963. Renamed 'Clapham High Street' 15/05/1989.
Clapham		G	25/08/1862	10/06/1963		
Clapham & North Stockwell						
Clapham						
CLAPHAM JUNCTION	38 / 5D		02/03/1863	N/A	LSWR / LBSCR	Replaced Clapham Common (LSWR) station to south.
	89					
Clapham Junction	38 / 5D		27/07/1846	N/A	LSWR	Junction between original LSWR line to Southampton and branch to Richmond.
Battersea Junction	89					
CLAPHAM NORTH	39 / 5B		03/06/1900	N/A	CSLR	Closed 28/11/1923 - 01/12/1924, Renamed 13/09/1926.
Clapham Road						
CLAPHAM SOUTH	39 / 6A		13/09/1926	N/A	UERL (NOR)	
CLAPHAM YARD	38 / 5C		c.1850s	N/A	LSWR	Sidings had appeared in angle between lines between 1850 and 1863.
	89					

Name	Page / grid		Date opened	Date closed	Opened by	Notes
CLAPTON	27 / 1B		01/07/1872	N/A	GER	Goods yard remote to north (see separate entry).
Clapton Curve	15 / 6B	P	01/07/1872	N/A	GER	
		G	01/07/1872	N/A		
CLAPTON GOODS	27 / 1B		??/??/1898	07/12/1964	GER	Yard enlarged 02/07/1900.
Clapton Junction	27 / 1B		01/08/1872	N/A	GER	
Clapton Tunnel	27 / 1B		01/07/1872	N/A	GER	
CLARENCE YARD GOODS	26 / 2C 81		c.1874	13/06/1960	GNR	Yard enlarged 1881, upon closure replaced by Finsbury Park Diesel Depot.
Clarence Yard Junction	81		c.1874	N/A	GNR	Formerly divergence of Clarence Yard goods, currently junction between Down goods and down line ex-Canonbury.
CLAYGATE Claygate for Claremont Claygate & Claremont	63 / 3B	P G	02/02/1885 02/02/1885	N/A c.1965	LSWR	Named 'Claygate & Claremont' until 1913, then '- for Claremont' until 1955, when suffix dropped.
Clerkenwell Tunnels	26 / 5C 32 / 2B		10/01/1863	N/A	MET	Quadrupled 17/02/1868.
CLOCK HOUSE	54 / 5C	P G	01/05/1890 01/05/1890	N/A 19/04/1965	SER	Named 'Penge Road' until opening. Goods yard closed 19/04/1965.
COBHAM & STOKE D'ABERNON Cobham for Stoke D'Abernon Cobham & Stoke D'Abernon	69 / 1D	P G	02/02/1885 02/02/1885	N/A c.1965	LSWR	Opening notice referred to 'Stoke D'Abernon & Cobham', but never appeared as such in Bradshaw. 'for' was substituted for '&' 1913 - 09/09/1953.
COBORN ROAD Coborn Road (Old Ford) Old Ford	27 / 5C		01/02/1865	08/12/1946	GER	Opened as 'Old Ford', renamed 'Coborn Road (Old Ford)' 01/03/1879, but suffix usually omitted. Re-sited west 02/12/1883. Closed 22/05/1916 - 05/05/1919, then for good 08/12/1946.
COCKFOSTERS	6 / 4A		31/07/1933	N/A	LPTB (PIC)	
COCKFOSTERS DEPOT	6 / 5A		31/07/1933	N/A	LPTB (PIC)	
Coleman Street Tunnel	41 / 2D		30/07/1849	N/A	SER	
COLINDALE	12 / 4C		18/08/1924	N/A	UERL (CCEHR)	
COLLIERS WOOD	52 / 4C		13/08/1926	N/A	UERL (NOR)	
COLNBROOK	34 / 3A	P G	09/08/1884 09/08/1884	29/03/1965 03/01/1966	GWR	Terminus of branch from West Drayton 09/08/1884 - 02/11/1885. Passing loop and 'up' platform opened 02/05/1904. Passenger service withdrawn between West Drayton and Staines West 29/03/1965 and Colnbrook station closed; goods yard remained open until 03/01/1966. Oil terminal opened on site 01/03/1990.
COLNBROOK ESTATE HALT	34 / 3A		01/05/1961	29/03/1965	BR	
COLNBROOK LOGISTICS CENTRE	34 / 3A		c.2003	N/A	PRIV	Terminal for Heathrow Airport construction materials built for Terminal 5 construction.
COLNBROOK OIL TERMINAL (ELF)	34 / 3A		01/03/1990	N/A	PRIV	Aviation Fuel terminal for Heathrow Airport.
Colne Junction	2 / 5C		10/02/1913	19/09/1966	LNWR	Last train on Colne Junction to Croxley Green Junction spur 06/06/1966, date is that of official closure / removal.
COLNE VALLEY WATERWORKS RAILWAY	2 / 6B		1931/1932	??/??/1967	PRIV	2 foot gauge light railway conveying coal, salt, and chlorine. Coal to Eastbury Pumping Station ceased 1956.
COLNEY HATCH CEMETERY	14 / 1A		10/07/1861	03/04/1863	GNR	Funeral traffic only (see King's Cross Funeral Station). May have re-opened 1866-7 during a cholera epidemic.
COMMERCIAL DOCKS	40 / 2B 79		01/05/1856	01/01/1867	SER	
COMMERCIAL ROAD GOODS	27 / 6A 74 / 1C		17/04/1886	03/07/1967	LTSR	
Connaught Bridge	41 / 1C 62 / 3B	P G	26/11/1855 26/11/1855	??/06/1976 ??/10/1967	ECR	Crossing of channel between Victoria and Albert Docks, passenger traffic diverted via Connaught Tunnel from June 1876 but route retained for heavier goods trains (1/50 gradients associated with Connaught Tunnel). Passenger services restored 30/09/1935 - 28/03/1936 due to temporary Connaught Tunnel closure. Last goods movement October 1967, line dismantled soon afterwards.
CONNAUGHT ROAD	41 / 1C 62 / 3B		03/08/1880	08/09/1940	LSKD	Gallions branch single until 14/11/1881. Operated by GER after 1896, ownership later transferred to PLA. Branch closed from 09/09/1940 due to 'Black Saturday' air raid 07/09/1940 (no trains on Sundays since 27/06/1915). Listed as 'Royal Albert Dock, Connaught Road' in Borley.
Connaught Tunnel	41 / 1C 62	P G	??/06/1876 ??/06/1876	10/12/2006 29/03/1993	GER	North Woolwich Branch diverted underground due to construction of Royal Albert Dock. No service 30/09/1935 -28/03/1936, 08/09/1940 - 01/01/1941 and 29/05/1994 - 29/10/1995. Passenger route singled 25/08/1969, the original 'up' road then becoming bi-directional and the original 'down' becoming a siding accessing the 'Silvertown Tramway' (taken out of use 29/03/1993). Stratford to North Woolwich closed by Network Rail 10/12/2006. Currently being refurbished to be re-used by Crossrail 1 Abbey Wood branch opening 2018.
COOMBE LANE	67 / 3B		10/05/2000	N/A	CTL	
COOMBE ROAD Coombe Lane	66 / 3D		10/08/1885	16/05/1983	LBSCR / SER	Closed 01/01/1917 - 30/09/1935, Renamed upon re-opening, closed again 16/05/1983.
Coopersale	8 / 1B		27/03/2005	N/A	EOR	Current limit of Epping Ongar Railway operation, no platform. Service from North Weald commenced Easter 2005. Service suspended 31/12/2007 - 25/05/2012 (engineering works).
Copenhagen Junction	75 / 76		??/??/1853	N/A	GNR / NLR	Also referred to as 'Belle Isle Junction'.
Copenhagen Tunnels	26 / 3B 75 / 76		07/08/1850	N/A	GNR	Middle bore first, West bore opened 1877, East bore 1886. East bore abandoned c.1977.
Coppermill Curve	15 / 6B	P G	01/08/1885 01/08/1885	06/09/1926 11/06/1960	GER	Regular passenger service ceased 06/09/1926, freight use ceased and curve abandoned 11/06/1960.
Coppermill North Junction	15 / 6B		01/07/1872	N/A	GER	Junction between Lea Valley Line and Clapton Curve.
Coppermill South Junction	15 / 6B		01/08/1885	11/06/1960	GER	Junction between Lea Valley Line and Coppermill Curve (see notes for latter).
Corbett's Lane Junction	40 / 3B 79 / 80		05/06/1839	N/A	LGR / LCRR	Junction between LGR and LCRR.
CORY OIL (SELSDON)	66 / 3D		c.1968	??/03/1993	PRIV	On site of Selsdon goods yard (closed 07/10/1968). Closed March 1993, track remains in situ.
Cottage Junction	66 / 1D 86		??/10/1983	N/A	BR	Created through remodelling of Gloucester Road Triangle 1983.
COULSDON NORTH Coulsdon West	73 / 1B	P G	05/11/1899 05/11/1899	03/10/1983 07/10/1968	LBSCR	Renamed 'Coulsdon & Smitham Downs' 01/06/1911, renamed 'Coulsdon West' 09/07/1923 for 3 weeks, then finally renamed

Name	Page / grid		Date opened	Date closed	Opened by	Notes
Coulsdon & Smitham Downs Stoat's Nest & Cane Hill						'Coulsdon North' 01/08/1923. Goods yard closed 07/10/1968. Opened as two through and two terminal platforms (with goods yard beyond terminal platforms), weekend services ceased September 1965, then peak hours only from May 1970. Closed altogether 03/10/1983.

COULSDON SOUTH
  Coulsdon East
  Coulsdon & Cane Hill
  Coulsdon
	73 / 2A	P
		G
			01/10/1889
			01/10/1889
				N/A
				01/10/1931
					SER	Suffix '& Cane Hill' added 1896. Renamed 'Coulsdon East' 09/07/1923 for 3 weeks then 'Coulsdon South' 01/08/1923. Goods yard closed 01/10/1931.

COULSDON TOWN
  Coulsdon Town (Smitham)
  Smitham
	73 / 1A	P
		G
			01/01/1904
			01/01/1904
				N/A
				07/05/1962
					SECR	Closed 01/01/1917 - 01/01/1919. Goods yard closed 07/05/1962. Renamed 22/05/2011, initially 'Coulsdon Town (Smitham)' on TfL map and Southern timetable, while station nameboards displayed both 'Coulsdon Town' and 'Coulsdon Town (formerly Smitham)' after renaming. Winter timetable 11/12/2011 became 'Coulsdon Town'.

Courthill Loop	40 / 5D	P G	07/07/1929 07/07/1929	N/A N/A	SR	
Courthill Loop North Junction	40 / 5D		07/07/1929	N/A	SR	Junction at north end of Courthill Loop.
Courthill Loop South Junction	40 / 6D		07/07/1929	N/A	SR	Junction at south end of Courthill Loop.
COVENT GARDEN	26 / 6B		11/04/1907	N/A	UERL (GNPBR)	
Cow Lane Junction	40 / 4A		01/08/1865	N/A	LCDR / LBSCR	Boundary between LCDR & LBSCR ('End-on' Junction).
COWLEY	21 / 5C		01/10/1904	10/09/1962	GWR	Passenger services withdrawn from Uxbridge Vine Street Branch 10/09/1962.
COXES LOCK MILL (FLOUR)	61 / 3C		c.1901	c.1970	PRIV	Mill rebuilt 1901, siding assumed to have been laid then (appeared between 1896 and 1914 OS). Removed c.1970.
CRANLEY GARDENS	14 / 5A	P G	02/08/1902 29/06/1897	05/07/1954 08/05/1957	GNR	Opened to goods first, passenger station opened 02/08/1902. Closed to passengers when Alexandra Palace to Finsbury Park service withdrawn 05/07/1954 after a previous closure period 29/10/1951 - 07/01/1952. Branch had been intended for electrification and transfer to LT Northern Line, but works abandoned post-WW2. Goods yard closed 08/05/1957 and route to Park Junction abandoned
CRAYFORD	57 / 1C	P G	01/09/1866 01/09/1866	N/A 04/01/1965	SER	Goods yard closed 04/01/1965
Crayford Creek Junction	43 / 5D		01/05/1895	N/A	BHR / SER	
Crayford Spur	43 / 6D	P G	11/10/1942 11/10/1942	N/A N/A	SR	Borley refers to spur opening in 1918 and closing to regular traffic c.1920, before re-opening 11/10/1942, however contemporary OS maps show no evidence of the line before WW2.
Crayford Spur 'A' Junction	43 / 6D		11/10/1942	N/A	SR	Junction at north end of Crayford Spur.
Crayford Spur 'B' Junction	43 / 6D		11/10/1942	N/A	SR	Junction at south end of Crayford Spur.
CREEKMOUTH	29 / 6C		TBA	N/A	DLR	Gallions Reach to Dagenham Dock was proposed to open c.2017, but funding removed November 2008.
Cremorne Bridge	38 / 4C		02/03/1863	N/A	WLER	
Crescent Wood Tunnel	54 / 2A		01/08/1865	20/09/1954	LCDR	Nunhead to Crystal Palace (High Level) closed 20/09/1954 (Passengers and Goods).
CREWS HILL	6 / 1C	P G	04/04/1910 04/04/1910	N/A 01/10/1962	GNR	Goods yard closed 01/10/1962.
CRICKLEWOOD Childs Hill & Cricklewood	25 / 2A 85	P G	02/05/1870 02/05/1870	N/A 06/10/1969	MID	Renamed 01/05/1903. Goods yard closed 06/10/1969.
Cricklewood Curve	25 / 1A 85	P G	03/08/1875 03/08/1875	01/10/1902 N/A	MID	Opened to passenger & goods traffic 03/08/1875. No passenger traffic between 01/07/1886 - 01/03/1893. Passenger traffic withdrawn for good 01/10/1902, freight traffic remains.
Cricklewood Curve Junction	25 / 1A 85		03/08/1875	N/A	MID	
CRICKLEWOOD DEPOT	25 / 1A 85		04/11/1979	N/A	BR	Built for Midland main line electrification, completed Bedford - Moorgate May 1982 and into St Pancras Summer 1982. Depot and associated signal box commissioned 04/11/1979 but only used for storage of class 317 EMUs between delivery and their entry into passenger service October 1983 (delayed by trade union dispute). Following introduction of 'Thameslink' service 16/05/1988, maintenance moved to Selhurst Depot and Cricklewood Depot became largely disused and the EMU shed rented out (Jerich's Warehouse – now disused). Some FCC EMU and Midland Mainline HST/DMU stabling remains on site.
CRICKLEWOOD DOWN SIDINGS	25 / 2A 85		c.1870s	c.1960s	MID	Had appeared by late 19th century, possibly laid in association with Cricklewood Curve. Lifted by 1970s.
CRICKLEWOOD ENGINE SHED	25 / 1A 85		??/??/1882	14/12/1964	MID	1st shed 1882, 2nd added 1893. After steam stabling ceased, sheds used for diesel stabling for a short while.
CRICKLEWOOD FREIGHT SIDINGS Cricklewood Brent Sidings	25 / 1A 85		c.1870	N/A (disused)	MID	First sidings on 'up' side had appeared by early 1870s, greatly expanded in late 19th and early 20th centuries. Most of goods sidings removed to allow construction of the TMD then EMU depot, some retained but now disused.
CRICKLEWOOD RECESS SIDINGS	25 / 1A 85		c.1870s	N/A (disused)	MID	Had appeared by late 19th century, possibly laid in association with Cricklewood Curve. Hosted Redland (now Lafarge) aggregate terminal until early 2000s. Shown in situ on 2005 Trackmaps edition, but now all overgrown / blocked.
Cricklewood South Junction Watling Street Junction	25 / 2A		25/06/1899	N/A	MID	
CRICKLEWOOD TMD	25 / 1A 85		c.1965	??/07/1983	BR	Replaced Cricklewood Engine Shed, maintained diesel locos and DMUs for Midland main line.
CROFTON PARK	40 / 6C		01/07/1892	N/A	LCDR	
Crofton Road Junction	40 / 4A		?	N/A	LCDR / LBSCR	
Cromwell Curve	38 / 2C 84	P G	03/07/1871 03/07/1871	12/02/1956 12/02/1956	MDR	Opening coincided with MDR's platforms at High Street Kensington.
Cromwell Curve North Junction	38 / 2C 84		03/07/1871	12/02/1956	MDR	Junction at north end of Cromwell Curve.
Cromwell Curve South Junction	38 / 2C 84		03/07/1871	12/02/1956	MDR	Junction at south end of Cromwell Curve.
Cromwell Road Junction	38 / 2B 84		03/07/1871	N/A	MDR	Remodelled as 'flying' junction 01/02/1878.

Name	Page / grid		Date opened	Date closed	Opened by	Notes
CROSSHARBOUR Crossharbour & London Arena Crossharbour	40 / 2D		31/08/1987	N/A	DLR	On site of former Millwall Docks station. '& London Arena' suffix added 14/08/1995, not dropped until 2007 despite The London Arena having been demolished in June 2006. Closed by IRA bomb at South Quay 09/02/1996 -15/04/1996. Southern terminus of DLR during Lewisham extension works 11/01/1999 - 20/11/1999.
Cross Street Tunnel	42 / 2A		30/07/1849	N/A	SER	
CROUCH END	14 / 6B		22/08/1867	05/07/1954	GNR	Closed when Alexandra Palace to Finsbury Park service withdrawn 05/07/1954 after a previous closure period 29/10/1951 - 07/01/1952. Branch had been intended for electrification and transfer to LPTB Northern Line, but works abandoned post-WW2.
CROUCH HILL	14 / 6C		21/07/1868	N/A	THJR	Closed 31/01/1870 - 01/10/1870.
CROWLANDS	18 / 6B		N/A	N/A	GER	Platform foundations built west of Jutsums Lane 1900, but station never completed.
CROXLEY Croxley Green	2 / 5A	P G	02/11/1925 02/11/1925	N/A 14/11/1966	MET / LNER	LNER services ceased 04/05/1926. 'Green' suffix dropped 23/05/1949. Goods yard closed 14/11/1966.
CROXLEY DEPOT	2 / 5C		16/04/1917	??/09/1985	LNWR	Facilities shared by Bakerloo Line and mainline until 24/09/1982.
CROXLEY GREEN	2 / 5A	P G	15/06/1912 15/06/1912	25/03/1996 14/11/1966	LNWR	Goods yard closed 14/11/1966. Platform relocated east 1989 (temporary structure due to subsidence). Last train ran on Croxley Green Branch 22/03/1996 (no weekend service so Monday 25/03/1996 is given as closure date), initially closed 'temporarily' for bridge work, replaced by bus service which ran until 26/09/2003.
Croxley Green Junction	2 / 5C		10/02/1913	19/09/1966	LNWR	Last train on Colne Junction to Croxley Green Junction spur 06/06/1966, date is that of official closure / removal.
CROXLEY TIP	1 / 6D		??/??/1902	1980s	MET	LT refuse tip, former gravel pit. Regular use into 1980s per Horne 'Metropolitan Line - an illustrated history'.
CROYDON 'A' POWER STATION	66 / 2C		??/??/1896	??/??/1973	PRIV	
CROYDON 'B' POWER STATION	66 / 1B		??/??/1950	??/??/1981	PRIV	
CRYSTAL PALACE Crystal Palace Low Level Crystal Palace	54 / 4A	P G	10/06/1854 10/06/1854	N/A 06/12/1965	LBCSR	Suffix 'Low Level' 01/11/1898 - 13/06/1955 to distinguish from LCDR station. Goods yard closed 06/12/1965. Original (eastern) section of station remodelled to accommodate LOROL services, commenced 23/05/2010.
CRYSTAL PALACE HIGH LEVEL Crystal Palace & Upper Norwood Crystal Palace High Level & Upper Norwood Crystal Palace High Level	54 / 3A	P G	01/08/1865 01/08/1865	20/09/1954 20/09/1954	LCDR	Suffix '& Upper Norwood' added 01/11/1898 after which time 'High Level' was sometimes omitted. Renamed 'Crystal Palace High Level' 09/07/1923. Closed 01/01/1917 - 01/03/1919 and 22/05/1944 - 04/03/1946. Nunhead to Crystal Palace (High Level) closed 20/09/1954 (Passengers and Goods).
Crystal Palace Tunnel	54 / 3A		01/12/1856	N/A	WELCPR	
Crystal Palace Tunnel Junction	54 / 4A		01/10/1857	N/A	LBSCR / WELCPR	
CUSTOM HOUSE Custom House Victoria Dock Victoria Dock, Custom House Custom House	41 / 1B 62		26/11/1855	N/A	ECR	Bay platform provided on 'down' side for terminating trains ex-Gallions. Station became temporary terminus from 08/09/1940 due to 'Black Saturday' air raid the previous day, North Woolwich service not restored until 01/01/1941 and Gallions service was never restored. Also referred to as 'Victoria Dock, Custom House' and 'Custom House Victoria Dock'. DLR Platforms opened 28/03/1994. NR platforms closed 10/12/2006, to re-open 2018 (Crossrail 1).
Custom House Junction	62 / 3B		??/06/1876	??/10/1967	GER	Junction between routes via Connaught Bridge and Connaught Tunnel.
CUTTY SARK	40 / 3D		03/12/1999	N/A	DLR	
CYPRUS	41 / 1D 62 / 5C		28/03/1994	N/A	DLR	

D

Name	Page / grid		Date opened	Date closed	Opened by	Notes
DAGENHAM DOCK	30 / 5A	P	01/07/1908	N/A	LTSR	Goods yard closed 02/11/1964; site became East London Waste Terminal. Proposed terminus of DLR extension from Gallions Reach.
DAGENHAM DOCK	30 / 6A		??/??1887	c.1980s	PRIV	Rail-served dock, sidings still apparent on OS maps until mid-1980s.
Dagenham Dock East Junction (Down)	30 / 5A		14/11/2007	N/A	LCOR / NR	
Dagenham Dock East Junction (Up)	30 / 5B		14/11/2007	N/A	LCOR / NR	
DAGENHAM EAST Dagenham	30 / 3B	P G	01/05/1885 01/05/1885	N/A 06/05/1968	LTSR	Served by District Railway trains 02/06/1902 - 01/10/1905, then by excursion trains to Southend (later Shoeburyness) from 01/06/1910. Regular District Line service reintroduced 12/09/1932 when route quadrupled, District Line trains utilising the new 'local' platforms. 'East' suffix added 01/05/1949. British Rail services withdrawn by 15/06/1962 and 'fast' platforms abandoned. Goods yard closed 06/05/1968. Ownership of 'local' platforms transferred to LTB 01/01/1969.
DAGENHAM HEATHWAY Heathway	30 / 3A		12/09/1932	N/A	LMS	Barking to Upminster quadrupled and 2 new stations opened by LMS 12/09/1932, but LMS service never provided, served solely by District Line from opening. Renamed 01/05/1949, ownership transferred to LTB 01/01/1969.
Dalston Eastern Curve	27 / 3A 6	P G	01/11/1865 ??/05/1868	15/05/1944 02/01/1966	NLR	Opened to passengers 01/11/1865, goods May 1868. Passenger service suspended 15/05/1944 (enemy action), was never reinstated. Regular goods traffic ceased 01/03/1965, points removed 02/01/1966. Route safeguarded for possible future re-opening for LOROL services.
Dalston Eastern Junction	27 / 3A 6		01/11/1865	02/01/1966	NLR	Junction at north end of Dalston Eastern Curve.
DALSTON JUNCTION	27 / 3A 6		01/11/1865	N/A	NLR	Platforms 5 & 6 closed 15/05/1944, 3 & 4 closed 08/11/1976. Closed completely 30/06/1986 - 27/04/2010.
Dalston Junction	27 / 3A 6		01/11/1865	02/01/1966	NLR	Junction at south end of Dalston Western and Eastern Curves.
DALSTON KINGSLAND Kingsland	27 / 3A 6		09/11/1850	N/A	BR	Opened as 'Kingsland' 09/11/1850, closed 01/11/1865 when Broad Street extension opened by NLR and platforms subsequently demolished. Goods yard to east (see 'Kingsland Goods'). Re-opened as 'Dalston Kingsland' 16/05/1983. Closed 20/02/2010 - 01/06/2010 (LOROL upgrade works).
Dalston Western Curve	27 / 3A 6	P G	01/11/1865 ??/05/1868	N/A 11/04/1969	NLR	Carried goods traffic from May 1868 to 11/04/1969. Closed with Broad Street and Dalston Junction Stations 30/06/1986 and dismantled, but subsequently reinstated (06/01/2011 test train, 28/02/2011 passenger service).
Dalston Western Junction	27 / 3A 6		01/11/1865	N/A	NLR	Junction eliminated 30/06/1986 - 06/01/2011 (date of first test train), no physical connection at present.

Name	Page / grid		Date opened	Date closed	Opened by	Notes
DARTFORD Dartford Junction for Farningham Dartford Junction Dartford	58 / 1A	P G	30/07/1849 *30/07/1849*	N/A *01/05/1972*	SER	Suffix 'Junction' added 1870, 'for Farningham' added 1871, reverted to 'Dartford' 1879/80. Remodelled 1895 to three through lines with the third road extending to Dartford Junction, carriage sidings expanded to current five at this time (there were previously two). Goods yard closed 01/05/1972. Remodelled to four bidirectional through lines / four platform faces 05/08/1973.
Dartford Junction	43 / 6D		01/09/1866	N/A	SER	
DATCHET	33 / 4D	P G	22/08/1848 *22/08/1848*	N/A *17/01/1965*	LSWR	Terminus of extension from Richmond until 01/12/1849. Goods yard closed 17/01/1965.
DAY & SONS GRAVEL (PURLEY)	66 / 5C		?	N/A	PRIV	Established on site of Purley goods yard, closed 06/01/1969.
DEBDEN Chigwell Lane Chigwell Road	8 / 4A	P G	24/04/1865 *24/04/1865*	N/A *18/04/1966*	GER	Opened as 'Chigwell Road', renamed 'Lane' 01/12/1865. Closed 22/05/1916 - 03/02/1919. Ownership and majority of passenger services transferred to LTE and station renamed 'Debden' 25/09/1949. First Trains in the morning remained British Rail services until 01/06/1970. Goods yard closed 18/04/1966.
Delta Junction	31		31/08/1987	N/A	DLR	Northern side of original triangular 'flat' junction eliminated at time of Beckton Extension. Eastbound trains ex-Bank diverted via new diveunder 24/08/2009.
DENHAM Denham for Harefield Denham	9 / 6B	P G	02/04/1906 *02/04/1906*	N/A *06/01/1964*	GCR / GWR	Suffix 'for Harefield' 01/10/1907 - 1955. Projected terminus of Central Line extension from West Ruislip, but works cancelled during WW2. Goods yard closed 06/01/1964. Through roads removed 12/12/1965 (up) & 19/12/1965 (down). Down platform relocated to north of track 27/07/2008 due to subsidence under original.
Denham East Curve	9 / 6C	P G	N/A *01/05/1907*	N/A *??/??/1917*	GWR	Denham East curve only saw occasional goods traffic and was lifted during WW1.
Denham East Junction	9 / 6C		01/05/1907	??/??/1917	GWR	Junction between Denham East Curve and GWR / GCR main line.
Denham South Junction	9 / 6C		01/05/1907	30/04/1965	GWR	Junction eliminated when East curve lifted c.1917, but reinstated 14/05/1942 - 30/04/1965 for access to oil depot.
Denham West Curve	9 / 6C	P G	01/05/1907 *01/05/1907*	01/09/1939 *30/04/1965*	GWR	Uxbridge High Street branch closed 01/09/1939 (passengers) & 24/02/1964 (goods), but northern portion remained open to serve an oil depot until 30/04/1965.
Denham West Junction	9 / 6B		01/05/1907	30/04/1965	GWR	Junction between Uxbridge High Street branch and GWR / GCR main line.
DENMARK HILL	39 / 5D		01/12/1865	N/A	LBSCR	Entire station owned by LBSCR, but the northern platforms used exclusively by LCDR opened first on 01/12/1865, line through station having opened 4 months earlier on 01/08/1865. Southern (LBSCR) platforms added 13/08/1866.
Denmark Hill Tunnels	39 / 5D		01/08/1865	N/A	LBSCR	North bore opened 01/08/1865, south bore 13/08/1866.
DENTON HALT Denton Road Denton Halt	60 / 1C		01/07/1906	04/12/1961	SECR	Named 'Denton Road' 1914 - 1919, otherwise 'Denton Halt'.
DEPTFORD	40 / 3C		08/02/1836	N/A	LGR	Country terminus of LGR 08/02/1836 - 24/12/1838. 3-road engine shed provided on 'up' side, with an incline down to carriage storage under the viaduct arches (incline still in situ, and 'listed'). Shed closed 1904. Station closed 15/03/1915 as a WW1 economy, did not re-open until 19/07/1926.
DEPTFORD BRIDGE	40 / 4D		20/11/1999	N/A	DLR	
Deptford Lift Bridge Junction	40 / 3B 79		15/05/1869	01/01/1964	LBSCR	Junction where Deptford Wharf branch split into lines to Old Kent Road (added 05/05/1869) and separate 'up' and 'down' lines to New Cross (Gate). Separate 'up' line added 01/10/1884 (until this date Deptford Wharf branch joined LBSCR main line on 'down' side only). Entire branch and connection virtually closed 14/10/1963, officially 01/01/1964.
DEPTFORD WHARF	40 / 2C 79		*02/07/1849*	*01/01/1964*	LBSCR	Was virtually closed by 14/10/1963, 01/01/1964 is official date of closure.
DEVONSHIRE STREET, MILE END	27 / 5C		20/06/1839	c.1841	ECR	London Terminus of ECR 20/06/1839 - 01/07/1840. Definitely remained open after line extended to Bishopsgate, but exact closure date unknown; late 1840 or early 1841 coinciding roughly with Mile End (ECR) opening to west.
DEVONS ROAD	27 / 5D 88		31/08/1987	N/A	DLR	Poplar to Stratford no service 18/04/2014 until 22:00 25/04/2014.
DEVONS ROAD DEPOT	27 / 5D 88		*??/??/1882*	10/02/1964	NLR	Locomotive Depot, upon losing last steam allocation 25/08/1958, became Britain's first diesel-only depot.
DEVONS ROAD GOODS	27 / 5D 88		*??/07/1874*	02/11/1964	LNWR	Originally coal only, opened to general goods February 1891.
District Junction (South Acton)	37 / 1B 51 / 1B		15/05/1899	??/??/1915	MDR / NSWJR	Points 'clipped' out of use since 1915 (last traffic the year before), but not physically removed until c.1930.
Dock Junction North	75 / 76		01/10/1868	N/A	MID	Junction between MID routes to St Pancras terminus and MET 'Widened Lines'.
Dock Junction South	75 / 76		01/11/1887	N/A	MID	Formerly divergence of line to Somers Town goods, currently crossovers on Midland main line.
Dockyard Tunnel	41 / 2D		30/07/1849	N/A	SER	
DOLLIS HILL Dollis Hill & Gladstone Park Dollis Hill	24 / 2D		01/10/1909	N/A	MET	Suffix '& Gladstone Park' in use 1931-1933. First served Bakerloo Line 20/11/1939. Last served Metropolitan Line 07/11/1940. Bakerloo Line service replaced by Jubilee Line 01/05/1979.
Dolphin Junction	33 / 1B		01/06/1879	N/A	GWR	Junctions between 'fast' and 'slow' lines between Langley and Slough.
DOWN EMPTY CARRIAGE SHED (EUSTON)	26 / 4A		?	c.2007	LNWR	In situ but disused, last train movements thought to be early 2007 to remove stored vans.
DOWN SIDINGS (PLUMSTEAD)	42 / 2B		c.1900	N/A	SER	No sidings apparent on 1896 OS, but had appeared by 1914. Three electrified stabling sidings & two unelectrified. East end access and unelectrified sidings to be removed due to construction of Plumstead Portal (Crossrail 1).
DOWN SIDINGS (SHENFIELD)	20 / 1C		*01/01/1934*	N/A	LNER	Not in regular use.
DOWN SIDINGS (WIMBLEDON)	52 / 3B		c.1895	N/A	LSWR	Berthing sidings, apparent on 1895 OS, one greatly extended 1898 to access Wimbledon Borough Council siding. Electrified c.1935, shortened 1984.
DOWN STREET Down Street, Mayfair	39 / 1A		15/03/1907	22/05/1932	UERL (GNPBR)	Opened with 'Mayfair' suffix, subsequently dropped.
DOWN YARD (REDHILL)	73 / 6C		c.1900	N/A	SECR	Not depicted on 1896 OS, but appeared on 1913 survey.
DOWN YARD (SOUTHALL)	35 / 1D		01/05/1839	N/A	GWR	On site of first goods yard at Southall.
DRAYTON GREEN Drayton Green Ealing Halt	23 / 6C		01/03/1905	N/A	GWR	Renamed 'Drayton Green' 05/05/1969.

Name	Page / grid		Date opened	Date closed	Opened by	Notes
Drayton Green Junction	23 / 6C		03/06/1903	N/A	GWR	
Drayton Green Tunnel	23 / 6C		??/04/1974	N/A	BR	Covered Way erected over line in connection with housing development
above, completed April 1974.						
DRAYTON PARK	26 / 2C 81		14/02/1904	N/A	GNCR	Opened by GNCR, absorbed by Metropolitan Railway 01/07/1913, transferred to LPTB Edgware - Morden Line (later Northern Line) 01/07/1933. Became northern terminus of line from Moorgate 04/10/1964 (Victoria Line works). Closed by LTE 05/10/1975, re-opened by British Rail 16/08/1976.
DRAYTON PARK DEPOT	26 / 2C 81		14/02/1904	05/10/1975	GNCR	GNCR depot, closed when Northern City Line closed by LTE prior to transfer to BR. Was connected to GNR.
DUDDING HILL FOR WILLESDEN & NEASDEN Dudding Hill Dudding Hill for Church End Willesden Willesden & Dudden Hill	24 / 2D	P G	03/08/1875 01/01/1872	01/10/1902 06/07/1964	MID	Opened to goods traffic 01/01/1872, passenger station opened 03/08/1875 as 'Willesden & Dudden Hill'. Renamed 'Dudding Hill for Church End Willesden' 01/02/1876, then 'Dudding Hill' 01/05/1878, then 'Dudding Hill for Willesden & Neasden' 01/06/1880. Closed to passengers 02/07/1888 - 01/03/1893, then for good 01/10/1902. Goods yard closed 06/07/1964.
Dudding Hill Junction	24 / 2D		02/05/1870	N/A	MID	
DUNDONALD ROAD	52 / 4A		30/05/2000	N/A	CTL	
DURNSFORD ROAD POWER STATION	52 / 2B		25/10/1915	??/??/1965	LSWR	LSWR power station, opening date denotes first section of route to be supplied (Wimbledon - East Putney). After closure and demolition, Wimbledon Traincare Depot inspection shed erected on site 1976.
DURNSFORD ROAD SIDINGS	52 / 2B		??/??/1914	N/A	LSWR	Originally 15-road shed built to stable LSWR's first fleet of electric multiple units, which entered service 25/10/1915. 1914 shed demolished c.1974 and replaced by Wimbledon Traincare Depot inspection shed to south.

E

Name	Page / grid		Date opened	Date closed	Opened by	Notes
EAGLE LANE GOODS	16 / 5B		15/05/1899	18/04/1966	GER	
EALING BROADWAY Ealing	23 / 6D		01/12/1838	N/A	GWR	Suffix 'Broadway' added 1875. Served by District Railway since 01/07/1879. Served by Central London Railway since 03/08/1920. Connection between LTE and BR east of station removed 17/09/1972 (disused since ??/05/1945). Connection between District / Central Lines last used 02/05/2010, removed by start of traffic 31/05/2010. Served by Piccadilly Line 26/12/2013 – 30/12/2013 (Engineering works).
EALING COMMON Ealing Common & West Acton Ealing Common	37 / 1A		01/07/1879	N/A	MDR	Suffix '& West Acton' 1886 - 01/03/1910. Served by Piccadilly Line since 04/07/1932.
EALING COMMON DEPOT Mill Hill Park Depot	37 / 1A		13/06/1905	N/A	MDR	District Line Depot built 1904-1905 for stabling electric trains; date quoted is that of the first section electrified. Used also for Piccadilly Line stabling 04/07/1932 - 10/10/1964, but had carried out overhaul work for GNPBR trains since that line's opening (15/12/1906).
EARDLEY CARRIAGE SIDINGS	53 / 4A		c.1900	post-1960	LBSCR	Exact opening date unknown; do not appear on 1898 OS, but had appeared by 1909. Never electrified. Regular use ceased c.1960, sidings remained in situ, used occasionally for several more years.
EARL'S COURT	38 / 2B 84		30/10/1871	N/A	MDR	Resited to west side of Earl's Court Road 01/02/1878 after first structure destroyed by fire 30/12/1875. GNPBR platforms opened 15/12/1906. Closed 22/11/1997 - 06/04/1998 and 23/11/2001 - 05/03/2002 (both Piccadilly Line only, escalator works).
Earl's Court Junction	38 / 2B 84		01/02/1872	03/03/1958	MDR / WLER	Junction between MDR and WLER, removed when segregated District Line track provided to Kensington Olympia.
EARLSFIELD Earlsfield & Summerstown Earlsfield	52 / 1C		01/04/1884	N/A	LSWR	Suffix '& Summerstown' 1884 - 01/06/1902. Originally two platforms, one on each side of four-track formation (before up slow flyover opened at Wimbledon 17/05/1936, slow lines were outside fast). Island platform constructed between former 'fast' lines for 17/05/1936 reconfiguration ('slow' south of 'fast'), original 'up' platform on 'up fast' line subsequently abandoned and further demolished. 'Down fast' platform remains, but is not regularly used.
Earlswood North Junction	73 / 6C		05/11/1899	N/A	LBSCR / SER	
EAST ACTON	24 / 6C		03/08/1920	N/A	CLR	Viaduct Junction to North Acton opened by GWR 16/04/1917, but no passenger service until CLR opened.
EAST BRIXTON Loughborough Park & Brixton Loughborough Park	39 / 5C		13/08/1866	05/01/1976	LBSCR	Terminus of LBSCR extension from Corbett's Lane Junction until 01/05/1867 high level route to Shepherd's Lane Junction opened. Renamed 'Loughborough Park & Brixton' ??/01/1870, then 'East Brixton' 01/01/1894. Closed 19/05/1926 - 20/09/1926, then for good 05/01/1976 (lack of patronage).
EAST CROYDON East Croydon Local / East Croydon Main New Croydon / East Croydon Croydon East Croydon	66 / 2D	P G	12/07/1841 12/07/1841	N/A 07/05/1973	LBRR	Opened as 'Croydon', 'East' suffix added ??/02/1850, reversed to 'East Croydon' 01/05/1862. Adjoining station for local traffic named 'New Croydon' opened 01/05/1862, renamed 'East Croydon Local' 01/06/1909, on which date the adjoining original station was renamed 'East Croydon Main'. Two stations combined as 'East Croydon' ??/07/1924. Goods yard closed 07/05/1973. Croydon Tramlink opened 10/05/2000 at street level outside station entrance.
EAST DULWICH Champion Hill	39 / 5D	P G	01/10/1868 01/10/1868	N/A 10/09/1962	LBSCR	Renamed 01/06/1888. Goods yard closed 10/09/1962.
EAST FINCHLEY East End Finchley	13 / 5D	P G	22/08/1867 22/08/1867	N/A 01/10/1962	GNR	Renamed 01/02/1887. First served by, and ownership transferred to, LPTB Northern Line 03/07/1939 (terminus of LPTB Northern Line extension from Archway 03/07/1939 - 14/04/1940). Became terminus of LNER service from Finsbury Park 14/04/1940 when LPTB took over High Barnet service. All LNER passenger trains withdrawn 02/03/1941. Goods yard closed 01/10/1962.
East Finchley Junction	13 / 5D		03/07/1939	N/A	LPTB / LNER	Junction of Northern Line with former LNER route to Finsbury Park (now depot access).
EAST GOODS YARD (FINSBURY PARK)	81		??/??/1877	13/06/1960	GNR	
EAST GREENWICH GAS WORKS	41 / 2A		??/??/1886	??/??/1976	PRIV	Constructed 1881-1886, initially internal railway network only but connection to SER Angerstein Wharf branch added c. early 20th century (between 1899 and 1916 per OS maps). Narrow gauge 2ft 5½in system present at northern end of site, closed 1933. Production at works ceased 1976.
EAST HAM	28 / 4D	P	31/03/1858	N/A	LTSR	First served by District Railway 02/06/1902, line quadrupled 1905,

Name	Page / grid		Date opened	Date closed	Opened by	Notes
		G	31/03/1858	??/04/1962		District trains then using 'slow' platforms to north. Served by Metropolitan Line since 30/03/1936 ('Hammersmith & City Line' since 30/07/1990). Bay platform ex-Kentish Town via TFGR and THJR abandoned 26/10/1958 (last train 15/09/1958). Main line services non-stopped since 15/06/1962 and 'Fast' platforms abandoned. Goods yard closed ??/04/1962.
EAST HAM DEPOT	28 / 3D		06/11/1961	N/A	BR	Built for LTSR electrification on Site of former District Line Little Ilford Depot, date is that of first AC electric service.
East Ham Loop	28 / 3D	P G	09/07/1894 01/09/1894	15/09/1958 30/11/1958	LTSR	First goods use 01/09/1894, last passenger use 15/09/1958 (TFGR trains diverted to Barking).
East Ham Loop North Junction	28 / 3D		09/07/1894	30/11/1958	LTSR	Junction at north end of East Ham Loop.
East Ham Loop South Junction	28 / 3D		09/07/1894	30/11/1958	LTSR	Junction at south end of East Ham Loop.
EAST INDIA	41 / 1A 31 / 5D		28/03/1994	N/A	DLR	
EAST INDIA DOCKS GOODS	41 / 1A 31 / 4D		??/??/1859	??/??/1961	GER	
East London Down Junction	40 / 4C 79		01/04/1880	16/04/1966	SER / ELR	SER service to Liverpool Street via ELR commenced 01/04/1880. Rolt Street Junction to New Cross (SER) became bi-directional (former 'down' only spur) 01/10/1884 when ELR bay platform opened at New Cross. 'Up' spur remained in use for goods / through traffic until 16/04/1966 when this and the connection on the 'down' side were both taken out of use (removed 1968).
East London Up Junction	40 / 3C 79		01/04/1880	16/04/1966	SER / ELR	See notes for 'East London Down Junction' above.
EAST LONDON WASTE TERMINAL	30 / 5A		?	N/A	PRIV	Shanks & McEwan, on site of former Dagenham Dock goods yard (closed 02/11/1964).
EAST PUTNEY	38 / 5A		03/06/1889	N/A	LSWR	Platforms to / from Putney Bridge opened first (built by LSWR but operated by MDR from outset). Platforms on curve to Wandsworth Town opened 01/07/1889, regular service withdrawn 05/05/1941, although some services called on occasions until 1969. Point Pleasant Junction to Wimbledon still used for empty stock working / diversions.
East Putney Junction	38 / 6A		01/07/1889	N/A	LSWR	First use East Putney Junction to Point Pleasant Junction 01/07/1889.
East Putney Tunnel	38 / 6A		03/06/1889	N/A	LSWR	Built by LSWR, but first use by MDR 03/06/1889. Ownership transferred to LU 01/04/1994.
EAST SIDINGS (ACTON TOWN)	37 / 1B 51 / 1A		04/07/1932	N/A	UERL	Current layout since 1932 quadrupling Turnham Green - Acton Town.
EAST SMITHFIELD / LONDON DOCKS GOODS	40 / 1A 74 / 2C		17/06/1864	01/09/1966	GER	
EAST TILBURY East Tilbury Halt	46 / 3D		07/09/1936	N/A	LMS	Suffix 'Halt' dropped February 1949.
EASTCOTE Eastcote Halt	10 / 6C	P G	26/05/1906 26/05/1906	N/A 10/08/1964	MET	Served by District Line Trains 01/03/1910 - 23/10/1933, Piccadilly Line thereafter. Suffix 'Halt' until 1934/5. Goods yard closed 10/08/1964
EASTERN DISTRICT OFFICE	27 / 6B 90		02/01/1928	31/05/2003	POR	POR Mothballed 31/05/2003.
EBBSFLEET INTERNATIONAL	59 / 1B		19/11/2007	N/A	LCOR	Opened five days after line. Two International and two Domestic platforms at low level, two Domestic platforms at high level. Latter did not receive regular train service until 13/12/2009 (Faversham to St Pancras).
EDEN PARK	54 / 6D		29/05/1882	N/A	SER	
EDGWARE (GNR)	12 / 2B	P G	22/08/1867 22/08/1867	11/09/1939 01/06/1964	GNR	Closed to passengers 11/09/1939, goods 01/06/1964.
EDGWARE (UERL)	12 / 2B		18/08/1924	N/A	UERL (CCEHR)	Built for through running to Bushey Heath, but extension abandoned c.1940 along with construction of additional terminating platforms to west.
EDGWARE ROAD (MET)	25 / 6D		10/01/1863	N/A	MET	Rebuilt 01/11/1926.
EDGWARE ROAD (UERL)	25 / 6D		15/06/1907	N/A	UERL (BSWR)	Northern terminus of Bakerloo Line 15/06/1907 - 01/12/1913.
EDGWARE SIDINGS	12 / 2B		18/08/1924	N/A	UERL (CCEHR)	Northern Line stabling sidings. Southern fan on site of aborted curve to GNR Edgware branch.
EDMONTON GREEN Lower Edmonton Lower Edmonton (High Level) Edmonton (High Level)	15 / 1B		22/07/1872	N/A	GER	Opened as 'Edmonton (High Level)' as distinct from the existing 01/03/1849 station (which became 'Low Level'). Both stations renamed 'Lower Edmonton' ('High Level' and 'Low Level' respectively) 01/07/1883. Suffix 'High Level' dropped when 'Low Level' station closed to passengers 11/09/1939 (remained open for goods). Renamed 'Edmonton Green' 28/09/1992.
Edward Street Junction	80		?	N/A	BR	
EFFINGHAM JUNCTION	69 / 4B		02/07/1888	N/A	LSWR	
Effingham Junction	69 / 4B		02/02/1885	N/A	LSWR	
EFFINGHAM JUNCTION MPV DEPOT	69 / 4B		c.1926	N/A	SR	Originally EMU stabling shed commissioned for electrification of route (1926), became disused c.mid-1990s. Used by AMEC as a base for MPVs since late 2003, fully commissioned as an MPV maintenance depot 2005.
EGHAM Egham for Englefield Green Egham	47 / 2C	P G	04/06/1856 04/06/1856	N/A c.1960s	LSWR	Suffix 'for Englefield Green' 17/07/1902 - 1955. Date of goods yard closure unknown.
ELEPHANT & CASTLE	39 / 2D		06/10/1862	N/A	LCDR	Initially temporary, replaced by permanent structure ??/02/1863. Terminus until 01/06/1864. CSLR station opened 18/12/1890 (closed 29/11/1923 - 01/12/1924), BSWR station opened 05/08/1906 (closed 10/11/1996 - 14/07/1997). Original BSWR 'over-run' tunnels headed due east under New Kent Road, diverted to head due south under Newington Butts in 1940 as initial works for the aborted Camberwell extension.
ELEPHANT & CASTLE COAL	39 / 2D		??/??/1871	01/07/1963	GNR	GNR coal depot accessed via LCDR.
ELM PARK	30 / 2D		13/05/1935	N/A	LMS	Barking to Upminster quadrupled by LMS 12/09/1932, new station opened at Elm Park 13/05/1935, served by District Line exclusively from opening. Ownership transferred to LTB 01/01/1969.
ELMERS END	54 / 6B	P G	01/04/1864 01/04/1864	N/A 06/05/1963	MKR	Goods yard closed 06/05/1963. 'Down' bay secured out of use 1985. Branch to Addiscombe closed 02/06/1997. Croydon Tramlink opened 30/05/2000 using former bay platform on 'up' side.
Elmers End Junction	54 / 6B		29/05/1882	02/06/1997	SER	Resited 50m south 1956 (platform extension). Elmers End to Addiscombe closed by RT 02/06/1997.
ELMSTEAD WOODS Elmstead	55 / 4C		01/07/1904	N/A	SECR	Renamed 01/10/1908.

Name	Page / grid		Date opened	Date closed	Opened by	Notes
ELSTREE & BOREHAMWOOD Elstree Elstree & Borehamwood Elstree Elstree & Boreham Wood Elstree	4 / 4B	P G	13/07/1868 13/07/1868	N/A 19/06/1967	MID	Opened as 'Elstree'. Suffix '& Boreham Wood' added 01/06/1869, dropped 01/04/1904, added again as '& Borehamwood' 21/09/1953, dropped again 06/05/1974, restored again by mid-1988. Goods yard closed 19/06/1967.
ELSTREE SOUTH	3 / 6D		N/A	N/A	LPTB (NOR)	On Northern Line extension to Bushey Heath from Edgware. Construction abandoned 1940.
Elstree Tunnels	4 / 5B		09/09/1867	N/A	MID	
ELTHAM Eltham Well Hall Well Hall & North Eltham Well Hall	41 / 6D	P G	01/05/1895 01/05/1895	N/A 07/10/1968	BHR	Opened as 'Well Hall', suffix '& North Eltham' added 01/10/1916. Renamed 'Eltham Well Hall' 26/09/1927. Goods yard expanded 1915, closed 07/10/1968. Relocated east and renamed 'Eltham' 17/03/1985 due to construction of A2 Rochester Way Relief road through original station site, adjacent Eltham Park station closed on same date due to proximity of resited station.
ELTHAM PARK Shooters Hill & Eltham Park	41 / 6D		01/07/1908	17/03/1985	SECR	Renamed 26/09/1927. Replaced by Eltham Station 17/03/1985 (see note above).
ELVERSON ROAD	40 / 5D		20/11/1999	N/A	DLR	
EMBANKMENT Charing Cross Embankment Charing Cross	39 / 1B 19		30/05/1870	N/A	MDR	BSWR platforms added 10/03/1906 (closed 10/11/1996 - 14/07/1997). CCEHR Loop platform added 06/04/1914, southbound platform on Kennington extension opened 13/09/1926. Renamed 'Charing Cross Embankment' 04/08/1974, shortened to 'Embankment' 12/09/1976.
EMERSON PARK Emerson Park & Great Nelmes	31 / 1A		01/10/1909	N/A	LTSR	Suffix '& Great Nelmes' only appeared on one station nameboard and was not published elsewhere. Loco run-around loop installed for terminating trains 14/10/1909, subsequently removed.
EMPIRE PAPER MILLS	45 / 6A		??/??1908	c.1970	PRIV	Connection to North Kent line appears to have been removed with 08/11/1970 resignalling of Greenhithe area, but internal railway network within works remained active for at least a decade longer.
Engine Shed Junction	26 / 2A 9		16/12/1900	05/01/1981	MID	Junction at south end of Low Level Curve, abandoned after diversion of Barking Trains to Gospel Oak.
ENFIELD	6 / 4D	P G	01/04/1871 01/04/1871	04/04/1910 01/07/1974	GNR	Original terminus of branch from Wood Green (Alexandra Palace). Passenger station closed 04/04/1910 when extension from Grange Park to Cuffley opened (replaced by present day Enfield Chase). Goods yard closed 01/07/1974, carriage sidings remained in use on west side of former station until 1979.
ENFIELD CHASE Enfield	6 / 4D		04/04/1910	N/A	GNR	Replaced original Enfield (GNR) station when line extended from Grange Park to Cuffley. Suffix 'Chase' added 01/07/1923.
Enfield Goods Junction	6 / 5D		04/04/1910	??/??/1979	GNR	Formed when route opened from Grange Park to Cuffley, eliminated when carriage sidings at first Enfield (GNR) station abandoned 1979.
ENFIELD LOCK Enfield Lock for Enfield Wash Enfield Lock for Enfield Highway Ordnance Factory	7 / 3C	P G	??/04/1855 ??/04/1855	N/A 07/12/1964	ECR	Exact opening date unknown. First reference to 'Ordnance Factory' in timetable April 1855. Renamed 'Enfield Lock for Enfield Highway' 01/04/1886. Suffix altered to 'for Enfield Wash' 01/11/1910, dropped 1955. 'Down' platform originally sited north of level crossing, rebuilt to south c.1890/91. Goods yard closed 07/12/1964.
ENFIELD TOWN Enfield	7 / 4A	P G	01/03/1849 01/03/1849	N/A 14/09/1959	ECR	Suffix 'Town' added 01/04/1886. Goods yard closed 14/09/1959.
EPPING	8 / 2B	P G	24/04/1865 24/04/1865	N/A 18/04/1966	GER	Ownership and majority of passenger services transferred to LTE 25/09/1949. First Trains in the morning remained British Rail services until 01/06/1970 (last train 31/05/1970). Goods yard closed 18/04/1966.
EPPING GLADE	8 / 2B		N/A	N/A	EOR	Proposed western terminus of Epping-Ongar Railway.
EPSOM Epsom High Street Epsom	64 / 6B	P G	01/02/1859 01/02/1859	N/A 02/01/1928	LSWR / LBSCR	Opened as temporary terminus of LSWR / LBSCR Epsom & LeatherheadRailway to Leatherhead, became a through station when line to LSWR main line at future site of Raynes Park opened 04/04/1859. When connection to LBSCR Epsom (Town) station opened 08/08/1859, LBSCR trains continued to call at Epsom (Town) and passed LSWR station without stopping. Sometimes referred to as 'Epsom High Street' 1874-1884 to distinguish from LBSCR's 'Town' and 'Downs' stations. Platforms opened on LBSCR line 03/03/1929, allowing Epsom Town station to close. Goods yard closed 02/01/1928, with goods traffic being transferred to Epson (Town).
EPSOM DOWNS	71 / 1D		22/05/1865	N/A	LBSCR	Station had 9 platform faces at its peak, from 01/05/1972 all but platforms 4 & 5 (re-numbered 1 & 2) abandoned. Resited 300 metres east 14/02/1989 as a single platform, site of original station sold for housing development.
EPSOM TOWN Epsom	64 / 6C	P G	10/05/1847 10/05/1847	03/03/1929 03/05/1965	LBSCR	Terminus 10/05/1847 - 01/02/1859. Suffix 'Town' used at times c.1870-1900 and again permanently after 09/07/1923. Closed to passengers 03/03/1929 when platforms opened at Epsom (former LSWR). Goods yard closed 03/05/1965.
ERITH	43 / 3C	P G	30/07/1849 30/07/1849	N/A 07/10/1968	SER	Original layout was of platforms staggered either side of a foot crossing; subsequent platform lengthenings have resulted in slight overlap of facing platforms. Goods yard closed 07/10/1968.
Erith Loop	43 / 5C	P G	01/05/1895 01/05/1895	N/A N/A	BHR	Opened with rest of BHR.
ERITH WHARF	43 / 3C		c.1880	c.1970	SER	Not on 1872 OS map, but had appeared by 1895. Depicted on OS into the 1970s, but date of abandonment unknown.
ESHER Esher for Sandown Park Esher for Claremont Esher & Claremont Ditton Marsh	63 / 1A	P G	21/05/1838 21/05/1838	N/A c.1965	LSWR	Opened as 'Ditton Marsh' (per opening notice; also referred to as 'Esher & Hampton Court' in some timetables). Renamed 'Esher & Claremont' 1844, 'Esher for Claremont' 1912/3, then 'Esher for Sandown Park' 1934, suffix dropped 13/06/1955. Additional pair of platforms on 'up' side added for returning race traffic from Sandown Park racecourse 20/04/1882, closed 18/10/1965.
Essex Portals	44 / 5D		14/11/2007	N/A	LCOR	
ESSEX ROAD Canonbury & Essex Road Essex Road	26 / 3D		14/02/1904	N/A	GNCR	Opened by GNCR, absorbed by Metropolitan Railway 01/07/1913, transferred to LPTB Edgware - Morden Line (later Northern Line) 01/07/1933. Closed by LTE 05/10/1975, re-opened by British Rail 16/08/1976. 'Canonbury & -' prefix 20/07/1922 - 11/07/1948.
EUROPEAN METAL RECYCLING (BRENTFORD)	36 / 3C		?	?	PRIV	Formerly Perry Metals, sidings shown in situ in Quail, but have been removed.
EUSTON	26 / 5A		20/07/1837	N/A	LBIR	London & Birmingham Railway terminus, referred to as 'Euston Square' or simply 'London' at times in early history. CSLR platforms opened 12/05/1907 (closed 09/081922 - 20/04/1924), terminus until 20/04/1924. CCEHR platforms opened 22/06/1907, Victoria Line 01/12/1968.

Name	Page / grid		Date opened	Date closed	Opened by	Notes
EUSTON SQUARE Gower Street	26 / 5B		10/01/1863	N/A	MET	Renamed 01/11/1909.
Euston Square Junction	76		15/03/1926	27/04/1935	MET	Link between Metropolitan and City Widened Lines using aborted 'Widened Lines' tunnel to Euston (eastbound only). Name given as 'Euston Square Junction' in Borley, Clives Underground Line Guides gives 'Chalton Street Junction'.
EWELL EAST Ewell for Worcester Park Ewell	64 / 5D	P G	10/05/1847 10/05/1847	N/A 04/04/1960	LBSCR	Suffix 'for Worcester Park' in use after 1871. Renamed 'Ewell East' 09/07/1923. Goods yard closed 04/04/1960.
EWELL WEST Ewell	64 / 4C	P G	04/04/1859 04/04/1859	N/A 01/05/1961	LSWR	Renamed 'Ewell West' 09/07/1923. Goods yard closed 01/05/1961.
EWER STREET DEPOT (LOCOMOTIVES)	39 / 1D 87		??/??/1901	??/??/1961	SECR	Adjacent to Southwark Depot (goods). No engine shed provided, but turntable, coaling stage, water tower present. Closed 1961, in advance of 18/06/1962 introduction of full electric timetable.
EXPRESS DAIRY (MORDEN)	52 / 6B		??/??/1954	30/12/1978	PRIV	Milk bottling plant.

F

Name	Page / grid		Date opened	Date closed	Opened by	Notes
Factory Junctions	39 / 4A 82		01/07/1863	N/A	LCDR	
FAIRFIELD YARD	66 / 2D		01/09/1890	??/02/1933	LBSCR	Permanent Way yard on truncated Central Croydon branch.
FAIRLOP	17 / 4B	P G	01/05/1903 01/05/1903	N/A 24/03/1958	GER	Fairlop Loop closed to LNER passenger services 30/11/1947 to allow electrification and transfer to LTE Central Line. First served by LTE Central Line Trains 31/05/1948. Goods yard closed 24/03/1958.
Falcon Junction	38 / 6D 89		02/03/1863	N/A	LBSCR / WLER	
FALCON LANE GOODS	38 / 5D 89		01/06/1869	03/06/1968	LNWR	
FALCONWOOD	42 / 5A		01/01/1936	N/A	SR	
FAR TOTTERING & OYSTERCREEK RAILWAY (later LAKESIDE MINIATURE RAILWAY)	38 / 3D		??/??/1951	??/??/1975	PRIV	15 inch gauge railway open 1951-1953, opened for Festival of Britain in Battersea Park. Relocated within park, re-opening 1954 as Lakeside Miniature Railway, closed 1975.
FARNINGHAM HOME FOR LITTLE BOYS	58 / 5C		11/10/1870	c.1939	LCDR	Unadvertised station, served home for destitute boys, opened 15/06/1867 (station first use 11/10/1870). Home closed 1961, but station had been demolished in 1939 although date of last use unknown.
FARNINGHAM ROAD Farningham & Sutton-at-Hone Farningham Farningham & Sutton-at-Hone Farningham	58 / 5B	P G	03/12/1860 03/12/1860	N/A ??/05/1968	LCDR	Opened as 'Farningham', suffix '& Sutton-at-Hone' added 01/04/1861, dropped 01/08/1861, renamed 'Farningham Road' 1869. Became 'Farningham & Sutton-at-Hone' again 1872, renamed 'Farningham Road' again 05/05/1975. Goods yard closed May 1968, siding served adjacent British Steel works in use until 1980.
FARRINGDON Farringdon & High Holborn Farringdon Street	26 / 5C 32 / 2C		23/12/1865	N/A	MET	Replaced original Farringdon Street station. City Widened Lines platforms added 01/03/1866 (now 'Thameslink'). Suffix '& High Holborn' replaced 'Street' 26/01/1922, dropped 21/04/1936. NR platforms extended to 12 cars and new entrance hall opened 12/12/2011. Platforms for 'Crossrail 1' expected to open 2018 (linking to Barbican station).
FARRINGDON GOODS	26 / 5C 32 / 2B		01/11/1909	01/07/1936	MET	Also referred to as 'Vine Street' Goods.
Farringdon Junction	32 / 3C		01/01/1866	23/03/2009	LCDR / MET	Junction eliminated 24/03/1969 (date of closure, last train 23/03/1969 but junction not disconnected until 03/05/1971). Reinstated 16/05/1988 (introduction of 'Thameslink'), service Farringdon - Moorgate withdrawn 23/03/2009 (last train 20/03/2009).
FARRINGDON STREET	26 / 6C 32 / 3C		10/01/1863	01/03/1866	MET	Original City terminus of Metropolitan Railway, partially abandoned when new station opened 23/12/1865, but not closed to passengers until 'Widened Lines' platforms opened at new station 01/03/1866. Became GNR goods station (see entry below).
FARRINGDON STREET GOODS	26 / 6C 32 / 3C		02/11/1874	16/01/1956	GNR	On site of original Metropolitan Railway passenger terminus (see entry above).
Fawkham Junction	59 / 5A		10/05/1886	N/A	LCDR	Originally junction for Gravesend West Branch, disused 24/03/1968 - 1972 and 1976 - 28/09/2003.
FELTHAM	49 / 1B	P G	22/08/1848 22/08/1848	N/A 09/09/1968	LSWR	Goods yard closed 09/09/1968.
Feltham Junction	35 / 6D		01/02/1850	N/A	LSWR	
FELTHAM LOCO SHED	35 / 6D		??/??/1922	09/07/1967	LSWR	Steam shed closed 09/07/1967. Diesel shed built on site of former coal stacking ground, closed 06/01/1969.
FELTHAM MARSHALLING YARD	35 / 6C		1921-1922	06/01/1969	LSWR	Opened in stages 1921-1922.
FENCHURCH STREET	27 / 6A 74 / 2B		29/07/1841	N/A	LBLR	Advertised opening 02/08/1841, but services actually commenced 29/07/1841. Redeveloped into current layout April 1935.
FERME PARK DOWN SIDINGS	14 / 5C		??/01/1888	N/A	GNR	Former Ferme Park goods yard, opened ??/01/1888 and effectively closed by 1973.
Ferme Park Flyover	14 / 6C		pre-1895	N/A	GNR	Appeared between 1876 and 1895 OS, originally 'Harringay Engine Viaduct', and double track (now single).
FIELDWAY	67 / 4D		10/05/2000	N/A	CTL	
FINCHLEY CENTRAL Finchley (Church End) Finchley Finchley & Hendon	13 / 4B	P G	22/08/1867 22/08/1867	N/A 01/10/1962	GNR	Opened as 'Finchley & Hendon', '& Hendon' suffix dropped 01/02/1872, 'Church End' suffix added 01/02/1894. Renamed 'Finchley Central' 01/04/1940, first served by and transferred to LPTB Northern Line 14/04/1940, closed to LNER passenger services on same date. Goods yard closed 01/10/1962.
Finchley Central Junction	13 / 3B		01/04/1872	N/A	GNR	Divergence of High Barnet Branch from original Edgware Line (now Mill Hill East Branch).
FINCHLEY ROAD (MID) Finchley Road & St John's Wood	25 / 3C		13/07/1868	11/07/1927	MID	Renamed 01/09/1868. Re-sited 03/02/1884.
FINCHLEY ROAD (MSJWR) Finchley Road (South Hampstead) Finchley Road	25 / 3C	P G	30/06/1879 01/01/1894	N/A 01/08/1941	MSJWR	Suffix 'South Hampstead' 11/09/1885 - c.1914. Served by Bakerloo Line 20/11/1939 - 01/05/1979, Jubilee Line replacing Bakerloo Line after 01/05/1979. Goods yard opened 01/01/1894, closed 01/08/1941.
FINCHLEY ROAD & FROGNAL Finchley Road St John's Wood	25 / 2C	P G	02/01/1860 c.1870	N/A 02/01/1967	HJR	Renamed 01/10/1880. Goods yard open c.1870 - 02/01/1967. Closed 29/10/1995 - 29/09/1996.
FINSBURY PARK Seven Sisters Road	26 / 1C 81	P G	01/07/1861 ??/??/1865	N/A 01/04/1968	GNR	Renamed 15/11/1869, also referred to as 'Seven Sisters Road, Holloway' before re-naming. GNCR opened 14/02/1904, closed 04/10/1964. GNPBR opened 15/12/1906, southbound tunnel diverted

Name	Page / grid		Date opened	Date closed	Opened by	Notes
						through abandoned northbound GNCR tunnel 03/10/1965. LTB Victoria Line opened 01/09/1968 using former southbound GNCR & GNPBR platforms. Goods yard opened 1865, closed 01/04/1968.
FINSBURY PARK DIESEL DEPOT	26 / 2C		*??/??/1960*	*??/10/1983*	BR	On site of Clarence Yard. First purpose-built diesel Traction Maintenance Depot in UK, downgraded ??/06/1981.
Finsbury Park North Junctions	26 / 1C 81		22/08/1867	N/A	GNR	Originally junction between GNR main line and branch to Edgware, now a series of crossovers.
Finsbury Park South Junctions	26 / 1C 81		14/12/1874	N/A	GNR	Junction of Great Northern main Line with routes ex-Canonbury & Moorgate.
FIRESTONE TYRES (BRENTFORD)	36 / 3C		*??/??/1928*	*31/05/1964*	PRIV	
FORD FREIGHTLINER TERMINAL (DAGENHAM)	30 / 5B		*c.1967*	*N/A*	PRIV	
FORD MOTOR WORKS (DAGENHAM)	30 / 6A		*??/10/1932*	*N/A*	PRIV	Production commenced October 1932, continues to manufacture diesel engines.
FOREIGN CATTLE MARKET	40 / 3C 79		*15/12/1900*	*??/??/1914*	PRIV	Accessed via tramway along Grove Street. Market purchased by War Office 1914 and became an army depot remaining in use until at least WW2, Ordnance Survey maps depict tramway in situ up until 1960s.
FOREST GATE	28 / 3B		??/??/1840	N/A	ECR	Exact opening date unknown. Closed 01/06/1843 - 31/05/1846. Goods yard east of station (see entry below).
FOREST GATE GOODS	28 / 2C		*c.1890s*	*07/12/1970*	GER	Site closer to Manor Park station than Forest Gate, adjacent to LTSR route to Barking. Although Borley states Forest Gate opened to 'all' traffic 1840 (i.e. including goods), the yard does not appear on OS maps before 1895, so may have been opened at approximately same time as GER quadrupling work (c.1894).
Forest Gate Junction	28 / 2C		13/04/1854	N/A	ECR / LTSR	
FOREST HILL	54 / 1B	P	05/06/1839	N/A	LCRR	Named 'Dartmouth Arms' until 03/07/1845, when renamed 'Forest Hill'.
Forest Hill for Lordship Lane		G	05/06/1839	04/05/1964		Suffix 'for Lordship Lane' in use c.1877 to c.1943. Goods yard closed 04/05/1964. Island platform serving the middle 'fast' roads was present, partially staggered to the south of the 'slow' side platforms, but since demolished. Present on 1970 OS, but had been removed by 1983.
Forest Hill						
Dartmouth Arms						
Fork Junction	28 / 3A 77		15/08/1854	01/06/1969	ECR	
Fulham Bridge	38 / 5A		03/06/1899	N/A	LSWR	Built by LSWR but only ever used by District Railway trains. Purchased by LUL 01/04/1994.
FULHAM BROADWAY	38 / 3B		01/03/1880	N/A	MDR	Renamed 01/03/1952. Rebuilt 1905 & 2003 (at latter rebuilding almost entirely covered over).
Walham Green	84					
FULWELL	50 / 2B		01/11/1864	N/A	TVR	Suffix '(New Hampton)' added 1874, changed to '& Hampton Hill' 1887, dropped 01/06/1913.
Fulwell & Hampton Hill						
Fulwell (New Hampton)						
Fulwell						
Fulwell Junction	50 / 2B		01/07/1894	N/A	LSWR	Junction at west end of Shepperton Spur (Fulwell Curve).
Fulwell Tunnel	50 / 2B		01/11/1864	N/A	TVR	

G

Name	Page / grid		Date opened	Date closed	Opened by	Notes
GALLIONS	42 / 1A 62 / 3D	P G	*late 1880* *late 1880*	*09/09/1940* *17/04/1966*	LSKD	Initially 'Central' (opened 03/08/1880) was branch terminus per Quick, Connor and Jackson ('for first few weeks' in latter), so precise date of services to Gallions commencing unknown, had appeared in Bradshaw by November 1880. Gallions branch single until 14/11/1881. Re-sited east 12/12/1886, then again 1924/5 (per Quick). Operated by GER after 1896, ownership later transferred to PLA. Branch closed from 09/09/1940 due to 'Black Saturday' air raid 07/09/1940 (no Sunday service after 27/06/1915). Listed as 'Royal Albert Dock, Gallions' in Borley. Branch continued to be used to access coal wharf at Gallions (Cory Brothers) until 17/04/1966.
GALLIONS REACH	42 / 1A 62 / 4D		28/03/1994	N/A	DLR	
GANTS HILL	17 / 6A		14/12/1947	N/A	LPTB (CEN)	
GARDNER'S PLEASURE RESORT RAILWAY	66 / 6C		*??/??/1893*	*By 1934*	PRIV	Circular miniature railway in Gardner's Pleasure Resort, Riddlesdown. Gauge unknown.
GARSTON	2 / 1D		07/02/1966	N/A	BR	
Gas Factory Junction	27 / 5D 88		26/09/1850	N/A	LBLR / NLR	Junction with curve to Bow (NLR) established 26/09/1850, eliminated 29/12/1967. Junction with LTSR added 31/03/1858 (only extant junction). Junction with access to Bow Road Goods added 1885, eliminated 07/12/1964.
Bow Common Junction						
Gasworks Tunnels	26 / 4B 75 / 76		14/10/1852	N/A	GNR	Tunnels under Regent's Canal approaching King's Cross. Middle bore first, East bore added 1878, West bore 1892. East bore abandoned Spring 1977.
George IV Tunnel	41 / 2D		30/07/1849	N/A	SER	
GEORGE STREET	66 / 2C		10/05/2000	N/A	CTL	
GIBBS CEMENT WORKS (WEST THURROCK)	45 / 4A		*c.1880*	*c.1965*	PRIV	Formerly Thames Cement works. Not on 1873 OS map, but present in 1897. Removed between 1961 and 1966
GIDEA PARK	18 / 5D	P	01/12/1910	N/A	GER	Opened as 'Squirrels Heath & Gidea Park', renamed 'Gidea Park & Squirrels Heath' 01/12/1913, '& Squirrels Heath' suffix dropped 20/02/1969. Goods yard in use 06/02/1911 - 07/12/1970 (sited to east of station, page 19 / 5A).
Gidea Park & Squirrels Heath		G	06/02/1911	07/12/1970		
Squirrels Heath & Gidea Park						
GIDEA PARK CARRIAGE SIDINGS	19 / 5A		*c.1930*	*N/A*	LNER	
Gidea Park Country End Junction	19 / 5A		01/01/1934	N/A	LNER	Dates from Romford to Brentwood quadrupling.
Gifford Street Portals	76		14/11/2007	N/A	LCOR	
GIPSY HILL	53 / 3D	P	01/12/1856	N/A	WELCPR	Sometimes referred to as 'Gypsy Hill' in early years. Suffix 'for Upper Norwood' in use c.1911 - c.1955. Goods yard closed 07/12/1968.
Gipsy Hill for Upper Norwood		G	01/12/1856	07/12/1968		
Gypsy Hill						
GLOBE ROAD & DEVONSHIRE STREET	27 / 5B		01/07/1884	22/05/1916		
GLOBE WORKS	45 / 4D		*c.1870s*	*??/??/1940*	PRIV	Chalk pit, established in 1870s, railway system not used after 1940.
GLOUCESTER ROAD	38 / 2C 84 & 45		01/10/1868	N/A	MET	Initially terminus of MET extension from Praed Street Junction, extended east to Westminster (Bridge) 24/12/1868. MDR platforms opened 12/04/1869 (initially terminus, extended east 01/08/1870). UERL (GNPBR) platforms opened 15/12/1906 as 'Gloucester Road', this name applying to entire station from 1907. Platforms re-arranged 28/07/1957 such that former MET platforms both became eastbound,
Brompton (Gloucester Road)						

Name	Page / grid		Date opened	Date closed	Opened by	Notes
						and former MDR both became westbound. Middle eastbound track removed 01/03/1970 and eastbound former platform 2 (now 3) widened into vacated space and former platform 1 abandoned. Piccadilly Line platforms closed 30/08/1987 - 21/05/1989 (lift replacement works). District / Circle platforms rafted over due to development above, completed June 1993.
Gloucester Road Junction	66 / 1D 86		c.1865	N/A	LBSCR	Originally junction at north end of 'New Croydon Line', now junction at south end of Selhurst Spur.
GOLDERS GREEN	13 / 6B		22/06/1907	N/A	UERL (CCEHR)	Northern terminus of CCEHR from opening to 19/11/1923.
GOLDERS GREEN DEPOT	13 / 6B		22/06/1907	N/A	UERL (CCEHR)	Northern Line depot.
GOLDHAWK ROAD	37 / 1D 83		01/04/1914	N/A	MET / GWR	Replaced first Shepherd's Bush MET / GWR station to North.
GOODGE STREET Tottenham Court Road	26 / 5B		22/06/1907	N/A	UERL	Renamed 09/03/1908.
GOODMANS YARD GOODS	27 / 6A 74 / 2B		01/02/1861	01/04/1951	LBLR	Sometimes referred to as 'Minories Goods'.
GOODMAYES	29 / 1C	P G	08/02/1901 03/06/1901	N/A 31/07/1962	GER	Goods yard opened 03/06/1901, closed 31/07/1962.
GOODMAYES MARSHALLING YARD	29 / 1C		??/??/1899	31/07/1962	GER	Enlarged 1911.
Goods & Mineral Junction	75		14/10/1852	05/03/1973	GNR	Divergence of route into King's Cross terminus from original route to Maiden Lane station / King's Cross Goods.
GORDON HILL	6 / 3D		04/04/1910	N/A	GNR	
GORESBROOK	29 / 5D		TBA	N/A	DLR	Gallions Reach to Dagenham Dock was proposed to open c.2017, but funding removed November 2008.
GOSPEL OAK Kentish Town	26 / 2A 9	P G	02/01/1860 ??/??/1862	N/A 07/08/1972	HJR	Renamed 01/02/1867. Platform for THJR opened 04/06/1888, closed to regular traffic 06/09/1926, some excursion traffic remained until ??/08/1939 and platform subsequently demolished. Platform re-opened 05/01/1981 when Barking trains diverted from Kentish Town. Goods yard in use 1862 - 07/08/1972. Became temporary terminus of Richmond trains 20/02/2010 - 01/06/2010 due to engineering works.
Gospel Oak Junction	26 / 2A 9		30/01/1916	N/A	HJR / THJR	Junction established 30/01/1916, eliminated 03/09/1922. Re-established 11/03/1940.
GRAHAME-WHITE AVIATION CO. WORKS	12 / 4B		15/06/1918	28/01/1921	PRIV	Dates of first & last trains on branch unknown, dates quoted are for the opening / closing of Hendon Factory signalbox, which controlled the junction between the branch and Midland main line. Branch lifted c.1930, but engine shed in Montrose Park and tunnel under Northern Line still remain.
Graham Road Curve	27 / 3B	P G	30/06/1986 30/06/1986	28/09/1992 N/A	BR	Opened for diverted trains ex-Watford Junction upon closure of Broad Street station. Regular passenger services withdrawn 28/09/1992, but curve retained for empty stock workings.
GRAHAM ROAD GOODS	27 / 3B		??/05/1894	04/10/1965	GER	
GRANGE HILL Grange Hill for Chigwell Row Grange Hill	17 / 2B	P G	01/05/1903 01/05/1903	N/A 04/10/1965	GER	Suffix 'for Chigwell Row' added July 1912, probably used until closure by LNER. Fairlop Loop closed to LNER passenger services 30/11/1947 to allow electrification and transfer to LTE Central Line, re-opening 21/11/1948. Goods yard closed 04/10/1965.
Grange Hill Tunnel	17 / 2B		20/04/1903	N/A	GER	
GRANGE PARK	6 / 5D		04/04/1910	N/A	GNR	
GRAVEL HILL	67 / 4C		10/05/2000	N/A	CTL	
GRAVESEND (GRR)	60 / 1B	P G	10/02/1845 10/02/1845	30/07/1849 30/07/1849	GRR	Terminus of Gravesend & Rochester Railway, situated on south side of Thames & Medway canal basin. Closed 13/12/1846 - 23/08/1847 by SER due to line improvement works. Closed for good 30/07/1849, replaced by Gravesend (SER) station on their North Kent line, opened the same day.
GRAVESEND (SER) Gravesend Central Gravesend	60 / 1A	P G	30/07/1849 30/07/1849	N/A 03/12/1961	SER	Replaced Gravesend (GRR) station. Carried suffix 'Central' 01/06/1899 – 14/06/1965. Goods yard closed 03/12/1961. Originally laid out with two platform roads either side of a pair of central reversing sidings (one west-facing, one east facing) altered to two 'through' roads c.1899. Bay was present on up side (abolished by 14/03/1971 resignalling?).
GRAVESEND WEST Gravesend West Street Gravesend	60 / 1A	P G	10/05/1886 10/05/1886	03/08/1953 24/03/1968	LCDR	Suffix 'West Street' added 01/06/1899, 'Street' dropped 26/09/1949. Closed to passengers with entire branch 03/08/1953, goods withdrawn and branch abandoned 24/03/1968.
GRAYS	45 / 4C	P G	13/04/1854 13/04/1854	N/A ?	LTSR	Sometimes referred to as 'Grays Thurrock' in early years. Bay on down side opened 05/11/1900. Closure date of goods yard unknown. Not noted in Borley which suggests it was open in some capacity into the 1980s, goods shed still depicted on 1974-7 OS, removed by 1984-7.
GRAYS CEMENT WORKS	45 / 4B		c.1880	??/??/1920	PRIV	Not on 1873 OS map, but present in 1897. Closed 1920 (Middleton Press 'Tilbury Loop').
Grays East Junction	45 / 4C		c.1960	N/A	BR	Junction providing access to Tilbury Docks via Seabrook Sidings, replaced former Tilbury North Junction.
GREAT PORTLAND STREET Great Portland Street & Regent's Park Great Portland Street Portland Road	26 / 5A		10/01/1863	N/A	MET	Opened as 'Portland Road', renamed 'Great Portland Street' 01/03/1917, '& Regent's Park' suffix added 1923, dropped 1933.
GREEN PARK Dover Street	39 / 1A		15/12/1906	N/A	UERL (GNPBR)	Renamed 18/09/1933. Victoria Line platforms opened 07/03/1969, Jubilee Line 01/05/1979.
GREENFORD (GWR)	23 / 3B	P G	01/10/1904 01/10/1904	17/06/1963 23/05/1980	GWR	Platforms on loops off GWR Birmingham Main line, closed 17/06/1963. Goods yard closed 23/05/1980, subsequently becoming a cement depot.
GREENFORD (LPTB)	23 / 3B		30/06/1947	N/A	LPTB (CEN)	Terminus of Central Line extension from North Acton from opening until 21/11/1948, incorporating central bay for BR Greenford Loop trains (first served 21/11/1948).
Greenford Bay Junction	23 / 3B		21/11/1948	N/A	BR	Greenford Loop passenger services diverted into bay platform in LTE station 21/11/1948.
Greenford East Curve	23 / 4B	P G	15/06/1903 03/06/1903	10/10/1905 N/A	GWR	Initially used by temporary goods (03/06/1903) and passenger (15/06/1903) services serving the Park Royal Royal Agricultural showground, disused 04/07/1903 (passenger) 10/08/1903 (goods) - 01/05/1904. Regular passenger services ceased 10/10/1905, singled ??/06/1970.
Greenford East Junction	23 / 4C		01/10/1904	N/A	GWR	
GREENFORD S & T	23 / 3B		??/??/1989	N/A	BR	Sidings formerly served Rockware Glass works.
Greenford South Junction	23 / 4B		01/10/1904	N/A	GWR	

Name	Page / grid		Date opened	Date closed	Opened by	Notes
Greenford West Curve	23 / 4B	P	01/10/1904	N/A	GWR	Passenger service north of Greenford Bay Junction ceased 21/11/1948.
		G	01/10/1904	N/A		Partially singled 29/05/1990.
Greenford West Junction	23 / 3B		01/10/1904	N/A	GWR	
GREENHITHE FOR BLUEWATER Greenhithe	44 / 6D		30/07/1849	N/A	SER	Renamed c.1999 (Bluewater shopping centre opened 16/03/1999). Rebuilt 14/03/2008.
Greenhithe Tunnel	45 / 6A		30/07/1849	N/A	SER	
GREENWICH	40 / 4D		24/12/1838	N/A	LGR	Originally temporary station to west of current, sometimes referred to as 'Church Row', replaced by current station to east 12/04/1840, which originally had two central engine release roads. Terminus until 01/02/1878, when extension to Maze Hill opened (former engine release roads retained as two through roads until first half of 20th century, when removed). DLR platforms opened 20/11/1999, space created using former through roads' track beds to realign 'up' main line road northwards and reposition platform.
GREENWICH PARK Greenwich	40 / 4D		01/10/1888	01/01/1917	LCDR	Renamed 01/07/1900. Passenger service withdrawn Nunhead to Greenwich Park 01/01/1917.
GREYSTONE LIME WORKS	73 / 6A		24/07/1805	28/09/1838	CMGR	Terminus of CMGR, last day of operation 27/09/1838.
Grosvenor Bridge	39 / 3A 82		01/10/1860	N/A	VSPR	
GROSVENOR ROAD	39 / 3A		01/11/1867	01/10/1911	LCDR / LBSCR	Open from January 1867 as ticket platforms, full opening 01/11/1867. LBSCR platforms closed before LCDR, on 01/04/1907. LBSCR platforms sometimes referred to as 'Grosvenor Road & Battersea Pier'.
Grove Junction (LSWR)	37 / 2D		01/06/1870	01/01/1911	LSWR	Junction at south end of link between MET / GWR Hammersmith & City Railway and LSWR Kensington & Richmond Railway.
Grove Junction (MET / GWR)	37 / 2D		01/06/1870	01/01/1911	LSWR	Junction at north end of link between MET / GWR Hammersmith & City Railway and LSWR Kensington & Richmond Railway. Junction severed November 1914, track lifted along link May 1916.
GROVE PARK	55 / 2B	P	01/11/1871	N/A	SER	Became a junction station with opening of Bromley (North) branch 01/01/1878, at which point the station was two through platforms with
		G	01/11/1871	04/12/1961		an up side bay. Rebuilt with three island platforms (six faces) for quadrupling of main line (complete 18/06/1905). Goods yard on up side (closed 04/12/1961), carriage sidings on down (closed 06/11/1976).
GROVE PARK CARRIAGE SERVICE SHED	55 / 2B		??/??/1959	N/A	BR	Commissioned coinciding with Kent Coast electrification scheme.
GROVE PARK DOWN (BRAMDEAN) SIDINGS	55 / 1B		c.1900	N/A	SECR	EMU stabling sidings (x 8) and unelectrified freight sidings (x 5). On site of SECR Hither Green marshalling yard, established c.1900.
Grove Park Junction	55 / 2B		01/01/1878	N/A	SER	
GROVE PARK UP (ST MILDRED'S) SIDINGS	55 / 2A		c.1900	N/A	SECR	EMU stabling sidings. On site of SECR Hither Green marshalling yard, established c.1900.
Grove Tunnels	39 / 4D		01/08/1865	N/A	LBSCR	North bore opened 01/08/1865, south bore 13/08/1866.
Guildford Line Junction	73 / 5C		04/07/1849	N/A	SER	
GUINNESS (PARK ROYAL)	24 / 4A		??/??/1936	06/07/1995	PRIV	Brewery, production started 1936 and ended Summer 2005. Last rail consignment left 06/07/1995.
GUNNERSBURY Brentford Road	37 / 2B 51 / 2A		01/01/1869	N/A	LSWR	Renamed 01/11/1871. First served District & Metropolitan Railways 01/06/1877 & 01/10/1877 respectively. Last served Metropolitan Railway 01/01/1907. Last served LSWR 05/06/1916. Originally had 5 platforms, 3 of which were abandoned in 1930. Remodelled 1932 (SR).
Gunnersbury Junction Gunnersbury East Junction	37 / 2B 51 / 2A		01/01/1869	N/A	LSWR	Renamed 24/07/1932 when 'West' junction eliminated.
Gunnersbury West Junction	37 / 2B 51 / 3A		01/01/1869	24/07/1932	LSWR	Chiswick Curve last use 24/07/1932.
GWR CREOSOTING WORKS (HAYES)	35 / 1C		06/06/1877	??/??/1965	GWR	GWR works for creosoting wooden sleepers, creosote being a by-product from Southall Gas works.

H

Name	Page / grid		Date opened	Date closed	Opened by	Notes
HACKBRIDGE	65 / 2D	P	01/10/1868	N/A	LBSCR	Goods yard closed 04/01/1965.
		G	01/10/1868	04/01/1965		
HACKNEY CENTRAL Hackney	27 / 3B	P	26/09/1850	N/A	EWIDBJR	First station opened to east of current site 26/09/1850 as 'Hackney',
		G	20/10/1850	04/10/1965		with goods yard opening 20/10/1850. Re-sited west 01/12/1870, train service suspended 15/05/1944 (enemy action) but remained open to sell tickets, full closure 23/04/1945. Goods yard closed 04/10/1965. Re-opened to passengers 12/05/1980 as 'Hackney Central'. Closed 20/02/2010 - 01/06/2010 (LOROL upgrade works).
HACKNEY DOWNS Hackney Downs Junction	27 / 3B		27/05/1872	N/A	GER	Suffix 'Junction' usually added until 1897/8. Rebuilt with 2 central through roads 01/06/1876, further rebuilt with 4 platforms 1894. Interchange walkway to Hackney (NLR) in use 01/12/1885 - 15/05/1944.
Hackney Downs North Junction	27 / 2B		01/07/1872	N/A	GER	
Hackney Downs South Junction	27 / 3B		01/06/1876	N/A	GER	Date given is that of quadrupling through Hackney Downs station.
Hackney Downs Tunnel	27 / 2B		01/07/1872	N/A	GER	
HACKNEY WICK	27 / 3D		12/05/1980	N/A	BR	Closed 20/02/2010 - 01/06/2010 (LOROL upgrade works).
HACKNEY WICK GOODS	27 / 3C		25/03/1877	06/11/1967	GNR	Closed ??/06/1967 - 01/03/1878.
HADLEY WOOD Beech Hill Park (goods yard only)	5 / 3C	P	01/05/1885	01/03/1950	GNR	Goods yard opened at some point in 1884 as 'Beech Hill Park',
		G	??/??/1884	01/03/1950		passenger station opened 01/05/1885. Goods yard closed 01/03/1950. East Coast main line quadrupling through Hadley Wood Station / tunnels completed 03/05/1959.
Hadley Wood North Tunnels	5 / 2C		07/08/1850	N/A	GNR	Original bore is today's 'Up' tunnel, 'Down' bore added 03/05/1959.
Hadley Wood South Tunnels	5 / 3C		07/08/1850	N/A	GNR	Original bore is today's 'Up' tunnel, 'Down' bore added 03/05/1959.
HAGGERSTON (NLR)	27 / 4A		02/09/1867	06/05/1940	NLR	Closed 06/05/1940, current Haggerston (TFL) slightly to the north.
HAGGERSTON (TFL)	27 / 4A		27/04/2010	N/A	TFL (LOROL)	Built by TFL for LOROL services.
HAINAULT	17 / 3B	P	01/05/1903	N/A	GER	Closed to passengers & goods 01/10/1908, re-opened to passengers
		G	01/05/1903	01/10/1908		03/03/1930 (goods yard remained closed). Fairlop Loop closed to LNER passenger services 30/11/1947 to allow electrification and transfer to LTE Central Line. First served by LT Central Line Trains 31/05/1948 (terminus until 21/11/1948).
HAINAULT DEPOT	17 / 3B		14/12/1947	N/A	LPTB (CEN)	Ostensibly complete by 1939, used ??/06/1943 - ??/01/1945 for temporary wartime use (rolling stock assembly for US Army

Name	Page / grid		Date opened	Date closed	Opened by	Notes
						Transportation Corps). Central Line depot since 14/12/1947 (partial opening), 31/05/1948 (full opening).
Halfpence Lane Tunnel	60 / 5D		28/09/2003	N/A	LCOR	
Hall Farm Curve	15 / 6B	P G	26/04/1870 26/04/1870	04/10/1914 06/11/1967	GER	Part of original GER branch from Lea Valley Line to Shern Hall Street Walthamstow. Passenger service withdrawn 04/10/1914, closed to freight and abandoned 06/11/1967.
Hall Farm North Junction	15 / 6B		01/08/1872	06/11/1967	GER	Junction between original Shern Hall Street Walthamstow branch and 01/08/1872 line to Hackney Downs, eliminated when Hall Farm Curve abandoned 06/11/1967.
Hall Farm South Junction	15 / 6B		01/08/1885	11/06/1960	GER	Junction at north end of Coppermill Curve (refer to Coppermill Curve notes).
HAM RIVER GRIT Co.	50 / 2C		??/??/1904	??/??/1952	PRIV	2 foot narrow gauge network within gravel pits, also serving a riverside wharf.
HAMMERSMITH (MDR)	38 / 2A 72		09/09/1874	N/A	MDR	MDR terminus 09/09/1874 - 01/06/1877. GNPBR terminus opened to north 15/12/1906, entire station rebuilt with Piccadilly Line platforms between District Line platforms for Piccadilly Line westward extension 04/07/1932.
HAMMERSMITH (MET / GWR)	38 / 2A 72	P G	13/06/1864 13/06/1864	N/A 01/02/1960	MET / GWR	Relocated slightly south 01/12/1868. Goods yard closed 01/02/1960.
HAMMERSMITH & CHISWICK Hammersmith	37 / 2C 51 / 2D	P G	08/04/1858 01/05/1857	01/01/1917 03/05/1965	NSWJR	Opened to goods traffic 01/05/1857, passenger traffic 08/04/1858. '& Chiswick' suffix added 01/07/1880. Passenger traffic withdrawn 01/01/1917, goods remaining until 03/05/1965, branch formally abandoned 01/01/1966.
HAMMERSMITH DEPOT Metropolitan Railway electric trains.	38 / 2A		05/11/1906	N/A	GWR	Hammersmith & City Line depot, built by GWR but used exclusively for
HAMMERSMITH (GROVE ROAD)	37 / 2D 72		01/01/1869	05/06/1916	LSWR	Served by GWR 01/06/1870 - 01/11/1870, MET 01/10/1877 - 01/01/1911.Addison Road to Studland Road Junction closed 05/06/1916.
HAMPSTEAD	25 / 2C		22/06/1907	N/A	UERL (CCEHR)	Was named 'Heath Street' up until point of opening, when renamed 'Hampstead'. Former name still appears on tiles at platform level.
HAMPSTEAD HEATH	25 / 2D	P G	02/01/1860 01/03/1863	N/A 30/09/1972	HJR	Closed 04/12/1984 - 15/04/1985 (cutting wall collapse) & 29/10/1995 - 29/09/1996 (engineering works). Goods yard opened 01/03/1863, closed 30/09/1972.
Hampstead Heath Tunnel	25 / 2D		02/01/1860	N/A	HJR	Closed 29/10/1995 - 29/09/1996 (engineering works).
HAMPSTEAD ROAD	26 / 3A 58		09/06/1851	05/05/1855	EWIDBJR	Replaced by new station of same name (opened on same date),later to become Primrose Hill (see entry for that station). Location believed to be at the point where the railway crossed Hampstead Road on the west side (source = Cross' New Plan of London 1861).
Hampstead Tunnel	25 / 3C		15/03/1899	N/A	GCR	
HAMPTON	49 / 4D	P G	01/11/1864 01/11/1864	N/A 03/05/1965	TVR	Originally passing point on single line until 17/07/1878 doubling. Goods yard initially on 'down' side only, additional sidings on 'up' side added 1899. Closed 03/05/1965.
HAMPTON & KEMPTON WATERWORKS RAILWAY	49 / 3B		17/05/2013	N/A	PRIV	Currently a 2-foot gauge loop with a single platform, with future plans to re-open the original Metropolitan Water Board Railway route between Bunny Lane and the Upper Shepperton Road.
HAMPTON COURT Hampton Court for East & West Molesey Hampton Court for East Molesey Hampton Court for East Moulsey Hampton Court & East Moulsey Hampton Court	50 / 5B	P G	01/02/1849 01/02/1849	N/A 03/05/1965	LSWR	Suffix '& East Moulsey' added 1869, became 'for East Moulsey' 1897/8, spelling changed to 'for East Molesey' 1903/4 (suffix also '& East Molesey' at this time). Suffix then changed to 'for East & West Molesey' at some point until 1955, when it was dropped and the station became simply 'Hampton Court' again. Goods yard closed 03/05/1965.
HAMPTON COURT GAS WORKS	50 / 4C		c.1895	??//??/1961	PRIV	Hampton Court Gas Co. Works founded in mid-19th century, but no rail connection apparent on OS before 1896.
Hampton Court Junction	63 / 1C		01/02/1849	N/A	LSWR	Line to Guildford added 02/02/1885. Remodelled with an 'up' diveunder on Guildford line 1908, further 'down' flyover to eliminate 'flat' junction for Hampton Court branch added 04/07/1915.
HAMPTON WATERWORKS	49 / 3B		??/??/1897	??/07/1964	PRIV	Waterworks at riverside site established c.1855, receiving coal by river. In 1897 a pumping station was built at Kempton Park, with a standard gauge rail connection. In 1915 a 2-foot narrow gauge railway system approx. 5km in length was constructed connecting the three pumping station complexes and riverside wharves. The narrow gauge system was dismantled in 1947 due to a switch from coal to oil, with the standard gauge sidings ceasing to be used after July 1964.
HAMPTON WICK	50 / 4D		01/07/1863	N/A	LSWR	
HANDLEY'S BRICKWORKS	54 / 6A		c.1930	c.1970	PRIV	1 foot gauge internal railway installed in existing brick works c.1930, still in situ on 1968 OS but had disappeared by 1974/5 (works closed 1976).
HANGER LANE	24 / 4A		30/07/1947	N/A	LPTB (CEN)	
Hanger Lane Junction	24 / 6A		23/06/1903	N/A	MDR	Divergence of MDR South Harrow branch from line to Ealing Broadway.
HANSON AGGREGATES (DAGENHAM DOCK)	30 / 6A		?	N/A	PRIV	
HANSON AGGREGATES (WEST DRAYTON)	34 / 1D		?	N/A	PRIV	
HANWELL Hanwell & Elthorne Hanwell	23 / 6B		01/12/1838	N/A	GWR	Served by District Railway trains 01/03/1883 - 01/10/1885. Suffix '& Elthorne' 01/04/1896 - 06/05/1974. Southern entrance and platform 1 demolished 1977.
HANWELL BRIDGE SIDINGS	36 / 1A		?	N/A	GWR	Currently used by DBS.
Hanwell Junction	23 / 6B		03/06/1903	N/A	GWR	Converted to 'single lead' junction 1974.
HAREFIELD ROAD	9 / 6C		N/A	N/A	LTE (CEN)	Station to have been built on aborted Central Line extension to Denham, adjacent to former South Harefield Halt.
HARLESDEN	24 / 4C 68 / 6D		15/06/1912	N/A	LNWR	Adjacent to site of LBIR 'Willesden' station open 1842 - 01/09/1866. Served by Bakerloo Line trains since 16/04/1917.
HARLESDEN FOR WEST WILLESDEN & STONEBRIDGE PARK Stonebridge Park for West Willesden & Harlesden Harrow Road for Stonebridge & Harlesden Harrow Road Harrow Road for Stonebridge Park & Harlesden Harrow Road for Stonebridge Park & West Willesden	24 / 3C	P G	03/08/1875 03/08/1875	01/10/1902 06/07/1964	MID	Opened as 'Harrow Road for Stonebridge Park & West Willesden', 'Harlesden' substituted for 'West Willesden' ??/02/1876. Renamed 'Harrow Road' 01/05/1878, suffix 'for Stonebridge & Harlesden' added 01/11/1880. Renamed 'Stonebridge Park for West Willesden & Harlesden' 01/07/1884. Closed to passengers 02/07/1888, re-opened 01/03/1893. Re-named 'Harlesden for West Willesden & Stonebridge Park' 01/02/1901. Closed to passengers for good 01/10/1902, goods 06/07/1964.
Harlesden Junction	24 / 4C 91 & 92		02/01/1860	N/A	LNWR / HJR	

Name	Page / grid		Date opened	Date closed	Opened by	Notes
HAROLD WOOD	19 / 4B	P	01/02/1868	N/A	GER	Was named 'Heril Wood' until point of opening. Rebuilt due to
		G	01/02/1868	04/10/1965		quadrupling 01/01/1934, platforms were staggered previously ('up' west of 'down'). Goods yard closed 04/10/1965.
HARRINGAY	14 / 6C	P	01/05/1885	N/A	GNR	Suffix 'West' in use 18/06/1951 - 27/05/1971. Goods yard closed
Harringay West		G	01/05/1885	01/01/1968		01/01/1968.
Harringay						
Harringay Curve	14 / 6C	P	N/A	N/A	GNR /	Harringay Curve possibly laid April 1864 (junction recorded as having
		G	??/04/1864	N/A	THJR	been established, but eliminated 5 months later, according to GNR records) then lifted by 1881 perhaps without being used. As the THJR did not open until 21/07/1868, if it were used, it could have been in connection with the THJR's construction. Laid again 15/05/1916 then lifted ??/04/1920, again possibly without having been used. Laid for a third time 08/01/1940.
HARRINGAY GREEN LANES	14 / 6D	P	01/06/1880	N/A	THJR	Opened as 'Green Lanes' 01/06/1880, Goods yard probably opened
Harringay East		G	c.1882	03/02/1964		1882. 'Harringay Park' prefix added 30/08/1884. 'Green Lanes' suffix
Harringay Stadium						dropped 09/06/1951, renamed 'Harringay Stadium' 27/10/1958. Goods
Harringay Park						yard closed 03/02/1964. Renamed 'Harringay East' 14/05/1990, then
Harringay Park, Green Lanes						'Harringay Green Lanes' 08/07/1991.
Green Lanes						
Harringay Junction	14 / 6C		??/04/1864	N/A	GNR / THJR	See notes re: Harringay Curve (junction at north end of curve).
Harringay Park Junction	14 / 6C		21/07/1868	N/A	THJR	See notes re: Harringay Curve (junction at south end of curve).
HARRINGTON ROAD	54 / 5B		23/05/2000	N/A	CTL	
HARROW LANE SIDINGS	31 / 4B		??/??/1866	30/08/1981	NLR	Scrap metal from Harrow Lane represented the last traffic on the Victoria
Park - Poplar route.						
Harrow North Junction	11 / 6B		04/07/1904	N/A	MET	Divergence of Uxbridge Branch, became a 'flying' junction with opening of Uxbridge Branch diveunder 14/10/1925.
HARROW-ON-THE-HILL	11 / 6B	P	02/08/1880	N/A	MET	Country terminus of Metropolitan Railway 02/08/1880 - 02/05/1885.
Harrow		G	02/08/1880	03/04/1967		Renamed 01/06/1894. Served by GCR since 15/03/1899. Goods yard closed 03/04/1967.
HARROW & WEALDSTONE	11 / 4B	P	20/07/1837	N/A	LBIR	Renamed 01/05/1897. First served by Bakerloo Line trains 16/04/1917,
Harrow		G	20/07/1837	03/04/1967		service withdrawn after 24/09/1982, reinstated 04/06/1984 as terminus. Goods yard closed 03/04/1967.
HATCH END	11 / 3A		08/08/1842	N/A	LBIR	Suffix '& Hatch End' added 01/02/1897. Renamed 'Hatch End (for
Hatch End (For Pinner)						Pinner)' 01/02/1920, suffix dropped 11/06/1956. Served by London
Pinner & Hatch End						Underground Bakerloo Line trains 16/05/1917 - 24/09/1982. Platforms
Pinner						3-6 abandoned 07/01/1963. Goods yard to the south, adjacent to future Headstone Lane station (see entry below).
HATCH END GOODS	11 / 3A		08/08/1842	14/11/1966	LBIR	Adjacent to Headstone Lane station.
HATTON CROSS	35 / 5B		19/07/1975	N/A	LTE (PIC)	Terminus 19/07/1975 - 16/12/1977 (empty trains ex-Hounslow West commenced reversing here from 14/07/1975).
HAVERSTOCK HILL	25 / 2D		13/07/1868	01/01/1916	MID	Platforms repositioned from original (now 'fast') to new (now 'slow') lines when these opened 03/02/1884.
Hawkswood Junctions	55 / 5D 56 / 5A		??/??/1992	N/A	BR	Physical junctions formed 1992 when Tonbridge Slow Loop doubled, leading to short section of bidirectional track.
HAYDON SQUARE GOODS	27 / 6A 74 / 1B		??/02/1853	02/07/1962	LNWR	Temporary opening February 1853, full opening 12/03/1853.
Haydon Square Junction	74 / 2C		??/02/1853	02/07/1962	LNWR / LBLR	
HAYDONS ROAD	52 / 3C	P	01/10/1868	N/A	LBSCR /	Renamed 01/10/1889. Closed to passengers 01/01/1917 - 27/08/1923.
Haydens Lane		G	01/10/1868	05/12/1966	LSWR	Goods yard closed 05/12/1966.
HAYES	68 / 2B	P	29/05/1882	N/A	SER	Initially single platform (current platform 2). Station rebuilt 1933,
		G	29/05/1882	19/04/1965		turntable removed at this time and built over. Goods yard closed 19/04/1965, but sidings retained until January 1971 for engineering purposes.
HAYES & HARLINGTON	35 / 1D	P	01/05/1864	N/A	GWR	Served by District Railway trains 01/03/1883 - 01/10/1885.
Hayes		G	01/05/1864	02/01/1967		Renamed 22/11/1897. Goods yard closed 02/01/1967.
HEADSTONE LANE	11 / 3A		10/02/1913	N/A	LNWR	Served by London Underground Bakerloo Line trains 16/05/1917 - 24/09/1982. Hatch End goods yard adjacent.
Heathrow Airport Junction	35 / 1A		19/01/1998	N/A	RT	Being remodelled for commencement of 'Crossrail' services 2018, estimated completion of works September 2017.
HEATHROW EXPRESS / CONNECT DEPOT	24 / 5C 91		19/01/1998	N/A	BAA	
HEATHROW JUNCTION	34 / 1D		19/01/1998	25/05/1998	BAA	Temporary terminus due to delayed opening of HEX tunnel (collapse during construction 21/10/1994). Closed 31/01/1998 - 03/02/1998 (operational problems), closed for good 25/05/1998 when HEX opened fully.
HEATHROW TERMINALS 1, 2 & 3	34 / 4D		16/12/1977	N/A	LTE (PIC)	Terminus 16/12/1977 - 12/04/1986. Suffix 'Terminals 1, 2 & 3' added
Heathrow Central Terminals 1, 2 & 3						03/09/1983, 'Central' dropped 12/04/1986. Heathrow Express platforms
Heathrow Central						opened 25/05/1998.
HEATHROW TERMINAL 4	34 / 5D		12/04/1986	N/A	LUL (PIC)	LUL platform closed 21/10/1994 - 04/12/1994, then again 06/01/2005 - 17/09/2006 (Terminal 5 Extension). Heathrow Express platforms opened 25/05/1998.
HEATHROW TERMINAL 5	34 / 4B		27/03/2008	N/A	BAA	Entire station owned & operated by BAA. Platforms for 'Airtrack' built but project cancelled 11/04/2011.
Heathrow Tunnel Junction	34 / 1D		25/05/1998	N/A	RT / BAA	Crossover at mouth of tunnel to Heathrow Airport, current BAA / NR boundary.
HENDON	12 / 5D	P	13/07/1868	N/A	MID	Goods yard opened 09/03/1868, passenger station 13/07/1868.
		G	09/03/1868	01/01/1968		Goods yard closed 01/01/1968.
HENDON CENTRAL	12 / 5D		19/11/1923	N/A	UERL (CCEHR)	Terminus of extension from Golders Green 19/11/1923 - 18/08/1924.
HENDON FACTORY PLATFORM	12 / 4D		19/05/1918	??/??/1919	PRIV	Station to cater for workers of the Grahame-White aircraft factory. Possibly never used.
HENDON RAILTRANSFER STATION	25 / 1A 85		c.1979	N/A	PRIV	Originally GLC facility (30 year lease signed March 1979), subsequently
Brent Waste Terminal						operated by Shanks & McEwan Ltd until expiry of lease. Now operated by Waste Recycling Group, proposed to be moved to site of 'Bestway' on west side of Midland main line (Brent Cross development).
HERNE HILL	39 / 6C	P	25/08/1862	N/A	LCDR	Terminus of line from Elephant & Castle until 01/07/1863.
		G	25/08/1862	01/08/1966		Goods yard closed 01/08/1966.
Herne Hill North Junction	39 / 6C		25/08/1862	N/A	LCDR	
Herne Hill South Junction	39 / 6C		01/01/1869	N/A	LCDR	
HERNE HILL SORTING SIDINGS	39 / 5C		c.1860s	01/08/1966	LCDR	Didn't open with line in 1862, but sidings appeared by 1870

Name	Page / grid		Date opened	Date closed	Opened by	Notes
HERON QUAYS	40 / 1D		31/08/1987	N/A	DLR	Closed 09/02/1996 - 22/04/1996 (IRA bomb) and 01/10/2001 - 18/12/2002 (reconstruction).
HERSHAM	62 / 2D		28/09/1936	N/A	SR	
HIGH BARNET	5 / 4B	P	01/04/1872	N/A	GNR	First served by and transferred to LPTB Northern Line 14/04/1940, closed to LNER passenger services on same date. Goods yard closed 01/10/1962.
		G	01/04/1872	01/10/1962		
HIGH BARNET SIDINGS	5 / 4B		01/04/1872	N/A	GNR	Originally GNR carriage sidings, became stabling sidings for Northern Line.
High Level (or Tottenham South) Curve	26 / 2A 9	P	01/07/1870	19/01/1964	MID	Connection between THJR and MID goods lines. First passenger use 01/07/1870, closed 19/01/1964.
		G	03/01/1870	19/01/1964		
High Meads Curve	27 / 3D 77 / 78	P	N/A	N/A	GER	No regular passenger service.
		G	??/??/1881	N/A		
High Meads Junction	27 / 3D 77 / 78		??/07/1891	N/A	GER	Junction at north end of Lea & High Meads Curves.
High Meads Loop	27 / 3D 77 / 78	P	N/A	N/A	GER	No regular passenger service. Northern portion now under covered way (Stratford City development).
		G	??/??/1881	N/A		
HIGH STREET KENSINGTON Kensington (High Street)	38 / 1B 84	P	01/10/1868	N/A	MET	Metropolitan District Railway platforms opened 03/07/1871. Renamed gradually by 1880. Adjacent goods yard opened by Midland Railway 04/03/1878, closed 25/11/1963. Terminus 23/07/2011 - 23/08/2011 (engineering work).
		G	04/03/1878	25/11/1963	MID	
HIGHAMS PARK Highams Park & Hale End Highams Park (Hale End) Hale End	16 / 3A	P	17/11/1873	N/A	GER	Renamed 'Highams Park (Hale End)' 10/10/1894, then became '& Hale End' 01/05/1899. Suffix dropped 20/02/1969. Goods yard closed 04/10/1965.
		G	17/11/1873	04/10/1965		
HIGHBURY & ISLINGTON Highbury (*GNCR*) Highbury or Islington (*NLR*) Islington (*EWIDBJR*)	26 / 3C	P	26/09/1850	N/A	EWIDBJR	Opened as 'Islington', renamed 'Highbury or Islington' 01/06/1864, then 'Highbury & Islington' 01/07/1872. GNCR station (separate from NLR premises) opened 28/06/1904 as 'Highbury', '& Islington' suffix added 20/07/1922. LTB Victoria Line platforms opened 01/09/1968, with the southbound using the former northbound GNCR platform, and a new northbound GNCR platform built alongside the northbound Victoria Line. Interchange provided with BR at this time and original GNCR entrance closed. GNCR platforms closed by LTE 05/10/1975, reopened by BR 16/08/1976. Goods yard opened for coal only 20/10/1851, transferred to LNWR and opened to general goods traffic 22/12/1872, closed 04/08/1969. LOROL platforms closed 20/02/2010 - 01/06/2010, upon re-opening formerly abandoned northern platforms used (now numbered 7 & 8), with southern 1 & 2 re-opening 06/01/2011 as terminus.
		G	20/10/1851	04/08/1969		
Highbury Vale Junction	26 / 2C 81		??/??/1988	N/A	BR	Junction formed when line through Canonbury Tunnel singled due to 1988 electrification works.
HIGHBURY VALE GOODS	26 / 2C 81		??/??/1876	05/04/1971	GNR	
HIGHGATE (GNR)	14 / 6A		22/08/1867	05/07/1954	GNR	Nominally opened by Edgware, Highgate & London Railway, which was absorbed by GNR a month before opening. Original layout of central siding and side platforms replaced by island platform c.1883. Closed when Alexandra Palace to Finsbury Park service withdrawn 05/07/1954. Had been intended for electrification and transfer to LPTB Northern Line, but works abandoned post-WW2.
HIGHGATE (LPTB)	14 / 6A		19/01/1941	N/A	LPTB (NOR)	Line through station opened 03/07/1939, but station itself did not open until 19/01/1941.
Highgate East Tunnel	14 / 6A		22/08/1867	05/10/1970	GNR	Last passenger use 05/07/1954, remained in use for Northern Line Stock transfer until 05/10/1970.
HIGHGATE ROAD HIGH LEVEL Highgate Road for Parliament Hill Highgate Road	26 / 2A 9		21/07/1868	01/03/1918	THJR	Closed 31/01/1870 - 01/10/1870. Carried suffix 'for Parliament Hill' ??/11/1894 - 01/07/1903, after which suffix 'High Level' added to distinguish from Low Level station. Most use ceased 01/10/1915, although some MID trains started from here until complete closure 01/03/1918.
Highgate Road Junction	26 / 2A 9		03/01/1870	19/01/1964	THJR / MID	Junction at north end of High Level Curve, although route toward Gospel Oak saw no traffic before 04/06/1888.
HIGHGATE ROAD LOW LEVEL	26 / 2A 9		17/12/1900	01/03/1918	MID	
Highgate West Tunnel	14 / 6A		22/08/1867	05/10/1970	GNR	Last passenger use 05/07/1954, remained in use for Northern Line Stock transfer until 05/10/1970.
HIGHGATE WOOD DEPOT	13 / 5D		01/10/1962	N/A	LTE (NOR)	On site of GNR Wellington Sidings, nominal opening date is that of withdrawal of BR usage of sidings, as Northern Line trains had stabled there since 1940. Remodelled 1969-1970, closed 25/03/1984 - 23/01/1989.
HILLINGDON Hillingdon (Swakeleys) Hillingdon	21 / 2D	P	10/12/1923	N/A	MET	Served by District Line from opening until 23/10/1933, Piccadilly Line thereafter. 'Swakeleys' suffix added ??/04/1934, gradually dropped. Goods yard closed 10/08/1964. Re-sited west 28/06/1992 (road scheme). Closed 18/07/2014 – 11/08/2014 (track renewal).
		G	10/12/1923	10/08/1964		
HINCHLEY WOOD	63 / 2B		20/10/1930	N/A	SR	
HITHER GREEN	41 / 6A		01/06/1895	N/A	SER	Rebuilt for St Johns to Elmstead Woods quadrupling (completed 18/06/1905) with six platforms. Dartford Line platform roads had a central through road between them, removed 1937.
HITHER GREEN DEPOT	41 / 6A		10/09/1933	N/A	SR	Opened by SR 10/09/1933 as a traction maintenance depot with 6-road engine shed. BR Engineering depot established on part of site 1991. Half of original shed demolished 1993 (reduced from 6 roads to 3). TMD transferred to EWS (now DBS) and engineering depot transferred to Balfour Beatty 24/02/1996.
Hither Green Junction	41 / 6A		01/09/1866	N/A	SER	
HOGSMILL CORN MILLS	64 / 4C		c.1890	??/??/1955	PRIV	Siding serving corn mills on Hogsmill River.
HOLBORN Holborn (Kingsway) Holborn	26 / 6B		15/12/1906	N/A	UERL (GNPBR)	Suffix 'Kingsway' added 22/05/1933, then Central Line platforms opened 25/09/1933, suffix gradually dropped. Platform for Aldwych service in use 30/11/1907 - 21/09/1940, then 01/07/1946 - 30/09/1994.
HOLBORN VIADUCT Holborn Viaduct (High Level) Holborn Viaduct	26 / 6C 32 / 4C		02/03/1874	29/01/1990	LCDR	Suffix 'High Level' 01/05/1912 - 01/06/1916. Some platforms closed and track removed 1967.
HOLBORN VIADUCT (LOW LEVEL) Snow Hill	26 / 6C 32 / 4C		01/08/1874	01/06/1916	LCDR	Renamed 01/05/1912.
HOLLAND PARK	38 / 1B		30/07/1900	N/A	CLR	
HOLLOWAY & CALEDONIAN ROAD Holloway	26 / 2C		??/??/1852	01/10/1915	GNR	Originally open for alighting 'up' passengers only, opened fully 01/08/1856. Renamed 06/05/1901.

Name	Page / grid		Date opened	Date closed	Opened by	Notes
HOLLOWAY CATTLE	26 / 2C		*??/??/1854*	*c.1930s*	GNR	Platforms later used by Holloway Motorail Terminal.
HOLLOWAY MOTORAIL TERMINAL access from Caledonian Road.	26 / 2C		30/05/1960	15/09/1968	BR	Used platforms of former Holloway Cattle Station (see above), road
Holloway North Junctions	26 / 2C 81		14/12/1874	N/A	GNR	
HOLLOWAY ROAD	26 / 2C		15/12/1906	N/A	UERL (GNPBR)	
HOMERTON	27 / 3C		01/10/1868	N/A	NLR	Train service suspended 15/05/1944 (enemy action), station fully closed 23/04/1945, subsequently demolished. Station rebuilt and re-opened 13/05/1985 on same site as original (coinciding with electrification of route). Closed 20/02/2010 - 01/06/2010 (LOROL upgrade works).
HONOR OAK	40 / 6B 54 / 1B	P G	01/12/1865 *01/12/1865*	20/09/1954 *20/09/1954*	LCDR	Closed 01/01/1917 - 01/03/1919 and 22/05/1944 - 04/03/1946. Nunhead to Crystal Palace (High Level) closed to 20/09/1954 (goods yard depicted on page 54 / 1B).
HONOR OAK PARK	40 / 6B		01/04/1886	N/A	LBSCR	
Hoo Junction	60 / 3C		01/04/1882	N/A	SER / HHR	Junction between SER and HHR branch to Sharnal Street.
HOO JUNCTION SIDINGS	60 / 3C		20/02/1926	N/A	SR	Laid out as a marshalling yard by SR, opening 20/02/1926, although some sidings were present on site before this.
Hoppity Tunnel	71 / 4D		01/07/1900	N/A	SECR	
HORNCHURCH	31 / 2A	P G	01/05/1885 *01/05/1885*	N/A *??/??/1981*	LTSR	Served by District Railway trains 02/06/1902 - 01/10/1905, then by excursion trains to Southend (later Shoeburyness) from 01/06/1910. Regular District Line service reintroduced 12/09/1932 when route quadrupled, District Line trains utilising the new 'local' platforms. British Rail services withdrawn by 15/06/1962 and 'fast' platforms abandoned. Ownership of 'local' platforms transferred to LTB 01/01/1969. Goods yard closed 1981.
HORNSEY	14 / 5C	P G	07/08/1850 *07/08/1850*	N/A *07/04/1975*	GNR	Goods yard enlarged 01/05/1885, closed 07/04/1975.
HORNSEY ROAD	26 / 1B		01/01/1872	03/05/1943	THJR	Suffix 'for Hornsey Rise' added in MID timetable 01/02/1880 - 01/07/1903.
HORNSEY STEAM SHED	14 / 5C		*??/11/1899*	*??/07/1961*	GNR	Shed remains as a store building within Hornsey TMD.
HORNSEY TMD	14 / 5C		*16/08/1976*	N/A	BR	Built for electrification of King's Cross suburban routes, first electric service Drayton Park-Old Street 16/08/1976 followed by remainder of suburban lines 08/11/1976. On site of Ferme Park 'Up' Yard and Hornsey steam shed.
HORNSEY THAMESLINK DEPOT *Hornsey Up Carriage Sidings*	14 / 4C		?	N/A	GNR	Former carriage sidings currently being developed into a Thameslink Depot by Siemens, expected to open Summer 2016.
HORSLEY *Horsley & Ockham & Ripley* *Horsley & Ockham*	69 / 5A	P G	02/02/1885 *02/02/1885*	N/A *c.1965*	LSWR	Originally listed in Bradshaw as 'Horsley & Ockham', then became 'Horsley & Ockham & Ripley', sometimes 'for' substituted for '&'. Settled on 'Horsley' 1955.
Hotel Curve	26 / 4B 75	P G	01/10/1863 *01/10/1863*	08/11/1976 *24/03/1969*	GNR	Curve in 'down' direction connecting MET with GNR, originally to 10/01/1863 MET lines but later to 'Widened Lines'. Carried goods traffic 20/02/1866 - 24/03/1969. Rebuilt with an easier radius 1892, closed when Moorgate trains diverted via GNCR 08/11/1976.
HOUNSLOW *Hounslow & Whitton* *Hounslow*	36 / 5A	P G	01/02/1850 *01/02/1850*	N/A *06/05/1968*	LSWR	Suffix '& Whitton' 1852 - 06/07/1930 (date that Whitton station opened). Original goods yard closed 06/05/1968. Second goods yard north of the original (also on 'up' side) opened by SR 1931, closed 06/02/1967.
HOUNSLOW CENTRAL *Heston-Hounslow*	36 / 4A		01/04/1886	N/A	MDR	Originally single platform, line doubled 01/11/1912 (station rebuilding completed 19/10/1912). Renamed 01/12/1925. First served by Piccadilly Line 13/03/1933. District Line service ceased 10/10/1964.
HOUNSLOW EAST *Hounslow Town*	36 / 4A		02/05/1909	N/A	MDR	Opened to replace original Hounslow Town terminal station (closed on same day). Renamed 01/12/1925. First served by Piccadilly Line 13/03/1933. District Line service ceased 10/10/1964.
Hounslow Junction	35 / 6D		01/01/1883	N/A	LSWR	Junction at north end of Hounslow Spur.
Hounslow Spur	35 / 6D	P G	01/01/1883 *01/01/1883*	N/A N/A	LSWR	Service reduced significantly May 1987 ('Roundabout' service around Hounslow Loop ceased).
HOUNSLOW TOWN *Hounslow*	36 / 4A		01/05/1883	02/05/1909	MDR	Original country terminus of MDR branch from Mill Hill Park (Acton Town). Arranged for through running for never- realised extension to junctions with LSWR on Hounslow Loop and at Strawberry Hill. Suffix 'Town' added 1884. Closed 01/04/1886 - 01/03/1903, then for good 02/05/1909.
HOUNSLOW WEST *Hounslow Barracks*	35 / 4D		21/07/1884	N/A	MDR	Opened by District Railway, renamed 'Hounslow West' 01/12/1925. First served Piccadilly Line 13/03/1933, District Line service ceased 10/10/1964. Closed 12/07/1975 and replaced by new station at lower level to north which opened 14/07/1975. New station terminus until 19/05/1975 when Hatton Cross extension opened (between 14/07/1975 and 19/07/1975 trains detrained at Hounslow West and ran empty to Hatton Cross to reverse).
HOWARD TENENS DISTRIBUTION CENTRE	29 / 4C		?	N/A	PRIV	Logistics, formerly 'Stora'.
HOXTON	27 / 4A		27/04/2010	N/A	TFL (LOROL)	Built by TFL for LOROL services.
HST STABLING & MAINTENANCE SHED (OLD OAK COMMON)	24 / 5C 91		*??/09/1976*	N/A	BR	Formerly GWR carriage shed, stabling for First GreatWestern stock. To close and relocate to North Pole Depot.
HYDE PARK CORNER	39 / 1A		15/12/1906	N/A	UERL (GNPBR)	

I

Name	Page / grid		Date opened	Date closed	Opened by	Notes
ICKENHAM	22 / 1A		25/09/1905	N/A	MET	Served by District Line 01/03/1910 - 23/10/1933, Piccadilly Line thereafter. Closed 18/07/2014 – 11/08/2014 (track renewal).
ILFORD	29 / 2A	P G	20/06/1839 *20/06/1839*	N/A *06/05/1968*	ECR	Goods yard to east of station, closed to general goods traffic 06/05/1968 but milk dock remained open until c.1980.
ILFORD DEPOT	29 / 1A		*c.1900*	N/A	GER	First carriage sidings on site c.1900, car sheds added for EMUs March 1949, 'New Shed' opened 1959.
Ilford Carriage Sidings Junction	29 / 1B		20/04/1903	30/11/1947	GER	West-facing junction between GER main line and Fairlop Loop.
Ilford Depot Country End Junction *Seven Kings West Junction*	29 / 1B		20/04/1903	19/03/1906	GER	Junction at south end of Seven Kings curve.
Ilford Depot London End Junction	29 / 2A		??/??1949	N/A	BR	
IMPERIAL PAPER MILLS (GRAVESEND)	60 / 1A		*c.1912*	*c.1968*	PRIV	Mills founded 1912, closed 1981. Connected to Gravesend West branch, so external traffic must have ceased by 24/03/1968, although OS maps depict internal railway network in situ until closure of mills.

Name	Page / grid		Date opened	Date closed	Opened by	Notes
IMPERIAL WHARF	38 / 4C		27/09/2009	N/A	NR (LOROL)	
International Junction	39 / 2C		14/11/1994	N/A	RT	Divergence of lines into platforms 20-24 Waterloo. Disused after 14/11/2007, reinstated when platform 20 re-opened 23/10/2013, to be followed by 21-24 by 2019.
Intersection Tunnel	24 / 3A 68 / 2A		15/06/1912	N/A	LNWR	
ISLAND GARDENS	40 / 3D		31/08/1987	N/A	DLR	One terminus of original DLR system. First station partially built on MER North Greenwich branch viaduct, two platforms present but platform one seldom used after train sets lengthened to two units. Closed on the night of 09/02/1996 by IRA bomb at South Quay, did not re-open until 15/04/1996. Closed 11/01/1999 due to works on the Lewisham extension, new subterranean station opened with extension 20/11/1999, original abandoned.
ISLEWORTH Spring Grove & Isleworth Isleworth	36 / 4B		01/02/1850	N/A	LSWR	Replaced Smallberry Green to east (closed same day). Named 'Spring Grove & Isleworth' 01/10/1855 - ??/08/1911(Borley). Quick refers to station opening as 'Isleworth', having '& Spring Grove' suffix added 1854/5, name then reversed 1874/5 (Spring Grove & Isleworth), reversed back 1895/6, then 'Isleworth for Spring Grove' 1912/3, before becoming 'Isleworth' again 1955.
IVER	34 / 1A	P G	01/12/1924 01/12/1924	N/A 06/01/1964	GWR	Goods yard closed 06/01/1964; sidings remained on site until c.1989.

J

Name	Page / grid		Date opened	Date closed	Opened by	Notes
J PARISH & Co. LOAM & BALLAST PITS	43 / 4B		c.1850	??/??/1957	PRIV	4 foot gauge system connecting loam & ballast pits with a riverside wharf.
JOHNSONS PORTLAND CEMENT WORKS	44 / 6D		??/??/1877	c.1970	PRIV	Originally 3 foot 9½ inches narrow gauge internal system, converted to standard gauge 1928 and connected to main line.
JUNCTION ROAD Junction Road for Tufnell Park	26 / 2A 9		01/01/1872	03/05/1943	THJR	Suffix 'for Tufnell Park' dropped 01/07/1903. Has been proposed to be re-opened as 'Tufnell Park'.
Junction Road Junction	26 / 2A 9		02/04/1883	N/A	THJR / MID	Junction between THJR and MID line to Carlton Road Junction.

K

Name	Page / grid		Date opened	Date closed	Opened by	Notes
KEMPTON PARK	49 / 3B		18/07/1878	N/A	LSWR	At first platform on 'down' side only, 'up' platform added 1879. Initially members only, opened to public 1890. Bay platform on 'up' side removed 1964. Race Days only until 06/03/2006, when full passenger service commenced (unadvertised service started from 05/03/2006).
KENLEY Coulsdon	73 / 1C	P G	05/08/1856 05/08/1856	N/A 03/04/1961	CR	Renamed December 1856. Goods yard closed 03/04/1961.
KENNINGTON	39 / 3C		18/12/1890	N/A	CSLR	Sometimes had suffix 'New Street' added 1890-1894. Closed 01/06/1923 - 06/07/1925 (tunnel widening). Charing Cross Branch platforms opened 13/09/1926.
KENSAL GREEN	25 / 4A		01/10/1916	N/A	LNWR / UERL	Served by Bakerloo Line from opening.
KENSAL GREEN & HARLESDEN	24 / 4D 91		01/11/1861	01/07/1873	HJR	Platforms were staggered on either side of present Wrottesley Road bridge (down on west, up on east). Replaced by Kensal Green (later Kensal Rise) station to east, opened on same date as closure.
Kensal Green Junctions	24 / 4D 91 & 92		02/01/1860	N/A	HJR	
Kensal Green Tunnels	24 / 4D 91 & 92		20/07/1837	N/A	LBIR	Quadrupled by LNWR 1879. DC lines tunnels (2 single track bores) added 10/05/1915.
KENSAL RISE Kensal Green	25 / 4A		01/07/1873	N/A	LNWR	Renamed 24/05/1890. Closed 29/10/1995 - 29/09/1996 (engineering works).
KENSINGTON & CHELSEA DISTRICT SCHOOL	65 / 6A		??/??/1880	c.1930	PRIV	School near Banstead for poor children of Kensington & Chelsea, served by siding from Epsom Downs branch. Established 1880, siding apparent on 1913 OS but had been removed by 1934-5.
KENSINGTON (OLYMPIA) Kensington (Addison Road) Kensington	38 / 2A 84		27/05/1844	N/A	WLR	Opened by WLR as passenger terminus, but passenger services withdrawn and station closed 01/12/1844. Note that prior to the WLR opening, a platform was built on Kensington Canal basin itself, but this was never served by trains. Re-opened by WLR slightly to north 02/06/1862, again as terminus (extended to Clapham Junction 02/03/1863). First served MET 01/07/1864, renamed 'Kensington (Addison Road)' 01/10/1868. LNWR trains to Earl's Court started 01/02/1872. Station closed to all services 21/10/1940 (enemy action). Re-opened after WW2 for workers' shuttle service to Clapham Junction (in operation by summer 1946), also to exhibition traffic via District Line starting 19/12/1940, on which date station renamed Kensington (Olympia). District Line bay platform and segregated track towards Earl's Court opened 03/03/1958. Mainline platforms regularly served 01/04/1963 - 15/06/1965 (diversions due to WCML electrification), then again 15/10/1967 - 20/12/1967 (diversions due to Paddington rebuilding). Workers' shuttle to Clapham Junction advertised after 16/05/1983, regular District Line service started 07/04/1986. Mainline station fully re-opened 12/05/1986 (long distance trains), local service Clapham Junction to Willesden Junction restored 31/05/1994. Regular weekday District Line service withdrawn 12/12/2011 (weekend and exhibition traffic remain).
KENSINGTON OLYMPIA MOTORAIL TERMINAL	38 / 2A 84		24/05/1966	late 1982	BR	Service withdrawn at end of Summer timetable 1982.
KENSINGTON SIDINGS	38 / 5C 89		02/03/1863	N/A	WLER	Formerly 7 sidings used primarily for goods traffic, currently a solitary siding used by LOROL.
KENT HOUSE	54 / 4B		01/10/1884	N/A	LCDR	Line through station quadrupled 10/05/1886.
KENT PORTLAND CEMENT WORKS	44 / 6D		??/??/1922	c.1970	PRIV	
KENTISH TOWN	26 / 2A 9		13/07/1868	N/A	MID	UERL (CCEHR) station opened 22/06/1907.
KENTISH TOWN ENGINE SHEDS	26 / 2A 9		08/09/1867	??/??/1963	MID	No.2 and No.3 sheds added 1899.

Name	Page / grid		Date opened	Date closed	Opened by	Notes
Kentish Town Junction	26 / 2A9		03/01/1870	19/01/1964	MID	Junction at south end of High Level Curve to Highgate Road Junction.
KENTISH TOWN WEST Kentish Town	26 / 3A		01/04/1867	N/A	HJR	Suffix 'West' added 02/06/1924. Closed 18/04/1971 - 05/10/1981 (arson), again 29/10/1995 - 29/09/1996 (engineering works), and again 20/02/2010 - 01/06/2010 (LOROL upgrade works).
KENTON Kenton (for Northwick Park) Kenton	11 / 5D	P G	15/06/1912 *13/03/1911*	N/A *03/05/1965*	LNWR	Goods yard opened 13/03/1911, passenger station opened later; 15/06/1912. Goods yard closed 03/05/1965. Suffix 'for Northwick Park' in use 01/10/1927 - 07/05/1973. Served by London Underground Bakerloo Line trains since 16/04/1917, but no service 27/09/1982 (last train 24/09/1982) - 04/06/1984.
KEW	37 / 2A19	P G	01/08/1853 *??/07/1856*	01/02/1862 *?*	NSWJR	Initially terminus, through services onto Hounslow Loop commenced 01/06/1854. Passenger service effectively ceased when NSWJR trains to Richmond diverted via Kew and Barnes Curves 01/02/1862, but a once weekly service between Windsor and the Metropolitan Cattle Market at Caledonian Road continued to call until October 1866. Coal yard south of down platform opened July 1856, later incorporated into Kew Bridge North Goods.
KEW BRIDGE Kew	37 / 2A19	P G	22/08/1849 *c.1890*	N/A *03/04/1967*	LSWR	Platforms on Kew Curve opened 01/02/1862 (initially had separate NSWJR entrance, which closed 01/07/1918), closed 12/09/1940. Entire station re-named 'Kew Bridge' December 1868. Adjacent goods yard re-named 'Kew Bridge South' 1948 (as distinct from the former MID yard in the Kew Bridge triangle, which became 'North', and the 1929 SR 'New' yard adjacent to Old Kew Junction), goods yard closed 03/04/1967. Per Borley goods facilities opened with passenger station, but none evident on OS before 1895 when a single siding had appeared behind down platform.
KEW BRIDGE NEW GOODS	37 / 2A19		*??/??/1929*	*??/??/1977*	SR	Expanded 1930.
KEW BRIDGE NORTH GOODS	37 / 2A19		*??/??/1863*	*?*	NSWJR	NSWJR, later MID, goods yard situated in Kew Bridge triangle. Named 'Kew Bridge North' 1948. Closure date not known, possibly c.1980s (still extant in Borley). Note 1863 opening date is sourced from Borley; no evidence is seen of yard until 1895 OS (not present on 1870 1:1,056 or 1882-94 1:2,500 surveys).
Kew Curve (LSWR)	37 / 2A19	P G	01/02/1862 *01/02/1862*	12/09/1940 *N/A*	LSWR	Regular passenger service (Kew Bridge to Willesden Junction) withdrawn 12/09/1940.
Kew Curve (LNWR)	24 / 5C91 & 92	P G	20/07/1885 *20/07/1885*	N/A *N/A*	LNWR	Link built to connect NSWJR and HJR, allowing closure of original HJR high level route / platforms to passengers.
Kew East Junction	37 / 2A19		01/02/1862	N/A	NSWJR / LSWR	Junction at north end of Kew Curve.
KEW GARDENS	37 / 4A		01/01/1869	N/A	LSWR	Served by GWR 01/06/1870 - 01/11/1870, first served MDR 01/06/1877, served by MET 01/10/1877 - 01/01/1911. Sidings and Bay platform in use until 04/07/1931, crossover north of platforms until 31/01/1954.
Kew Railway Bridge	37 / 3A		01/01/1869	N/A	LSWR	Also known as Strand-on-the-Green bridge.
KIDBROOKE	41 / 5C	P G	01/05/1895 *01/05/1895*	N/A *07/10/1968*	BHR	Goods yard a single siding on 'down' side, west of station. In 1917 a large military depot was established to the south of the station, remaining in situ until at least the early 1960s (subsequently redeveloped as the Ferrier Estate). Goods yard closed 07/10/1968.
Kidbrooke Tunnel	41 / 5B		01/05/1895	N/A	BHR	
KILBURN Kilburn & Brondesbury	25 / 3B		24/11/1879	N/A	MSJWR	First served by Bakerloo Line 20/11/1939, last served Metropolitan Line 07/12/1940. Suffix '& Brondesbury' until 25/09/1950. Transferred from Bakerloo Line to Jubilee Line 01/05/1979.
KILBURN HIGH ROAD Kilburn & Maida Vale Kilburn	25 / 4B	P G	c.1851/1852 *c.1851/1852*	N/A *05/11/1962*	LNWR	Opening date unknown, late 1851 or early 1852. Renamed 'Kilburn & Maida Vale' 01/06/1879. Closed 01/01/1917, re-opened 10/07/1922, then renamed 'Kilburn High Road' 01/08/1923. Closed 17/09/2004 - 22/08/2005 (fire). Goods opened with passenger, closed 05/11/1962.
KILBURN PARK	25 / 4B		31/01/1915	N/A	UERL (BAK)	Terminus from opening until 11/02/1915.
KING EDWARD BUILDING	26 / 6D32		*19/12/1927*	*c.1996*	POR	King Edward Building ceased operation 1996, so POR station below presumed to have closed at same time.
KING GEORGE V	41 / 1D62 / 5C		02/12/2005	N/A	DLR	Terminus until 10/01/2009 extension to Woolwich Arsenal.
KING HENRY'S DRIVE	67 / 5D		10/05/2000	N/A	CTL	
KING WILLIAM STREET	26 / 6D87		18/12/1890	25/02/1900	CSLR	Original terminus of CSLR from Stockwell. Abandoned when line extended from Borough to Moorgate.
KING'S CROSS	26 / 4B75 / 76		14/10/1852	N/A	GNR	Replaced original terminus to north (see Maiden Lane GNR). 'Suburban' portion of station to west of main station was separate from opening on 18/12/1874 until being incorporated into main station 05/03/1977. Platform 16 of the Suburban station on gradient ascending from the 'Hotel Curve' in use 01/02/1878 - 08/11/1976.
KING'S CROSS FUNERAL STATION	75		10/07/1861	03/04/1863	GNR	Funeral traffic to Colney Hatch Cemetery only, last recorded departure 03/04/1863.
KING'S CROSS GOODS	26 / 4B75		*18/11/1850*	*05/03/1973*	GNR	Amalgamation of various facilities, including Potato market, Granary, Eastern & Western Coal drops, and MID goods shed.
King's Cross Junction	75		01/10/1863	08/11/1976	GNR / MET	
King's Cross Loop	76	P G	N/A *27/03/1927*	N/A *N/A*	UERL	Connection between Northern and Piccadilly Lines for stock transfer / engineering use. No passenger service ever provided.
KING'S CROSS ST PANCRAS King's Cross for St Pancras King's Cross	26 / 5B75 / 76		15/12/1906	N/A	UERL (GNPBR)	UERL GNPBR (Piccadilly Line) Platforms opened 15/12/1906 as 'King's Cross', 'for St Pancras' added 1927, became 'King's Cross St Pancras' 1933. CSLR (Northern Line) Platforms opened 12/05/1907 as 'King's Cross for St Pancras', became 'King's Cross St Pancras' 1933, closed 09/08/1922 - 20/04/1924 (tunnel widening), 19/11/1987 - 05/03/1989 (fire) and 16/10/1995 - 17/06/1996 (escalator works). Relocated Metropolitan Line platforms opened 14/03/1941 (see entry for 'King's Cross Thameslink'), initially had a central 'bay' platform that was subsequently lifted late 1940s and later filled in. Victoria Line platforms opened 01/12/1968.
KING'S CROSS THAMESLINK King's Cross Midland City King's Cross Midland King's Cross St Pancras	26 / 4C75		10/01/1863	09/12/2007	MET	Original MET station at King's Cross, platforms on 'Widened Lines' added 17/02/1868. '& St Pancras' after 1925, '&' dropped 1933. Original MET platforms replaced by current station to the west 14/03/1941 (last train 09/03/1941), but platforms on 'Widened Lines' remained open

Name	Page / grid		Date opened	Date closed	Opened by	Notes
King's Cross & St Pancras King's Cross						after this date. BR trains ceased to call 03/10/1977 (down) and 14/05/1979 (up), with the station closed from this date. Platforms on 'Widened Lines' re-opened 11/07/1983 as 'King's Cross Midland', also referred to as 'King's Cross Midland City'. Renamed 'King's Cross Thameslink' 16/05/1988, closed again 09/12/2007 (last train 08/12/2007), replaced by platforms under St Pancras International.
KING'S CROSS 'TOP SHED'	26 / 4B		??/??/1851	17/06/1963	GNR	One of three engine sheds at King's Cross, the others being the Midland roundhouse (opened February 1859) and the 'Main Line Running shed' (opened 1862).
King's Cross Tunnel	75 / 76		13/07/1868	N/A	MID	Connection between MID and MET 'Widened Lines', currently used by 'Thameslink' services.
KING'S CROSS YORK ROAD	26 / 4B 75		01/01/1866	05/03/1977	GNR	Up (Southbound) only, at north end of York Road Curve toward the Metropolitan Railway. Rebuilt slightly to east 04/03/1878 (due to new bore of Gasworks Tunnel opening). Closed 08/11/1976 when Moorgate trains diverted along GNCR at Finsbury Park, but briefly re-opened 31/01/1977 - 05/03/1977 for use of terminating trains.
KINGSBURY	12 / 5B		10/12/1932	N/A	MET	Opened by Metropolitan Railway. Transferred to Bakerloo Line 20/11/1939, Jubilee Line 01/05/1979.
KINGSLAND GOODS	27 / 3A 6		*20/10/1851*	*07/08/1972*	EWIDBJR	
Kingsley Road Junction	36 / 4A		13/06/1905	02/05/1909	MDR	Junction at north end of curve linking Hounslow Town and Heston-Hounslow.
KINGSTON (1st)	51 / 6A		21/05/1838	??/??/1845	LSWR	Situated east of King Charles Road. Replaced by Kingston (2nd station, later Surbiton) to west in 1845.
KINGSTON (2nd)	50 / 4D	P G	01/07/1863 *01/07/1863*	N/A *05/09/1966*	LSWR	Opened as terminus of branch from Twickenham (Low level station). High level platforms opened on extension to New Malden 01/01/1869, although low level platforms remained open. Station rebuilt 1935 with a new bay platform at the high level, allowing the original low level platforms to close (track retained for a period as carriage sidings). Engine shed became goods shed 1898, goods yard closed 05/09/1966.
Kingston Bridge	50 / 4D		01/07/1863	N/A	LSWR	
KINGSWOOD Kingswood & Burgh Heath	72 / 4A	P G	02/11/1897 *02/11/1897*	N/A *07/05/1962*	CVR	02/11/1897 is given as opening date for Chipstead Valley Railway (Purley to Kingswood) in Borley, but it also states regular passenger service 'probably' commenced 09/11/1897, Quick states first train 09/11/1897, so 02/11/1897 may have been official / ceremonial opening. Country end terminus until 01/07/1900 SECR extension to Tadworth. Goods yard closed 07/05/1962. Suffix dropped 01/12/1968.
Kingswood Tunnel	72 / 4A		01/07/1900	N/A	SECR	
KNIGHT'S HILL GOODS	53 / 1D		*16/05/1892*	*07/10/1968*	LNWR	
Knight's Hill Tunnel	53 / 1C		01/10/1868	N/A	LBSCR	
KNIGHTSBRIDGE	38 / 1D		15/12/1906	N/A	UERL (GNPBR)	Reconstructed, with new Sloane Street entrance, 18/02/1934.
KUEHNE + NAGEL LOGISTICS (DAGENHAM DOCK)	30 / 5A		?	N/A	PRIV	Replaced 'Hays Distribution'.

L

Name	Page / grid		Date opened	Date closed	Opened by	Notes
LADBROKE GROVE Ladbroke Grove (North Kensington) Notting Hill & Ladbroke Grove Notting Hill (Ladbroke Road) Notting Hill	25 / 6A		13/06/1864	N/A	MET / GWR	Opened as 'Notting Hill', sometimes had '(Ladbroke Road)' suffix added 1869 - 1880. '& Ladbroke Grove' suffix added 1880, renamed 'Ladbroke Grove (North Kensington)' 01/06/1919, suffix dropped 1938.
LADYWELL Lady Well	40 / 6D		01/01/1857	N/A	MKR	Built by the Mid Kent Railway, but operated by SER from opening. 'Lady Well' used at times as late as 1960.
Ladywell Junction	40 / 6D		01/09/1866	N/A	SER	Junction at south end of Ladywell Loop.
Ladywell Loop	40 / 5D	P G	01/09/1866 *01/09/1866*	N/A N/A	SER	
LAFARGE AGGREGATES (WEST DRAYTON)	21 / 6B		*post-1999*	N/A	PRIV	On site of former coal yard.
LAMBETH NORTH Lambeth (North) Westminster Bridge Road Kennington Road	39 / 2C 89		10/03/1906	N/A	UERL (BSWR)	Opened as 'Kennington Road', renamed 'Westminster Bridge Road' 05/08/1906, renamed 'Lambeth (North)' 15/04/1917, renamed 'Lambeth North' c.1928. Closed 10/11/1996 - 14/07/1997 (Bakerloo Line tunnel strengthening).
Lampton Junction	36 / 4A		21/07/1884	02/05/1909	MDR Hounslow	Junction between original MDR Hounslow Town route and subsequent Barracks extension.
LANCASTER GATE	25 / 5C		30/07/1900	N/A	CLR	Closed 02/07/2006 - 13/11/2006 (lift works).
LANGDON PARK	27 / 6D		10/12/2007	N/A	DLR	Slightly to south of site of South Bromley station (NLR). Poplar to Stratford no service 18/04/2014 until 22:00 25/04/2014.
LANGLEY Langley Marsh	33 / 1C	P G	01/12/1845 *01/12/1845*	N/A *06/01/1964*	GWR	Served by MDR trains 01/03/1883 - 01/10/1885. Suffix 'Marsh' dropped 1849. Goods yard closed 06/01/1964.
LANGLEY OIL TERMINAL	33 / 1C		*15/06/1969*	*c.2000*	PRIV	Operated by Total, lease expired December 2002 but usage ceased c.2000, purchased by EWS but now abandoned.
Latchmere Curve	38 / 5D 89	P G	02/03/1863 *02/03/1863*	N/A N/A	WLER	Singled at time of electrification July 1993, restored to double track 26/04/2011.
Latchmere No.1 Junction	38 / 4D		02/03/1863	N/A	WLER	
Latchmere No.2 Junction	38 / 4D		02/03/1863	N/A	WLER	
Latchmere No.3 Junction	38 / 4D		06/07/1865	N/A	WLER	Junction eliminated 21/01/1936 - 17/08/1994.
LATIMER ROAD	25 / 6A 83		16/12/1868	N/A	MET / GWR	Closed 17/01/2011 - 24/04/2011 (platform lengthening).
Latimer Road Junction Kensington Junction	25 / 6A 83		01/07/1864	01/03/1954	MET / GWR	Originally 'Kensington Junction' before Latimer Road station was opened.
LCC CENTRAL TRAM REPAIR WORKS	41 / 3B		*??/??/1909*	*05/07/1952*	LCC	
LEA BRIDGE Lea Bridge Road	27 / 1C	P G	15/09/1840 *15/09/1840*	08/07/1985 *07/12/1970*	NER	Suffix 'Road' dropped 1841. Goods yard closed 07/12/1970. Closed with Tottenham Hale to North Woolwich service. Per DfT announcement 15/05/2013, will re-open by end of 2014.
Lea Bridge Junction	27 / 1C		26/04/1870	06/11/1967	GER	Southern junction of Hall Farm Curve.
Lea Curve	27 / 3D 77 & 78	P G	N/A *N/A*	N/A *??/07/1891*	GER	No regular passenger service.
Lea Junction	27 / 3D 77 & 78		??/07/1891	N/A	GER	Junction at south end of Lea Curve.
LEATHERHEAD (LBSCR)	70 / 3C	P G	04/03/1867 *04/03/1867*	N/A *c.1965*	LBSCR	Replaced joint station to north. Combined with former LSWR station by SR 10/07/1927.

Name	Page / grid		Date opened	Date closed	Opened by	Notes
LEATHERHEAD (LBSCR & LSWR)	70 / 3C	P	01/02/1859	04/03/1867	LBSCR / LSWR	First station in Leatherhead, at country end of LBSCR / LSWR joint line. Replaced by separate LBSCR and LSWR termini to south, opened on same day as closure 04/03/1867.
		G	*01/02/1859*	*04/03/1867*		
LEATHERHEAD (LSWR)	70 / 3B	P	04/03/1867	10/07/1927	LSWR	Replaced joint station to north. Closed when new connection made between former LSWR and LBSCR by SR 10/07/1927. Track through station remained in situ until at least 1970s (rolling stock storage), with northern portion of former LSWR route remaining in situ until c.1985.
		G	*04/03/1867*	*c.1965*		
Leatherhead Joint Line Junction	70 / 3C		04/03/1867	10/07/1927	LBSCR / LSWR	Junction between branches to separate LBSCR / LSWR termini. LSWR ceased to be through route 10/02/1927, but sidings on former route diverged at this location until c.1985.
Leatherhead Junction	70 / 4C		10/07/1927	N/A	SR	Connection installed between former LSWR and LBSCR by SR, allowing LSWR station at Leatherhead to close.
LEATHERHEAD NORTH	70 / 2C		N/A	N/A	SR	One of two intermediate stations on Chessington South to Leatherhead route, works abandoned at outset of WW2.
LEBANON ROAD	66 / 2D		10/05/2000	N/A	CTL	
LEE	41 / 6B	P	01/09/1866	N/A	SER	Goods yard closed 07/10/1968.
		G	*01/09/1866*	*07/10/1968*		
Lee Loop Junction	41 / 6A		c.1900	N/A	SECR (?)	Junction at north end of Lee Spur.
Lee Spur	41 / 6A	P	N/A	N/A	N/A	Opened c.1900, coinciding approximately with opening of Hither Green marshalling yards.
		G	*c.1900*	*N/A*	SECR (?)	
Lee Spur Junction	55 / 1A		c.1900	N/A	SECR (?)	Junction at south end of Lee Spur.
LEICESTER SQUARE	26 / 6B		15/12/1906	N/A	UERL (GNPBR)	(UERL) CCEHR platforms opened 22/06/1907.
Leigham Court Tunnel	53 / 2B		01/12/1856	N/A	WELCPR	
Leigham Junction	53 / 2C		01/08/1871	N/A	LBSCR	
Leigham Spur	53 / 2C	P	01/08/1871	N/A	LBSCR	
		G	*01/08/1871*	*N/A*		
Leigham Tunnel	53 / 2B		01/10/1868	N/A	LBSCR	
LEMAN STREET	27 / 6A 74 / 2C		01/06/1877	07/07/1941	LBLR	Originally built 1872 but Board of Trade refused to sanction opening, so reconstructed and opened 01/06/1877, closed 22/05/1916 - 01/07/1919.
Leman Street Junction	74 / 2C		17/06/1864	01/09/1966	LBLR / GER	Divergence of East Smithfield / London Docks branch from LBLR line.
LEWISHAM Lewisham Junction Lewisham	40 / 5D	P	30/07/1849	N/A	SER	Suffix 'Junction' 01/01/1857 - 07/07/1929. Goods yard to east of station on Blackheath line, closed 06/05/1963. DLR platforms opened 20/11/1999.
		G	*30/07/1849*	*06/05/1963*		
Lewisham Crossover Junctions Lewisham Junction	40 / 5D		01/01/1857	N/A	MKR / SER	Originally simple junction between SER and MKR routes, developed into crossovers following 30/06/1929 opening of SR connection from former LCDR Greenwich Park branch to Lewisham.
LEWISHAM ROAD	40 / 5D		18/09/1871	01/01/1917	LCDR	Passenger service withdrawn Nunhead to Greenwich Park 01/01/1917.
Lewisham Vale Junction	40 / 5D		29/03/1976	N/A	BR	Junction at south end of Tanners Hill Flydown.
LEY STREET YARD SIDINGS	29 / 1A		c.1900	N/A	GER	Part of Ilford Depot complex.
LEYTON Low Leyton	28 / 2A	P	22/08/1856	N/A	ECR	Prefix 'Low' dropped 27/11/1867. First served by LPTB Central Line trains 05/05/1947, first trains in the morning remained British Rail services until 01/06/1970 (last train 31/05/1970). Goods yard (P27 / 2D) closed 06/05/1968.
		G	*22/08/1856*	*06/05/1968*		
Leyton Junction	28 / 2A		05/05/1947	03/05/1971	LPTB / LNER	Junction of ECR Loughton Branch and LPTB Central Line ex-Stratford. Closed 03/05/1971, dismantled 29/10/1972.
LEYTON MIDLAND ROAD Leyton	27 / 1D	P	09/07/1894	N/A	TFGR	Renamed 01/05/1949. Goods yard (P28 / 1A) open 01/09/1894 - 06/05/1968.
		G	*01/09/1894*	*06/05/1968*		
LEYTONSTONE	28 / 1A	P	22/08/1856	N/A	ECR	Original layout with 'down' platform south of 'up' and a small goods yard on 'up' side. 'Down' platform relocated north 1891 and new goods yard opened partially on site of original 'down' platform. First served by LPTB Central Line trains 05/05/1947 (terminus until 14/12/1947). Goods yard closed 02/09/1955. First trains in morning remained British Rail services until 01/06/1970 (last train 31/06/1970).
		G	*22/08/1856*	*02/09/1955*		
LEYTONSTONE HIGH ROAD Leytonstone	28 / 1A	P	09/07/1894	N/A	TFGR	Renamed 01/05/1949. Goods yard opened 01/09/1894, closed 06/05/1968.
		G	*01/09/1894*	*06/05/1968*		
Leytonstone Junction	28 / 1B		14/12/1947	N/A	LPTB / LNER	Divergence of 1947 route to Newbury Park from Epping Line.
LILLIE BRIDGE DEPOT	38 / 3B 84		*Mid-1872*	N/A	MDR	Originally built by MDR to house their first fleet of locos / coaches (delivered mid-1871), depot complete by mid-1872. Became UERL GNPBR (Piccadilly Line) depot between 15/12/1906 - 04/07/1932. Subsequently used for engineering purposes, but again became a District Line stabling point after 11/12/2010 (S7 Stock upgrade works).
LIMEHOUSE (1st)	27 / 6C		06/07/1840	04/05/1926	LBLR	Passenger service to Blackwall and North Greenwich withdrawn 04/05/1926.
LIMEHOUSE (2nd) Stepney East Stepney	27 / 6C		03/08/1840	N/A	LBLR	Opened as 'Stepney', renamed 'Stepney East' 01/07/1923, platforms to/from Blackwall closed 04/05/1926. Renamed 'Limehouse' 11/05/1987. Former Blackwall platforms re-opened by DLR 31/08/1987, RT platforms closed 22/07/1994 - 12/09/1994 (engineering works).
Limehouse Curve	27 / 6C	P	01/09/1880	01/03/1881	LBLR	Saw passenger use 01/09/1880 - 01/03/1881, not officially closed until 10/05/1963 (date given is last use).
		G	*05/04/1880*	*05/11/1962*		
Limehouse Junction	27 / 6C		05/04/1880	05/11/1962	LBLR	Junction at south end of Limehouse Curve.
Linford Street Junction	39 / 4A 82		17/08/1994	N/A	RT	Date quoted is start of trial Eurostar service, advertised service commenced 14/11/1994. Largely disused since 14/11/2007 (diversion of Eurostar to St Pancras), but chord still in situ and traversed by test trains.
LION CEMENT WORKS (WEST THURROCK)	45 / 4B		c.1880	??/??/1976	PRIV	Originally Wouldham works. Not on 1873 OS map, but had appeared by 1897. Closed 1976.
Lismore Circus Tunnel	9		09/09/1867	N/A	MID	
LITTLE ILFORD DEPOT	28 / 3D		20/08/1905	01/12/1959	UERL (MDR)	District Railway depot. Closed when Upminster Depot opened, replaced by East Ham BR Depot on same site.
LIVERPOOL STREET Bishopsgate *(Metropolitan Railway only)*	26 / 6D 90		02/02/1874	N/A	GER	First served by Metropolitan Railway 01/02/1875 (direct into GER station, platforms 1 & 2). Separate MET platforms opened as 'Bishopsgate' 12/07/1875, terminus until 18/11/1876 (became 'Liverpool Street' 01/11/1909). CLR platforms opened 28/07/1912 (terminus until 04/12/1946). POR station opened 19/12/1927, trains had ceased calling before POR was mothballed 31/05/2003, but subsequent to 1987 re-branding to 'Mail Rail'. Platforms for 'Crossrail 1' expected to open 2018.

Name	Page / grid		Date opened	Date closed	Opened by	Notes
Liverpool Street Junction	90		12/07/1875	??/??/1907	MET / GER	Junction between MET and connection to GER at Liverpool Street platforms 1 & 2. Last through train 1904, junction severed 1907.
LLOYD PARK	67 / 3A		10/05/2000	N/A	CTL	
LONDON BRIDGE Tooley Street London	39 / 1D 87		14/12/1836	N/A	LGR	Replaced Bermondsey Street temporary terminus to east. Separate terminus opened by LCRR to north of LGR one 05/06/1839. Initially referred to as simply 'London', or also as 'Tooley Street', in timetables before 1844. Station rebuilt as joint terminus July 1844 (opened while incomplete), and rearranged with LGR / SER trains using the northern (ex LCRR) portion and LCRR / LBRR the southern (ex LGR) portion to eliminate conflicting train movements at Corbett's Lane Junction. Joint station divided into SER and LBSCR portions 02/08/1850 (during this rebuilding period, temporary stations were provided), enlarged 1854. Original LCRR station demolished 1863 to make way for line to Charing Cross (through platforms opened 11/01/1864). Goods traffic handled between 1864 – 1901 (when transferred to Ewer Street). Station combined by SR 1928, rebuilt 1971 - 1977, again 2010 – 2018. CSLR Platforms opened 25/02/1900 (closed 16/07/1922 - 23/02/1925, 01/07/1996 – 21/10/1996 [southbound line diverted via new tunnel] and 02/07/1999 - 05/09/1999 [further tunnel works]). Jubilee Line platforms opened 07/10/1999.
LONDON CITY AIRPORT	41 / 1D 62 / 5C		02/12/2005	N/A	DLR	
LONDON FIELDS	27 / 3B		27/05/1872	N/A	GER	Closed 22/05/1916 - 01/07/1919 and 13/11/1981 - 29/09/1986* (fire) *per Quick, Connor states 25/09/1986.
LONDON MUSEUM OF STEAM & WATER	37 / 3A		??/??/1986	N/A	PRIV	2 foot gauge demonstration railway (formerly Kew Bridge Steam Museum).
LONDON ROAD DEPOT	39 / 2C		10/03/1906	N/A	UERL (BSWR)	Bakerloo Line depot.
LONG GROVE HOSPITAL	64 / 4A		20/05/1905	??//??/1950	PRIV	Horton Estate Light Railway opened to supply building materials, later fuel, to hospitals.
LONGFIELD Longfield for Fawkham and Hartley Longfield Fawkham for Hartley and Longfield Fawkham Fawkham Road	59 / 6A	P G	12/06/1872 12/06/1872	N/A ??/05/1962	LCDR	Opened as 'Fawkham Road', 'Road' dropped by 1875. Became 'Fawkham for Hartley and Longfield' 1895/6. Renamed 'Longfield for Fawkham and Hartley' 12/06/1961, then 'Longfield' 1968/72. Single carriage siding present on 'up' side, two-road goods yard on 'down', all closed May 1962 (eleven months after June 1961 re-naming per kentrail.org.uk).
LONGFIELD HALT	59 / 5A		01/07/1913	03/08/1953	SECR	Opened by SECR on existing LCDR Gravesend West branch, closed with entire branch 03/08/1953.
Longhedge Junctions	39 / 4A 82		02/03/1863	N/A	WLER / LBSCR	
LORD'S St John's Wood St John's Wood Road	25 / 5D		13/04/1868	20/11/1939	MSJWR	Opened as 'St John's Wood Road', 'Road' suffix dropped 01/04/1925, renamed 'Lord's' 11/06/1939, closed 20/11/1939 and replaced by St John's Wood Station (Bakerloo Line) to north.
LORDSHIP LANE	54 / 1A		01/09/1865	20/09/1954	LCDR	Closed 01/01/1917 - 01/03/1919 and 22/05/1944 - 04/03/1946. Closed for good 20/09/1954.
LOUGHBOROUGH JUNCTION Loughborough Road	39 / 5C		??/10/1864	N/A	LCDR	First platforms opened on Brixton Spur October 1864 as 'Loughborough Road'. Platforms on lines to Herne Hill and Cambria Spur added 01/12/1872 and station renamed 'Loughborough Junction'. Line to Herne Hill originally quadruple track, one 'up' track removed to make room for island platform while two 'down' roads retained. Post-1925 middle 'down' road removed, side 'down' platform closed, and island platform widened into space vacated by middle 'down' road. Brixton Spur platforms closed 03/04/1916, Cambria Spur platforms closed 12/07/1925. *Note: The above dates are per Borley and Quick; Mitchell & Smith in 'Holborn Viaduct to Lewisham' state that the Brixton Spur platforms were named 'Brixton Junction' upon opening, and the platforms on the Herne Hill route and Cambria Spur opened 01/07/1872 as 'Loughborough Road', before the entire station complex was renamed as 'Loughborough Junction' 01/12/1872.*
Loughborough Junction	39 / 5C		01/05/1863	N/A	LCDR	North end of Brixton and Cambria Spurs (latter added 01/07/1872).
LOUGHTON (ECR)	8 / 5D	P G	22/08/1856 22/08/1856	24/04/1865 18/04/1966	ECR	Original terminus of ECR branch from Stratford, sited just south of the High Road. Closed to passengers when line extended to Ongar 24/04/1865. Line lifted beyond a relocated goods station c.1866, second goods yard remaining open until 18/04/1966.
LOUGHTON (GER)	8 / 6D		24/04/1865	N/A	GER	Station built to replace original ECR terminus on extension to Ongar, re-sited to east 28/04/1940 by LNER in readiness for LTE services. Majority of passenger services transferred to LTE 21/11/1948 when LTE service commenced (terminus until 25/09/1949), but first trains in the morning remained British Rail services until 01/06/1970.
Loughton Junction	27 / 2D		22/08/1856	03/05/1971	ECR	Divergence of ECR Loughton Branch from NER Lea Valley Line. Closed 03/05/1971, dismantled 29/10/1972.
LOUGHTON SIDINGS	8 / 6D		21/11/1948	N/A	LTE (CEN)	Stabling Sidings for Central Line.
Low Level Curve	26 / 2A 9	P G	17/12/1900 17/12/1900	05/01/1981 05/01/1981	MID	Curve between THJR and MID 'slow' passenger lines at Kentish Town, abandoned when Barking trains diverted from Kentish Town to Gospel Oak.
LOW STREET	46 / 4C	P G	??/07/1861 ??/07/1861	05/06/1967 28/09/1964	LTSR	Exact opening date unknown; first appeared in Bradshaw July 1861. Goods yard closed 28/09/1964, passenger station followed 05/06/1967.
LOWER EDMONTON (LOW LEVEL Edmonton (Low Level) Edmonton	15 / 1B	P G	01/03/1849 01/03/1849	11/09/1939 07/12/1964	ECR	Opened as 'Edmonton' on original ECR Enfield Branch from Angel Road. 'Low Level' suffix added 22/07/1872 with opening of 'High Level' station. Renamed 'Lower Edmonton (Low Level)' 01/07/1883. Became passenger terminus 01/08/1872 when High Level platforms commenced Enfield (Town) service, closed to passengers 11/09/1939, goods yard closed 07/12/1964 along with entire Angel Road to Lower Edmonton Junction route.
Lower Edmonton Junction	15 / 1B		01/08/1872	07/12/1964	GER	Angel Road Junction to Lower Edmonton Junction closed to goods 07/12/1964.
LOWER SYDENHAM	54 / 3C	P G	01/01/1857 c.1857	N/A 20/06/1966	MKR	Station re-sited south 1906 (no more precise date known). Goods yard opened 'probably' 1857 per Borley, but is not apparent on 1863 OS map, and cannot be discerned before 1895 survey. Originally short

Name	Page / grid		Date opened	Date closed	Opened by	Notes
						siding north of 'down' platform, much extended through site of original 'down' platform after 1906. Yard closed 20/06/1966.
LOWER SYDENHAM GASWORKS	54 / 2C		*??/??/1878*	*22/04/1969*	PRIV	Works established 1854, rail connected since 1878. Closed 22/04/1969, rail connection severed 1971.
Lucas Street Tunnels	40 / 4C		30/07/1849	N/A	SER	
LUDGATE HILL	26 / 6C 32 / 5B		21/12/1864	02/03/1929	LCDR	Terminus until extension to Farringdon opened 01/01/1866. Two island platforms until 1910, when eastern island removed and western island widened.
Ludgate Hill Junction	32 / 4B		02/03/1874	29/01/1990	LCDR	Divergence of Holborn Viaduct Branch.
Ludgate Junction	38 / 5D 89		02/03/1863	N/A	LSWR / WLER	
LYONS WORKS (GREENFORD)	23 / 3B		*??/??/1920*	*??/??/1970*	PRIV	

M

Name	Page / grid		Date opened	Date closed	Opened by	Notes
MAIDA VALE	25 / 5C		06/06/1915	N/A	UERL (BSWR)	
MAIDEN LANE (GNR)	26 / 4B 75		07/08/1850	14/10/1852	GNR	London terminus of GNR until King's Cross opened. Also referred to as 'King's Cross'. Trainshed roof retained after closure to passengers as Potato market.
MAIDEN LANE (NLR)	26 / 3B 75		01/07/1887	01/01/1917	NLR	Platforms only ever provided on unelectrified northern 'No.1' NLR lines (original southern lines were 'No.2').
Maiden Lane Curve	75	P G	10/01/1863 10/01/1863	10/01/1863 10/01/1863	GNR	West-facing curve between MET and GNR York Road Curve. Crossed Hotel Curve on level. Possibly never used.
Maiden Lane Junction	75		24/06/1867	??/05/1968	NLR	Junction accessing Maiden Lane goods (later York Way Freightliner terminal)
MAIDEN LANE GOODS	26 / 3B 75		*24/06/1867*	*??/??/1965*	NLR	Initially cattle only, general goods from 07/01/1868. Site subsequently occupied by York Way Freightliner terminal.
MALDEN MANOR	64 / 1C		29/05/1938	N/A	SR	
MANOR HOUSE	14 / 6D		19/09/1932	N/A	UERL (GNPBR)	
MANOR PARK	28 / 2C	P G	06/01/1873 ??/??/1882	N/A 01/01/1968	GER	Suffixes 'for Little Ilford' or '& Little Ilford' sometimes used 1895 - 1940. Goods yard opened 1882, closed 01/01/1968.
Manor Park & Little Ilford						
Manor Park for Little Ilford						
MANOR ROAD GOODS	27 / 1A		*??/12/1872*	*07/12/1964*	GER	
MANOR SIDINGS	44 / 4D		*c.1960s*	*N/A*	BR	Disused.
MANOR WAY	42 / 1A 62 / 3D		??//07/1881	09/09/1940	LSKD	Opened July 1881 as 'Manor Road', renamed 'Manor Way' June 1882. Initially single track, doubled 01/04/1882. Original station west of road bridge demolished and replaced by new station east of bridge c.1887. Operated by GER after 1896, ownership later transferred to PLA. Branch closed from 09/09/1940 due to 'Black Saturday' air raid 07/09/1940 (no trains on Sundays since 27/06/1915). Listed as 'Royal Albert Dock, Manor Way' in Borley.
Manor Road						
MANSION HOUSE	26 / 6D 32 / 5D		03/07/1871	N/A	MDR	Terminus until 06/10/1884. Northern bay platform abolished 04/02/1968. Closed 29/10/1989 - 11/02/1991 (rebuilding).
MARBLE ARCH	25 / 6D		30/07/1900	N/A	CLR	
MARLBOROUGH ROAD	25 / 4C		*13/04/1868*	*20/11/1939*	MSJWR	Replaced by St John's Wood (then Bakerloo Line) to south.
MARSH FARM SEWAGE WORKS	46 / 6B		*c.1940*	*by 1979*	PRIV	First appeared on 1940 OS, railway had ceased operating by 1979.
MARYLAND	28 / 3A		06/01/1873	N/A	GER	Renamed 28/10/1940.
Maryland Point						
Maryland East Crossovers	28 / 3A		?	N/A	BR	
MARYLEBONE	25 / 5D		15/03/1899	N/A	GCR	Terminus of Great Central Railway. UERL BSWR platforms opened as 'Great Central' 27/03/1907, were terminus until 15/06/1907, renamed to 'Marylebone' 15/04/1917 ('Great Central' tiling remains at platform level). NR station closed 15/08/2011 - 22/08/2011 (engineering work at Neasden South Junction).
Great Central (UERL only)						
MARYLEBONE GOODS & COAL	25 / 5C		*11/04/1899*	*28/03/1966*	GCR	Coal & minerals traffic commenced 11/04/1899, general goods commenced 27/04/1899.
MAYER-PARRY SCRAP (WILLESDEN)	24 / 5D 91 & 92		*c.1960s*	*N/A*	PRIV	Car-crushing plant. Opened in 1960s on site of former LNWR electric carriage sidings.
MAZE HILL	41 / 3A		01/01/1873	N/A	SER	Opened as terminus of short branch from Charlton 01/01/1873 as 'Greenwich (Maze Hill)'. Through line to original Greenwich station opened and station renamed 'Maze Hill & East Greenwich' 01/02/1878. Became 'Maze Hill & Greenwich Park' 01/07/1878, reverted to 'Maze Hill & East Greenwich' (or 'Maze Hill [East Greenwich]') 01/01/1899. Suffix dropped and became 'Maze Hill' ??/04/1937 (Borley), although alternative suffix 'for National Maritime Museum' referred to in Quick, with this being dropped in 1955. Two 'down' roads flanked an island platform, with 5 carriage sidings on the 'down' side and 6 on the 'up' (including a 2-road carriage shed). Carriage sidings were never electrified and had ceased to be used by North Kent Line full electrification (1962). Signal box abolished 29/11/1969.
Maze Hill (for National Maritime Museum)						
Maze Hill & East Greenwich						
Maze Hill & Greenwich Park						
Maze Hill & East Greenwich						
Greenwich (Maze Hill)						
Maze Hill Tunnel	41 / 3A		01/02/1878	N/A	SER	
MCVITIE & PRICE'S SIDING	24 / 4B		*??/??/1902*	*?*	PRIV	Later United Biscuits.
MERSTHAM	73 / 3D	P G	early 1842 early 1842	N/A c.1965	LBRR	Quick states opened with line 12/07/1841, but LBRR Board minute of 01/07/1841 refers to tender for construction being delayed, and a further minute from 16/12/1841 refers to permission being granted for construction spoil to be deposited on adjacent land owned by The Countess of Warwick. An SER board minute from 30/05/1842 refers to consideration of 'pulling down' or 'shutting up' Merstham, so it appears to have opened by this date. Closed by SER 02/10/1843, re-opened 04/10/1844 pending completion of new (current) station to north, re-sited c.1845.
Merstham Tunnel	73 / 5A		12/07/1841	N/A	LBRR	
MERTON ABBEY	52 / 4C	P G	01/10/1868 01/10/1868	03/03/1929 01/05/1972	LBSCR / LSWR	Closed to passengers 01/01/1917 - 27/08/1923, then again for good 03/03/1929 (passenger service Tooting Junction to Merton Park withdrawn). Goods yard remained open until 01/05/1972 (Borley), although the closure date of line from Merton Park to Merton Abbey is given as 05/05/1975 in Borley, so private goods traffic may have remained until latter date, or this may merely be the date of official closure of the route by BR.

Name	Page / grid		Date opened	Date closed	Opened by	Notes
MERTON PARK Lower Merton	52 / 4B		01/10/1868	N/A	LBSCR / LSWR	Opened by LBSCR & LSWR on their joint loop line from Streatham to Wimbledon as 'Lower Merton', initially platforms on this route only (none on WCRR route), single platform on WCRR route added 01/11/1870. Renamed 'Merton Park' 01/09/1887. Platforms on route to Tooting Junction closed 01/01/1917 - 27/08/1923, then again for good 03/03/1929. Platform on Wimbledon to Croydon route sometimes had 'Halt' added on timetables / tickets 1918 - 1923/4. Closed 02/06/1997 (last train 31/05/1997, no Sunday service), re-opened by Croydon Tramlink 30/05/2000.
Merton Park Junction	52 / 4B		01/10/1868	05/05/1975	LBSCR / LSWR	
MERTON SEWAGE WORKS	52 / 3C		c.1915	??/??/1963	PRIV	Opened by Wandle Valley Joint Sewerage Board, 2 foot gauge internal railway in operation c.1915 – 1963.
Metropolitan Junctions	39 / 1D 87		01/09/1866	N/A	SER	Junction with curve to Blackfriars opened 01/06/1878.
Mickleham Tunnel	70 / 6C		11/03/1867	N/A	LBSCR	
MIDDLE SIDINGS (SHENFIELD)	20 / 5B		01/01/1934	N/A	LNER	
MILDMAY PARK	26 / 3D		01/01/1880	01/10/1934	NLR	
MILE END (ECR)	27 / 5B		c.1841	24/05/1872	ECR	Replaced Devonshire Street, Mile End station to east, later replaced by Bethnal Green Junction station to west.
MILE END (MDR)	27 / 5C		02/06/1902	N/A	MDR / LTSR	Served by Metropolitan Line since 30/03/1936 ('Hammersmith & City Line' since 30/07/1990). Central Line platforms opened 04/12/1946.
MILE END GOODS Mile End & Devonshire Street Goods Devonshire Street Goods	27 / 5C		??/??/1850	06/11/1967	ECR	Opened as 'Devonshire Street Goods', prefix 'Mile End &' added 01/09/1922, suffix '& Devonshire Street' dropped 01/01/1939.
MILEAGE YARD Crimea Yard	25 / 6B 67 / 5A		c.1850s	17/07/1967	GWR	Yard was in situ by 1863, originally referred to as 'Crimea Yard' which may suggest opening date between October 1853 and February 1856 (Crimean War). Closed 17/07/1967.
MILL HILL BROADWAY Mill Hill	12 / 2C	P G	13/07/1868 09/03/1868	N/A 03/08/1964	MID	Goods yard opened first; 09/03/1868, passenger station opened 13/07/1868. Suffix 'Broadway' added 25/09/1950, although goods yard was renamed previously (01/07/1950). Goods yard closed 03/08/1964.
MILL HILL EAST Mill Hill East for Mill Hill Barracks Mill Hill for Mill Hill Barracks Mill Hill	13 / 3A	P G	22/08/1867 22/08/1867	N/A 01/10/1962	GNR	Opened as 'Mill Hill', suffix 'for Mill Hill Barracks' added 17/04/1916, renamed 'Mill Hill East for Mill Hill Barracks' 01/02/1928. Closed by LNER 11/09/1939 to allow transfer to LPTB, doubling, and electrification (reopened by LPTB 18/05/1941 as terminus), but electrification only reached Mill Hill East and second track to Mill Hill (The Hale) dismantled without being used. Goods yard closed 01/10/1962.
MILL HILL (THE HALE) The Hale Halt	12 / 2C	P G	11/06/1906 18/07/1910	11/09/1939 29/02/1964	GNR	Goods yard opened 18/07/1910. Originally opened as 'The Hale Halt', renamed 'Mill Hill (The Hale)' 01/03/1928. Closed to passengers 11/09/1939 to enable doubling and electrification of Finchley Central to Edgware prior to transfer to LPTB Northern Line. Works abandoned and station did not re-open. Goods yard closed 29/02/1964.
MILLWALL DOCKS	40 / 2D		18/12/1871	04/05/1926	MER	Terminus until 29/07/1872, before this date a temporary station served by horse-drawn trains, after this date reconstructed as a permanent station south of Glengall Road. Often also referred to as 'Millwall Dock'. Passenger service to Blackwall and North Greenwich withdrawn 04/05/1926. Crossharbour DLR on same site.
MILLWALL GOODS	40 / 2D		18/12/1871	01/06/1925	MER	Goods station closed 01/06/1925, but goods trains continued to serve the adjacent dock.
MILLWALL JUNCTION	40 / 1D 31 / 4B	P G	18/12/1871 18/12/1871	04/05/1926 14/11/1927	LBLR / MER	Opening coincided with that of Millwall Extension Railway to Millwall Docks. Rebuilt & re-sited 1888, two platform faces on Blackwall route, one on route to North Greenwich. Passenger services withdrawn from both 04/05/1926.
MILTON RANGE HALT	60 / 2D		01/07/1906	17/07/1932 (see notes)	SECR	Removed from timetables 17/07/1932, only served 'as required' for adjacent rifle ranges thereafter. Rebuilt in concrete 1954 (previously wood), continued to be served until at least 1956, local services ceased on route 04/12/1961, even then station did not 'officially' close and platforms remained standing until 2008 (up) / 2009 (down).
MILTON ROAD HALT	60 / 1B		01/07/1906	01/05/1915	SECR	Closed as a WW1 economy, did not re-open.
MINORIES	27 / 6A 74 / 2B		06/07/1840	24/10/1853	LBLR	Original LBLR London terminus. Replaced by Fenchurch Street, although both open until 15/02/1849 (Minories closed) then again 09/09/1849 - 24/10/1853 (Minories re-opened, then closed again for good).
Minories Junction	27 / 6A 74 / 1B		06/10/1884	N/A	MDR / MET	
MITCHAM	52 / 6D	P G	22/10/1855 22/10/1855	N/A 01/05/1967	WCRR	Station opened by WCRR as only intermediate station between Wimbledon and Croydon, 2 platforms from outset (passing loop on single line), following a landslip in 1971 'up' (northern) abandoned. Goods yard closed 01/05/1967, passenger station closed 02/06/1997 (last train 31/05/1997, no Sunday service), re-opened on a new site slightly to east by Croydon Tramlink 30/05/2000.
MITCHAM EASTFIELDS	52 / 5D		02/06/2008	N/A	NR	Opened during afternoon of 02/06/2008, platforms staggered either side of level crossing.
MITCHAM JUNCTION	52 / 6D		01/10/1868	N/A	LBSCR	Station opened with Streatham - Sutton line (no station on WCRR line prior to this). Separate Croydon Tramlink platforms opened 30/05/2000 following withdrawal of Wimbledon - West Croydon NR trains 02/06/1997.
Mitre Bridge Curve	24 / 5D 91 & 92	P G	02/09/1867 02/09/1867	N/A N/A	LNWR	Loop built to connect WLR with HJR.
MITRE BRIDGE EXCHANGE PLATFORMS	24 / 5D 91		27/05/1844	01/12/1844	GWR / WLR	Exchange platforms built for traffic between WLR / GWR, abandoned when WLR passenger services ceased. Location of GWR platforms uncertain, WLR and GWR crossed each other on the level at this location until 1860.
MITRE BRIDGE GOODS	24 / 5D 91		c.1870	c.1965	LNWR	Sidings had appeared by 1870 OS and been removed by 1975, dates not listed in Borley.
Mitre Bridge Junction	24 / 5D 91 & 92		02/09/1867	N/A	LNWR	
MONUMENT The Monument Eastcheap	26 / 6D 87		06/10/1884	N/A	MDR / MET	Opened as 'Eastcheap', renamed 'The Monument' 01/11/1884, 'The' prefix gradually dropped.

Name	Page / grid		Date opened	Date closed	Opened by	Notes
MOOR PARK Moor Park & Sandy Lodge Sandy Lodge	10 / 1A	P G	09/05/1910 09/05/1910	N/A ??/06/1938	MET / GCR	Opened as 'Sandy Lodge', 'Moor Park' prefix after 18/10/1923, 'Sandy Lodge' suffix dropped 25/09/1950. Goods yard closed ??/06/1938. Rebuilt with two new island platforms for quadrupling 23/04/1961.
MOORGATE Moorgate Street	26 / 6D		23/12/1865	N/A	MET	City Widened Lines platforms opened 01/07/1866, closed 23/03/2009 (last train 20/03/2009), CSLR platforms opened 25/02/1900. GNCR (later Northern Line, then British Rail) platforms opened 14/02/1904. Station renamed 24/10/1924.
MORDEN	52 / 5B		13/09/1926	N/A	UERL (NOR)	Southern terminus of LU Northern Line.
MORDEN DEPOT	52 / 6B		13/09/1926	N/A	UERL (NOR)	
MORDEN ROAD Morden Road Halt Morden Halt Morden	52 / 4B		??/03/1857	N/A	WCRR	Did not open with WCRR, first appeared in timetables March 1857 as 'Morden'. Removed from timetables October & November 1918, upon re-appearing in December 1918, became 'Morden Halt'. Further renamed 'Morden Road Halt' 02/07/1951. 'Halt' dropped 1968. Closed 02/06/1997 (last train 31/05/1997, no Sunday service), re-opened by Croydon Tramlink 30/05/2000. In its mainline guise, was always a single platform on north side of single track.
MORDEN SOUTH	52 / 6B		05/01/1930	N/A	SR	
MORNINGTON CRESCENT	26 / 4A		22/06/1907	N/A	UERL (CCEHR)	Closed 23/10/1992 - 27/04/1998 for lift replacement works.
Mortimer Street Junction	26 / 2A 9		17/12/1900	05/01/1981	MID	Junction at north end of Low Level Curve, abandoned after diversion of Barking Trains to Gospel Oak.
MORTLAKE Mortlake & East Sheen Mortlake	37 / 5B		27/07/1846	N/A	LSWR	Carried '& East Sheen' suffix 01/04/1886 - 30/01/1916.
Mortlake Junction	37 / 5C		01/02/1862	01/01/1869	LSWR	Junction at south end of Barnes Curve. Barnes Curve disused since 01/01/1869 but not dismantled until 1881.
MOTSPUR PARK	51 / 6D		12/07/1925	N/A	SR	
Motspur Park Junction	64 / 1D		29/05/1938	N/A	SR	
MOTTINGHAM Eltham & Mottingham Eltham for Mottingham Eltham & Mottingham Eltham	55 / 1D	P G	01/09/1866 01/09/1866	N/A 07/10/1968	SER	Opened as 'Eltham', suffix '& Mottingham' added 01/01/1892. '&' became 'for' 1914, reverted to '&' 1922. 'Eltham' dropped and station became 'Mottingham' 26/09/1927. Six carriage sidings were laid west of the station c.1900, all but one were decommissioned along with the goods yard 07/10/1968. The remaining siding was usually left 'clipped' out of use and eventually lifted.
MOUNT PLEASANT	26 / 5C		05/12/1927	31/05/2003	POR	POR mothballed 31/05/2003, but re-opening of a portion of the route centred upon Mount Pleasant and the adjacent depot as part of a British Postal Museum & Archive has been approved by Islington Council, expected opening 2016.
Mount Street Tunnel	41 / 2C		30/07/1849	N/A	SER	
Mountnessing Junction	20 / 4C		01/01/1934	N/A	LNER	Dive-under for Southend Victoria Branch built by LNER 01/01/1934.
MUDCHUTE	40 / 2D		31/08/1987	N/A	DLR	Closed on the night of 09/02/1996 by IRA bomb at South Quay, did not re-open until 15/04/1996. Closed 11/01/1999 due to works on the Lewisham extension, new station at a lower level opened with the extension 20/11/1999.
MUSEUM DEPOT	37 / 1A		??/10/1999	N/A	LUL	Opened on part of Ealing Common Depot site (and accessible by rail from there) to house LT Museum exhibits.
MUSWELL HILL	14 / 4A	P G	24/05/1873 24/05/1873	05/07/1954 14/06/1956	GNR	Nominally opened by Edgware, Highgate & London Railway, which was absorbed by GNR a month before opening. Closed to passengers 01/08/1873 - 01/05/1875 and again 29/10/1951 - 07/01/1952 along with entire branch. Had been intended for electrification and transfer to LT Northern Line, but works abandoned post-WW2. Finally closed to passengers when Alexandra Palace to Finsbury Park service permanently withdrawn 05/07/1954. Goods yard remained in use until 14/06/1956 after which time branch abandoned beyond Cranley Gardens.

N

Name	Page / grid		Date opened	Date closed	Opened by	Notes
Navarino Road Junction	27 / 3A		30/06/1986	N/A	BR	Junction at north end of Graham Road Curve.
NEASDEN Neasden & Kingsbury Kingsbury & Neasden	24 / 2C 22	P G	02/08/1880 01/01/1894	N/A ??/04/1958	MET	Opened as 'Kingsbury & Neasden', renamed 'Neasden & Kingsbury' 01/01/1910, suffix dropped 01/01/1932. Goods yard opened 01/01/1894, closed April 1958. Served by Bakerloo Line 20/11/1939 - 01/05/1979, Jubilee Line thereafter. Last served regularly by Metropolitan Line 07/12/1940.
NEASDEN COAL	24 / 2C 22		25/07/1898	04/03/1968	GCR	
Neasden Curve	24 / 2C 22	P G	N/A 01/08/1899	N/A N/A	GCR	Curve only regularly used for freight services, originally double track but subsequently singled.
NEASDEN DEPOT	24 / 2C 22		??/??/1882	N/A	MET	Originally Metropolitan Railway Works & Power Station. Substantially rebuilt in 1930s. Stabled Bakerloo Line Trains 20/11/1939 - 01/05/1979, Jubilee Line trains thereafter.
NEASDEN ENGINE SHED	24 / 3C 22		15/03/1899	18/06/1961	GCR	
NEASDEN FREIGHT TERMINAL	24 / 2B 22		05/04/2002	24/03/2007	PRIV	Tibbett & Britten, terminal for imported mineral water. Dates quoted are for beginning of / break in lease of building. Sidings remain in situ and connected to main line despite 2011 junction remodelling, but are obstructed. Current owner Seneca (recycling) website states an aim to recommission sidings, but 'early 2012' is the given date.
Neasden Junction	24 / 2C 22		01/08/1899	N/A	GCR	Junction at southern end of Neasden Curve.
Neasden North Junction	24 / 2B 22		28/04/1923	18/05/1968	LNER	Junctions between Wembley Stadium Loop and former GCR main line.
NEASDEN POWER STATION	24 / 1B 22		??/12/1904	21/07/1968	MET	Metropolitan Railway Power Station, commissioned December 1904, electric services commenced 01/01/1905.
Neasden South Junction	24 / 2C 22		20/11/1905	N/A	GCR	Junction between GCR lines to Aylesbury and 1905 High Wycombe route (first passenger use 01/03/1906). Extensively remodelled 15/08/2011 - 22/08/2011.

Name	Page / grid		Date opened	Date closed	Opened by	Notes
NEASDEN SOUTH SIDINGS	24 / 2B 22	?	N/A	GCR		
NECROPOLIS	39 / 2C 89		13/11/1854	11/05/1941	LSWR	Station for funeral traffic to Brookwood Cemetery. Resited south 16/02/1902 (Waterloo station expansion). Last recorded funeral departure 11/04/1941. Partially destroyed by air raid night of 16-17/04/1941, officially declared closed 11/05/1941.
NEVER STOP RAILWAY	24 / 1B 22		23/04/1924	??/10/1925	PRIV	The system had four stations; North End, Tree Top, Mid Way and South End.
NEW ADDINGTON	67 / 5D		10/05/2000	N/A	CTL	
NEW BARNET Barnet	5 / 5D	P G	07/08/1850 *07/08/1850*	N/A *22/08/1966*	GNR	Prefix 'New' added 01/05/1884. Goods yard closed 22/08/1966.
NEW BECKENHAM	54 / 4C		01/04/1864	N/A	MKR	Opening coincided with MKR route from here to Addiscombe. Original site south of current station and junction, it is thought that there were four platform faces serving the Addiscombe and Beckenham Junction routes. Replaced by current 2-platform station to north c.1868 (Borley) / 1866-8 (Quick) / 1866 (Mitchell & Smith). Jackson provides the most detail; with the original station closing 'autumn 1866' and the replacement opening 'from October 1866, if not a little earlier'. There was a central through road in use 1904 - 1926* to facilitate joining / dividing of trains. *Jackson states track removed 1926, Mitchell & Smith states road eliminated 1929*
New Beckenham Junction	54 / 4C		01/04/1864	N/A	MKR	
NEW CROSS (SER)	40 / 4C 79 / 80		??/10/1850	N/A	SER	Precise opening date unknown, October 1850. SER began running own trains over ELR 01/04/1880, separate bay platform for ELR added on 'down' side 01/10/1884. Served by MDR 01/10/1884 - 06/10/1884 only. Served by MET 06/10/1884 - 03/12/1906, then again 31/03/1913 onwards, gaining separate 'East London Line' identity during 1980s No LUL service 25/03/1995 - 25/03/1998 (engineering work), withdrawn for good 23/12/2007. Former LUL bay re-opened by TfL (LOROL) 27/04/2010.
NEW CROSS (ELR)	40 / 4C 79		07/12/1869	01/09/1886	ELR	Original ELR southern terminus. Closed 01/11/1876 - 01/10/1884, MDR service commenced 06/10/1884, station closed entirely 01/09/1886 and all services diverted to adjacent New Cross (Gate). Sometimes differentiated from New Cross (Gate) by use of 'Low Level' suffix. At times ELR used both this and New Cross (Gate) station for terminating services.
NEW CROSS DEPOT	40 / 3C 79		31/03/1913	23/12/2007	MET	Carriage shed built for ELR electrification, MET EMU stabling. Closed with ELL prior to transfer to TfL (LOROL).
NEW CROSS GATE New Cross	40 / 4C 79 / 80		05/06/1839	N/A	LCRR	Served by ELR 01/11/1876 - 01/10/1884. Served by MDR 01/09/1886 - 01/08/1905. Served by MET 31/03/1913 onwards, gaining separate 'East London Line' identity during 1980s. 'Gate' suffix added 09/07/1923. No LUL service 25/03/1995 - 25/03/1998 (engineering work), withdrawn for good 23/12/2007. Served by TfL (LOROL) services since 27/04/2010 (terminus until 23/05/2010).
NEW CROSS GATE DEPOT	40 / 3C 80		27/04/2010	N/A	TFL (LOROL)	LOROL depot opened coinciding with re-opening / transfer of ELL 27/04/2010, replaced former New Cross Depot.
New Cross Gate Down Junction	40 / 4C 79 / 80		01/11/1876	N/A	NR	Re-established 23/05/20120 due to LOROL extension to West Croydon / Crystal Palace. Connection between ELR and LBSCR first formed 01/11/1876 to north of New Cross (Gate) station, junction for 'down' trains relocated to present site in late 19th century. Direct connection between LTE and BR removed 17/09/1972. Indirect connection between LTE and BR carriage / permanent way sidings removed 12/01/1975. Access to sidings remained from south until their abandonment c.1990, current junction established on same site.
New Cross Gate Up Junction	40 / 4C 79 / 80		23/05/2010	N/A	NR	Junction eliminated after 27/04/1966, re-established 23/05/2010 for new flyover (LOROL).
NEW CROSS GOODS	40 / 4C 79		05/06/1839	06/11/1967	LCRR	Goods yard opened with New Cross (Gate) passenger station, expanded over the years and became GER owned, occupying site of New Cross (ELR) station and area to immediate east. Closed 06/11/1967, carriage sidings then occupying part of site until c.1990.
NEW CROSS LOCO WORKS & ENGINE SHEDS	40 / 4C 79		05/06/1839	14/06/1947	LCRR	LCRR's original loco works / shed, first shed being an octagonal 'roundhouse'. Loco works subsequently transferred to Brighton by LBSCR. Additional engine sheds added ('Middle' and 'New'), as well as carriage works and sidings. Depot officially closed 14/06/1947, but locos continued to stable until 1951. Sheds demolished 1957, replaced by carriage sidings which remained until c.1990 when removed for supermarket development (opened 1996).
New Croydon Line	66 / 1D 86		c.1865	??/10/1983	LBSCR	In situ by 1870 OS, eliminated during 1983 remodelling of Gloucester Road Triangle.

NEW ELTHAM
  New Eltham & Pope Street
  Pope Street
	56 / 2A	P
		G
			01/04/1878
			01/04/1878
				N/A
				13/05/1963
					SER	Opened as 'Pope Street', prefix 'New Eltham &' added 01/01/1886, suffix 'Pope Street' dropped 26/09/1927. Goods yard closed 13/05/1963 (Borley), Jackson states November 1965.

New Guildford Line Junction	63 / 1B		02/02/1885	N/A	LSWR	
New Kew Junction	37 / 3A 19		01/02/1862	N/A	LSWR	Junction at south end of Kew Curve. 'Up' road extended 220 metres west 1932.

NEW MALDEN
  Malden
  Malden for Coombe
  Coombe & Malden
  New Malden & Coombe
  Malden
	51 / 5C		??/12/1846	N/A	LSWR	Opened as 'Malden', exact opening date uncertain, first in timetable December 1846. Renamed 'New Malden & Coombe' May 1859, then 'Coombe & Malden' March 1862, 'Malden for Coombe' November 1912, 'Malden' 1955, then finally 'New Malden' 16/09/1957. Goods yard was remote from station (see separate entry).

NEW MALDEN GOODS	51 / 5B		c.1869	03/08/1964	LSWR	Borley states goods opened with passenger station, but no facilities are evident on contemporary OS maps. Remote from passenger station, accessed from Kingston Loop, which precludes an opening date before 01/01/1869. Single siding evident on 1868 OS (Kingston loop depicted although not opened until 01/01/1869). Closed 03/08/1964.
New Malden Junction	51 / 5C		??/??/1883	N/A	LSWR	Junction between LSWR main line and Kingston Loop. No physical connection until 1883.

Name	Page / grid		Date opened	Date closed	Opened by	Notes
NEW SOUTHGATE 　New Southgate & Friern Barnet 　New Southgate for Colney Hatch 　New Southgate & Colney Hatch 　Southgate & Colney Hatch 　Colney Hatch & Southgate	14 / 2A	P G	07/08/1850 07/08/1850	N/A 07/12/1970	GNR	Opened as 'Colney Hatch & Southgate', reversed to 'Southgate & Colney Hatch' 01/02/1855. Prefix 'New' added 01/10/1876, became 'New Southgate for Colney Hatch' 01/03/1883. Platforms originally staggered with 'up' south of 'down', rearranged April 1890. Renamed 'New Southgate & Friern Barnet' 01/05/1923, suffix dropped 18/03/1971. Closed 25/12/1976 - 14/02/1977 (fire), goods yard closed 07/12/1970.
NEW WANDSWORTH	38 / 6C	P G	29/03/1858 29/03/1858	01/11/1869 07/10/1968	WELCPR	Passenger station closed 01/11/1869, goods yard 07/10/1968.
NEWBURY PARK	17 / 6B	P G	01/05/1903 01/05/1903	N/A 04/10/1965	GER	LNER Fairlop Loop closed to passengers 30/11/1947 to allow electrification and transfer to Central Line. Station re-opened by LPTB Central Line as terminus from Leytonstone 14/12/1947 (until Hainault extension opened 31/05/1948). Goods yard closed 04/10/1965.
Newbury Park Junction	29 / 1B		20/04/1903	30/11/1947	GER	Junction at north end of Newbury Park Junction to Ilford Carriage Sidings Junction curve.
NEWBURY PARK SIDINGS	17 / 6B		14/12/1947	?	GER	Opened for Central Line extension from Leytonstone, but lightly used after Hainault Depot's full opening 31/05/1948.
NEWINGTON VESTRY DEPOT	39 / 3D		?	?	LCDR	
NINE ELMS (LSWR)	39 / 3B 57	P G	21/05/1838 21/05/1838	11/07/1848 29/07/1968	LSWR	LSWR London terminus until Waterloo opened. Remained in use for goods traffic until 29/07/1968 ('North' goods).
NINE ELMS (LUL)	39 / 3B		??/??/2020	N/A	LUL (NOR)	Intermediate station on proposed Northern Line extension from Kennington to Battersea.
NINE ELMS DEPOT	39 / 4A 57		??/??/1885	??/??/1967	LSWR	Locomotive sheds.
NINE ELMS GAS WORKS	57		c.1879	??/??/1970	PRIV	Works opened 1853 but had no standard gauge railway connection until c.1880 (not present on 1874 OS, had appeared by 1895). Narrow gauge internal system opened c.1879, initially 3 foot gauge but then some 2 foot gauge lines laid. Narrow gauge system function replaced by conveyors 1926-7 and probably disused thereafter. Works closed 1970.
Nine Elms Junction	39 / 3A 82		17/08/1994	N/A	RT	Date quoted is start of trial Eurostar service, advertised service commenced 14/11/1994. Little used since 14/11/2007 (diversion of Eurostar to St Pancras), but chord still in situ and traversed by test trains.
NINE ELMS ROYAL STATION	39 / 3B 57		??/??/1854	??/??/1876	LSWR	Station provided for exclusive use of Queen Victoria.
NINE ELMS SOUTH GOODS (formerly locomotive works)	39 / 4B 57		??/??/1843	29/07/1968	LSWR	Opened as LSWR's loco works, which transferred to Eastleigh in 1909. Site then became 'South' goods yard.
NINE ELMS, SOUTH LAMBETH GOODS 　South Lambeth Goods	39 / 4A 82		??/??/1911	??/??/1980	GWR	Renamed 29/07/1968.
NOEL PARK & WOOD GREEN 　Green Lanes & Noel Park 　Green Lanes	14 / 4C	P G	01/01/1878 01/01/1878	07/01/1963 07/12/1964	GER	Initially terminus of branch from Seven Sisters, until Palace Gates extension opened 07/10/1878. Opened as 'Green Lanes', Suffix '& Noel Park' added 01/05/1884, renamed 'Noel Park & Wood Green' 01/01/1902. Station and entire Palace Gates Branch closed to passengers 07/01/1963, goods yard closed 07/12/1964.
NORBITON 　Norbiton for Kingston Hill 　Norbiton for Kingston Hill and Richmond Park 　Norbiton 　Norbiton and Kingston Hill	51 / 4A	P G	01/01/1869 01/01/1869	N/A 03/05/1965	LSWR	Various suffixes used from opening; 'and Kingston Hill' initially, dropped 1890. 'for Kingston Hill and Richmond Park' 1894, 'for Kingston Hill' 1914, dropped again and became 'Norbiton' 1955. Goods yard closed 03/05/1965.
NORBURY	53 / 4B		01/01/1878	N/A	LBSCR	
NORTH ACTON	24 / 5C 91 & 92		05/11/1923	N/A	UERL / GWR	Platforms built on GWR Birmingham main line and electrified lines used by UERL Central Line. Central pair of GWR goods lines did not have platform faces provided. GWR Birmingham main line platforms closed 30/06/1947, after this date station served by Central Line only. Central pair of goods-only lines abandoned 09/03/1964, the 'down' line subsequently being re-used as the LU Central Line Eastbound road, allowing the original eastbound to become a central reversible road after 22/03/1993.
NORTH ACTON HALT	24 / 5B		01/05/1904	01/02/1913	GWR	
North Acton Junction (1)	24 / 5B		30/06/1947	N/A	LPTB (CEN)	Junction between Central Line and extension to Greenford (later West Ruislip).
North Acton Junction (2)	24 / 5B		16/04/1917	09/03/1964	GWR	Junction between GWR Birmingham Main Line and route ex-Viaduct Junction.
NORTH DULWICH	39 / 6D		01/10/1868	N/A	LBSCR	
NORTH EALING 22/10/1933.	24 / 6A		23/06/1903	N/A	MDR	First served Piccadilly Line 04/07/1932, last served District Line
NORTH END (or BULL & BUSH)	25 / 1C		N/A	N/A	UERL (CCEHR)	Platforms built but station buildings and platform access never completed. Access stairway sunk c.1950s.
NORTH GREENWICH (LUL)	41 / 1A		14/05/1999	N/A	LUL (JUB)	Three platform faces from outset, layout to facilitate possible future branch towards Royal Docks.
NORTH GREENWICH (MER)	40 / 3D		29/07/1872	04/05/1926	MER	Suffix '(Cubitt Town)' or '& Cubitt Town' sometimes used. Services to North Greenwich and Blackwall ceased 04/05/1926, subsequent DLR station at Island Gardens to north (north side of Manchester Road).
NORTH HARROW	11 / 5A		22/03/1915	N/A	MET / GCR	
North Junction (Mitcham)	52 / 6D		01/10/1868	02/06/1997	LBSCR	Junction eliminated when Wimbledon to West Croydon line closed 02/06/1997 prior to conversion to Tramlink.
North Kent East Junction	40 / 3C 79 / 80		30/07/1849	N/A	LGR / SER	
North Kent Line Connection	45 / 6B		14/11/2007	N/A	LCOR / NR	Junction between HS1 and North Kent Line.
North London Incline (GNR)	75 / 76	P G	N/A ??/??/1853	N/A N/A	GNR	No regular passenger service. Originally double track. Re-aligned during HS1 works to a more southerly route.
North London Incline (MID)	75	P G	N/A ??/??/1867	N/A 31/12/1975	MID	No regular passenger service.
North London Incline Junction	75		??/??/1867	31/12/1975	MID	
NORTH MIDDLESEX GASWORKS	13 / 3A		??/??/1869	01/10/1962	PRIV	Jackson gives dates as 1886-1956 (Borley dates quoted).
NORTH POLE DEPOT (disused) To become HITACHI IEP DEPOT	24 / 5D 91 & 92		11/11/1992	14/11/2007	ES	Official opening 11/11/1992 although revenue earning Eurostar operations did not begin until 14/11/1994. Closed when Temple Mills Depot opened 14/11/2007. To be converted for use by First GreatWestern's fleet of Hitachi IEP trains, expected introduction 2017.

Name	Page / grid		Date opened	Date closed	Opened by	Notes
North Pole Junction	24 / 5D / 91 & 92		??/10/1860	N/A	WLR / GWR	Formerly provided connection to GWR Main Line, now only North Pole Depot (currently disused).
NORTH SHED (QUEENS PARK)	25 / 4A		11/02/1915	N/A	UERL (BAK)	Stabling Shed for Bakerloo Line also traversing running lines.
NORTH SHEEN	37 / 5A		06/07/1930	N/A	SR	
NORTH SURREY SEWAGE BOARD RAILWAYS	51 / 5A		*??/??/1939*	*post-1965*	PRIV	Three separate systems opened 1939 (Malden & Berrylands) and 1953 (Hogsmill). Amalgamated 1961.
NORTH SURREY WATER (WALTON ON THAMES)	62 / 1A		*c.1970*	N/A	PRIV	3ft 6in gauge line alongside semi-treated reservoirs, still sees occasional use.
NORTH WEALD	8 / 1C	P	24/04/1865	N/A	GER	Epping to Ongar transferred to LTE 25/09/1949, Electrified 18/11/1957. Between these dates passenger services provided by BR (steam). Line closed by LUL 30/09/1994, re-opened by Epping-Ongar Railway between Ongar and North Weald 10/10/2004, closed 31/12/2007 for engineering works, re-opened 25/05/2012. Goods yard closed 06/01/1964.
		G	*24/04/1865*	*06/01/1964*		
NORTH WEMBLEY	23 / 1D	P	15/06/1912	N/A	LNWR	Referred to as 'East Lane' before opening. Goods yard opened before passenger station 31/10/1910, passenger station opened 15/06/1912, goods yard closed 05/05/1965. Served by Bakerloo Line since 16/04/1917, no service 27/09/1982 (last train 24/09/1982) - 04/06/1984.
		G	*31/10/1910*	*05/07/1965*		
NORTH WOOLWICH	41 / 2D	P	14/06/1847	10/12/2006	ECR	Closed 08/09/1940 - 01/01/1941 (air raid damage), 29/05/1994 - 29/10/1995 (Jubilee Line extension works), then permanently 10/12/2006 (closure of North Woolwich branch for partial conversion to DLR). Formerly three platform faces with a central run-around siding and turntable. Reduced to one platform after 25/08/1969 singling east of Custom House, platform then switched from 'down' to 'up' side with 1979 rebuilding. Goods yard closed 07/12/1970.
	62 / 4D	G	*14/06/1847*	*07/12/1970*		

NORTHFIELDS
    Northfields & Little Ealing
    Northfield (Ealing)
	36 / 1D		16/04/1908	N/A	UERL (MDR)	Opened as 'Northfield (Ealing)', renamed 'Northfields & Little Ealing' 11/12/1911. Relocated east and renamed 'Northfields' 18/12/1932 due to opening of Northfields Depot. First served by Piccadilly Line 09/01/1933 (terminus), District Line service ceased 10/10/1964.

NORTHFIELDS DEPOT	36 / 2C		*early 1932*	N/A	UERL (MDR)	Opened first half of 1932 (before July). Used by Piccadilly Line since 09/01/1933. Ceased to be regularly used by District Line Trains from 10/10/1964.
NORTHFLEET	59 / 1C	P	01/11/1849	N/A	SER	According to Quick does not appear to have opened with line (30/07/1849), first recorded in timetable alteration 01/11/1849 (kentrail.org.uk states opened with line 30/07/1849). Goods yard closed 09/09/1968.
		G	*01/11/1849*	*09/09/1968*		
NORTHFLEET CEMENT WORKS	59 / 1C		*14/12/1970*	*13/03/1993*	PRIV	APCM (later Blue Circle) works, rail consignments 14/12/1970 - 13/03/1993, Crossrail logistics centre now on site (see below).
NORTHFLEET CROSSRAIL LOGISTICS CENTRE	59 / 1C		*27/04/2012*	N/A	PRIV	Crossrail spoil terminal, re-connected to mainline 10-11/09/2011, commissioned 01/02/2012, first test train 27/04/2012, first spoil train 18/05/2012. To become Lafarge aggregates terminal after Crossrail use ceases.
NORTHFLEET HOPE CONTAINER TERMINAL	45 / 6C		*??/??/1978*	N/A	BR	
NORTHFLEET PAPER MILLS	45 / 6B		*c.1886*	*c.1970*	PRIV	Mills erected 1884-1886, appeared to retain rail connection into 1970s.
NORTHOLT (GWR) *Northolt Halt*	23 / 3A	P	01/05/1907	21/11/1948	GWR	Suffix 'Halt' until 23/09/1929. Closed to passengers 21/11/1948 (replaced by LTE station), goods 01/09/1952. Suffix 'for West End Halt' referred to in Dewick, but no reference in Borley or Quick.
		G	*01/05/1907*	*01/09/1952*		
NORTHOLT (LTE)	23 / 3A		21/11/1948	N/A	LTE (CEN)	Replaced BR (former GWR) station closed on same day.
Northolt Junction	22 / 2C		02/04/1906	N/A	GCR / GWR	New 'down fast' road commissioned alongside original 'up' 30/08/2011.

NORTHOLT PARK
    Northolt Park for Northolt Village
    South Harrow & Roxeth
	23 / 2A		19/07/1926	N/A	LNER	Opened as 'South Harrow & Roxeth', renamed 'Northolt Park for Northolt Village' 13/05/1929 suffix 'for Northolt Village' dropped 13/06/1955.

Northolt Park Junction	22 / 2D		30/08/2011	N/A	NR	Junction between original 'down' line (now slow) and new down fast (parallel to 'up'), commissioned 30/08/2011.

NORTHUMBERLAND PARK
    Park
    Marsh Lane
	15 / 3B		01/04/1842	N/A	NER	Opening date given as 01/04/1842 in Borley, April / October 1841 in Quick. Probably closed for a period late 1842 / early 1843. Opened as 'Marsh Lane', renamed 'Park' 01/06/1852, 'Northumberland Park' 01/07/1923.

NORTHUMBERLAND PARK DEPOT	15 / 4B		*01/09/1968*	N/A	LTB (VIC)	Sole Depot for Victoria Line. Formerly BR sidings on part of site, laid c.1900s.
NORTHWICK PARK Northwick Park & Kenton	11 / 6C		28/06/1923	N/A	MET	Suffix '& Kenton' dropped 15/03/1937.
NORTHWOOD	10 / 3B	P	01/09/1887	N/A	MET	Goods yard closed 14/11/1966.
		G	*01/09/1887*	*14/11/1966*		
NORTHWOOD HILLS	10 / 4B		13/11/1933	N/A	MET / GCR	
Norwood Fork Junctions	54 / 6A 86		01/12/1862	N/A	LBSCR	
Norwood Fork Spurs	86	P	01/12/1862	?	LBSCR	Originally both single-directional, single-track routes forming a 'flying' junction at the Norwood Junction end. Southerly spur was doubled during pre-WW1 remodelling and northerly spur became depot access. Southerly spur abandoned in 1983 remodelling. Passenger traffic was carried from outset, but final use for this purpose unknown.
		G	*01/12/1862*	N/A		

NORWOOD JUNCTION
    Norwood Jcn & South Norwood for Woodside
    Norwood Junction
    Norwood
    Jolly Sailor
	54 / 6A
	86
		P	05/06/1839	N/A	LCRR	Opened with line as 'Jolly Sailor', renamed 'Norwood' October 1846. Re-sited south 01/06/1859 and 'Junction' suffix added. Further suffix '& South Norwood for Woodside' added 01/10/1910, dropped 13/06/1955. Date of goods yard closure unknown, not stated in Borley (presumably on account of Norwood Yard still being in operation at that time).

		G	*05/06/1839*	?		
NORWOOD JUNCTION LOCO SHED	54 / 5A		*??/??/1935*	*??/01/1964*	SR	
Norwood North Junctions	54 / 5A		01/10/1857	N/A	WELCPR / LBSCR	
Norwood Spur	54 / 5A	P	18/06/1862	01/01/1917	LBSCR	Passenger services ceased 01/01/1917. Singled 1928. All use ended 30/10/1966, but not dismantled until 1972.
		G	*18/06/1862*	*30/10/1966*		
NORWOOD YARD	86		*c.1870s*	*c.1980s*	LBSCR	Extensive freight sidings; traffic continued into 1980s but date of last use unknown.
NOTTING HILL GATE	38 / 1B		01/10/1868	N/A	MET	CLR station opened 30/07/1900 (no interchange provided). Served by District Line since 01/11/1926. Interchange facilities between Central and Circle / District Lines completed 31/07/1960. Circle / District lines platforms closed 23/07/2011 - 23/08/2011 (engineering work).

Name	Page / grid		Date opened	Date closed	Opened by	Notes
NUNHEAD	40 / 5B	P	18/09/1871	N/A	LCDR	Opened as junction station for Blackheath Hill branch, original advertised opening date 01/09/1871, hence Borley gives this as opening date. Quick states that station opening coincided with the delayed opening of the branch, on 18/09/1871. Originally three through tracks / five platform faces with reversing siding to west of station. Relocated West 03/05/1925 by SR, as a new single island platform on the site of former reversing siding. Goods yard closed 02/04/1962.
		G	18/09/1871	02/04/1962		
Nunhead Junction	40 / 5B		18/09/1871	N/A	LCDR	Crystal Palace (High Level) branch junction eliminated 20/09/1954.

O

Name	Page / grid		Date opened	Date closed	Opened by	Notes
OAKLEIGH PARK	5 / 6D		01/12/1873	N/A	GNR	

OAKWOOD
    Enfield West (Oakwood)
    Enfield West
	8 / 5B		13/03/1933	N/A	UERL (GNPBR)	Opened as 'Enfield West', 'Oakwood' suffix added 03/05/1934, renamed 'Oakwood' 01/09/1946.

OCKENDON	32 / 5A	P	01/07/1892	N/A	LTSR	Goods yard closed 06/05/1968. Passing loop out of use 24/12/1977 - November 1978 (signal box fire).
		G	01/07/1892	06/05/1968		
OLD FORD	27 / 4C	P	01/07/1867	N/A	NLR	Goods yard opened 1868, transferred to LNWR 01/11/1870. Passenger service Dalston Junction to Poplar withdrawn 15/05/1944, 'officially' closed 23/04/1945. Goods yard closed 06/11/1967.
		G	??/??/1868	06/11/1967		
OLD KENT ROAD & HATCHAM Old Kent Road	40 / 4B 79		13/08/1866	01/01/1917	LBSCR	Renamed 01/02/1870.
OLD KENT ROAD GAS WORKS	40 / 3A		??/??/1892	??/05/1953	PRIV	South Metropolitan Gas Company, 3 foot gauge internal railway system.
Old Kent Road Junction	40 / 4B 79 / 80		13/03/1871	N/A	LBSCR / ELR	Junction formed 13/03/1871, ELR route abandoned 30/06/1911, Old Kent Road Spur abandoned 02/11/1964 and junction eliminated. Re-established 24/06/2012 (date of line being energised to allow testing to begin).
Old Kent Road Spur	40 / 3B 79	P	N/A	N/A	LBSCR	Opened at some point in 1871, never saw regular passenger traffic (if any). Although engineered for double track, continuous double track never appears to have been present. Closed 02/11/1964.
		G	??/??/1871	02/11/1964		
Old Kew Junction	37 / 2A 19		15/02/1853	N/A	NSWJR / LSWR	Remodelled ??/11/1981 to a single-lead junction.
OLD OAK COMMON	92		??/??/2026	N/A	NR	Proposed HS2 / Crossrail 1 interchange, platforms on latter dependant on former being built. London Overground platforms also proposed.
OLD OAK COMMON CROSSRAIL DEPOT	92		??/??/2018	N/A	NR	Crossrail depot to open on site of Old Oak Common Diesel Depot.
OLD OAK COMMON DIESEL DEPOT	24 / 5D 91		c.1964	??/04/2009	BR	Established on site of former steam shed. Closed April 2009 to allow future use of site as 'Crossrail' tunnel ring manufacturing facility, then depot.
Old Oak Common East Junction	24 / 5D 91 & 92		??/11/1912	N/A	GWR	
Old Oak Common Flyover	24 / 5D 91		??/11/1912	N/A	GWR	Built for light engine / empty carriage access to Old Oak Common Depot, singled 04/09/1967. May become obsolete when First GreatWestern depot transferred to North Pole 2017.
OLD OAK COMMON STEAM SHED	24 / 5C 91		17/03/1906	??/03/1964	GWR	After shed's demolition one turntable retained as part of diesel depot.
OLD OAK COMMON SIDINGS	91		c.1880	N/A	GWR	First sidings appeared on site c.1880 (between 1871 and 1896 OS), initially named 'West London Sidings' adjacent to GWR main line.
Old Oak Common West Junction	24 / 5C 91 & 92		03/06/1903	N/A	GWR	
Old Oak Junction	24 / 5C 91		20/07/1885	??/??/1977	NSWJR / LNWR	Junction abolished 1977 (effectively moved south to Acton Wells Junctions).
OLD OAK LANE HALT	24 / 5C 91		01/10/1906	30/06/1947	GWR	Closed 01/02/1915 - 29/03/1920. 'Bay' platform on down side in use 20/06/1932 - 02/06/1940.
OLD OAK SIDINGS	24 / 4C 91 & 92		c.1890	N/A	NSWJR	Sidings had appeared on site by 1893 OS.
OLD STREET	26 / 5D		17/11/1901	N/A	CSLR	GNCR (later Metropolitan Railway, then Northern Line, then British Rail) platforms opened 14/02/1904. CSLR platforms closed 09/08/1922 - 20/04/1924. GNCR platforms became southern terminus 06/09/1975, closed 04/10/1975, re-opened by British Rail 16/08/1976 (terminus until 08/11/1976).
ONGAR	8 / 1D	P	24/04/1865	N/A	GER	Epping to Ongar transferred to LTE 25/09/1949, Electrified 18/11/1957. Between these dates passenger services provided by BR (steam). Line closed by LUL 30/09/1994, re-opened by Epping-Ongar Railway between Ongar and North Weald 10/10/2004, closed 31/12/2007 for engineering works, re-opened 25/05/2012. Goods closed 18/04/1966.
		G	24/04/1865	18/04/1966		
ORIENT WAY SIDINGS	27 / 1C		30/05/2008	N/A	NR	On site of Stratford Traction Maintenance Depot. Replaced Thornton Fields Sidings. First test train 19/05/2008, was to open 29/05/2008, but no trains stabled until 30/05/2008.
ORPINGTON	56 / 4C	P	02/03/1868	N/A	SER	Initially two platform faces on double track, although Borley states goods facilities opened with passenger station, kentrail.org.uk website states goods facilities not provided until c.1890, corroborated by contemporary OS maps. Extensively remodelled 1904 for quadrupling; engine shed and four carriage sidings provided on 'down' side and passenger facilities expanded to four through platforms and London-facing bays on the 'up' and 'down' sides. At time of electrification (c.1925), 'down' carriage sidings covered by shed and engine shed abandoned (becoming permanent way depot). Goods yard closed 07/10/1968, site then occupied by 'up' carriage sidings. Additional 'down' bay platforms 7 and 8 opened and 'down' carriage shed demolished 1992, 'up' carriage sidings lifted weekend of 13-14/03/1993.
		G	c.1890	07/10/1968		
Orpington North Junction	56 / 3C		06/06/1904	N/A	SECR	Junction formed through Chislehurst to Orpington quadrupling.
Orpington South Junction	56 / 4C		06/06/1904	N/A	SECR	Junction formed through Chislehurst to Orpington quadrupling.
OSTERLEY Osterley & Spring Grove	36 / 3B		01/05/1883	N/A	MDR	First served by Piccadilly Line 13/03/1933. Re-sited west and renamed 'Osterley' 25/03/1934. District Line service ceased 10/10/1964.
OVAL The Oval	39 / 3C		18/12/1890	N/A	CSLR	Opened as 'The Oval', prefix dropped c.1894. Also known as 'Kennington Oval' between 1890-1894. Closed 29/11/1923 - 01/12/1924 (tunnel widening).
OXFORD CIRCUS	26 / 6A		30/07/1900	N/A	CLR	UERL (BSWR) station opened 10/03/1906 (combined with original CLR station 16/08/1925), further new concourse opened c.1967 / 1968 in anticipation of Victoria Line opening. Victoria Line platforms opened 07/03/1969.

Name	Page / grid		Date opened	Date closed	Opened by	Notes
OXSHOTT Oxshott & Fair Mile	63 / 6A	P G	02/02/1885 02/02/1885	N/A c.1965	LSWR	Variously '- & Fair Mile', '- & Fairmile', '- for Fair Mile' and 'for Fairmile' until becoming 'Oxshott' 13/06/1955.
OXSHOTT BRICK WORKS	62 / 6D		c.1885	??/??/1958	PRIV	Works established 1866 but could not have been rail served before 02/02/1885 opening of adjacent line. Sidings present on 1895 OS, the previous 1884 OS pre-dated line opening. Production ceased 1958.
OXTED LIME WORKS	74 / 6D		c.1890	??/??/1971	PRIV	Standard gauge branch from the main line appeared between 1883 and 1896 OS, had disappeared by 1961 OS. Internal 2 foot narrow gauge system appeared between 1896 and 1912 OS, much truncated then closed in 1971 (per Middleton Press 'Industrial Railways of the South-East').
Oxted Tunnel	74 / 6C		10/03/1884	N/A	SER / LBSCR	

P

Name	Page / grid		Date opened	Date closed	Opened by	Notes
PADDINGTON (GWR 1st)	25 / 6C 67 / 5C	P G	04/06/1838 04/06/1838	29/05/1854 29/12/1975	GWR	Original GWR terminus. Replaced by Paddington (2nd) 29/05/1854 (passengers), closed to goods traffic 29/12/1975.
PADDINGTON (GWR 2nd)	25 / 6C 67 / 6C		16/01/1854	N/A	GWR	Replaced 1st station (passengers only), opened to departures 16/01/1854, arrivals 29/05/1854. Post Office Railway station opened 05/12/1927, mothballed 31/05/2003.
PADDINGTON (MET 1st) Paddington (Bishop's Road)	25 / 6C 67 / 5C		10/01/1863	N/A	MET / GWR	Suffix 'Bishop's Road' dropped, station designated 'Paddington Suburban', and rebuilt as 4 through roads / 2 island platforms 10/091933. 2 middle roads became terminal 1966. Northernmost platforms 15 & 16 became LTB only and southernmost platforms 13 & 14 became BR only, and terminal, 12/11/1967. Connections between LTB and BR removed and subsequently connecting footway built between platform 12 and 13 across old trackbed.
PADDINGTON (MET 2nd) Paddington (Praed Street)	25 / 6C 67 / 6C		01/10/1868	N/A	MET	Platforms on District / Circle Lines, subway to GWR station built 22/10/1887. UERL BSWR platforms added 01/12/1913 (terminus until 31/01/1915). Suffix 'Praed Street' dropped 11/07/1948 (never applied to Bakerloo Line). Circle / District lines platforms closed 23/07/2011 - 23/08/2011 (engineering work).
PADDINGTON NEW YARD	25 / 5B 67 / 4A		13/04/1908	29/12/1972	GWR	Goods yard opened on site of former engine shed (open 02/03/1852 - 18/03/1906). Replaced by stone terminal 1975.
PALACE GATES WOOD GREEN	14 / 4C	P G	07/10/1878 14/10/1878	07/01/1963 05/10/1964	GER	Entire Palace Gates Branch closed to passengers 07/01/1963. Goods yard opened 14/10/1878, closed 05/10/1964.
PALACE GATES COAL CONCENTRATION DEPOT	14 / 4C		??/07/1958	??/??/1984	PRIV	Charringtons Ltd.
PALACE OF ENGINEERING	24 / 2B 22		23/04/1924	03/12/1962	PRIV	Originally rail-served exhibition hall, later goods station
PALMERS GREEN Palmers Green & Southgate Palmer's Green	14 / 2C	P G	01/04/1871 01/04/1871	N/A 01/10/1962	GNR	Suffix added 01/10/1876, dropped 18/03/1971. Goods yard closed 01/10/1962.
Park Junction	13 / 5D		24/05/1873	18/05/1957	GNR	Junction between Alexandra Palace Branch and original line to Edgware. Goods traffic ceased to Cranley Gardens 18/05/1957, after which time junction eliminated.
PARK ROYAL (GWR)	24 / 5B		15/06/1903	27/09/1937	GWR	Opened to special traffic 25/05/1903, public traffic commenced 15/06/1903. Closed 05/07/1903 - 01/05/1904 then again 01/02/1915 - 29/03/1920. Large goods yard to north (see separate entry below).
PARK ROYAL (UERL) Park Royal (Hanger Hill) Park Royal	24 / 5A		06/07/1931	N/A	UERL (DIS)	Replaced original station to north. Served by Piccadilly Line since 04/07/1932, last served District Line 22/10/1933. Suffix 'Hanger Hill' in use 01/03/1936 – 1947.
PARK ROYAL GOODS	24 / 5B		03/06/1903	??/??/1982	GWR	
PARK ROYAL & TWYFORD ABBEY Park Royal	24 / 4A		23/06/1903	06/07/1931	MDR	Suffix '& Twyford Abbey' added 01/05/1904. Replaced by current Park Royal station to south.
PARK ROYAL WEST HALT	24 / 5A		20/06/1932	15/06/1947	GWR	
Park Street Tunnels	26 / 4A		20/07/1837	N/A	LBIR	
Parks Bridge Junction	40 / 5D		01/09/1866	N/A	SER	Junction at north end of Ladywell Loop.
PARSONS GREEN	38 / 4B		01/03/1880	N/A	MDR	
PARSONS GREEN SIDINGS	38 / 4B		01/03/1880	N/A	MDR	District Line stabling sidings. 29 road adjacent to westbound platform disused since withdrawal of C Stock June 2014.
Paxton Tunnel	54 / 3A		01/08/1865	20/09/1954	LCDR	Nunhead to Crystal Palace (High Level) closed 20/09/1954.
PECKHAM COAL	40 / 4A		23/03/1891	??/08/1961	LNWR / MID	High and low level sidings connected by a wagon hoist. Traffic ceased in 1958, officially closed August 1961.
PECKHAM RYE	40 / 4A		01/12/1865	N/A	LBSCR	Entire station built by LBSCR, but LCDR-served platforms (to / from Crystal Palace H.L.) opened first 01/12/1865. LBSCR-served platforms (to / from London Bridge) opened 13/08/1866, originally 3 platforms (two up, one down), additional 'up main' platform and track removed 1933, new island platform constructed in vacant space and original side 'up local' and 'down' platforms abandoned 1961.
PECKHAM RYE DEPOT	40 / 5A		01/02/1909	c.1961	LBSCR	Originally built to accommodate stock for LBSCR South London Line overhead electrification. Site previously occupied by berthing sidings for East London Railway trains. Overhaul work transferred to Selhurst 31/12/1958, Lighter repairs continued for a further two years.
Peckham Rye Junction	40 / 5A		01/10/1868	N/A	LBSCR	
PENGE	54 / 4C		03/05/1858	c.1860	WELCPR	Probably opened with WELCPR Bromley Junction to Shortlands line 03/05/1858. Closure date unknown, 'by end of 1860' per Quick, c.1861 per Cobb. Also referred to as 'Beckenham Road', Tramlink station of that name on site today.
PENGE EAST Penge Lane Penge	54 / 3B	P G	01/07/1863 01/07/1863	N/A 07/11/1966	LCDR	Opened as 'Penge', but listed as 'Penge Lane' in Bradshaw 1864-79 (Borley), Quick states 1864-9 & 1867. Renamed 'Penge East' 09/07/1923. Goods yard closed 07/11/1966.
Penge Junction	54 / 4C		01/07/1863	N/A	LCDR / WELCPR	
Penge Tunnel	54 / 3A		01/07/1863	N/A	LCDR	
PENGE WEST Penge Bridges Penge	54 / 4B	P G	05/06/1839 01/07/1863	N/A 04/05/1964	LCRR	Opened as 'Penge' with line 05/06/1839, closed c.1841 (Borley), or 'probably by mid-1840' (Quick). Re-opened 01/07/1863, listed as 'Penge Bridges' in Bradshaw 1864 - 1879. Suffix 'West' added 09/07/1923. Goods yard closed 04/05/1964.
Pepper Hill Tunnel	59 / 3C		14/11/2007	N/A	LCOR	
PERIVALE (GWR) Perivale Halt	23 / 4C		01/05/1904	15/06/1947	GWR	Closed 01/02/1915 - 29/03/1920 and again for good 15/06/1947 (replaced by Perivale [LPTB] to the east). Carried 'Halt' suffix until 1927.

Name	Page / grid		Date opened	Date closed	Opened by	Notes
PERIVALE (LPTB)	23 / 4C		30/06/1947	N/A	LPTB (CEN)	
Perry Street Fork Junction	43 / 5C		01/05/1895	N/A	BHR	Junction at south end of Erith Loop.
PETTS WOOD	56 / 6A	P G	09/07/1928 09/07/1928	N/A 07/10/1968	SR	Goods yard closed 07/10/1968.
Petts Wood Junctions 　Orpington Junction	56 / 6A		08/09/1902	N/A	SECR	Junctions at southern ends of Tonbridge Loops, originally 'Orpington Junction', renamed 'Petts Wood' upon opening of latter station (09/07/1928). 'Slow' junction made 08/09/1902, 'Fast' 14/09/1902.
Petts Wood South Junction	56 / 2B		?	N/A	BR?	
PHIPPS BRIDGE	52 / 5C		30/05/2000	N/A	CTL	
PICCADILLY CIRCUS	26 / 6A		10/03/1906	N/A	UERL (BSWR)	UERL (GNPBR) platforms opened 15/12/1906, extensively rebuilt 10/12/1928 (original buildings closed 21/07/1929).
PIG HILL SIDINGS	89		c.1868	N/A	WLER	Laid at approximately same time as Falcon Lane Goods' opening.
PIMLICO (LTE)	39 / 3B		14/09/1972	N/A	LTE (VIC)	
PIMLICO (WELCPR)	39 / 3A 82		29/03/1858	01/10/1860	WELCPR	Original terminus of WELCPR (later LBSCR). Closed when VSPR route to Victoria station opened.
PINNER	10 / 4D	P G	25/05/1885 25/05/1885	N/A 03/04/1967	MET	Country terminus of Metropolitan Railway until 01/09/1887. Goods yard closed 03/04/1967.
PITLAKE	66 / 2C		26/07/1803	31/08/1846	SIR	Croydon terminus of SIR and junction with CMGR.
PLAISTOW	28 / 4B	P G	31/03/1858 31/03/1858	N/A 01/05/1953	LTSR	First served by District Railway 02/06/1902, line quadrupled 1905, District trains then using 'slow' platforms to north. Served by Metropolitan Line since 30/03/1936 ('Hammersmith & City Line' since 30/07/1990). Main line services non-stopped since 15/06/1962, and 'Fast' platforms abandoned. Goods yard closed 01/05/1953.
PLAISTOW MOTIVE POWER DEPOT	28 / 5B		30/09/1911	??/06/1962	LTSR	Steam shed replacing original 1899 shed adjacent to Plaistow Works, closed when steam traction withdrawn.
PLAISTOW WORKS	28 / 4B		??/??/1880	??/??/1932	LTSR	LTSR locomotive works, ceased servicing locos 1925, remained as servicing point for wagons until 1932.
PLAISTOW & WEST HAM GOODS	28 / 6A		01/10/1906	06/08/1984	GER	Connection to main line taken out of use 13/06/1984, 'official' closure date 06/08/1984. Date of last train unknown.
PLASSER WORKS (WEST EALING)	23 / 6C		??/??/1969	N/A	PRIV	Assembly of railway equipment, manufacture since 1977. Formerly GWR signal engineers works (c.1900s).
PLUMSTEAD	42 / 2B	P G	16/07/1859 16/07/1859	N/A 04/12/1967	SER	Goods yard closed 04/12/1967. Re-opened 08/12/1971, mainly for paper traffic. Connection in situ and yard is 'not in regular use', but will be lifted in connection with 'Crossrail' works. Date of last use unknown.
Plumstead Portal	42 / 2B		??/??/2018	N/A	NR (XRAIL)	
Point Pleasant Junction 'Down' line bi-directional since 11/02/1991.	38 / 5B		01/07/1889	N/A	LSWR	'Up' line abandoned 04/04/1987, bridge demolished 1990 (unsafe).
PONDERS END	7 / 5C	P G	15/09/1840 15/09/1840	N/A 02/11/1964	NER	Goods yard closed 02/11/1964.
PONTOON DOCK	41 / 1C 62 / 5B		02/12/2005	N/A	DLR	
POPLAR (LBLR)	41 / 1A 31 / 4C		06/07/1840	04/05/1926	LBLR	Passenger service to Blackwall withdrawn 04/05/1926.
POPLAR (EWIDBJR - Did Not Open)	40 / 1D 31 / 4B		N/A	N/A	EWIDBJR	Platforms constructed 1851 but station did not open.
POPLAR (NLR) 　Poplar (East India Road)	27 / 6D 31 / 4B		01/08/1866	15/05/1944	NLR	Station initially carried suffix '(East India Road)' to distinguish from the first, unopened, EWIDBJR station to the south. Operated as terminus for service ex-Broad Street except between 01/09/1870 - 01/07/1890 when some trains continued to Blackwall. Passenger service Dalston Junction to Poplar withdrawn 15/05/1944, 'official' closure did not occur until 23/04/1945. Present-day DLR 'All Saints' station built on same site.
POPLAR (DLR)	40 / 1D 31 / 6B		31/08/1987	N/A	DLR	Reconstructed with four platforms 28/03/1994 (Beckton extension).
POPLAR DEPOT	40 / 1D 31 / 6B		31/08/1987	N/A	DLR	Original DLR Depot.
POPLAR DOCK GOODS (GNR)	40 / 1D 31 / 5C		01/09/1878	??/??/1968	GNR	
POPLAR DOCK GOODS (GWR)	40 / 1D 31 / 4C		01/04/1878	??/??/1940	GWR	
POPLAR DOCK GOODS (MID)	41 / 1A 31 / 5C		01/12/1882	04/05/1956	MID	Suffix 'Riverside' added by BR January 1951.
Portobello Junction	25 / 5B		16/01/1854	N/A	GWR	Originally divergence of routes into original and current Paddington termini.
Potters Bar Tunnels	5 / 1C		07/08/1850	N/A	GNR	Original bore is today's 'Up' tunnel, 'Down' bore added 03/05/1959.
Pouparts Junction	38 / 4D 82		01/12/1867	N/A	LBSCR	Junction between original WELCPR route to Pimlico and subsequent route to Victoria.
POYLE ESTATE HALT	34 / 4A		04/01/1954	29/03/1965	BR	
POYLE FOR STANWELL MOOR HALT 　Stanwell Moor & Poyle Halt	34 / 5A		01/06/1927	29/03/1965	GWR	Renamed 26/09/1927.
Praed Street Junction	25 / 6C		01/10/1868	N/A	MET	No service towards High Street Kensington 23/07/2011 - 23/08/2011 (engineering works).
PRESTON ROAD 　Preston Road for Uxendon 　Preston Road for Uxendon and Kenton	12 / 6A		21/05/1908	N/A	MET	Opened with 'for Uxendon and Kenton' suffix, 'and Kenton' dropped 01/07/1923, 'for Uxendon' dropped c.1924. Southbound / Up platform re-sited north 22/11/1931, Northbound re-sited north 03/01/1932.
PRIMROSE HILL 　Chalk Farm 　Hampstead Road	25 / 3D 58		05/05/1855	23/09/1992	NLR	Replaced 'Hampstead Road' station to east. Renamed 'Chalk Farm' 1862. Re-sited to west and rebuilt 1871-1872 (works complete 24/05/1872). Closed 01/01/1917 - 10/07/1922, northern island platform closed 1922 per Borley (presumably simply did not re-open). Renamed 'Primrose Hill' 1950. Due to close when Watford Junction to Liverpool Street service withdrawn, but trains ceased calling prematurely due to flooding (last eastbound 18/09/1992, last westbound 22/09/1992).
Primrose Hill Junction	58		10/07/1922	N/A	LNWR	
Primrose Hill Tunnels	25 / 3D 58		20/07/1837	N/A	LBIR	2nd tunnel added 02/06/1879, 3rd tunnel added 10/07/1922.
PRINCE REGENT	41 / 1C 62 / 5B		28/03/1994	N/A	DLR	
PRINCESS ROYAL DISTRIBUTION CENTRE	24 / 3B 68 / 3D		??/??/1996	N/A	PRIV	Royal Mail depot.

Name	Page / grid		Date opened	Date closed	Opened by	Notes
PUDDING MILL LANE	27 / 4D 88		15/01/1996	N/A	DLR	Planned opening 02/01/1996, but delayed. Closed 14/07/2012 - 13/09/2012 (Crossrail works) and again 18/04/2014, re-opening 28/04/2014 on a new site to the south on a new alignment.
PURFLEET	44 / 3B	P G	13/04/1854 13/04/1854	N/A 02/11/1964	LTSR	Goods yard closed 02/11/1964 (although adjacent oil terminal remained open significantly longer).
PURFLEET STONE TERMINAL (FOSTER YEOMAN)	44 / 4C		?	N/A	PRIV	Deep Water Wharf.
PURFLEET RIFLE RANGE HALT	44 / 2B		??/10/1921	31/05/1941	LTSR	Opened to public October 1921, but had been served as required since July 1910 for military traffic.
PURFLEET THAMES TERMINAL	44 / 4C		c.1960s	N/A	PRIV	Deep Water Wharf (containers).
PURLEY Caterham Junction Godstone Road, Caterham Junction Godstone Road	66 / 5C	P G	12/07/1841 12/07/1841	N/A 06/01/1969	LBRR	Opened as 'Godstone Road', closed to passengers 01/10/1847 - 05/08/1856. Re-opened 05/08/1856 as 'Godstone Road, Caterham Junction'. Renamed 'Caterham Junction' October 1856, then 'Purley' 01/10/1888. Goods yard closed 06/01/1969, aggregates terminal established on part of site (Day & Sons).
Purley Chipstead Line Junction	66 / 6C		21/11/1897	N/A	SER	
Purley North Junction	66 / 5C		?	N/A	LBSCR	
PURLEY OAKS	66 / 5D		05/11/1899	N/A	LBSCR	
Purley South Junction	66 / 5C LBSCR		05/08/1856	N/A	CR /	
PUTNEY	38 / 5A		27/07/1846	N/A	LSWR	Expanded to four platforms 1886 (quadrupling).
PUTNEY BRIDGE Putney Bridge & Hurlingham Putney Bridge & Fulham	38 / 5A		01/03/1880	N/A	MDR	Opened as 'Putney Bridge & Fulham' as terminus of MDR extension from West Brompton. Extension to Wimbledon opened 03/06/1889 by LSWR, although no LSWR trains used route. Suffix '& Fulham' replaced by '& Hurlingham' 01/09/1902, station re-arranged 1910. Suffix '& Hurlingham' dropped 1932. Bay platform 2 last used 02/06/2014, decommissioned thereafter (withdrawal of C Stock trains).

Q

Name	Page / grid		Date opened	Date closed	Opened by	Notes
QUAKER OATS (SOUTHALL)	36 / 1A		?	?	PRIV	
Quarry Tunnel	73 / 5A		05/11/1899	N/A	LBSCR	
QUEENS PARK Queens Park (West Kilburn)	25 / 4B	P G	02/06/1879 02/06/1879	N/A 06/07/1964	LNWR	Served by Bakerloo Line since 11/02/1915 (terminus until 10/05/1915). LNWR mainline platforms closed 01/01/1917 but retained for occasional use. Suffix 'West Kilburn' dropped by 1954 (never applied to Bakerloo Line). Goods yard (to west of station between DC lines and LNWR main lines) opened with passenger station, closed 06/07/1964.
QUEEN'S ROAD	27 / 2B		N/A	N/A	GER	Platforms built 1875 but station did not open, formally abandoned 1895. Also referred to as 'Queen's Down Road' and 'Down Road, Clapton'. Platforms demolished c.1965.
QUEENS ROAD GOODS Boundary Road Goods	15 / 6D		*01/09/1894*	*06/05/1968*	MID	Opened as 'Boundary Road Goods', but renamed 'Queen's Road Goods' late in 1894.
QUEENS ROAD PECKHAM Peckham	40 / 4B		13/08/1866	N/A	LBSCR	Renamed 01/12/1866. Opened with 3 platform faces / tracks, middle track / platform taken out of use 1933. Rebuilt with island platform on vacant space 1977, side platforms demolished.
QUEENSTOWN ROAD BATTERSEA Queens Road Battersea	39 / 4A 82		01/11/1877	N/A	LSWR	Renamed 12/05/1980.
QUEENSBURY	12 / 4A		16/12/1934	N/A	LPTB (MET)	Opened by LPTB Metropolitan Line. Transferred to Bakerloo Line 20/11/1939, Jubilee Line 01/05/1979.
QUEENSWAY Queens Road	25 / 5C		30/07/1900	N/A	CLR	Renamed 01/09/1946. Closed 07/05/2005 - 14/06/2006 for lift replacement.

R

Name	Page / grid		Date opened	Date closed	Opened by	Notes
RADLETT	3 / 1C	P G	13/07/1868 c.1867	N/A 25/03/1968	MID	Goods yard opened before passenger station (date unknown), and was initially named 'Aldenham' prior to passenger opening. Goods yard closed 25/03/1968.
Radlett Junction	3 / 2D		?	N/A	?	
RAINHAM	30 / 6C	P G	13/04/1854 13/04/1854	N/A 04/10/1965	LTSR	Station re-sited south 1962, new platforms on original goods yard site. Replacement goods yard closed 04/10/1965.
RANELAGH BRIDGE DEPOT	25 / 6C 67 / 5B		??/??/1907	??/??/1980	GWR	Depot for stabling locomotives, converted from steam to diesel April 1964.
RAVENSBOURNE	55 / 4A	P G	01/07/1892 01/07/1892	N/A 04/09/1961	LCDR	Goods yard closed 04/09/1961.
RAVENSCOURT PARK Shaftesbury Road	37 / 2D		01/04/1873	N/A	LSWR	Opened by LSWR. First served MDR 01/06/1877. Served by MET 01/10/1877 - 01/01/1911 (MET / GWR joint after 01/01/1894). Renamed 01/03/1888. Rebuilt from 2 side platforms to 2 island platforms when route quadrupled 03/12/1911 (LSWR northern island, MDR southern island). LSWR service ceased and northern island abandoned 05/06/1916. Eastbound District Line started using north face of north island from 05/06/1932. Piccadilly Line started running non-stop through middle platforms 04/07/1932. Served by Piccadilly Line 26/12/2013 – 30/12/2013 due to District Line engineering works.
Ray Street Gridiron	32 / 2B		17/02/1868	N/A	MET	Widened Lines dive-under, replaced by a concrete raft 1960.
RAYNERS LANE Rayners Lane Halt	10 / 6D	P G	26/05/1906 26/05/1906	N/A 10/08/1964	MET	Served by District Line Trains 01/03/1910 - 23/10/1933, Piccadilly Line thereafter. 'Halt' suffix dropped 1934/5. Goods yard closed 10/08/1964.
Rayners Lane Junction	11 / 6A		01/03/1910	N/A	MET / MDR	Rayners Lane to South Harrow built by Metropolitan Railway 1904, but no regular trains until MDR service commenced in 01/03/1910.
RAYNES PARK	51 / 4D	P G	30/10/1871 c.1900	N/A 04/12/1967	LSWR	From the 04/04/1859 opening of the LSWR Epsom route there was a junction at this location with no station (initially 'Wimbledon Junction'). Subsequent to station opening 30/10/1871, new 'up' platforms constructed due to diveunder for up Epsom line (opened 16/03/1884). Date of goods yard opening uncertain: Borley states open with passenger station, but no yard is apparent on 1897-8 OS (had appeared on 1913 OS). Yard closed 04/12/1967, but sidings retained for use as a permanent way depot until late 1983.
Raynes Park Junction Wimbledon Junction	51 / 4D		04/04/1859	N/A	LSWR	Junction between LSWR main line and Epsom line. Initially named 'Wimbledon Junction'.
Reading Lane Junction	27 / 3B		30/06/1986	N/A	BR	Junction at south end of Graham Road Curve.

Name	Page / grid			Date opened	Date closed	Opened by	Notes
RECTORY ROAD	27 / 2A			27/05/1872	N/A	GER	Closed 09/12/1972 - 17/01/1973 (fire).
REDBRIDGE	16 / 6D			14/12/1947	N/A	LPTB (CEN)	

REDHILL
   Red Hill Junction
   Reigate
	73 / 5C			29/01/1844	N/A	SER	First served by SER trains 29/01/1844 as 'Reigate', allowing original SER Reigate station south of the SER / LBRR junction to close. Building from original station moved to this location during February 1844, fully opened 05/03/1844. LBRR trains began calling here 15/04/1844, allowing their original station to south to close. Rebuilt 1858 and renamed 'Red Hill Junction'. Became 'Redhill' 07/07/1929 (before this date variously 'Red Hill' / 'Redhill' / 'Reigate' with 'Junction' sometimes added per Quick). Separate goods yards associated with original LBRR and SER stations (see entries for 'Reigate'), supplemented by larger yard in vee between Tonbridge and Brighton Lines, appeared on OS between 1896 and 1913 surveys so presumably opened c. time of Quarry Line opening 1899.

Redhill Tunnel	73 / 5C			05/11/1899	N/A	LBSCR	
REEDHAM Reedham Halt	66 / 6B			01/03/1911	N/A	SECR	Closed 01/01/1917 - 01/01/1919. 'Halt' dropped 05/07/1936.
REEDHAM SIDINGS	73 / 1B			c.1899	N/A	LBSCR	Appear to have been laid c. time of Quarry Line opening.
REEVES CORNER	66 / 2C			10/05/2000	N/A	CTL	
Regent's Canal Junction	76			14/11/2007	N/A	LCOR / NR	
REGENT'S PARK	26 / 5A			10/03/1906	N/A	UERL (BSWR)	Closed 10/07/2006 - 13/06/2007 (lift replacement).

REIGATE (LBRR)
   Red Hill
   Red-Hill & Reigate Road
	73 / 6C	P
		G
				12/07/1841
				12/07/1841
					15/04/1844
					c.1965
						LBRR	First station in Reigate area, opened with LBRR route Croydon Junction to Haywards Heath, situated on Hooley Lane. Closed when LBRR trains began serving present-day Redhill station north of junction with SER 15/04/1844. Opened as 'Red-Hill & Reigate Road', before being shortened to 'Red Hill', named 'Reigate' at point of closure. Goods yard depicted on OS until 1963-8, unknown when public goods traffic ceased.

REIGATE (SER)	73 / 6C	P G		26/05/1842 26/05/1842	29/01/1844 c.1965	SER	Second station in Reigate area, situated immediately south of SER / LBRR junction. Closed when SER trains first began to serve present-day Redhill station, allowing first station building to be dismantled and rebuilt at new site. Goods yard depicted on OS until 1935 (shed demolished by 1963-8), unknown when public goods traffic ceased.
REMENHAM SIDING	33 / 5B			c.1920s	c.1930s	PRIV	Served a gravel pit. Does not appear on OS maps before 1926 or after 1938.
Renwick Road Junction	29 / 5D			14/11/2007	N/A	LCOR / NR	
RICHMOND	36 / 5D	P G		27/07/1846 27/07/1846	N/A 06/05/1968	LSWR	Opened as country terminus of branch from Battersea Junction (east of current Clapham Junction station), goods facilities assumed to have opened at same time as passenger station. Original terminus given over wholly to goods traffic and new through platforms built to north on extension to Datchet 22/08/1848. New 5-platform terminus opened to north of 22/08/1848 station 01/01/1869 to coincide with opening of line from Kensington (Addison Road). First served MDR 01/06/1877, then MET 01/10/1877. MET service ceased from 01/01/1907. Original 1846 terminus closed to goods traffic 1936 and demolished, new goods station opening north-east of 1869 passenger station November 1936. 1848 and 1869 portions of station rebuilt and combined 01/08/1937. November 1936 goods station (on page 37 / 5A) closed 06/05/1968. Centre road between platforms 3 and 4 taken out of use 1970.
Richmond Bridge	36 / 5D			22/08/1848	N/A	LSWR	
RICHMOND GASWORKS	37 / 5A			??/??/1882	??/??/1933	PRIV	
Richmond Junction (Kensington)	38 / 1A 83			01/01/1869	05/06/1916	LSWR / WLR	Junction between WLR and LSWR Richmond branch.
Richmond Junction (Richmond)	37 / 5A			01/01/1869	28/12/1972	LSWR	Direct connection between lines ex-Kew Gardens and ex-North Sheen eliminated 28/12/1972, but indirect link via Richmond station platform 3 established 1985 for stock transfer between North London Line and Selhurst Depot.
RICKMANSWORTH	1 / 6C	P G		01/09/1887 01/09/1887	N/A 14/11/1966	MET	Country terminus of MET until 08/07/1889. Goods yard closed 14/11/1966.
RICKMANSWORTH (CHURCH STREET) Rickmansworth	1 / 6C	P G		01/10/1862 01/10/1862	03/03/1952 02/01/1967	WRR	Branch from Watford Junction; closed to passengers 03/03/1952, goods 02/01/1967. Suffix 'Church Street' in use from 25/09/1950 until closure.
RICKMANSWORTH NORTH SIDINGS	1 / 5C			c.1890	N/A	MET	Stabling Sidings for Metropolitan Line, first siding on site by 1896 OS.
RICKMANSWORTH SOUTH SIDINGS	1 / 5C			c.1960	N/A	LTE (MET)?	Not present on 1938 OS, but had appeared by 1961/2 (possibly commissioned for 1960 Amersham electrification?).
RIDDLESDOWN	66 / 6D			05/06/1927	N/A	SR	
Riddlesdown Tunnel	66 / 6D			10/03/1884	N/A	LBSCR / SER	
RIPPLE LANE DIESEL DEPOT	29 / 5D			c.1960	??/??/1993	BR	4-road shed, closed 1993.
RIPPLE LANE FREIGHTLINER TERMINAL	29 / 5D			??/??/1972	N/A	BR	Partially on site of Ripple Lane 'Hump' marshalling yard (closed 1968).
RIPPLE LANE YARD	29 / 5D			c.1940	N/A	LMS	Opened c.1940, main line tracks diverted around site 27/05/1960, reconstructed as 'Hump' marshalling yard 1961, closed 1968 and replaced by Freightliner Terminal (opened 1972).
RODING VALLEY	16 / 2C			03/02/1936	N/A	LNER	Fairlop (later Hainault) Loop closed by LNER 30/11/1947 to allow electrification and transfer to LTE Central Line. Station re-opened 21/11/1948 by LTE following electrification.
Rolt Street Junction	40 / 3C 79 / 80			01/04/1880	N/A	ELR	SER service to Liverpool Street via ELR commenced 01/04/1880. Rolt Street Junction to New Cross (SER) became bi-directional (former 'down' only spur) 01/10/1884 when ELR bay platform opened at New Cross. 'Up' spur remained in use for goods / through traffic until 16/04/1966. After this date junction was point where double track ex-Canal Junction became single bi-directional track to New Cross.
ROMFORD	18 / 6C	P G		20/06/1839 20/06/1839	N/A ?	ECR	Carried the suffix 'for Hornchurch, Upminster & Corbet's Tey' according to Dewick, but no other reference found. Platform for Upminster originally a separate LTSR station, opening 07/06/1893, combined 01/04/1934. Goods yard remains partially in use as engineers depot, date of closure to general goods traffic unknown.

Name	Page / grid		Date opened	Date closed	Opened by	Notes
ROMFORD FACTORY	19 / 5A		??/??/1843	?	ECR	ECR's locomotive works until 1847 (when relocated to Stratford) then wagon cover factory after 1854.
Romford Junction	18 / 6C		07/06/1893	N/A	LTSR / GER	Removed 1930s, reinstated 21/07/1940.
ROSHERVILLE HALT Rosherville	60 / 1A		10/05/1886	16/07/1933	LCDR	Suffix 'Halt' added 17/06/1928.
ROTHERHITHE	40 / 1B		07/12/1869	N/A	ELR	First served MET & MDR 01/10/1884, last served MDR 01/08/1905, no service MET 03/12/1906 - 31/03/1913. Separate 'East London Line' identity introduced during 1980s. Closed 25/03/1995 - 25/03/1998 & 23/12/2007 -27/04/2010 (engineering work), upon latter re-opening became TfL (LOROL) station.
ROYAL ALBERT	41 / 1C 62 / 5B		28/03/1994	N/A	DLR	
ROYAL ARMY SERVICE CORPS DEPOT (FELTHAM)	49 / 1B		c.1930	??/??/1958	PRIV	Not present on 1920 OS, but had appeared by 1932. Branch partly tramway, passing west side of 'The Green' and along Browells Lane. Not used after 1958.
ROYAL ARSENAL RAILWAY (WOOLWICH)	42 / 2C		??/??/1859	??/??/1967	SER	A network of Standard, 18 inch, and Mixed gauge lines covering the Plumstead and Erith Marshes. First Standard gauge lines laid by SER 1859, followed by 18 inch Narrow gauge from 1871 onwards. After a zenith during World War I, operations were wound down until eventual closure in 1967. Passenger trains ran within the system for workmen
ROYAL BETHLEM HOSPITAL	67 / 1C		??/??/1928	??/??/1930	PRIV	1.2km siding from Eden Park in use during construction of the Hospital, abandoned when construction completed.
Royal Curve	33 / 1C	P G	N/A 08/10/1849	N/A 26/07/1970	GWR	Not used for regular passenger traffic; Royal and excursion trains only.
ROYAL DOCKYARD (WOOLWICH)	41 / 2D		c.1880	c.1962	PRIV	Branch to dockyard not apparent on 1873 OS, but had appeared by 1896, so approximate 1880 opening assumed. Still in use 11/07/1961 (Middleton Press album 'Charing Cross to Dartford'), but abandoned by 1962 and the tunnel under Woolwich Church Street blocked.
ROYAL MINT STREET GOODS	74 / 2B		01/08/1858	01/04/1951	LBLR	Tower Gateway DLR station occupies much of site.
Royal Mint Street Junction	27 / 6A 74 / 2C		29/07/1991	N/A	DLR	Divergence of DLR Bank extension from original route to Tower Gateway.
ROYAL OAK	25 / 6C 67 / 5B		30/10/1871	N/A	MET / GWR	Last GWR service called 01/10/1934. Ownership transferred to LTE 01/01/1970.
ROYAL SHOWGROUND	24 / 4B		23/06/1903	27/06/1903	LNWR	Only open for duration of Royal Agricultural Society show 1903.
ROYAL VICTORIA	41 / 1B 62 / 5A		28/03/1994	N/A	DLR	
RUGBY ROAD	37 / 1C		08/04/1909	01/01/1917	NSWJR	
RUISLIP	10 / 6B	P G	04/07/1904 04/07/1904	N/A 10/08/1964	MET	Served by District Line Trains 01/03/1910 - 23/10/1933, Piccadilly Line thereafter. Goods yard closed 10/08/1964.
RUISLIP DEPOT	22 / 1B		21/11/1948	N/A	LTE (CEN)	Depot for Central Line and Transplant (Engineering).
RUISLIP GARDENS	22 / 1B		09/07/1934	N/A	GWR / LNER	Platforms on 'slow' GWR / LNER lines only (South Ruislip to West Ruislip formerly quadruple). LTE Central Line platforms added 21/11/1948, BR platforms closed 21/07/1959.
RUISLIP MANOR Ruislip Manor Halt	10 / 6B		05/08/1912	N/A	MET	Served by District Line trains from opening to 23/10/1933, Piccadilly Line thereafter. Closed 12/02/1917 - 01/04/1919. Suffix 'Halt' until 1934/5.
RUSHETT	63 / 5D		N/A	N/A	SR	One of two intermediate stations on Chessington South to Leatherhead route, works abandoned at outset of WW2.
RUSSELL SQUARE	26 / 5B		15/12/1906	N/A	UERL (GNPBR)	

S

Name	Page / grid		Date opened	Date closed	Opened by	Notes
ST ANN'S ROAD	14 / 6D		02/10/1882	09/08/1942	THJR	
ST HELIER	52 / 6B	P G	05/01/1930 05/01/1930	N/A 06/05/1963	SR	Goods yard closed 06/05/1963.
ST HELIER ESTATE RAILWAY	65 / 1C		??/??/1928	??/??/1936	LCC	Railway system built by the LCC to convey building materials to the then under construction St Helier Estate.
St James Road Junction	66 / 1D 86		22/05/1865	??/10/1983	LBSCR	Junction at southern end of West Croydon Spur.
ST JAMES'S PARK	39 / 1B		24/12/1868	N/A	MDR	Also spelt 'St James' Park'. Rebuilt 1927 - 1929 (construction of 55 Broadway above).
ST JAMES STREET WALTHAMSTOW	15 / 5C		26/04/1870	N/A	GER	Originally single platform on 'up' side, Shern Hall Street to Clapton Junction doubled 1873 and 'down' platform built.
ST JOHNS	40 / 4D		01/06/1873	N/A	SER	Originally had three island platforms with six faces onto five tracks, southernmost island abandoned 1926, then middle ('fast') island demolished 1973 and 'fast' roads straightened. Now only 'slow' island remains, with two faces.
ST JOHN'S WOOD	25 / 4C		20/11/1939	N/A	LPTB (BAK)	Replaced Marlborough Road Station to north. Named 'Acacia Road' until opening. Opened by Bakerloo Line, transferred to Jubilee Line 01/05/1979.
St John's Wood Tunnel	25 / 4C		15/03/1899	N/A	GCR	
ST MARGARETS	36 / 6C		02/10/1876	N/A	LSWR	Additional 'up' platform added 26/11/1899.
ST MARY CRAY	56 / 6C	P G	03/12/1860 03/12/1860	N/A 07/10/1968	LCDR	Rebuilt with four platforms due to quadrupling 31/05/1959. Goods yard closed 07/10/1968.
St Mary Cray Junctions	56 / 5A 56 / 6A		19/06/1904	N/A	SECR	Junctions at southern end of Chatham Loops.
ST MARY'S (WHITECHAPEL ROAD) St Mary's	27 / 6B 90		03/03/1884	01/05/1938	SER	First served by SER trains ex-ELR (terminus), withdrawn 01/10/1884. MDR / MET joint line to Whitechapel did not open until 06/10/1884. Renamed 26/01/1923. Closed when Aldgate East relocated eastwards.
St Mary's Curve	27 / 6B 90	P G	03/03/1884 03/03/1884	06/10/1941 23/12/2007	MDR / MET	Built as part of MDR / MET Whitechapel extension, but first used by SER between 03/03/1884 - 01/10/1884. MET use commenced 01/10/1884, MDR 06/10/1884. Closed to passenger services 01/08/1905 (MDR) and 06/10/1941 (MET), retained for stock transfer thereafter until 23/12/2007 when ELL closed for extension.
St Mary's Junction	27 / 6B		01/10/1884	23/12/2007	MDR / MET	Junction at north end of St Mary's Curve, MDR service to Whitechapel commenced 06/10/1884 although empty stock workings to Whitechapel commenced 5 days before with the MET service to New Cross.

Name	Page / grid		Date opened	Date closed	Opened by	Notes
ST PANCRAS INTERNATIONAL St Pancras	26 / 4B 75 / 76		01/10/1868	N/A	MID	Extensively rebuilt for Eurostar services; last Midland mainline train left trainshed 09/04/2004, temporary station to northeast opened 12/04/2004. Main trainshed reopened for international trains and suffix 'International' added 14/11/2007. Platforms below original station opened for 'Thameslink' 09/12/2007 (see 'King's Cross Thameslink').
ST PANCRAS GOODS	26 / 4B 75 / 76		??/07/1862	29/04/1968	MID	Initial access via GNR, then also NLR (GNR connection subsequently severed) full opening 09/09/1867.
St Pancras Junction (MID)	75		??/??/1867	31/12/1975	MID / NLR	
St Pancras Junction (GNR)	75		??/??/1853	14/11/2007	GNR / NLR	
ST PAUL'S Post Office	26 / 6D		30/07/1900	N/A	CLR	Renamed 01/02/1937.
St Paul's Bridge	32 / 6C		10/05/1886	N/A	LCDR	Built alongside original Blackfriars Bridge.
St Paul's Road Junction	26 / 3B 75 / 76		13/07/1868	N/A	MID	Junction providing access to St Pancras Goods (MID route to MET 'Widened Lines' opened 13/07/1868.) Access to St Pancras goods removed 29/04/1968, Churchyard sidings remain as truncated route.
ST QUINTIN PARK & WORMWOOD SCRUBS Wormwood Scrubs	24 / 5D 91		01/08/1871	03/10/1940	LNWR / GWR	Opened as 'Wormwood Scrubs', renamed 'St Quintin Park & Wormwood Scrubs' 01/08/1892. 'Scrubs' sometimes spelt 'Scrubbs' in both titles. Platforms relocated north 01/11/1893. Destroyed by fire 03/10/1940 and ceased to be served by trains, not officially closed until 01/12/1940.
Salmons Lane Junction	27 / 6C		05/04/1880	05/11/1962	LBLR	Junction at north end of Limehouse Curve.
SANDERSTEAD	66 / 4D	P G	10/03/1884 10/03/1884	N/A 20/03/1961	LBSCR / SER	Goods yard closed 20/03/1961.
SANDILANDS	67 / 2A		10/05/2000	N/A	CTL	
Sandilands Tunnels (Woodside, Park Hill & Coombe Road)	67 / 2A		10/08/1885	N/A	LBSCR / SER	Line through tunnels closed by BR 16/05/1983, re-opened by CTL 10/05/2000.
SEABROOK SIDINGS	45 / 4C		??/??/1884	N/A	PRIV	Sidings initially provided access to Seabrookes Brewery (see below). Now provide access to Tilbury Docks following abolition of Tilbury North Junction c.1960.
SEABROOKES BREWERY	45 / 4C		??/??/1884	??/??/1940	PRIV	Brewery established 1799, acquired siding 1884. Sold to Charringtons 1929, siding lifted 1940.
SELHURST	53 / 6D 86		01/05/1865	N/A	LBSCR	
SELHURST DEPOT	53 / 6D 86		??/??/1911	N/A	LBSCR	Sidings first laid on site c.1890 (not on 1879-1887 OS but had appeared by 1896). Became a depot 1911.
Selhurst Junctions	53 / 6D 86		01/12/1862	N/A	LBSCR	
Selhurst Spur	86	P G	c.1910 c.1910	N/A N/A	LBSCR	
SELSDON Selsdon Road Selsdon Road Junction	66 / 3D	P G	10/08/1885 10/08/1885	16/05/1983 07/10/1968	LBSCR / SER	For first month 'Selsdon Road Junction', then 'Selsdon Road'. Woodside platforms closed 01/01/1917 - 01/05/1919. Renamed 'Selsdon' 30/09/1935. Oxted Line platforms closed 14/06/1959, Woodside platforms 16/05/1983. Goods yard closed 07/10/1968, but oil depot established on site (latterly Cory), remaining open until March 1993.
Selsdon Road Junction	66 / 4D		10/03/1884	??/03/1993	LBSCR / SER	Last traffic to Selsdon oil depot March 1993, but junction remains in situ.
SEVEN KINGS	29 / 1B		01/03/1899	N/A	GER	
Seven Kings Curve	29 / 1B	P G	N/A 20/04/1903	N/A 19/03/1956	GER	Never used for regular passenger traffic, route obliterated by Ilford Depot 'New Shed' 1959.
SEVEN SISTERS	15 / 5A		22/07/1872	N/A	GER	Platforms for Palace Gates Branch open 01/01/1878 - 07/01/1963. Victoria Line station opened 01/09/1968. Borley refers to goods yard opening c.1878 (no closure date), may refer to cold store to north.
Seven Sisters Chord	15 / 5A	P G	01/01/1880 ??/??/1879	N/A N/A	GER	Open to goods 1879, passengers 01/01/1880. Closed to passengers 07/01/1963 – 1989 (when electrified), singled ??/05/1977.
Seven Sisters Junction Seven Sisters South Junction	15 / 5A		??/??/1879	N/A	GER	Junction at north end of Seven Sisters Chord (see notes above).
Seven Sisters North Junction	15 / 5A		01/01/1878	07/02/1965	GER	Junction of Palace Gates branch.
Shacklegate Junction	50 / 2B		01/07/1894	N/A	LSWR	Junction at east end of Shepperton Spur (Fulwell Curve).
SHADWELL Shadwell & St George's East (LBLR) Shadwell & St George-in-the-East (ELR) Shadwell	27 / 6B		01/10/1840	N/A	LBLR	LBLR station opened 01/10/1840 as 'Shadwell', suffix '& St George's East' added 01/07/1900. Closed 22/05/1916 - 05/05/1919, and again 07/07/1941. Rebuilt as an island platform and re-opened by DLR 31/08/1987 as 'Shadwell'. ELR station opened 10/04/1876 as 'Shadwell', first served MET & MDR 01/10/1884. Suffix '& St George-in-the-East' added 01/07/1900, last served MDR 01/08/1905, suffix dropped 1918. No service MET 03/12/1906 - 31/03/1913. ELL platforms closed 25/03/1995 - 25/03/1998 & 23/12/2007 - 27/04/2010 (engineering work).
Sheet Factory Junction	28 / 4A 77		29/04/1846	12/03/1973	ECTJR	Junction at south end of Stratford Eastern Curve.
Sheepcote Lane Curve	38 / 4D	P G	06/07/1865 06/07/1865	25/05/2004 14/11/2007	WLER	Opened 06/07/1865 (all traffic), passenger services ceased 13/03/1912, goods 21/01/1936, track lifted 1937. Re-laid for Eurostar access to North Pole Depot (commissioned in advance of 17/08/1994 commencement of 'demonstration' service), Eurostar connecting service to Cardiff commenced 24/10/1994, regular passenger services ceased with effect from 25/05/2004 (last train 21/05/2004), shadowed by token bus service until 'official' closure 14/12/2004 (last bus 07/12/2004). Curve effectively redundant since 14/11/2007 opening of St Pancras International and closure of North Pole Depot, but remains in situ.
SHENFIELD Shenfield & Hutton Shenfield & Hutton Junction Shenfield	20 / 5B	P G	29/03/1843 29/03/1843	N/A 04/05/1964	ECR	Opened as 'Shenfield', but closed to passengers ??/03/1850 due to lack of patronage. Re-opened by GER 01/01/1887 as 'Shenfield & Hutton Junction', with the suffix 'Junction' being dropped later that year. Rebuilt 01/01/1934 due to quadrupling work. Goods yard closed 04/05/1964. Suffix '& Hutton' dropped 20/02/1969.
Shenfield Country End Junction	20 / 4C		01/01/1934	N/A	LNER	
Shenfield London End Junction	20 / 1C		01/01/1934	N/A	LNER	
Shenfield Southend Line Junction	20 / 5C		01/10/1889	N/A	GER	
SHEPHERD'S BUSH (CLR)	38 / 1A 83		30/07/1900	N/A	CLR	Terminus of Central London Railway until 14/05/1908. Sometimes had suffix 'Green' added. Closed 01/02/2008 - 05/10/2008 (reconstruction).

Name	Page / grid		Date opened	Date closed	Opened by	Notes
SHEPHERD'S BUSH (MET / GWR) (1st)	37 / 1D 83		13/06/1864	01/04/1914	MET / GWR	Replaced by Shepherd's Bush (now Shepherd's Bush Market) to north and Goldhawk Road to south.
SHEPHERD'S BUSH (MET / GWR) (2nd)	38 / 1A 83		01/07/1864	01/11/1869	MET / GWR	Existence of this station is unclear: appeared on contemporary maps. Presumably opened 01/07/1864 on spur between MET / GWR Hammersmith & City Railway and WLR (no platforms apparent on WLR). If opened, was soon replaced by Uxbridge Road Station to south of junction between spur and WLR 01/11/1869.
SHEPHERD'S BUSH (LSWR)	38 / 1A 83		01/05/1874	05/06/1916	LSWR	Addison Road to Studland Road Junction abandoned 05/06/1916.
SHEPHERD'S BUSH (WLR)	38 / 1A 83		27/05/1844	N/A	WLR	Inaugural WLR passenger service withdrawn 01/12/1844 and station closed, when services to Kensington recommenced 02/06/1862, station did not re-open but was subsequently replaced by Uxbridge Road to south 01/11/1869 (later closing 21/10/1940). New NR (LOROL) station named Shepherd's Bush built on original 1844 station site, opening 28/09/2008. Present 'down' platform occupies approximate site of 27/05/1844 platform Present 'up' platform partially built upon site of southern end of MET / GWR spur to Latimer Road.
SHEPHERD'S BUSH MARKET Shepherd's Bush	37 / 1D 83			01/04/1914	N/A	MET / GWR Replaced Shepherd's Bush (MET / GWR) (1st) to south. Renamed 12/10/2008.
Shepherd's Lane Junction	39 / 5B		01/01/1867	N/A	LCDR	Initially junction between 25/08/1862 LCDR Herne Hill to Stewarts Lane route and new line to Factory Junction (quadrupling), but the junction was eliminated when 01/05/1867 high level route to Denmark Hill via East Brixton was opened. Connection reinstated through late 1970s / early 1980s Victoria resignalling.
SHEPPERTON Shepperton for Halliford	48 / 6D	P G	01/11/1864 01/11/1864	N/A 01/08/1960	TVR	Suffix 'for Halliford' sometimes used 1914 - 1955. 'Up' platform road designated a siding after 05/02/1915 and all passenger traffic reversed via 'down' platform. Turntable removed August 1942, goods yard closed 01/08/1960 (Borley), Jackson states 07/10/1960.
Shepperton Spur Fulwell Curve	50 / 2B	P G	01/07/1894 01/07/1894	N/A N/A	LSWR	Curve opened 01/07/1894, but possibly saw no regular traffic until 01/02/1895 (Borley). Utilised for race specials to Kempton Park from opening (as well as goods), but no ordinary passenger services used curve before 01/06/1901.
SHERN HALL STREET, WALTHAMSTOW	15 / 5D		26/04/1870	17/11/1873	GER	Terminus of single track branch from Lea Bridge Junction, replaced by Wood Street when line extended to Chingford.
SHERWOOD HOSPITAL & POWER STATION	64 / 5A		??/??/1918	??//??/1950	PRIV	Horton Estate Light Railway opened to supply building materials, later fuel, to hospitals.
SHOREDITCH (NLR)	27 / 5A 90		01/11/1865	04/10/1940	NLR	Closed by enemy action, booking office remained open until 17/11/1941.
SHOREDITCH (ELR)	27 / 5A 90		10/04/1876	11/06/2006	ELR	Became northern passenger terminus of ELR upon electrification 31/03/1913 (through goods traffic remained). 'Down' platform abandoned 1928 and all services reversed off 'up'. Through goods traffic, connection to GER main line, and down through road abandoned 17/04/1966. Closed 25/03/1995 - 27/09/1998 (engineering works). Closed for good 11/06/2006 (last train 09/06/2006) to allow East London Line Extension works to commence.
SHOREDITCH (DUNLOE STREET) GOODS DEPOT	27 / 4A		??/03/1893	03/06/1968	LNWR	
SHOREDITCH HIGH STREET	27 / 5A 90		27/04/2010	N/A	TFL (LOROL)	On site of northern portion of Bishopsgate Goods yard (formerly Bishopsgate High Level station).
SHORTLANDS Bromley	55 / 5A		03/05/1858	N/A	WELCPR	Opened as 'Bromley' at terminus of WELCPR extension from Bromley Junction. Renamed 'Shortlands' 01/07/1858, line then extended to Southborough Road (now Bickley) four days later 05/07/1858.
Shortlands Junction	55 / 5A		01/07/1892	N/A	LCDR	Remodelled 1958-9 then again as a 'flying' junction June 2003.
SIDCUP	56 / 2C	P G	01/09/1866 01/09/1866	N/A 15/08/1966	SER	Opened with line 01/09/1866 according to Borley, Quick & Jackson, but kentrail.org.uk website states station did not open until the following month (i.e. October 1866). Goods yard closed 15/08/1966, partially replaced by new siding 1967 to facilitate reversal of trains. According to Quick carried suffix 'for Halfway Street' in Bradshaw 1867 – 1893.
Silk Stream Junction	12 / 4D		14/09/1890	N/A	MID	Junction between Midland Main Line and freight flyover.
Silo Curve	76	P G	N/A 14/11/2007	N/A N/A	LCOR / NR	No regular passenger service.
Silo Curve Junction	76		14/11/2007	N/A	LCOR / NR	
SILVER STREET Silver Street for Upper Edmonton Silver Street	15 / 2A		22/07/1872	N/A	GER	Suffix 'for Upper Edmonton' in use c.1883 – 1933.
SILVERTOWN Silvertown & London City Airport Silvertown	41 / 1C 62 / 4B	P G	19/06/1863 19/06/1863	10/12/2006 early 1993	ECR	Closed 08/09/1940 - 01/01/1941 (air raid damage), 29/05/1994 - 29/10/1995 (Jubilee Line extension works), then permanently 10/12/2006 (closure of North Woolwich branch for partial conversion to DLR). Former 'up' platform closed 25/08/1969 when passenger route singled (former 'up' line became bidirectional goods line, taken out of use 29/03/1993). Goods yard to west of station accessed via Silvertown Tramway, scrap metal traffic remained until early 1993 (formally abandoned 29/03/1993). '& London City Airport' suffix added 04/10/1987, removed 24/09/2000. Line through station site to re-open 2018 (Crossrail 1 Abbey Wood branch), but station not planned to re-open on this site (but may re-open to east).
Silvertown Tramway Woolwich Abandoned Line	41 / 1B 62 / 4B	P G	14/06/1847 14/06/1847	26/11/1855 29/03/1993	ECR	Part of original ECR extension from Thames Wharf to North Woolwich. After opening of diversionary route via Custom House 26/11/1855, line became goods only but remained a through route. Swing Bridge across entrance to Royal Victoria Dock removed c.1950 and line became accessible from Silvertown end only. Last goods movement took place in early 1993 and line abandoned 29/03/1993. Route now partially followed by DLR Woolwich Arsenal line. Officially became 'Woolwich Abandoned Line' in 1855, but more commonly referred to as 'Silvertown Tramway'.
Silwood Junction Deptford Road Junction	40 / 2B 79 / 80		13/03/1871	N/A	ELR	Junction established 13/03/1871, further junction for 'up' road to New Cross Gate added 01/07/1876. Old Kent Road route closed 30/06/1911, lifted 1913. Junction eliminated 01/11/1964 with 'up' road to New Cross. Gate closing. Remodelled to a 'flying' layout and re-established 24/06/2012 as 'Silwood Junction' (date line energised to allow testing to begin).

Name	Page / grid		Date opened	Date closed	Opened by	Notes
SILWOOD SIDINGS	80		*??/09/2014*	N/A	TFL (LOROL)	At the point of producing this edition, the predicted opening is September 2014. First test train used sidings 19/08/2014.
SINGLEWELL MAINTENANCE DEPOT	60 / 4B		*??/04/2007*	N/A	LCOR	
SLADE GREEN Slades Green	43 / 5C		01/07/1900	N/A	SECR	Renamed 01/08/1953.
SLADE GREEN DEPOT	43 / 5D		27/10/1899	N/A	SECR	Current EMU berthing shed is original 27/10/1899 steam shed (extended June 1954). Maintenance shed added 1925, demolished and completely rebuilt on same site 08/04/1991.
Slade Green Junction	43 / 5C		01/05/1895	N/A	BHR / SER	Junction at north end of Erith Loop.
SLOANE SQUARE	38 / 2D		24/12/1868	N/A	MDR	
SLOUGH	33 / 1C	P G	01/06/1840 *01/06/1840*	N/A *27/07/1975*	GWR	Trains began calling at Slough 01/05/1839, although objections from Eton College initially prevented the construction of a station. Station opened 01/06/1840, initially with a single platform to the south of the main line. Served by MDR trains 01/03/1883 - 01/10/1885. Station rebuilt and relocated west 08/09/1884. Goods yard closed 27/07/1975.
Slough West Junction	33 / 1C		08/10/1849	N/A	GWR	Originally junction at northern end of Royal Curve (closed 26/07/1970), today set of junctions between the 'fast' and 'slow' roads west of Slough.
SMALLBERRY GREEN Hounslow	36 / 4C		22/08/1849	01/02/1850	LSWR	Temporary country terminus of LSWR Hounslow Loop until 01/12/1850 completion, situated at Wood Lane level crossing. Officially named 'Hounslow' (timetable, and almost certainly tickets and station nameboards), but was so remote from Hounslow that 'Smallberry Green' was more commonly used. Replaced by Isleworth to west.
Smithfield Curve	32 / 3C	P G	01/09/1871 *01/09/1871*	01/04/1916 *01/04/1916*	LCDR	
SMITHFIELD GOODS	26 / 6C 32 / 3C		03/05/1869	30/07/1962	GWR	
Smithfield Junction	32 / 3C		01/09/1871	01/04/1916	LCDR	Junction at northern end of Smithfield Curve.
Smithfield Sidings	32 / 3C		c.1885	N/A	LCDR	Laid originally c.1885 (portion of Smithfield market above built 1886-8). Abandoned with rest of Snow Hill Tunnel but 2 sidings (originally 4) re-laid as part of 'Thameslink' project. Used by services terminating at City Thameslink.
Smithfield Tunnel	32 / 3C		01/07/1866	22/03/2009	MET	Farringdon to Moorgate (NR) closed 22/03/2009 due to platform lengthening at Farringdon.
SNARESBROOK Snaresbrook for Wanstead Snaresbrook & Wanstead Snaresbrook	16 / 5B	P G	22/08/1856 *22/08/1856*	N/A *01/08/1949*	ECR	Opened as 'Snaresbrook', suffix '& Wanstead' added ??/11/1898, became 'for Wanstead' 1929, dropped 14/12/1947. Bay platform on 'down' side added 1893. Majority of passenger services transferred to LPTB 14/12/1947. Goods yard closed 01/08/1949. Bay platform on down side abandoned 1950. First trains in the morning remained British Rail services until 01/06/1970 (last train 31/05/1970).
Snow Hill Junction	32 / 3C		01/09/1871	01/04/1916	LCDR	Junction at southern end of Smithfield Curve.
Snow Hill Tunnel	32 / 3C		01/01/1866	N/A	LCDR	Line closed through tunnel 24/03/1969 - 16/05/1988.
SOMERS TOWN GOODS St Pancras New Goods	26 / 4B 75		*01/11/1887*	*23/04/1968*	MID	Renamed 01/08/1892. British Library now occupies site.
SOUTH ACTON	37 / 2B		01/01/1880	N/A	NSWJR	UERL (MDR) platform opened 13/06/1905, closed 02/03/1959 (last train 28/02/1959). Bay on 'down' side for Hammersmith & Chiswick Branch.
South Acton Junction	37 / 2B 51 / 1B		01/01/1869	N/A	NSWJR / LSWR	
SOUTH BERMONDSEY Rotherhithe	40 / 3B 79 / 80		13/08/1866	N/A	LBSCR	Renamed 01/12/1869. Closed 01/01/1917 – 01/05/1919. Relocated south by SR 17/06/1928.
South Bermondsey Junction	40 / 3B 79 / 80		01/01/1871	N/A	LBSCR	Spur to Bricklayers Arms Junction opened 01/01/1871.
SOUTH BROMLEY	27 / 6D		01/09/1884	15/05/1944	NLR	Passenger service Dalston Junction to Poplar withdrawn 15/05/1944, 'official' closure 23/04/1945.
SOUTH CROYDON	66 / 3D		01/09/1865	N/A	LBSCR	
South Croydon Junction	66 / 3D		10/03/1884	N/A	LBSCR / SER	
SOUTH DOCK South West India Dock South Dock	40 / 1D		18/12/1871	04/05/1926	MER	Island platform between single passenger line and passing loop. Due to locomotives not being permitted to work through West India Docks initially, trains were horse-hauled through station until August 1880. Traction was switched to steam at boundary of Millwall Dock Company until this date for final stretch to North Greenwich. Sometimes known as 'South West India Dock' 1881 - 1895. Passenger service withdrawn 04/05/1926.
SOUTH EALING	36 / 1D		01/05/1883	N/A	MDR	First served by Piccadilly Line 09/01/1933. District Line ceased from 10/10/1964. Rebuilt with 4 platforms 1932.
SOUTH GREENFORD South Greenford Halt	23 / 4B		20/09/1926	N/A	GWR	Suffix 'Halt' dropped 05/05/1969. 'Up' platform removed early 1990s due to embankment instability, not reinstated until 26/10/1999.
SOUTH HAMPSTEAD Loudoun Road	25 / 3C		02/06/1879	N/A	LNWR	Closed 01/01/1917, re-opened and renamed 10/07/1922.
SOUTH HAREFIELD HALT Harefield Halt	9 / 6C	P G	24/09/1928 *27/06/1929*	01/10/1931 *01/01/1953*	GCR / GWR	Renamed 29/05/1929. Goods yard opened 27/06/1929. Closed to passengers and general goods 01/10/1931. Goods siding served Peerless wire fence co. between 1933 and 01/01/1953.
SOUTH HARROW	23 / 1B		28/06/1903	N/A	MDR	Terminus 28/06/1903 - 01/03/1910. First served Piccadilly Line 04/07/1932. Last served District Line 23/10/1933. Re-sited to north 05/07/1935.
SOUTH HARROW GASWORKS	23 / 1B		*??/??/1910*	*04/04/1954*	PRIV	
SOUTH HARROW SIDINGS	23 / 1B		28/06/1903	N/A	MDR	Stabling sidings (formerly depot) for Piccadilly Line (previously District Railway).
South Harrow Tunnel	23 / 2B		02/04/1906	N/A	GCR	
South Junction (Mitcham)	52 / 6D		01/10/1868	02/06/1997	LBSCR	Junction eliminated when Wimbledon to West Croydon line closed 02/06/1997 prior to conversion to Tramlink.
SOUTH KENSINGTON	38 / 2C 45		24/12/1868	N/A	MET	Opened by MET as part of 24/12/1868 MET / MDR extension to Westminster (Bridge) - boundary between two companies was east of station (South Kensington East Junction). MDR opened own platforms to south of MET 10/07/1871. UERL (GNPBR) platforms opened 08/01/1907. Middle bay road removed & filled in 28/07/1957, tracks reconfigured at same time such that former MET = eastbound and former MDR = westbound. Northernmost platform road (eastbound Circle) removed 08/01/1967, southernmost (westbound District) removed 30/03/1969, station reconstruction completed 21/10/1973.

Name	Page / grid		Date opened	Date closed	Opened by	Notes
South Kensington East Junction	38 / 2D 45		10/07/1871	28/07/1957	MDR / MET	Initially site of 'end on' junction between MET and MDR, became traditional junction when MDR opened its own lines through South Kensington 10/07/1871. Junction eliminated when tracks reconfigured 28/07/1957.
SOUTH KENTISH TOWN	26 / 3A		22/06/1907	05/06/1924	UERL (CCEHR)	
SOUTH KENTON	23 / 1D		03/07/1933	N/A	LMS	Served by Bakerloo Line since opening, except 27/09/1982 (last served 24/09/1982) - 04/06/1984.
SOUTH MERTON	52 / 5B		07/07/1929	N/A	SR	Temporary country terminus of Wimbledon - Sutton line until full opening 05/01/1930.
SOUTH QUAY	40 / 1D		31/08/1987	N/A	DLR	Closed 09/02/1996 - 15/04/1996 (IRA bomb adjacent to station). Closed again 23/10/2009, re-opening 125m east 26/10/2009 to facilitate longer platforms (original site constrained by adjacent curves).
SOUTH RUISLIP South Ruislip & Northolt Junction Northolt Junction	22 / 2C	P G	01/05/1908 01/05/1908	N/A 27/01/1964	GCR / GWR	Opened as 'Northolt Junction'. Renamed 'South Ruislip & Northolt Junction' 12/09/1932. Suffix dropped 30/06/1947. First served by Central Line Trains 21/11/1948. Goods facilities closed 27/01/1964, although milk traffic remained until 1972. Up slow track removed and up platform widened to abut former up fast track 1973.
SOUTH SHED (QUEENS PARK)	25 / 4B		11/02/1915	N/A	UERL (BAK)	Stabling Shed for Bakerloo Line.
SOUTH TOTTENHAM South Tottenham & Stamford Hill	15 / 6A	P G	01/05/1871 01/05/1871	N/A 04/07/1966	THJR MID	Goods yard opened by MID on same date as passenger station. Suffix '& Stamford Hill' dropped 01/07/1903. Goods yard closed 04/07/1966 (usually referred to as 'Tottenham Goods').
South Tottenham East Junction	15 / 5A		09/07/1894	N/A	TFGR / THJR	Junction between THJR and TFGR.
South Tottenham West Junction	15 / 5A		??/??/1879	N/A	GER	Junction between THJR and Seven Sisters Chord (refer to notes for latter).
SOUTH WEST SIDINGS	24 / 5C 91 & 92		c.1870	N/A	NSWJR	Sidings had appeared on site by 1871 OS.
SOUTH WIMBLEDON South Wimbledon (Merton) South Wimbledon	52 / 4B		13/09/1926	N/A	UERL (NOR)	(Merton) suffix added c.1928, but gradually dropped. Still appears on some station signage at platform level.
SOUTH WOODFORD South Woodford (George Lane) George Lane	16 / 4B	P G	22/08/1856 22/08/1856	N/A 06/01/1964	ECR	Opened as 'George Lane', Renamed 'South Woodford (George Lane)' 05/07/1937. Ownership and majority of passenger services transferred to LPTB 14/12/1947, when 'George Lane' suffix dropped. Goods yard closed 06/01/1964. First Trains in the morning remained British Rail services until 01/06/1970.
SOUTHFLEET	59 / 3C	P G	10/05/1886 10/05/1886	03/08/1953 11/06/1962	LCDR	Opened as an island platform with Gravesend West branch. Closed to passengers 03/08/1953, goods 11/06/1962. Line through station site closed 24/03/1968, but was re-opened due to establishment of APCM (later Blue Circle) coal terminal on station site 1972 – 1976.
Southfleet Junction	59 / 3D		14/11/2007	N/A	LCOR	Route to Fawkham Junction rarely used after 14/11/2007.
SOUTHALL	35 / 1D	P G	01/05/1839 01/05/1839	N/A 02/01/1967	GWR	Sometimes had suffix 'Brentford Junction' added. Served by District Railway 01/03/1883 - 01/10/1885. Goods yard closed 02/01/1967.
SOUTHALL EAST SIDINGS	36 / 1A		??/07/1859	N/A	GWR	First engine shed on site ??/07/1859 (single road). Rebuilt 1884 & 1954, steam allocation withdrawn 31/12/1965. Became DMU depot 03/01/1966, until November 1986. Taken over by GWR Preservation Group 1988 (became 'Southall Railway Centre'), further taken over by Flying Scotsman Railways July 1997.
SOUTHALL GAS WORKS	35 / 1C		??/??/1869	??/??/1961	PRIV	Opened by Brentford Gas Company.
Southall West Junction	35 / 1D		18/07/1859	N/A	GWR	Junction between GWR main line and Brentford Branch. Direct access from branch to main line restored March 1995 (shunt move via Down Yard had been necessary previously).
SOUTHBURY Churchbury	7 / 5B	P G	01/10/1891 01/10/1891	N/A 07/12/1970	GER	Opened as 'Churchbury', closed to passengers 01/10/1909 - 01/03/1915 then again 01/07/1919. Re-opened as 'Southbury' 21/11/1960, goods yard closed 07/12/1970.
SOUTHFIELDS	52 / 1A		03/06/1889	N/A	LSWR	Putney Bridge to Wimbledon built by LSWR, initially operated by MDR only, LSWR services commenced 01/07/1889. Last regular main line passenger service withdrawn 05/05/1941, although services called on occasions until 1969. Station ownership transferred to LUL 01/04/1994 along with entire Putney Bridge to Wimbledon route.
SOUTHGATE	6 / 6B		13/03/1933	N/A	UERL (GNPBR)	
SOUTHWARK	39 / 1C		20/11/1999	N/A	LUL (JUB)	
SOUTHWARK DEPOT (GOODS)	39 / 1D 87		??/??/1901	03/10/1960	SECR	Provided goods facilities transferred from London bridge, adjacent to Ewer Street locomotive depot. General goods ceased 03/10/1960, parcels 1969. Became EMU stabling sidings after 1969, decommissioned May 1983.
SOUTHWARK PARK	40 / 2B 79		01/10/1902	15/03/1915	SECR	
SPA ROAD, BERMONDSEY Spa Road & Bermondsey	40 / 2A		08/02/1836	15/03/1915	LGR	Temporary London terminus of LGR until 10/10/1836 extension to Bermondsey Street. Closed 14/12/1836 (Quick), 'end of 1838' (Mitchell & Smith) or 'probably' February 1843 (Borley). Re-opened as permanent structure 'probably' 30/10/1842 (Quick - also Mitchell & Smith), or 'probably' February 1843 (Borley). Resited east 01/09/1872. Usually 'Spa Road & Bermondsey' until 1877, after 1877 usually 'Spa Road, Bermondsey'. Closed to passengers 15/03/1915, but used by railwaymen until 21/09/1925.
SPENCER ROAD HALT	66 / 3D		01/09/1906	15/03/1915	LBSCR / SER	
SPITALFIELDS GOODS Whitechapel Coal Brick Lane Goods	27 / 5B 90		c.1840	06/11/1967	ECR	Brick Lane Goods (opened ECR c.1840) amalgamated with Whitechapel Coal (opened GER 01/11/1866) 01/01/1881 to form Spitalfields Goods. Closed 06/11/1967.
Springhead Junctions	59 / 1C		13/12/2009	N/A	NR	Regular services Faversham to St Pancras commenced 13/12/2009.
Spur Junction	54 / 5A		18/06/1862	30/10/1966	LBSCR	Junction at north end of Norwood Spur.
STAINES Staines Central Staines Junction Staines Old Staines	48 / 2A	P G	22/08/1848 22/08/1848	N/A ??/??/1973	LSWR	Opened as 'Staines', suffix 'Old' added 1885, changed to 'Junction' 1889, suffix dropped 1920/1. Suffix 'Central' added 26/09/1949, dropped 18/04/1966. Two goods yards (west and east) had ceased to be used by 1973.

Name	Page / grid		Date opened	Date closed	Opened by	Notes
Staines Bridge	48 / 2A		04/06/1856	N/A	LSWR	
STAINES CARRIAGE SIDINGS	48 / 2B		??/??/1974	N/A	LSWR	
Staines Curve	48 / 2A	P	01/07/1884	30/01/1916	LSWR	Utilised by a Windsor to Weybridge (via Staines High Street) passenger service.
		G	07/04/1877	18/03/1965		
Staines East Junction	48 / 2A		04/06/1856	N/A	LSWR	
STAINES HIGH STREET	48 / 2A		01/07/1884	30/01/1916	LSWR	Served by Windsor – Weybridge services only (Waterloo to Windsor services did not call).
Staines High Street Junction	48 / 2A		07/04/1877	18/03/1965	LSWR	Junction at north end of Staines Curve.
STAINES LINOLEUM WORKS	48 / 2A		??/??/1887	??/??/1957	PRIV	Extensive internal network of narrow gauge lines as well as standard gauge lines connected to GWR and LSWR.
Staines Moor Junction	47 / 1D		23/06/1940	16/12/1947	SR	Curve between GWR and SR established as a diversionary route during WW2, little used.
STAINES WEST	48 / 2A	P	02/11/1885	29/03/1965	GWR	Suffix 'West' added 26/09/1949. Passenger service West Drayton to Staines West withdrawn 29/03/1965, but traffic to Staines West oil terminal remained. Goods yard closed 02/11/1953, but re-opened as oil terminal 24/06/1964.
Staines		G	02/11/1885	02/11/1953		
Staines West Junction (1st)	48 / 2A		07/04/1877	18/03/1965	LSWR	Junction at south end of Staines Curve.
Staines West Junction (2nd)	47 / 1D		24/01/1981	24/06/1991	BR	Established for access to Staines West oil terminal after M25 severed GWR route to West Drayton. First train special passenger service 24/01/1981, last use 24/06/1991. Still in situ but disused.
STAINES WEST OIL TERMINAL (SHELL / BP)	48 / 2A		24/06/1964	24/06/1991	PRIV	On site of former Staines West goods yard (closed 02/11/1953). Accessed by GWR Staines West branch from West Drayton until 16/01/1981. New connection to LSWR Windsor branch commissioned 24/01/1981, when a special passenger train became last train to traverse length of GWR Staines West branch. Oil trains ran via LSWR route after this date, and GWR branch subsequently severed by M25 motorway south of Colnbrook.
STAMFORD BROOK	37 / 2C 51 / 2D		01/02/1912	N/A	UERL (MDR)	Island platform built only for District Line (LSWR trains non-stopped). Due to forthcoming Piccadilly Line extension, eastbound District Line diverted via former 'up' LSWR road so new platform opened on that line 05/06/1932. Served by Piccadilly Line 26/12/2013 – 30/12/2013 due to District Line engineering works.
STAMFORD HILL	15 / 6A		22/07/1872	N/A	GER	
STANMORE	11 / 2D	P	10/12/1932	N/A	MET	Opened by Metropolitan Railway. Transferred to Bakerloo Line 20/11/1939, Jubilee Line 01/05/1979. Goods yard closed 31/03/1936 (Now stabling sidings). Third platform opened 26/06/2011.
		G	10/12/1932	31/03/1936		
STANMORE VILLAGE	11 / 2D	P	18/12/1890	15/09/1952	LNWR	'Village' suffix added 25/09/1950. Stanmore Village to Belmont closed to passengers 15/09/1952, goods 06/07/1964.
Stanmore		G	18/12/1890	06/07/1964		
Stanmore Branch Junction	11 / 4C		18/12/1890	05/10/1964	LNWR	Southern quarter mile of branch retained as head shunt for Harrow & Wealdstone goods until 03/04/1967.
Star Bridge	73 / 3A		05/11/1899	N/A	LBSCR	Point where LBSCR 'Quarry Line' crosses original LBRR.
STAR LANE	28 / 6A		31/08/2011	N/A	DLR	
STEPNEY GREEN	27 / 5B		23/06/1902	N/A	MDR / LTSR	Served by Metropolitan Line since 30/03/1936 ('Hammersmith & City Line' since 30/07/1990).
Stepney Green Junction	27 / 6C		??/??/2018	N/A	NR (XRAIL)	
Stepney East Junction *Stepney Junction*	27 / 6C		02/04/1849	??/??/1951	LBLR	Junction points removed 1951, although original LBLR route along north side of Limehouse Basin remained accessible from east end (Limehouse Junction) as a siding until 1962.
STEWARTS LANE (LCDR)	39 / 4A 82		01/05/1863	01/01/1867	LCDR	
STEWARTS LANE (WELCPR)	39 / 4A 82		29/03/1858	01/12/1858	WELCPR	Opened by WELCPR, but operated by LBSCR from outset.
STEWARTS LANE DEPOT *Longhedge Locomotive Works*	39 / 4A 82		??/02/1862	N/A	LCDR	Land purchased by LCDR 1861. Roundhouse opened February 1862, erecting shop in operation 1869 – 1904 (work then transferred to Ashford, Kent). Renamed 'Stewarts Lane' after 1933-4 rebuilding. Steam ceased 1963.
STEWARTS LANE GOODS	39 / 4A 82		15/01/1862	02/11/1970	LCDR	
Stewarts Lane Junction	39 / 4A 82		25/08/1862	N/A	LCDR	
STEWARTS LANE STONE TERMINAL	82		?	N/A	PRIV	
STOKE NEWINGTON	27 / 1A		27/05/1872	N/A	GER	Terminus from opening until 22/07/1872. Goods yard to north of Stoke Newington Tunnel (see 'Manor Road Goods').
Stoke Newington Tunnel	27 / 1A		22/07/1872	N/A	GER	
STOAT'S NEST	73 / 1B		12/07/1841	01/12/1856	LBRR	Opened with LBRR Croydon Junction to Haywards Heath route as request stop, permanent premises opened 1842.
Stoat's Nest Junction	73 / 1B		05/11/1899	N/A	LBSCR / SER	Junction former by opening of LBSCR 'Quarry Line'.
STOAT'S NEST QUARRY	73 / 2B		*pre-1868*	*c.1970*	PRIV	Quarry began to be worked c.1805, rail connection depicted on 1868 OS, last shown 1965-7, absent 1975.
Stockley Park Flyover	34 / 1D		19/01/1998	N/A	RT	Flyover carrying 'up' line ex-BAA Heathrow Airport branch.
STOCKWELL	39 / 4B		18/12/1890	N/A	CSLR	Terminus of CSLR 18/12/1890 - 03/061900. Line closed for tunnel widening 28/11/1923, station re-opened to south 01/12/1924. Victoria Line platforms opened 23/07/1971.
STOCKWELL DEPOT	39 / 4B		18/12/1890	29/11/1923	CSLR	Original CSLR Depot, accessed by a steep incline (cable haulage), later replaced by hydraulic lift (one car capacity). Closed with rest of CSLR 29/11/1923 for tunnel widening works, remained closed when CSLR re-opened 1924 due to access having become available to Golders Green Depot via 20/04/1924 Euston to Camden Town link.
STONE CROSSING *Stone Crossing Halt*	44 / 6D		02/11/1908	N/A	SECR	Suffix 'Halt' dropped 05/05/1969.
STONEBRIDGE PARK	24 / 3B 68 / 6B		15/06/1912	N/A	LNWR	Served by Bakerloo Line Trains since 01/08/1917. Terminus of Bakerloo Line services 24/09/1982 - 04/06/1984. Goods station site remote (to north west), see separate entry below.
STONEBRIDGE PARK DEPOT	24 / 3A 68 / 3B		09/04/1979	N/A	LTE (BAK)	Bakerloo Line Depot, on site of former LNWR power station.
STONEBRIDGE PARK GOODS	24 / 3A 68 / 4B		19/08/1912	??/06/1951	LNWR	Heavy Repair shop later built on same site.
STONEBRIDGE PARK POWER STATION	24 / 3A 68 / 3B		24/02/1916	30/07/1967	LNWR	LNWR power station, Stonebridge Park Depot later built on same site.
STONELEIGH	64 / 3C		17/07/1932	N/A	SR	

Name	Page / grid		Date opened	Date closed	Opened by	Notes
STRATFORD Stratford (West Ham) Stratford	28 / 3A 77 / 78	P G	20/06/1839 20/06/1839	N/A ?	ECR	NER platforms opened 22/11/1841 (initially separate station, combined with ECR station 01/04/1847). 'Low Level' ECR platforms opened 16/10/1854. Sometimes had suffix '(West Ham)' appended 1898 - 1923. LPTB Central Line platforms opened 04/12/1946 (terminus until 05/05/1947). First DLR platform 4 opened 31/08/1987 (until then a never utilised BR bay platform), closed and replaced by platforms 4a & 4b 18/06/2007 & 09/12/2007 respectively. LUL Jubilee Line platforms opened 14/05/1999. 'Low Level' NR platforms closed and replaced by new platforms 1 & 2 14/04/2009 before being converted for DLR use (opened 31/08/2011 as platforms 16 & 17). Central Line westbound platform 3a opened 05/09/2010. Goods yard to east of station, date of closure unknown (not stated in Borley).
Stratford Central Junction East	28 / 3A 77 / 78		15/09/1840	N/A	ECR / NER	
Stratford Central Junction West	28 / 3A 77 / 78		15/08/1854	N/A	ECR	
Stratford Country End Crossovers	28 / 3A 78		?	N/A	BR	
Stratford Eastern Curve	28 / 3A 77	P G	N/A 29/04/1846	N/A 12/03/1973	ECTJR	Never saw regular passenger services.
Stratford Eastern Junction	28 / 3A 77		29/04/1846	12/03/1973	ECTJR / ECR	Junction at north end of Stratford Eastern Curve.
STRATFORD FREIGHTLINER TERMINAL	27 / 3D		04/07/1967	??/??/1998	BR	
STRATFORD HIGH STREET	28 / 4A 78		31/08/2011	N/A	DLR	On site of former Stratford Market station.
STRATFORD INTERNATIONAL	27 / 3D 78		30/11/2009	N/A	LCOR	Opened with advent of Southeastern services into St Pancras International. DLR platforms opened 31/08/2011.
STRATFORD MARKET Stratford Market (West Ham) Stratford Market Stratford Bridge	28 / 4A 77		14/06/1847	06/05/1957	ECR	'Stratford Bridge' until 01/11/1880 when renamed 'Stratford Market'. Relocated slightly to east 1892 (quadrupling). Carried suffix '(West Ham)' 1898 - 1923. Current Stratford High Street DLR station occupies same site. Large goods yard to south of station (see separate entry below).
STRATFORD MARKET DEPOT	28 / 4A		14/05/1999	N/A	LUL (JUB)	Jubilee Line Depot, on site of former Stratford Market Goods.
STRATFORD MARKET GOODS	28 / 4A		01/10/1879	05/11/1984	GER	Fruit & Vegetable Market, with adjacent goods depot. Sidings retained for engineering use until 1988, then lifted.
Stratford Southern Curve	28 / 4A 77	P G	14/06/1847 14/06/1847	28/10/1940 03/11/1984	ECR	Closed to passenger services 28/10/1940, fell into disuse by early 1980s, junctions eliminated 03/11/1984.
Stratford Southern Junction	28 / 4A 77		14/06/1847	03/11/1984	ECR	Junction at east end of Stratford Southern Curve.
STRATFORD TMD (1st) Stratford Works	77		c.1847	??/??/2001	ECR	ECR locomotive works. Overhaul work continued until 31/03/1991 (closure of diesel repair shop), loco stabling continued. Relocated to Temple Mills 2001 due to Channel Tunnel Rail Link works at Stratford (see Stratford TMD [2nd]).
STRATFORD TMD (2nd)	27 / 1C		??/??/2001	??/??/2007	EWS	Relocated depot closed and replaced by Orient Way Sidings.
Stratford Western Junction	28 / 4A 77		14/06/1847	03/11/1984	ECR	Junction at west end of Stratford Southern Curve.
STRAWBERRY HILL	50 / 1B		01/12/1873	N/A	LSWR	
STRAWBERRY HILL DEPOT Fulwell Depot	50 / 2B		01/05/1897	N/A	LSWR	Fulwell Depot opened 01/05/1897 with a six-road engine shed (current 'A' shed). In 1908 the shed was extended by three roads with the addition of the 'B' shed. The shed roads were electrified 30/01/1916, the steam allocation subsequently being transferred to the new Feltham shed in 1923. EMU depot always referred to as 'Strawberry Hill Depot'. Site of former coal dump sidings became additional stabling sidings ('Field Sidings') in 1936.
Strawberry Hill Junction Thames Valley Junction	50 / 2B		01/11/1864	N/A	LSWR / TVR	Junction between LSWR Kingston Branch (now Loop) and Thames Valley Railway (Shepperton Branch).
STREATHAM	53 / 3B	P G	01/10/1868 01/10/1868	N/A 07/10/1968	LBSCR	
STREATHAM COMMON Streatham Common (Greyhound Lane) Streatham Common	53 / 4B	P G	01/12/1862 01/12/1862	N/A 07/10/1968	LBSCR	Suffix 'Greyhound Lane' in use 01/09/1868 - 01/01/1870.
Streatham Common Junction	53 / 3A		01/10/1868	N/A	LBSCR	Spurs at Streatham thought to have opened at same time as Peckham - Sutton line (01/10/1868) (Borley).
STREATHAM HILL Streatham & Brixton Hill Streatham	53 / 2B	P G	01/12/1856 c.1856	N/A ??/??/1938	WELCPR	Opened as 'Streatham', became either 'Streatham & Brixton Hill' or simply 'Brixton Hill' 01/09/1868, further renamed 'Streatham Hill' 01/01/1869. Coal yard was present on 'down' side west of station as early as 1869 OS, possibly opened with passenger station, closed and converted to EMU stabling sidings 1938 (no mention in Borley).
STREATHAM HILL DEPOT	53 / 2B		c.1890	N/A	LBSCR	Carriage sidings had appeared by 1895 OS on 'up' side (not present on 1874-5 OS). Shed added in mid-20th century (not apparent before 1951-2 OS). Sidings on down side originally coal yard, converted for stabling 1938.
Streatham Junction	53 / 3B		01/10/1868	N/A	LBSCR	Spurs at Streatham thought to have opened at same time as Peckham - Sutton line (01/10/1868) (Borley).
Streatham North Junction	53 / 3A		01/10/1868	N/A	LBSCR	Spurs at Streatham thought to have opened at same time as Peckham - Sutton line (01/10/1868) (Borley).
Streatham South Junctions A & B	53 / 3A		01/10/1868	N/A	LBSCR	Spurs at Streatham thought to have opened at same time as Peckham - Sutton line (01/10/1868) (Borley).
Streatham South Junction C	53 / 3A		01/10/1868	N/A	LSWR / LBSCR	Spurs at Streatham thought to have opened at same time as Peckham - Sutton line (01/10/1868) (Borley).
Streatham Tunnel	53 / 2B		01/10/1868	N/A	LBSCR	
STROUD GREEN	14 / 6C		11/04/1881	05/07/1954	GNR	Closed when Alexandra Palace to Finsbury Park service withdrawn 05/07/1954 after a previous closure period 29/10/1951 - 07/01/1952. Branch had been intended for electrification and transfer to LPTB Northern Line, but works abandoned post-WW2.
Studland Road Junction	37 / 2D		01/06/1877	03/12/1911	LSWR / MDR	Junction physically eliminated through 03/12/1911 quadrupling between there and Turnham Green.
Subway Tunnel	25 / 6B 67 / 5A		12/05/1878	N/A	MET / GWR	Diveunder provided to eliminate the Hammersmith & City Railway's original level crossing of the GWR main line.
SUDBURY & HARROW ROAD	23 / 2C	P G	01/03/1906 01/03/1906	N/A 03/05/1965	GCR	Goods yard closed 03/05/1965. Platforms originally provided on loops off two central 'fast' roads, which were subsequently removed. Original platforms then abandoned and replaced by 'island' on site of 'fast' roads.

Name	Page / grid		Date opened	Date closed	Opened by	Notes
SUDBURY HILL Sudbury Hill for Greenford Green	23 / 2B		28/06/1903	N/A	MDR	Suffix 'for Greenford Green' 1904 - 1938. First served Piccadilly Line 04/07/1932, last served District Line 23/10/1933.
SUDBURY HILL HARROW South Harrow	23 / 2B	P G	01/03/1906 01/03/1906	N/A 03/05/1965	GCR	Terminus from opening until 02/04/1906. Renamed 19/07/1926. Goods yard closed 03/05/1965. Platforms originally provided on loops off two central 'fast' roads. Loops and platforms later removed with new platforms being constructed alongside original 'fast' roads. Closed 22/09/1990 - 07/10/1990.
Sudbury Junction Brent Junction	24 / 3B 68 / 2C		c.1890	N/A	LNWR	Willesden Relief lines and diveunder added c.1890.
SUDBURY TOWN Sudbury Town for Horsenden Sudbury Town	23 / 3D		28/06/1903	N/A	MDR	Suffix 'for Horsenden' 1904 - 1938. First served Piccadilly Line 04/07/1932, last served District Line 23/10/1933.
SUNBURY	49 / 4B	P G	01/11/1864 01/11/1864	N/A 01/08/1960	TVR	Originally passing point on single line until 17/07/1878 doubling. Goods yard closed 01/08/1960 (Borley), Jackson states 07/10/1960.
SUNDRIDGE PARK Plaistow	55 / 4B		01/01/1878	N/A	SER	Renamed 01/07/1894.
SUNNYMEADS	33 / 4B		10/07/1927	N/A	SR	
SURBITON Surbiton & Kingston Kingston Junction Kingston	50 / 6D	P G	??/??/1845 ??/??/1845	N/A 01/11/1971	LSWR	Replaced Kingston (1st) station 1/2 mile to east at some point in 1845. Also initially named 'Kingston', suffix 'Junction' added December 1852. Renamed 'Surbiton & Kingston' 01/07/1863 (on same day that current 'Kingston' station opened). Renamed 'Surbiton' 01/10/1867. Goods yard closed 01/11/1971.
Surrey Canal Junction North Kent West Junction Bricklayer's Arms Junction	40 / 3C 79 / 80		01/09/1849	N/A	LGR / SER	Junction between Bricklayers Arms Branch and LGR, former disused since 1981, but junction remains in situ Easternmost portion of Bricklayer's Arms Branch to be re-used from 2018 as Bermondsey dive-under leading to junction being re-established in use. Originally 'Bricklayers Arms Junction', currently 'North Kent West Junction', to be named 'Surrey Canal Junction' when diveunder opens.
SURREY CANAL ROAD	40 / 3B 80		TBC	N/A	TFL (LOROL)	Proposed station on LOROL East London Line extension Phase 2. Did not open with line 09/12/2012, due to insufficient funds, but foundations for station building / platforms were constructed.
SURREY QUAYS Surrey Docks Deptford Road	40 / 2B 79 / 80		07/12/1869	N/A	ELR	First served MET & MDR 01/10/1884, last served MDR 01/08/1905, no service MET 03/12/1906 - 31/03/1913. Renamed 'Surrey Docks' 17/07/1911, then 'Surrey Quays' 24/10/1989. Closed 25/03/1995 - 25/03/1998 & 23/12/2007 – 27/04/2010 (engineering work), upon latter re-opening became TFL (LOROL) station.
SUTTON	65 / 3B	P G	10/05/1847 10/05/1847	N/A 07/10/1968	LBSCR	Originally two-platform through station, additional platforms on Epsom Downs branch added 22/05/1865. Goods yard closed 07/10/1968.
SUTTON COMMON	65 / 2B		05/01/1930	N/A	SR	
Sutton East Junction	65 / 3C		22/05/1865	N/A	LBSCR	Route to Mitcham Junction opened 01/10/1868.
Sutton West Junction	65 / 3B		05/01/1930	N/A	SR	
SWANLEY Swanley Junction Sevenoaks Junction	57 / 6B	P G	01/07/1862 01/07/1862	N/A 16/05/1964	LCDR	Opened by LCDR at divergence of Sevenoaks Railway (nominally independent by operated by LCDR) branch to Bat & Ball station from LCDR main line. Four platform faces, opened a month after branch line. Initially 'Sevenoaks Junction', renamed 'Swanley Junction' 01/01/1871, then 'Swanley' 16/04/1939. Rebuilt on a site west of the junction with two island platforms 02/07/1939. Goods yard closed 16/05/1964 to public traffic, but two sidings retained as part of Westinghouse training compound (sidings currently disused).
Swanley Junction Sevenoaks Junction	57 / 6B		02/06/1862	N/A	SOR / LCDR	Initially 'Sevenoaks Junction', presumably renamed in conjunction with Swanley (Junction) station 01/01/1871.
SWANSCOMBE Swanscombe Halt	45 / 6B		06/07/1930	N/A	SR	Replaced original Swanscombe Halt 770 metres west 06/07/1930. Suffix 'Halt' dropped 05/05/1969.
SWANSCOMBE HALT	45 / 6A		02/11/1908	06/07/1930	SECR	Replaced by new halt 770 metres to east (see 'Swanscombe').
SWANSCOMBE PORTLAND CEMENT WORKS	45 / 6B		??/??/1929	??/??/1982	PRIV	Britain's first cement works, opened 1825 with internal narrow gauge rail network. Connected to North Kent line and converted to Standard gauge 1929. Closed when chalk pits exhausted 1982.
SWISS COTTAGE (MSJWR)	25 / 3C		13/04/1868	18/08/1940	MSJWR	Terminus of MSJWR from Baker Street until 30/06/1879.
SWISS COTTAGE (LPTB)	25 / 3C		20/11/1939	N/A	LPTB (BAK)	Opened by Bakerloo Line, transferred to Jubilee Line 01/05/1979.
SYDENHAM	54 / 3B		05/06/1839	N/A	LCRR	Rebuilt 1853-4 (quadrupling).
Sydenham Down Junction	54 / 3B		10/06/1854	N/A	LBSCR	
SYDENHAM HILL	54 / 2A		01/08/1863	N/A	LCDR	
Sydenham Up Junction	54 / 3B		10/06/1854	N/A	LBSCR	
SYON LANE	36 / 3C		05/07/1931	N/A	SR	

T

Name	Page / grid		Date opened	Date closed	Opened by	Notes
TADWORTH Tadworth & Walton on the Hill	71 / 4D	P G	01/07/1900 01/07/1900	N/A 07/05/1962	SECR	Terminus until extension to Tattenham Corner opened 04/06/1901 (please see Tattenham Corner entry for pre-25/03/1928 service patterns beyond Tadworth). Goods yard closed 07/05/1962. Suffix dropped 01/12/1968.
Tanners Hill Flydown	40 / 5D	P G	29/03/1976 29/03/1976	N/A N/A	BR	Doubled for Thameslink upgrade, works completed 02/04/2013.
Tanners Hill Junction	40 / 5D		29/03/1976	N/A	BR	Junction at north end of Tanners Hill Flydown.
TARMAC STONE TERMINAL (HAYES)	35 / 1B		??/??/1968	N/A	PRIV	
TARMAC TOPMIX STONE TERMINAL (PADDINGTON)	25 / 5B 67 / 5A		??/??/1975	??/??/2010	PRIV	Opened 1975 on site of Paddington New Yard, closed 2010 to allow construction of 'Crossrail 1'. To re-open on same site upon completion of Crossrail 1 works c.2018.
TARMAC TOPMIX STONE TERMINAL (PARK ROYAL)	24 / 5B		?	N/A	PRIV	
TATTENHAM CORNER	71 / 2D	P G	04/06/1901 04/06/1901	N/A 02/04/1962	SECR	First use for a race meeting 04/06/1901, initially appears to have been race / excursion specials only. All day service commenced June 1902 (Bradshaw), albeit Summer only until end Summer 1914. Army camp use September 1914 to 1919. Race specials recommenced 29/04/1919, full public re-opening 25/03/1928 (electrification). Goods yard closed 02/04/1962. Reduced from original six platforms to three 29/11/1970. Original station building demolished by a train over-running buffers 01/12/1993, replacement opened March 1994.
TAYLOR'S LANE POWER STATION	24 / 3C		??/??/1903	c.1990	PRIV	Originally built by Willesden Urban District Council. Decommissioned

Name	Page / grid			Date opened	Date closed	Opened by	Notes
							1972 and replaced by current power station 1979, sidings connected until at least 1990 (Quail), and remain in situ at power station end.

TEDDINGTON
  Teddington for Bushey Park
  Teddington & Bushey Park
  Teddington (Bushey Park)
	50 / 3C	P
		G
				01/07/1863
				01/07/1863
					N/A
					03/05/1965
						LSWR	Suffix variously '(Bushey Park)', '& Bushey Park' or 'for Bushey Park' until August 1911 when station became simply 'Teddington' (Borley). Suffix carried until 1955 in Bradshaw (per Quick). 'Bushey' also spelt 'Bushy' at times. Goods yard closed 03/05/1965.

TEMPLE The Temple	26 / 6C			30/05/1870	N/A	MDR	Prefix 'The' dropped gradually by c.1883.
Temple Mills East Junction	28 / 2A 77 / 78			??/??/1881	N/A	GER	High Meads Loop opened 1881.
TEMPLE MILLS EUROSTAR DEPOT	27 / 1D			07/10/2007	N/A	LCOR	Partly on site of Temple Mills Marshalling Yard. Formal opening 02/10/2007, came into use 07/10/2007.
TEMPLE MILLS LOCO & WAGON WORKS	27 / 2D 27			??/??/1850	??/??/1963	ECR	
TEMPLE MILLS YARD	27 / 1D 27			??/??/1871	N/A	GER	First goods sidings opened 1871. Expanded 1877, 1893 & 1930, reconstructed as a 'hump' yard December 1958. No longer used as a Marshalling yard; some engineering use. Much of original site occupied by Eurostar Depot.
THAMES AMMUNITION WORKS	44 / 3A			??/??/1917	c.1918	PRIV	Connected to external rail network during latter stages of WW1 only, via 1½ mile light railway from Slade Green.
Thames Bridge (Windsor)	33 / 4B			08/10/1849	N/A	GWR	Track singled 09/09/1963.
THAMES DITTON	50 / 6B			??/11/1851	N/A	LSWR	Opened November 1851 (Jackson), Quick states first in timetable December 1851.
Thames Tunnel (ELR)	40 / 1B			07/12/1869	N/A	ELR	Opened to pedestrian traffic 25/03/1843, first trains ran through tunnel 07/12/1869.
Thames Tunnel (LCOR)	44 / 5D 45 / 5A			14/11/2007	N/A	LCOR	
THAMES WHARF	41 / 1B 62 / 4A			29/04/1846	04/10/1965	ECTJR	Midland Railway goods yard opened 1870 adjacent to existing GER / ECR (former ECTJR / ECR).
THAMES WHARF	41 / 1B 62 / 5A			N/A	N/A	DLR	Proposed station on DLR Woolwich Arsenal line, dependant on adjacent housing development.
Thames Wharf Junction	41 / 1B 62 / 3A			26/11/1855	04/10/1965	ECR	Junction between original line to North Woolwich and 1855 route via Custom House. Eliminated when Thames Wharf Goods closed (original North Woolwich route 'Silvertown Tramway' had been severed by then).
THEOBALDS GROVE	7 / 2A	P G		01/10/1891 02/04/1900	N/A 03/01/1966	GER	Closed 01/10/1909 – 01/03/1915 & 01/07/1919 – 21/11/1960. Goods yard opened 02/04/1900, closed 03/01/1966.
THERAPIA LANE	66 / 1B			30/05/2000	N/A	CTL	
THERAPIA LANE DEPOT	66 / 1B			10/05/2000	N/A	CTL	Sole depot for London Tramlink Croydon (first section opened 10/05/2000), on site of former permanent sidings.
THEYDON BOIS Theydon	8 / 3A	P G		24/04/1865 ??/??/1886	N/A 18/04/1966	GER	Suffix 'Bois' added 01/12/1865. Goods yard opened 1886. Majority of Passenger services transferred to LTE 25/09/1949, first trains in the morning remained BR until 01/06/1970. Goods closed 18/04/1966.
THORNEY MILL SIDINGS	34 / 1B			11/07/1943	N/A	GWR	Formerly used for Coal, Oil, Scrap metal and Stone traffic, today only Stone traffic remains.
THORNEY MILL STONE TERMINAL (BARDON)	34 / 1B			??/??/1986	N/A	PRIV	Current terminal opened 1986, stone traffic to site had been handled prior to this.
THORNTON FIELDS CARRIAGE SIDINGS	27 / 4D 77			??/??/1928	16/06/2008	GER	Points 'clipped' out of use and overhead wires de-energised 16/06/2008, 'officially' closed 30/06/2008. Site cleared for 2012 Olympic park. Replaced by Orient Way Sidings (opened 30/05/2008).
THORNTON HEATH	53 / 5C	P G		01/12/1862 01/12/1862	N/A 07/10/1968	LBSCR	Goods yard on 'up' side, coal yard on 'down' side, all closed 07/10/1968.
Three Bridges	36 / 1A			15/07/1859	N/A	GWR	Unusual feature where rail, canal, and road intersect (rail below canal, road above canal). Date stated is that of special passenger train run on Brentford Dock branch, regular goods trains followed three days later.
THURROCK AGGREGATES CENTRE (LAFARGE)	44 / 5C			??/12/2007	N/A	PRIV	
THURROCK CHALK & WHITING Co. WORKS	44 / 3C			?	c.1980	PRIV	
TIDAL BASIN	41 / 1B 62 / 3A			??/02/1858	15/08/1943	ECR	Borley gives name as 'Victoria Docks, Tidal Basin', this name also given in Quick in use 1882-1914 (GER timetables).
TILBURY EAST CONTAINER TERMINAL	45 / 5D			??/??/1970	N/A	BR	
Tilbury East Curve	46 / 6A	P G		14/08/1854 14/08/1854	??/??/1985 30/11/1992	LTSR	Opened as part of LTSR extension from Tilbury to Stanford-Le-Hope. Regular passenger trains ceased 1985 when trains from London to / from Southend ceased reversing at Tilbury Riverside.
Tilbury East Junction	46 / 6A			c.1855	30/11/1992	LTSR	Junction at east ends of Tilbury North / East Curves.
TILBURY GRAIN TERMINAL	45 / 5C			??/??/1969	N/A	BR	
TILBURY INTERNATIONAL RAIL FREIGHT TERMINAL	46 / 6A			c.2000	N/A	BR	Opened on site of former carriage sidings subsequent to closure of Tilbury Riverside station.
Tilbury Junction	27 / 5D 88			17/05/1869	13/09/1959	NLR	Junction at north end of curve between NLR at Bow and LTSR at Bromley.
TILBURY MARINE	46 / 6A			15/05/1927	01/05/1932	PLA	Platform adjacent to Tidal basin within Tilbury Docks opened by PLA to serve boat trains.
TILBURY MPD	46 / 6A			13/04/1854	18/06/1962	LTSR	Original 2 road engine shed adjacent to Tilbury South Junction, replaced by 4 road shed adjacent to Tilbury North Curve 1912 (original closed 1908). Rebuilt 1956, closed 18/06/1962 (LTSR electrification).
Tilbury North Curve	46 / 6A	P G		??/??/1985 c.1855	N/A N/A	LTSR	Opened c.1855. No regular passenger trains until 1985 when London to Southend services ceased reversing at Tilbury Riverside station and began to run direct from Tilbury Town to East Tilbury.
Tilbury North Junction	45 / 4D			17/04/1886	c.1960	LTSR	Primary junction giving access to Tilbury Docks (opened 17/04/1886), eliminated during resignalling c.1960 when access provided via Grays East Junction instead.
TILBURY POWER STATIONS	46 / 6B			??/??/1956	?	PRIV	Tilbury 'A' (oil fired) commissioned 1956, mothballed 1981, demolished 1999. Tilbury 'B' (coal & biomass fired) commissioned 1968, still in operation but rail connection severed (date unknown).
Tilbury Railport Junction Tilbury West Junction	46 / 5A			c.1855	N/A	LTSR	Junction at west end of Tilbury West / North Curves. Eliminated when Tilbury Riverside closed 30/11/1992, but re-established to provide access to Tilbury International Rail Freight Terminal.

TILBURY RIVERSIDE
  Tilbury
  Tilbury Fort
	46 / 6A	P
		G
				13/04/1854
				13/04/1854
					30/11/1992
					06/05/1968
						LTSR	Terminus of original LTSR line from Forest Gate Junction. Branch to Stanford-Le-Hope (and subsequently towards Southend) added 14/08/1854. 'Fort' suffix applied from opening until 1866 (although not always), 'Riverside' suffix added 1935 (in timetable with effect from 06/07/1936). Until 1985 all services reversed at station, after 1985 trains between London and Southend ran direct, with the only trains remaining being Upminster via Ockendon service. Upminster via

Name	Page / grid		Date opened	Date closed	Opened by	Notes
						Ockendon service truncated at Grays and station closed 30/11/1992. Goods yard closed 06/05/1968. Site partially occupied by Tilbury International Rail Freight Terminal.
Tilbury South Junction	46 / 6A		14/08/1854	30/11/1992	LTSR	Junction at south end of Tilbury West and East curves.
TILBURY TOWN Tilbury Town for Tilbury Docks Tilbury Docks	45 / 5D		17/04/1886	N/A	LTSR	Opened to public on same date as adjacent Tilbury Docks (17/04/1886) according to Quick (who also states had been open to dock construction workers from c. May 1884). Borley gives opening date of 15/06/1885. Renamed 'Tilbury Town for Tilbury Docks' 03/08/1934, 'for Tilbury Docks' suffix dropped 1958.
Tilbury West Curve		P G	13/04/1854 *13/04/1854*	30/11/1992 *N/A*	LTSR	Part of original LTSR route from Forest Gate to Tilbury (Riverside). After 1985 London to Southend trains ceased reversing via Tilbury Riverside, only Upminster via Ockendon trains remained, these withdrawn 30/11/1992. Curve remains as access to Tilbury International Rail Freight Terminal.
TOLWORTH	64 / 2A	P G	29/05/1938 *29/05/1938*	N/A *N/A*	SR	Initially temporary terminus with 'down' platform only in use; extended to Chessington South and 'up' platform opened 28/05/1939. Goods yard expanded 1940, ceased handling general goods traffic 03/05/1965, but dedicated coal terminal had opened 04/01/1965. Aggregates traffic commenced c.1981, then coal traffic ceased c.1989. Aggregates traffic then ceased July 1993 before re-starting c.1998 (Day Group).
Tonbridge Fast Loop	55 / 5D 56 / 6A	P G	14/09/1902 *14/09/1902*	N/A *N/A*	SECR	Referred to as 'Bickley Loop' until 1959. Originally single track, doubled in readiness for Eurostar services 1992.
Tonbridge Line Junction	73 / 6C		26/05/1842	N/A	SER / LBRR	
Tonbridge Slow Loop	55 / 5D 56 / 6A	P	08/09/1902	N/A	SECR	Referred to as 'Bickley Loop' until 1959. Originally single track, doubled in readiness for Eurostar services 1992.
		G	*08/09/1902*	*N/A*		
TOOTING Tooting Junction	52 / 3D	P G	01/10/1868 *01/10/1868*	N/A *05/08/1968*	LBSCR / LSWR	Opened as a 4-platform station at divergence of LBSCR / LSWR joint loop line from Streatham to Wimbledon. Named 'Tooting Junction' initially, original closed and replaced by 2-platform station east of junction 12/08/1894. Closed to passengers 01/01/1917 – 27/08/1923. Suffix 'Junction' dropped 01/03/1938 (physical junction had been severed 10/03/1934), after 10/03/1934 goods yard accessed via Merton Park, closed 05/08/1968.
TOOTING BEC Trinity Road (Tooting Bec)	52 / 2D		13/09/1926	N/A	UERL (NOR)	Renamed 10/10/1950.
TOOTING BROADWAY	52 / 3D		13/09/1926	N/A	UERL (NOR)	
Tooting Junction	52 / 3D		01/10/1868	10/03/1934	LBSCR / LSWR	Junction eliminated 10/03/1934 and Tooting (Junction) to Merton Park route became a siding accessed from latter.
TOTTENHAM COURT ROAD Oxford Street (CCEHR only)	26 / 6B		30/07/1900	N/A	CLR	UERL (CCEHR) platforms opened 22/06/1907 as 'Oxford Street', renamed 09/03/1908. Northern Line platforms closed 02/04/2011 – 28/11/2011 (engineering work). 'Crossrail 1' station to open 2018.
TOTTENHAM HALE Tottenham Tottenham Hale Tottenham	15 / 5B	P G	15/09/1840 *15/09/1840*	N/A *??/??1968*	NER	Opened as 'Tottenham', suffix 'Hale' added ??/06/1875, dropped ??/11/1938, reinstated 1968. LTB Victoria Line station opened 01/09/1968. Goods yard closed 1968.
Tottenham North Curve (MID)	9	P G	N/A *02/04/1883*	N/A *N/A*	MID	No regular passenger service.
Tottenham North Curve (THJR)	15 / 5B	P G	21/07/1868 *??/??/1886*	01/11/1925 *11/06/1961*	THJR	Opened with rest of THJR 21/07/1868 (passenger service), no regular freight until 1886. Closed to passengers 01/11/1925, closed to freight and abandoned 11/06/1961.
Tottenham North Curve Tunnels Nos. 1, 2 & 3	9		02/04/1883	N/A	MID	
Tottenham North Junction	15 / 5B		21/07/1868	11/06/1961	THJR / GER	Northern end of Tottenham North Curve (THJR) (see notes above).
Tottenham South Curve	15 / 5B	P G	01/01/1880 *??/??/1868*	N/A *N/A*	THJR	First trains 1868 (goods), passenger services commenced 01/01/1880, ceased 07/01/1963, reintroduced 1989.
Tottenham South Junction	15 / 5B		??/??/1868	N/A	THJR / GER	Junction between Tottenham South Curve and GER (see notes above).
Tottenham West Junction	15 / 5B		??/??/1868	11/06/1961	THJR	Southern end of Tottenham North Curve (THJR) (see notes regarding Tottenham North Curve THJR).
TOTTERIDGE & WHETSTONE Totteridge	5 / 6C	P G	01/04/1872 *01/04/1872*	N/A *01/10/1962*	GNR	Suffix '& Whetstone' added 01/04/1874. First served by and transferred to LPTB Northern Line 14/04/1940, closed to LNER passenger services on same date. Goods yard closed 01/10/1962.
TOWER GATEWAY	27 / 6A 74 / 2B		31/08/1987	N/A	DLR	Closed 30/06/2008 – 02/03/2009 (rebuilding from 2 tracks to 1 track to accommodate longer trains).
TOWER HILL (MDR / MET) Mark Lane	27 / 6A 74 / 2B 87		06/10/1884	05/02/1967	MDR / MET	Replaced former 'Tower of London' Station to East. Renamed 'Tower Hill' 01/09/1946, closed and replaced on original 'Tower of London' site to east by 'Tower Hill' (MET) 05/02/1967.
TOWER HILL (MET) Tower of London	27 / 6A 74 / 2B		25/09/1882	N/A	MET	Terminus of MET extension from Aldgate 25/09/1882 - 06/10/1884, replaced by Mark Lane station to west 06/10/1884 when MET / MDR route from Mansion House to Aldgate East opened, although 'Tower of London' did not close until 13/10/1884. Re-opened as 'Tower Hill' 05/02/1967, replacing 'Tower Hill' (MDR / MET) station (former 'Mark Lane'). Westbound trains used current bay platform as a through route until 03/09/1967, then diverted and bay commissioned 21/01/1968.
TREASURE ISLAND RAILWAY	48 / 5A		??/04/1984	??/??/1993	PRIV	2 foot gauge railway within Thorpe Park.
TRIANGLE SIDINGS	38 / 2C 84		*c.1915*	N/A	UERL (MDR)	Sidings laid between 1914 and 1916 Ordnance surveys. Closed for S Stock upgrade work 11/12/2010, trains stabled at Lillie Bridge instead. Re-opened with 3 longer roads 22/05/2011 (previously 5).
TRUMPER'S CROSSING HALTE Trumper's Crossing (for Osterley Park) Halte	36 / 1B		01/07/1904	01/02/1926	GWR	Closed 22/03/1915 – 12/04/1920. The full length former name stated is that which appeared on nameboards.
TUFNELL PARK	26 / 2A 9		22/06/1907	N/A	UERL (CCEHR)	
TUFNELL PARK GOODS	26 / 1B		*15/02/1886*	*06/05/1968*	GER	
TULSE HILL	53 / 1C	P G	01/10/1868 *01/10/1868*	N/A *07/09/1964*	LBSCR	Goods yard to south of station in triangle beyond Tulse Hill South Junction, closed 07/09/1964. Pair of sidings provided on 'down' side. Station had an overall roof spanning its four platforms until c.1900.
Tulse Hill North Junction	53 / 1C		01/01/1869	N/A	LBSCR / LCDR	
Tulse Hill South Junction	53 / 2C		01/11/1870	N/A	LBSCR	Junction at north end of Leigham and West Norwood Spurs.
TUNNEL CEMENT WORKS (THURROCK)	44 / 4D		?	?	PRIV	

Name	Page / grid			Date opened	Date closed	Opened by	Notes
TURKEY STREET Forty Hill	7 / 2B	P G		01/10/1891 *01/10/1891*	N/A *01/06/1966*	GER	Opened 01/10/1891 as 'Forty Hill', closed 01/10/1909 - 01/03/1915 and again 01/07/1919. Reopened 21/11/1960 as 'Turkey Street'. Goods yard closed 01/06/1966.
TURNHAM GREEN	37 / 2C 51 / 2C			01/01/1869	N/A	LSWR	Opened by LSWR. Served by GWR 01/06/1870 – 01/11/1870. First served MDR 01/06/1877. Served by MET 01/10/1877 – 01/01/1911 (MET / GWR joint after 01/01/1894). Rebuilt from 2 side platforms to 2 island platforms when route quadrupled 03/12/1911 (LSWR northern island, MDR southern island). LSWR service ceased and northern island abandoned 05/06/1916. Eastbound District Line started using north face of north island from 05/06/1932. Piccadilly Line started running non-stop through middle platforms 04/07/1932 (but started calling at these platforms at extremes of traffic day from 23/06/1963).
Turnham Green Junction	51 / 2C			01/07/1879	N/A	LSWR / MDR	Junction between LSWR route to Richmond and MDR branch to Ealing Broadway.
TURNPIKE LANE	14 / 5C			19/09/1932	N/A	UERL (GNPBR)	
TWICKENHAM	36 / 6C	P G		22/08/1848 *22/08/1848*	N/A *02/01/1967*	LSWR	Original station west of London Road. Engine shed added June 1850, rebuilt 01/07/1863, closed 1897. Additional 'up' platform added when junction to west of station became 'flying' 22/10/1883. New station to east of London Road with 2 bay platforms for rugby traffic opened 28/03/1954 (original station closed same day). Goods yard closed 02/01/1967.
Twickenham Junction	50 / 1B			01/07/1863	N/A	LSWR	Junction between LSWR Windsor Line and branch to Kingston. Was a 'flat' junction until flyover opened 22/10/1883.
TWYFORD ABBEY HALT	24 / 4A			01/05/1904	01/05/1911	GWR	Replaced by Brentham station to west. Slightly east of present Hanger Lane station.
TWYFORD ABBEY SIDINGS	24 / 4B			*26/03/1903*	*c.1955*	LNWR	Built to serve Royal Agricultural Showground, remained in situ until lifted by 1955.

U

Name	Page / grid			Date opened	Date closed	Opened by	Notes
Up Empty Carriage Tunnel	26 / 4A 58			*10/07/1922*	*c.2000*	LNWR	Colloquially known as the 'Rat Hole', abandoned circa resignalling in Euston area 1999 – 2000.
UP SIDINGS (EUSTON)	26 / 4A			?	N/A	LNWR	
UP CARRIAGE SIDINGS (VICTORIA)	39 / 3A			*c.1880s*	N/A	LBSCR	Not present on 1875 OS map, but had appeared by 1896.
Up Slow Flyover (Wimbledon)	52 / 2B			17/05/1936	N/A	SR	Allowed reconfiguration of LSWR main line between Wimbledon and Clapham Junction.
UP YARD (REDHILL)	73 / 5C			*post 1849*	N/A	SER	Sidings on site on 1871 OS, possibly laid at same time as Guildford Line c.1849.
UPMINSTER	31 / 2C	P G		01/05/1885 *01/05/1885*	N/A *07/12/1964*	LTSR	Served by District Railway trains 02/06/1902 - 01/10/1905, then by excursion trains to Southend (later Shoeburyness) from 01/06/1910. Regular District Line service reintroduced 12/09/1932 when route quadrupled, which also resulted in station rebuilding and relocation of original 1893 engine shed (demolished 1931, rebuilt 1935). District Line excursion trains beyond Upminster withdrawn 30/09/1939. Separate platform for Romford service opened 20/05/1957. Goods yard closed 07/12/1964.
UPMINSTER BRIDGE District Line trains from outset.	31 / 2B			17/12/1934	N/A	LMS	Opened by LMS on the 1932 'local' lines only, served exclusively by
UPMINSTER DEPOT	31 / 1C			01/12/1959	N/A	LTE (DIS)	South of site accommodated 5 stabling sidings for District Line trains since 12/09/1932. Depot construction commenced 01/12/1958, completed 29/06/1959, full opening 01/12/1959.
Upminster East Junction	31 / 2C			01/07/1892	N/A	LTSR	Junction between LTSR main line and Ockendon Loop.
Upminster West Junction	31 / 2C			07/06/1893	20/05/1957	LTSR	Junction between LTSR main line and Romford Branch, eliminated when LTE and BR segregated at Upminster.
UPNEY	29 / 4B			12/09/1932	N/A	LMS	Barking to Upminster quadrupled by the LMS 12/09/1932 and Upney station opened, served by UERL District Line from opening. Ownership transferred to LTB 1970.
Upper Abbey Mills Junction	28 / 5A			31/03/1858	27/07/1958	LTSR	Junction at north end of Abbey Mills Curve.
UPPER HALLIFORD Upper Halliford Halt Halliford Halt	49 / 4A			01/05/1944	N/A	SR	Opened as 'Halliford Halt', prefix 'Upper' added 22/05/1944. 'Halt' dropped 05/05/1969. Initially opened with only a 'down' platform (single line working), 'up' platform opened 06/05/1946.
UPPER HOLLOWAY Upper Holloway for St John's Park U.H. for St John's Park and Highgate Hill Upper Holloway	26 / 1B	P G		21/07/1868 *c.1870*	N/A *06/05/1968*	THJR	Closed 31/01/1870 – 01/10/1870. Opened as 'Upper Holloway', suffix 'for St John's Park and Highgate Hill' added 01/03/1871, '- and Highgate Hill' dropped 01/04/1875, then '- for St John's Park' dropped 01/07/1903 (i.e. returned to 'Upper Holloway' from this date). Goods yard opened c.1870, closed 06/05/1968.
UPPER SYDENHAM	54 / 2A			01/08/1884	20/09/1954	LCDR	Closed 01/01/1917 – 01/03/1919 and 22/05/1944 – 04/03/1946. Closed for good 20/09/1954.
UPPER WARLINGHAM Upper Warlingham for Riddlesdown Upper Warlingham Upper Warlingham & Whyteleafe Upper Warlingham	74 / 2A	P G		10/03/1884 *10/03/1884*	N/A *04/05/1964*	LBSCR / SER	Opened as 'Upper Warlingham', '& Whyteleafe' suffix added 01/01/1894, dropped 01/10/1900. 'for Riddlesdown' suffix added 1912 (LBSCR timetable), until 1926/7. Goods yard closed 04/05/1964.
UPTON PARK	28 / 4C			17/09/1877	N/A	LTSR	First served by District Railway 02/06/1902, line quadrupled 1905, District trains then using 'slow' platforms to north Served by Metropolitan Line since 30/03/1936 ('Hammersmith & City Line' since 30/07/1990). Main line services non-stopped since 15/06/1962, and 'Fast' platforms abandoned. Goods yard situated east of passenger station on a short branch line (see separate entry below).
UPTON PARK GOODS	28 / 4C			*01/04/1895*	*??/07/1989*	LNWR	
URALITE HALT	60 / 3C			01/07/1906	04/12/1961	SECR	Built to serve adjacent British Uralite plc. works; opened for workers only early 1901, to public 01/07/1906.
UXBRIDGE (1st)	21 / 2C	P G		04/07/1904 *04/07/1904*	04/12/1938 *01/05/1939*	MET	Served by District Line 01/03/1910 - 23/10/1933, Piccadilly Line thereafter until closure. Closed to passengers 04/12/1938 and replaced by Uxbridge (2nd) to west, goods yard remained open until 01/05/1939 (became sidings).
UXBRIDGE (2nd)	21 / 3C			04/12/1938	N/A	LPTB (MET / PIC)	Replaced 1st station, closed on same date. Closed 18/07/2014 – 11/08/2014 (track renewal).

Name	Page / grid		Date opened	Date closed	Opened by	Notes
UXBRIDGE HIGH STREET	21 / 2B	P G	01/05/1907 11/05/1914	01/09/1939 24/02/1964	GWR	Goods yard open 11/05/1914. No passenger service 01/01/1917 - 03/05/1920, withdrawn for good 01/09/1939 although 'official' closure not until 25/09/1939. Goods yard closed 24/02/1964 and most of branch abandoned.
UXBRIDGE ROAD	38 / 1A 83		01/11/1869	21/10/1940	WLR	Replaced Shepherd's Bush (MET / GWR) (2nd) to north, located to south of 1844 WLR Shepherd's Bush station. Shepherd's Bush (NR) station opened slightly to north of site 28/09/2008.
UXBRIDGE ROAD GOODS Shepherd's Bush Goods	38 / 1A 83		??/??/1844	01/11/1967	WLR	Goods yard to north of Shepherd's Bush (WLR) station, probably not open continuously in early years. Subsequently re-named after Uxbridge Road passenger station (opened 01/11/1869).
Uxbridge Road Junction	38 / 1A 83		01/07/1864	01/03/1954	WLR / MET/ GWR	Junction at southern end of spur to Latimer Road, 'up' platform of present-day Shepherd's Bush NR station occupies site of junction.
UXBRIDGE SIDINGS	21 / 3C		??/??/1942	N/A	LPTB (MET)	Metropolitan Line stabling sidings. On site of former Goods yard, closed 01/05/1939 (see Uxbridge [1st]).
UXBRIDGE VINE STREET Uxbridge	21 / 3C	P G	08/09/1856 08/09/1856	N/A 13/07/1964	GWR	'Vine Street' suffix added 01/05/1907. Passenger station closed with withdrawal of passenger services on branch10/09/1962, goods yard closed and branch abandoned 13/07/1964.

V

Name	Page / grid		Date opened	Date closed	Opened by	Notes
VAN DEN BURGHS & JURGENS (PURFLEET)	44 / 4C		?	N/A	PRIV	Stork margarine manufacturers, disused but still in situ.
VAUXHALL Vauxhall Bridge	39 / 3B		11/07/1848	N/A	LSWR	Victoria Line station opened 23/07/1971. No dedicated goods yard, but milk traffic was handled on platform 1.
VAUXHALL GAS WORKS	39 / 3B		c.1890	1958	PRIV	South Metropolitan Gas Company, 3 foot gauge internal railway system.
Ventnor Road	65 / 4B		03/10/1982	N/A	BR	Point where single track commences on Epsom Downs Branch (singled 03/10/1982).
Viaduct Junction	25 / 6A 83		16/04/1917	09/03/1964	GWR	Through goods route closed on quoted date, but access to Wood Lane milk depot remained until 1966.
VICTORIA	39 / 2A		01/10/1860	N/A	VSPR	Opened by Victoria Station & Pimlico Railway, a joint venture between the LBSCR, LCDR, GWR & LNWR. LBSCR portion opened first, served by LCDR trains from 03/12/1860. Separate LCDR station opened 25/08/1862. LBSCR and LCDR stations reconstructed 1908 and 1907-9 respectively, entire station combined by SR 1924 and platforms numbered consecutively 21/09/1925. MDR station opened 24/12/1868, connected to mainline termini via a subway 12/08/1878. Victoria Line platforms opened 07/03/1969 (terminus until 23/07/1971).
VICTORIA & ALBERT GOODS	41 /1C 62 / 3B		??/??/1902	?	GWR	GWR goods depot accessed via Gallions Branch, opened 1902, closure date unknown.
VICTORIA (GROSVENOR) CARRIAGE SHED	39 / 3A		c.1860s	N/A	LCDR	Was in situ by early 1870s.
VICTORIA PARK Victoria Park, Hackney Wick	27 / 3C		14/06/1856	08/11/1943	NLR	Initially opened for a single day 29/05/1856 (celebrations for end of Crimean War), date quoted is date of full opening. Sometimes referred to as 'Victoria Park, Hackney Wick' until c.1859. Resited South 01/03/1866 with four platforms at new site. Stratford-bound 'down' platform little used and removed 1895, with all GER trains reversing via the 'up' platform ex-Stratford. Former GER platform abandoned 01/11/1942 followed by former NLR platforms 08/11/1943.
VICTORIA PARK & BOW	27 / 4D 88		02/04/1849	06/01/1851	LBLR / ECR	Exchange platforms between ECR and LBLR (Blackwall Extension Railway), opened with latter route from Stepney (East) Junction. LBLR platforms closed 26/09/1850, ECR platforms closed 06/01/1851. Also referred to as 'Old Ford'.
Victoria Park Junction	27 / 3C		15/08/1854	03/10/1983	NLR / ECR	Poplar Branch singled 19/08/1979, officially closed 03/10/1983 (little or no traffic subsequent to Harrow Lane Sidings closure 30/08/1981). Junction points eliminated and remainder of branch dismantled 05/05/1984.
VICTORIA ROAD GOODS (ROMFORD)	18 / 6D		??/07/1896	04/05/1970	LTSR	
VIRGINIA WATER Virginia Water for Wentworth Virginia Water	47 / 5B		09/07/1856	N/A	LSWR	Suffix 'for Wentworth' January 1929 – 1955.
Virginia Water East Junction	47 / 5B		01/10/1866	??/06/1966	LSWR	Junction at east end of Virginia Water West Curve.
Virginia Water Junction Virginia Water North Junction	47 / 5B		01/10/1866	N/A	LSWR	
Virginia Water South Junction	47 / 5B		01/10/1866	??/06/1966	LSWR	Junction at west end of Virginia Water West Curve.
Virginia Water West Curve	47 / 5B	P G	N/A 01/10/1866	N/A ??/06/1966	LSWR	Opened 1866 as single track (at same time as line to Chertsey, 01/10/1866?). No regular passenger service. Had been doubled by 1914 per OS. Closed June 1966.
Voltaire Road Junction	39 / 5A		early 1980s	N/A	BR	Junction installed during Victoria resignalling late 1970s / early 1980s.
VOPAK (PURFLEET)	44 / 5D		?	?	PRIV	Formerly Van Ommeren. Petrochemical / liquid gas storage and distribution, still active but rail connection removed.

W

Name	Page / grid		Date opened	Date closed	Opened by	Notes
WADDON	66 / 2B	P G	??/02/1863 ??/02/1863	N/A 07/10/1968	LBSCR	Exact opening date unknown, first appeared in timetables February 1863. Goods yard closed 07/10/1968.
WADDON MARSH Waddon Marsh Halt	66 / 2B		06/07/1930	N/A	SR	Opened by SR at time of electrification with an island platform and passing loop on otherwise single passenger line. Suffix 'Halt' dropped 05/05/1969. Passing loop decommissioned 13/05/1984. Wimbledon to West Croydon closed by Railtrack 31/05/1997 (date of last train; official date of closure 02/06/1997). Re-opened by Croydon Tramlink on new site to the south 30/05/2000.
WALLINGTON Carshalton	66 / 3A	P G	10/05/1847 10/05/1847	N/A 06/05/1963	LBSCR	Renamed 01/09/1868. Goods yard closed 06/05/1963. Reversing siding west of station installed c.1916, present on 1956-7 OS, possibly decommissioned with signal box 26/11/1972. Station extensively rebuilt 13/09/1983.
WALTHAM CROSS Waltham Cross (& Abbey) Waltham Cross Waltham	7 / 1C	P G	15/09/1840 15/09/1840	N/A 04/07/1966	NER	Opened as 'Waltham', suffix 'Cross' added 01/12/1882. Passenger station closed and relocated South 1885 (exact date unknown). Suffix '& Abbey' in use 01/05/1894 – 20/02/1969. Goods yard closed 04/07/1966.

Name	Page / grid		Date opened	Date closed	Opened by	Notes
WALTHAMSTOW CENTRAL Hoe Street, Walthamstow Hoe Street	15 / 5D	P G	26/04/1870 26/04/1870	N/A 02/11/1964	GER	Originally single platform on 'up' side, Shern Hall Street to Clapton Junction doubled 1873 and 'down' platform built. Opened as 'Hoe Street'; suffix 'Walthamstow' added 1886, although this was often omitted. Goods yard closed 02/11/1964. Renamed 'Walthamstow Central' 06/05/1968. LTB Victoria Line terminus opened 01/09/1968.
WALTHAMSTOW QUEEN'S ROAD Walthamstow	15 / 5D		09/07/1894	N/A	TFGR	Suffix 'Queen's Road' added 06/05/1968, see 'Queen's Road Goods' entry for goods yard (remote from station).
WALTON-ON-THAMES Walton for Hersham Walton & Hersham Walton	62 / 2B	P G	21/05/1838 21/05/1838	N/A c.1965	LSWR	Opened as 'Walton', suffix '& Hersham' added 1849, became 'Walton for Hersham' 1913, then 'Walton-on-Thames' 30/09/1935.
WALWORTH ROAD Camberwell Gate	39 / 3D		01/05/1863	03/04/1916	LCDR	Renamed January 1865.
WALWORTH ROAD COAL	39 / 2D		16/11/1871	30/04/1973	MID	
WANDLE PARK	66 / 2C		30/05/2000	N/A	CTL	
WANDSWORTH BASIN	38 / 5B		01/06/1804	31/08/1846	SIR	Wandsworth terminus of SIR. Railway operational as far south as Summerstown by October 1802, but per Jackson the basin at Wandsworth was not in use until 01/06/1804.
WANDSWORTH COMMON Wandsworth	52 / 1D	P G	01/12/1856 c.1869	N/A 28/09/1964	WELCPR	Opened as 'Wandsworth', suffix 'Common' added January 1858. WELCPR's temporary London terminus until 29/03/1858 extension to Pimlico (WELCPR). After this date both Wandsworth Common and New Wandsworth to north were open concurrently, until Wandsworth Common's closure 01/06/1858. When New Wandsworth closed 01/11/1869, it was replaced by the second 'Wandsworth Common' slightly to the south of the 01/12/1856 station. Goods yard given as opening c.1869 in Borley (at same time as 2nd passenger station?), closed 28/09/1964.
WANDSWORTH ROAD	39 / 4A 82		01/03/1863	N/A	LCDR	Original (western) platforms opened by LCDR 01/03/1863 on 25/08/1862 route, closed 01/01/1867, re-opened by LBSCR 01/05/1867. Eastern platforms opened by LCDR with its 01/01/1867 route, closed 03/04/1916
WANDSWORTH ROAD GOODS	39 / 4A 82		??/??/1874	30/04/1973	MID	
WANDSWORTH TOWN Wandsworth	38 / 5C		27/07/1846	N/A	LSWR	Original site slightly to west of present (on current Smugglers Way, formerly North Street). Relocated to current site on Old York Road c.1860. Line quadrupled 1886. Renamed 07/10/1903.
WANSTEAD	16 / 6C		14/12/1947	N/A	LPTB (CEN)	
WANSTEAD PARK	28 / 2B		09/07/1894	N/A	TFGR	
WAPPING Wapping & Shadwell	40 / 1B		07/12/1869	N/A	ELR	Northern terminus of ELR until 10/04/1876, suffix '& Shadwell' also dropped on same date. First served MET & MDR 01/10/1884, last served MDR 01/08/1905, no service MET 03/12/1906 – 31/03/1913. Separate 'East London Line' identity introduced during 1980s. Closed 25/03/1995 – 25/03/1998 & 23/12/2007 – 27/04/2010 (engineering work), upon latter re-opening became TfL (LOROL) station.
WARREN STREET Euston Road	26 / 5A		22/06/1907	N/A	UERL (CCEHR)	Renamed 07/06/1908. Victoria Line platforms opened 01/12/1968 (terminus until 07/03/1969).
WARWICK AVENUE	25 / 5C		31/01/1915	N/A	UERL (BSWR)	
WARWICK ROAD GOODS Kensington Canal Basin	38 / 2B 84		27/05/1844	17/07/1967	WLR	Initially southern extremity of WLR (Kensington Canal Basin). In c.1865 basin filled in and site developed as Warwick Road goods yard accessed from south ex-WLER.
Warwick Road Junction	38 / 3B 84		01/02/1872	N/A	MDR	Curve towards Kensington (Addison Road) built 1869-1870, but no regular use until 01/02/1872. Remodelled as a 'flying' junction 1914.
WATERLOO	39 / 1C 89		11/07/1848	N/A	LSWR	LSWR terminus, replacing Nine Elms station. Known alternatively as 'Waterloo Bridge' until 1882. Expanded 03/08/1860 (Windsor or 'North' station), link to SER opened 11/01/1864 (only used July 1865 - December 1867). Expanded again 16/12/1878 ('South' station), further platforms added November 1885, 1909, 06/03/1910. Connection to SER removed 26/03/1911. Designations of 'North', 'Central' and 'South' stations removed and platforms renumbered 01/10/1912. Station rebuilt to pre-Eurostar form, official opening 21/03/1922. WCIR platforms opened 08/08/1898, UERL (BSWR) 10/03/1906, UERL (CCEHR) 13/09/1926, LUL (JUB) 24/09/1999 (terminus until 20/11/1999). Waterloo & City Line platforms closed 08/08/1992 – 06/09/1992 & 28/05/1995 – 19/07/1993, transferred to LUL 01/04/1994. Bakerloo Line platforms closed 10/11/1996 – 14/07/1997. Eurostar services terminated here 14/11/1994 – 14/11/2007 (unadvertised trial services commenced 17/08/1994), dedicated platforms 20-24 then abandoned until 23/10/2013, when platform 20 re-opened for domestic services (as a contingency), followed by timetabled services from 18/05/2014. Platforms 21-24 to re-open by 2019.
Waterloo Curve	82	P G	17/08/1994 17/08/1994	14/11/2007 N/A	RT	Date quoted is start of trial Eurostar service, advertised service commenced 14/11/1994. Disused since 14/11/2007 (diversion of Eurostar to St Pancras), but chord still in situ and traversed by test trains / railtours. Briefly blocked late 2011 but reinstated.
WATERLOO DEPOT	39 / 1C 89		08/08/1898	N/A	WCIR	Waterloo & City Line depot.
WATERLOO EAST Waterloo Waterloo Junction	39 / 1C 89		01/01/1869	N/A	SER	Replaced Blackfriars (SER) station to the east. Opened as 'Waterloo Junction', connection to Waterloo LSWR opened 11/01/1864, but only used July 1865 - December 1867 (i.e. before station opened), and taken out of use 26/03/1911. Suffix 'Junction' dropped 07/07/1935, renamed 'Waterloo East' 02/05/1977. Closed 24/07/1993 – 16/08/1993.
WATFORD	2 / 4B	P G	02/11/1925 02/11/1925	??/??/2017 14/11/1966	MET / LNER	Not intended to be terminus (see Watford Central below). Goods yard closed 14/11/1966. Proposed to close 2017 when 'Croxley Link' built (but to remain as stabling sidings).
WATFORD CENTRAL	2 / 4C		N/A	N/A	MET / LNER	Envisaged as terminus of MET / LNER Watford branch, station building remains ('Moon Under Water' pub).
WATFORD HIGH STREET	2 / 4C		01/10/1862	N/A	WRR	Served by London Underground Bakerloo Line Trains 16/04/1917 - 27/09/1982. Proposed to be served by Metropolitan Line from 2017.
Watford High Street Junction	5 / 5C		10/02/1913	25/03/1996	LNWR	Last train ran ex-Croxley Green 22/03/1996 (no weekend service), but junction not severed until 2005. To be re-established 2017.
Watford East Junction	1 / 5D		02/11/1925	N/A	MET / LNER	

Name	Page / grid		Date opened	Date closed	Opened by	Notes
WATFORD JUNCTION Watford	2 / 3C	P G	20/07/1837 20/07/1837	N/A ??/??/1965	LBIR	Opened as 'Watford', re-sited south and suffix 'Junction' added 05/05/1858 coinciding with opening of the St Albans (Abbey) branch. Served by London Underground Bakerloo Line Trains 06/04/1917 - 27/09/1982. Former goods yard (closed to public goods traffic 1965) now used as Civil Engineers' sidings. To become terminus of LUL Metropolitan Line from 2017 (diversion from Watford station via 'Croxley Link').
WATFORD NORTH Callowland	2 / 2C	P G	01/10/1910 01/10/1910	N/A ??/??/1988	LNWR	Renamed 01/03/1927. Goods yard situated to north, opened with passenger station. General goods traffic ceased 01/04/1970, but remained open for heating oil, later M25 construction materials, finally dog food, until 1988 closure.
Watford North Curve	1 / 5D	P G	02/11/1925 02/11/1925	N/A N/A	MET / LNER	Used by early morning and late night passenger services only. Normal daytime passenger service in operation 02/11/1925 - 31/12/1933 06/10/1941 - 03/01/1960, proposed to be reinstated for and an Aylesbury to Watford Junction service operated by Chiltern if 'Croxley Link' built.
Watford North Junction (1)	1 / 6D		02/11/1925	N/A	MET / LNER	
Watford North Junction (2)	2 / 3B		??/??/1874	N/A	LNWR	
Watford South Curve	1 / 6D	P	02/11/1925	N/A	MET / LNER	
		G	02/11/1925	N/A		
Watford South Junction (1)	1 / 6D		02/11/1925	N/A	MET / LNER	
Watford South Junction (2)	2 / 3C		01/10/1862	N/A	WRR / LNWR	
WATFORD STADIUM	2 / 5B		04/12/1982	14/05/1993	BR	Opened using funds from Watford FC. Only served on Match days, last recorded train 14/05/1993. Not proposed to re-open when 'Croxley Link' built (replaced by Watford Vicarage Road immediately to west).
Watford Tunnels	2 / 1B		20/07/1837	N/A	LBIR	Original tunnel used by 'fast' roads, second bore used by 'slow' roads added by LNWR 1874.
WATFORD VICARAGE ROAD	2 / 5B		??/??/2017	N/A	LUL (MET)	Proposed new station on re-opened Croxley Green branch (funding announcement 14/12/2011, expected opening 2017). Immediately to west of former Watford Stadium station, to replace this and former Watford West stations.
WATFORD WEST	2 / 5B		15/06/1912	25/03/1996	LNWR	Last train ran on Croxley Green Branch 22/03/1996 (no weekend service), initially closed 'temporarily' for bridge work, replaced by bus service which ran until 26/09/2003. Not proposed to re-open when 'Croxley Link' built (replaced by Watford Vicarage Road).
Watford West Junction	2 / 5C		15/06/1912	02/01/1967	LNWR	
WELLESLEY ROAD	66 / 2D		10/05/2000	N/A	CTL	
WELLING	42 / 5C	P G	01/05/1895 01/05/1895	N/A 03/12/1962	BHR	Goods yard closed 03/12/1962.
WELLINGTON SIDINGS	13 / 5D		??/??/1867	01/10/1962	GNR	Goods sidings in use in 1867, Carriage sheds opened 1881. Latter used by Northern Line Trains after 1940, BR use ceased 01/10/1962. Now Highgate Wood Depot (Northern Line).
WELSH HARP	12 / 6D		02/05/1870	01/07/1903	MID	For excursion traffic to Brent Reservoir (Welsh Harp).
WEMBLEY CENTRAL Wembley (for Sudbury) Sudbury & Wembley Sudbury	24 / 2A	P G	08/08/1842 08/08/1842	N/A 04/01/1965	LBIR	Opened as 'Sudbury', '& Wembley' suffix added 01/05/1882. Became 'Wembley for Sudbury' 01/11/1910, renamed 'Wembley Central' 05/07/1948. Served by Bakerloo Line Trains 16/04/1917 – 24/09/1982, 04/06/1984 – present. Goods yard closed 04/01/1965.
Wembley Central Junction	24 / 3A		15/06/1912	N/A	LNWR	
WEMBLEY DEPOT	24 / 2B 22		30/06/2005	N/A	NR	Chiltern Railways light maintenance depot.
WEMBLEY PARK	24 / 1B	P G	12/05/1894 12/05/1894	N/A 05/07/1965	MET	Additional pair of terminal platforms south of road bridge built for British Empire Exhibition 1924 ('Exhibition Station', after exhibition used for football traffic). Reduced to a single platform 1931, demolished 1937. Served by Bakerloo Line Trains 20/11/1939 - 01/05/1979, Jubilee Line thereafter. Goods yard Transferred to LNER 01/12/1937, closed 05/07/1965.
WEMBLEY PARK SIDINGS	24 / 1A		c.1894	N/A	MET	First two sidings laid to facilitate construction of adjacent station, so slightly predate 12/05/1894. Much expanded with 9-road carriage shed 1926, demolished 2005 and replaced by 5 open air sidings.
WEMBLEY STADIUM (LNER) Wembley Exhibition Exhibition Station, Wembley	24 / 2B 22	P G	28/04/1923 ??/??/1921	18/05/1968 03/12/1962	LNER	Renamed 'Wembley Stadium' 15/09/1927, name varied before this date. Loop last used 18/05/1968, officially closed 01/09/1969, dismantled 19/10/1969. Goods yard in use 1921 - 03/12/1962.
WEMBLEY STADIUM (GCR) Wembley Complex Wembley Hill	24 / 2A		01/03/1906	N/A	GCR	Opened as 'Wembley Hill', renamed 'Wembley Complex' 08/05/1978, renamed 'Wembley Stadium' 11/05/1987.
WEMBLEY YARD	24 / 3A 68 / 5A		c.1912	N/A	LNWR	First sidings appeared on site by 1912, subsequently expanded. New freight distribution centre opened 06/09/1993.
Wembley Yard South Junction	68 / 3C		c.1912	N/A	LNWR	
WEST ACTON	24 / 6B		05/11/1923	N/A	UERL (CEN)	Line through station opened by GWR 16/04/1917 (goods only) with UERL passenger trains commencing 03/08/1920. Station built by UERL, opening 05/11/1923.
WEST BROMPTON	38 / 3B 84		01/09/1866	N/A	WLER	MDR platforms opened 12/04/1869 as terminus from Gloucester Road, line extended to Putney Bridge 01/03/1880. Main line platforms closed 21/10/1940 and subsequently demolished, but rebuilt and re-opened 30/05/1999.
WEST BYFLEET Byfleet for Woodham & Pyrford Byfleet & Woodham	61 / 5A	P G	01/12/1887 01/12/1887	N/A c.1965	LSWR	Opened as 'Byfleet & Woodham', renamed 'Byfleet for Woodham & Pyrford' 1913, then 'West Byfleet' 05/06/1950.
WEST CENTRAL DISTRICT OFFICE	26 / 6B		13/02/1928	c.2000	POR	Had become disused prior to mothballing of POR on 31/05/2003.
WEST CROYDON Croydon	66 / 1C		05/06/1839	N/A	LCRR	Country terminus of LCRR until 10/05/1847, original terminus was 'up' bay, current through platforms added on Epsom extension on this date. Gained prefix 'West' 1850 (sometimes reversed to 'Croydon West') per Borley, Mitchell & Smith refer to opening as 'Croydon', becoming 'Croydon Town' May 1847, then 'West Croydon' April 1851. Engine shed closed 1935. No record of goods facilities. Bay platform for Wimbledon services closed 02/06/1997. Tramlink platform opened 10/05/2000.
West Croydon Junction (1st) Croydon Junction	86		12/07/1841	N/A	LBRR / LCRR	Divergence of original LBRR and LCRR routes, current junction location just south of Norwood Junction station, but original junction (Croydon Junction) was further south near present Norwood Fork Junction.

Name	Page / grid		Date opened	Date closed	Opened by	Notes
West Croydon Junction (2nd)	66 / 2C		22/10/1855	02/06/1997	LBSCR / WCRR	
West Croydon Spur	66 / 1D 86	P G	22/05/1865 22/05/1865	??/10/1983 ??/10/1983	LBSCR	Opened on same day as Epsom Downs Branch. Closed due to Gloucester Road Triangle remodelling October 1983.
WEST DRAYTON West Drayton & Yiewsley West Drayton	34 / 1C		04/06/1838	N/A	GWR	Served by MDR trains 01/03/1883 - 01/10/1885. Re-sited east 09/08/1884. Suffix '& Yiewsley' added 1895.
WEST DRAYTON COAL	21 / 6B		18/12/1963	07/04/1999	PRIV	Lafarge stone terminal now on site.
WEST DULWICH Dulwich	53 / 1D		??/10/1863	N/A	LCDR	Opened as 'Dulwich', first in Bradshaw October 1863. 'West' prefix added 20/09/1926.
WEST EALING Castle Hill, Ealing Dean Castle Hill	23 / 6C	P G	01/03/1871 01/03/1871	N/A 23/05/1980	GWR	Opened as 'Castle Hill', suffix 'Ealing Dean' added ??/06/1875. Served by District Railway 01/03/1883 – 01/10/1885. Renamed 'West Ealing' 01/07/1899. 'New' goods yard opened 03/02/1908, 'Old' goods yard closed ??/11/1968. Platform 1 removed ??/11/1973. Milk dock closed c.1978, 'New' goods yard closed 23.05.1980. Platform 4 (up slow) originally east of bridge, re-sited to west 1991.
West Ealing Junction	23 / 6C		03/06/1903	N/A	GWR	
West Ealing West Loop Hanwell Loop	23 / 6C	P G	15/06/1903 03/06/1903	10/10/1905 N/A	GWR	Initially used by temporary goods (03/06/1903) and passenger (15/06/1903) services serving the Park Royal Royal Agricultural showground, disused 04/07/1903 (passenger) 10/08/1903 (goods) - 01/05/1904. Regular passenger services ceased 10/10/1905. Originally 'Hanwell Loop', became 'West Ealing West Loop' in the 1950s. Singled at southern end 1974.
WEST END SIDINGS	25 / 3B		??/??/1868	??/??/1968	MID	
WEST FINCHLEY	13 / 3C		01/03/1933	N/A	LNER	First served by and transferred to LPTB Northern Line 14/04/1940, closed to LNER passenger services on same date.
WEST GREEN	14 / 5D	P G	01/01/1878 01/01/1878	N/A 05/10/1964	GER	Station and entire Palace Gates Branch closed to passengers 07/01/1963. Goods yard closed 05/10/1964.
WEST HAM West Ham Manor Road West Ham	28 / 5A		01/02/1901	N/A	LTSR	First served by District Railway 02/06/1902, line quadrupled 1905, District trains then using 'slow' platforms to north. Served by Metropolitan Line since 30/03/1936 ('Hammersmith & City Line' since 30/07/1990). Carried suffix 'Manor Road' between 11/02/1924 - ??/01/1969. 'Fast' platforms abandoned 01/01/1916, taken out of use 1940, demolished 1956. Low Level (BR) Platforms opened 14/05/1979, closed 29/05/1994 – 29/10/1995, then again 10/12/2006 for conversion to DLR, re-opening 31/08/2011. 'Fast' (former LTSR) Platforms re-built and re-opened 30/05/1999. Jubilee Line Platforms opened 14/05/1999.
WEST HAM SOUTH GOODS	28 / 6C 62 / 3B		c.1892	07/12/1964	GER	
WEST HAMPSTEAD (MSJWR)	25 / 3B		30/06/1879	N/A	MSJWR	Country terminus of MSJWR until 24/11/1879. Last served Metropolitan Line 07/12/1940. Served by Bakerloo Line 20/11/1939 - 01/05/1979, Jubilee thereafter.
WEST HAMPSTEAD (LNWR) West End Lane	25 / 3B		01/03/1888	N/A	LNWR	Renamed 05/05/1975. Closed 29/10/1995 - 29/09/1996 (engineering works).
WEST HAMPSTEAD THAMESLINK West Hampstead Midland West Hampstead West End & Brondesbury* West End West End (For Kilburn & Hampstead)	25 / 3B	P G	01/03/1871 01/03/1871	N/A 03/08/1970	MID	Opened as 'West End (for Kilburn & Hampstead)', suffix dropped 01/07/1903. Renamed 'West End & Brondesbury' 01/04/1904*, then 'West Hampstead' 01/09/1905. Renamed 'West Hampstead Midland' 25/09/1950, 'Thameslink' substituted for 'Midland' 16/05/1988. Goods yard closed 03/08/1970. Rebuilt with a new entrance on Iverson Road, opening 14/12/2011. *Discrepancy between Borley and Quick; Quick states 'West Hampstead & Brondesbury' 01/04/1904 - 01/09/1905
WEST HARROW	11 / 6A		17/11/1913	N/A	MET	
WEST HORNDON East Horndon	32 / 1D	P G	01/05/1886 01/05/1886	N/A 07/09/1964	LTSR	Country terminus of LTSR from opening until 01/06/1888. Served by District Line excursion trains between 01/06/1910 and 30/09/1939. Renamed 01/05/1949. Goods yard closed 07/09/1964.
WEST INDIA DOCKS	40 / 1D 31 / 4A	P G	06/07/1840 c.1892	04/05/1926 06/11/1967	LBLR	Goods yard to north east of passenger station on a lower level, Midland Railway coal yard adjacent.
WEST INDIA QUAY	40 / 1D 31 / 6A		31/08/1987	N/A	DLR	Closed 14/10/1991 (last train 11/10/1991) - 28/06/1993 due to reconstruction. Original platform 1 closed 2008 and demolished to make way for new diveunder, in consequence eastbound trains ex-Bank ceased serving after 24/08/2009.
WEST KENSINGTON North End (Fulham)	38 / 2B 84		09/09/1874	N/A	MDR	Renamed 01/03/1877. Adjacent goods yard opened by Midland Railway (see entry below).
WEST KENSINGTON GOODS & COAL	38 / 3B 84		25/03/1878	14/07/1965	MID	
West Kensington East Junction	38 / 2B 84		09/09/1874	N/A	MDR	Junction between 1872 route to WLER and 1874 extension to Hammersmith.
West Kensington West Junction	38 / 2A 84		25/03/1878	14/07/1965	MDR / MID	Junction allowing access to West Kensington Goods.
West London Extension Junction	84		02/03/1863	01/01/1923	WLR / WLER	'End on' junction between WLR and WLER, elimination given here nominally as date of Grouping.
WEST LONDON JUNCTION	24 / 4D 91		27/05/1844	01/12/1844	WLR / LBIR	Exchange platforms built for traffic between WLR / LBIR, abandoned when WLR passenger services ceased.
West London Junction (1st)	91		27/05/1844	N/A	WLR / LBIR	
West London Junction (2nd)	24 / 5D 91		??/10/1860	27/10/1990	GWR	Junction between 'West London Loop' (linking WLR and GWR) and GWR main line.
West London Junction (3rd)	38 / 4D		06/07/1865	N/A	WLER /	Junction eliminated 21/01/1936 - 17/08/1994.
West London Loop	91	P G	??/10/1860 ??/10/1860	27/10/1990 27/10/1990	GWR	Country-facing connection between GWR and WLR.
WEST LONDON WASTE TRANSFER STATION	22 / 2D		??/??/1980	N/A	PRIV	
WEST NORWOOD Lower Norwood	53 / 2C		01/12/1856	N/A	WELCPR	Opened as 'Lower Norwood', renamed 01/01/1886.
West Norwood Junction	53 / 2C		01/11/1870	N/A	LBSCR	Junction at south end of West Norwood Spur.
West Norwood Spur	53 / 2C	P G	01/11/1870 01/11/1870	N/A N/A	LBSCR	
WEST PARK HOSPITAL	64 / 5A		??/??/1918	??/??/1950	PRIV	Horton Estate Light Railway opened to supply building materials, later fuel, to hospitals.
WEST RUISLIP West Ruislip (For Ickenham)	22 / 1A	P G	02/04/1906 02/04/1906	N/A 06/10/1975	GCR / GWR	Opened as 'Ruislip & Ickenham', renamed 'West Ruislip for Ickenham' 30/06/1947. First served by LTE Central Line 21/11/1948 as terminus,

Name	Page / grid		Date opened	Date closed	Opened by	Notes
Ruislip & Ickenham						suffix 'for Ickenham' gradually dropped thereafter. Goods yard closed 06/10/1975. Down slow line removed and down platform widened to abut former down fast line ??/05/1990.
WEST SIDINGS (SOUTHALL)	35 / 1D		*c.1860*	N/A	GWR	First sidings on site by late 1860s, expanded to current layout in early 20th Century. Southernmost 3 sidings referred to as 'Down Yard'.
WEST SILVERTOWN	41 / 1B 62 / 5A		02/12/2005	N/A	DLR	
WEST SUTTON	65 / 3B		05/01/1930	N/A	SR	
West Thurrock Junction	45 / 4A		01/07/1892	N/A	LTSR	Third road added between here and Grays for Upminster trains early 1960.
WEST THURROCK POWER STATION	45 / 4A		*??/??/1962*	*??/??/1993*	PRIV	
WEST THURROCK SIDINGS	45 / 4A		*c.1940*	N/A	LMS	Not present on 1920 OS map, but had appeared by 1947. Officially 'disused' and still connected, but overgrown.
WEST WICKHAM	67 / 1D	P G	29/05/1882 *29/05/1882*	N/A *02/09/1963*	SER	Goods yard closed 02/09/1963.
WEST YARD (RIPPLE LANE)	29 / 5C		*c.1940*	N/A	LMS	See entry for 'Ripple Lane Yard'.
WESTBOURNE PARK Westbourne Park & Kensal Green	25 / 5B 67 / 5A		01/02/1866	N/A	MET / GWR	Opened as 'Westbourne Park & Kensal Green' (HCR only), re-sited west and suffix dropped 30/10/1871. GWR main line services not thought to call until 01/11/1871. BR platforms closed 16/03/1992, remaining platforms had previously transferred to LTE ownership 01/01/1970.
WESTCOMBE PARK Coombe Farm Lane	41 / 3B		01/05/1879	N/A	SER	Opened as 'Coombe Farm Lane', renamed later in 1879.
WESTERN DISTRICT OFFICE (1st)	26 / 6A		*05/12/1927*	*03/08/1965*	POR	Replaced by Western District Office (2nd) to east.
WESTERN DISTRICT OFFICE (2nd)	26 / 6A		*03/08/1965*	*31/05/2003*	POR	Replaced by Western District Office (1st) and Western Parcels Office, construction involved diverting POR route with original tunnels becoming abandoned. Open until POR mothballing 31/05/2003.
WESTERN PARCELS OFFICE	25 / 6D		*05/12/1927*	*03/08/1965*	POR	Replaced by Western District Office (2nd) to east.
WESTFERRY	40 / 1D		31/08/1987	N/A	DLR	
WESTMINSTER Westminster Bridge	39 / 1B		24/12/1868	N/A	MDR	Terminus until 30/05/1870. Renamed 1907. Jubilee Line platforms opened and station rebuilt 22/12/1999.
WEYBRIDGE Weybridge Junction Weybridge	61 / 3D	P G	21/05/1838 *21/05/1838*	N/A *c.1965*	LSWR	Carried suffix 'Junction' 1848 - 1858/9.
Weybridge Junction	61 / 3D		14/02/1848	N/A	LSWR	Junction between LSWR main line and branch to Chertsey (later Virginia Water).
Wharncliffe Viaduct	23 / 6B		04/06/1838	N/A	GWR	GWR main line crossing of the Brent Valley.
Wheeler Street (or Bishopsgate) Junction	27 / 5A 90		10/04/1876	N/A	GER / ELR	Originally junction between ELR and GER (severed 17/04/1966), crossovers remain on GER main line.
Whipps Cross Tunnel	16 / 6B		22/08/1856	N/A	ECR	
WHITE CITY (LPTB)	25 / 6A 83		23/11/1947	N/A	LPTB (CEN)	Replaced Wood Lane (CLR) Station.
WHITE CITY (MET / GWR) Wood Lane (White City) Wood Lane (Exhibition)	38 / 1A 83		*01/05/1908*	*25/10/1959*	MET	Opened as 'Wood Lane (Exhibition)', closed to regular traffic 01/11/1914, opened on special occasions thereafter including 12/12/1914 – 29/04/1915 (weekday evenings and weekends for servicemen). Renamed 'Wood Lane (White City)' 07/10/1920, renamed 'White City' 23/11/1947, closed for good 25/10/1959. LUL opened new station 12/10/2008 on opposite side of Wood Lane ('Wood Lane').
WHITE CITY SIDINGS *White City Depot* *Wood Lane Depot*	38 / 1A 83		*30/07/1900*	N/A	CLR	Opened as Wood Lane Depot, the CLR's sole depot. Rearranged as White City Depot 1949, replaced by new facility to west 15/01/2007 which was subsequently rafted over and covered by Westfield shopping centre. Referred to as 'White City Sidings' at current location.
WHITE HART LANE	15 / 3A	P G	22/07/1872 *22/07/1872*	N/A *02/07/1977*	GER	Goods yard closed to public traffic ??/01/1968, saw some private traffic until 02/07/1977.
WHITECHAPEL Whitechapel (Mile End)	27 / 6B 90		10/04/1876	N/A	ELR	MDR platforms opened 06/10/1884 (terminus until 02/06/1902). 'Whitechapel (Mile End)' until 13/11/1901, suffix then dropped. MDR platforms served by MET 03/12/1906 – 31/03/1913 then again 30/03/1936 – present ('Hammersmith & City Line' since 30/07/1990). ELR platforms first served by MET 31/03/1913, later became 'East London Line', closed 25/03/1995 - 25/03/1998 and 22/12/2007 - 27/04/2010 (engineering works). LUL platforms reduced from 4 to 2 31/01/2011. Platforms for 'Crossrail 1' to open 2018.
Whitechapel Junction	27 / 6B 90		01/10/1884	23/12/2007	SER / ELR	Junction at southern end of St Mary's Curve.
WHITECROSS STREET GOODS	32 / 3D		*c.1880*	*pre-1965*	MID	Appeared between 1875 and 1896 OS. Present on 1954 OS, but site cleared for 1965 re-alignment of railway.
WHITTON	36 / 6A		06/07/1930	N/A	SR	
Whitton Junction	36 / 6A		01/01/1883	N/A	LSWR	Junction at south end of Hounslow Spur.
WHYTELEAFE	73 / 2D	P G	01/01/1900 *01/01/1900*	N/A *28/09/1964*	SECR	
WHYTELEAFE SOUTH Warlingham	74 / 3A		05/08/1856	N/A	CR	Opened as 'Warlingham', renamed 'Whyteleafe South' 11/06/1956.
WILLESDEN	24 / 4C 68 / 6C		*early 1841*	*01/09/1866*	LBIR	Exact opening date unknown; thought to be 1841 before 10/06/1841. On Acton Lane Adjacent to current Harlesden station, replaced by Willesden Junction to east 01/09/1866.
WILLESDEN BRENT SIDINGS	24 / 4B 68 / 5C		*c.1890*	N/A	LNWR	First sidings appeared on site c.1890.
WILLESDEN EURO TERMINAL	24 / 4C 91 & 92		*??/??/1967*	N/A	BR	On site of Willesden North Carriage Sidings. Container traffic ceased c.2006, only engineering traffic remains.
WILLESDEN 'F' SIDINGS	24 / 3B 68 / 2C		*c.1940*	N/A	LMS	Sidings appeared between the late 1930s and mid-1950s.
WILLESDEN GREEN Willesden Green & Cricklewood Willesden Green	25 / 3A		24/11/1879	N/A	MSJWR	Country terminus of MSJWR until 02/08/1880 (by which time it had been absorbed by MET). Suffix '& Cricklewood' 01/06/1894 - 1938. Last served Metropolitan Line 07/12/1940. First served by Bakerloo Line 20/11/1939, transferred to Jubilee Line 01/05/1979. Goods yard remote from station (see separate entry below).
WILLESDEN GREEN GOODS	24 / 2D		*??/??/1899*	*03/01/1966*	MET	
Willesden High Level Junction	24 / 5C 91 & 92		20/07/1885	N/A	LNWR	
WILLESDEN JUNCTION	24 / 4D 91 & 92	P G	01/09/1866 *01/09/1866*	N/A *?*	LNWR / HJR	Replaced 'Willesden' station to west (closed on same date). Initially platforms on LNWR main line (low level) and original 1860 HJR

Name	Page / grid		Date opened	Date closed	Opened by	Notes
						route (high level). Further high level platforms added 02/09/1867 with opening of LNWR Mitre Bridge Curve linking HJR and WLR. Original high level platforms closed 20/07/1885 with opening of Kew Curve, which allowed all high level passenger traffic to pass through 02/09/1867 platforms, although the original high level line remained in use until 01/05/1892. Third high level platform (no.11) added 1894 for reversing trains ex-WLR. New low level platforms (2 through and 2 'bay') added for DC electric trains 15/06/1912, served by Bakerloo Line trains since 10/05/1915. Platform 11 abandoned 20/10/1940. All low level platforms except the 'DC line' platforms closed 03/12/1962. One of the low level bays taken out of use c.1964. Goods yard north of station off HJR route, after closure to general goods traffic, sidings remained open to serve works (MG gas products) until c.2000.
Willesden Junction (Acton Branch)	24 / 4C		21/07/1963	N/A	BR	
WILLESDEN SHED	24 / 4C 91		*??/??/1873*	*27/09/1965*	LNWR	Upon closure loco allocation transferred to Willesden TMD, Willesden Euro terminal built on site 1967.
Willesden Suburban Junction	24 / 4D 91 & 92		15/06/1912	N/A	LNWR	
WILLESDEN TRAINCARE CENTRE	24 / 4D 91 & 92		*c.1965*	N/A	BR	Built to replace Willesden Shed, opened on site of former South Carriage Shed.
WILLOW WALK GOODS	40 / 2A 4		*??/??/1847*	*07/03/1932*	LBSCR	Amalgamated with Bricklayers Arms by SR 07/03/1932, but fabric of depot remained in use until 01/08/1977 closure.
WIMBLEDON Wimbledon & Merton	52 / 3A	P G	21/05/1838 *c.1838*	N/A *05/01/1970*	LSWR	Opened as 'Wimbledon & Merton' south of Wimbledon Bridge. Upon its opening on 22/10/1855, the WCRR had a separate terminus, which was incorporated into main station during 1869 rebuilding. Entire station re-sited to north side of bridge 21/11/1881. Current LUL District Line platforms opened 03/06/1889 as a separate station, referred to as 'Wimbledon North' until amalgamated with rest of station 1929. Suffix '& Merton' dropped 01/06/1909. A platform remained in vicinity of original station, south of the bridge, on the north side of the formation, referred to as 'Volunteer Platform' due to military use pre-WWI, subsequently became a milk dock in 1926. There were 3 other goods facilities: Wimbledon West yard (see separate entry), a small yard on the east side of the station, and a larger yard adjacent to Wimbledon North station. All public goods traffic ceased 05/01/1970. Former island platforms 9 & 10 used by trains between Tooting and Sutton reduced to a single through platform 9 to allow formation of a terminal bay for Tramlink, opening 30/05/2000.
WIMBLEDON BOROUGH COUNCIL SIDING	52 / 2B		*??/??/1898*	*??/??/1965*	PRIV	Power station and refuse destructor.
WIMBLEDON CHASE	52 / 4A		07/07/1929	N/A	SR	
Wimbledon East 'A' Junctions	52 / 3B		01/10/1868	N/A	LSWR / LBSCR	
Wimbledon North Junction	52 / 3A		03/06/1889	N/A	LSWR	
WIMBLEDON PARK	52 / 2B		03/06/1889	N/A	LSWR	Putney Bridge to Wimbledon built by LSWR, initially operated by MDR only, LSWR services commenced 01/07/1889. Last regular main line passenger service withdrawn 05/05/1941, although services called on occasions until 1969. Station ownership transferred to LUL 01/04/1994 along with entire Putney Bridge to Wimbledon route.
WIMBLEDON PARK SIDINGS	52 / 2B		*c.1910*	N/A	LSWR	Part of Wimbledon Traincare Depot (SWT). Not present on 1899 OS but had appeared by 1913. Shed erected over six roads nearest the main line c. time of electrification (25/10/1915), now carriage cleaning shed.
Wimbledon South 'B' Junction	52 / 3A		22/10/1855	02/06/1997	LSWR / WCRR	Junction eliminated when Wimbledon to West Croydon line closed prior to conversion to Tramlink.
WIMBLEDON TRAINCARE DEPOT	52 / 2B		*c.1910*	N/A	LSWR	First carriage sidings appeared c.1910 (see 'Wimbledon Park Sidings'). Site expanded to north with Durnsford Road sidings & power station 1915 (see separate entries).
Wimbledon West 'C' Junctions	52 / 4A		07/07/1929	N/A	SR	
WIMBLEDON WEST YARD	52 / 4A		*c.1880*	*c.2000*	LSWR	Sidings on site appeared between 1869-77 and 1895 OS. S&T works and coal yard also on site. Some track remains in situ, but disconnected from running line.
WINCHMORE HILL	6 / 6C	P G	01/04/1871 *01/04/1871*	N/A *01/10/1962*	GNR	Goods yard closed 01/10/1962.
Windmill Bridge Junctions	66 / 1D 86		01/12/1862	N/A	LBSCR	
WINDSOR & ETON CENTRAL Windsor & Eton Windsor	33 / 4B	P G	08/10/1849 *08/10/1849*	N/A *06/01/1964*	GWR	Opened as 'Windsor', suffix '& Eton' added 01/06/1904, further suffix 'Central' added 26/09/1949. Served by MDR trains 01/03/1883 - 01/10/1885. Goods yard closed 06/01/1964. Platforms 3 & 4 decommissioned 17/11/1968, followed by platform 2 05/09/1969. Platform 1 subsequently truncated twice (station rebuilding).
WINDSOR & ETON RIVERSIDE Windsor & Eton Windsor	33 / 4C	P G	01/12/1849 *01/12/1849*	N/A *05/04/1965*	LSWR	Original station temporary, permanent station opened 01/05/1851. Opened as 'Windsor', suffix '& Eton' added 10/12/1903, further suffix 'Riverside' added 26/09/1949. Engine shed probably opened with station and remained in use for a while after electrification (1930). Goods yard closed 05/04/1965.
Windsor Branch Junction Slough East Junction	33 / 1C		08/10/1849	N/A	GWR	
WOLDINGHAM Marden Park	74 / 4B	P G	01/07/1885 *01/07/1885*	N/A *04/05/1959*	LBSCR / SER	Renamed 01/01/1894. Goods yard closed 04/05/1959.
WOOD GREEN	14 / 4C		19/09/1932	N/A	UERL (GNPBR)	
Wood Green North Junction	14 / 4B		01/04/1871	N/A	GNR	Divergence of GNR Enfield Branch (now Hertford Loop) from main Line
Wood Green Tunnels	14 / 3B		07/08/1850	N/A	GNR	
WOOD LANE (CLR)	38 / 1A 83		14/05/1908	23/11/1947	CLR	Terminus of CLR until 03/08/1920 (on terminal loop). After 03/08/1920 through platforms to Ealing Broadway open resulting in triangular formation. Replaced by White City (LPTB) to north 23/11/1947.
WOOD LANE (LUL)	25 / 6A 83		12/10/2008	N/A	LUL (HCL)	
Wood Lane Junction	24 / 6D		03/08/1920	19/06/1938	GWR	Eliminated when parallel freight lines opened to North Acton 19/06/1938
WOOD LANE MILK DEPOT	83		?	*??/??/1966*	PRIV	
WOOD STREET Wood Street, Walthamstow	16 / 5A	P G	17/11/1873 *20/04/1893*	N/A *06/05/1968*	GER	Goods yard in use 20/04/1893 - 06/05/1968. Also referred to as 'Walthamstow Wood Street'. Became 'Wood Street' 18/03/1971. Loco

Name	Page / grid		Date opened	Date closed	Opened by	Notes
						shed and carriage sidings opened ??/03/1897. Loco shed closed 1960 and Carriage Sidings abandoned 1986.
WOODFORD	16 / 3C	P	22/08/1856	N/A	ECR	Platforms originally 'staggered' (up south of down). Majority of passenger services transferred to LPTB 14/12/1947, terminus for Central Line from that date until 21/11/1948. Goods yard closed 18/04/1966. First trains in the morning remained British Rail services until 01/06/1970 (last train 31/05/1970).
		G	22/08/1856	18/04/1966		
Woodford Junction	16 / 2C		20/04/1903	N/A	GER	Divergence of Fairlop Loop (= Hainault Loop) from Epping Line.
WOODFORD SIDINGS	16 / 3C		c.1910	N/A	GER	Central Line stabling sidings, laid by the GER by 1920 (appear on 1920 Ordnance Survey map, but not on 1898).
WOODGRANGE PARK	28 / 3C	P	09/07/1894	N/A	LTSR	Goods yard opened 01/01/1895, closed 07/12/1964.
		G	01/01/1895	07/12/1964		
Woodgrange Park Junction	28 / 3C		09/07/1894	N/A	LTSR / TFGR	
WOODMANSTERNE	72 / 1D		17/07/1932	N/A	SR	
WOODSIDE Woodside & South Norwood Woodside	67 / 1A	P	??/07/1871	N/A	LBSCR / SER	Exact opening date unknown, first appeared in Bradshaw July 1871. Carried suffix '& South Norwood' 01/10/1908 – 02/10/1944. Goods yard closed 30/09/1963. Closed by RT 02/06/1997 (last train 31/05/1997, no Sunday service), re-opened by Croydon Tramlink 23/05/2000.
		G	??/07/1871	30/09/1963		
Woodside Junction	67 / 1A		10/08/1885	16/05/1983	LBSCR / SER	
WOODSIDE PARK Woodside Park for North Finchley Woodside Park Torrington Park, Woodside Torrington Park	13 / 2C	P	01/04/1872	N/A	GNR	Opened as 'Torrington Park', suffix 'Woodside' added 01/05/1872. Renamed 'Woodside Park' 01/05/1882. Suffix 'for North Finchley' added 01/02/1894, dropped by 1927. First served by and transferred to LPTB Northern Line 14/04/1940, closed to LNER passenger services on same date. Goods yard closed 01/10/1962.
		G	01/04/1872	01/10/1962		
WOODSTOCK ROAD	37 / 1C 51 / 1D		08/04/1909	01/01/1917	NSWJR	
WOOLWICH	42 / 2A		??/??/2018	N/A	NR (XRAIL)	Proposed station on Crossrail 1 Abbey Wood branch.
WOOLWICH ARSENAL	42 / 2A	P	01/11/1849	N/A	SER	Goods yard closed 17/05/1965. DLR platforms opened 10/01/2009 (official opening 12/01/2009).
		G	01/11/1849	17/05/1965		
WOOLWICH DOCKYARD Woolwich	41 / 2D		30/07/1849	N/A	SER	Initially simply 'Woolwich', suffix 'Dockyard' added when Woolwich Arsenal station opened 01/11/1849.
WORCESTER PARK Old Malden & Worcester Park	64 / 1C	P	04/04/1859	N/A	LSWR	Renamed February 1862. Goods yard closed 06/05/1963.
		G	04/04/1859	06/05/1963		
WORCESTER PARK BRICKWORKS	64 / 2C		??/??/1898	c.1950s	PRIV	
WRAYSBURY	33 / 6C	P	22/08/1848	N/A	LSWR	Village name formerly spelt 'Wyrardisbury', but station always appears to have used modern spelling. Re-sited south 01/04/1861. Goods yard closed 1962.
		G	22/08/1848	??/??/1962		

Y

Name	Page / grid		Date opened	Date closed	Opened by	Notes
YEOVENEY Runemede Runemede Range	33 / 6D		01/03/1892	14/05/1962	GWR	Opened as 'Runemede Range', suffix dropped 09/07/1934. Renamed 'Yeoveney' 04/11/1935. Suffix 'Halt' sometimes appended to all three names. Request stop in daylight hours only, closed prior to withdrawal of passenger services from branch. Mitchell & Smith ('Branch Lines of West London') gives opening date of c.01/04/1887.
YORK ROAD	26 / 4B 75		15/12/1906	17/09/1932	UERL (GNPBR)	
York Road Curve	75	P	01/10/1863	08/11/1976	GNR	Curve in 'up' direction connecting GNR with MET, originally to 10/01/1863 MET lines but later to 'Widened Lines'. Carried goods traffic 20/02/1866 - 24/03/1969. Closed when Moorgate trains diverted via GNCR 08/11/1976.
		G	20/02/1866	24/03/1969		
YORK WAY FREIGHTLINER TERMINAL	26 / 3B		15/11/1965	??/05/1968	BR	On site for former Maiden Lane goods yard.
York Way North Junction	76		14/11/2007	N/A	LCOR / NR	
York Way South Junction	76		14/11/2007	N/A	LCOR / NR	